新闻学与传播学经典丛书·大师系列

个性动力论
A Dynamic Theory of Personality
中文·英文(双语版)

[美]库尔特·卢因 著
何道宽 译

中国传媒大学出版社
·北京·

图书在版编目(CIP)数据

个性动力论:双语版:汉、英/(美)库尔特·卢因著;何道宽译.
—北京:中国传媒大学出版社,2016.10
(新闻学与传播学经典丛书·大师系列)
ISBN 978-7-5657-1758-1

Ⅰ.①个… Ⅱ.①库… ②何… Ⅲ.①实验心理学—汉、英
Ⅳ.①B84

中国版本图书馆 CIP 数据核字(2016)第 167467 号

新闻学与传播学经典丛书·大师系列

个性动力论
GEXING DONGLILUN

著　　者	[美]库尔特·卢因
译　　者	何道宽
策划编辑	姜颖昳　司马兰
责任编辑	姜颖昳　司马兰
封面制作	博采文案
责任印制	曹　辉
出版发行	中国传媒大学出版社
社　　址	北京市朝阳区定福庄东街 1 号　邮编:100024
电　　话	86-10-65450532 或 65450528　传真:010-65779405
网　　址	http://www.cucp.com.cn
经　　销	全国新华书店
印　　刷	北京艺堂印刷有限公司
开　　本	880mm×1230mm　1/32
成品尺寸	145mm×210mm
印　　张	19.5
字　　数	562 千字
版　　次	2016 年 10 月第 1 版　2016 年 10 月第 1 次印刷
书　　号	ISBN 978-7-5657-1758-1/B·1758　　定价 78.00 元

版权所有　翻印必究　印装错误　负责调换

总　序

　　新闻与大众传播事业在现当代与日俱增的影响与地位,呼唤着新闻学与传播学学术研究的相应发展和跟进。而知识的传承,学术的繁荣,思想的进步,首先需要的是丰富的思想材料的积累。

　　"新闻学与传播学经典译丛·大师系列"的创设,立意在接续前辈学人传译外国新闻学与传播学经典的事业,以一定的规模为我们的学术与思想界以及业界精英人士理解和借鉴新闻学与传播学在西方方兴未艾之际的精华,提供基本的养料,便于站在前人的肩膀上作进一步的探究,以免长期在黑暗中自行低效摸索。

　　将近十年前,在何道宽教授与我的发起和主持下,在司马兰女士的大力支持下,"新闻与传播学译丛·大师经典系列"开始启动,至今已推出十来种名著的中译本,在学界也较有影响。这首先是何道宽教授的贡献,作为英语科班出身、口译笔译俱佳的高手,依然投身于传播学经典的引进;退休后更是一发不可收,每天清晨起床开始工作,每年推出好几本译著,而且专攻技术学派(何老师称之为"环境学派"),不但包办了哈罗德·伊尼斯、马歇尔·麦克卢汉著作的所有中译本,而且还延伸到保罗·莱文森等当代名家。

　　记得何老师说过,他热爱传播学学术翻译到了这样的程度:"不给我钱(稿费)我也愿意翻译。"我当时就感慨,新闻传播学界要是多有一些像何老师这样外语水平高、热衷翻译的专才就好了。可是在目前的学术考核体制下,译著辛苦和稿费低暂且不提,在多数学校还是不被承认为科研工作量的。这就妨碍了许多为教学科研和生活所累的年轻学人接续这一事业，尽管也出现了像刘海龙这样的优秀青年译者。

好在随着新闻传播学的发展，越来越多的学人意识到了我九年多前说的两个80%：新闻学与传播学是舶来品，80%的学术和思想资源不在中国；而日见人多势众的研究队伍将80%以上的精力投放到虽在快速发展，但是仍处在"初级阶段"的国内新闻与大众传播事业的研究上。这两个80%倒置的现实，导致了学术资源配置的严重失衡和学术研究的肤浅化、泡沫化；专业和学术著作的翻译虽然在近几年渐成气候，但是其水准、规模和系统性不足以摆脱"后天失调"的尴尬。

如果说当年启动时，我们深感百余年前梁启超呼吁"国家欲自强，以多译西书为本；学子欲自立，以多读西书为功"对于当代新闻传播学的意义，如果说任公所言西学著述"今之所译，直九牛之一毛耳"的巨大落差，如果说新闻学与传播学相关典籍的译介比其他学科还要滞后许多，以至于我们的学人们对这些经典知之甚少，眼界相当狭窄，那么这种状况已经有所改观。如今的新闻传播学，虽然仍属小学科，但是近十年出版的图书数量猛增，其中译著的大量问世是最为引人瞩目的现象。

这些新闻传播学译著可能并非本本经典，事实上也出现了些许重复翻译。一些译本的翻译质量存在问题，译校也比较粗糙。但是总体而言，它们对于学术的推动和学科地位的提升功不可没，尤其是比较媒介理论、传播研究方法类译著，直接烘托了和滋养了年轻学子，令他们的研究水准迅速提升。回想十年前，尽管几乎所有新闻传播专业学生言必称传播学"四大奠基人"或"四大先驱"，可是当时他们的传播学译著一本也没有被翻译成中文。

本译丛将奉献新闻学与传播学大师的经典之作，如哈罗德·拉斯韦尔、埃尔·塔尔德、哈罗德·伊尼斯、马歇尔·麦克卢汉、库尔特·卢因、卡尔·霍夫兰等人的佳作。大部分名著是新近翻译出版的，部分名著是中文版的修订本。"译事之艰辛，惟事者知之。"从事这种恢弘迫切而又繁难备至的工作，需要好几代人作出不懈努力，幸赖同道和出版者大力扶持。我们自知学有不逮，力不从心，因此热忱欢迎中青年学人加入译者队伍，我们也将虚心聆听各界读者提出的批评和建议。

主编

目 录

中译者序   1
英译者序   5
作者前言   7

第一章　亚里士多德思维模式和伽利略思维模式在当代心理学里的冲突   1
   第一节　两种思维模式的一般特征   2
   第二节　亚里士多德的概念   2
   第三节　伽利略物理学   7
   第四节　两种思维模式在心理学里的差异   10
   第五节　动力论   20

第二章　论心理结构   32
   第一节　心理事件的动因   32
   第二节　心理能量与心理结构   39
   第三节　平衡趋势：心理系统边界的动态牢固与相对隔离   43
   第四节　心理过程即生命过程   46

第三章　环境在儿童行为及发展中的作用　49
第一节　引言　49
第二节　行动自由的地域,力量与力量场　60

第四章　奖励和惩罚的心理情境　87
第一节　兴趣情境　90
第二节　带惩罚性威胁的指令　91
第三节　带奖赏希望的指令　120
第四节　带惩罚威胁的禁令　124
第五节　惩罚真实度的偏离　127
第六节　带奖赏希望的禁令　129
第七节　奖赏、惩罚、真正的兴趣转变　130

第五章　为现实服务的教育　134
第一节　心理生活空间和时间的延伸　135
第二节　现实与非现实的分层　136

第六章　替代活动和替代价值　140

第七章　低能的动力学理论　151
第一节　低能儿童的顿悟　152
第二节　实验问题的设计　153
第三节　低能儿童和正常儿童的心理满足　154
第四节　被中断行为的恢复,替代行为的价值　157
第五节　个性动力差异的一般理论　160
第六节　低能的动力论　163

第八章　实验研究概述　186
第一节　历史概述　186

第二节　系统扫描　　　　　　　　　　　　　188
第三节　心理系统的一般规律　　　　　　　　189
第四节　环境问题　　　　　　　　　　　　　202
第五节　整体人的结构与状况　　　　　　　　211

附录：心理学家实验研究问题一览表　　　　　218
　　人名索引　　　　　　　　　　　　　　　221
　　主题索引　　　　　　　　　　　　　　　227

A Dynamic Theory of Personality　　　　　　247
Preface　　　　　　　　　　　　　　　　　　249
Translators' Preface　　　　　　　　　　　　253
Chapter Ⅰ　The Conflict Between Aristotelian and Galileian Modes of Thought In Contemporary Psychology　　257
Chapter Ⅱ　On The Structure of The Mind　　307
Chapter Ⅲ　Environmental Forces In Child Behavior And Development　　335
Chapter Ⅳ　The Psychological Situations of Reward and Punishment　　392
Chapter Ⅴ　Education For Reality　　466
Chapter Ⅵ　Substitute Activity and Substitute Value　　476
Chapter Ⅶ　A Dynamic Theory of The Feeble-Minded　　492
Chapter Ⅷ　Survey of The Experimental Investigations　　547
Index of Names　　　　　　　　　　　　　　590
Index of Subjects　　　　　　　　　　　　　594

中译者后记　　　　　　　　　　　　　　　　605
译者简介　　　　　　　　　　　　　　　　　607

中译者序

一、跨界的书

《个性动力论》是实验心理学和社会心理学的书,书名显示其领域归属,不言自明。既然如此,我们将其纳入"新闻学与传播学经典丛书·大师系列",有何根据呢?

首先,传播学是20世纪初酝酿、20世纪40年代正式创建的学科。从学术发展史看,后起的学科必然要撷取其他学科尤其是相邻学科的遗产。传播学和心理学相近,同为研究人的学科,当然有共性、相似性和交叉性,不可能相隔太远,所以,传播学"撷取"心理学成果势在必行,合情合理,亦无障碍。

其次,传播学是交叉学科,是多门学科碰撞、汇聚、融合的产物,凡是研究人与人关系的学科如政治学、经济学、人类学、社会学、心理学、哲学、语言学、语义学、神经病学等,都与传播学相关。

20世纪40年代,威尔伯·施拉姆与社会学家拉扎斯菲尔德、政治学家哈罗德·拉斯韦尔、心理学家库尔特·卢因和卡尔·霍夫兰等共同开拓传播学研究的新边疆。施拉姆更进一步,他将新闻学、社会学、心理学、政治学熔为一炉,创建了传播学。

1980年,施拉姆在《美国传播研究的开端》一文中,高度评价拉斯韦尔、拉扎斯菲尔德、卢因和霍夫兰等对传播研究的贡献,宣告他们为传播学奠基人。

卢因的代表作《个性动力论》《解决社会矛盾》《群体决定与社会变革》《拓扑心理学原理》《社会科学中的场论》等自然成为新兴传播学的重要资源。

我翻译的跨越心理学和传播学的经典著作有三种,《个性动力论》是其中之一,其他两本是《传播与社会影响》①《模仿律》②。塔尔德是法国社会学三大奠基人之一,活跃在19世纪和20世纪之交,是公认的刑法学家、社会学家和社会心理学家、创建法国社会学的三驾马车之一,曾对美国社会心理学的发展产生重大影响。

现代学术的发展趋势之一是,跨界的学者和著作越来越多了。

二、卢因成就

卢因对心理学和传播学的贡献广为人知,网上俯拾即是,这里的介绍仅限于他对传播学的贡献,他的心理学成就请见下文。为求简明,容我借用"百度百科"的扼要总结:"卢因对传播学的贡献主要表现在三个方面。一是他在把心理学的实验方法引入社会学研究的同时,实际上也给传播学研究提供了一种有效的手段。因为他研究的人类行为场理论和群体动力学,既属于心理学和社会学的范畴,也涉及传播学的一些基本问题。所以,在这个意义上,卢因是最早研究传播学的心理学家之一;二是他对人们行为和群体的研究,给传播学中的效果研究提供了一个重要启示:在研究大众传播媒介对个人的影响时,要充分注意社会环境和个人所属群体的作用;三是他提出了著名的'把关人'概念,为信息流动的复杂性等提供了圆满的解释。"

三、四大特色

《个性动力论》篇幅不大,内容却很丰赡。全书仅八章,但章以下几个

---

① 〔法〕加布里埃尔·塔尔德著,〔美〕特里·N. 克拉克编,何道宽译:《传播与社会影响》,北京:中国人民大学出版社,2005。

② 〔法〕加布里埃尔·塔尔德著,〔美〕埃尔希·克鲁斯·帕森斯英译,何道宽译:《模仿律》,北京:中国人民大学出版社,2008。

层级的分节却超过 140 个。最大的特色有四点：

(1) 科学手段与人文洞见的结合；

(2) 动力论、场论、拓扑学成为心理学研究的有力武器，对矢量、诱发力、场力、拓扑结构等概念得心应手的运用；

(3) 上百个图表彰显了它的"理科"色彩；

(4) 科学的实验设计和手段极富说服力，书末附录中的"心理学家实验研究问题一览表"是一座富矿，可供研究者和实验人掘金寻宝。

四、各章提要

第一章"亚里士多德思维模式和伽利略思维模式在当代心理学里的冲突"的题名彰显了本书的物理学灵感和源头。本章调动许多哲学、数学和物理学的概念，比如目的论、场论、统计、微分、矢量、张力、历史—地理等，推出作者本人的"心理动力论"和"行为场理论"。

第二章"论心理结构"引入了许多专用术语，比如心理(mind)、诱发力(valence)、心理统一性(unity of the mind)、张力系统(tension system)、心理能力(psychical ability)等。诱发力(valence)是卢因创造的专用语。

本章题名里的 mind 的意蕴丰富，需要作出说明。德语文本里用的是 Seele，英译者将其译为 mind，颇费思量，因为 Seele 兼有"心理"和"心灵"双重意蕴，但偏重英语的 soul(心灵、灵魂)。中译者也将其译为"心理"，我们同意英译者的判断：这里所用的 mind，指的是心理系统的整体，而不是狭义的心灵或灵魂。

第三章"环境在儿童行为及发展中的作用"区分一般环境与个人环境、外部环境和内在环境，辨析环境的现实分层，阐述和应用场域、场力、力量场、紧张状态、感应诱发力和社会场，把人所处的里里外外的环境都说透了。

第四章"奖励和惩罚的心理情境"依据作者及其同事主持的大量实验研究，论述奖惩的心理学，内容丰赡、图表众多，但明白晓畅、繁而不乱，无需详细介绍。

第五章"为现实服务的教育"主张心理学为教育服务，颇有论辩色彩。

第六章"替代活动和替代价值"篇幅不大，要言不烦，亦无需详细介绍。

第七章"低能的动力学理论"是本书的重中之重,篇幅最大,内容宏富、创新、新锐、闪亮,是唯一专辟"小结"的一章,可见其分量非凡。

兹将"小结"全文抄录如次,省得我们啰唆饶舌:

"本章开篇讲正常儿童和低能儿童心理满足的实验研究,接着讲被中断行为的恢复以及替代情境的替代价值,提出了一类低能现象的动力论。"

"低能儿童的行为是从心理系统的心理基质的动力特征衍生出来的,心理系统隐含着个性的结构特征,个性心理分化的程度和速度各有不同,结构各有特色。我们讨论了个性特征在智力、注意力、意志等领域的影响。最后,我们介绍了个性特征与正常儿童心理结构的关系,及其与老人的关系。"

第八章"实验研究概览"将诸多实验心理学家主持的心理实验一网打尽,精华在斯,无须赘言。为了突出本章附录"心理学家实验研究问题一览表"的核心价值,我冒昧将其升格为全书的附录,意在彰显这座"富矿"的持久价值。

何道宽

于深圳大学文化产业研究院

深圳大学传媒与文化发展研究中心

2016 年 4 月 18 日

英译者序

如果附上德语原文,这个译本里的一些术语就比较容易理解了。形容词 psychisch 和 seelisch 的译文都是 psychic 或 psychical(心理的),因为在我们看来,事件、过程和结构被称为 psychical,颇为妥当;然而,除非经过心理学或心理学家的加工,它们并不能被视为 psychological(心理学的)。借此可以避免因文字晦涩而导致不必要的误解,须知,物理学就有这样晦涩的文字和误解。比如,"the physical world"的意思就模棱两可,既可能是"经验的物质世界",也可能是"物质世界",两者之不同判若云泥。

Seele 一词被译为 mind,但我们对此仍然疑虑重重。我们曾想将其译为 soul,我们相信,重新将其引进英语的心理学术语的条件业已成熟。乍一看,soul 一词的心理学含义与神学含义是不会混淆的:心理学"心灵"演绎于具体的行为,相反,神学里"灵魂"的属性则不可能从具体的行为中演绎出来。然而,抽样调查的结果显示,美国心理学家反对将 seele 译成比较具体的 soul。因此,我们有必要指出,这里所用的 mind(心理系统的整体)不是指狭义的心智意义,而是更接近麦道孤①所指的"心理"。我们把卢因后期论文里的 psychologische person 译为 psychological person,如此看来,他后期所谓的 psychologische person 和早期论文里的 Seele 的意义是基本相同的。

其他需要说明的翻译请见正文或注释。

感谢克拉克大学卡里·莫奇森主任和克拉克大学出版社允许我重印本书第一章和第三章,这两篇文章分别原载《普通心理学杂志》(*Journal of General Psychology*,Volume 5,pages 141—177)和莫奇森主编的《儿童心理学手册》(*Handbook of Child Psychology*)。

本书第四章"奖励和惩罚的心理情境"(*Die Psychologische Situation bei Lohn und Strofe*)原为专论,由莱比锡的希瑟尔出版社印行。本书第七章"低能的动力学理论"(*Theorie des Schwachinns*)1933 年收入比利时一家出版社推出的《向德克罗利博士致敬》(*Hommage au Dr. Decroly*)。第五章"为现实服务的教育"(*Erziehung zur Realitat*)初版于 1931 年。第二章"论心理结构"取自柏林尤利乌斯·斯普林格书局出版的《感知、意志与需求》,第八章的大多数图表也取自该书,在此深表谢忱。这些图表根据卢因教授的《心理学研究》(*Psychologische Forschung*)制作。同时,我们还要感谢斯图尔特先生在制作这些图表中提供的慷慨帮助。

D. K. 亚当斯博士

卡尔·齐纳博士

北卡莱罗纳杜伦市

1935

---

① 麦道孤(W. Mcdougall,1871—1938),英裔美国心理学家、策动心理学的创建人,社会心理学先驱,著有《社会心理学导论》《群体心理》《生理心理学》《肉体与心灵:泛灵论研究》《人的能量》《人生之谜》等——译者。

作者前言

本书是一部论文集,各篇发表的时间和时机各不相同。故此,读者会发现,一些基本概念屡屡重现。本书旨在展现迄今心理学研究诸领域的总体景象,以及个人心理和环境的关系,同时显示各应用性研究领域的相互关系,尤其是儿童心理学、教育学、心理学、性格学和社会心理学的相互关系。

就在几年前,你可以看到,在心理学家中——至少是在德国心理学家中弥漫着一股悲观情绪。实验心理学初获成功之后,情况似乎越来越明显,在斩获感知和记忆研究的成功之后,再将其应用于心理分析之类的重大问题时,实验方法就越来越力不从心了。沉重的"哲学"和"方法论"问题似乎预先就决定了实验方法努力的失败。这个方向的第一批实证研究似乎证实了这样一个信念:意志、情感和人格的实验心理学注定要满足于表面的事实,而不得不把深层的问题留给学校,让人去猜想,它们并不能用实验方法去检测。

在这个领域探索时,我觉得,我启动了方法论上和技术上健全而必要的任务,穷数十年之功,拓宽这个领域的工作是可以期待的。至少不久以后就会清楚,解决这些问题虽然困难,但绝不是不能解决的。所需要的,无非是澄清一些陈旧的哲学问题,把科学目标设定在足够的高度,我们就能够进行解释和预测。比如,只要用稳妥的方法和恰当的概念,心理分析提出的问题就可以靠实验方法来澄清了,这一点今天已不容置疑。实际上,和感知心理相比,在需求和情感领域求得动力律似乎较为容易。在美国几所大学访学一年的经历向我显示,虽然其历史背景各有不同,但它们对探索的可能性抱有共同的信念,许多实验正在进行之中。诸多实验与心理病理学和比较心理学的关系研究,尤其有望结出累累硕果。我自然知道,我们才刚刚起步,但发展比我希望的快得多。原因首先在于心理学的历史地位,一种"伽利略式"的思维模式即将成熟。

有人问,我是否同意将这类研究命名为"拓扑心理学"。我说,只要突出以下几点,我不会反对这个术语。我相信,今天的心理学正处在超越陈旧意义"学派"的地位。推进诸如此类的研究是我们的主要目标,我们的工作要尽可能使用数学语言。这是因为和其他语言相比,数学语言不那么模糊,既"客观",又"少猜度",因为它只表达事物和事件的结构秩序。然而,我不会局限于拓扑学概念。另外,数学语言的使用,仅仅是更一般的"建构"方法的表现手段之一而已;"建构"方法的主要特征是,它更能弥合理论和具体事实之间的鸿沟。尽管如此,拓扑学仍然是表现心理学领域动力关系的最基础的理论。我坚信,拓扑学将超越这一功能,成为动力社会学坚实的框架。

亚当斯(D. K. Adams)博士和齐纳(Karl Zener)博士呕心沥血将这本文集译成英语。只有承担过科学新领域里艰难译事的人才知道,我对他们是多么心存感激。

库尔特·卢因
于纽约伊萨卡
1935 年 3 月

第一章 亚里士多德思维模式和伽利略思维模式在当代心理学里的冲突

探讨当前实验心理学和理论心理学几个紧迫的问题时,我建议重温物理学概念的发展史,尤其是物理学从亚里士多德思维模式向伽利略思维模式的转变。其目的不仅仅是重温历史,而是相信,在重建当今心理学的一些概念时,某些重要问题能得到澄清;在比较的过程中,这些问题能够得到更准确的表述。借此,我们提供超越当前困难的观点。

我无意从物理学历史中演绎出心理学应该做什么的结论。我不认为只有一种经验学科即物理学;也不认为,作为生物学的一部分,心理学能简化为物理学;亦不认为,这里敞开了一门独立学科的大门。

我们的出发点是研究者的观点。既然如此,在比较亚里士多德和伽利略的概念构成时,我们就不太关心其个人理论的细微差异,而是关心一些可以测量的思维模式的差异:正是这种思维模式的差异决定着中世纪亚里士多德学派的实际研究工作,以及后伽利略派物理学家的研究工作。至于在某一点上,某一位研究者是否在早期的研究中显露出某一种后期的思想,现代相对论的某些猜想是否应该与亚里士多德模式有一些吻合——这些问题就与我们当前的探讨无关了。

为了从理论研究上给这些动力关系问题提供一个具体的背景,我将首先考虑亚里士多德物理学和伽利略物理学的一般特征,以及现代心理学的一般特征。

第一节 两种思维模式的一般特征

一、两种思维模式的物理学特征

若要问"现代"的后伽利略物理学和亚里士多德物理学最典型的差异是什么,一般的回答是:亚里士多德物理学的概念是拟人式的、不精确的。这一回答对心理学家的科学理想产生了重大的影响。相反,现代心理学有量的精确性,如今,纯数学的、功能性关系取代过去的拟人式解释。这样的解释曾赋予物理学抽象的外观,现代物理学为此而感到特别骄傲。

诚然,有关物理学发展的这个观点是稳妥的。然而,如果我们把较少的注意力放在所用概念的形式上,把更多的注意力放在理解世界的工具的实际功能上,后伽利略物理学和亚里士多德物理学的差异似乎就是第二位的了,它们是世界与研究任务关系的深层差异所引起的后果而已。

第二节 亚里士多德的概念

一、亚里士多德概念的评价性质

如同一切学科一样,物理学从普世哲学与实践母体分离出来的过程是一个渐进的过程。亚里士多德物理学的许多概念今天被视为生物学概念,而且首先被视为评价性的概念。该物理学充斥着借用自伦理学的规范性概念,哲学概念介于评价性和非评价性之间:最高形态的运动形式是圆形的和直线的,只出现在天体即星星的运动中;地上世界的运动是低等的运动。同理,动因也有评价性差异:一方面是优等的力量,或所谓天体被赋予的权威力量,其力量来自其趋于完美的倾向;一方面是扰动的倾向,这样的扰动有偶然性,扰动的原因是其他天体方向的力量。

这种价值分类在中世纪物理学中起到了非常重要的作用。它把许多有细微关系或非重要关系的事物归于同一类别,把客观上有紧密关系或重要关系的事物归于不同类别。

显而易见,直至今天,这种极其"拟人式"的思维模式仍在心理学中发挥着重要的作用。如同天象和地象的分别一样,长期以来,同样评价性的"常态"和"病态"将心理事实区分为两个界限分明的领域。

同样重要的是,价值概念在具体问题的观念语境中占支配地位,直到最近都是如此。因此,心理学不久前才开始研究感知的结构(格式塔)关系,以取代视错觉(optical illusion)概念;视错觉不是衍生于心理学范畴,而是衍生于知识论范畴;视错觉毫无根据地把诸如此类的错觉归并在一起,将其与心理光学(psychological optics)的其他现象区别开来。心理学所讲述的儿童的"错误""实践"和"遗忘",是根据心理过程结果的价值对心理过程进行分类,而不是根据心理过程的性质进行分类。诚然,只有在谈论发展中的障碍、自卑感、优越感时,心理学才超越以价值为基础的分类。在各个方面,人们都倾向于研究实际的心理过程。但毋庸置疑,我们站在这个阶段的门口,我们所见到的亚里士多德物理学处在两级对子典型的评价性和非评价性之间,这些两级对子有:智能和低能、驱力和意志。心理学的概念结构与教育学、医学和伦理学的功利概念的分离,尚未完全实现。

稍后,功利或表现的概念,比如对"正确"认知与对"错误"认知的概念,也许能够获得符合规律的意义,这是可能的——实际上我认为是很可能的。如果真是这样,"幻觉"就必然带有知识论的特征,而不是生物学的特征。

二、抽象的分类

伽利略物理学和后伽利略物理学不区分天象和地象,因此极大拓宽了自然规律的领域,这不仅和它排除了价值概念有关系,而且和它的分类诠释变化有关系。对亚里士多德物理学而言,客体的类别身份极其重要,因为在亚里士多德看来,类别界定了客体的本质或本质属性,从而决定了客体正反两方面的行为。

这样的分类常常以二分对子的形式出现,比如冷和热、干和湿,和现今的分类相比,亚里士多德物理学的分类具有僵硬和绝对的性质。在现代的定量物理学里,二元分类完全被连续渐进等级的概念取而代之。实体概念已经被功能概念取代了。①

在这里同样不难看出,当代心理学走过了模拟式的发展阶段。智能、记忆、冲动的分化始终打上了亚里士多德分类的典型烙印;比如在情感(愉快和不愉快)分析、气质分析②或驱力分析③中,亚里士多德的二元分类仍然是极其重要的。然而,诸如此类的分类正在失去其重要性,正在让位于另一种概念:在以上所有领域中推衍出同样的规律,以功能差异为基础在整个心理学领域进行分类。

三、规律的概念

亚里士多德类别界定的绝对依据是一组事物共同特征的总和。这一情况不仅是亚里士多德逻辑的典型特征,而且决定着他的合规律性(lawfulness)和偶然性(chance)的概念。这两个概念对当代心理学很重要,需要更仔细地予以考察。

对亚里士多德而言,凡是无例外发生的事物就是有规律的。而且他特别强调,凡是频繁发生的事物就是合乎规律的。凡只出现一次的事物、单一的事件都被排除在可以理解的概念类别之外。实际上,既然事物的习性由其基本性质所决定,其基本性质正是绝对界定的类别(即一组事物共同特征的总和),所以,每一个事件,具体的事件就是由偶然决定的。因为在亚里士多德的类别里,个体差异是不存在的。

这一概念的真正根源寓于这样一个事实中:亚里士多德物理学认为,并非一切物理过程都具有后伽利略物理学赋予它们的规律性。对年轻的物理学而言,它所研究的宇宙,其包含的无序性和规律性一样多。在亚里士多德物理学时代,物理过程的规律性、可理解性仍然很有限,规律性和可理解性仅存在于某些过程中,比如星星的运行中,绝不会存在于地球上

---

① See E. CASSIRER, *Substanzbegriff und Funktionsbegriff*, *Untersuchungen über die Grundfragen der Erkenntniskritik*, B. Cassirer, Berlin, 1910.

② See R. SOMMER, Uber Personlichkeitstypen, *Ber. Kong, f, exper. Psychol*, 1925.

③ See LEWIN, *Die Entwicklung der experimentellen Willenspsychologie und die Psychotherapie*, S. Hirzel, Leipzig, 1929.

转瞬即逝的事件中。和其他的年轻学科一样,物理过程是否有规律制约,多大程度上受规律制约?这个问题在物理学中仍然悬而未决。虽然在哲学原理中,普遍规律性的观念业已存在,但物理学规律性悬而未决的问题对物理学概念的形成产生了很大的影响。在后伽利略物理学中,由于不区分规律性事件和偶发事件,考察的过程是否有规律就不必证明了。相反,对亚里士多德物理学而言,判断事件是否有规律的标准是必备的条件。实际上,自然界里类似事件发生的规律性就被当作一个基本的标准。只有天象之类事件受规律制约,因为历史业已证明,它们是有规律的,至少是频繁发生的;至少是因为它们频繁发生,而不是单个的事件,所以它们才是可以理解的。换言之,科学有解释复杂、混乱、费解世界的抱负,有信心最终破解这个世界的秘密,但其抱负和信心却被局限为历史反复证明的既持久又稳定的事件上。

这方面必须牢记,亚里士多德强调频率(这是绝对规律性之外的又一个规律性依据),和前人相比,这是他进一步拓展和具体应用规律性原理的倾向。"经验主义者"亚里士多德坚持认为,有规律和频繁发生的事情都是合理的。当然,这使他个性和规律的二分对子更加分明,因为单个事件未进入规律性事件的范围,因而也不在科学研究的范围之内。合乎规律仅限于反复发生的事件和类别(亚里士多德绝对意义上的类别),这样的事件和类别揭示了事件的本质。

对自然界规律性问题的这种态度主宰着中世纪物理学,连反对亚里士多德物理学的人,比如布鲁诺和培根也只能逐渐放弃反对的态度,这样的局面在几个方面产生了重大的影响。

上文清楚显示,规律性概念始终具有准统计学的性质。规律性被视为最高程度的普遍性,常常以同样方式发生的现象,极端地有规律可循,因而是不频繁发生事件或具体事件的完美对立面。规律性概念由统计数字决定,这个概念清楚地见于培根的思想,他试图用他的"白板"说来断定,一些属性的联想是真实的抑或是偶然的。比如,他用数字的频率来判定日常生活里温暖和干燥的程度。从数学上来看,这不太精确,但亚里士多德物理学的统计式思维方式的明晰度并不因此而逊色。

全无例外,"总是如此"的思维方式也进入了后来的物质规律性概念中。就其源头而言,这一思维方式寓于日常世界历史进程中,与类似事件实际发生的频率有关。简单一例足以将其说明得更加清楚:在日常生活中,轻物总是上扬,重物通常总是下降。在亚里士多德所知的情况下,火焰总是上扬。在气候、生活方式等亚里士多德所知的范围内,正是这样频繁的规律决定着物体的性质和倾向,使他得出结论:火焰和轻物有上扬的趋势。

亚里士多德概念的形成和另一个地理历史条件有直接的关系,正如上文提及的评价性概念一样,这个地理历史条件类似原始人和儿童的思维。

当原始人用不同的词语表示"走路"时(视不同情况而定,或指南北方向,或指走路人的性别,或指出门进门),①他参照的历史情况和亚里士多德推定的绝对化描写(上扬或下沉)类似,是一种真正意义上的地理描述,确定了物体与地球表面相对的位置。②

起初,上述概念与历史—地理条件的"现实情况"有关,也许这是亚里士多德物理学最重要的特征。也许,正是因为这一特征而不是因为其目的论,他的物理学获得了普遍的拟人式性质。显然,即使在理论推导的细节和实际的研究中,我们不仅对物理概念和规范概念尚未区分。而且对我们今天应该区分的问题和概念表述也尚未进行区分。其实,我们所区分的历史的范畴③和非历史的范畴(即系统的范畴)是纠缠不清的(顺便指出,在其他学科发展的早期,类似的混淆同样存在,经济学即为一例)。

---

① See L. LÉVY—BRUHL, *La Mentalité primitive*, Alcan, Paris, 1922, (5th ed., 1927).
② 在下文里,我们将频繁使用"historicgeographic"一词。这个词不常用,但我认为,就历史问题和系统问题进行对比是不准确的。真正的对比是将"类型"(客体、过程、情景等)和"发生的事情"进行对比。就发生的事情的概念而言,绝对地理空间坐标的参照和绝对时间坐标的参照一样典型,时间坐标由日期来决定。另一方面,地理概念应该参照以下的意义来理解:并置,与历史继承的关系,可用于心理事件。
③ 如今尚无一个通用语词来表示非历史性问题,所以作为权宜之计,我在这里用"系统的"一词予以表述,在这里,"系统的"的意思并非"整齐有序的"。"系统的"一词总体上用来指非历史性的问题和规律,当代物理学多半就是这样的问题和规律(参见 p.12)。

从这些概念出发,亚里士多德物理学还踏上了合乎规律性的一个新方向。只要其继续局限于以同样方式反复重现的机制,结果就很明显:年轻的物理学不仅缺乏推展其原理以涵盖一切物理现象的勇气,而且,合乎规律性的概念依旧维持着其历史意义即特定时间的意义。亚里士多德物理学强调的不是现代物理学所理解的规律性,而是强调特定的历史世界,而这样的世界所展现的是需要中的稳定。最大程度的规律性超乎单纯的频繁性,其特征是永远、永恒的理念。换言之,在延展的过程中,拥有常恒性的历史时间被引申为永恒了。规律的普遍有效性尚未与过程的永恒性区别开来。唯独永恒的频繁的重复才能证明其超乎短时间的有效性。永恒性的理念似乎超越历史性,但即使在这里,永恒性与历史现实的直接联系似乎也很明显。这样的紧密关系是亚里士多德"经验主义的"方法和概念的典型特征。

不仅在物理学里,而且在其他学科,比如经济学和生物学里,科学发展的早期总有一个倾向是显而易见的:经验主义的倾向、搜集和整理事实的倾向、总是带有建构历史概念的倾向、总是过高估计历史因素的价值。

第三节 伽利略物理学

用这种经验主义的观点来观照,伽利略物理学和后伽利略物理学概念的形成似乎是奇异难解的,甚至是颇为吊诡的。

如上所述,数学工具的使用及追求精确的倾向固然重要,但它们不能被视为亚里士多德物理学和伽利略物理学差异的实质。实际上,用数学形式重新表述亚里士多德物理学,比如其动态理念,是完全可能的。物理学用数学工具重新表述亚里士多德概念的路子,是可以想象的,就像今天的心理学正在走的路子一样。然而实际情况却是,这样的迹象寥寥无几,培根的准统计方法即为其一,已如上述。其主要走的是另一个发展方向,结果证明,那是内容的变化而不是形式的变化。

新物理学的精确性同样可以这样来分析。不要忘记,在伽利略的时代,没有我们今天这样的时钟:第一批时钟的出现是建立在伽利略力学研究成果的基础上。① 连法拉第早期研究电学的测量方法都罕有精确性,今天流行的到小数点后多少位的精确性,那时也不存在;他不得不在物理学发展的重要阶段凑合着运用这样的不精确性。

量化倾向的资源埋藏得很深,它们隐藏在物理学家对物质世界性质的新观念中,物理学必须要求自己进一步拓展理解世界的任务,并且增强自己完成这一任务的信念。这些变化是物理学基本理念重大而深远的变革,量化倾向只不过是这些重大变革的表现之一而已。

一、均质化

决定布鲁诺、开普勒和伽利略观点的是这样一个理念:物质世界是综合的、无所不包的统一体。对他们而言,同一个规律统揽星体的运行、自由下落的石头和鸟儿的飞行。物质世界是均质化的,规律是有效的,物体不能分为刚性、绝对抽象的类别;但对亚里士多德物理学而言,这样的分类却极为重要,它认为,观念的类别决定着物体的物理性质。

与此密切相关的是逻辑二分法和观念对立体重要意义的丧失。二分和对立的观念被流动过渡、渐进变化的观念取而代之,如此,二分术语的对立性就被剥夺,以逻辑形式表现的分类概念和系列概念之间的过渡就被取而代之了。②

二、遗传概念

僵化类别尖锐对立的消解,增加了两个过渡同时发生的可能性,一是向功能主义思维方式的转变,一是条件遗传概念(conditionalgenetic concepts)的使用。对亚里士多德而言,直接可感知的外观即今天生物学所谓的显型(phenotype)难以和决定物体动力关系的属性区别开来。比如,轻的物体常常上扬,足以使亚里士多德赋予它们上扬的趋势。由于显型和遗传类型(genotype)的分别,由于更一般的描写性概念和条件遗传概念③的分别,由于重点向条件遗传概念的转移,许多旧的分类就失去意义了。

---

① See E. MACH, *Die Mechanik in ihrer Entwicklung*, Leipzig, 1921.
② See E. CASSIRER, *op. cit.*
③ LEWIN, *Gesetz und Experiment in der Psychologie*, Weltkreis verlag, Berlin Schlachtensee, 1927.

如果使用显型来分类,行星的轨道、石头的自由下落、物体在斜面的运动、钟摆的摆动就会被分到迥然不同的类别,而且是对立的类别之中,然而事实证明,它们只不过是同一规律的不同表现而已。

三、具体性

强调量化的价值似乎赋予现代物理学一种形式和抽象的特征,但这一特征并非演绎着逻辑形式的倾向。相反,会对具体现实性甚至对具体例子的充分描写产生重大影响。谈及现代心理学时,这样的描写特别需要强调。一切学科的具体目标不仅有类的规定即量的规定,而且,科学的每一种属性都有其强度或确定的量度。只要你认为某一物体重要的、可以理解的属性是同一组物体共同的属性,个体程度的差异在科学上就无关紧要了,因为在抽象界定的类别里,这些度的差异或多或少都消失殆尽了。科学研究对现实事件和具体案例的兴趣日益高涨,描绘个案度量差异的任务必然会日益重要,最后,科学研究必然会要求量的确定性。

充分理解具体情况的欲望在增强,人的能力也在增强,加上物理世界均质性的理念以及物体属性连续性的思想,这些因素合在一起促成了物理学日益量化的主流冲动。

四、新经验主义悖论

尽可能贴近现实性的倾向,今天一般被视为反猜测倾向的特征。贴近现实性的倾向导致亚里士多德与现代物理学截然相对的概念模式,出奇的是,这一倾向还导致亚里士多德"经验主义"的对立面。

如上所见,亚里士多德概念表现出直接参照特定历史现实的趋势以及参照时间现实过程的趋势。现代物理学没有这样的趋势。一个过程只发生一次,在历史进程中常常重复或必然重复,这是亚里士多德极其重要的概念,但这一概念与现代物理学的大多数基本问题没有丝毫的关系。①现代物理学认为,这是偶然的现象,或纯历史的现象。

比如,自由落体定律并不强调物体频繁下落;亦不强调适用于自由落体公式 $s=1/2gt^2$ 的某一事件,在现实的世界历史中有规律地发生,或经

---

① 只要它和"天地的历史"或地理没有直接关系,它就和现代物理学没有关系。

常发生。至于自由落体定律是很难发生还是经常发生的,那和定律本身没有关系。实际上,在真实的事件进程中,该定律指向的情况从未实现过,或仅仅近似于实现过。只有在实验室里,在人为构建的条件下,近似与该定律相关的事件才发生过。现代物理学的命题常常被视为反猜想的、反经验主义的;和亚里士多德经验主义相比,现代物理学的命题无疑较少经验主义,较多建构主义;亚里士多德的概念直接建基于历史真实性。

第四节　两种思维模式在心理学里的差异

在这里,我们面对着一些实际研究的问题和理论问题,它们对心理学的发展产生了极大的影响,构成了心理学当前危机的基础。

就其内容而言,心理学的重要概念是彻底的亚里士多德学派的主张,不过,在许多方面,其表现形式比较温和。心理学界当前的争鸣和困难很像物理学界战胜亚里士多德思维方式所遭遇的困难。

一、亚里士多德的概念

(一)个案的偶然性

主导亚里士多德物理学概念形成的问题是频率性意义上的规律性,心理学概念的形成亦是如此。这个判断显然见之于心理学对规律性的态度,也见之于它对具体现象的态度。比如,如果你放映一部电影,表现一个儿童在某一事件中的行为,心理学家问你的第一个问题通常是:"所有的儿童都表现出这样的行为吗？这样的行为是常见的吗？"如果你的回答是否定的,那么,心理学家就认为这一行为就完全失去了或几乎完全失去了科学意义。对他而言,注意这种"例外"似乎是毫无科学意义的愚蠢之举。

也许,心理学研究者对具体事件和个体性问题的现实态度更明显地表现在他的行为中,而不是表现在那些理论问题上。对他而言,个体事件似乎是偶然的、不重要的、在科学上是无关紧要的。然而,个体事件也可能是异乎寻常的事件、重要的经验、影响命运的决定性事件,亦可能是一个成就历史人物的事件。在这样的情况下,研究者通常的态度是强调全然个性的和原创性的"神奇",那只能靠"直觉"去理解,至少不能靠科学去理解了。

这两种对具体事件的态度导致相同的结论:凡是不反复发生的事情都难以理解。

(二)规律性即频繁性

当今的心理学看重频繁性,因为这是关乎心理世界是否有规律的问题。和亚里士多德物理学一样,频繁性的地位盖源于物质世界中,与规律类似的不确定性。在此,我们无须赘述心理学规律性主题哲理探讨中的起起伏伏。只需回顾一点:即使在当前,许多形形色色的倾向也把规律的运行局限在心理事件的"低端"范围内。我们认为,更重要的是,心理学领域原则上并不被视为是有规律的;相反,在实际的研究中,即使在实验心理学中,心理学领域的拓展也是一个渐进的过程。心理学突破感知心理的边界,进入意志和情感的领域,缓慢渐进,颇为踟蹰。这不仅是因为技术上有困难,而且主要是因为这样一个事实:在心理学领域里,同一事件的重复并不在期待之中。正如亚里士多德物理学一样,这样的重复性在很大程度上是事件规律性的基础,是其可以被理解的基础。

实际上,任何心理学研究都必须承认,规律性寓于心灵的性质之中,寓于一切心理活动之中,包括那些只发生过一次的心理活动之中;即使不承认这一点,心理学也必须像亚里士多德物理学一样用标准去判断,它是否必须在特定的情况下才出现合乎规律的现象。另外,和亚里士多德物理学一样,心理活动的频繁性就被视为这样一个标准。频繁性证明,重复性和规律性的关系既深厚又有冲击力,甚至被用来界定实验,被视作一种科学工具;只要不和亚里士多德物理学直接抵牾,它至少已成为现代的重要工具。① 连冯特也认为,重复性寓于实验的概念之中。到了近年,心理学才放弃了这一必备的工具,把大片的心理领域挡在实验研究的门外。

然而,除了限制实验研究之外,更耐人寻味的也许是这样一个事实:过高估计重复性的趋势(认为重复性是规律性表达的标准)支配着心理学

---

① 希腊人当然知道实验工具。

概念的构建，这种情况在比较年轻的心理学分支里尤其如此。

正如亚里士多德物理学里发生过的情况一样，当代儿童心理学认为，一组个案共有的现象是一个年龄段的典型特征；情感心理学分析了特定情绪表达的典型特征。亚里士多德这一抽象的类别概念决定着种类的划分，主导着分类的程序。

（三）类别与实质

当代儿童心理学和情感心理学也清楚地证明，亚里士多德习惯性地把抽象界定的类别视为特定对象的本质，将其用来解释儿童的行为。凡是一个年龄段儿童常见的行为总是被视为那个年龄段的基本特征。三岁幼儿常常表现出违拗的行为，于是违拗就被视为其天性，如此，违拗年龄或阶段的概念就被用来解释（虽然不是完全的解释）特定情况下违拗的表现。

与此相似，驱力比如饥饿驱力或母爱本能只不过是一组频繁发生的行为中相同特征的抽象。这一抽象被视为行为的实质，反过来又被用来解释频繁发生的本能行为，比如呵护婴儿的本能行为。对表现、性格和气质的解释常常也与此类似。在这里，正如在能力、才能等基本概念以及智力测验里所用的类似概念一样，当代心理学实际上已经被简约为对亚里士多德术语的解释；很久以来，这种解释被斥为官能心理学和循环解释，但取代这种解释的思维方式尚付阙如。

（四）统计方法

当代心理学观念的分类性及其对频繁性的强调表现为极端重视统计学的方法论。至少就其在心理学里最常见的应用而言，统计方法是这种亚里士多德思维模式最显著的表现。求平均数值的目的是显示一组事实的共同特征。这一平均数需要一个代表性价值，并被用来表征2岁幼儿心理年龄的属性。从表面上看，当代心理学和亚里士多德物理学有些差异，因为当代心理学非常倚重数字和曲线。虽然这一差异比较典型，但它与其说是观念内容的差异，倒不如说是计算技巧的差异。基本上，统计分析是亚里士多德概念的必然结果，它在亚里士多德物理学里是显而易见的，亦如上文所见。由于数学和一般科学方法无与伦比的大发展，当代心理学和亚里士多德物理学的差异是：心理学的统计方法更清晰、更精确。

近年，心理学追求准确和精细的努力指向统计方法的提炼和延伸。只要它们显示充分理解精神生活的决心，付出这样的心血就有道理。至少在一定程度上，心理学基于证明其科学地位的抱负，使其研究方法尽可能使用数学，结果尽可能计算到小数点以后若干位。

这一方法在形式上的延伸并未改变其底层概念：心理学的概念仍然是彻底的亚里士多德概念。实际上，统计方法的数学表达只能是加强和延伸底层概念的主导地位。无疑，这使我们更难看清底层概念的真正性质，难以用其他概念取而代之。这是伽利略物理学难以解决的困难，因为扎根在数学里的是亚里士多德思维模式，而亚里士多德思维模式还受到数学的遮蔽。

（五）知识的有限，例外

据信，合乎规律性（lawfulness）与规律性（regularity）相关，而且被认为是个案的两个对立面（用当前流行的公式来表现，合乎规律性接近于这样公式：$r = \pm 1$）。只要赞同心理学命题的有效性，心理学家就只能认为，这些命题通常是有效的。他们接受其有效性的形式是：意识到简单规律性和充分规律性的差异，把规律性归之于生物学命题尤其心理学命题。否则，合乎规律性只能被视为规律性的极端表现。[①] 在那样的情况下，两者的一切差异原则上都消失殆尽，判断规律性的需要被保留下来了。

个性被视为合乎规律性的反义词，这对实际的研究工作产生了两种影响。首先，这意味着研究工作的局限性。所以，尝试理解一种情绪真实而独特的轨迹、试图理解某人个性的现实结构，看来是毫无希望的。因此，人只能以平均的方法来应对诸如此类的问题，测试和问卷调查就用的是这样的方法。凡认为这类方法不科学的人都遭遇了令人生厌的怀疑主

---

① 众所周知，在物理学的探讨中，可能例外的概念、规律统计有效性的概念又复活了。即使这个观点最终被采纳，也不意味着回归亚里士多德的概念。指出一点足矣：即使出现了这样的回归，那也不可能根据规律性的程度在物质世界里分离出一类事件；整个物质世界只受制于一个统计学合法性。关于统计学观点与精确测量的关系，见 Lewin, *Gesetz and Experiment in der Psychologie*, Weltkreisverlag, Berlin, 1927。

义的质疑,否则,他对心理学里个性和原理的理解只能是很肤浅的;如此,如果有足够多的相似个案重现的可能性被排除,那么就不可能求得科学的解释,就需要求助于直觉。在这两种情况下,心理学领域都远离了实验研究,因为质的属性被视为规律性的对立面。在实验心理学的讨论中,这个观点不断地、反复地被提出来,这样的情况酷似伽利略物理学不得不苦苦申论的主张。彼时,伽利略物理学拷问,怎么可能用一条运动定律来统揽性质不同的现象,比如星体的运动、树叶在风中的飞扬、鸟儿的飞翔、石头在山坡上的滚动呢?但规律和个案的对立与亚里士多德物理学的概念非常吻合,也符合日常生活哲理的原始思维方式,这些都存在于物理学家的著作里——不是在他们的物理学著作里,而是在他们的哲学著作里。①

由于知识有限和确信不可能完全理解个案的思想暗示,研究条件可以适当宽松:可以满足于提出单纯的规律性。心理学对命题严格性的要求是"大体上的""平均的"或"一般的"有效性。据说,既然生命过程是"复杂的"和"短暂的",如果要求心理学研究完全有效,且没有例外,那岂不荒唐?古谚云,"例外反证规则",只要频发性不是太高,心理学并不认为例外是反论据。

心理学对合乎规律性的态度还清晰而突出地显示出亚里士多德思维模式的特征。这一态度的基础是对心理事件合乎规律性乏善可陈的自信,这使得研究者对自己命题的有效性要求不高,或使之不证明命题的有效性。

(六)历史—地理概念

合乎规律性的观点、对重复的强调和刚才提及的动机是亚里士多德物理学的特征;对这样的观点和动机而言,历史—地理意义上的实际参照至关重要。这样的参照证明,这些思维方式关系密切;与此相似,当代的心理学很大程度上也直接参照历史—地理数据,研究也是由这样的参照主导的。但心理概念的历史倾向并非总是一目了然的,历史倾向常常与

---

① 为免误解,我们必须强调:我们批评心理学习惯将个案和规律对立,并不等于说,我们没有意识到个性概念的复杂性。

非历史的、系统的概念纠缠不清、难以区分。我认为,这种准历史的特定形式是理解和批评概念这种模式如何形成的原因。

我们批评了统计学思维模式,其公式对我们在这里讨论的问题并非至关重要。我们批评的目的不是搞算术,不是加法和除法。无疑,未来的心理学还要继续广泛运用这样的运算。关键问题不在于应用统计方法,而是在于如何应用统计方法,是什么样的个案结合成群组。

当代心理学参照历史—地理数据,其结论依靠频发性,这一倾向引人注目。实际上,就直接参照历史数据而言,1～3岁幼儿的天性的结论就是靠统计平均数得出的,刚好与培根洛克在"白板说"中严格搜集的个案相吻合。诚然,这样的平均数对一些非历史概念作了让步:明显的病理个案、处于异常环境的个案被排除在外。除了这样的考虑之外,对于极端反常的个案纳入哪个统计组别进行计算,基本上是依据历史—地理因素决定的。用历史—地理因素界定组别时,比如界定1928年在美国纽约和越南1岁儿童这个年龄组时,平均值的计算对史学家和务实的学人无疑是极其重要的。但平均值与特定历史—地理条件下所发生的事情相关联,研究者还可能继续研究德国、欧洲、世界各地儿童的平均值,或者研究10年期的平均值,而不是1年的平均值。历史—地理基础面的拓宽并不放弃历史—地理对具体个案频发性的依赖,个案是在历史—地理界定的场域里发生的。

我们还应该提及统计数字提炼的问题,数字提炼的基础是对历史—地理因素的限制,在第一次世界大战后的几年里,对德国柏林贫民区1岁婴儿的研究可为一例。这样的分组通常基于个案的个性,又基于历史—地理的界定因素。如果连这些限定性因素也和基于频发性之上的统计学相矛盾,也就意味着在方法论上向具体细节的迁移。顺便指出,切不可忘记,即使在极端精细化的个案中,比如在独生子的统计研究中,实际的界定仍然是依靠历史—地理因素,至多是参考了社会学的范畴。换言之,按照组合分类的标准,被纳入同一组的个案有可能是迥然不同的,甚至有可能是决然对立的。

直接参照历史真情是亚里士多德概念形成的典型特征;在讨论实验

的或真实的条件时,这样的直接参照也是显而易见的。当然,你可以批评简单反应的实验,可以批评研究意志的实验心理学起步时的举措,还可以批评反射学实验,理由是它们与实际生活情况相去甚远。产生这样的距离在很大程度上是基于这样的研究倾向:研究的过程不被视为个案的个体特征,相反,这些"简单元素"(也许是最简单的运动)是一切行为共同的元素,或一切事物共同的元素。与此相对,有些心理学研究比如意志研究则要求贴近现实生活。这就是说,心理学不应该只研究用实验生成的情况,因为最重要的生活决策是难以用实验来研究的。

在这里,我们又遭遇到偏重历史意义的倾向。如果把这个要求迁移到物理学里,其可能意味着:在实验室里研究流体力学是错误的,研究对象应该是大江大河。如此,两个问题就凸现出来:(1)在理论和规律领域,高估历史因素的重要性、轻视一般的因素;(2)在实验领域,挑选频繁发生的过程(或对大多数事件相同的过程)。两种倾向都显示了亚里士多德方法论混淆了历史问题和系统问题,搞乱了历史类别和系统类别与抽象类别的关系,从而忽视了对具体个案真实情况的充分展示。

二、伽利略概念的形成

上文简略描绘了亚里士多德概念的形成。如今的心理学里出现了一个显而易见的形势:有时激进,或比较激进,但通常以细碎的半步前进,有时则陷入谬误(尤其在它亦步亦趋地追随物理学案例的时候)。然而总体上,这一势头似乎正向着适当修正的方向前进,这个势头显而易见、势不可挡,最终会完成从亚里士多德概念表述向伽利略概念表述的过渡。

(一)无价值概念,无二分术语,场域的统一

为伽利略物理学铺平道路的最重要的环境条件见之于当代心理学,这一走势清晰而明确。

在这个过程中,以心理现象为基础而不是以心理过程的性质为基础的方法败下阵来,评价性、拟人式的分类法失败了,但并没有完全彻底地失败。在许多领域尤其在感知心理学中,至少最困难的时刻已经过去了。

和物理学一样,心理学也处在一个过渡期:事件和客体被分为成对的对立面和类似的逻辑二分对子这种理论正在消退,取而代之的是容许连

续变异的成系列的概念。这种改变的部分原因是积累了更多的经验,过渡期存在的认识也是这一转折的原因之一。

在这一转折中,取得最大成就的领域是感知心理学领域,尤其是心理光学和心理声学;近年,嗅觉领域的研究也卓有成效。变革的趋势还见于其他领域,比如情感领域的研究。

弗洛伊德的学说贡献良多,最大的贡献之一是关于常态和病态、正常和异常界线的消弭,这使得心理学各领域进一步的均质化得以实现。虽然这一变革远未完结,但它堪比现代物理学里天地运行过程统一的变革。

另外,在儿童心理学和动物心理学中,二者必选其一的方式正在逐渐消失:儿童被视为小大人或动物即低劣人的观点正在退场,换言之,试图确立儿童与成人、动物与人类难以弥合鸿沟的倾向正在消失。这种均质化倾向在一切领域都越来越清晰;这不是在纯哲学概念上坚持某种抽象的基本统一性,均质化影响着具体的差异充分得到保留的研究。

(二)心理律无条件的普遍有效性

从类别概念到系列概念的过渡是均质化的表现,此外,最清楚、最重要的均质化表现是,具体心理律的有效性不再局限于具体的领域。过去,心理律曾被局限于表现正常的成年人,其理由是,精神变态者或天才人物可能什么事情都干得出来,心理律不适合于表现他们的异常行为。如今,人们逐渐认识到,每一条心理律都有效,无一例外。

就实际内容而言,无例外的、合乎规律性的过渡有这样的含义:出现了整个领域终极的、无所不包的均质化与协调化的走向。均质化与协调化赋予伽利略物理学令人神往的无限广阔性;和抽象的类别概念不同,均质化与协调化并不能铲平世界的丰富多样性,使一条定律适用于整个世界。

均质化建基于心理律无例外有效性的概念。均质化的走势在心理学领域明朗化是近年的事情,但这样的走势开辟了非常广阔的视野。①

结构规律研究、尤其对整体的实验研究证明,统一的心理律不仅在心理光学的领域里有效,而且总体上在听觉心理学和感知心理学领域也有效。这一研究本身就是迈向同质性的一大步。

再者,光学数据规律和智能洞见规律被证明是密切相关的。实验研究发现了行为整体、意志过程和心理需求的重要规律。在记忆和表达领域,心理学也有类似的研究。总之,心理律普遍有效性在主题方面变得非常具体了,心理律普遍有效性适用于表面上迥然不同的领域,所以,心理生活同质性的主题与其定律的关系活力大增,正在破除老死不相往来的领域的边界。②

(三)高扬的抱负

从方法论来看,心理律普遍有效性也有深远的意义。对证据的要求也随之大大增加,以轻慢的态度对待例外再也行不通了。例外绝不能"证明规则",相反,例外是完全有效的反证。即使很少有例外,但只有一个例外也可以斥为反证。普遍有效性的主题在整个心理学领域都是适用的,

---

① 联想心理学就有瞄准这样的均质化的尝试,并已经在这个方向作出了重要的贡献。同理,当代的反射学和行为学对人与动物、身体和心灵的均质化作出了贡献。但亚里士多德合乎规律性即规律性的观点(没有这一观点,联想律就得不到支持),一无所成。因此,在19世纪末,实验联想心理学试图从一条单一的规律演绎出全部心理生活领域,展现出循环、抽象的特征,这一特征是学科发展早期阶段猜测性的典型特征,亦是亚里士多德类别概念的典型特征。

实际上,由于频率和重复对亚里士多德的方法论概念极其重要,联想律旨在将频率和重复用作心理原理的实际内容,因为频繁的重复被视为心理现象最重要的动因。

② 这一节尤其需要注意的参考文献是:M. Wertheimer, Untersuchungen zur Lehre von der Gestalt, II, *Psychol. Forsch.*, 1923, 4, 301—350, W. Köhler, *Gestalt Psychology*, Liveright, New York, 1929. K. Koffka, *The Growth of the Mind: An Introduction to Child Psychology*(trans, by R. M. Ogden), Harcourt, Brace, New York; Kegan Paul, London, 1924, (2d ed., 1928), and Lewin, *Vorsatz Wille und Bedurfnis, mit Vorbemerkungen uber die psychischen Krafle und Energien und die Struktur der Seele*, Springer, Berlin, 1926. 各种研究的文献述要见 W. Kohler, Gestaltprobleme und Anfänge einer Gestalttheorie, *Jahresber. d. ges. Physiol.*, 1924。

无论是在儿童心理学或成人心理学,还是在常态心理学或病态心理学,这个主题都是适用的。

另一方面,心理律普遍有效性的主题使人在研究尤其实验中注意那些不经常以相同形式重现的心理过程,比如情感心理过程。

(四)从平均情况到单纯的个案

对心理律普遍有效性主题的理解尚未成为学习心理学的习惯。实际上,从较早前亚里士多德的观点看,这个新的方法论似乎掩盖了上文提及的基本矛盾。一方面,人们宣示,他们想要在更高层次上充分理解具体的现实,另一方面,他们又认为,实际历史进程和特定地理背景中的现实情况确实是偶然出现的。比如,斜面上物体的滚动律不是靠尽可能多地滚石下山并求其平均数确立的,这样的观察并不被视为最可能出现的情况。① 相反,这一观察的基础是:一个理想圆球在绝对平直和硬质的平面上无摩擦滚动。即使在实验室里,那样的过程也只能接近现实,在日常生活里是不可能出现的。人们声称——人们竭力求证规律是普遍有效的和具体的,但人们使用的方法是上一个时代使用的方法,它不顾历史事实,全靠个别偶然的情况,实际上全靠最明显的例外。

这样的研究程序使人觉得,当代心理学的亚里士多德观点是双重的悖论,这个研究程序是如何达成的?如果你设想合乎规律性广度的变化,并设想所引起的必然的方法论后果,这个问题就容易看清了。当合乎规律性不再局限于频繁发生的案例,而是指每一个物理事件的特征时,就没有必要再用特别的标准,比如发生的频率来证明其合乎规律性了。即使具体的案例也会被视为合乎规律性的。历史上的罕见性不是合乎规律性的反证,历史上的常见性也不是合乎规律的例证。这是因为合乎规律的概念远离了经常性;规则无例外的观念与历史常恒性(亚里士多德所说的

---

① 心理学常特别强调,也许在婴儿测试的构建中,我们能获得"一般人"心理的表征,因为日常生活中儿童更多、更频繁的心理活动过程被选中了。如此,你就能指望,儿童自然会在测试中展示出类似的行为,而且这样的或然率是很高的。

"永久")严格区别开来了。①

第五节 动力论

一、物理学基本动力概念的变化

物理学的动力论问题不仅见于亚里士多德的思维模式。相反,对伽利略物理学而言,动力论问题始终都意义重大,我们能把动力论视为伽利略思维模式的典型后果。② 伽利略思维模式不仅能引起表层的兴趣转移,而且产生了理论内容的变革。和前人相比,亚里士多德还强调"生成"(becoming)。也许更正确的说法是,在亚里士多德的概念里,统计学和动力论尚未分家,这特别要归因于一些基本的设想。

二、目的论与物理矢量

我们今天觉得,亚里士多德动力论的一个主要特征是,它赖以解释事件的概念是生物学和生理学概念:只要不受其他物体阻挡,每个物体都趋于完美,都趋于实现自己的本质。如上文所见,亚里士多德认为,这一本质是同类物体的共性。于是,对他而言,类别既是客体的概念,又是其想要达到的目的。

这一物理事件的目的论不仅显示了,生物学和物理学尚未分离。它还显示了,亚里士多德物理学的动力论在某些方面类似万物有灵论和原始人的思维模式。原始人的思维模式把一切运动视为生命,把人工制造物当作生存的原型。这是因为在人工制造物身上,制造人对这个物体的

---

① 亚里士多德合乎规律性的观点和伽利略合乎规律性的观点的对比,以及两者方法的差异,可用下表显示:

	亚里士多德	伽利略

(1) 经常的是
   经常的是
   个案的是
	合乎规律的
	合乎规律的
	偶然的
		合乎规律的
		合乎规律的
		合乎规律的

(2) 合乎规律性的标准是	经常的、频繁的	非必需的
(3) 历史案例常见的现象是	事物本然性的表现	偶然的,仅仅由历史条件决定

② See E. MACH, *The Science of Mechanics* (Eng. trans., 2d ed., rev.), Chicago, 1902.

理念在一定程度上既是事件的原因,也是事件的目的。

再者,对亚里士多德概念而言,物理事件的原因和心理的"驱力"密切相关:物体达到一个目的,就运动而言,它就趋于逼近它本性的地方。如此,沉重的物体向下降——越重的物体势能越大;轻盈的物体向上扬。

人们常习惯性地贬斥这些亚里士多德的物理概念,说它们是拟人式的。然而,正是这些基本的动力论理念在具体的心理学和生物学中占主导地位,考虑到这一事实,更好的态度也许是:尽可能考察亚里士多德论题的实际内容,而不管其表达方式。

人们常习惯性地说,目的论假设了事件向目标运动的方向,而因果论解释并不承认这一趋向;人们又习惯性地认为,这是目的论解释和因果论解释最重要的差异。但这种观点并不正确,因为现代物理学的因果论解释使用定向量,即数学描绘的矢量。物理力被定义为"物理变化的原因",被视为定向的矢量因素。矢量因素被用作动力论的基础,在这一点上,现代观点和亚里士多德的观点没有区别。

真正的区别在于,在亚里士多德动力论里,物体矢量的类别和方向预先由物体的性质所决定。与之相反,在现代物理学里,物理矢量的存在总是取决于几种物理事实的相互关系,尤其取决于客体与环境的关系。①

三、亚里士多德和伽利略动力论的意义

就亚里士多德概念而言,环境起一定的作用,环境会被扰动,扰动会修正运动过程,而运动过程是由物体的性质决定的。物体运动的矢量完全由该物体决定。换言之,物体运动的矢量不取决于它和环境的关系,它们与该物体捆绑在一起,一劳永逸,和任何给定时间的环境都没有关系。轻盈物体上扬的趋势寓于物体本身;沉重物体下沉的倾向也定在物体本身。现代物理学的概念相反,它认为,轻盈物体上扬的趋势不仅源自它与环境的关系,而且,其重量本身还取决于它与环境的关系。

这个革命性的标志清楚地表现在伽利略对自由落体的经典研究中。他没有研究自由落体的重物本身,其研究的是物体在"在斜面上的自由下

---

① 自然,这一规律也适用于内部关系,涉及物理系统各部分的相互关系。

落或运动"。这标示了一种观念转变:概念只能靠参照情景来界定。这里的情景是:有一定倾斜度平面的存在,或一个无障碍的垂直下落空间。自由落体下落速度太快,不可能进行令人满意的观察;用斜面上较慢的运动研究自由落体的思想有这样一个预设:事情的动态关系不再与孤立的物体相关,而是取决于事情发生时的总体情况。

实际上,伽利略的研究方法包含了情境因素的精细研究,穿透力很强。斜面的坡度、高与宽之比有明确界定。情境因素清楚罗列(自由落体、斜面运动和水平面运动),予以穷尽,坡度分门别类。事件的基本特征(如速度)依靠情景的基本属性(平面的斜坡),这些因素成为重要的概念和方法论核心。

动力论观点并不意味着,物体的性质微不足道。对动力论而言,物体的属性和结构始终非常重要,但情景比物体的性质重要得多。总体情况包含物体的性质和情景,凭借具象的总体情况,决定事件动态关系的矢量才得以界定。

为了贯彻这一观点,伽利略物理学尽可能具体而精确地描绘总体情况的特殊性,这就把亚里士多德的原理颠倒过来了。亚里士多德思维模式是寻求许多个案的相似性,借以确定普遍性。对其而言,事件对情景的依靠比干扰的力量更重要。变化中的情景是偶然因素,扰乱并遮蔽着事物的根本性质。因此,为了理解物体的性质和目标的方向,以便进行有效的工作,就要尽可能排除情景的影响并对情境进行抽象,这也成了习惯的程序。

四、摆脱历史倾向

对这种矢量的实际研究显然有一个预设:过程涉及某种规律性或频繁性。否则,情境差异的排除将排除相似性。如果从亚里士多德动力论的基本观点出发,过程动态的研究会更加困难——你可以设想以心理学里的情感为例,过程动态的研究会更倚重相关情景的性质。于是,单一事件在原则上就不合乎规律性了,因为我们没有办法研究单一事件的动态关系。

决定过程动态的伽利略方法与这种亚里士多德的研究方法截然相

对。既然过程的动态不仅取决于物体，更首先取决于情景，那么，试图求得过程的一般规律岂不荒唐？（因为亚里士多德的研究方法尽量排除情景的影响。）既引入尽可能多的情景，又认为在一切和任何情景下都看到的因素才具有普遍的有效性，那岂不愚蠢？相反，领悟其总体情况，尽可能把握其全部特征就至关重要了。

从具体个案到规律，从"这一"事件到"这类"事件，就不再需要亚里士多德思维模式典型的历史规律性。由于物理事件无例外合乎规律性的原理，迈向"普遍性"这一步自然而然就立即完成了。① 对动力论研究，重要的问题不是从情景中去抽象，而是搜寻总体独立结构里决定性因素的各种情景。不参照尽可能多的历史个案的抽象平均值，而是参照具体情境中充分展现的具体情况。

在这里，我们不可能详细检视，为何并非一切情景对动态关系的研究都有同等作用，为何有些情景具有方法论的优势，为何这些优势的方法论用实验手段来设计。只有一种情况需要详细阐述，人们似乎很难正确看待它，它造成了许多误解，而这些误解又给心理学造成了严重的后果。

如上所见，伽利略的概念把以前未分化的问题分离开来：一方面是事件的历史进程，另一方面是事件的规律性。伽利略的概念在研究系统问题时放弃了对历史—地理数据的直接参照。乍一看，这样确立的研究程序与充分理解显示的经验主义倾向矛盾，但实际上却没有矛盾。我们刚才探讨的问题就清晰地显示出，这里没有矛盾：亚里士多德直指历史常例及其平均值，实际上放弃了具体的、情景决定的事件。当这样的直接参照完全被弃之不顾时，当历史—地理的常恒性被情景里的具体事件的地位取而代之时，换言之，无论当情景频繁而恒久，抑或罕见而短暂（如实验方法里那样），我们都有可能去承担理解真实的、终极独特的事件的任务。

五、过程微分的意义

从方法论来看，这里会产生一个理论上的困难，这个困难最好用实例

---

① 这里不可能展开讨论归纳法问题。(Cf. Lewin, *Gesetz and Experiment in der Psychologie*.)

来解释，而不是用泛泛的讨论来阐述。为了把基本要素表述得更加明白，这个例子没有取自广为人知的物理学，而取自问题尚多的心理学。如果你把儿童的行为归之于心理场力量——为何进行这样的追溯并不是这里探讨的主题，很可能会引起异议。儿童面对两个诱人的物体(如玩具 T 和巧克力 C)，而两个物体又在不同的地方(见图 1-1)。根据这一假设，那么存在两个方向的场力(a 和 b)。两者的比例关系不重要，力的平行四边形的物理定律是否适用于心理场的力量也不重要。在这里，两种力作用的结果是合力，合力必然走向 r，而不是 T 或 C。①

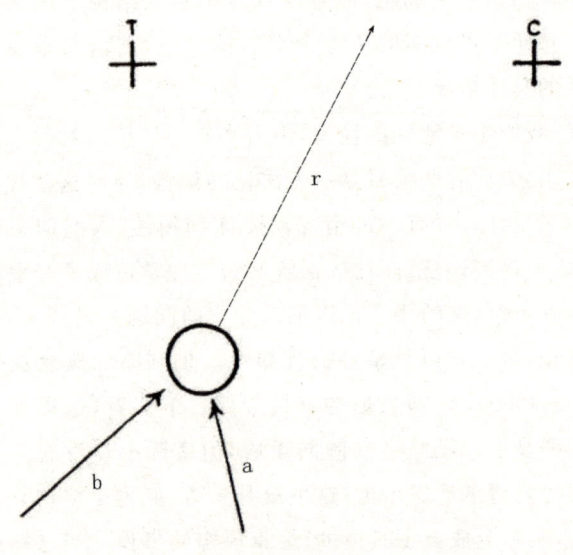

图 1-1

实际上，这样下结论未免太匆忙，因为即使矢量是起初的方向，那也不等于说，实际的过程永远维持那个方向 r。相反，总体情况随着过程而变化，其力度和方向都在变，每一刻的多个矢量决定着动态关系。即使你假设，存在着力的平行四边形，且儿童内在情境维持不变，但由于总体情况

---

① 我这里忽略了一种可能性：其中一种力完全消失。

的变化,实际的过程总是会把儿童引向其中一个诱人的物体(图1-2)。①

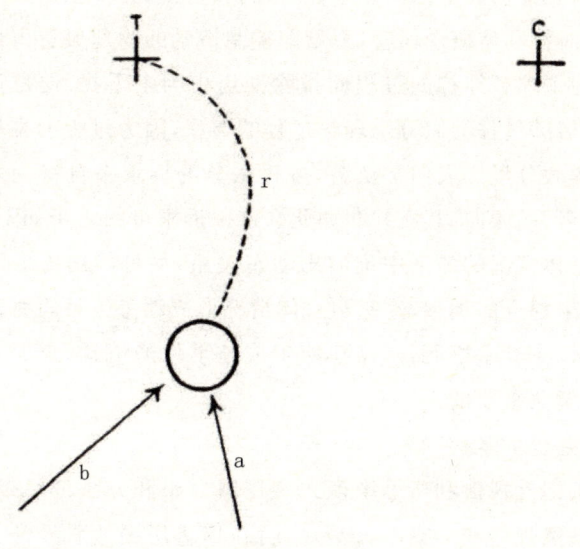

图 1-2

我想用这个例子显示:如果你试图用实际的事件演绎过程的动态,尤其是从决定过程的矢量去演绎,你就不得不诉诸过程的微分。在这个例子里,你只能把过程初始的那一刻视为情景初始矢量的表达,而不能把全过程视为这一矢量的表达。

众所周知,一切物理律或至少大多数物理律都是微分律(differential laws)。人们常想,这似乎证明,物理学试图把一切都变成最小的"元素"来进行分析,并将其视为最完美的分析,我则不以为然。这个想法源自伽利略以降物理学的境况:一个过程的历史进程不被视为决定动态关系的矢量的直接表达。对亚里士多德而言,运动显示了整个运动过程的某种趋势,比如完美圆环运动的趋势。相反,即使在一个具体的过程中,伽利

---

① 即使两个诱人物体的距离相等,吸引力也相等,但由于平衡的不稳定性,冲突情景会产生同样的结果。

略的概念也把准历史因素和决定动态关系的因素区别开来。伽利略物理学概念指向总体情况中的具体个性,指向每一刻的具体情况。

再者,对伽利略概念而言,力量即控制情景的物理矢量由最终的结果来证明。为了求解纯粹的过程而排除准历史因素干扰,便是正当的。因此,有必要借助过程的微分来理解过程的类型,因为过程的类型表现在不混杂的过程微分里。人们常认为,过程微分的诉求来自将一切事件化解为"终极元素"的倾向,其实并非如此。这一诉求可归之于如下倾向:从具体情况和总体情况的关系中推演出动态关系,尽可能用历史因素判定事件纯粹的、未混合的类型,这是与总体情况形成动态关系的类型。

再次,以实验手段而言,构建能生成纯事件的情景,至少要容许重建概念,这是至关重要的。

六、方法论的意义

更仔细地检视伽利略思维模式之逻辑后果和方法论后果,尚待进一步展开。既然规律和个案不再是对立面,倚重历史地看异常、罕见、短暂的事件,将其视为证据的干扰就不复存在了,大多数物理实验就不会成为障碍。即使并非为了展示鲜为人知的个案,用系统概念展示这样的个案也给人启示,其原因就在于障碍不复存在。

尽可能充分而具体地理解实际情景甚至其个性特征的倾向,使可能最精确的质和量的确定成为必需和有益的。但不要忘记,赋予精确性重要意义的正是理解实际情景的任务,而不是为精确而精确。

有两种最基本的定量知识表征模式和广义的数学表征模式:(1)用连续性过渡而不是用二分法描绘知识,从而使描绘大大细化;(2)凭借这些功能性概念,从具体到一般,同时又不失去一般中的具体,因而使一般回到具体成为不可能。

最后应提及的是描绘客体和情景的近似法,在这里,连续性的官能思维模式是显而易见的。

七、心理学的基本动力论概念

今天,心理学的动力论概念仍然是彻头彻尾的亚里士多德思维模式。① 实际上,我觉得,当代心理学的内在关系和动机都展现出亚里士多德的思维模式,甚至到每一个细部亦是如此。

八、亚里士多德的思想:不依附情景;本能

就其内容而言,心理学动力论很容易展示,几乎是不需要揭示的。在这一点上,心理学动力论与亚里士多德概念吻合:这是亚里士多德意义上的目的论。传统的错误是把随意性的解释当作恰当的解释,不借助其指向明确的力量;显而易见,这是迟滞了的动力论的进步,这是因为如果不像物理动力论那样借助矢量概念,心理动力论是难以理解的。赋予心理动力论亚里士多德性质的,不是其中所用的定向的量,而是将研究过程归之于和研究对象相关的矢量,比如和具体的人相关的矢量,以及相对独立于情景的矢量。

也许,经典的本能概念是最突出的一例。本能据信是必须归之于一个人的预设条件所决定的矢量。基本上,本能是这样决定的:发现一个人或一群相似的人在实际生活中频繁发生的行为。这些行为(如迷失、争斗、互助等)的共同特征被视为行为过程的基本性质。而且,在亚里士多德的意义上,这些抽象的类别概念既被视为行为的目标,也被视为过程的原因。实际上,如此求得的本能是历史现实的平均值;类别概念越抽象,本能概念就越重要,平均值的实例就越多。唯有这样看问题,具体个案和具体情景里的"偶然"才能被克服。这是因为主导心理学领域研究目的之根基依然是:心理学试图摆脱与具体情景的关联。

九、亚里士多德思维定势固有的困难与无规律性

从严格的伽利略规律概念来看,一旦明白本能与个人紧密而牢固的关系以及随之而来的结果,亚里士多德思维模式和伽利略思维模式的差异就一清二楚了。如此,本能(如母亲本能)必然不断起作用,不会中断,

---

① 顺便指出,今天的生物学也深受亚里士多德的影响;虽然我认为心理学总体上是生物学领域的一部分,但我在此不能细致考察生物学对心理学的影响。

就像伽利略式的心理学把违拗说成是三岁幼儿的"天性"那样,其结论是:所有的三岁幼儿都违拗,而且一天 24 小时都违拗。

总体上,心理学的亚里士多德定势能规避这样的结果。即使为了解释矢量存在的证据,并用矢量来解释行为,心理学也可以满足于倚重规律的概念。如此,亚里士多德定势就可以不必假设矢量存在于每一种情境中。根据严格的规律概念,如果证明本能在具体的个案中不存在,就可以反驳本能存在的假设。亚里士多德概念不惧怕这样的反证,单纯凭借对统计数字有效性的倚重,它们就能回答有关具体个案的问题。

当然,亚里士多德概念并不能解释具体个案的发生,这里所谓个案不是指抽象界定的"一般儿童"的行为,而是指某个儿童某时的行为。

如此,心理学动力论的亚里士多德倾向有两重含义:对频繁发生、足以在情境中进行抽象的个案进行解释时,倾向有一定的局限;这一倾向意味着任何个案、甚至频繁发生的事件都存在着任何的可能性。

十、自我矫正的尝试:一般的情况

亚里士多德思维模式动力论遭遇到的固有困难,可能会危及该理论的解释价值,因为它排除情景。这些困难常见于当代心理学中,最终将导致最独特的杂交方法,从而进行以某种方式去纳入情景概念的尝试。这一趋势清楚地见于定量测定的尝试。试举一例,用实验手段测定小白鼠驱力(饥饿、干渴、性欲和母爱)的力量,以比较各种驱力;如果提出这样的问题有意义(相当于物理学里问:重力和电力,哪一个更大),那就必须有一个前提:这些矢量全都归之于小白鼠,而且完全独立于具体的情景之外,不依靠小白鼠的状态,与环境无关。当然,这样的固化关系说到底是不可能求得的,我们不得不至少在一定程度上放弃这种思维方式。如此,朝这个方向迈出的第一步就是考虑小白鼠在那一刻驱力的状况,即小白鼠餍足的程度;测定其驱力的强度,比较不同驱力的最大值。

当然,这样的测算只能使亚里士多德式的态度略有改善。曲线表现了大批个案统计的平均值,但这样的平均值对个案并没有束缚力。最重要的是,这种思维模式应用矢量时并不考虑情景的结构。

当然,无可否认的是,在实验个案中,决定小白鼠本能行为的是情景,但论及这些行为时,正如实验观察婴儿的自发行为一样,实验所追求的规律仅限于行为的平均值。因此,规律仅适用于平均的情景。但我们在实验中忘记了,世上根本就没有所谓"平均的情况",就像根本就无所谓"平均的儿童"一样。

实际上但并非原则上,比所谓"最佳"情景略进一步。即使到了这一步,情景的具体结构仍然是不确定的:仅仅达到了某一个方向结果的最大值。

然而,在这些概念里,亚里士多德思维模式的两个基本缺陷并没有被消除:(1)决定过程动态的矢量仍然归之于孤立的个体,不考虑总体的情况;(2)对心理学原理有效性的要求很低,对理解个体过程的实际情况的要求也很低。

连与情景意义直接相关的概念也不是很明朗。已如上述,讨论情景时的核心问题是,就亚里士多德思维模式的意义而言,情景在多大程度上起妨碍或促进作用。情景甚至被视为一种常恒的客体,讨论的问题是:哪一个更重要:遗传还是环境? 在这里,问题的基础同样是抽象得来的情景概念,本来要处理一个动态问题,处理的办法却只是统计所得的历史意义。围绕遗传还是环境的讨论显示,即使在具体问题上,这些概念也使客体和情景彻底分离,只从孤立的客体本身演绎动态关系。

参照绘画的演变,上述概念里情景的作用就能清楚地得到展现。在中世纪的画作里,早期作品一般是没有环境的,只有一个空洞的背景(常为金黄色)。即使在画作中环境逐渐出现以后,通常也只在环境中表现主角之外的几个人或物;画作最多只能说是几个人的集合,每个人实际上有独立的存在。

稍后,画作里才出现了空间,才成为一个总体的情景。与此同时,情景总体上占支配地位,各部分独立且维持其个性(伦勃朗那种极端),但只能位于总体情境中,并通过总体情境来获得各自的地位。

十一、伽利略思维模式的滥觞

种种迹象表明,与上述亚里士多德动力论概念相对的一种伽利略式的思维模式初露端倪。在这个方面,感知心理学走在最前面。

起初,即使在感知心理学里,解释也指向孤立的感知甚至孤立的感知要素。近年来它的发展带来了基本动力论理念的一场革命,这场革命初期发展缓慢,稍后的变化则比较急剧:它显示,心理过程不能从单个的感知要素去演绎,只能从感知的总体结构上去推衍。只考虑一幅画的要素,并据此界定其意义,那是不可能的。比较准确地说,感知心理过程的整体动态要依靠背景,而且要依靠整个场域的结构。感知的动态关系不能用亚里士多德的抽象方法去理解,那种方法排除了一切偶发的情况。今天,考虑一切情景的原理正在深入感知心理学的场域;它要在界定分明的环境中去确立一种界定分明的结构。①

近年,基本的动力论思想超越了感知的领域,被用于分析较高级的心理过程,用于研究本能、意志、情感和表达,还被用来研究发生心理学。遗传因素或环境因素循环往复的讨论一无所获,以个人特征为基础去讨论遗传和环境的分割就钻进了死胡同:这两种现象显示,原来的基本设想失之偏颇。一种思维模式逐渐清晰,其概念相当于生物学里的表现型和遗传型概念;判定心理倾向时,它正在尝试不排除环境的影响,而是接受这样一个观点:研究心理倾向时,必须要参照一组具体界定的情景。

如此,在对生物总体行为研究最重要的心理学领域里,向伽利略式的动力论观点的转变必然发生。按照这一理论,动力场的矢量不是来自单个的客体,而是来自具体情境中的各种因素的相互作用,换言之,动力场的矢量基本上来自个人的状态和心理情景的结构。心理过程的动态总是从个人和具体情景的关系中演绎出来的,就内在力量而言,心理过程的动态源自个人内在功能系统的相互关系。

贯彻情景原理的任务刚刚起步,任重道远。我们的任务是:根据个人特征及其相关的功能属性提出一个具体心理情景可行的表征;表征人的心理及其内在动力因素的具体结构。这样的表征是物理情景和心理情景的表征。也许,不借助最年轻的数学分支拓扑学,表征的手法是难以获取的。目前,随着该学科的不断发展,心理动力学进入到了心理学最重要的

---

① See E. RUBIN, *Visuelwahrgenommene Figuren*, Gyldenalske, Copenhagen, 1921.

领域,并维持了亚里士多德的思维模式。然而,比这些技术性问题更重要的也许是总体的实质性和哲理性预设:在心理学规律性问题上缺乏勇气,对心理学原理的有效性要求太低;倾向于纯规律性问题,同时又倾向于具体的历史—地理概念。

如果排除变化中的情景,不进行系统的考虑,历史偶然性问题就不能克服。唯有充分地考虑具体个案的独特性,偶然性问题才能解决。问题的解决端赖以下条件:规律的普遍有效性和个案的具体性不是对立面;参照具体的总体情况,借以取代收集尽可能多的频繁重复的历史个案。换言之,从方法论来看,以个案的重要性、有效性作为重要的证据,不能用其发生的频率来评估。对心理学而言,正如对物理学一样,这是从抽象分类式程序向具体的建构主义方法的转折。

目前,心理学正处在一个过渡期,亚里士多德式概念被伽利略式思维模式取代的时刻,为期不远了。心理研究一个更加外在的问题似乎是这一转折的迹象。

这个迹象是一切学科初期猜想性阶段的典型特征。代表不同系统的学派互相对立的方式和程度尚不为人所知,当代物理学就是一例。当代物理学涌现出不同的假说,却有一个共同的基础,这是猜想性阶段各个学派尚不熟悉的基础。这仅仅是一个外在的迹象,学科领域的概念引入了一种方法,使人逐步接近对该领域的理解。由此而推进物理学不断向前发展,使研究结果的范围逐渐收窄,各种理论分歧的整体结构则更加分明。

我觉得,许多迹象表明,当代心理学虽然学派林立,但学科的转折已初露端倪,正在经历类似物理学的稳步发展,不仅感知心理学在发展,而且心理学的整个领域都在发展。

第二章 论心理结构[①]

第一节 心理事件的动因

迄今为止，实验心理学寻求心理事件动因时注意的关系几乎都是一种非常独特的关系。你不妨用其指称某类客体或过程的黏附力（adhesion）。一些客体相互关联时，一个事件粘连在一起时，就被视为这一个心理事件的动因。

这种关联最显著的例子见于两个心理事件的联想，这就是传统联想理论所指的那种关联。事件 a 和 b 由于过去的邻接性而进入联想的关系。经验 a 发生时，经验 b 随即产生，据认为，这种联想现象就是两种经验因果关系的原因。

有时，经验并不被视为联想的原因，人们未必认为，有些力量比如决定性倾向[②]或自然黏着力要服从于联想律；[③]即使这样，一种基本的联想

---

① 关于"mind"（心理）的用法，见英译者序。
② See N. ACH, *Über den Willensakt und das Temperament*, Quelle u. Meyer, Leipzig, 1910.
③ See G. E. MÜLLER, *Komplextheorie und Gestalttheorie*, Vanderhoeck u. Ruprecht, Göttingen, 1923.

还是被保留下来了:刺激拥有与某种反应关联的附着力。

在心理学里,这种耦合现象多半机械地被视为僵化的关联,也就是刺激与积习反应的联想。与之对立的一种思想初露端倪:通常,我们不必应对明显的碎片或元素,而是应对时间上延展的整体(比如曲调的类型),时刻或时段只能用整体来解释。近年出现了对格式塔理论基本思想的误解,令人遗憾。这一误解大概可以表述为:过程 b 的原因不要被放进它与此前事件 a 严格的耦合关系里去看。正确的表述是,如果 a 构成更大整体里的一个独立时刻,a 就与那个整体偕行。因此,被视为事件"原因"的不是成分对成分的链式反应的耦合,而是部分与整体的关系。①

对习惯(联想)的实验研究证明,习惯造成的耦合绝不是心理事件的动机。② 如果习惯和实践形成的过程不是被视为零碎联想的形成过程,而是被视为特定行为统一体重新构建的过程,那也是误解。正确的表述是,无论心理事件是如何发生的,心理能量总是心理事件发生的必要条件;所谓心理能量就是紧张的心理系统;一般来说,心理系统是在意志或需求压力下衍生出来的。毋庸赘言,这并不意味着,一方面存在心理格式塔完形,另一方面存在无明确定位的心理场所。

有时,由于需求的增加,习惯比如"强制性习惯"可能会产生新的心理能量。有时,习惯能获得以前不曾获得的能量;以瘾君子为例,单一、偶尔的愉悦体验"被纳入重要的需求"③,其人格里更宽广和更深的层面就陷入了毒瘾。

然而,单说"习惯表现出来"(即某些行为的融合、形成和重构)时,原

---

① 如此看来,这样的表述仍然没有提及动态整体里的张力。
② See LEWIN, *Zeitschr. f. Psychol.*, 1917, 77, 212—247; *Psychol. Forsch*, 1922, 1, 191—302; 1922, 2, 65—140. SIGMAR, Über die Hemmung bei der Realisation eines Willensaktes, *Arch f. d. ges. Psychol.*, 1925, 52, 92.
③ E. JOËL and F. FRÄNKEL, Zur Pathologie der Gewöhnung, II in *Theraple der Gegenwart*, 1926, 67, 60. Further *Der Kokainismus*, Springer, Berlin, 1924. Cf also W. MCDOUGALL, *Social Psychology*, Methuen, London, 1908.

则上就不可能将其视为心理事件(任何充分意义上的)的原因了。①

这些命题适用于习惯和联想,但不能推广到每一种耦合。这是因为无论连接采取何形式、如何发生,它们绝不是事件的原因。准确地说,为了让捆绑或耦合复合体即过程发生(同样适合于机器系统),那就必须释放能做功的能量。因此,在探查心理事件时,你必须问,作为动因的能量来自何方。

我们说耦合不能被视为能量的源头,但绝不意味着不存在耦合,也不意味着耦合的存在不重要。虽然耦合不是事件的能量之源,但事件的形式很大程度上取决于耦合。比如,耦合对一些常见行为统一体的重构就发挥着重要的作用。(毫无疑问,如果我们要探索规律,我们就必须放弃统揽一切的习惯,不能把以前发生的一切都纳入"经验"的概念之下。这种囫囵一体的概念毫无意义,我们应该区分不同的现象,因为它们遵循的规律是迥然不同的:丰富或改变知识的储存;学习并执行不同类型的任务;我们应该区分不同性质的现象,这是描绘冲动或需求固化的过程。)

我们在这里用能力的概念,稍后还要用紧张、系统等概念,至于是否应该最终回归物理学力量和能量的概念,这个问题可以非常开放。无论如何,我认为,这些概念是一切动力论通用的基本逻辑概念(可惜逻辑学非常忽视这些概念)。它们不是物理学专属的概念,比如经济学就常用这些概念(虽然迄今阐述得不那么精准),我们不需要这样的假设:经济学必须在一定程度上从物理学演绎而来。

所以,姑且不论心理学是否演绎自物理学的终极问题,因果动力问题

---

① 前人早已述及,除了将联想视为心理事件的原因之外,还要考虑其他因素。在这方面取得进展的实验心理学家首先当推阿赫(N. Arch)和波普尔路特(W. Poppelreuter)。塞尔兹(Selz, O.)展现了非联想力量的意义,并且说,"即使在记忆研究中,现存的决定因素也不能老是被忽略。"迟至20世纪20年代,塞尔兹在应对联想心理学的论战时明确指出,知识复合体的表现"在没有施之于它们的决定因素时,也能出现"。加上其他论述,他似乎毫不含糊地指出,联想作为心理事件的原因,是不容否定的。既然塞尔兹在以上言论和其他类似论断里提出了优先因素的问题,我不想在此深入探讨,只想说,我可以这样理解他的意思:他认为,我的基本论断已被实验所证明。换言之,除了联想之外,心理事件的其他意义也必须得到承认,而且,联想原则上不表现心理事件的动机。

的研究迫使心理学不得不启用动力论的基本概念,虽然使用不像过去那样频繁,但亦不像过去那样暧昧,而是借用其概念表明动力场形成的基本理论。我们可以借鉴物理学的类比,这也并不会伤害分类研究。另外,我们必须随时避免粗枝大叶造成的错误,比如,对场力量一知半解的解读就必须避免;必须时刻牢记,我们研究的是心理场的力量,而不是物理环境的力量。

至于能量的心理源头问题,应该在这里予以简要说明。

许多感知过程中的刺激可以同时被视为感知领域(如视域)能量的源头,一定程度上,这一结论是正确的。然而,在实际行为和情绪中,刺激的物理强度显然不发挥重要的作用,收到电报以后踏上旅途的行为,遇到问题时勃然大怒的情绪都是例子。因此,我们常说"释放",这是借用电火花引爆炸药的类比。

然而,这个结论必须在以下两个方向做一些基本的修正。

1. 感知世界的概念即是感知成分的总和——这一概念必须被放弃。既然如此,感知呈现给我们的就是真实的物件和事件,它们具有明确的意义,所以,对感知刺激(如因伤病变形的面孔)的衡量就必须根据物理强度,而不是根据心理现实了。这种感知经验立即带上了某种目的或需求,这是过去不曾出现的目的或需求。根据目前的研究水平,探讨这样的感知经验能否被视为能量之源,以及在多大程度上被视为能量之源,大概不会有多大的收获。无论如何,重组及重新分层是有可能发生的,相关的能量会这个过程中得到释放;换言之,过去不存在的紧张的心理系统可能会出现,至少以这种形式出现。然而,许多证据表明,心理过程的基本能力并不会从短暂的感知中流淌出来。

2. 无疑,这不等于说,我们在这里要研究的就是像弹药筒爆炸、蒸汽机传动杆"释放"能量那样的意义。

a. 比如,一个儿童想要拿到一块巧克力,如果有一件利器、一条狂犬或其他什么东西挡住了他的道路,他就会改变移动的方向。最简单的情况是,他绕道而行,改到新的方向上前进。简言之,心理场里的全部力量,包括吸引他的巧克力,将控制他移动的方向,决定这个过程的规律是可以详细阐明的。至此,我们只需注意广为人知的、基本的事实:多种力量决定了运动的过程。

过程中力量的大小和能量的多少之间不存在确定不变的关系,这一规律既适用于物理学,也适用于心理学。相反,场域的构成相宜时,相对弱小的力量能控制相对强大的力量。反过来,强大力量的高度紧张状态可以和弱小的力量并行。于是,这些力量在类别和方向上的轻微变化就会把过程引向其他的路径。(这在社会支配技术中起重要作用。)

在每一个过程中,过程本身会改变内外环境的力量。然而,在不同的过程中,控制过程的力量发生的变化可能会有很大的差异,所以,在许多过程中,这一变化对于过程的轨迹影响不大;在其他过程中,这一变化的轨迹则受到很大的影响。

心理学常常不得不研究上述第二种情况,其研究过程属以下类型:感知某客体起步运动的同时改变了其在场域里的位置,改变了控制其行为的场力。这就规定了运动过程的新方向,比如,儿童在遇到障碍后就改变了起初移动的方向。如此,由感知场确定过程航向的问题就出现了。[①]

有时,人的活动不是内源性的,寓于过程的力量相对于场力很弱小时,外在心理环境力量持续控制过程轨迹的情况就会发生。比如,儿童受到多方面的威胁时,他所面对的就是不愉快的处境。如果他不能在冲动之下一走到底,同时又不能在内心隔绝外来的影响,他就会在正诱发力和副诱发力的场地里缓慢地穿行。此时,场力对过程航向的作用就表露无遗了,其作用在运动过程中的每一个细小阶段都彰显出来了。

然而,一般来说,行为过程不能被视为一个连续的流动过程。比较准确地说,其典型的展开方式是连续的小步运动,每一个步子在很大程度上都是一个内源性的整体:儿童奔向巧克力,直至第一个障碍;因气愤而伸

---

① See W. KÖHLER, Gestaltprobleme und Anfänge einer Gestalttheorie, *Jahresbericht d. ges. Physiol.*, 1922—1924, 537 ff. Compare also as a concrete example from tes oculomotor system: K. Lewin and K. Sakuma, Die Sehrichtung monokularer und binokularer Objekte bei Bewegung und das Zustandekommen des Tiefeneffektes, *Psychol Forsch.*, 1925, 6, 339.

手去拿巧克力,却停下来;他绕过障碍走向巧克力。这个行为过程表现出总体的特征(寓于其中的力量是一个内源性过程,大于外界的场力),此间,场力没有表现出对整体内源性每个阶段连续不断的控制。但场力的导航作用大体上维持下来了,尤其在行为整体(action wholes)连续发生的过程中维持住了。这一结果意义重大,对迂回行为说就很有意义。

场力对过程的控制以迂回的方式出现,抑或在继续不断导航的意义上出现,这个问题取决于两个因素:一个是整体的坚韧和行为过程本身的力量,另一个是场力的大小。因此,这两种变化都导致了过程轨迹的变化。无论如何,对冲动行为和受控行为的整体场而言,导航过程都至关重要。(无疑,导航概念还有一个更狭隘的意义:相对独立的导航过程同时又改变场力,从而启动了另一个同步的过程。物理学的例子有电子管放大器。)

b. 如以上所举例的巧克力,构成目标的客体同时又被视为需要绕行接近的对象,引导过程的力量避开利器、易碎的物品,或避开沿途对称、不对称的物体布局,为儿童开道。[①] 此外,客体又可能诱发需求,需求是能量的储蓄所,由此而流淌出运动的过程(这个过程未必适用于利器挡道的情况)。如果儿童吃过糖果已很满足,搜求巧克力的过程就不可能发生。在这个程度上,巧克力也有第二个功能。

能量的储蓄存在与否,换言之,需求或类似需求的紧张态,在意志和冲动心理学的整个场域里以各种形式反反复复出现,引人注目。当心理需求得到满足时,对目标的兴趣随即失去,奔向目标的努力也随即停止,能量的储蓄就开始起作用;有意为之的行为(或替代性行为)完成,并不在另一个类似的场合重现时,能量的储蓄就起作用了。即使在习惯性刺激发生而习惯性行为又不出现时,即使某些能量不迫使个人行动,能量的储蓄也要起作用。最后要说的是,这一事实对情感过程至关重要。上文所

---

① Cf. A. HERMANN-CZINER, Zur Entwicklungspsychologie des Umgehens mit Gegenständen, *Zeitschr. f. angew. Psychol.* ,1923,22,337. BARTELT and LAU, Beobachtungen an Ziegen, *Psychol. Forsch.* ,1924,5,340. DEXLER, Das Gestalt-prinzip und die moderne Tierpsychologie, *Lotos*,1921,69,143.

述感知场和过程轨迹的密切关系我们不应该忘记:当心理能量不存在时,当维持过程的紧张心理系统不相关时,控制过程轨迹的力量就不起作用了。

如上例所示,释放需求能量的时机是过程轨迹的决定性力量。这一双重功能常常在心理学里得到验证。它和场域的重构关系密切,场域的重构是由活动过程决定的。

c. 拿到并吃掉巧克力对场域力量的变化特别重要,这是因为巧克力的占有和满足过程的开始不仅意味着场域力量地位的变化,而且产生行为的心理张力也随之发生深刻的变化。

因此,对器物或事件的感知:

1. 产生一个明确的心理张力系统,这是以前不存在的系统,至少不是以那种形式存在的系统。这一经验立即生成一个意向,唤醒一个欲望——过去不存在的意向或欲望。

2. 业已存在的张力状态可以归因于一个目的、一种需求或一种尚未完成的活动,这一心态使人对某一客体或事件感兴趣,觉得它有吸引力,致使运动器官受到控制。于是我们说,这样的客体具有诱发力(valence)。

3. 像其他经验一样,这种诱发力和场力一道起作用,就是说,它们为心理过程导航,尤其为运动器官导航。

4. 一定程度上靠诱发力生成的某些活动引起满足的过程,或使意向得以实现。如此,基本心理系统的紧张随之减少,下一层次的张力状态就实现平衡了。

由于篇幅限制,看见巧克力启动的过程所引起的行为,这里不再赘述。大概是这样一种情况:在心理系统里短暂逗留的张力状态得以突破,进入运动器官。也可能是这样一种情况:诱发力存在时,未能起作用的心理系统突变,使能量得以释放。你甚至可以设想有时出现的共鸣等现象,但有一点是不可能的:纯机器那种特殊意义的释放发挥重要的作用。通常,冲动吸收心理能量,表现出与心理能量内在的真实关系,这一事实就不支持纯机器式释放的假设。

自然,释放能量的诱发力与控制过程的场力之间存在各种过渡形态。

但这不影响我们随时探究心理过程中所涉及的能源。

这同样适用于狭义的导航。同理,你不能忽略一个事实:启动导航所需的微弱力量和能量不等于受引导的系统拥有的能量;启动过程的能量流不足时,效果就不能实现。(如:电子放大管里的电路板。)

在此,我们不能根据内容来讨论心理能量源。无论如何,意志的需求和核心目标在这里至关重要。尽管如此,有关心理能量结构的一般问题仍然是恰当的论题,也是必须在这里考虑的。

第二节 心理能量与心理结构

当前,更强调心理统一性(unity of the mind)已成为习惯。无疑,此举旨在反对原子论,不同意把心理切割成具体感知、情感和其他经验的碎片。然而,心理统一性仍然非常暧昧。为了避免误解,我们稍后将在这方面提出若干问题。这里只需指出,我们不讨论"心理统一性"这个含糊术语的全部复杂问题,而只讨论心理能量这个具体的问题。

首先,我们需要考虑以下一些问题:当统一性问题成为核心问题时,必须注意尽力拓宽整体外貌的倾向;最重要的是必须明白,具体的研究总是要超越模糊的总体情况,以便将整体的结构分解成子系统,从而探究决定具体个案的超级系统的特殊疆界。

有一个倾向认为,构成个体心理场域的统一性大于心理性质的统一性,这个倾向大概是正确的。"任何心理现象与其他一切心理现象相关"的命题远不能充分描绘心理性质的具体情况,[①]这个命题也不完全适合心理统一性,虽然在这两种情况下,该命题有一定的正确性。

25 年前的一天早上,我醒来时很高兴,因为我不必去上学。我出去放风筝,过了午饭时间才回家吃饭,吃了很多甜食,下午又在花园里玩耍。那天的经验,以及接着几天、几个星期的经验在某些情况下(或许被催眠时)会重现,在这个意义上,那些经验并没有完全消逝。无疑,童年时代的全部经验会对后来的成长产生决定性的影响,对我们当前的行为也会产

---

① See W. KOHLER, *Die physischen Gestalten*, Weltkreisverlag, Erlangen, 1920.

生影响。而且,某些特殊的经验对我们当前的心理过程还有深刻的意义。如此,过去的每一点日常经验都对当前的精神生活有影响。但在大多数情况下,评估这种影响的方式与评估星星对我们心理的影响是相仿的:不能说这种影响不存在,但这种影响极其微小,接近于零了。

影响缺乏的情况绝不限于被时间分隔了的遥远的经验。我抬头看窗外,注意到了一缕炊烟。诚然,这一次经验又可能深刻地影响我的精神生活;但一般而言,并非每一个心理事件都和数以千万计的其他日常经验相联系。无论其他经验是否存在,行为都可能发生变化,也可能不发生变化,变与不变都在不知不觉间发生。

然而,"任何心理现象与其他一切心理现象相关"的命题并不充分,原因倒不是有必要区别重要的和不重要的。另一种说法也不充分:"虽然不是每一次经验都与其他心理事件相关,但深刻的或重要的经验与其他心理事件都有关系。"这是个经量化后改进的命题,但这个命题也不充分。

心理事件的相互关系,每一次经验对其他心理过程影响的广度并不仅仅取决于其力度,甚至不取决于其重要性。更准确地说,单个的心理体验、行为与情绪、目的、愿望和希望都嵌入了特定的心理结构、个性范围和总体过程。比如,你和他人交谈时被电话打断,这个电话并不重要,三言两语就结束了。在这样的情况下,总体的情景使电话很快结束了。但接电话之前交谈时的主要经验、愿望和目的也好,打完电话接着交谈时的经验、愿望和目的也好,对电话上的交谈都不重要——通常是这样的,除非面对面交谈时心理上有强烈的投入。

两个心理事件是否互相影响?如果互相影响,又是如何影响的呢?这都取决于两个因素:它们是否嵌入了相同的或不同的总体过程及这两个心理复合体的关系。因此,对时间上相对遥远的心理事件而言,一个微弱的经验反而颇有意义;相反,另一个系统的经验,即使强有力,对时间上比较邻近的心理过程也不会产生影响。

同理,基于记忆的语境并不取决于经验强度和时间的关系,而是主要取决于其相同总体过程的归属。①

在很大程度上,不同心理系统的归属性同样以基本的心理紧张和能量为典型特征。

当然,过程和经验产生的心理需求和心理紧张常常是互相联系的。因此就可能出现这样的情况:一个系统的情感能量可能会进入另一个系统(职业生活产生的情感能量也许会进入家庭生活的心理过程中),在另一个系统中表现出来。还可能出现另一种情况:意志需求的满足使功能上邻近的需求也得到满足。然而,在不同张力状态的心理系统中,传播亲近性可能千差万别。在某些心理状态下,在不同的个体身上,传播的总体倾向在强度上也千差万别。但不能忘记,并非所有的动态心理系统都有明显的交流;许多情况下,系统之间的交流极其微弱,甚至根本就不存在。

倘若不同心理系统没有令人吃惊的隔绝,而是存在所谓永恒的心理统一性,倘若某一时刻存在的心理张力被视为始终如一、单一和封闭的系统,那么,井然有序的行为就不可能了。井然有序的行为必须具备两个条件:同步存在的大多数心理张力必须是彻底排除例外的,其中一些还很强烈;运动器官和一个特定领域的心理张力形成排他性的关系。特定行为宗旨的专一性可能发生,但这未必需要借助其他心理张力来消除;心理张力在一些心理结构或区域里自然而然发生;凭借一些动态的心理过程,这些结构或区域,或已形成或正在形成,我们不拟在此介绍这些心理过程。

在此,我们将这一节思考的问题做个小结。心理常被视为统一性的原型。意识的统一、个性的统一常被视为深刻思考的基础和不言自明的预设。个体的整合,尤其是个体心理的整合与个体的特殊性情和绝对特性联系在一起,我们习惯上把绝对特性归之于个人。

然而仔细一看,我们就会首先发现大量涉及统一性的问题。意识统一性和大量心理形式和过程的统一性不能画等号,和紧张的、非紧张的心理系统也不能画等号,心理系统加在一起可以被命名为心理。此外,对许

---

① See W. POPPELREUTER, Über die Ordnung des Vorstellungslaufers, *Arch. f. d ges. Psychol.*, 1912, 25, 208—349.

多问题至关重要的所谓自我(ego or self)的统一性,究竟是单一的系统还是系统的复合体,抑或是心灵总体里的一个功能区,这个问题至少可以存疑。

我们在这里讨论的不是自我统一性的问题,而是仅限于探讨心理动态同质性的问题。

其次,X 先生的心理统一性至少不同于 R 先生的心理统一性,也不同于儿童 Q 的心理统一性。这样的差异构成人的个性(individuality),所谓个性就是使个人有别于其他人的性质,个性大概是某种显而易见的性质,是心理过程、成分和表达的特征。至于这个意义上的个性问题,比如某人心理过程的特征是否可以展示的问题,以及这些特征如何构成的问题(个性心理学的基本问题),我们也不拟在此探讨。即使心理未表现出坚实的统一性,一个人的心灵整体(心理)的个性或独特性也是可能存在的。即使心灵整体宛若一个心理世界,不具有心理有机体的统一性,甚至不具有单一的、同质的封闭系统的统一性,心理的个性或独特性也是可能存在的。我们在这里讨论的不是心理过程同一的、属于同一心灵整体的特征,我们只探讨心灵的因果—动态同质性问题,以及相对分隔的能量系统存在的问题。

最后,应该指出的是,相对分隔的心理能量系统和心理能力的区分没有关系,这就是所谓的心理能力有记忆、意志和领悟力。相反,我们批判将这些研究领域一刀切的疆界分割,这就是我们当前研究思路的一个预设。

兹将本节思考的最后一个结果略加说明。无疑,有些领域比如运动器官里存在相当高的统一性。至于心理的统一性,无论你的估计有多高,心灵存在程度不一致的观点尚需更深入的心理学研究,这个现状很重要。我们要研究的不是单一的系统,而是许多显著的形貌,其中一些与其他形貌有交流,成为一个更大的、但形貌不那么分明的构造成分。我们重申,其他的心理结构可能没有表现出值得一提的关系。心理是单一的整体,其各部分是一致的,这是一种概念;心理是经验的总结,这是另一种概念,两者的区别仅仅是形式上的区别,和认真的研究丝毫不搭界。然而,我们要承认心理的自然结构,承认心理系统、分层和范围。我们需要判定,何处要研究心灵整体、何处不研究心灵整体。

在一定程度上,边界分明的心理系统的形成和心理的个体发生有关系。与个体发生的过程一样,心理系统的形成还清楚地显示了一个特殊的历史元素。

第三节　平衡趋势:心理系统边界的动态牢固与相对隔离

在心理结构的动态方面,以下思考也会得出类似上一节的结论。

借用某些观点,心理过程常常能从平衡趋势中演绎而来,正如生物、物理、经济等过程能由此演绎而来一样。从静态到动态过程的过渡、静态过程里的变化都可以这样来演绎:某些点上的平衡被打破,一个新方向平衡态的过程随之来临。

但循着这条思路走下去,你还必须特别注意以下几点。

1. 所谓走向平衡态,那仅仅是对系统整体而言。其中一部分过程可能会反向运行,[①]这种情况对迂回行为理论很重要。因此,考察系统的整体至关重要,系统是主导平衡走向的基础。实际上,具体的研究任务正是寻找这个决定意义的系统及其边界和内部结构。根据上述的总命题,具体的事件就可以从系统及其边界和内部结构中推衍出来了。

2. 此外,系统的平衡态并不等于说系统里没有张力。相反,系统也在张力中实现着平衡(比如压紧的弹簧、受压的油罐)。然而,这种系统的出现有一个前提:边界的牢固、系统与环境的隔离。如果系统各部分的内聚力不足以抗衡可能取代它的力量(系统未展现足够的内在牢固性,系统有流动性),如果系统没有牢固的围墙与环境隔离,而是常向临近的系统开放,那么,平衡的张力状态是不可能出现的。相反,力的指向就会出现这样一个过程,能力的扩散就会侵蚀相邻的区域,就会在这个区域里的下一个张力层级中走向平衡。因此,这种静态张力存在的预设是:系统的相对牢固、系统内部的牢固或系统围墙的牢固。

---

① See KOHLER, *Die physischen Gestalten*.

在这里，我们所谓系统的牢固仅仅是功能—动态意义上的牢固，对系统的物质材料我们不作特别的论述。自然，系统牢固围墙的周围可能有一个张力的系统。在这样的情况下，上述预设总体上对两个系统都适用。

张力心理系统的出现在心理过程中非常典型，至少过了婴儿期后就常有这一现象。立即释放张力状态的趋势（走向下一个层级张力状态的平衡）是很容易看到的。然而，由于全局的性质，这样的平衡（比如通过愿望的实现而寻求的平衡）常常是不可能立即达成的。也许平衡只能逐渐实现，比如通过长期努力来实现，而且平衡永远不能实现的可能性也是存在的。严重失衡时，一连串静态张力系统至少一个系统可能会囊括许多心理层级。儿童的愿望不被满足时，他可能会倒在地上，紧张、僵挺、绝望、一动不动。不过，一般地说，稍过一会儿，一个特殊的张力系统随之产生。比如，未满足的愿望或未完成的活动并不会瘫痪所有的运动器官，也不会使整个心理绷紧，而是使一种特殊的张力状态保存下来，长期不发作，仅仅对其他心理过程产生小小的影响。然而，一旦时机恰当，张力状态就可能猛然显身，比如，未完成的活动可能会继续下去。

在许多心理系统里，即使直接的张力状态平衡（愿望的满足、稍后才完成的活动）没有发生时，张力的释放也可能最终发生。也许，张力状态平衡是替代性（补偿）完成的结果；也许，系统的隔离不完全，不排除与相邻系统的平衡（略有扩散意味）。但常见的情况是，这类特殊系统的张力长时间稽延，或仅仅是略有缓解而已。

在成年人身上，通常有许多相对分离的张力心理系统，它们受全身总体张力释放的影响，却罕有真正得到释放的机会，其释放通常是不完全的。它们形成行为能力的储备所，倘若没有它们的相对独立性，井然有序的行为是不可能发生的。

心理学家对未完成活动所做的实验研究，[①]也给人留下深刻的印象：心理是动态的结构，绝不是完全封闭的统一体。即使一系列的实验任务并未完成，也很少产生总体的紧张状态，紧张情绪也不随未竟任务的增加

---

① Cf. OVSIANKINA and ZEIGARNIK. below, Chap. VIII, p. 242.

而增加。促发随意释放的单一紧张状态(继续未完成任务)也不会出现,此时产生的是若干相对独立的心理张力系统,它们会在多个方向上表现出分离的性质。只有在非常紧张的情况下,紧张状态才会蔓延,进入相邻的区域。

心理是单一均质的、各部分相连的系统吗?其中有相对分离的动力系统吗?这个问题并不等于自我统一体的问题;在分裂人格的现象里,自我的统一成为尖锐的问题,虽然这两个问题有一些关联。

由此提出的问题极为尖锐,且影响深远。其具体的探讨有一个必要的前提:心理结构实验研究的更高级阶段。一些讨论只能被视为初步的探索,既是旨在避免容易产生的误解,也是意在表明一些探讨中的理论可能性,我们常常要提及在这些问题上的具体实验研究。

从格式塔心理学理论考虑问题,将心理统一性视为其结构特性是很自然的。实际上,这样一个观念是性格的基本概念,为了充分理解,我们不能从孤立的特性(特质)出发,而是要从人格的整体出发。如果由此出发而研究心理动力系统的问题,这样的尝试很可能会将自我与心理统一体的整体画等号。

然而,若干事实使人得出相反的观点:在心理统一体里,一个特殊的区域必须被界定为狭义的自我。并非每一个心理系统都属于这个核心的自我。并非每一个我称之为"你"的人,我了解并对我重要的一切事物、人物和环境区域都构成自我属性。这个自我系统还有功能方面的某种独特地位,这一点很重要。并非每一个紧张的心理系统和自我都有交流。在总体的心理有机体(见下一节)里,与自我有关系的诸多紧张心理系统还有功能上的特殊意义;在这个区域里,不同的紧张状态走向平衡的趋势很强烈,其中相对孤立的动力系统走向平衡的趋势就弱小得多。

除非动力学的重要事实证明了类似的假设,比如某种情绪迫使人们走向这个假设,否则你就不必借重这个假设或类似的假设。只需在这里指出,相对分离的心理系统的区分为自我统一性和同质性的问题提供了各种各样的可能性。

总之,无论如何都要作出如下判断:我们看到,在因果关系和动力关系的研究中,必须特别注意心理张力和能量源。张力状态和能量是心理系统,心理系统是动态统一体,显示出或多或少的分离性。因此,动力系统的结构、动力系统和其他心理系统的交流和边界情况的变化都极为重要;对心理过程而言是如此,对心理张力也是如此,对心理能量的流动亦是如此。

因此,在研究心理能量和张力状态时,我们决不能忘记:它们在心理系统里有特定的地位,必须用格式塔理论的观点来研究。格式塔理论是研究诸如此类系统的有效理论。

第四节 心理过程即生命过程

将心理能量源视为彼此密切交流的动力系统时,我们不能忘记,研究心理过程就是在研究生命过程。我们在上一节讨论心理过程时,这一现象自然被置于背景中,因为在心理力量问题和能量问题中,我们必须首先解决一些初级的问题。为了避免误解,我们应该强调这一现状,至少要简略地提一提。

仅仅区分动力系统间不同程度的交流,可能不足以描绘心理结构。我们还必须区分不同功能意义的层次或层级。

比如,运动过程对心理紧张的平衡具有特殊的意义,运动器官与某些心理系统交流的方式亦是如此,这一交流变化的环境赋予了运动领域相对独特的功能地位。同理,也赋予了探究清醒思维或清晰意象的功能意义。(即使在感知领域,你可能也不得不超越核心过程和周边过程的区分,而进入特殊功能层级的细分领域。)

另外,发展类型的变化——成熟、成长和心理需求的变化也发挥了重要的作用。

与此相似,心理能量源,比如心理需求的变化也发挥了重要的作用。心理需求表现出显著的个体发育过程。这种变化不仅特别表现在性需求上,而且表现在一般的需求上。幼儿喜欢扔东西,稍后,他把东西藏在地毯下;稍大的儿童喜欢藏猫猫,儿童的撒谎也多半是"掩藏"。幼儿喜欢开关小盒子,稍后,他喜欢由妈妈抱着去开门、关门;蹒跚学步后,开门、关门的游戏无限延伸,他喜欢开关所有的抽屉。在这些案例及类似的情况下,除了追踪儿童动作能力的发展外,我们还要追踪其意向、需求和兴趣的发展。① 在追踪具体的需求和儿童个体的变化时,重要的是注意需求内容的发展,哪里的需求有增有减,起初宽泛的需求在哪里收窄到很小的诱发力范围;同时要注意特别的意向在哪里延伸到相邻的区域。在这个方面,我们不能把表现的同一性当作同样需求的唯一标准。表面上迥然不同的行为可能关系紧密,反之,表面上非常相似的行为,比如玩玩具、叠积木等在不同年龄儿童身上的归属却不一样,两岁和四岁儿童相同行为的归属就不同。

这一点发展常常表现出某种节律,仿佛鸡蛋的生物发展节律:表现出很大程度上自主的阶段性。成熟概念和危机概念成为基本的概念。

叠印在个体发育上的是意向和需求消长比较快的节律,也就是心理满足和回归不满足的节律。

生理学研究有机体能量节省的基本问题,迄今为止,它被视为"生命物理学"。人们对能量交换做了精细的研究,却忘了能量交换过程中嵌入的有机体,从而忽略了能量交换过程中真正的生物学问题。作为生命过程的时刻,能量交换取得了生物学的独特地位,一些独特的问题由此而生;人们将其称为"一般的有机体现象"。

用这些问题去研究具体材料时,类比的危险和类比的困难显而易见,研究心理能量也存在类似的危险和困难。比如,研究表明,具有某些张力状态和平衡速度的心理系统可以用以下方式来推导:与相邻系统的交流,与其张力状态的关系;在研究这些心理系统时,原则上可以在上述概念或相关的能量过程概念的研究中有所收获。但偶尔也会发生调节现象(常常被称为自制或意志的干预),原有被视为基础的足以说明问题的原理并不能推导出这样的现象。在这样的情况下,向更全面领域(被视为总体系统时,这种领域能澄清起初令人困惑的现象)的过渡有时会大有裨益。至

---

① See K. G. LAU, *Beiträge zur Psychologie der Jugend in der Pubertatszeit*, 2d ed., Beltz Langensalza, 1924.

于借助不同程度和不同力度的总体研究是否能使人作出这样的解释,至于心理成长和成熟过程是否需要借助有别于上述概念的结构,是因篇幅有限而难以在此探讨的问题,因为我们在这里面对的问题是涵盖整个生命领域的问题。无论如何,格式塔意义上的动力整体的概念至关重要,它指明了心理实验研究的广阔领域;这样的研究有望产生累累硕果,并澄清一般生命问题的研究路径。

第三章 环境在儿童行为及发展中的作用[①]

我们在这里研究环境对心理的影响。这并不意味着,环境比如营养或气候仅对身体产生影响,而不会对心理产生重大的影响。相反,环境对身体和心理产生的影响都无时无刻地表现在儿童的各方面。

第一节 引言

环境对儿童行为和发展产生的心理影响极为重要,这一点早已广为人知。[②] 实际上,儿童行为的各个方面都受到现有环境的影响,因此,其看似本能和随意的行为、游戏、情绪、言语、表情都由现在的环境来决定。晚

---

① See reprinted from CARL MURCHISON, *Handbook of Child Psychology*, Clark Univ. Press, Worcester, Mass., 2d ed. rev., Chap. 14, 1933, by permission.
② See H. TAINK, Dc l'Intelltgence (2 vols) Paris, 1870 (3d ed., 1878) On Intelligence (trans, by T. D. Haye and rev. with additions by the author, 2 vols.), Holt & Williams, New York, 1889.

近一些的理论,尤其是华生①和阿德勒②赋予了环境影响主导地位,却常常忽略了遗传因素的影响。③ 相反,斯腾④⑤的融合论(theory of convergence)强调,心理倾向和环境影响必须在同一方向上起作用才能产生特定的行为样式。

一、一般环境与个人环境

近年,对各种环境的心理学研究已经用多种方式相当透彻地确定了环境的影响。比如,对乡村儿童和城市儿童进行智力比较⑥,对同胞兄弟

---

① 华生(John Broadus Watson,1878—1958),行为主义心理学的创始人,曾任美国心理学会主席,著有《行为主义心理学》《行为主义》《婴儿及儿童的心理护理》等——译者注。
② 阿尔弗雷德·阿德勒(Alfred Adler 1870—1937),奥地利精神病学家,个体心理学创始人,人本主义心理学先驱,现代自我心理学之父。他反对弗洛伊德的心理学体系,主张由生物学定向的本我转向社会文化定向的自我心理学,著有《论神经症性格》《自卑感》《理解人类本性》《个体心理学的实践与理论》《生活的科学》《神经症问题》等——译者注。
③ See J. B. WATSON, Behaviorism, *People's Instit. Publ. Co.*, New York, 1924—1925 (rev. ed., Norton, NewYork, 1930); AADLI-R, *Über den nervosen Charakter. Grundznge cincr vergleichenden Individual psychologie und Psychotherapie*, Bergmann, Munich and Wiesbaden, 1912 (4th ed., 1928). *The Neurotic Constitution; Outlines of a Comparative Individualistic Psychology and Psychotherapy* (trans by B. Glueck and J. E. Lind), Moffat, Yard, New York, 1917.
④ 威廉·斯腾(J. W. Stern, 1871—1938),德国心理学家、人格心理学和智力心理学先驱,著有《智力测试的心理学方法》《从人格论看普通心理学》等——译者注。
⑤ See W. STERN, *Psychologie der frnhen Kindheit, bis zum sechslen Li'bcnijahre*, Quelle & Meyer, Lcipzig, 1914(6th ed., rev., 1930). *Psychology of Early Childhood, up to the Sixth Year of Age* (trans. from the 3d German ed. by A Harwell), Holt, NewYork, Allen, London, 1924(2d ed., rev., 1930).
⑥ E HAUCK, Zur difTerenticllen Psychologie des Industrie und Landkindes, *Jenacr Beitr. z. Jugend-und Erzichnngspychol*. Beltz, Langensals, 1929, H E JONES, H S CONRAD, and M. B. BLANCHARD, Environmental Handicap in Mental Test Performance, *Univ. Calif, Psutbl. Pychol*, 1932, 5, pp. 63—99.

姐妹的多少和排行的影响进行研究。① 在对领养儿童②和孪生子③的研究中,环境心理学也起了重要的作用。对同卵双生子的研究使人确信同等的遗传能力和倾向。面对环境差异表现出来的相似性所得出的重要信息表明:一方面是环境影响的类型和力度,另一方面是遗传影响的类型和强度。

当代的环境研究主要用统计方法。比如,尽力搜集独生子以及三孩家庭里老大、老二、老三的学习成绩并进行比较。比如,研究子女人数和排行,同时也研究经济地位大致相当的独生子,这样具体的环境因素就可以被排除。这类研究揭示了大量有趣的事实,比如,在德国的某些社会阶层里,学业成绩最佳的孩子一般有两三个兄弟姐妹;相反,在无产者家庭里,独生子一般表现出最好的成绩。④

这些事实固然有价值,且必不可少,但它们只不过能暗示环境力量问题的趋势。因为在研究个人与环境的动态关系时,都要根据实际上总体的具体特征。统计法界定群体时,通常不是依据纯心理特征,而是或多或少依据非本质的特征(比如同胞兄弟姐妹的人数),其结果迥然不同甚至相反结构的案例可能被纳入相同的群组。特别要指出的是以下几个方面:一般情况(比如一岁婴儿)的设计旨在消除环境的"偶然性";一般情况(比如情景对独生子的一般影响)的确定旨在排除个体的变异。如此,对动态研究起决定作用的关系——儿童个人在实际、具体、总体情境中的地

---

① See A. BUSFMANN, Die Familie als Erlebnismilieu des Kindes, *Zsch. f. Kinderforsch*, 1929, 36, pp. 17—32.

② See B. S. BURKS, The Relative Influence of Nature and Nurture upon Mental Development: A comparative study of foster parent-foster child resemblance, *27th Yearbook*, N. S. S. E, 1928, Pt. i, 219—316; F. N. FREEMAN, *et al.*, The Influence on the Intelligence, School Achievement and Conduct of Foster Children, *27h Yearbook*, N. S. S. E., 1928, Pt. 1, pp. 103—218.

③ See A. GESELL, The Developmental Psychology of Twins, in *A Handbook of Child Psychology*, ed. by C. Murchison, Worcester, 1st ed., 1931.

④ See A. BUSEMANN, *op. cit.*

位——却因此被搞抽象了。[1] 结果,从一般向具体案例演绎就不可能了。一般儿童的概念和一般情景的概念是抽象概念,对动态关系的研究毫无用处。[2] 当研究目的是求得数量价值以描绘群体里某个孩子的地位时,平均概念和分布曲线并非例外。然而,如果只分离单个的属性或显型界定的时间,却不注意总体的结构,如果不用统计手段研究展示这一特征的尽可能多的情景,那就不足以发现动态规律。

如果不研究实际的自由落体,比如树叶、石头等物体,物理学里的自由落体定律是发现不了的。同理,只有从简单但清楚界定了具体个性的全局出发,我们才能在心理学里发现环境力量及其规律对儿童的影响。这就需要进行实验,需要研究环境条件的规律性变异,只有这样才能提出带普遍性的主张,并使之适合儿童的实际个案和具体的案例研究。

当然可以拷问的是,科学地(用严谨的概念)言说动态属性是否可能,尤其科学地界定心理环境的力量是否可能。[3] 比如,对儿童的虐待使之压抑,表扬儿童使之飘飘然,这样的言论显然只具有比喻的意义。

在生物学领域,雅克·洛布[4]试图以严谨的科学方式确定环境刺激和动物行为的动态关系。然而科学家的研究显示,动物学习的环境受到很大的修正,[5]而且,动物的行为取决于其瞬间的"情绪"。[6]

目前,生物学家在一定程度上已经回归非决定性的观点,至少已回归非动态的观点,据此,再说环境力量对个人产生影响的观点有严格的科学

---

[1] See LEWIN, Conflict between Aristotelian and Galileian Modes of Thought in Psychology, Jour. Gen. *Psychol.*, 1931, 5, pp. 141—177(Chap I of this volume).

[2] 由此可见,越是注意具体的总体情况而不是若干案例,环境研究总体上就越有成效。

[3] 这里不考虑相反观点的思辨哲学基础。在美国,这样的动态属性一般被视为物理属性;在德国,它们被视为兼有物理性和艺术性。

[4] 雅克·洛布(1859—1924),美国动物学家和心理学家,著有《普通生理学》《作为整体的有机体》——译者注。

[5] See H. S. JENNINGS, *Behavior of the Lower Organisms*, Columbia Univ. Press, New York, 1906.

[6] See F Au ERDES, *Neue Bahnen in der Lehre vom Verhalten der niederen Tiere*, Springer, Berlin, 1922.

性就不可能了。环境影响基本上已经简化为尝试—错误原理。换言之，就其与环境的关系而言，基本动作的发生基本上是偶然的。可见，这一生物学理论表现出了达尔文主义的特征：它排除了环境与个人直接的动态关系，把环境影响限定在唤起相宜经验和不相宜经验的范围。可以认为，这一理论试图避免令人不舒服的心理意义上的环境力量概念，它尽可能从有机体自身解释有机体的行为。

同样，儿童心理学将尝试—错误原理视为儿童行为发展的基本原理。[1] 另外，近年来科学家又确定了两个观点：(1)除了经验因素，内在的成熟对儿童的发展具有重大的意义；[2](2)除了盲目的试错之外，儿童还表现出有富有洞见的行为。[3] 这些行为发生时，个人回复到与情境结构的直接关系中。

二、个人、环境与规律

我们要先简要地说一说环境、个人和规律的关系，然后再详细介绍心理学里的环境力量问题。心理学里的环境有时被理解为儿童的瞬间情景，有时被理解为外部环境，即持久性情景的主要部分。以下几方面的思考适用于这两种环境概念。

在一切情况下，儿童的实际行为都取决于他的个性特征和那一刻的情境结构。我们不可能单独挑出一部分情境并将其归之于环境，而把另一部分情境归之于个人，这一点越来越明显。然而，假若放弃了第一步提出的问题："遗传和环境相比，哪一个因素更重要？"而提出这样一个命题："为了达成某一行为模式，遗传和环境必须在同一方向上起作用。"那又如何呢？即使这样，我们还是要假定，遗传倾向可以被界定为真实行为模式的倾向，而不必提及具体的环境。实际上，倾向的概念必然涉及具体的环

---

[1] See K. BtUILKR, *Die geistige Entitleklung des Kindes*, Fischer, Jena, 1918(new ed., 1929). *The Mental Development of the Child*, Harcourt, Brace, New York, Kegan Paul, London, 1930.

[2] See W. STERN, Psydiologie der fruhcn Kindheit, *bis zitm sechsten Lebensjahre*; K. KOFFKA, *The Growth of the Mind*; K. BUHLER, *op. cit.*

[3] See K. KOFFKA, op. cit.

境,实际上是涉及若干环境的聚合体。倾向或曰个人的个性特征(P_a)不能用一个具体的行为模式来界定,而是要用行为模式的聚合体来界定;不同的外部情景(E_1,E_2等)和不同的行为模式($B_α$,$B_β$等)相关。因此,研究动态关系问题时,个人的倾向和瞬间状态特征就不能用显型特征来界定,而是要用属型特征来界定。

与个人特征相关的行为变异($B_α$,$B_β$等)极其多样。儿童在一种情境中消极,在另一种情境中可能会羞涩,在第三种情境中却很轻松自如。克莱默(Kramer)研究了许多儿童的行为,在他的所有案例里,他发现,只要被带进适当的情境里,粗野的儿童就百分之百、彻彻底底地失去了野蛮的行为;他认为,这些儿童被描述为乖巧的儿童更合适一些。

个体对环境的敏感性差异颇大,总体上说,精神病儿童比正常儿童更敏感。①

为了区分一个人的个性特征②(P_a)和另一个人的个性特征(P_b),就必须将其与相同情境(E_1,E_2,E_n)中不同的行为模式(B)联系起来看。

$$P_a \begin{cases} E_1 & B_α \\ E_2 & B_β \\ E_3 & B_γ \\ . & . \\ . & . \\ . & . \\ E_n & B_ν \end{cases} \qquad P_b \begin{cases} E_1 & B_g \\ E_2 & B_o \\ E_3 & B_a \\ . & . \\ . & . \\ . & . \\ E_n & B_μ \end{cases}$$

于是,总体上看,不同的人可能会表现出相同的(或很相似)行为模式(B)。华生和阿德勒强调这样的相似性;也许,许多人的终极行为模式即使不呈现出完全的相似性,也至少呈现出相当程度的相似性。但行为的相似性并不意味着个性的相似性,因为产生大致相似的行为还需要不同

---

① See A. HOMHURG. ER,*Vorlesungen ubcr Psychopathologie des Kindesalters*,Springer,Berlin,1926.
② 这一点思考同样适用于单个的特征或人格特征,也适用于总体的人格特征。

的情境。① 行为(B)的相似性和差异性都不会直接而明确地指向个性特征或情境因素的相似性和差异性。只有在外部情境(E)相同时,推导个性特征才有可能;只有在个体相似时,推导情境才有可能。②

这种情况下的推导无疑是明确的。实际上,心理规律用另一种方式表述相同的意思:某一总体情况的组合(含一个情境和一个人)产生某一行为,可用如下的公式来表示:$(E_1, P_a) \rightarrow B_a$ 或 $B = f(PE)$。

一方面,环境影响的动力学研究只能与个体差异的研究同步进行,只能与一般心理规律的研究同步进行;另一方面,心理规律的发现使人洞察环境因素和个体特征的意义。以上诸多思考明示,对同一人环境变化的系统研究——尤其实验研究,③对环境力量的研究具有极其重大的意义。

三、环境的结构与需求

环境因素的分析必须从总体情况的思考入手。因此,这样的分析有一个预设:对总体心理情境有充分的理解,用动力论的语言加以表述,并视之为最重要的任务。

大体上,洛布的理论将生物环境和物理环境视为同一环境:环境的动态因子含有特定波长和强度的光线、重力等因素。④ 其他学者尤其是于克斯屈尔⑤持相反的观点,他从迥然不同的角度去描绘生物环境:环境是食物、敌害、防护手段等因子的复合体。针对不同的动物,同样的环境必须被描绘为不同的现象世界和功能世界。

在儿童心理学中,同样的环境也必须根据儿童的年龄、个性和瞬间状态来描绘。婴儿的社会空间极度狭窄,尚未分化,其感知空间和情感空间

---

① 总之,个体差异越大,情境就越是不同。
② 即使华生和阿德勒有关人类绝大多数个体都能完成大多数任务的命题是正确的,那也不意味着先天的相似性,亦不意味着环境因素的决定性意义。
③ 只有面对同一个体或同卵双生子时,你才能肯定,你研究的是同样的个体特征。
④ See W. J CROZIER, The Study of Living Organisms, Chap. II, *The Foundations of Experimental Psychology* (ed. by C. Murchison), Clark Univ. Press, Worcester, Mass., 1929, pp. 45—127.
⑤ 冯·于克斯屈尔(Jakob Johann von Uexküll, 1864—1944),德国生物学家,研究肌肉生理学、生命控制论和动物行为,创建生物符号学——译者注。

也是如此。① 随着社会空间的延伸和分化,广阔的环境和不同的事实获得了心理的存在,动态的因素也获得了心理的存在。儿童学会了越来越多地掌控环境。同时,在心理上,他越来越倚重圈子、倚重越来越大的环境,其意义不逊于他对环境的掌控。

比如,有人在距婴儿几英尺外损坏了一个布娃娃时,婴儿不会受到丝毫的影响;相反,如果在三岁幼儿身边发生这样的事情,他就会立即进行有力的干预。

稍后,儿童的生活空间超越了房间和家人的圈子。这意味着,他能在智能上测量更广阔的关系,而且尤为重要的是,这使他环境里的事物和事件得到延伸,事物和事件是他心理上直接倚重的东西。

单纯对某物(如外国地理、经济形势和政治形势或家事)的了解未必会深刻改变儿童的生活空间。另外,心理上重要的环境事实(如某一成人的友好与否)却可能会对儿童的生活空间产生重要的影响,无论他是否清楚理解这种事实的意义。

为了研究动态问题,我们不得不从儿童真实的心理空间着手。

在"客观"意义上,对生活能力尚不能满足自己重要生物需求的儿童而言,社会纽带是必须的条件。通常这是与妈妈的纽带,功能上,这是婴儿需求至上的纽带。

然而,作为心理环境基本要素的社会事实很早就获得了主导的意义。当然,这并不意味着,三个月大的婴儿对人的声音和友好的微笑作出回应时,和某些人的关系业已成为他心理环境稳定的要素。这一现象发生的年龄很大程度上取决于儿童的先天条件和后天经验。

有些活动(如耍玩具)被允许,有些活动(如扔东西、触摸属于成人的

---

① See E. LAU, Beiträge zur Psychologic der frühen Kindheit II. *Zeittschr. Kinderforieh.*, 1931, 31, 481−501; C. BÜHLER, Kindheit und Jugend: Genese des Bewusstseins, *Psychol. Monographien*, 3, Hirzel, Leipzig, 1928. *From Birth to Maturity.* (In preparation. S. FAJANS, Die Bedeutung der Entfernung fur die Stärke eines Aufforderungscharakters beim Säugling und Kleinkind, *Psychol. Forsch.*, 1933, 17, pp. 213−267.

物品)不被允许,① 这种事情在儿童两岁之前就已开始,这是儿童心理环境结构中重要的动力要素。随着年龄的增长,社会事实在儿童心理环境结构中的作用越来越重要。

社会事实比如与妈妈的情谊、对成人的依靠也必须用动态的观点去看待,就像用动力论的观点去看待物理事实一样。当然,在描绘儿童的心理环境时,我们不能像社会学家或法学家那样去罗列现象。而是要根据它们对儿童的影响去进行描绘。② 这是因为客观的社会事实与儿童心理的关系模糊不清,就像客观的物理事实与儿童心理的关系一样模糊。对不同的儿童,对不同情境里的同一儿童,同样的物体可能意味着迥然不同的心理存在。一个木方块某个时间可能是一枚火箭,另一个时间可能是一块积木,也可能是一个火车头。一个物体某时为何物?这个问题取决于总体的情境及其瞬间情况。社会因素的意义也可以从类似的角度去思考。

在这种依赖关系中,一个事实具有至关重要的心理意义就是显而易见的了。这个事实是:个人的瞬间状态与心理环境结构的直接关系。③ 即使客观上同样的心理环境也依存于儿童的个性和发展阶段,而且取决于儿童瞬间的状态;考虑环境与需求的关系时,这种依存关系就显而易见了。

除了准物理和准社会环境外,精神活动或幻想有时也要用动态的观点去描绘环境。活动(如游戏)可能会带有儿童能进入或走出的区域的性质。同样,数学题也可能有这样的性质。如果不包括整个魔幻世界,儿童环境的描绘就不完全。这是因为魔幻世界对儿童的行为极其重要,与儿童的理想及其目标的关系极其密切。

---

① See G. WEISS, Aufgabegebundenes und aufgabefreies Verhalten von Fürsorgezöglingen, *Zeiltschr. f. Kinderjorsch*, 1930, 36, 195ff.

② See LEWIN, Vectors, Cognitive Processes and Mr. Tolman's Criticism, *Jour. Gen Psychol.*, 1933, 8, pp. 318—345.

③ See Ibid. ; LEWIN, Vorsatz, *Wille und Bedurfnis mil Vorbemerkungen uber die psychischen Kraftc und Encrgicn und die Struktur der Seele*.

我们看到,环境中有许多物体,还有许多准物理和准社会性的事件。物体有房间、走道、桌子、椅子、床、帽子、刀叉等;物体掉地上、翻转、启动、移动;周围有小狗、朋友、大人、邻居;有人生气,有人发脾气,有人很随和。有些地方能避雨,有些地方能躲避大人,有些地方任何情况下都不能去。对儿童而言,对以上事物和事件的界定一定程度上靠的是外观,但首先靠的是于克斯屈尔所谓的功能世界。楼梯是可以(或不可以)爬上爬下的东西,或者是某人昨天才第一次爬过的东西。因此,在儿童的经验里,历史也是环境事物中重要的心理要素。

以上诸多方面,要言不烦,但心理环境的某些主要属性尚未涉及。客体事物对儿童的影响并非中性,而是对儿童产生了直接的心理影响。许多食物吸引儿童去吃,有些物体吸引儿童去爬,有些物体吸引他去抓拿、摆弄、吮吸,另一些物体使他发怒,如此等等。我们将这些必不可少的环境事实称为诱发力,[1]它们决定行为的方向。从动力论的角度看,诱发力及其类型(符号)、力度和分布必须被归属于环境最重要的属性。

事物的诱发力盖源于这一事实:它是满足一种需求的手段,或者与满足一种需求有间接的关系。由此可见,事物诱发力的类型(符号)和力度直接取决于个人瞬间需求的状况;环境事物的诱发力和个人的需求相互关联。[2] 即使在客观环境相同的情况下,诱发的力度对饥饿儿童的作用胜过饱餐儿童,对健康儿童的作用胜过生病儿童。

诱发力和环境的相互关联使环境发生重大变化,随着年龄增长,儿童的需求发生变化而导致环境的变化。具有诱发力的事物对婴儿、蹒跚学步的幼儿、幼稚园儿童和青春期儿童的吸引力是不一样的。[3]

诱发力还随着需求的瞬间状态的改变而改变。当营养需求、玩耍需

---

[1] 诱发力不能和一般理解的"刺激"混淆,因为诱发说的是刺激反应过程。从动力关系来说,诱发力更接近于指令、召唤或要求。

[2] See LEWIN, *Vorsatz, Wille und Bedurfnis mit Vorbemerkungen uber die psychischen Krafte und Energien und die Struktur der Seele.*

[3] See LEWIN, Vectors, Cognitive Processes and Mr. Tolman's Criticism, *Jour. Gen. Psychol.*, 1933, 8, pp. 318−345.

求或阅读需求处在饥饿状态或未满足状态时，一点食物、一件玩具、一本历史书就能吸引儿童，也具有正面的诱发力。相反，当这一需求处在满足阶段或状态时，事物对儿童的诱发力就很小；如果需求处在过分满足的阶段，事物就会使儿童感到不舒服，换言之，它就获得了负面的诱发力。①

心理环境并不等同于物理环境或社会环境，对儿童尤其如此。所以，在研究环境的力量时，就不能从物理力量着手，不能像洛布研究生物学那样。如果我们首先从心理环境着手，注意其对个人瞬间状态的倚重，我们就可以发现环境动态影响的普遍原理。无疑，我们有必要随时将现存环境的整体结构铭记在心。②

心理环境的力量可以用其对儿童行为的影响来界定，可从经验和功能的角度来界定，但需排除一切形而上的问题。③ 心理环境的力量既适用于儿童暂时的情境，也适用于永久性的环境。

兹就本节所论作一小结。为了理解或预测心理行为（B），我们必须判定每一种心理事件（动作、情绪、表情等）瞬间的总体情境，也就是个人（P）心理的瞬间结构和状态以及心理环境（E）。用公式来表述就是：$B = f(PE)$。心理存在的每一个事实在心理场里必须各司其位，已居其位的事实方能产生动力效应，方能成为事件的动因。环境的一切属性（方向、距离等）都不能用物理属性来界定，而是必须用心理属性来界定，换言之，环境的一切属性都要根据准物理、准社会和准心理的结构来界定。

用数学概念来表现人和环境的动力结构是有可能的。数学表征及其心理动力意义的协调性必须是严格的，没有例外的。

我们将首先描绘心理场力量及其运行模式，至于具体情况下的客体

---

① See A. KARSTEN, Psychische Sattigung, *Psychol. Forsch.*, 1928, 10, pp. 142 − 254; D KATZ, Psychologische Probleme des Hungers und Appetits, insbesondere beim Kinde, *Zeitschr f. Kinderforsh.*, 1928, 34, pp. 158 − 197; LEWIN, Die Bedeutung der "psychischen Sättigung" für einige Probleme der psychotechnik, *Psychoteechn. Zritsehr.*, 1928, 3, 182.
② 这里所谓情境指的是心理情境，尤其指心理情境的动力属性。
③ 目前，心理动力的基本概念纯粹从心理学和生物学的观点来界定。至于其形式逻辑结构是否与物理学的基本动力概念协调，在这里则不必讨论。

是否通过以前的经验或其他方式获得诱发力,则暂时不予考虑。

第二节　行动自由的地域,力量和力量场

理解儿童的第一个预设是判断儿童的心理场所、他行动的自由区域——也就是他能活动的地方,以及心理上存在却不能去的地方。之所以不能去或是因为社会不允许(成人禁止,或模仿其他儿童等),或是因为社会、能力、体力和智力的局限。自由活动的区域,无论大小,均会对儿童的行为产生决定性的影响。[①]

借助拓扑学概念,我们可以描绘每一个环境点上的心理动力运动(准物理、准社会、准心理运动);拓扑学是一门非定量学科,研究"空间"及其构成部分的关系。

就环境问题而言,数学概念和心理动力概念协调的基础是拓扑路径和心理动力运动。拓扑学判定将拓扑路径引向什么空间点,路径在什么空间里交叉。借助空间与相邻空间的障碍,我们可以界定儿童不能去的地方。动力学里的障碍概念与数字里的边界概念对应,我们必须区分不同力度的障碍。

一、场力的基本属性

为了判定什么样的运动(路径)可能发生,哪些运动可能在给定时刻发生,就必须要用力量的概念。

力量用三种属性来界定:(1)方向;(2)力度;(3)施力点。前两种属性用矢量来表示,施力点由图式(如物理学惯用的图式)里的箭头方向来表现。

从动力论看,力量和心理运动有一对一的相关性。任何情况下,真实运动方向的依据都是瞬间力量共同作用而产生的方向和力度。在任何情况下,运动的方向都是多力作用的结果。

诱发力注入儿童行为的方式五花八门,随其欲望和需求的内容而变

---

① See F WIKHE, *Die Grenzen des Ichs*. (In preparation.) LEWIN, *Die psychologische Situation bci Lohn und Strafe*, Hirzcl, Leipzig, 1931 (Chap. Ⅳ of this volume).

化多样。但我们可以区分两大类诱发力,根据其诱发的初始行为的类比来划分,一是正诱发力(+),一是负诱发力(-)。正诱发力是产生趋近的力量,负诱发力是产生退缩的力量。

跟随诱发力的动作有两种形式:一是无控制的冲动行为,一是定向、有意的活动。动作可能"恰当",也可能"不恰当"。

从动力论来看,给人留下追求目标印象的过程通常要借助正诱发力来描绘。

我们要区分两种驱动力:一是正诱发力或负诱发力,一是与障碍对应的约束力。

(一)场力的方向

诱发力不仅与方向的主观感觉有关系,而且与界定行为的定向力有关系,这就要归之于诱发力。场力的方向可以这样来理解:吸引人的事物位置的变化导致(其他条件不变的情况下)儿童运动方向的变化。

一个很简单的例子见图 3-1 和图 3-2,它们显示正诱发力引起的动作方向。一个 6 个月的婴儿手脚并用,沿着矢量(V)爬向一锅粥或一勺粥。

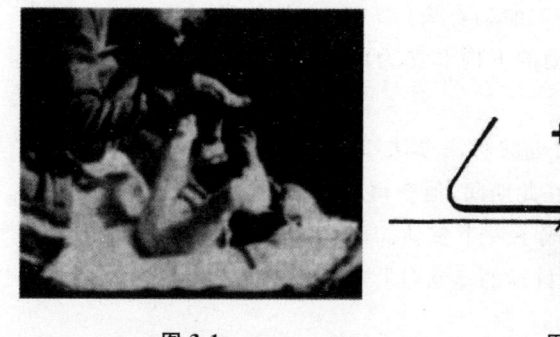

图 3-1

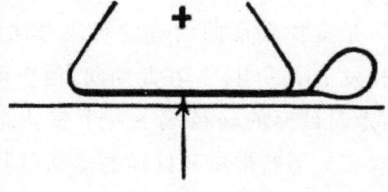

图 3-2

场力方向在智能驱动行为中发挥重要作用,就像迂回前进时场力的方向所起的作用一样。也许,儿童想要拿到椅子另一端的一块巧克力(图 3-3)的困难主要不在于迂回(D)的力度,而是在于恰当路径的初始方向与诱发力产生的矢量不一致。在其他条件相同的情况下,迂回前进的困难更大,因为在儿童迂回前进时,起步的方向和诱发力所指的方向是相反的(图 3-4)。

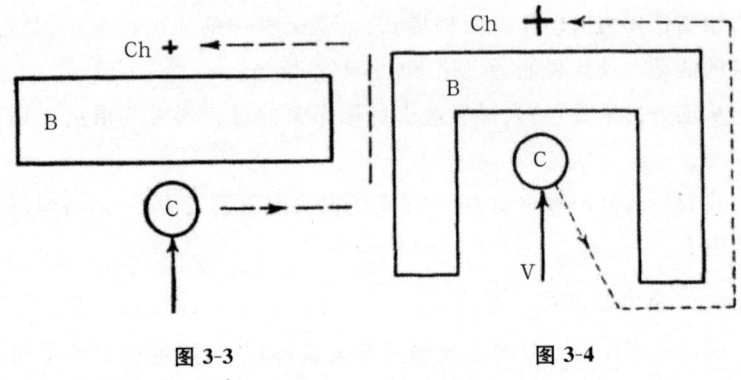

图 3-3　　　　　图 3-4

说明:C=儿童;Ch=巧克力;B=椅子

儿童想要取下木棍上的圆环时,情况也类似。木棍扎在地上,他不能朝怀里拉,只能往上拔,往外推。儿童想要坐在椅子或石头上,会遭遇困难,其中也有类似的因素。儿童面朝石头(S)走,坐下之前,他不得不转身,他运动的方向和场力的方向刚好相反(图 3-5)。①

儿童找到迂回前进的解决办法,那是因为场的结构发生了重组。② 在此期间,他获得了对全局的感知:走向目标的路径成了一个整体。路径的初始部分客观上仍然是离开目标的运动(图 3-4),心理上失

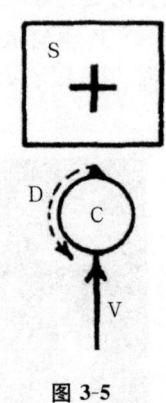

图 3-5

---

① See LEWIN, Die Auswirkung von Umwettkräften, *Proc. 9th Inc. Cong. Psychol.*, 1929, pp. 286—288.
② See W. KÖHLER, *The Mentality of Apes* (trans, by E. Winter), Harcourt, Brace, New York, 1925.

去了走向目标的属性,成了走向目标的整个运动的初始阶段。①

在这里,你不能靠增大诱发力的力度来加强迂回路径的选择。这就说明力量场里的方向是多么重要。如果目标的吸引力太弱,无疑就很难成功,因为儿童不会表现出足够的兴趣。② 但如果我们继续加大诱发力,儿童会从对抗场力的方向起步,他完成任务时就会遭遇双倍的困难。反之,儿童会沿着诱发力的方向采用情感意义的动作。③ 最重要的是,有利于感知全局并有利于整体场转化的相对超脱、背离诱发力的内向退隐,就更加困难了,因为超脱和退隐是在洞悟之中发生的。同理,重奖或重罚也可能妨碍智力任务的完成。

对稍大一点、智力正常的儿童而言,上述迂回前进的问题没有困难,因为他们应对这样情境的相应经验已足够充足了。对他们而言,这不需要特别的动作,功能方向取代了空间方向,成为运动轨迹的决定性因素。

在此,我们不妨注意一个具有普遍意义的现象:心理生理场的方向未必就等于物理方向,它要用心理学的术语来界定。心理方向和物理方向的差异在稍大一点儿童的身上更加凸显。年龄稍小的儿童去拿工具,或向实验者求助时,即使有背离目标方向的身体运动,那也不意味着他在背离目标,而是意味着他在向目标前进。这是因为儿童环境的功能分化比较少,对其而言,社会结构尚不具有压倒性的意义;对年龄稍长的儿童,社会结构才具有这样的意义。

比如,法扬斯(Fajans)就发现,在某一情境中,三四岁的幼儿向实验者求助(间接前进);而婴儿则转向妈妈,这是他失败后的退隐,而不是求助。

在上述例子中,场力的方向由事物决定,由于视觉距离和听觉距离的感知,场力在环境中确定场所。如果研究对象是新生儿,只要心理环境的结构有足够的可靠性,我们就可以描述这种准确定向的力量。

---

① 这一变化通常不是立即完成的,它首先维持了双重性。
② 博根(Bogen)发现,即使在资源参与实验的学童中,如果加一块巧克力以加强目标的诱发力,找到完成任务的办法也更加多了。
③ 桑代克(Thorndike)实验小白鼠冲动行为的部分原因常常归之于这样的情境(See E. L. THORNDIKE, *Animal Intelligence*, Macmillan, New York, 1911)。

回应触觉刺激的定向动作很早就出现在婴儿身上。妈妈用乳头触碰婴儿的小脸蛋,他的头就会转到相应的方向。

在稍大儿童的身上,自我与诱发力的(心理)分离是许多方面的必要条件,决定着指向诱发力的动作。许多时候,这一动作并不立即导致物件的使用。然而,一旦"占有"了物件,场力就随之消失(至少是被大大削弱)。我们摄制的电影里有这样一个例子:两个拨浪鼓放在九个月大的婴儿面前,婴儿抓到其中一个后,并不玩耍,而是对另一个没有拿到的拨浪鼓感兴趣。定向的场力与自我和目标物件关系密切,在稍大的儿童身上,有多种办法证明这样的关系。

(二)场力的强度

就诱发力的强度而言,内在因素——尤其是儿童瞬时状态的需求,是极端重要的。此外,诱发力的强度取决于它对个人而言的相对地位,亦取决于其他诱发力是否存在。

法扬斯[①]的实验显示,如其他条件相同,诱发力的强度随着其邻近性而增加,至少在某些情况下是这样。这种增加表现在指向目标的时长和努力的强度(在这样的实验里,目标的实现是不可能的)。

比如,在 10 个月大的一组婴儿中,起初 3 分钟,在距离为 9.40 米和 100 厘米的情况下,爬向目标的平均时长分别为 75.39 秒和 27 秒。在 3 岁的幼儿组里,走向目标的平均时长,在"近"距离和"远"距离的实验中分别为 28 秒和 58 秒。

活动时间与接近目标的时长随着诱发力的邻近程度而增加。在年龄小和年龄大的儿童身上,变化的原因有所不同。

无疑,我们在这里也不能假设,心理距离对应物理距离。只有在窄小而有限的范围内,心理距离的差异才重要,心理距离差异与儿童生活空间的狭小是吻合的:正如法扬斯的实验所示,一岁婴儿的生活空间比三岁幼儿的生活空间小得多。感知空间的视觉广度(就感觉空间大小的规律而

---

① See S. FAJANS, Die Bedeutung der Entfernung für die Stärke eines Aufforderungscharakters beim Säugling und Kleinkind, *Psychol. Forsch.*, 1933, 17, pp. 213—267.

言)随着年龄而加大;同理,在动态方面,儿童的生活空间也随着年龄增长而分化。心理距离不能只用物理距离来界定还有一个原因,儿童在"差一点"获得想要的物件时有一个质的特征。这种"差一点"达到的目标情境有一种特别的标志性意义,比如关乎成败的经验,所以这种"差一点"的情境不能仅仅被视为短一点的距离。

她在四岁儿童小组的实验里发现,空间距离和心理距离的差异明显。儿童的经验是,实验的情境与其说是客观的任务,不如说是与实验者的社会关系。他们面对的只不过是一个不愿意送玩具给他们玩的成年人。对他们而言,接近目标的路径类型和所花时间与诱发力的距离都没有关系。实际上,就走向诱发力(由实验者发出)的社会路径而言,任何情况下的心理距离都是一样的。

在更大年龄组的实验里,儿童对功能关系尤其社会关系的理解(也许是对自己所依靠的其他儿童和成人的社会关系的理解)大大提高了,所以心理距离发挥的作用就大大缩小了。①

怀斯(Weiss)在五岁儿童小组的实验里发现,在不太受抑制的情况下,桌子上玩具的距离不再重要,他们选择自己想要的玩具。当然,在抑制存在的情况下,距离还是有相当重要的作用,即使年龄再大一点的儿童也受到抑制的影响。

随着年龄的增长,时间久远的事件获得日益重要的意义。不仅实际上感知到的、客观存在的事实归属于心理情境,而且过去和未来的一些事件也纳入心理情境了。责备或夸奖可能是儿童初期保存在记忆里的历史事实,期待中的事件在未发生之前就可能提前成为心理事实了。

一个例子说明,诱发力的强度随事件的临近而增加。不妨指出,在少年犯教养所、工读学校和类似的机构里,少年犯获释前特别难以管教,这种现象是很常见的。我们指出,这种吊诡的行为和他们直接的利益截然对立。②这种现象在曾经表现良好的少年犯身上尤其常见。研究发现,重

---

① 当然,如有强大的诱发力存在,或有非常重要的需求时,初期的物理距离通常起重要作用,即使在成年人身上也发挥重要的作用。

② 即将获释的决定被撤销,难管教的情况也并非罕见。

要的原因是:即使起初在教养所(H)表现好的少年犯,重获自由(F)的愿望也是其行为的重要动机。起初,这样的自由是想象的遥远目标,最重要的是,表现好是最终实现目标的办法。等到获释即将来临时,那渴望中的、却未必肯定的自由世界就在眼前时(图3-6),教养所就具有了明显的障碍(B)特性,这一障碍把他和几乎达到的目标隔离开来。如此,教养所就获得了显著的负诱发力。他很紧张,紧张使他情绪焦虑,引发叛逆动作;半自由的感觉也促成了这样的行为。① 在拓扑结构相似的实验情境中,在障碍背后的目标方向上,场力得到加强,张力状态因而加重,95%的参试婴儿的易感性都有所增加。② 在许多情况下,这些婴儿的焦躁情绪都可以用相似的环境结构来解释。

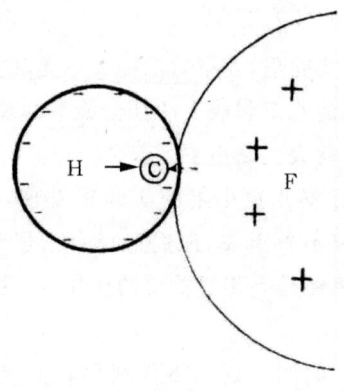

图 3-6

说明:C=儿童;F=场力

法扬斯的实验表明,障碍背后的诱发力增加时,与障碍对应的约束力随之增加。

(三)力量群,冲突

自然,在同一情景里,不同诱发力互动的方式千差万别。我挑选冲突

---

① 有案例表明,三年刑期的少年犯在即将获释的前一周试图越狱。
② 参见 S. FAJANS, Erfolg, Ausdauer und Aktivität, beim Säugling und Kleinkind, *Psychol. Forsch*, 1933, 17, pp. 268—305.

的方式来讨论,因为它具有特殊的意义。

从心理上说,冲突可以定义为大致相等的场力的对立。

1. 儿童位于两个正诱发力之间(图 3-7)。也许,他不得不在野餐(P)和与小伙伴玩游戏(Pl)之间作出选择。在这种冲突情境中,选择通常是相当容易的。选择以后,目标常常显得略为逊色(原因稍后讲),所以有时会出现摇摆。

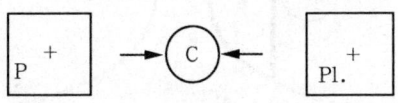

图 3-7

说明:儿童(C)位于两个诱发力之间

2. 儿童面对的情况常常是正负诱发力同时并存(图 3-8)。比如,他想要爬树(Tr),但又害怕;参加活动(比如做功课)会有奖赏,但他不想参加,这样一组正负交织的力量就产生了重要的作用。①

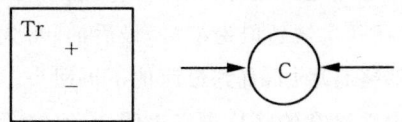

图 3-8

说明:儿童(C)处在正负两个诱发力之间

在上文法扬斯的迂回路径的实验里,在目标达成的过程中遭遇障碍情境时,这样的冲突情境通常发展得很快。起初,儿童看见障碍(B)挡在他和目标(G)之间,障碍妨碍他完成场力指示方向的动作(图 3-9)。在遭遇了几次障碍,或受伤,或遭遇失败体验之后,障碍就成了负诱发力(图 3-10)。此时,除了正矢量,还出现了负矢量,于是,第二类冲突情境随之产生。通常,负矢量逐渐加大,并最终大于正矢量。于是,儿童就退场不

---

① 关于这段话和紧随其后的几段话的意义,参见第四章。

玩了。

退缩可能是身体上的,儿童退场,离开,走出房间或游戏场所;退缩也可能是心理的退场,他开始玩另一种游戏,或做其他的事情。

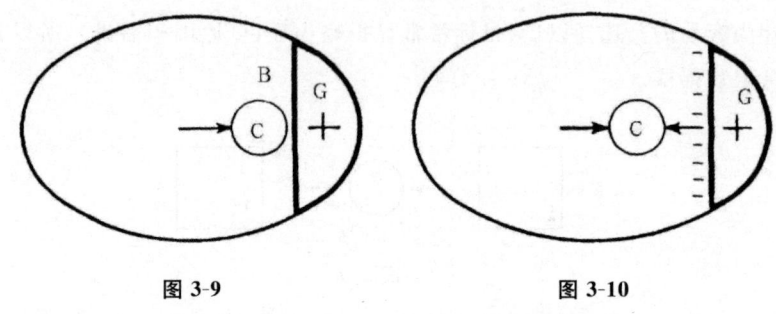

图 3-9　　　　　　　　　图 3-10

说明:C=儿童;B=障碍;G=目标　　说明:C=儿童;B=障碍;G=目标

难为情时,儿童的身体朝目标移动,心里却在想其他事情,这样的情况并不罕见。此时,身体动作或多或少带有既定姿态的性质。①

在这样的情况下,退缩起初总是短暂的。儿童转身,不一会儿又回到障碍跟前再试。只有在几次短暂的退缩后,最后的、永久性的退缩才会发生;每次退缩的时间都略有增加,直到最后他不再回头。

在这种情境中,异乎寻常的坚持未必表明活动的继续。相反,活跃的儿童往往比不活跃的儿童更早退场。表明活动会继续的不是时间的持续,而是活动方式的类型。

与此有关的现象是,某些情况下,这种冲突情境中的单一动作持续的时间和年龄有关系:婴儿单一动作持续的时间比幼儿长。但总体上看,行为单位持续的时间随着儿童年龄的增长而延长。

3. 儿童位于两个负诱发力之间时,第三种冲突情境发生。例如,用惩罚(P)胁迫儿童完成他不想执行的任务时,就会发生冲突(图3-11)。

第三种冲突情境和第一种冲突情境有很大的区别。我们着手表现力

---

① See LEWIN. Kindlicher Ausdruck, *Zeitschr. f. pad. Psychol*, 1927, 28, pp. 510－526; S. FAIANS, Erfolg, Ausdauer und Aktivitat bcim Saugling und Kleinkind.

量场里力量的总体分布时,整个差别就显而易见了。

（四）力量场

力量场旨在表现,人在场域里的某一点时,哪一股力量在哪里。与一个负诱发力对应的是一个会聚场(convergent field)(图 3-12)。

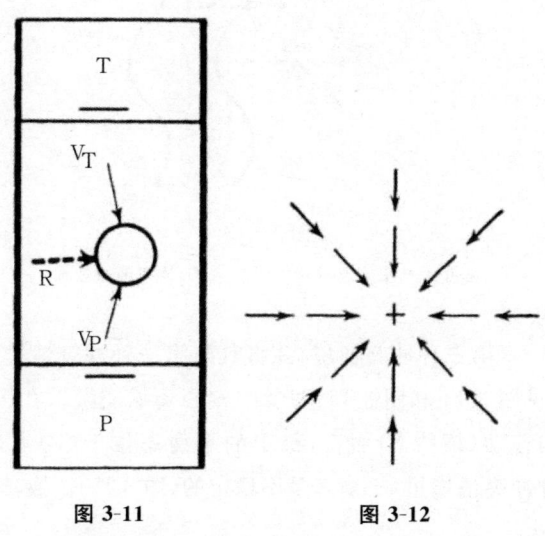

图 3-11　　　　　图 3-12

现从我制作的电影里撷取一例,以说明第二种冲突情境的力量场结构。一个三岁男童想要抓住水里的橡皮天鹅并把它拖到岸上,但他怕水。和天鹅(S)正诱发力对应的是会聚场(图 3-13),这个会聚场之上叠加着与另一个波浪对应的会聚场,乃是负诱发力。重要的是,这种情境经常是：随着空间距离的增大,和负诱发力对应的场力减弱得很快,相反,和正诱发力对应的场力的减弱却要慢得多。从位于场域里若干点的场力的方向和力度中,我们可以推导出儿童必须到达的某一点(P),那就是平衡发生的地方。(在其他地方,都存在一个最后导向这个平衡点的结果。)这个平衡点和情境里的瞬间摇摆相对应,尤其和有一点威胁的波浪对应,他在水里来来回回、进进退退。实际上,这样的摇摆反映在儿童在水里进进退退的动作中。

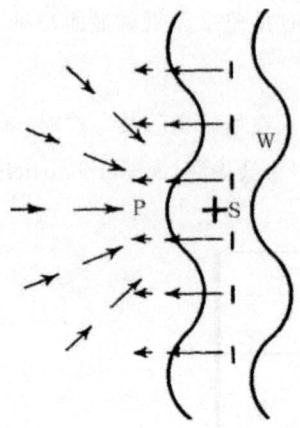

图 3—13

说明:P=儿童位置;S=目标天鹅;W=障碍波浪

回头看一下第三种冲突情境,并将其与第一种冲突情境相比较,两者的主要差异见图 3-14 和图 3-15:两者的核心场域交叠。在第一种冲突情境里,就横向移动(横线 S)而言,稳定的平衡态位于(P)点(图 3-14);相反,在第三种冲突情境里,平衡态是不稳定的(图 3-15)。换言之,这里存在

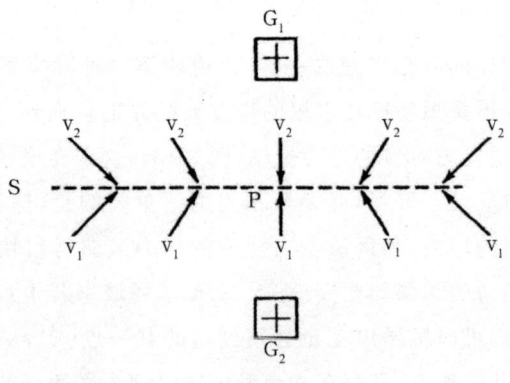

图 3-14

说明:第三种冲突情景(平衡态稳定)

箭头→=对应目标(G)的驱力(V);虚线(S)......=平衡线

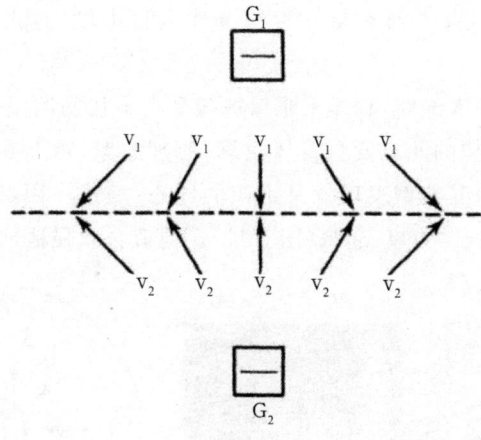

图 3-15

说明：第三种冲突情景（平衡态不稳定）

箭头→＝对应目标（G）的驱力（V）；虚线......＝平衡线

在惩罚的威胁（图 3-11），激发一个往旁边退却的倾向，其依据是两个矢量强有力（Vp and Vt）拉动的结果（R）。结果，除非受其他情况的阻止，儿童总是要退场的。如此，如果要惩罚生效，那就必须用障碍（B）把儿童圈起来；于是，他如果逃离就要接受惩罚，或完成那不合心意的任务。① 也就是说，除了要求他完成任务外，还有必要限制他的行动自由，借以（用物理或社会手段）形成或多或少有约束力的环境。

在冲突环境中，只要情境并非不稳定的平衡，两种大致相等的力量对立就会导致一个典型的后果：在两种场力之间，儿童的两种行为发生快速的交替。如果其行为不摇摆，说明儿童有比较典型的自控力；在冲突尚未解决时，他表现出相当平静的行为。②

忍受未解决冲突情境的能力是意志教育的主要目标。当然，冲突情境的发生有一个预设：两种对立的场力大致对等。倘若惩罚的威胁、成人

---

① 障碍的心理刚性可能源于成人的权力、儿童自己的荣誉感或其他诸如此类的因素。
② 在这些思考中，我们看到以下原理的理论依据：自制力不是自制的结果，而是顺从的表现。

的压力或其他约束力没有给儿童留下什么自由度,真正的冲突就不会发生。

如果情境令人绝望,总体上难以逃避令人不快的困境,在四面八方矢量的压力下,绝望的儿童就会身体收缩,心理收紧,就会在他和情境之间筑起一道高墙。其典型表现就是绝望的体态:缩成一团,以手掩面等(图3-16),或者把自己"包裹"起来(图 3-17)。他就会顽强地抗拒了。

图 3-16　　　　　　　　图 3-17

(五)紧张状态

在冲突情境中,两种场力的对立直接导致紧张状态[①]的加重,这是可以详细推导的。遭遇外部障碍时,儿童尤其紧张。(见图 3-11:惩罚威胁存在的情境。)

自我和环境的心理分野仍然不清晰时,环境里任何紧张状态的加重都立即反映在儿童身上。这样的敏感性可源于环境里的泪眼、愉悦的情绪、收拾行装的繁忙、妈妈不好的心情,或任何其他激动的情绪,这些紧张的情绪都会传染给儿童,无论大人如何掩盖这样的情况。

最简单的例子是,一般紧张状态的加重表现为儿童的焦躁不安。焦躁是紧张状态弥散的、无指向的释放,同时释放的还有具体情境中的定向力,焦躁最终可能会导致情绪的爆发,比如大发雷霆。[②]

---

① 紧张可以界定为:四面八方场力的对抗。
② See T. DEMBO, Der Ärger als Dynamisches Problem, *Psychol. Forsch*, 1931, 15, pp. 1—144.

焦躁行为的基本情况在婴儿身上是一目了然的,无论其期待愉悦与否,焦躁的形式都很相似。如果有人在他跟前摇晃拨浪鼓或奶瓶(婴儿的心理状态和图3-2相似),他都会伸展手脚,把嘴巴转向诱发力的方向。但他不会这样保持平静,他要开始摇晃蹬打。

在稍大的儿童身上,和一般紧张状态对应的最轻微的焦躁行为是迅速改变正在做的事情。兹举一例:在一所实施蒙台梭利[1]教学法的幼稚园里,一个三岁的幼儿喜欢画画,有一天,老师没有拿纸给他画画。于是他就出现了几种替代行为:抚弄铅笔、看小伙伴画画等。最后,他就去玩其他游戏了,但他玩其他游戏的时间平均只有3.5秒。而他前一天玩其他游戏的时间长达14.6秒,后一天玩其他游戏的时间也长达12.3秒。儿童在他和目标之间遭遇不可逾越的障碍时,他的紧张状态随之加重,结果,他变换所玩游戏的频率会加快四倍。

乌柯(Ucko)的实验显示,稍大的儿童在类似情境中变换所玩游戏的频率也比较高。[2] 此外,紧张度的加重使他们的玩耍也更加敷衍。

标志性的焦躁行为基本上是弥散的释放,但其形式却取决于具体的情境。如果焦躁行为发生时,儿童和正诱发力之间存在障碍,虽然他有焦躁的动作,但他和正诱发力之间的距离没有增加,焦躁行为也不会增加。换言之,焦躁行为沿着平衡线发生,就是说,当前进路线遭遇障碍时,焦躁行为的方向会与场矢量垂直相交。

以儿童有困难坐到石头上为例(图2-5),他可能会绕着石头走。如果强大的正诱发力被一个篱笆(F)圈定(图3-18),除了沿着正诱发力前进的动作外,焦躁行为(R)可能是环绕障碍走的形式。另一方面,如果儿童在圈子里面,而诱发力在圈子外面,典型的行为就是沿着圈子边沿走,指向诱发力,但其动作略有摇摆(图3-19)。

---

[1] 蒙台梭利(Maria Montessori,1870—1952),意大利医生、教育家,创办"儿童之家",提出蒙台梭利教育法,强调儿童潜能的自由发展,著有《蒙台梭利教育法》《启发人的潜力》等——译者注。

[2] 这些实验里,实验者打断儿童喜欢玩耍的游戏,借以产生紧张状态。

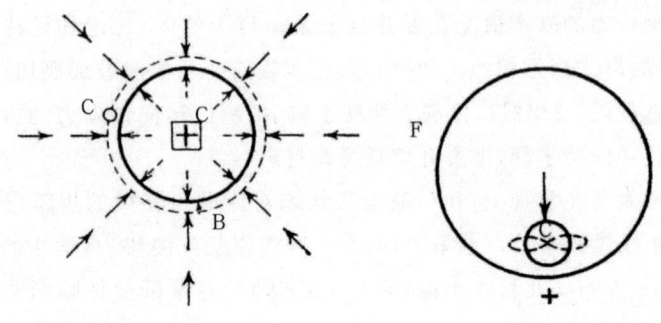

图 3-18　　　　　　　　　图 3-19

说明：→＝对应目标（G）的驱力；实线圆环＝对应障碍的约束力；虚线圆环＝平衡线

（六）感应诱发力

如上所述，诱发力在一定程度上对应儿童的瞬间需求。然而，由于其他环境因素的影响，正诱发力或负发力是可以从事件里演绎出来的。感应诱发力对儿童特别重要。

（七）社会场

童年的一个基本事实是，环境是不受儿童控制的。他会面对许多要求和困难。这些困难来自环境的物理事实和儿童自身有限的能力。物体太重，他举不起来；楼梯太陡，他爬下不去；铅笔在纸上不听使唤。更重要的是社会因素，尤其是成人和其他儿童的权威或权力。

在新生儿的生活中，这些权力的有效性仅仅产生于对他身体上的控制（他被沐浴、被用浴巾擦干、被用奶瓶喂奶）。但不久之后，权力对婴儿心理环境的影响就获得了越来越大的意义。成人禁止或允许他摆弄一些东西，把有些行为说成是好的或坏的，区分受表扬的行为和受责备的行为。

对几个星期或几个月大的婴儿而言，诱发力基本上取决于他自己的需求和瞬间的状态。如果他不需要食物，你就不能用心理手段强制他吃下去，[①]他会吐出来。儿童稍大后，用心理手段影响的他可能性不成比例

---

① 简单的干扰除外。

地加大了。令人不安的动作被嵌入游戏时，其意义（及其诱发力）就大大改变了。

对儿童直接的影响与他接触的社会事实所含的心理存在的日益增加相关联，尤其与他和别人力量的接触相关联。① 环境里的许多物件、许多行为方式、许多目标获得了或正或负的诱发力，获得了障碍的属性，这不是直接来自他本人的需求，而是来自另一个人。然而，更重要的是示范效应，那是儿童所见成人身上典型的或正或负的诱发力。即使是幼儿也会对社会评价和力量非常敏感。

儿童的负面诱发力（O，图 3-20）来自成人催生诱发力的力量场（A）。如果这个力量场对儿童来说失去了它的心理存在（成人离开或失去权威），负面诱发力就同时消失了。

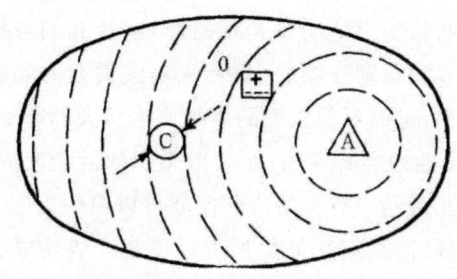

图 3—20

说明：C＝儿童；A＝力量场；O＝被禁目标

除了成人的力量场之外，其他儿童或一组儿童的行为和力量场对诱发力的类型和强度也至关重要。

在儿童的环境里，其他人的力量场的强度和范围千差万别，其变异尤其取决于经济情况、父母的性格、同胞兄弟姐妹的人数和性别，以及朋友的人数和性别。

一般地说，儿童环境里的"自由"范围（即基本上取决于他个人的力量

---

① 从动力论的观点看，这些影响范围构成儿童的力量场。

范围)是相当狭小的。太强大、太宽广的外来力量场可能会引起儿童的压抑,或猛烈地反叛。太严厉、太溺爱尤其会造成这样的后果。太严厉也好,太溺爱也好,儿童都没有足够的生活空间;在他的生活空间里,心理环境的诱发力和其他动力属性是由他的需求决定的。维赫(Wiehe)[1]研究陌生环境或陌生人的效应,研究这种场域里的各种力度,探寻力度与不同行为量的相关性,看看靠近或远离陌生人的不同行为所产生的力量场不同程度。除了儿童和陌生人的个性之外,这种力量场的力度就是儿童与陌生人距离、陌生人在场的时间以及他的行为的函数。最大的压力表现为儿童的呆住不动,较小的压力表现为他的哭叫,或逃避的倾向,他可能会跑到妈妈身边,或跑到另一个力量场中,在那里他会感觉比较舒服自在。在儿童行为中,强烈的陌生感也会使他感到压抑,稍小的压力会使他很激动或做出很过分的行为(见第八章图 8-9)。

兹举一例说明陌生力量场对儿童的影响,让我们考虑外在要求这个层次的意义。正如阿德勒强调的那样,成功或失败的经验对儿童有显著地激励和打击作用,进而对他以后的表现产生重大的影响。法扬斯对 3～4 岁幼儿成功或失败的实验发现:如果把儿童的活跃度分为四级(从最活跃到最不活跃),儿童同一行为的活跃度就可以简约为三个失败的等级。[2]另外,不活跃儿童的活跃度又可能相应地增加。成功或失败的经验对儿童自觉程度的影响也是相当大的。

霍普(Hoppe)[3]的实验证明,成功或失败的经验取决于短时间的"渴望水平"。反过来,渴望水平和个人的能力有关:"太困难"和"太容易"的任务不会产生成功或失败的经验。比如,儿童做成人或少男少女才能做的事情时,他不会产生什么成功或失败的经验。然而,渴望水平绝不仅仅是由个人能力所决定的。相反,成人的要求或小伙伴的表现可能会使儿童产生超过(或低于)他真实能力的渴望水平。因此,他可能产生优越感或自卑感,这对他的日常举止和实际成绩都可能造成严重的影响。

---

[1] F. WIEHE, *op. cit.*
[2] 这一关联主要适用于一定时间内所重复的同样动作。
[3] F. HOPPE, Erfolg und Misserfolg, *Psychol. Forsch.*, 1930, 14, pp. 1-62.

法扬斯发现,安慰话可以大大减轻失败对儿童的影响(图 3-21)。在这里,我们又看到,社会场对自我意识的意义是显而易见的。成人替代性的满足比安慰话更有效。

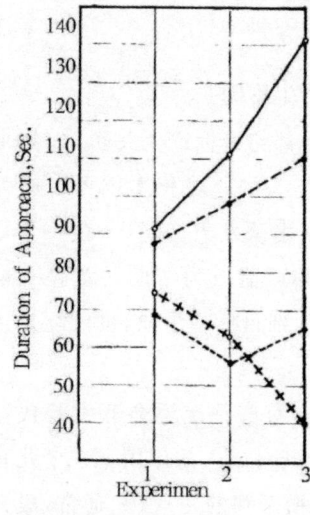

说明:成功、鼓励、替代和失败对走向目标时长的影响;实线(——)表示成功与鼓励相伴。在第 1～3 场实验里,时长增加 48%;虚线(- - -)表示成功。时长增加 25%;…表示替代性成功。走向目标的时长减少等于 6% 的失败;走向目标的时长减少 48%。

图 3-21

即使对六七个月大的婴儿,成功或失败的经验也会影响其活跃度和指向目标的时长。不过,在这个年龄段,成功以后的重复行为会使指向目标的时长缩短(图 3-22)。

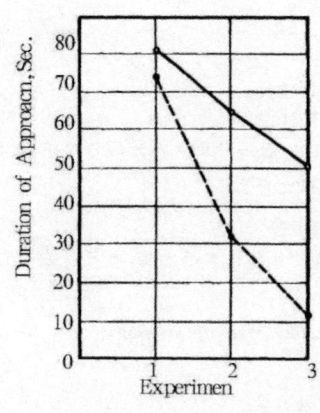

说明:实线(——)表示成功对儿童的影响;
虚线(- - -)表示失败对儿童的影响。

图 3-22

第三章 环境在儿童行为及发展中的作用 **77**

朱克纳特(Jucknat)①对数百名儿童的实验研究发现,在某些情况下,一个区域的失败可能会改变其他区域的渴望水平。就是说,当两个区域有足够的动力互动,儿童在一个区域的目标水平又不太受拘束时,该区域的失败就可能会使另一个区域的目标水平发生变化。

(八)手段与替代

和社会场一样,特别的事物也会对环境产生影响。

特别强调的目标使环境剧变,使一切事物都与目标产生关联。② 如果儿童想要把木棍敲进洞里,刚才被他用作火车头的一块积木就可以成为有用的锤子了。如此,成为工具的事物就衍生出诱发力。同样,在一个目标前,椅子可能是障碍,在另一个目标前,它却可能成为帮助儿童爬上桌子的手段。③ 环境里其他事物的属性可能是达到目标的手段,也可能是达到目标的障碍。

环境总体指向主要目标的另一个效应是,有些情况下会产生替代性目标。④ 替代现象对儿童的作用很重要,大于其对成人的作用。一个儿童想要摸摸宠物狗,却又害怕,其替代动作是摸摸牵狗的儿童。⑤ 通常,成人千方百计用替代方式满足儿童,使儿童的愿望转向替代目标。一般来说,这样的办法产生的摩擦比较少,抑制儿童渴望的动作则会引起较大的摩擦。抑制产生另一种后果(不在此细说),那是或明或暗的相反动作,即所谓儿童的负面行为,负面行为事关重大,因为他渴望行为的心理重心反而被成人的抑制大大强化了。⑥

---

① JUCKNAT, Leistung und Anspruchsniveau. (In preparation.)
② 这不仅将一种好的性质延伸到一个较大的场域,而且,在一种正诱发力的作用下,围绕事物迥然不同的正诱发力、负诱发力和其他变化也随之产生了。
③ See T. DEMBO, op. cit; W. KOIILER, *The Mentality of Apes.*
④ 我们在这里关心的不是替代理论,替代理论在弗洛伊德理论里很重要;之所以关心它,那是因为它涉及环境力量的问题。
⑤ See LEWIN, K. *Die Entwicklung der experimentcllen Willenpsychologic und die Pschotherapie*, Hirzel Leipzig, 1929.
⑥ 有可能,"动作和反应对等"的命题同样适用于心理动力学。

在假装的动作或表扬行为中,这样的替代过程常常是非常重要的。一个儿童想要打另一个儿童,最后却只满足于动嘴威胁。他想要把一个皮球高高抛起,但只做了一个夸张的动作。

拉扎尔把有些孩子称为"手势儿童"(gesture children)。他们用手势替代真实的表扬或真正动作的倾向非常强烈,一种重要的人格特质就这样被取代了。

对儿童总体上来说,认真和嬉闹、真实和假装的流动性很大,不像成人眼里那样界限分明。这个现象和心理环境的一种属性有关系,下文将予以简要的介绍。

二、环境里的现实分层

成人的心理环境在现实中表现为若干层级,分化程度不同,但分化鲜明。简言之,现实的层面可以说就是"事实",即独立于个人愿望的存在。这是现实行为的领域——难以逾越的领域。

更加非现实的领域是希望和梦幻的领域,常常是意识形态的领域。从动力学来看,一种更加非现实的层次特征是更大的流动性。[1] 非现实层次里的界线和障碍不那么牢固,自我和环境的边界更富有流动性。在非现实的层次里,人可以做自己喜欢做的事情。[2]

完整的心理环境描绘不仅必须厘清现实层次的结构,而且必须廓清非现实层次的结构。如果现实层次的情况太不尽人意,无论基于什么原因产生如此高的紧张度,告别现实层次而进入非现实层次的倾向都会非常强烈,逃离现实遁入梦境、幻想甚至产生疾病的现象就会随即发生。

原则上,这些事实同样适用于成人和儿童。不过,儿童心理环境的特征是:(1)心理层级的分化不那么明显;(2)心理现实和非现实层次的转化比成人容易。

幼儿的心理环境既不能说是现实世界,也不能说是非现实世界,相对

---

[1] See J. F. BROWN, Über die dynamischen Eigenschaften der Realitats-und Irreal; tätsschichten, *Psychol. Forsck.*, 1933, 18, 1−26.

[2] See T. DEMBO, *op. cit.*

而言,这两个世界的分化尚未完成。让舍①研究的感知心理学证明,儿童的遗觉像有尚未分离的属性,不像成人的感知和想象分离得那样清楚。皮亚杰②证明,幼儿的世界观念,尤其因果观念仍然是"巫术的"和"万物有灵"的,在儿童身上,名与物、行为和巫术语词尚未清晰地分离。③

儿童的感知特征和世界观特征仅仅是以下事实的表现:在他的心理环境中,现实层次和非现实层次的分化还微不足道。儿童游戏时那股认真劲儿也表现了他心理环境分化不足的事实。由此衍生出了愿望和现实区分的不足,比如"虚假"和"真实"的区分就不清晰。④ 儿童了不起的"暗示性"也与此有关。这是因为儿童的身体机能紧紧依靠其身体状况(如生病),而且这一现象常常被人忽视;反过来也是这样:身体状况紧紧依靠其身体机能。身体状况可能深受心理情况的影响,儿童的情况尤其如此。于是我们看到,幼儿喊痛时,大人吹吹他疼痛的部位,他就不痛了;有人"把马扔出窗外"时,马就"不见"了。

现实和非现实不太清晰的分化甚至能延伸到青春期:有时,除了现实生活外,有些人多年生活在另一种幻想生活中,幻想生活的事件对儿童具有极其重大的意义。即使对青少年而言,思想意识拥有的力量也远远超过了成人。

当然,如果你认为,现实和非现实分化完全不见于儿童,那就错了。⑤在他的真实需求里,情况基本上就是这样的,身体需求和心理需求都是这样的。在某些情况下,儿童会满足于幻想的糖果而不是真实的糖果,他喜欢积木块胜过玩偶。尽管如此,幼儿从很小的时候就表现出区分现实和

---

① See E. JAENSCH, *Übbcr den Aufbau der Wahrnehmungswelt und die Grundlagen der menschlichen Erkenntins*, Barth, Leipzig, 1927.

② 让·皮亚杰(Jean Piaget, 1896年8月9日—1980年9月16日),瑞士人,近代著名儿童心理学家,著有《儿童的语言和思想》《发生认识论》《儿童的物理因果概念》等——译者注。

③ See also D. KATZ and R. KATZ. *Gcsprache mit Kindern. Untersuchungen znr Sozi— alpsychotogie und Padagogik*, Springer, Berlin, 1928.

④ See C. STERN and W. STERN, Errinnerung, Aussage und Lüge in der ersten Kindheit. (*Monog, u. d. seel Entwick. d. Kinds*, Vol. 2), Barth, Leipzig, 1910.

⑤ 即使对儿童的世界观,皮亚杰的论点也可能必须要做一些限定。

非现实的迹象,至少在许多方面是这样的。

斯里奥伯格(Sliosberg)发现,只有在游戏情境中,儿童才会把这种非现实的物件当作替代物。①

(一)游戏

我认为,以下情况是游戏动力论的基础:一种行为(如沙箱里的游戏X)描绘为游戏或非游戏,不取决于成人的立场,相反,它完全由儿童的生活空间来界定。游戏动力论的基本特征是,一方面,与它相关的事件属于现实层次,就是说,其他人也能看到这样的游戏活动(它不同于白日梦)。另一方面,游戏行为受现实规律制约的程度大大低于非游戏行为:目标的设定和达成在很大程度上受制于游戏人的喜好。在这种动态流动中,游戏场近似于非现实的状态,其显著特点是:事物的意义容易改变,儿童的身份(扮演的角色)也容易改变,这是其他现实层面难以企及的特征。就现实性而言,游戏场或多或少受限,这说明,即使就内容而言,游戏与空中楼阁和空想的非现实也有极为密切的关系。

游戏可以根据其动态流动性来分类。不同的游戏的动态流动性差异很大;游戏规则可能会非常严格,以至其使游戏的动态性接近现实的僵硬性。

人逃离现实进入非现实的倾向是非常强烈的,这是现实中主导因素的作用所致,当现实的压力太强时,这一倾向尤其强烈。

心理环境分离的进程不仅取决于儿童的个人特征,而且取决于儿童的境遇和命运。在劳工子女的身上,这一分化通常发展得较早。② 现实和非现实较早且鲜明的分化似乎不利于儿童的发展。当然,层次之间足够充分的分化也很重要,但层次之间的关系却具有决定性意义;这些关系对创新行为产生决定性影响;理想目标属于非现实层次,它们或多或少直接影响现实层次的行为,层次之间的关系都具有决定性意义。

---

① See S. SLIOSBERG, Zur Dynamik des Ersatzes in Spielund Ernstsituationen. *Psychol. Forsch.*, 1934, 19, pp. 122—181.
② See H. HETZER, Kindheit und Armut, *Psychol. d. Fursorge*, 1, Hirzel, Leipzig, 1929.

(二)自我的边界

儿童心理环境仅仅略微分化成现实、次现实和非现实三个层次。与此相关的还有一个因素:对儿童而言,自我与环境及边界的划分不如成人那样分明。就环境对儿童的影响而言,这一现象极为重要。

从动态角度来看,个人是一个相对封闭的系统。因此,除了情境的结构和力量外,环境对个人的影响很大程度上取决于个人和环境之间的边界在功能上的牢固程度。儿童个人的内结构的动态特征是:心理区域的分化相对少,心理系统边界的牢固程度低。[1]

换句话说,相比成人,儿童在很大程度上是一个动态统一体。[2] 比如,婴儿起初的动作是全身动,逐渐才学会了部分肢体动,[3]之后才学会了分化环境,将注意力集中在部分环境上。

儿童内在心理系统的分界不分明,与此相似,他个人与心理环境的边界在功能上也不牢固,一般不如成人。例如,"我"或"自我"是逐渐形成的,大约在两三岁时出现。直到那时,财产观念、某物属于自己的观念才开始形成。自我边界欠明晰的状态还表现在这样一个事实上:外在印象对儿童核心个性的影响更直接,显然超过其对成人的影响。反过来,需求或内在心理系统的紧张状态很容易失控,其形式是冲动行为和无控制的情感展示。

自我与环境边界较小的牢固程度对现实和非现实较少的分离产生了直接的影响。自我与环境边界较小的牢固程度隐含着这样一个命题:儿童心理环境与其瞬时的需求和愿望的关系比成人更紧密,儿童心理环境也是对其需求和愿望的回应。

儿童与环境之间的限制性层面在功能上的联系不那么牢固,其程度会有很大变异。即使在同一个孩子身上,其牢固程度也因不同的情境而

---

[1] 这里不全面展开介绍人格内结构。
[2] 此所谓苛勒(Köhler)意义上的"强势格式塔"。
[3] 柯格希尔(Coghill)研究证明,在胚胎发育期,连反射行为也是在反应动作分化中形成的,起初的反射行为是整个有机体的行为。

有很大的差异;面对不同的人时,这样的功能变异也迥然不同。同理,儿童对外界的感知程度亦迥然有别,内部心理状态,尤其是紧张状态的外在表现,也因时、因地、因人而异。

心理学研究还发现,在有些情况下,不穿衣服时,儿童更容易受诱导而说出自己个人的事情。① 晚间上床睡觉时,他们通常更容易说出自己在其他情况下保密的事情。②

自我与环境之间墙壁功能的牢固性不仅取决于儿童的年龄,而且取决于其人格特征。在一些精神病儿童的身上,这个特点尤其明显。其原因可能是人格分化具有更大的流动性,同时,相对心理年龄而言,精神病儿童人格分化的程度也比较低。就环境的动态受心理影响而言,流动性在环境动态中也是显而易见的。低能儿童的特点也是人格分化的程度低。

和上述精神病儿童相比,某些类型的低能儿童的特点是心理系统的流动性较低。这样的刚性导致了"非此即彼"的行为,并显著表现在意志心理学领域,在此,某些诱发力和行为样式(倔强、固守)尤其牢固。同时,精神病儿童的功课之所以困难,其决定性的因素是心理系统和环境心理结构的牢固性。

即使在自我与环境分化明显的情况下,自我与他人特别的动态合并也可能发生,比如,儿童与妈妈朋友的联系。这样的联系表现为多种形式:在妈妈跟前表现坏,在他人面前表现比较好;看不见妈妈就大闹;遇到不愉快的情况就奔向妈妈——"躲到妈妈的裙子背后"。在此,母亲是否在场是儿童心理环境结构改变的决定因素,儿童的安全感由此完全改变。母亲和儿童人格的心理关系密切,所以,母亲的能力、她抗御环境事物和情感的效应对儿童具有功能性意义,那就是儿童抗御环境而获得安全感的力量增强。因此,母亲的离场意味着儿童抗御环境力量的削弱。③

---

① 詹姆斯(W. James)强调衣服与社会心理人格的密切关系,因此,可以理解的是,在有些情况下,赤条条的状态使儿童与环境之间心理墙的牢固性削弱了。
② 儿童入睡前的坦承可能与现实和非现实边界的部分消减有关系,这是睡眠和梦境的特征。
③ 儿童往往喜欢抱布娃娃或玩具上床,这也说明了这些东西与自我的紧密关系。

在儿童世界观里万物有灵的特点和另一个事实有关：总体上，他的心理环境有个人特有的力量场，这是他心理环境结构里凸显的动态特征。

他人和他物都与儿童有密切的心理关系。归属于"我"这个意义的不仅有儿童的身体，还有他的玩具、椅子等。从动力学来看，这样的物件宛若他的身体的一部分，因为它们表征的是他对环境力量入侵特别敏感的方面。维赫认为，物件属于自我抑或属于外部世界，取决于儿童的需求和内在紧张状态，并且随着这些因素的变化而变化。比如，如果儿童制作的一样东西尚未完成即被毁坏，由于这件东西属于他的自我，所以他就感觉这是对他的严重侵犯。相反，如果毁坏行为在事后才发生，他就不会受到多大的影响。内在紧张状态的释放常伴有自我附属物被放松的结果，这在儿童身上表现得尤其明显。

三、环境力量对儿童发展的影响

儿童瞬间情境的主要因素同样影响着他长期生活总体环境的特征。这些因素对儿童的人格发展和行为也产生着重要影响，其影响和瞬间情境力量对瞬间行为的影响相类似。通常，环境的具体特征对儿童发展的影响与环境总体特征的影响相同；具体来说，环境对儿童人格分化的速度和样式产生影响。过分严厉或残酷的环境可能会导致儿童自我封闭，他把自己和环境隔离开来，他变得倔强、抗拒。最佳的环境条件比如最佳的张力水平因人而异，差别很大。

众所周知，从总体上看，保育院喂养的婴幼儿在许多方面比在家庭里养育的孩子成长得慢。这和父母的具体要求、他们的性格以及相处方式有关系。一旦在合适的环境里生活一段时间以后，训练这些孩子的困难就会消失。当然，如果回到原来的环境，他们通常会旧态复萌。

尿床常常用换环境的办法来治愈。当然，这样的治疗效果常常是短暂的。格里希(Grisch)报告了环境变化治愈"聋哑症"的一个病例。

迄今为止，我们描绘了当前情境对儿童发展的影响。这样的影响随着情况的改变而停止。然而，环境的影响总是使个人产生或多或少的变化，进而改变他对以后一切情境回应的基础。当前情境对将来的行为举止产生影响，这一点对儿童发展特别重要。同时，这样的影响又在时间上延伸到将来,这不仅影响到儿童智能经验的获得,而且最重要的是,儿童的整个人格在许多方面都被改变了。

当前情境对未来情境的间接影响既可能表现为有利的方式,也可能表现为不利的方式。其特别重大的意义表现为这样一个观点:自我与环境的循环因果关系。比如,与小伙伴相比,低能儿在两个方面处于不利的地位。首先,他不能胜任面前的任务(给瓶口塞上软木塞、用铅笔写字等),即使他和正常小伙伴面对的条件相同,即使实验者手把手教他们握铅笔、给瓶子塞上软木塞,他也不能胜任。然而,在实际生活中的一些情况下,还存在第二种困难:比较聪明的孩子面对任务时知道,他必须寻找在现有条件下最容易的方法来操作。不那么聪明的孩子视野比较狭窄,他看到环境的内在关系比较少。比如,他没有发现,最方便的办法是他手握的瓶子要尽可能靠近嘴巴。一般地说,他找到最容易解决问题的办法的可能性比较小。

由此可见,不那么聪明的孩子不仅能力比较差,而且同样问题对他提出的要求实际上大于对聪明孩子的要求。所以,情况通常是,较弱孩子较差的解决办法就具有这样的双重性:面对更困难任务会有更差的表现。

如上所见,如果不那么聪慧的孩子遭遇失败,他以后面对问题时就会更加懦弱。失败使他更加恐惧,除了低下的能力外,加大的恐惧感会造成更加不利的心理状态。在新情况下,本来就比较弱的儿童就可能会容易失败,就更容易放弃努力。他通常在比较难的任务面前发愣(心理意义上如此),由于过去失败的经验,总体的形势对他就更加不利了。

这样就造成了恶性循环,十分类似的例子可见于精神病儿童,亦可见于在社会群体里交往有困难的儿童。过度兴奋的儿童、不太合群的儿童在社会情境中能力较差,这使他完成任务比较困难;而且,因为其他儿童不接受他,促使他抱有防卫心理,如此等等。这样的孩子可能会难以应对社会情境;这样的情况下,连很小的冲突造成的困难也难以应对,甚至社会能力比较强的儿童也会被搞得筋疲力尽。因果关系循环也类似于恶性循环,这是能力与环境的因果循环,例如,口吃。反过来,聪慧儿童为未来创造有利的环境条件,这是他成长最有利的条件之一。

我认为,教育学根本的任务之一就是为困难儿童创造环境,以避免或矫正因果关系循环造成的严重损害。这里至少存在着真正的教育学的可能性,我们不再需要改变儿童的"能力"。

第四章 奖励和惩罚的心理情境

本章的讨论不准备涵盖奖惩的全部范围。如果提出完全避免奖惩可能性的问题,那就进入了教育根本的辩证问题。因此,基于奖惩教育原理的教育学体系正确与否的问题与其说是心理学问题,不如说是生活哲学问题。

本讨论主要限于心理学领域,从心理学角度看,我有意将其限定在技术问题上:奖惩手段可能会催生或压制儿童的某种行为。

这里不会把奖惩视为社会学问题或司法学问题,而是将其视为心理学问题。因此,同一种行为在某一情况下可能是惩罚,在某一情况下可能是奖赏,这要取决于儿童所处的总体情境。

只有当儿童被要求完成的动作或行为的方式不符合他那一刻的喜好时,奖惩才可能发生。要求儿童解答的问题、做的功课或从事的活动使他反感,他不感兴趣,对要完成的任务他了无兴趣。他被迫做算术题,但他不喜欢计算。他被迫吃东西,但那不是他喜欢的食物。

如果老师希望儿童参与的活动本身有足够的吸引力,奖惩就不必要。儿童在他自己需求的推动下沿着老师希望的方向前进。

可见,奖励或惩罚引导儿童去完成老师给他的指令或遵守老师的禁令:换言之,他克制自己不去完成自己想要做的活动。

所以,奖励或惩罚的情况与另一种情况相对:主导儿童行为的是原生或派生的兴趣本身。①

从纯心理的角度,我们可以提出这样一个问题:哪一个因素更有利于完成任务:对任务本身的兴趣,抑或是可能的奖惩?乍一看,你可能会判定,兴趣更有利。你的根据是:儿童的需求直接提供了足够的心理能量,相反的情况则使儿童缺乏足够的动力。然而,自然的兴趣能提供较大心理能量的论断却未免太轻率。相反,在某些情况下,有力的惩罚或渴望的奖赏能使更大、更持久的力量发挥作用,其作用胜过兴趣的作用。

有人试图证明,在一种情况下,兴趣"自然性"的心理优势胜过在另一种情况下兴趣的"人为性"。这样的尝试至少需要对概念作更精准的表述,以避免心理学意义上的含糊其辞。即使儿童对物体本身感兴趣,其兴趣也可能是从图形或文字里派生出来的,比如从他对电车的线条、门牌号码或商店招牌的兴趣中派生出来的。

即使儿童对数字或文字感兴趣,给它贴上"自然"的标签恐怕也有些牵强。它可能是在大都会环境中形成的,有一定的间接性,也可能是从更原生的需求中派生出来的。即使在兴趣活跃的大多数人的例证中,这样的派生性也是事实。

根据上述观点,奖惩可能纯粹是一种手段,老师有意借此强化儿童不曾有的兴趣。实际上,我们常常发现,儿童心理学和发展心理学(而不是反射论)有这样一种观点:在幼儿身上,奖惩的重要功能是产生老师想要附带强调的东西。这个观点使深层的心理差异模糊不清,混淆了兴趣教育学和基于奖惩原理的教育学。对有些老师而言,这样的混淆固然方便使用,但其他老师却认为,这会产生致命的心理后果。

为了理解其间涉及的心理过程的性质和范围,有必要深入洞察具体

---

① 我的讨论局限于奖惩的一般情境,不涉及儿童实际体验的奖惩。因此,不考虑因为这样那样的情境儿童希望得到的惩罚,比如使他减轻难以忍受的情境,或使他有可能和某一位小伙伴联系的情境。同样,讨论奖励时,我不考虑使他吃惊的奖励,因为那本来就是他很想做的事情。这里讨论的根据是我们的实验研究。

心理情景的结构。儿童回应奖惩的行为不能从孤立的刺激或分离的心理过程中演绎出来,就像任何希望都不能从受环境影响的心理意义推导出来一样。把儿童行为归之于"自然"或衍生的需求,那样的描述是不充分的。相反,只有把心理过程放进它与联系的整个情境的关系中去考虑,我们才能理解环境干扰对实际动作的影响。事实上,只有考虑个人与当前整个情境的结构关系,对实际发生的事情作概念的演绎才有可能。[1]

在工作和游戏中,在标签、动作和情绪中,事实上在一切言行中,实际发生的事情都受到当前环境结构的影响。所谓环境,不仅指狭义的瞬间情境,而且涵盖了心理生活空间。所以,科学表达心理环境的任务极为重要,最重要的心理学问题即科学解释心理动力的问题。然而迄今为止,我们仍然缺乏研究其所必需的恰当工具。除了其特殊主题外,本章的讨论可以被视为一种应用方法的初步尝试,我将其视为完成这一任务的重要一步。

下文的情境分析中,我尝试着对整体情境和重要的动力学因素作精确的拓扑图表征。分析的结果将直呈读者,相信其中的术语一目了然,我不准备对以下表征情境心理特征的术语进行解释:"障碍""矢量"(力量)、"地域"等。

无论结果看起来多么简单,这里都有一个研究问题需要解决——表征的重大困难问题。在这样的拓扑图表征中,我们不必考虑相对孤立的情境细节,不能像口头描绘那样啰嗦。整个研究过程迫使我们从当前的情境出发,将其视为一个统一体。因此,由于这种表征概念手段的精确,我们必须随时注意大量隐性的共同决定的结果。

另外,由于同样的原因,这样的表征使我们能在很大程度上整合大量貌似无关或矛盾的细节,使我们能澄清其相互关系。下面的讨论将局限于瞬时全局的主要特征,这些特征为理解许多案例分化的层次提供了基础。

---

[1] See LEWIN, The Conflict between Aistotelian and Galileian Modes of Thought in Contemporary Psychology, Chap. I above; Zwei Grundtypen von Lebensprozessen, *Zeitschr. f. Psychol.*, 1929, 113, 209 ff.

我将介绍兴趣本身决定的情境的若干特征,然后考虑奖惩的心理情境,首先我介绍涉及指令的情境。

数学拓扑学是非量化科学,研究一般性质的关系。借用其概念是否合理,这个问题不宜在此讨论。然而,我想强调指出,这不是表征物理—地理问题,也不是表征社会情境问题,而是表征心理情境的结构问题,即儿童心理情境的问题。毋庸赘言,以下图表里的矢量并不代表物理的力量。

第一节 兴趣情境

从动力学的观点看,儿童由于兴趣而转向他感兴趣的事情(如玩布娃娃)时,其心理结构的情境相对简单。这个情境由兴趣主导,用我们的术语说,就是由正诱发力主导(图 4-1)。① 儿童(C)看见一个布娃娃(D),玩布娃娃产生正诱发力。这里有一个心理场力量即矢量,其方向是从儿童指向玩布娃娃。如果吸引力大于情境中的其他物理力量,儿童顺着矢量方向的动作就会发生。

如果儿童顺着这个方向的动作遭遇困难,他会怎么办呢?比如,椅子挡路、大人禁止、另一个儿童的力量范围阻挡他达到目标时,他会怎么办呢?从心理学来说,无论这一困难是物理的或社会的,它都是儿童和布娃娃之间的障碍(B,图 4-2),这妨碍儿童指向目标的活动。一般来说,困难不能完全阻止儿童的活动,而是以

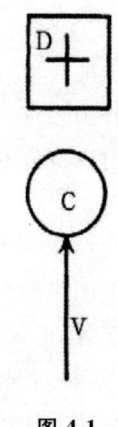

图 4-1

说明:C=儿童;D=布娃娃;
V=矢量

---

① 我们用加号"+"表示正诱发力,用减号"—"表示负诱发力。重要的是注意任何心理意义上的物件,如具体的物理客体、社会理想、活动、行事的方式、状态(如睡觉)或任何目标都带有诱发力。

某种方式迫使他脱离原来的方向。① 他可能会绕过椅子,"绕过"大人,或向小伙伴借布娃娃玩,"至少是借来玩一会儿"。

总之,对目标本身感兴趣而发生的事情表现出以下典型的动态特征。如果困难迫使儿童偏离原来的方向(图4-3),场力的方向随之变化,变化的依据是个人和目标关系的变化。再者,方向变化的性质是:指向目标的矢量出现,并启动相应的行为。如此,儿童行为给人留下了明显追求目标的印象。一个自然而然的目的论由此而生。

一般所谓目的论的、被视为生物行为标准的无非是以下事实:一个正诱发力控制着局势,以至于随着人位置的变化,力量场的方向亦随之变化,如上所示。

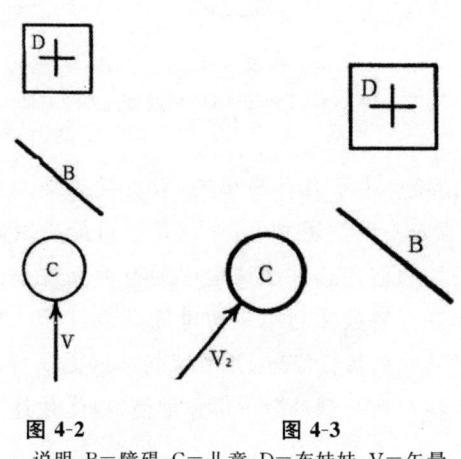

图 4-2　　　　图 4-3
说明:B=障碍;C=儿童;D=布娃娃;V=矢量

第二节　带惩罚性威胁的指令

一、诱发力的性质和倾向

在奖励或惩罚情境中,儿童做事情时所包含的诱发力——其一切行

---

① 至于具体会发生什么事情,这取决于障碍的牢固程度和形式,以及矢量的方向;最重要的是,障碍是否把目标包围得严严实实,或者是留下了接近目标的路径。

为所包含的诱发力,都不是正面的,而是负面的,已如上所述。比如,儿童不想抄满满一页纸的字母"i",或不想做算术。于是,偏离任务的矢量(V_t)就在他的身上起作用了(图4-4)。

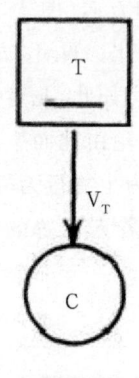

图 4-4

说明:C=儿童;T=任务;V_t=偏离任务的矢量

奖励或惩罚情境产生了几种简单的、教育学意义上重要的事实。儿童表现出的倾向对应一种负诱发力,那就是尽可能冷淡超脱,远离任务。在此,他逃脱的行为和他在感兴趣情境中的行为反差很大。在其感兴趣的情境中,他使尽浑身解数并利用一切可能贴近目标;相反,在奖励或惩罚情境中,他主动防止向目标靠近,并尽可能推迟去执行任务。无路可逃时,他万般无奈才在最后一刻奉命行事。即使这样,他还是有尽可能放弃的倾向。

倘若在他不愿意时,我们仍然希望他做算术题,那就要让他放下正在做的游戏,转向做算术题。其动力学意味是,我们必须想办法生成一种场力(C_t),新的场力要和原来的场力截然相反,而且要胜过它。

一种办法就是惩罚。至于惩罚是一望而知的,抑或遮遮掩掩的,那并不要紧。

你可能会说,如果你不做算术题,我就要揍你,就不让你去野餐,放学后你就得留堂,不能回家。说这些话时,你用上了第二种诱发力,加重了不愉快的气氛。再者,为了调动一个新的场力,使之与第一个负诱发力矢量逆向而行,你就必须在儿童的背后启动第二个负诱发力。

惩罚性威胁基本情况的拓扑结构表征(见图 4-5)。儿童夹在两个负诱发力之间:做算术题(T)和受惩罚(P)。若要使惩罚性威胁起作用,由它启动的矢量(V_P)就要大到足以压倒矢量(V_T);即使儿童接受那不愉快的任务,第二个矢量也要大到足以把儿童控制在任务场里。①

以下的抽象思考有助于澄清奖励或惩罚情境和兴趣情境两者的差异。在兴趣情境里,儿童受阻时,矢量的方向随即改变,但我们看到,儿童继续向着原定的目标前进。然而,在奖励或惩罚情境里,儿童因困难而被迫改变方向时,他运动的方向往往和完成任务的方向相反。

如果你要他重新启动,向完成任务的方向走,第二个负诱发力即惩罚就势在必行,其位置就必须和现有的矢量(V_T,图 4-6)逆向而行。这里就缺乏兴趣情境中那种教育学意义的特征;在兴趣情境中,儿童受阻时它会根据自己的兴趣继续前进(图 4-3),只要困难不使他太难受。

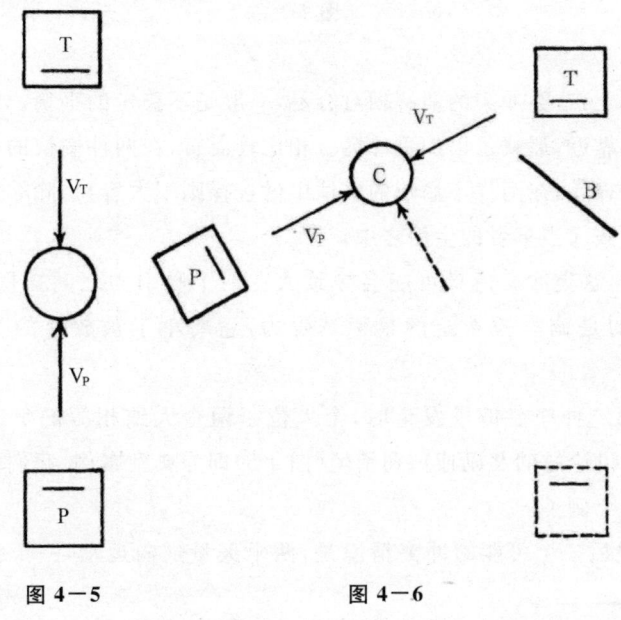

图 4—5　　　　　　图 4—6

---

① 儿童一旦进入任务场,其他因素也随之起作用。

然而，即使执行任务没有特殊困难，奖励或惩罚情境里始终存在着这样一种动态形貌：儿童总是被迫偏离任务。任务的负诱发力本身就有一种动态机制，它就像一个障碍。在许多情况下，它阻碍儿童走向目标的力度更大。第二个负诱发力的存在使情况更加复杂，造成了一个冲突的情境，使儿童感到困惑。

二、冲突类型

心理学所谓的冲突是，两种逆向、同步、大致相等的力量在同一个人身上起作用。因此，基本的冲突类型有以下三种：

1. 个人位于两个大致相等的正诱发力之间（图 4-7），例子有布里丹的驴子①，饿死在两堆干草之间。

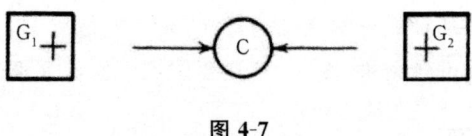

图 4-7

总体上，这类冲突的消解相对容易，一般是不稳定的平衡。如果向一个诱发力靠近，那就足以加重冲突。相比较而言，在两件愉快的事情中做选择比较容易，在两件不愉快的事情中做选择则不太容易，除非设计的问题深深地嵌入当事者的生活之中。

有时，这类冲突情景可能会导致人在两个吸引力之间摇摆不定；此时，重要的是调整被选定的目标诱发力，它要小于被放弃的目标的诱发力。

2. 第二种冲突情景发生时，个人位于两个大致相等的负诱发力之间。刚才讨论过的奖励或惩罚情境（图 4-5）即为典型案例，我们稍后将充分考察这个例子。

3. 最后一个可能的冲突情景是，两个矢量逆向运动，一个源于正诱

---

① 法国哲学家布里丹（Jean Buridan, 1300 ? —1358?）笔下的驴子喜欢思考，在两堆干草之间不知如何选择，以至于被饿死。故事寓指优柔寡断的哲学困境。

发力,一个源于负诱发力。在这里,只有两个诱发力处在同一位置时,冲突才会发生。比如,孩子想要抚摸宠物狗,却又害怕;想要吃巧克力,但得不到允许。这样的冲突用图 4-8 表示,我们有机会比较详细地介绍这样的冲突情景。

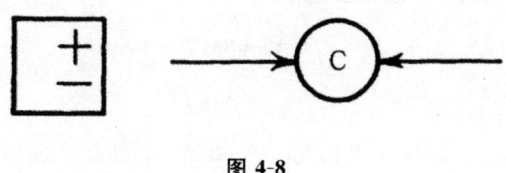

图 4-8

三、逃避倾向,外部障碍

惩罚性威胁造成的冲突情景见图 4-5,儿童位于两个负诱发力和相应的场力之间。为了回应来自两边的压力,他的倾向必然是,两件不愉快的事都要避免。不稳定的平衡由此而生,侧向的移位 C 会产生一个很强大的矢量(VR)。该矢量与惩罚任务的方向垂直相交(图 4-9)。如此,既规避任务又躲避惩罚的儿童将试图逃离这个力量场(沿着图 4-9 里虚线箭头的方向逃)。

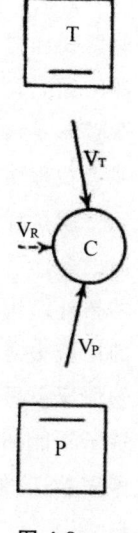

图 4-9

不妨补充说,儿童进入威胁性惩罚情境时,未必立即处在惩罚和不愉快的任务中。通常的情况是,起初他发现自己完全置身事外。比如,对他的要求是半个月内完成令人讨厌的作业。在这样的情况下,惩罚和任务构成相对统一的、未分化的整体,这是双倍的讨厌。在这样的情况下(图 4-9a),逃跑的倾向就很强烈,结果是惩罚的威胁胜过讨厌任务的威胁。更准确地说,由于惩罚性威胁,总体的复杂情况更令人讨厌。

同时躲避任务和惩罚的最初的尝试是身体退场,跑开,躲起来。离场的形式常常是推迟几分钟或几个小时去执行任务。在反复严惩的情况下,新的威胁可能使儿童试图离家出走。对惩罚的恐惧常常在儿童逃学

第四章　奖励和惩罚的心理情境　95

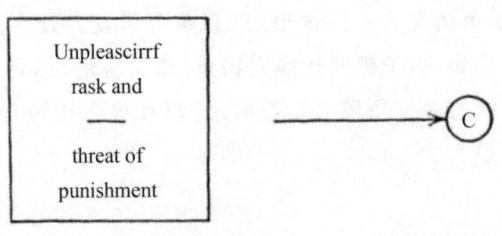

图 4-9a

的初期起很大的作用。①

另一种形式的离场是去做另一件事情,儿童常常选择做的是成人没有理由反对的事情,借此,他掩盖离场的行为。如此,他可能做另一种更令人愉快的功课,利用以前获得的允许,或诸如此类的东西。

最后,儿童有时会或多或少地欺骗大人,借以逃避惩罚和讨厌的功课。大人难以检查时,他可能说功课已做完,实际上并没有完成;他还可能说(更机灵的欺骗形式),另一个人接过了那不太令人愉快的任务;或者找理由说,那个任务不再需要做了。

就这样,源于惩罚性威胁的冲突情景造成了逃离的倾向(图 4-5 和图 4-9)。儿童离场的倾向因情境的拓扑结构和场力而变化,难以避免,除非采取特别的措施去防止。如果大人想要孩子在负诱发力干扰的情况下做功课,单纯的威胁是不够的。大人要确保孩子不能离场。就是说,他必须设置障碍(B):只有做完功课,他才能自由活动,否则他就要受到惩罚(图 4-10②)。

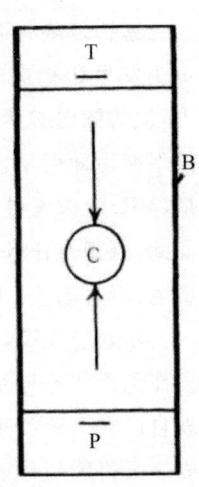

图 4-10

实际上,意在使儿童做完功课的惩罚性威胁总是在构建一个滴水不

---

① See G. HOMBURGER, *Psychopathologie des Kindesalters*, Berlin, 1926, p. 508.
② 在图 4-10 和以后的示意图里,障碍用粗线条来表示。粗线条用来圈定界限分明的区域,比如任务区,任务区的边界心理上并不是很牢固。区分边界的牢固程度既有可能,也是必须。

漏的框框,任务场和惩罚场一起把他围得水泄不通。大人被迫设置障碍,不留任何漏洞,儿童溜不出去。倘若大人太笨拙,或者在他这方面的能力不足,只要觉察到任何一点漏洞,儿童就会溜出去。

最原始的障碍是身体禁闭,儿童可能会被关在屋子里,直到他做完功课。①

但障碍一般是社会性的,②儿童周围的障碍是成人因其社会地位而握有的权力工具,以及他和儿童的内在关系。这样的社会障碍和物理障碍是同样重要的。

社会因素导致的障碍可能会把儿童的天地限制在狭小的空间里。比如,他没有被关起来,但在完成作业之前不准他离开房间。③ 在另一些情况下,他到外面活动的自由不受限制,大人常常监督他,不准他走到大人看不见的地方。因为大人不可能时时刻刻跟着他,所以大人常常利用儿童的魔幻世界,时常把控制儿童的能力赋予警察或怪物。上帝知道他的一举一动,他无处可逃,父母常用上帝教训他,效果也不错。比如,偷吃糖果的行为就可以这样来控制。

在社会环境里,障碍是由生活直接构建,或者由家庭生活习惯养成,或者由学校的组织机构设置的。

若要有效,社会性障碍就必须要有足够的牢固性。如果在某一点上不够坚实,儿童就会冲破障碍。比如,如果他知道,大人的惩罚仅仅是说说而已;如果他有把握用甜言蜜语哄父母不兑现惩罚,他就相信,不做完功课是可能突破的障碍。还有一个类似的障碍,母亲把看孩子做功课的责任交给保姆、老师、大孩子,但这些人不像她,不足以抗压,他们不能防

---

① 还应该指出,若要儿童完成任务,你就必须为他设定明确而狭隘的界线。用示意图表现情境时,你只能局限于当前的心理状态(原因难以在此细说)。如此,一连串发生的事情只能用示意图来表示。因此,时间的约束就用单一的线条来表现,儿童在当前情景中对时间限制性的感觉如同受约束的自由走动。
② 构成心理场的大多数概念和现象都是由社会现象决定的,而不是由物理事实决定的。
③ 对行动自由的限制常常被用作惩罚。即使这样,约束常常也是用非物质的、社会的或准魔术的手段实施的。比如,儿童可能被惩罚待在屋角不准动,也可能被捆绑在椅腿上。

止孩子逃离做功课的场域。

与物理障碍和社会障碍并行的第三种障碍紧紧依靠社会事实,但和上述几个例子有重要的区别。比如,你可以诉诸儿童的自尊心("记住,你不是小混混""你不是坏孩子");你可以利用群体的社会标准("记住,你是女孩子""你是男子汉")。在这里,你可以借助于孩子能懂的意识形态、目标和价值。儿童对意识形态的诉求暗含着威胁:他要当心被群体排斥的危险。同时最重要的是,意识形态构成外部障碍,它界定了意识形态允许儿童自由活动的边界。只有他感觉到受束缚时,惩罚性威胁才有效。如果他不再承认意识形态,不承认替代意识形态的道德限制,惩罚性威胁就常常失效,他就不接受道德的限制和约束。

障碍在具体情况下的强度取决于儿童的性格,以及功课和惩罚的负诱发力。负诱发力越大,障碍就越坚固;障碍越坚固,侧向运动的力量就越大。因此,成人要儿童的行为符合自己的意愿而施加的压力越大,障碍就越坚固、越难以穿透了。

四、情境受约束的性质

包围惩罚环境的障碍不仅构成与外部环境隔绝的圈子,而且也多多少少限制了儿童的自由活动。这样的限制不仅意味着,他必须完成功课,而且对他的自由活动的广泛性也构成了约束。

这一事实最明显地表现在儿童被关在房间里的情境。但即使表面上只要求他做一件事,其他的自由活动还是允许的,实际的障碍还是对他的自由活动形成了普遍的限制。如果不是这样而是相反,如果他在游戏的范围即障碍圈定的拓扑空间(图4-11)里能随心所欲,那么在做完功课之前,他爱做多少其他的事情都可以。实际上,儿童当然会利用这样的可能性。结果,只要他留在圈子里,就奖励和惩罚而言,他是可以"离场"的。换言之,就心理上而

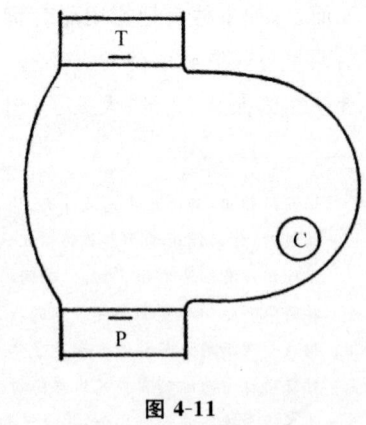

图 4-11

言,障碍则会大大退却,就变得不那么真实了。

在心理学和教育学里,物理障碍或社会障碍留给儿童的自由活动范围当然意义重大。但必须强调,惩罚性威胁总是而且必然会产生一个约束情境的结构。情境约束的显著性和成人压力的严厉性成正比,成人的压力是迫使儿童完成任务的手段。约束力的大小一方面取决于障碍的坚实和严密程度;另一方面取决于成人限定障碍、避免薄弱点、极力减少儿童游戏空间的倾向。成人的威胁性惩罚越严厉,儿童生活所受的限制就越大,成人回归原始物理障碍的倾向就越强烈。儿童的环境越是建立在惩罚性威胁的基础上,惩罚越严厉,他所处的环境就越像监狱或教养院,其约束性标记是禁闭室和随时随地的监督。

围绕惩罚情境的障碍并非总是特别有形的。儿童自由走动的地方即自由活动范围所受的约束,和他受限的权力范围对应。成人尤其是有组织的成人权力范围极其强大,他们把儿童自由活动的范围限制得严严实实。在儿童的生活里,他不受成人立即干涉及威胁的地方是有限的。与小伙伴秘密结成小集团、与小伙伴的友情和闲聊,这些活动和游戏场所可能就是自由活动的地方。然而,即使在这些范围里,儿童的自由、儿童免于成人监管的时间也是有限的。实际上,儿童的心理状态、营养状态和居住状态都受成人控制,所以,儿童的自由活动范围通常都位于成人的权力范围之中。

惩罚性威胁是否必然造成特别的障碍,这是一个特别需要注意的问题。通常,轻微的惩罚性威胁使限制的增加成为必然。成人的生活方式、同一个屋檐下的生活情况和习惯,过去不觉得是限制,但在惩罚性威胁之下,这些情况都获得了障碍的意义,限制了儿童的自由活动范围。

五、无障碍的惩罚情境

有些情况下,除了惩罚性威胁,并不见得有特别的障碍。面对不愉快的任务,即使是不折不扣的负诱发力,儿童也能完成任务,并不见得有明显的障碍促使他退场,甚至连惩罚性威胁似乎也没有。成人吩咐他做功课,这就足以使他规规矩矩地完成任务。

这里讨论的不是儿童出于对大人的爱而执行任务,那是将要被奖赏时讨论的问题。相反,我们关注的情况是,训诫背后有一个未言明的惩罚性威胁。准确地说,儿童与成人的关系格格不入,甚至对成人产生敌视,却必须出于自愿似的去执行不愉快的任务。在这样的情况下,设置特别狭窄的障碍似乎就没有必要了。实际上,在这样的环境里,常有人骄傲地指出,儿童被赋予了很多自由,但没有给他设定狭隘的限制。

图 4-10 用拓扑结构所示的情境并不完全正确。障碍圈定的场域用拓扑学形式表现的事实是,儿童的心理场被完全圈定了。除此之外,图 4-10 还显示,一个特殊的区域即围障把儿童圈定起来了。

如上所述,相对于一个内在范围的圈定区,也就是围障圈定的区域,儿童自由行动的内在范围可大可小。当然,我们不能认为,内在范围内的自由等同于没有外部障碍的范围内的自由。相反,由于障碍的存在,整个场域的性质及其动态特征在许多重要的方面都发生了质的变化。稍后,我们将予以细说。然而,在上述惩罚情境里,还是要有一个相对自由的活动区,这是内在的场域,我们要将其与感觉到的障碍区别开来。即使小孩被限制在房间里,如果他顽强,内心没有被压垮,他基本上还是能做自己想做的事情。

然而,在刚才勾勒的情境中,这种特殊的障碍和内在范围实际上是不存在的。成人的权力和惩罚的威胁渗透在儿童生活的全部领域,他能自由而独立活动的区域是不存在的。用外部障碍阻止儿童离场之所以不需要,那是因为这一障碍的功能遍及他生活的整个场域。儿童发现,他的生活场域被控制在围墙内,成人权力对他的控制无孔不入(图 4-12[①])。

自然,无孔不入的控制并未完全实现,若要生存,儿童就必须保留最低限度的行动自由。我们希望的状况并不简单地对应百密一疏的控制环境,外部障碍圈定的行动范围并没有降低到最低限度。这种手段并不能造成限制行动范围的状况,这种情况的发生更可能是因为成人用非常严

[①] 从动力学来看,与成人权力场(A)对应的儿童心理场如图 4-12 所示,亦如本章后续示意图中的同心圆所示。当然实际上,成人的权力场不会以均质的方式渗透到儿童的行为场,而是在不同的地方有不同的密度。就当前的目的而言,我们不必考虑这个不均等的现象。

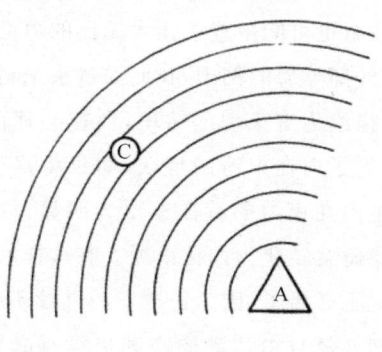

图 4-12

厉的惩罚手段或清晰的意识形态压倒了儿童,以至于他不敢反抗。儿童爽爽快快地完成了令他讨厌的任务,那是因为他的行动范围(C)处处都受到成人的控制,这是对他内心的控制。既然他对成人的依靠非常彻底,惩罚性威胁就没有必要了。在极端情况下,成人根本就不必提自己对孩子的希望。

当然,惩罚手段在整个场域里渗透的程度不只取决于环境,还取决于儿童的性格。但即使在没有极端限制他行动自由的情况下,也必须记住,整个情境的结构是对应图 4-9 的拓扑结构,或是对应图 4-12 的拓扑结构。[①] 我们特别要强调图 4-12 的拓扑结构,因为正是在最严格束缚的情景里,儿童的心理特征才最明显。因为在这些例子里,儿童内心起到决定性的作用,所以成人实际上施加的压力就难以显现。然而,成人从外到里的压力约束越明显,其强度就越大。在许多被视为强制的行为里,在一些考察中,它们表现出来的特征可能正好是相反情境里的特征。在这里,我指的是儿童明显自愿的行为,这是他感兴趣时的典型表现:对任务感兴趣时,他会无拘无束地根据需要行事,这是没有障碍的情境。

上文勾勒的情境有时会变得相当复杂。当成人对孩子过度溺爱与呵护时,成人的管束渗透在他的整个生活空间,其转化为约束情境就成为必

---

① 自然,过渡性和混合性的情况也是有的。你可以想象,图 4-12 表现的是障碍渗透在整个场域的情境。这个观点可以成立,因为障碍始终是以其功能界定的。

然的结果。如此,儿童也可能被置于强大无比的力量场里。

暂别以上无需外部障碍的例子,我们回过头来讨论典型的惩罚情境。这种情境也可以被描绘为有束缚的情境,内在心理范围很小的情境尤其如此。外部障碍产生了内在束缚的特征,如果将这种情境与另一种情境比较,外部障碍产生内在束缚的特征就更为明显。当主导因素不是惩罚而是兴趣时,外部障碍就转化为内在束缚。在这样的情况下(图 4-1,图 4-3),设置外部障碍就不必要了,因为正诱发力继续不断地引导儿童回归任务;在任何方面限制儿童自由活动的空间也没有必要了。和处罚情境相反,在兴趣情境中,儿童在整个场域里就能自由行动,无拘无束了。

六、紧张状态

带惩罚威胁的情境的拓扑图一般有这样的特征:两个负诱发力(一是任务,一是惩罚),以及阻止侧向移动的外部障碍。为了对情境作全局性描绘,还有必要判定场域里的紧张状态。

如上所见,冲突在惩罚情境里发生:两个负面、反向的诱发力会产生两个矢量(V_T和V_P),两个矢量作用于儿童(图 4-10)。两个矢量并非场域里孤立的力量,场域也并非不受到影响;矢量导致全局产生紧张状态。

这就意味着,影响儿童的矢量并不局限于来自任务和惩罚的两种矢量。其他一切方向上都存在着矢量,它们大致相等,影响着运动。在场域里的一切地方,儿童都受制于有所增加的总体压力。

场域里加大的紧张状态是惩罚情境里两个负诱发力作用的必然结果,这一点很容易从一般原理中推导出来。[①] 我们已经介绍过两个矢量(VT 和 VP)产生的侧向运动结果(VR),侧向运动指向对外部障碍的突破(图 4-9)。换言之,冲突情境产生离场的倾向,如果儿童决定循侧向运动,他就会撞击外部障碍,而且可能会突破障碍。如果这样,整个情境的拓扑结构就会变化,惩罚就不再有效,稍后我们会讨论这一后果。另外,障碍可能会岿然不动,如此,障碍本身就获得一个负诱发力。这就可能产

---

① 接着探讨的场力和全局张力的关系虽然基于惩罚情境,但对大量类似的情境具有普遍的心理学意义。

生多种结果:儿童受伤,可能是因撞击障碍而受伤;他会体会到自己的无能;如此等等。此外,大部分由禁令构成的非物理障碍会直接成为障碍,因为它们具有负诱发力。

如此,在维持惩罚情境的情况下,障碍产生的一个矢量(VB,图 4-13)和侧向移动的矢量(VR)逆向而行。逆向而来的矢量导致冲突,也就是说,两个逆向的场力在同一条线上起作用。

儿童试图在任一点突破障碍时,同样的动态情境随之产生。对立的场力存在于场域里的每一个地方,在每一个方向上起作用(图 4-14①),场域里的紧张状态随之而起。②

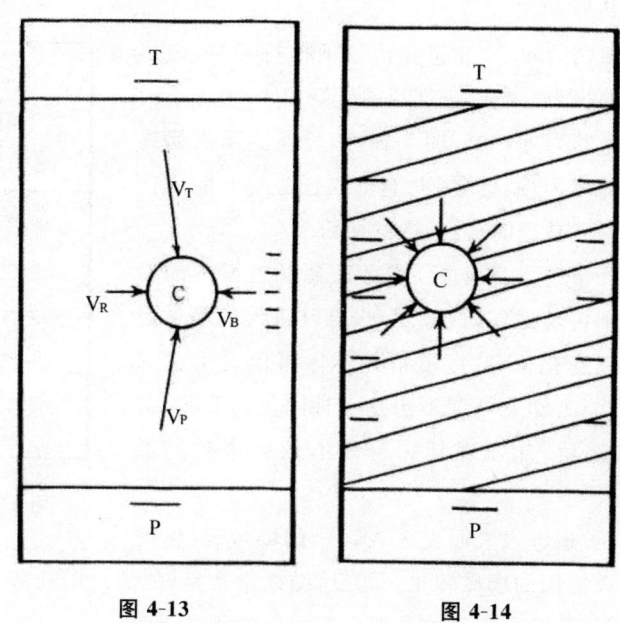

图 4-13   图 4-14

场域里状态的紧张程度取决于惩罚性负诱发力、任务和障碍的力度。在决定惩罚性负诱发力大小的因素中,一个重要的影响因素是儿童过去

---

① 图 4-14 的交叉线表示张力。
② 作为动力学概念,张力的定义是逆向运动的矢量。

的经验或者是过去与障碍冲突的经验。如果儿童曾经因为试图离场而遭到严厉的惩罚,负诱发力的力度就很大。然而,在很大程度上,障碍的负诱发力对个人的影响取决于任务和惩罚性负诱发力的大小。归根结蒂,使这种威胁起作用所必需的触发点取决于任务所具有的负诱发力的大小。

七、惩罚情境里的行为样式

在上一节里,我们讨论了以下情境中拓扑结构和场力的一般特征。在那种情景里,成人试图用惩罚威胁来迫使儿童以某种方式行事。现在,我们简要地考虑这种情境中儿童的实际行为。

(一)执行指令

通过惩罚的威胁,儿童在诱导下执行任务,做出成人希望的行为。起因于惩罚的矢量(VP)表现出大于反向矢量的力度(VT,图 4-15)。外在的障碍始终维持足够的牢固性,于是,儿童进入任务场。完成任务对他的意义是通向自由,逃避惩罚。

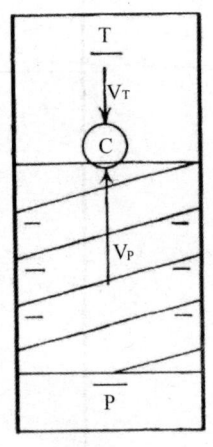

图 4-15

一旦儿童进入任务场,情况就会发生根本的变化。任务不再与他作对,他发现,自己进入的场域足以产生这一变化。有时,事情并不像事前看上去那样可怕。比如,幼儿可能不想吃一种陌生的食物,但尝过一口之后,却发现其味道并不像原来想的那样糟。

然而,被迫进入表面上令人讨厌的场域时,情况未必向令人愉快的场域转化。相反,结果常常是,他面对的任务一直令人讨厌。况且,儿童早已经熟悉那令人讨厌的任务。

无论如何,身处任务场里感觉到的情境和惩罚性威胁的情境是迥然不同的。①

---

① 在刚刚过去的那场世界大战中,我们可以清楚看到的是,重返战场比身在战场是更令人不快的情境。

(二)接受惩罚

起因于任务的矢量比源自惩罚的矢量强(图4-16),在一定意义上,这一情境是惩罚情境的反面。如果外部障碍足够强大,儿童就愿意接受惩罚。他走进惩罚场域,因为惩罚是通向自由之路,和上一节里讲述的任务提供的自由之路有相似之处。

兹举一例。爸爸对三岁儿子说:"如果你不收拾洒在地上的东西,我就要打你屁股。"儿子走到爸爸跟前,转过身,准备挨揍,并且说:"好吧。"显然,孩子理解爸爸的话有两种意思,有两种可能。

值得注意的是,这个孩子没有挨过鞭子。爸爸不久前买了一根鞭子,曾经用鞭子威胁他。但家里的教育氛围是自由活泼的,买鞭子是相当孤立的事件。

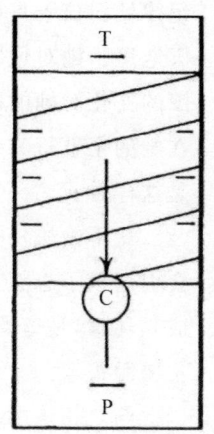

图 4-16

而且还可能,好奇心在儿童的角色里起到了决定性的作用,因为不久前过圣诞节时,爸爸老是说圣诞老人和鞭子。

在此,孩子受惩罚时,情况又为之一变。他注意到,实际挨揍并不像大人事前所说的那样严重。

一个10岁的女孩大吵大闹,被宠爱她的老师关进小黑屋。她坐在吸尘器上,用腿敲打吸尘器,大声唱歌。老师放她时,不禁大吃一惊,因为她很高兴,她向老师回嘴时有说有笑,一点也不难堪。

实际上,她成功地把惩罚变成找乐子的机会。一旦决定不把惩罚当作道德上的训诫以后,不愉快的感觉就不是很严重了。

屡屡受罚的孩子积累了经验,对不同处罚不舒服的程度略有所知。他不再从外面去看成人威胁的惩罚,而是从内部去看,并权衡任务和受罚令人不快的程度。他对惩罚麻木了,对威胁不再那么敏感了。他回头看受惩罚和与之相关的道德堕落时,试图将其降低到最低限度。

一个聪明、活泼的6岁女孩上学已经3个月了。上课时,她懒洋洋地仰面靠在椅子上,老师罚她下跪。放学回家时,她一点也不伤心,反而对妈妈说:"我喜欢跪。"

对老师和孩子而言,每件事都有一个大背景。老师觉得,用更严格的纪律处罚孩子是可取的。孩子起初喜欢上学,后来,慢慢退缩到自己的小天地里。她对惩罚的态度同时也是她对老师权力场的初步抗争。学校氛围的变化对她的影响很大,她的冷漠仅仅是抗争的表现,结果清楚地表现在她的全部行为中。她害怕黑暗,老是做噩梦,睡梦中惊叫,"老师,别老是这样看我!"

比不愉快任务更重要的是上述环境,在这些例子里,惩罚的实施可能会引起孩子思想上的剧变。他的价值系统可能会变,老师总是把惩罚说成是坏事,是道德上的降格。这种道德羞耻通常是儿童功课负诱发力的主要源头。

与之相连的事实是,公开的惩罚是特别要避免的。惩罚损害社会地位,不仅对成人有重大影响,而且也是儿童害怕惩罚的主要原因之一。

一个5岁男孩生病在床,每当他调皮时,挂在床头的黑人小玩偶就掉过头去面对墙,不看他。如此,孩子的调皮就一目了然,人人都能看到。这样的曝光给他的痛苦雪上加霜,小玩偶耷拉着脑袋,面对墙壁不看他。顺便补充一句,男孩从来不把小玩偶转过身来,虽然它就在床头,伸手就够得着。

一旦价值观变化发生,一旦处罚失去了羞辱的作用,其负诱发力就大大减弱。如此,威胁的背后就只剩下当前惩罚令人不快的具体情况,在整个惩罚场面前的胆怯就不复存在。儿童再也不觉得那是什么惩罚了。最后,他可能会想,不做完功课比做完功课更值得骄傲了。

在这一变化的源头上,以下现象具有动力学上的重要意义。如果功课的负诱发力很大,儿童宁可受处罚,那么,惩罚就是小恶,并具有了相对正面的意义。属于道德低下范围的东西似乎属于道德高尚的范围了,那是成人希望看到的道德上不令人讨厌的行为。惩罚成为小恶的变化使儿童更难调教。这种结果发生时,惩罚氛围特有的道德地位就出现了一个漏洞,原则上就分崩离析了。

然而,试图通过受罚在拓扑结构里获取自由的儿童常常会感到希望的幻灭。一般地说,成人不满足于单纯的惩罚,而是再次要求儿童继续做使他反感的任务。同时,成人还常常用更严厉的惩罚威胁他(P_2)。

如此,接受惩罚实际上并不意味着儿童有了通向自由之路。事后,他发现自己仍然受到束缚(图 4-17),面对越来越重的处罚,这些处罚最后总要把他搞得服服帖帖。这大概可以解释一个耐人寻味的事实:儿童很少心甘情愿地接受处罚。

然而有的时候,处罚实际上成了通向自由之路。原因可能是,大人不忍心采取更加极端的措施,儿童要完成的任务后来就难以实施了。

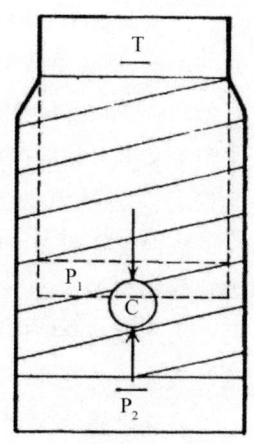

图 4-17

以下例子显示,接受惩罚真的成了逃避受约束情境的出路。屈戈尔根(Kügelgen)5 岁时被送到一所女子学校去读书。女孩子们的阴柔令他恶心,第二天他对妈妈说,他不去了。"最后,我倔强的反抗使她震怒,她就打出王牌,要我选择,是吃鞭子还是回女校。母亲战败了,一想到那些女孩子的面孔和柔性身姿,我就不再犹豫,我选择挨揍。我记得,她出手相当狠,那出乎了我的预料。但和那一群令人讨厌的女孩子相比,那又算什么呢。挨打以后我就自由了,母亲再也没有要我做类似的选择。"

(三)抗拒障碍

与执行任务、接受惩罚并行的第三种行为选择是抗拒障碍。

在这样的情况下,源自任务和惩罚的诱发力太强大,儿童就可能侧向移动(V_R)。接下来的行为既可能是对障碍发起盲目的、不克制的冲击(被关在屋子里的儿童可能以头撞门,用脚踹门),也可能经过仔细盘算后尝试的突围。儿童在具体情况下所用的行为方式取决于现存障碍的性质,他试图求得自由的策略有奉承、挑战或欺骗。

如果障碍牢固,儿童就无路可逃了。在这样的情况下,整个场域里的紧张状态达到足够高的程度时,儿童就可能表现出自杀倾向。于是,自杀似乎是逃离场域的最后一种可能。

由于父母十分严厉,10岁的玛莎整天提心吊胆,总是怕成绩不好。[1]复活节前,她显得特别恐惧,因为那是决定升、留级的时间。她的恐惧与日俱增,时常在睡梦中惊叫,跑到妈妈的床边,想和妈妈一起睡,因为她很害怕。父母对她很严厉,妈妈曾经威胁说,如果你不能升级,就不用再回学校了。"这次惊叫后,孩子想要自杀。"她亲近父母以改善在父母心中地位的倾向也很明显。她"帮助妈妈做家务,不需要她帮助时她也干活,她要让妈妈高兴。"

大多数破除障碍的尝试不仅显示了逃亡的倾向,而且或多或少表现为与成人的公开斗争。

破除障碍的大多数尝试与儿童对成人的抗争有关,我们接着详细讲述。

(四)与成人斗

上文业已提及,一般地说,外部障碍基本上是社会性的,它依托的是成人控制儿童生活的真实权力。归根结蒂,儿童对外部障碍的反抗就是对成人权力的反抗,因为障碍是成人设置的。

此外,惩罚的威胁以及任务本身都是成人设定的。控制情境的一切矢量和障碍最终都可以追溯到成人身上,因为正是他们在维护这些矢量和障碍。如果成人的权力丧失,整个情境就会随之分崩离析,任务、惩罚和障碍都将不复存在。如此,决定情境的一切诱发力盖源于一种现象:场域是成人控制的(图4-18)。与儿童权力对应的场力不足以维护儿童的权力,不足以抗衡成人的力量场。儿童对成人的斗争是站稳脚跟抗拒优势力量的尝试。

我们曾经讨论过成人对整个场域的支配(图4-12)。在那里,我们关心的是特别粗暴的约束情境;在那里,惩罚性威胁有效,似乎没有特殊的障碍。现在我们看到,一般来说,惩罚性威胁与那种情况的关系是相当普遍的。

---

[1] See A. DOHME, Beitrag zur Psychologie und Psychopathologie typischer Schulkonflikte auf den verschiedenen Altersstufen, *Zeitschr. f. Kinder forsch.*, 1930, 36, 458.

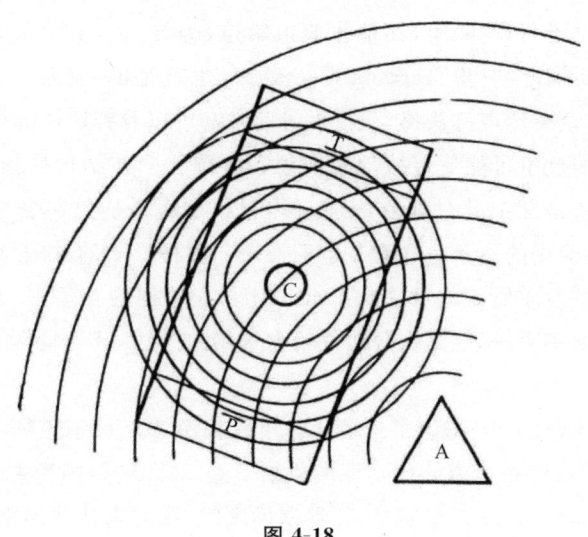

图 4-18

但那里的情况和这里考虑的情况不同。由于成人掌握实际的权力，外部障碍显得异常坚固；尽管如此，在圈定的区域里，儿童也享有明显的行动自由，这种情况也是可能的。在这里，惩罚的威胁特别指向一个任务。并非整个情境里的每一个点都具有约束性质，以上的例子就是明证。

成人与任务、惩罚和障碍的实际关系如何，儿童从思想上未必清楚；但即使是幼儿，也对生活领域里的社会关系非常敏感，所以儿童清楚地感觉到成人与任务、惩罚和障碍的关系。

因此，惩罚情境往往引起源自中心部位的抗拒，从动力学上看，那里放射出负诱发力，整个痛苦的情境基于负诱发力，将反抗的矛头指向了成人。

由此可见，惩罚的威胁必然造成儿童与成人对立的情况，使儿童与成人敌对。正是在这里，惩罚情境与兴趣情境存在很大的分歧：儿童出于兴趣去完成任务时，他和成人的关系就不再敌对了。

斗争的性质及其指向千差万别，取决于儿童、成人和情境的特征。大体上，儿童斗争的矛头可能指向任务、惩罚或阻止他离场的障碍。

直接反抗任务时，如前所述，儿童可能会摆出成人应该看到的困难：

笔记本不见了,铅笔断了,其他作业很紧迫,等等。一个常用的斗争手段是阿德勒所谓的"安排"(arrangements)。① 也就是说,成人应该意识到的困难有:儿童突然声称头疼,学校大考前常常可以看到这样的现象。

儿童的抗争可能更直接地指向惩罚。预料会在学校挨揍时,他通常喜欢的办法是穿上几件厚衣服应对体罚。小病小痛是防备惩罚的好办法,成人很受用的奉承也含有斗争的性质。各种形式的欺骗每每发生,且往往与斗争性质所需的难易状况成正比。在这样的斗争中,儿童毫不犹豫地采用欺骗手段,这是在敌对气氛中采用的方法,其他情况下大概不至于如此。

舒尔茨(Schurz)描绘了自己儿时用欺骗手法以后避免惩罚的一个例子。② 他的成绩单上有一门功课的成绩不好。"无论是因为失败的羞辱或害怕父亲的惩罚,反正事实是,礼拜六回家时,我竭力让父亲坚信,老师忘记填写我的成绩了,或者是诸如此类的原因吧。我不自然的举动使父亲坚信,有什么事情不对劲。他几个连珠炮似的问题很快就让我坦白了真相。"

"以下是我和父亲的对话:'你该做的事没有做,还想隐瞒。你不认为该吃鞭子吗?'"

"'该吃。但求你让我们去牛棚,那里没人看,谁也听不见。'父亲同意了。我在隐蔽的牛棚里挨了揍,他打得不凶,而且谁也不知道。父亲原谅了我,还像原来一样爱我。但我心里被羞辱的感觉长期挥之不去,沉甸甸地压在我心头,那是活该。很长一段时间,我都不去牛棚,躲得远远的,那是令我蒙羞之地。"

这个例子清楚地说明了儿童试图不让别人知道自己所受的惩罚。

最后,儿童的抗争还可能特别针对防止他离场的外部障碍。

无论这些反抗活动特别针对的是任务、惩罚还是障碍,它们都具有双

---

① Cf. ALFRED ADLER, *Über den nervosen Charakter*, Bergmann, Wiesbaden, 1912. (English trans, *The Neurotic Constitution*, Moflat, Yard, New York, 1917.
② See KARL SCHURZ, *Lebenserinnerungen*, cited by BAÜMER and DROESCHES, *Vonder Kinderseele*, Leipzig, 1908, p. 236.

重性,造就这个特征的是情境的结构和场力的源头。它们既是逃离成人控制的尝试,又是针对成人的斗争。实际上,只有穿越障碍、完成任务或接受惩罚后,儿童才能离场;归根结蒂,这一切抗争形式只不过是对成人反抗的不同体现而已。

如果总体的环境使儿童相信,他经常会遭到惩罚,他的反抗就可能超越具体的惩罚情境,他就会试图动摇或瓦解成人的权力。师生之争、纪律问题、积极和消极的破坏就属于这样的斗争。对特别强调权威的父母和老师,儿童经常用这样的方式进行反抗。

(五)自闭,违抗

离场未必以冲破惩罚情境的边界告终,儿童把自己包裹在场域里,也能够达到离场的目的。在不离场的情况下,儿童试图把自己包裹起来,避免受罚,至少暂时不受惩罚;他在任务、惩罚和自己之间筑起高墙。从功能和意义上看,这样的自我包裹在许多方面相当于离场。

紧张度越高、逃亡的希望越小时,自闭的倾向越明显。上文出于害怕而想要自杀的儿童就表现出这样的自闭倾向。"玛莎没有好朋友,除了放学回家的路上和同班同学玩耍之外,她都是独来独往。在邻居的孩子们中,她也没有朋友,偶尔才和他们一道玩,她喜欢和比她小的孩子玩耍。"[1]

和自闭关系密切的违抗反应实际上是自闭的一种特殊形式。

自闭的孩子退守、孤僻,但他不试图规避环境的压力,不躲避不愉快的接触。相反,这里所谓的自闭是对环境采取蔑视和对抗的姿态。[2] 比如,刚受过惩罚,新惩罚的威胁接踵而至时,儿童就可能表现出自闭的倾向;违抗的反应既是痉挛性的力量调动,又是在紧张环境里强调自信的表现。它显示的是,对威胁不反应过敏,对成人的权力场进行反抗。反应过敏主要是因为,格格不入的场力不再被视为一种约束力。和自闭与斗争一样,违抗也意味着他的思想在一定程度上发生了巨变。

儿童的违抗倾向常常是独立性的一个征兆,表明他要打破压倒他的

---

[1] A. DOHME, *loc. iit.*
[2] Cf. FAJANS, *loc. cit.*, and WINKLER, *Der Trotz*, Munich, 1929.

社会场域。在受压制的、被动的儿童身上,初露端倪的活跃征兆含有粗鲁的意味。

(六)遁入非现实,情绪爆发

在惩罚情境里发生的实际行为中,还有一些机制需要介绍,它们与情境的紧张状态有直接的关系,这就是遁入非现实和情绪的爆发。

在心理生活领域里,除了现实层面外,还有多种非现实层面。非现实层面(梦想层面、幻想层面和姿态层面)的特征大致是,如果遁入非现实,你就能做你想做的事情。从动力学上看,这些情境缺乏牢固的边界,流动性很大,[1]自我和环境的边界也是流动的。

心理过程及其现实层级是一个基本范畴,而且被用作一切更精确的心理环境特殊表征的第三维(图 4-18)。用更细致的奖惩问题表征来考虑这个第三维问题无疑是至关重要的,它与儿童的道德和意识形态关系密切。

如果威胁性惩罚情景太紧张、太难受、没有出路,就会出现从现实遁入非现实的强烈倾向。当然,身陷其中的儿童不是身体逃离难受的场域,他仅仅是在心理上出逃了。

心理环境分为现实层面和非现实层面,儿童起初并不清楚这样的划分。分层的情况表现在儿童世界观里的魔幻结构中,[2]表现在游戏里;在这个结构里真和假、梦境与现实、倾向和行动的边界是不牢固的。再者,从现实到非现实的转换也很容易。

对惩罚的惧怕也许不仅主宰了梦境,而且可能会引起尿床和类似的现象,[3]还可能产生深度的白日梦。

在非现实层面上,基于现实层面的痛苦都被移除了。儿童不再身陷成人权力的约束环境中,他自由了。讨厌的任务已经完成,或者被搁置在

---

[1] See J. F. BROWN, Über die dynamischen Eigenschafften der Realitatsund Irrealitatss-chichten, *Psychol. Forsch.*, 1933, 18, pp. 1—26.

[2] See J. PIAGET, *La representation du monde chez Venfant*, Alcan, Paris, 1926. (Engiish trans., *The Child's Clncepion of lhe World*, Harcourt, Brace, New York, 1929.)

[3] Cf. HOMBURGER, *op. cit.*, and DOHME, loc. cit.

一边了。儿童自己成了主宰,成人则不是,当需求和希望在现实层面被堵死时,在游戏或白日梦的非现实层面里就会出现需求的替代性满足①。

以下大段引用列夫·托尔斯泰笔下的一个故事,主人公展示的不是讨厌功课和惩罚之间冲突的情境,而是犯错误以后害怕受惩罚时跌宕起伏的情境。故事后半部分情境的拓扑结构和惩罚情境的拓扑结构相对应。儿童被关在屋子里,面对惩罚的威胁,这是地地道道受束缚的情境。

尼古拉的历史考试不及格,老师说他什么也没学。他怕家庭教师杰罗姆的责备和惩罚,他的哥哥因为考试分数撒谎就吃过杰罗姆的苦头。而且,他还在做功课的时候跑出去玩了一会儿。他姐姐的家庭教师米米发现尼古拉逃学,就向他的奶奶告状。尼古拉偷偷打开奶奶的公事包,偷看了奶奶的私信,而且把公事包的小钥匙扭坏了。因此,他预料爱他的父亲要惩罚他。

"米米在抱怨!分数又不及格!钥匙还搞坏了!事情再糟糕不过了,奶奶——米米告状,圣杰罗姆——零分,爸爸——钥匙……过不了今天晚上,这一切会使我大难临头!""我会遭到什么惩罚呢?"

"唉,我掉进什么陷阱了?"我自言自语,在自修室的地毯上来来回回地踱步。"唉,"我心里想,抓了一把糖果和香烟,"该来的一定会来!"这样想以后,我跑回了家。

这是我童年时代从尼古拉身上学到的听天由命的感伤。尼古拉给我抚慰,让我在繁忙的人生中,获得了短暂的宁静。我进屋时,有一点兴奋,神情不太自然,心情却很快活。

晚餐后,游戏开始,我们玩猫捉老鼠的游戏。我想表现得很活泼,但我笨手笨脚,踩在客人的裙子上,把她的裙子撕烂了;她是科马考家的家庭教师,常和我们一起玩。我看到,所有的女孩

---

① 众所周知,替代理论在心理分析中很重要。关于替代机制的动力学和类型,见 Dembo, op. cit.。

子,尤其是索尼契卡,都被这事儿逗乐了;客人很生气,匆匆走进女孩子的房间去缝裙子。我决定重复一遍那样的"事故",让女孩子们再乐一乐。

拿定了这个主意,看见那位家庭教师回到房间后,我立即上前围着她跳来跳去,抓住一个好时机,踩住她的裙子,把裙子撕烂了。索尼契卡和老师的孩子们都忍不住笑出声来,我感到得意洋洋。但我的老师杰罗姆看穿了我的把戏,他走到我跟前,紧皱眉头(使我受不了),说我调皮、不本分。虽然那天是欢庆的日子,但如果我不守规矩,就要吃苦头。

"但我很兴奋,玩过头了,口袋里没有几张牌了;我怕算账,绝望中打出新牌,没有希望赢,只是不让自己回过神来。我大笑,抬头看他,很无礼;接着转身就走,让他站在那里发愣。"

从动力学来看,上述情境的特点可以示意如下(图 4-18a)。主导那个孩子(C)生活空间的力量场首先是父亲(F)、奶奶(G)和老师杰罗姆(J)。他觉得杰罗姆的场力和他相斥;由于他自己的过错,父亲、奶奶的矢量场都和他相斥。他觉得这些力量场紧紧束缚了他,控制着这个家,老师杰罗姆的力量场说到底来自这个家。在那一刻,所有这些力量场都具有了威胁的意义。

由于四面八方的威胁,那孩子的内心极度紧张,他的第一个举动是离场,走向非现实。他用听天由命的思想安慰自己,弱化现实("该来的一定会来")。自然,这不足以减压,现实层面欢庆的气氛使他更紧张,明显焦躁不安的举动和情感爆发接踵而至。

这样的举动很快就导致他和老师杰罗姆的冲突。此间,老师发现,他的历史考试成绩不及格,并当众宣布了。他打了老师,被关进了阁楼。

他很绝望,坐在阁楼里,害怕即将到来的惩罚,这一情境的现实层面(LR)可示意如下图(图 4-18b)。

从旋涡状的场景中出来,他被带到外面安静的环境中。但与此同时,那样的情境又是地地道道的身体约束、身体的囚笼。这个囚笼是杰罗姆

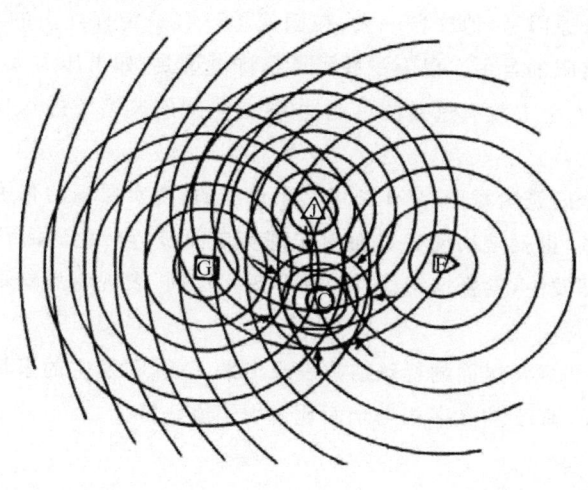

图 4-18a

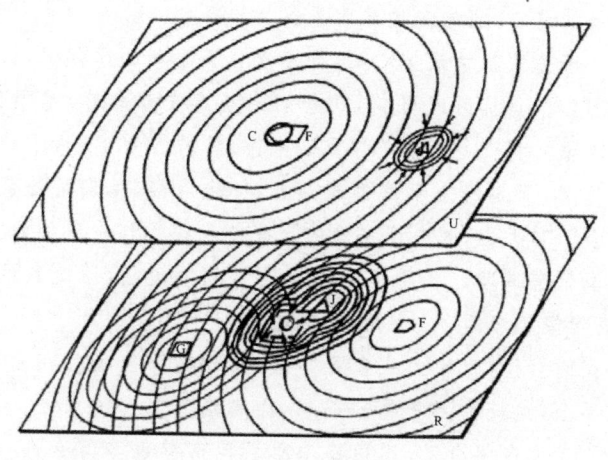

图 4-18b

老师敌视他的表现，也是与他作对的权力场力量的表现。杰罗姆把他关进了睡房，沉重的压力使其更压抑，因为他预料父亲和奶奶那最高权威、极端敌视的举动即将到来。

虽然他极度紧张，却不见前不久那样的情绪爆发。从表面上看，他很平静。部分原因是,他独自一人,在囚笼里享有一定程度上的自由,虽然那是非常有限的自由。以下一些思考也许更重要,如果压力太大,且来自四面八方,看上去没有逃避的可能性(这是绝望的典型条件),身体的僵硬就处处发生。①

在这个囚笼困境里,身体离场是不可能的,现实层面的张力就导致了内心的离场,也就是从现实层面向非现实层面进行转化。活跃的幻想和白日梦随即发生,紧张情绪就反映在非现实层面,表现为焦躁不安的胡思乱想。

如此,非现实层面的特殊结构表现出来了,其间发生的事情表现出了典型的特征,以下的文字相当全面地再现了这些特征。

  我没有哭泣,但千钧巨石压在心上,千头万绪,来回冲撞,一片混乱。但不幸的遭遇时时打断这奇怪的思绪,我又跌进了没有尽头的迷宫,我的命运悬而未决。

  一个想法很快涌上心头:肯定有什么不明的原因吧,世间缺乏爱啊,人人(那时我坚信,从奶奶到马车夫菲利普)都恨我,都幸灾乐祸。我心想,也许我不是爸爸、妈妈的亲生子,不是沃洛加的兄弟,而是一个不幸的流浪儿,一个弃婴,他们可怜我才把我收下。实际上,这个傻乎乎的念头使我在忧伤中感到慰藉,而且好像蛮有道理。我不幸的原因不是我的过错,而是我的命不好,我就像悲惨的卡尔·伊万诺维奇。

  我问自己,为什么一直不知道这个秘密,但我现在看穿了。明天早上,我就去问爸爸,"爸爸,你隐瞒我出生的秘密,不让我知道。我现在明白了,你白费心思。"他回答说,"怎么办,孩子?你早晚会发现的,你不是我亲生的。但我一直把你当成亲儿子,如果你能证明你值得我爱,我就绝不遗弃你。"我回答说,"爸爸,

---

① See LEWIN, Kindliche Ausdrucksbewegungen, in W. STERN, *Psychologic der fruhen Kindheit*, 6th ed., Quelle u. Meyer, Leipzig, 1930, p. 502(Engiish trans., *Psychology of Early Childhood*, Holt, New York, 1930).

虽然我没有权利这样称呼你,我还是最后一次叫你爸。我一直爱你,永远爱你。我绝不会忘记,你是我的恩人。但我再也不能待在这里。这里没有人爱我,杰罗姆发誓要毁了我。不是他离开这个家,就是我离开,我自己找不到答案。我恨他,什么事都干得出来,我要杀了他。是的,爸爸,我发誓,我要杀他。"爸爸给我讲道理,但我伸出手说,"不,我的朋友,我们不共戴天,让我走。"我在黑屋子里,坐在箱子上,越想越难受,哭出声来。突然,我又想起等待我的惩罚。现实又回到身边,露出真相,我的胡思乱想立即烟消云散了。

主观感觉里的情境压迫在很大程度上取决于一个事实:它可以追溯到孩子自己的过错。第一次遁入非现实的胡思乱想在于,他把这些过错与自我剥离开来。失败以后经常发生的现象是,个人对不愉快事情的责任用行为的合理化推卸掉了。要怨的是命——谁也不能解答的命。他心里觉得与奶奶尤其与父亲格格不入,他害怕他们。他的解释是,他不是父亲的亲生子,而是一个弃婴。他悲痛至极,放弃了一切自我安慰,得出了一个悲惨(而不是愧疚)的结论:离开家,心想,我就要死了。逃离囚笼的过程完成了,即使那是在非现实的层面上的。

他渐渐悟出了非现实层面上的真相,实现了非现实层面上的重组。这个过程持续进行,直到他在非现实层面上找到了现实层面中缺少的东西,他的社会地位大变,实际上完全颠倒了。

"不久,我发现自己获得了自由,离家很远。我当上了轻骑兵,参加战斗。四面八方的敌人向我压过来,我抽出马刀,第一刀劈死了第一个迎面扑来的敌人,第二刀劈死了第二个,第三刀劈死了第三个。最后因战伤和疲惫而倒在地上,却还在高喊'赢啦!'将军骑马路过我身边,问道,'谁在喊?'战友们都指着我。他翻身下马,搂着我的脖子,泪流满面,高兴地呼喊'胜利啦!'后来,我去养伤,在大街上散步。我当上将军啦!沙皇召见我,问道,'这个受伤的年轻人是谁?'有人告诉他,'著名的英雄,尼古拉。'沙皇走到我跟前说,'谢谢你,告诉我,你有什么愿望。我将赏赐你想要的任何东西。'我恭恭敬敬地向他鞠躬,挂着军刀说,'伟大的陛下,我能为祖国流血,深感荣幸,为国捐躯,亦万死不辞。既然陛下赐我许愿,请容许我宰了我的敌人,外国佬杰罗姆。'我走近心里想象的杰罗姆,拿出威胁的架势说,'你要为我的痛苦负责,跪下!'但突然之间,我意识到真正的杰罗姆任何时候都可能拿着棍棒闯进屋来。于是,我不再把自己当成拯救祖国的将军,而是最悲惨的可怜虫了。"

"不一会儿,上帝的念头又涌上心来。我问上帝为什么惩罚我。我早上晚上都祈祷啊。为什么我该受苦受难呢? 我可以肯定地说,我童年时代怀疑宗教的第一步就是在那一刻迈出的。不是痛苦使我抱怨,使我不信教,而是因为上帝不公平的思想涌上心头。在那 24 小时的禁闭和精神错乱里,上帝不公的念头像邪恶的种子,落在湿润松软的泥土里,很快就发芽生根了。不一会儿,我又想自己死了,我清清楚楚看见了杰罗姆的震惊,他在阁楼里找到我的尸体。我想起娜塔利娅·索维查的故事,她的鬼魂在家里游荡了 40 天。我死后也会在奶奶家的屋子里游荡,谁也看不见,我听见柳巴契卡的痛哭,奶奶的抱怨,听见爸爸对奥古斯特·安托诺维奇说,'他是好孩子。'他眼里充满泪花。杰罗姆顶嘴说,'他是不错,但他是无赖。'爸爸指责他说:'你应该尊重死者。他的死就是因为你,你恐吓他,他受不了你的羞辱……滚出我家,你这可怜虫!'"

"杰罗姆跪下,请求爸爸的宽恕。40 天过后,伟大的灵魂飞到天堂。我看见美妙无比、雪白、透明的东西,我觉得那是我妈妈。"

非现实里的情境把现实情境完全颠倒过来。儿童的力量场在现实情境(R,图 4-18b)里很弱,到了非现实里,由于他的英勇壮举,他的力量场成了占主导地位的社会场域。同时,分离的痛苦也被克服了。在现实情境里,最强大的社会场力就是父亲的力量(F),它与那孩子作对;到了非现实的情境,由于父子重逢,最强大社会场力就掌握在儿童的手里了——父亲惩处了杰罗姆。

在非现实层面上,白日梦也造就了一个非常相似的情境。在这个白日梦中的是沙皇——世界上最有权势的君主,他把自己的力量场赋予了那个男孩。两个幻想都导致杰罗姆的毁灭,他在现实层面里的力量是把男孩囚禁在阁楼上。在非现实的层面上,男孩并不弱小,也没有被囚禁,他孔武有力,行动自由;现实世界里最强大的敌人都虚弱无力,败下阵来。

幻想的画面无限延伸,进入超凡力量和自由的境界,故事的高潮是与仙逝的母亲重逢。

我们不在这里考察现实层面上后继的事情。男孩拒绝向老师道歉,离家出走的尝试被父亲挫败了。

如果控制冲突情境互相对立的矢量非常强大,由此引起的张力可能以弥散的方式释放,这就是所谓的情绪爆发。上述故事显示了这样的情绪爆发,男孩胡言乱语、大哭大闹、低声抽泣。惩罚情境里的情绪爆发,一般是在逃亡受挫时发生的。

即使没有非常明显的情绪爆发(上述故事中的情绪爆发就不明显),紧张状态的加重肯定会影响工作质量。我们将讨论教育学上特别有趣的一种情况:智力任务的求解。无疑,智力任务的完成需要一定程度的紧张状态,需要完成任务方向上的一个矢量。智力任务所带的正诱发力,创造了解决问题的条件,比在厌恶情绪下更有利于任务的完成,前文已经解释,这里不必再费笔墨。在正诱发力主导的情况下,虽然有困难或障碍,但在完成任务的过程中,儿童会继续朝着完成任务的方向前进。

还应该注意,冲突情境——尤其是走向全面紧张的情境特别不利于智力任务的完成。在总体的心理结构里,智力问题的解决基本上就是问题领域里格式塔关系的转换,也就是所谓脑子里那"咔嚓"一声的快闪。① 这种快闪发生的必要条件是,个人要总揽全局。场域结构的决定性转变要求个人要能够驾驭全局。他要尽可能地与任务保持一定的距离。只有这样,他才能鸟瞰总体的系统,而不是只看见场域里几个孤零零的事实。

身处高度紧张的冲突情境中,儿童就觉得,冲突凌驾于他的头上,他不能俯瞰全局。显然,这个不利的情境不利于他平静地解决智力问题。

带有指令性惩罚情境的拓扑结构,这里就讲完了。我们不立即转向

---

① W. KÖHLER, *Intelligenzpruffungen an Menscliena f fen*, Springer, Berlin, 1924. (English trans., *The Mentality of Apes*, Harcourt, Brace, New York, 1925.)

带抑制的惩罚情境,而是先研究带奖赏希望的惩罚情境。

第三节 带奖赏希望的指令

从教育学的角度看,奖赏似乎与惩罚相对。

然而,在某些方面,奖赏和惩罚发生的情境一般是类似的。在惩罚情境中,儿童在引导之下表现出来的行为是自然场力作用下不会产生的行为,只有这样,才有可能获得奖赏。此时,儿童所做的事情是他不希望的,或者,他控制住了自己不去做他想做的事情。我们先考虑以下情境:儿童在奖赏的引诱下去完成他不想执行的任务。

一、诱发力和障碍的性质和倾向

儿童(C)身处带负诱发力任务(T)的对立面。在惩罚情境中,儿童尝试用另一个负诱发力去克服源自任务的矢量;相反,在带奖赏的惩罚情境中,被调动的是一个正诱发力。这个正诱发力可能是一个好分数、一个玩具、一块糖、一次升级,或被称为好孩子,以及诸如此类的东西。源自正诱发力的诱惑必须胜过任务引起的反感,所以奖赏(R)必须和任务(T)的方向一致。奖赏必须放在任务的背后(图 4-19)。

如此,我们又面对一个冲突情境了。如上所示,两个旗鼓相当的对立的场力在影响儿童。在这样的情况下,冲突情境属于上文讨论过的第三种类型。

源自奖赏的矢量(V_R)必须胜过源自任务的矢量(V_T),其力度随任务引起的反感的程度而变化。

然而,这样的情况绝不足以推动儿童去完成任务。虽然被奖赏所诱惑,但对他而言,令人不快的任务还是一道障碍,横亘在他和目标(G)之间。在这个方面,此间的拓扑结构与另一种情境下的拓扑

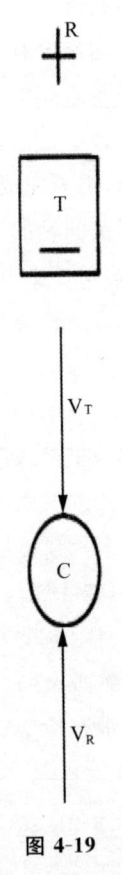

图 4-19

结构对应：困难妨碍儿童达到目标(图 4-20)。在这种奖赏(R)情况下，目标通常会受到阻碍，儿童会尝试绕过障碍。在这里，迂回是典型的行为，或者，儿童试图找到障碍的弱点。如此，正如惩罚情境一样，由于提供了奖赏，儿童会尝试在不完成任务的情况下得到吸引他的目标，如糖果(图 4-20)。如果采取上述措施的情况发生，儿童就会想方设法地得到奖赏，比如，他可能会奉承成人，或掩盖他没有完成任务。

由此，在有奖赏的情况下，设置障碍也是必要的，这样做的目的是确保只有完成任务才可能得奖(图 4-21)。

发生图示这种情境时，也可能不借助具体的障碍。我们可以把任务描绘为一个环绕奖品的区域(图 4-22)，只有完成任务才能得奖。从拓扑结构来看，这两个示意图有相似之处：奖赏(R)都在圈内。两者的差异在于：在图 4-22 里，圈里的场域具有相当大的同质性，其中只有任务(T)；反之，在图 4-21 圈定的两个成分中，一是任务(T)，一是障碍(B)。大多数情况下，图 4-21 表现的情境大概会更准确一些：通常有特别的障碍，比如成人坚定的态度。一般来说，其他预防措施——包括物质的和社会的措施都是有必要的，只有这样，才足以保证儿童只有完成任务才能获得奖赏。

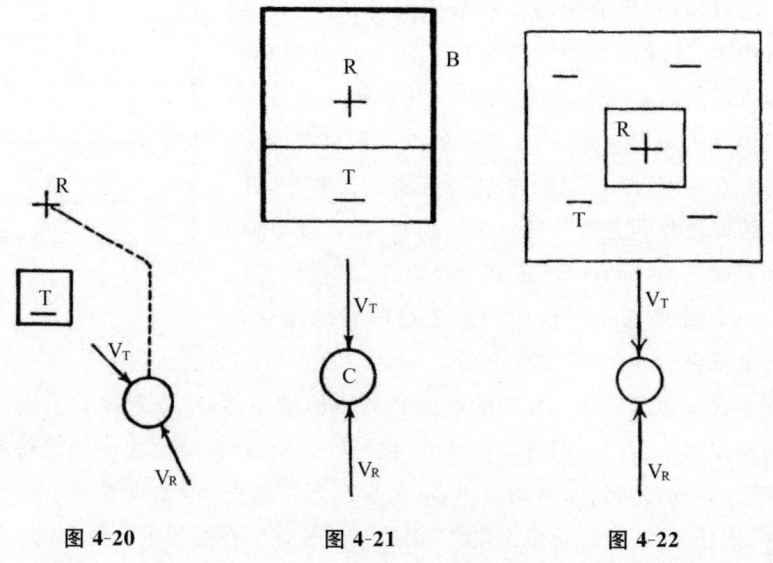

图 4-20　　　　　图 4-21　　　　　图 4-22

第四章　奖励和惩罚的心理情境　**121**

二、奖赏和惩罚总体情况的比较

奖赏情境和惩罚情境的比较显示,两者有相似之处。两者都是冲突情境,都产生了冲突的后果:紧张状态加大,有偏离任务方向的倾向。两种情况都缺乏自然目的论,自然目的论是兴趣情境的特征。

然而,两者亦有区别。考虑两者的差异时,我们首先关心的不是奖惩的道德问题,也不是两者对自我意识的影响,亦不是伴随这两种情境的鼓励或劝阻。一个主要的差异是,在惩罚威胁的情境中,儿童被困在障碍里;相反,在奖赏的情境中,他处在障碍和任务组成的圈子外。因此,获奖的希望在总体上不限制儿童的行动自由!更准确地说,在儿童的生活领域里,只有一个目标即奖赏是难以达到的(当然,完成任务是可以达到目标的)。

此外,如果获奖纯粹是为了达到完成任务的目的时,奖赏情境就缺乏惩罚情境常有的特征。

(一)奖赏情境里的行为

1. 如果奖赏的吸引力足以抗衡任务的不快及其持续的时间,如果奖赏周围的障碍相当坚固,儿童就会完成任务。

然而,和惩罚情境一样,奖赏情境也缺乏自然的目的论,目的论是兴趣情境的特征;在兴趣情境中,儿童的行为时常指向实际的任务目标。即将进入或实际进入任务场时,儿童移动的方向很快就表现出差异:任务目标的方向和奖赏的方向略有不同(图 4-23)。在执行任务的过程中,儿童转向任务的方向。只要能得到奖赏,在任务尚未完成之前,一有可能他就会停留。

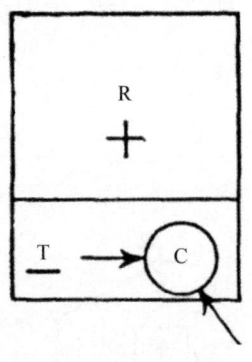

图 4-23

2. 如果任务不快的程度超过奖赏的激励,儿童就会放弃奖赏,接受惩罚。

常常会出现儿童行为的改变和对价值的重估,任务常被赋予道德的基调。这个道德基调时常意味着,他是好孩子,社会地位比小伙伴略胜一筹。如果放弃奖赏,那就意味着,至少在那个情况下,他被置身于那一奖赏(如好分数)的意识形态之外,而奖赏则被认为在道德上是可取的。

不过,刚才勾勒的奖赏情境和惩罚情境之间还是有重大的差异。在奖赏情境里,由于约束减轻,行为过程总体上就比较轻松。此外,儿童把惩罚视为小恶接受时,接受小恶的道德重估与他不努力得奖的道德重估是两种不同的类型。

奖赏成为儿童某种行为必然结果的情况并不多见,这并不取决于成人的意志。① 在心理上,奖赏情境与兴趣情境决定行为的做法在许多方面都有关系。

3. 任务很不愉快,但奖赏很吸引人时,儿童就会尝试冲破障碍,比如他会希望获奖参与郊游,仿佛他没有完成功课也可以这样。

在某些方面,这一情境类似于惩罚情境。当然,这时冲破障碍的结果是奖赏而不是自由,但类似之处在于,这里的障碍取决于儿童的力量。因此,这时的突破带有儿童斗争的性质,他的斗争不那么艰苦,这显然和缺乏束缚的情况是一致的。此外,一个强烈的倾向是,他的斗争往往用奉承或其他可以被接受的手段进行,因为他引诱成人允许他享受一点斗争的乐趣。

(二)奖赏和惩罚的结合

高潮勾勒的奖赏情境很少以单纯的形式出现。通常,成人所采取的教育方法既不是单纯的奖赏,也不是单纯的惩罚,而是奖惩的结合,即所谓"糖果加鞭子"。一般地说,如果奖赏的程度不够有效的话,奖赏提出的同时,多多少少隐藏着惩罚性威胁。

学校成绩的记分制,也许是最简单、最典型的例子。好分数有奖赏性,差分数有惩罚性:总体的情况是,二者必有其一。儿童面对老师要打分数的不快的任务时,尽量解决问题的倾向既源自低分的负诱发力,又源自高分的正诱发力(图 4-24)。

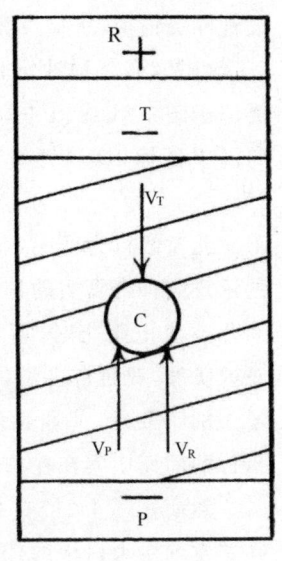

图 4-24

---

① 在有些情况下,惩罚也带有自然制裁的特征,违背指令或禁令时自然就要受到制裁。

既害怕惩罚,又希望奖赏,这就是许多奖惩结合的情境的特征。

第四节 带惩罚威胁的禁令

迄今为止,我们介绍了为了让儿童完成任务所用的奖赏或惩罚手段。我们现在简略地论述另一种情境下的拓扑结构:确保儿童做成人希望的事情,所用的手段是禁令而不是指令。我们首先讨论带惩罚性的威胁禁令。

在一些威胁性的惩罚里,有一种指令被称为禁令。如果老师威胁儿童:不听话就要受惩罚,那么儿童面对禁令,就首先表现出某些行为,比如大笑、假装"不懂"等。此外,老师还期待儿童表现出良好的正面行为,其中有一些是遵守禁令所不能回避的最低限度的行为。可见,这里也有指令。以下情况并非总是容易进行非此即彼的归类,但为了阐明心理动力学,最好还是从这些基本情况着手。

儿童面对着他渴望的目标——一个正诱发力。如果负诱发力要成为有效的反制力量,负诱发力就必须与目标的方向相同。在此发生的是第三种冲突情境,它与带奖赏的指令情境有相似之处。

可见,第三种冲突情境最明显的表征类似于图 4-21 或图 4-22:惩罚性的威胁是与渴望目标(DG)针锋相对的力量(图 4-25)。

儿童的行为证明,在一定程度上,这样的示意图符合真实的情境。当一个 2 岁的幼儿被禁止摘花时,请看他的行为。他在花前犹豫,威胁自己说,"不,不。"他的行为给人的印象是,惩罚性威胁是挡在他渴望目标的前面实实在在的障碍。

然而实际上,挡在目标前的惩罚与挡在奖赏前令人讨厌的任务不同。惩罚并不在时间上处于目标的前面,惩罚不是达到目的可能路径,惩罚在时间上处于目标的

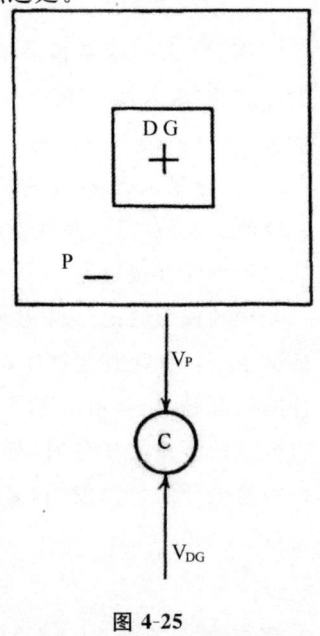

图 4-25

后面。

然而,在表征时间关系时,你不可能把惩罚(P)紧贴在渴望的目标(DG)之后(图 4-26)。这一表征的结果就是:目标唾手可得,儿童立刻即可获得自由,远离惩罚。但实际情况刚好相反,如果他从事既定的活动,就可能遭到惩罚。一旦进入既定目标的场域,他就发现自己被惩罚紧紧包围了。图 4-27 用拓扑结构表征了进入既定活动(第二阶段)以后的情况。儿童仿佛钻进了一个笼子,他千方百计地想要逃出这个笼子。

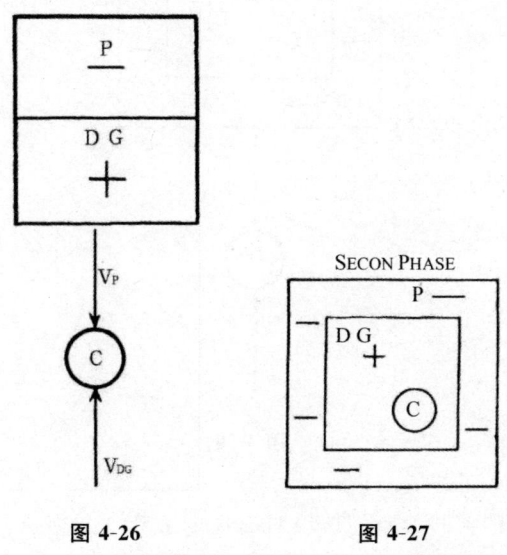

图 4-26   图 4-27

有时我们看到,儿童试图在目标场域里逗留,但这样的逗留不能使他逃避惩罚,这样的逗留没有用示意图表现出来。在这里,惩罚不能阻碍儿童从一种活动转入另一种活动,总体上,没有任何东西阻碍这样的转换。更确切地说,惩罚的到来未必是他向某一方向移动的结果。

因此,图 4-27 拓扑结构的变化是禁令情境的特征。行动(第一阶段,图 4-28)之前,儿童把惩罚(TP)当作他和目标之间的障碍,但这一障碍和我们以前介绍的障碍有本质区别。他可以通过这一障碍,不与现实的困难遭遇,他没有不愉快的感觉。因此,这一障碍并不代表实际的、真正的惩罚;只有等到他进入渴望的活动场域以后,这个障碍才成为现实。由此可见,在活动的第一阶段,那个障碍多多少少具有一切未来事件的非现实性,是尚未笃定到来的一切事件的非现实性。①

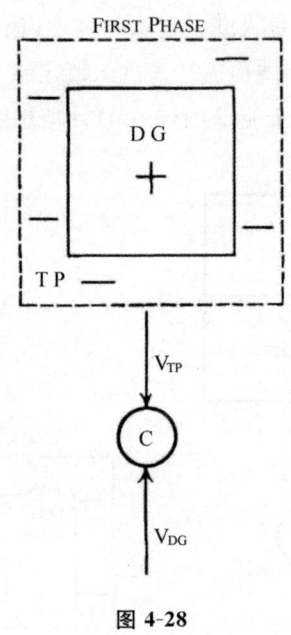

图 4-28

带惩罚性的威胁禁令的情境明确规定了禁令必须执行的时间。② 这就提供了一个约束要素,儿童处在障碍的包围中(图 4-10)。在带惩罚性的威胁禁令的情境里,这种时间限制未必存在,约束性一般不那么明显。在既定的禁区之外,儿童可以自由活动。然而,如果禁区很大,或触及到核心的生活领域时(比如,禁止与好友联系,喜欢的活动被禁),情境的约束性就加大了。

---

① 未来事件的现实性和思想的现实性并不相同,我们在这里不予考虑。
② 指令也可能是带有条件的。比如,某一动作在某种情况发生时才采取。因此,"有人迎面走来时,你说'您好'很得体。"

第五节 惩罚真实度的偏离

奖惩真实度在儿童的实际行为中起到了很大的作用,真实度取决于一系列因素。首先,它是儿童预料奖惩必然性的一个函数(成人实际的权力、同情心等的函数)。其次,它还取决于儿童的性格和当时的状态(比如,沉湎于梦境、其世界观的真实度)。我很清楚地记得我童年时代对鞭打的态度。因为我在家里从来没有吃过鞭子,所以虽然老师经常用鞭子抽人,但学校里藤条手柄鞭子对于我来说仍是不可思议的、不真实的东西。这样的非真实性给我的印象很深,因此面对鞭打时,我总是感到震惊。老师也感到震惊,我奇怪地看着他,一鞭又一鞭地打在我身上,我很疼,但不叫喊。

惩罚真实度的重要性首先表现出这种现象:面对惩罚威胁时,受过惩罚的儿童和没有受过惩罚的儿童的行为往往是大不相同的。被火烧过的儿童躲避火,受过重罚的儿童面对新的惩罚威胁时一般较少抗拒,其原因不能只到挨揍时的疼痛中去找。更重要的原因是惩罚的真实度增加了,在想象中可能出现的惩罚从非现实层面转变成了现实层面的一部分。上文业已指出,这种真实度的变化并非总是加重对惩罚的恐惧,而是导致惩罚的贬值,并最终导致恐惧从以前的思想意识中释放出来。从非现实层面降到现实层面不仅使惩罚更严厉,而且使之更赤裸裸、更简单、更容易全面考察。

真实度在时间上的变化在上述各种奖惩情境中都可以看到。惩罚和不愉快的任务越接近,它们就越真实,此间发生的一切都可以导致真实度的突变。成人对另一个儿童的惩罚、另一种惩罚的提及、任何使成人看似特别危险或无害的事情都是可能发生的事情。在决定儿童选择的性质上,诸如此类的突变都发挥着重要的作用,如果惩罚和任务的真实度相差太大,明显的冲突情境一般是不会发生的。①

在带惩罚性的威胁禁令的情境中,只要任务尚未完成,惩罚就逐渐逼

---

① 我们不妨回忆,真正冲突情景出现的必要条件是对立的矢量大体上旗鼓相当。

近。在带惩罚性的威胁禁令的情境中,惩罚是典型的事后现象,尤其被禁的渴望目标(如诱人的糖果)在场并具有更大的真实度时是这样的。"机会成全小偷。"正诱发力和负诱发力的真实度相差较大时,这些情境中自然会出现惩罚越邻近就越加重的特征。儿童难以抗拒诱惑的主要原因就在这里。

从心理上看,惩罚是使渴望得到满足的进一步的润滑剂;与此相关的是,心智成长是威胁性惩罚有效的必要条件。幼儿的时间范围和空间范围都很小,他们在过去或未来方向上能看到的事件,成为短暂情境的组成部分,决定着婴儿生命第一年的行为发展。初生婴儿的空间范围是非常狭小的,等到足够大的时间范围成为真实的心理存在时,惩罚性的威胁因为这样的拓扑结构而才成为有效的威胁。[①]

在最后这种情境中,可以见到惩罚性威胁的一个普遍属性,它与惩罚和渴望目标的真实度的自然差异有关系。正是由于惩罚性威胁,起初中性的事件首次获得了正面的吸引力。[②] 指令中也可以看到诱发力发生的相应反向转变,这样的过程和抗拒密切相关。这里存在重要心理意义上的领域,只要它对总体情境的拓扑结构有影响,我就会探讨这个领域。

禁令从儿童的生活范围中分离出一个区域,并用障碍把这个区域包围起来,它是限制儿童自由活动的区域。这就对儿童的权力场形成干扰,儿童自然会释放出对抗的行为并借此彰显自己,反对成人的权力场。指令尤其是禁令对事物的诱发力产生反常的影响,从这个观点看问题,反常的影响可以被理解为儿童为争取生活空间里的行动自由所做的努力。这也可以解释为何儿童在两三岁的时候,这种抗拒的反应特别常见。幼儿在这个年龄开始具有明显的自我意识,例如私有财产的观念开始产生。[③]

至于约束的程度,带惩罚性的威胁禁令情境与希望奖赏的指令情境

[①] 稍后,我们将探讨惩罚有效的另一种情况。
[②] 我在这里不是说,惩罚本身就具有正诱发力。
[③] 夏洛特·布勒(Challotte Bühler)提出"抗拒的年龄"。抗拒反应底层心理过程可能具有普遍性。当然,抗拒反应不能只用年龄层来解释。我们的观察和实验研究似乎说明,抗拒反应反映的是社会领域里非常普遍的心理规律,相当于"作用相当于反作用"的命题。

有关系。总体上,儿童保留了行动自由,只有一个区域即渴望接近目标的区域是封闭的。然而,如果不是孤立地看这一现象,而是将其放进总体的包围情境中去看,前一种情境里的约束显然是更加明显。成人在场域里的主导地位似乎更清晰地凸显在前台。

第六节 带奖赏希望的禁令

控制自己不做某事就可能得到奖赏,这样的情境性质很特别。允诺的奖赏总是有一个条件:在特定时间内自始至终要避免某一行为,而这一行为(如吃糖果)却难以避免。可能是因为它对儿童有直接的吸引的原因,更可能是由于某种间接的原因。如此,成人常常用奖赏来防止儿童尿床;父母可能会向孩子的同胞兄弟姐妹许诺奖赏,使他们不要再互相取乐。

这种情境的特点是用正诱发力或同等的压力来引导某种行为。奖赏是成人用的第二种诱发力,旨在防止儿童循着第一种诱发力的方向前进,如此就产生了第一种冲突情景(图 4-7)。

但这里的关系没有这么简单。一般地说,节制欲望就能获奖的希望是有的,因沉溺于某事而受惩罚的可能也是存在的。而且在一般情况下,第一种诱发力随着时间的流逝而增强,短时抗拒容易,长期抗拒则难。以下例子虽然简单,却能表征许多类似情境的拓扑结构。一个儿童试图在游泳池里来回游一百公尺,这个目标有很大的吸引力。在游泳池边,每隔一段就有绳子让他握住休息一下。在过去的尝试中,他多次依靠这些绳子。而他现在面对的问题是,他游过这些绳子时,不能休息,他要直达游泳池的另一端。

在这里,心理情境的拓扑结构和物理—地理的拓扑结构相对应。儿童被眼前供他休息的绳子吸引(R,图 4-29),与此同时,他渴望的目标(游一百公尺)吸引着他。任务越来越困难,人越来越疲倦,使他屈服的诱惑就越来越大了(图 4-30)。

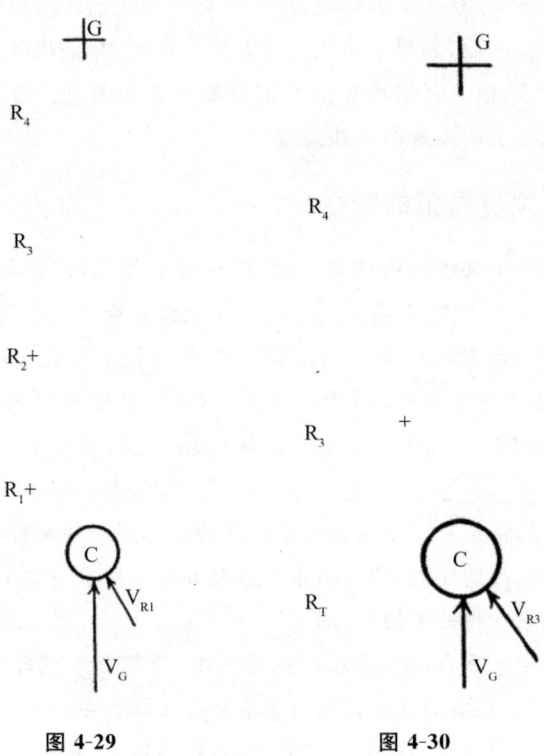

图 4-29　　　　　　　图 4-30

离目标尚有一段距离时,随着最终目标的逼近,其吸引力越来越大。终极行为的变化随着矢量的相对力度而变化,也随着儿童的状况而不同。

允诺在特定时间里靠自制力避免某一活动而给予奖赏时,我们还得考虑一些使人违反禁令的诱惑力。只有在成功地抵御了这些诱惑力以后,儿童才能得到奖赏。

第七节　奖赏、惩罚、真正的兴趣转变

奖励和惩罚情境结构的总体介绍到此为止,我们转向一个与心理学和教育学密切相关的问题。前面已经指出,只有在渴望的行为不是自然倾向诱发的行为时,奖励和惩罚手段的使用才会成为一个尖锐的问题。在这样的情况下,除了可能产生两种渴望的行为之外,还有第三种可能

性,那就是唤起一种兴趣,产生一种倾向。这是现代教育学特别强调的可能性,如何描绘这一情境的心理特征的问题由此而生。这个问题很重要,在理论上很有趣,深入探讨需要大量的篇幅。在此,我不得不先简要地进行论述。

使人对无趣的事物或活动感兴趣,那有许多办法,比如把任务嵌入另一个语境(如扮售货员做算术题),五花八门的办法还有许多。经常,儿童对一个目标的兴趣有赖于老师的个性。

这样就出现了这样一个问题:这样的情境是否与奖励和惩罚情境有本质的差异。

乍一看,而且从心理学的角度上看,因为喜欢售货游戏而做算术题的儿童所处的情境和奖赏的情境有相似之处。

算术含有一个负诱发力,但由于玩游戏,游戏背后的目标引导儿童去计算,这个情境对应图 4-21 的情境。

这样的情况无疑是存在的,但在这些情境里,第三种可能性的心理要素,即事物本身诱发力的转变并没有实现。奖励和惩罚情境拓扑结构的特征维持不变:计算的负诱发力维持不变,只不过紧挨着它出现了第二个正诱发力。从根本上看,做算术题的诱发力没有出现真正的转变。

然而,从心理学的角度看,除非活动的诱发力成功地实现了真正的转变,否则我们就难以讨论兴趣教育学的问题。

很可能有人反驳说,事物本身诱发力的变化是难以达成的;无论如何,为了实现兴趣的转变,我们总是要给情境加上新的因素。我们不会忽视其中极大的实际困难,也无意暗示,诱发力的变化总是能实现的,但我们仍然想要强调,时间的"追加"可能会产生不同于上面所示的结果。

如果不想要的活动被置于儿童喜欢的另一物件(如配图的低幼儿读物)的旁边,虽然两者邻近,但其愉快和不愉快的性质不会改变。然而另一种情况也是有的,一件任务、一种活动被嵌入时,任务的意义和与其相伴的诱发力会完全改变。如果要孩子吞下勺子上的小妖精,或者要他把勺子像火车进站那样送进嘴里,即使不喜欢,他也会痛快地把食物吃下,不会磨蹭了。在这两个例子中,原来的吃饭动作成了一个大动作的附属成分,最后成为这个大动作整体的表层。这些附属成分的心理现实和效应首先是由它们嵌入的整体决定的,这是行为和需求心理以及感知心理的基本事实。①

正是由于这一基本情况,当一件任务嵌入另一种心理场(比如把学校作业领域的一种活动带进实用目的领域)时,就会彻底改变活动的诱发力。

另一种关系的确定是否引起诱发力的变化？这个问题基本上取决于由此而生的一个真实的整体,即一个动态的格式塔,或者仅仅是一个累积性的组合体。② 累积性的组合体和强势格式塔的整合体之间,有一个连续不断的渐进过渡(动态上的弱势格式塔);在格式塔结构里,构造成分的独立性荡然无存。对于兴趣转变的议题,这一特点意义重大。对抄写字母表不感兴趣的儿童,如果允许他尽快学习抄写有意义的句子,而不是让他读页边配图的识字本,诱发力的变化就会更快。这是可以期待的结果,③因为抄写字母时,字母很容易在心理上难以区别。

然而,如果单独读写字母很困难,每写一个字母都成为独立的任务,整体活动意义的结构转化就会受到阻碍。

由此可见,当(外部所见的)"相同成就"被植入另一个行为整体或心理领域时,一件任务或一种活动的诱发力就可能产生。(比如重要的是,某件事是准备为老师庆贺生日的一部分,而另一件事情则是为这位或那位老师。)如果应用于教育学,这就意味着,对幼儿而言,学校的整体氛围不仅重要,而且分离活动的动力关系有可能成为构造成分了。

---

① For references, see K. KOFFKA, Psychol ogie der optischen Wahrnehmung, Handuch der normalen uid pathologischen Physiologic, 1931, 12, 2 Hefte, pp. 1215—1271; and KOHLER, Gestalt Psychology, Liveright, New York, 1920. For au especial experimental investigation of wholes behavior and in systems of needs, see BIRKN-BAUM, Das Vergessen ciner Vornahme, Psydiol. Forsch., 1930, 13, 218 ff.

② Cf. the concept of Und-Summe in M. WFRTHE. IMKR, Psychol Forsch., 1921, 1, p. 47; 1923, 4, p. 301.

③ 这就是德克罗利提出的读写训练的"整体"法的优势之一。

我们对兴趣转化与奖励和惩罚情境作了比较。但如果忽视过渡情况的存在,那就是错了,而且也太粗略了。在特定情况下,在一定程度上,惩罚威胁和奖赏希望都可能导致事物本身诱发力的转变。惩罚威胁可能会使被禁目标的价值减少,奖赏可能会使儿童起初不想要的事物成为有价值的东西。

诱发力从奖赏和惩罚扩散到事物本身,这一现象在幼儿的生活中特别起作用,而且符合其心理系统的功能边界比较弱的事实。可见,奖赏和惩罚从外部加上时,可能会加强指令或禁令;虽然对儿童而言,没有可以理解的理由来解释奖赏为何有这样的功能。然而,对稍大的儿童而言,只有在指令或禁令被视为有道理时,事物本身的诱发力转变才有可能发生。换言之,此时的行为被植入于一个整体的关系中:这个整体或吸引他,使他觉得有价值;或使他厌恶,使他觉得没有价值。采用惩罚性的威胁或允诺奖赏来支持指令或禁令,说明了这样一个事实:那个指令或禁令没有道理,或理由不足。由此可见,惩罚性的威胁事实上和诱发力的转变刚好对立。奖惩手段很随意,缺乏足够的理由,同时又和责备儿童结合起来时,这种适得其反的效应最为明显。

第五章 为现实服务的教育

在这篇有关教育的论文里，我不希望讨论蒙台梭利体系教育学宗旨和方法在目前社会、经济、政治全局中的地位问题，虽然这是一个十分有趣的问题，我也不希望讨论教育在这方面有何作用。相反，我希望从心理学的角度探究教育对当今生活的意义。

我记得和一位蒙台梭利体系老师的谈话。她告诉我，有一个六年级的学生不知道应该学什么。接着她颇为感慨地说："在蒙台梭利体系里受教育的儿童不可能出现这样的情况。"

凡是了解蒙台梭利体系的人都知道她这句话的意思。她所说的这个六年级学生在各种可能性和欲望中踟蹰徘徊，不能在恰当的时机做恰当的事情。这个学生在当下失败了，因为他不能在世界呈献给他的事务中作出选择，不能头脑清醒地作出决定。相反，蒙台梭利体系学校里的儿童首先学习的正是这样的能力：独立决策，在呈现给他的可能性中自由选择。无疑，这是蒙台梭利体系教育最积极的方面之一。

由于成长的总体环境，美国学生一般能自己决策，脚踏实地，其能力高于德国学生；今天德国学生的能力高于战前的德国学生。这样的生活态度虽然可取，但却有危险。今天需要注意的是：我们现实生活很容易变得太狭隘,生活方式太肤浅,志向太低,事实太赤裸裸。

熟悉蒙台梭利体系教育学的人一望而知,上述后果与压缩游戏时间从至想象力萎缩有关系。我不希望在这里讨论儿童想象力的问题,因为想象力本身是美好的。即使对现实生活所需的很实在的考虑也必须认识到在这个要求里的一个固有问题。

第一节 心理生活空间和时间的延伸

讨论教育为现实服务的问题时,这个固有的问题就更清楚了。

如果从儿童心理学入手讨论这个问题,我们首先要把这一任务视为地道的悖论。实际上,对于6个月大的婴儿来说,他生活的主要特点就是"现在",而且只有现在。黑格尔的名言略加变换就可以说,"儿童的生活基本上就是现在。"(The child is essentially present.)儿童的世界不仅空间狭小(摇篮、托儿所),而且在时间上也有限。他的动作单位范围小、时间短。在他的心理环境里,过去和未来几乎不起作用,即使起作用也很短暂。因此,在婴儿身上,对当前生活的要求在很小的程度上实现了。

与此相关的是在当下独立决策的要求;在某种意义上,这个要求在婴儿身上,在很小的程度上实现了。婴儿的动作符合瞬间的需求:味道不好的东西他不吃;如果强迫他吃,他也会吐出来。

在这里,为现实服务的教育似乎绝对没有必要。更准确地说,教育学的任务似乎与此截然相反,那就是在空间(含社会)和时间维度上拓展现实的狭隘视野。今天,歌德的名言似乎仍然有效:"不能描绘上下三千年的人停留在无经验的黑暗中,他只能活一天算一天。"

看起来,这种空间—时间延伸的发展基本上依托于这样一个事实:儿童通过经验学会观察越来越广阔的关系。于是,成人就肩负起进一步加速这个自然过程的任务。今天,生活对成人的要求纷然杂陈,他们的实际任务仍然很繁重,但教育学理论有一个共同的特征:简单获取和记住知识的教学法,不可能引导儿童走出狭小的世界;完成这个任务有一个先决条件:儿童的自主活动和创造能力是自然而然的基础。

然而,如果把儿童现实心理生活空间的拓展只看成智力问题,那就忽视了一个决定性的问题。

无疑,若要儿童世界超越瞬间的现实进入未来,至少在一定程度上意味着,世界表征的感知整体结构逐渐扩大,思想扫描的范围更宽广;在他的总体的经验中,雷暴紧接着闪电,打碎杯子后就要挨骂。然而,在许多方面,更重要的是"行为整体"(action wholes)的发展:儿童不再仅限于索求现实的事物,它不仅有必须立即实现的愿望,而且也希望能够把握未来。年岁稍长后,不仅过去几个月的发生的事情很重要,而且将来几个月将要发生的事情在他当前的行为里也起着相当重要的作用。决定儿童行为的目标继续不断地被推向未来,儿童当下的心理生活空间决定性的延伸就建立在这种目标的时间位移上。

然而,这就提出了一个教育学的重大问题。当儿童的感知空间从摇篮延伸到房间再延伸到街道,时间从几小时到几天再到几个月时,这样的延伸主要还是在同一现实层面上的空间(社会)或时间延伸。然而,这一行为目标深入到未来的同时又具有某种非现实的属性。这是产生于希望和梦想领域的属性,通常是一个理想的目标,尚不具有当前事件那种充分的现实性。与此同时,远程的希望目标使生活空间在另一个维度上延伸,它指向心理环境中一个非现实的层面;实际上,目标越遥远,这个指向就越明显。即使在成人身上,大胆的、目光远大的计划也接近乌托邦和幻想,偏离现实滑进非现实的危险也是存在的。

第二节　现实与非现实的分层

我们现在对现实与非现实的差异略说一二。[①] 从心理动力学的观点来看,非现实、梦境和空中楼阁呈现出柔和灵动媒介的风姿。其特点是,人可以在此随心所欲,非现实不限于思想方面,[②] 行为也可以是非现实的。由于某种原因,幼儿园里的一个孩子被禁止用铅笔画画时,他会看其他小

[①] Cf. DEMBO, Der Arger als dynamisches Probem, *Psychol. Forsch.*, 1931, 15, pp. 1—144; HOPPE, Erfolg und Misserfolg, *Psychol. Forsch.*, 1930, 14, pp. 1—62; LEWIN, above, pp. 145—153.

[②] 当然还有非现实的思想。

朋友画画,也可能用蜡笔画。一个手势、一句话甚至一个替代性(补偿性)动作都可能属于非现实的层面,且与梦境无异。

现实分为大大小小的层面,这是心理环境的普遍属性。当现实层面太紧张、太不合时宜时,成人就会遁入非现实。对这个行为最重要的、教育学最基本的一个事实是现实层面的真实程度,成人生活的重心就寓于现实层面中。

就儿童而言,现实和非现实的分化初露端倪,比如,他的思想显露出魔幻的痕迹。现实和非现实在多大程度上分离,如何分离?这在儿童生活里是至关重要的问题。两者的分离清晰、界限分明——这是教育学最重要的假设之一。这不仅是儿童魔幻—万物有灵世界观的形成过程,也是智力成长的过程。更准确地说,现实和非现实的分离主要源于行为的领域,它依托的是他的经验,这里所指的经验是不按照他主观意愿运行的经验。

儿童心理现实的构成依托的是两个基本条件:(1)另一个人的意志,(2)客观情况对此人意志的抗拒。

(一)社会力量场

婴儿的心理环境基本上是由他自己的需求决定的。在第一年的发展过程中(容我不赘述),婴儿心理环境的形成、吸引力与恐惧、可能性和困难多半不是他自己的需求决定的,他生活在其他人的社会场力中。父母和小伙伴的意志引导着他形成目标、评价、友情和敌意。最重要的是,儿童现实和非现实的分离就是通过其他人的力量场实现的。

成人的意志几乎总是儿童生活里最强大、最严厉的现实。实际上,由于实际的权力优势,成人总是有一种自然而然的倾向,总是想使自己的意愿成为儿童现实里的决定性因素。用教育学的话来说,儿童必须服从。教育学越是建立于服从的基础上,这一外来意志就越成为儿童现实的支撑。即使在服从成人意志的情况下,儿童的现实和非现实也是分离的,不过,这时的分离相当简单。儿童面对现实的自控也是这样学会的,但这样的纪律依托着这样一个事实:成人引导着孩子。一种约束情境得以确立的最明显表征是,偶尔在街上还能看到幼儿套着安全绳或背带绳。在这样的情况下,倘若成人权力场及其权威突然坍塌,儿童在生活、心理上依托的现实层面结构就必然会坍塌。儿童独立时通常会发生这样的坍塌,坍塌最迟发生在青春期。坍塌会产生不良后果,因为他生活中的约束情境不仅是巨大的压力,也是他生存的拐杖。

由于儿童的目标和价值与成人的目标和价值密切相关,儿童生活其中的现实无疑超越了瞬间的狭小情境;在这个情境中,他实现了现实和非现实的分离。但现实的层面坍塌了,因为它和儿童的需求没有根本的关系。

现实层面的坍塌意味着什么?如果考虑心理现实和非现实分离的其他条件,其意义就十分清楚了。这里所指的其他条件是:外界情况抵御其个人意志的实施。

(二)客观障碍

从教育学的角度看,现实和非现实分离的第二条路径在许多方面和第一条路径刚好相反。在此,儿童在达到自己选定目标的过程中遭遇到了客观困难。换句话说,只有在他对目标的渴望非常强烈时,独立于自己愿望的现实才会发生。从教育学的角度来看,客观现实与需要层面的形成当然是合意的,其前提条件是总体情境的存在;在这个总体情境里,儿童也可以根据自己的需求和判断确定目标,自由行动。客观性不可能在约束情境中产生,只能在自由情境中产生。教育学认为,儿童自己的强烈需求和行动自由不会抑制现实和非现实,这是两者分离的必要条件。

当然,在达到目标的路上,选定自己目标的儿童可能会受到困难的阻挠,这是必然的。他也可能会遭遇社会生活的困难和物质条件的困难。另外,这些困难不应该把他压垮,不应该使他完全放弃设定的目标,逃离难以忍受的现实而遁入非现实。

我们知道,一方面自由选择自己想要做的事情,另一方面在所做事情物质材料的特殊结构的基础上进行自我控制,这正是蒙台梭利体系教育的基本原理。所用物质材料的特殊性引起的困难也许是清楚的,这使儿童特别幸运地体会到困难的客观性。通常,儿童不能理解达到目标的障碍,容易掉进不确定的、可怕而神秘的非现实的领域;因此,我们可能希望,达到目标的障碍可以被用来构建一个清晰的客观现实的层面。我相信,让儿童在幼儿园里按照自己的节奏玩耍对大多数儿童是完全适合的;这是因为餍足和满意的心理需求因人而异,天天不同,在不同的儿童身上难以预测;除非儿童实际上顺应自己的需求,否则我们就不能指望,目标路上的强大张力成为彰显现实层面发展的有利条件。

对于稍大的儿童而言,按照自己的选择和节奏提供休整的间隔是十分重要的。虽然融入社会群体在许多方面占据主导地位,在个人关系中形成一个客观现实层面更加重要,但毫无疑问,多重的嵌入使情况更加复杂。因此,在儿童的心理生活空间中,我们要赋予心理现实和非现实层面恰当的功能地位——这个问题就是教育学最大的困难之一;非现实层面一般叫作幻想,它与肢体表达和各种艺术表达的关系极为密切。这是因为清楚地分离现实和非现实的需求不能有这样的含义:儿童心理生活空间要彻底清除非现实层面,心理现实和非现实的功能联系会被摧毁殆尽。这是因为现实生活空间的广度如何、现实行为的实现与否,都取决于现实和非现实层面关系的类型和深度,前者对后者的倚重是非常重要的。

(三)自由与责任

为当前服务的教育不能说就是为在瞬间情境中生活服务的教育。儿童心理生活空间拓展的问题超乎心智问题和说教问题,这个问题与心理现实层面和非现实层面的分离的关系极为密切。心理现实层面的发展为儿童顺利进入成年提供了坚实的基础,这个发展过程要求——儿童的自由生活空间不能太小。在穷孩子身上,现实和非现实的分离通常较早发生。但我们知道,这并非总是一个优势,太严酷的环境容易导致发育障碍。与此相似,威权主义的、要求服从的、约束性的情境的建构使现实和非现实的分离过早发生。但武断的、操之过急的现实和非现实的分离常伴有这样的危险:虽有隐蔽的替代性满意,但稍后却是整个现实层面的坍塌。只有在足够自由的生活空间里,儿童才有可能根据自己的需要选择目标,他才能体会到走向目标过程中的客观困难。只有这样,清晰的现实层面才能形成,负责任的选择能力才能培养出来。

第六章 替代活动和替代价值

行为动力律和个性结构的实验研究迫使我们越来越注意思考复杂的问题。我们不再研究单一的心理逻辑系统,它们与简单的需求和欲望对应;而是研究这些系统的相互关系,研究其分化与转化,研究建基于这些系统的不同种类的更高一级的整体。这些相互关系和更高一级的整体极容易生变,其中的关系又显得很微妙。然而,我们必须用实验手段把握它们,因为这对理解行为的潜隐现实和个性差异,把握心理系统的相互关系和大系统的整体结构极其重要。在实验过程中,我们常常发现,弗洛伊德给我们指出了一些事实,虽然他没有用动力律清晰勾勒出这些事实,但他无意之中对动力学作出了很大的贡献。

弗洛伊德广泛使用替代的概念来解释正常行为和异常行为,而且他认为,与替代的密切关联是我们整个文化生活重要的基石。我们发现替代关系有多种多样的形式。比如,有人梦想殿堂般的生活,就用一些大理石装饰他的厨房;有人无钱买钢琴,就搜集钢琴的广告目录。我们还发现,一个少年犯知道他不被允许离开教养所,他就希望得到一个旅行袋作为生日礼物。数以百计的例子使我们相信,无论是心理需求还是饥饿和性欲之类的身体需求,替代都极为重要,且意义深远。需求越大,替代的倾向似乎就越强烈。连儿童广阔的游戏场都和替代形成了特殊的关系,这些替代形式或为物件,或为活动。

众所周知,目前尚无解释替代机制动态关系的理论。弗洛伊德规避替代的定义,诸多杰出的心理分析学家认为,他没有提出什么替代理论。

倘若你研究替代行为出现的必要条件和充足条件,研究其后果,你就遭遇一个悖论。替代行为常常发生在不能达到目标的情境里,以及存在心理紧张的情境里。让我们从登博①的实验里选取一个关于愤怒的例子。受试者尝试扔圆环去套瓶子,老是套不上。最后,她眼含泪水走到门边,把圆环吊在衣帽钩上。在另一个实验里,受试者尝试去摘花,但老是够不着;她突然转过身来,从身旁的花瓶里抓了一枝花。

乍一看,这些事件很容易理解,但如果从情境动力学的立场上来看这个问题,它们其实不那么简单。显然,替代行为生于张力系统,张力系统与初始行为对应。因此,我们自然希望,通过替代行为,初始行为的张力系统会得到完全释放或部分释放。然而,在许多情况下,当事人反而更不满意、更情绪化了,以上例子已然彰显了这个道理。但如果替代行为没有使主要的心理系统得到释放,那么,从动力学的观点来看,替代行为为什么会产生问题就可以理解了。

为了研究这个问题和其他动力学问题,我们做了一连串的实验,分别以成人、低能儿童和患精神病儿童为研究对象。我们选取了一些实验结果在这里介绍。

如果你尝试界定替代可能发生的范围,你将会遭遇重重困难。比如,在研究禁令的效应时,你拿走了一个孩子的布娃娃,她就自己动手做布娃娃,你称之为替代活动;但在另一个实验中,如果她开始玩火车,你就不敢肯定说,那就是替代活动,因为即使她的布娃娃没有被拿走,她也可能会玩火车。初始行为和后继行为的相似度有多大,你才能肯定地说,后继行

---

① 塔玛拉·登博(Tamara Dembo,1902—1993),俄裔美国心理学家,师从卢因,以研究愤怒著称——译者。

为就是替代行为呢？另一个例子是：如果受试者不是用圆环去套瓶子，而是用圆环去套身边的一块积木，那可能是替代行为吗？但如果他把圆环套在自己的一只手臂上，然后又把它套在另一只手臂上，或者把圆环扔到地板上，那是替代行为呢，抑或是简单的焦躁行为呢？

你若想把替代概念局限于在内容上和初始行为很相似的行为，就必须界定该概念的范围。一方面，因为有些替代行为在形式上和初始行为大不相同，比如我们从法扬斯的实验里获悉，儿童拿不到巧克力时，布娃娃可以成为实实在在的替代品。或者，儿童能把妈妈的同情当作巧克力真实的替代品。另一方面，我们从下文中可以看到，两个行为可能很相似，却不是替代关系。就心理学家的例子而言，更要注意的是，要有足够的证据证明两件事的相似性，两者一定要有替代关系。替代关系是否存在不能从事件的外观来判定，在每一个具体情况下，两件事是否存在某种动力论关系是进行判定的必要条件。

从动力论关系来看，只有替代行为与对应初始目标的张力系统有直接关系时，换言之，只有在替代行为生于初始系统时，我们才能说替代关系成立了。从动力论关系来看，我们发现了一个意料之外的关系：替代行为与达到目标所用的工具或手段有关系。一个人想向另一个人传达信息时，如果电话坏了，他就发电报；如果儿童不能直接走向目标，他就会绕道走。在这种情况下，意向的实现随环境而变化，新行为派生于对应初始目标的心理系统。

实验证明，我们的确发现，新工具或新方法的使用和特别的替代行为之间存在着流动性的过渡关系。比如，受试者用一根棍子挑着圆环去套瓶子，这一工具的使用就改变了任务的意义，于是我们就看到一个新的任务。如果使用广义的替代概念，我们就可以用心理学的观点说明替代目标或替代行为，我们稍后再说相似性问题。首先，只有新行为生于初始的张力系统，而新目标和初始目标颇为不同时，我们才能说，替代发生了。有必要区分不同的替代关系，但我们在这里将讨论这个问题：替代行为是否带来了替代满足？如果带来了替代满足，那又是在什么情况下带来了什么样的满足呢？

我们尝试用实验方法判定,心理张力系统是否能通过替代行为而得到释放。我们从奥甫桑吉纳(Ovsankina)的实验获悉,一种活动被打断时,心理张力系统就产生回复这一活动的强烈倾向,这个系统和完成任务的准需求相对应。我们对替代行为做了实验研究。在我们的研究中,受试者的第一个活动被打断以后,他又接受了第二个任务,第二个任务似乎在替代第一个活动。如果第一个任务是用橡皮泥做一匹马,第二个任务可能是做另一种动物,或一个球。如果打断他正在讲的故事,我们可能叫他为故事的结局画一幅画;如果受试者画画时被打断,我们可能叫他用讲故事的方法来完成这幅画。

我们的实验研究设置了以下一些情况:初始活动和替代活动所用的物质材料相同;活动的内容相似,但物质材料不同。如果第二个任务真的具有替代价值,被打断的初始任务中的张力系统就必然会得到完全或部分释放。如果第二个任务有替代价值,能产生替代满足,受试者就不会再去完成初始任务。相反,如果第二个任务没有替代价值,受试者就频频回头再去完成初始任务。在有些实验里,我们不直接给受试者第二个任务,而是创造一种情境,提供他自发替代活动的可能性。

事实上,里斯纳[1]发现,在有些情况下,第二个任务有替代价值,再去完成初始任务的可能性比较小。他很快发现,不仅两个任务的相似性对替代价值有重要意义,而且替代活动的难度也对替代价值有重要意义。比如,第一个马赛克拼图的任务被中断,而第二个马赛克拼图任务比较容易,那么,再去完成第一个任务的可能性就是100%,换言之,第二个任务的替代价值就是零。然而,如果第二个任务比较难,再去完成第一个任务的可能性就下降到42%。为了让较高的替代程度数值上对应较高的百分比,我们用无恢复(nonresumption)的术语来表达实验结论。根据这一循环关系,容易替代行为的无恢复价值用0%来表示;困难的替代行为价值是58%。再举一例,受试者的第一个任务是用橡皮泥做一只狗,第二个任

---

[1] See K. LISSNER, Die Entspannung von Bedürfnissen durch Ersatzhandlungen, *Psychol. Forsth.*, 1993, 18, pp. 218—250.

务可能是做另一种动物;如果第二种动物如蛇做起来比狗容易,其替代价值就比较小(58%);如果第二个任务困难,其替代价值就比较大(70%)。因此我们可以说,第二个任务越困难,其替代价值就越大。任务的难度对替代价值起到至关重要的作用,因为它和执行者自定的标准有关系。由此可见,替代价值和我们所谓的志向高低有关系。

替代行为是否与初始任务有直接的动态接触,对替代价值关系重大。在当时的情况下,如果这两种活动在心理上分隔了一段距离,我们就发现,替代价值几乎不存在。这样的心理距离有时可以这样来实现:实验者打断受试者时说,"我们现在去完成一个全新的任务。"如果替代任务从初始任务衍生而来,由于从事的是同一种任务,所以替代价值就大。在心理分隔的情况下,无恢复的百分比低至15%;相反,在两个任务有动态接触的情况下,无恢复的百分比高达57%。

初始任务和替代任务之间的关系意义重大,突出表现在对低能儿童的实验中。柯普克(Köpke)和蔡加尼克(Zeigarnik)对7~8岁的低能儿童所做的实验发现:如果实验者不提供替代行为,低能儿童一定会恢复被打断的任务,就是说,无恢复价值为0%。同样的情况下,比低能儿童小一岁的正常儿童的无恢复价值为18%。如果实验者提供一个替代任务,低能儿童的无恢复价值仅为5%,正常儿童的无恢复价值则高达70%。这就是说,同样的行为在正常儿童身上的替代价值很高,在低能儿童身上可以忽略不计。柯普克增加了第二种活动与初始活动的相似性,直至两者近乎相同。比如,如果第一个任务是在红纸上画一种动物,第二个任务就是在绿纸上画同一种动物;如果第一个任务是用积木搭一座桥,第二个任务就是搭一座相似的桥。在这样的情况下,低能儿童的无恢复行为从来不超过20%,这一耐人寻味的数值结果似乎与我们的其他经验相冲突。我们常常看见,当低能儿童不能达到目的时,很容易满足于尚未达标的成就。戈茨沙特(Gottschaldt)在一些特殊的实验中观察到同样的表现。低能儿童用积木搭建高塔遇到困难时,比较容易满足于转向替代行为,比如建一座小塔或其他简单的建筑。他们很容易满足于替代行为,还可以从以下例子看出来。一个低能幼儿想要把皮球扔得很远,却不行,但他很高兴，因为他用了劲。如果真实的行为不可能达到目的，他就往往满足于做一个姿态。拉扎尔用一个术语来描述这样的儿童，这就是他所谓的"手势儿童"(gesture children)。由此可见，低能儿童比正常儿童更容易满足于替代行为，这种例子是很多的。另一方面，其他人的实验也显示，有的时候，替代价值对低能儿童的价值远不如对正常儿童的价值。为了澄清这两种情况的冲突，我们必须研究低能儿童心理系统的性质。无疑，在性质上，并非所有低能儿童的心理系统都相同，我只描绘最常见的类型。

当前普遍的设想是，低能儿童不仅心智有缺陷，而且个性结构也与正常儿童不同。然而在总体上，我们尚不能给人格个性下定义。近年来，我们使用多种方法研究这个问题，我在这里简要介绍一下从中提炼出的理论。

从动力学的观点来看，人与人的差异基于三个方面。从这个观点来看，人是由若干系统组成的一个整体。首先，可以研究整体的结构，也就是系统分化的程度，以及在整体中系统分化的类别。比如，一岁婴儿动力学上的系统分化就不如三岁幼儿。儿童身上没有分化出许多系统，事物之间的联系比较紧密，看不出显著的边缘和中心的分化。其次，在相同的结构中，系统的动力学材料可能不一样；系统可能比较固化，或者或多或少有一点流动性；如此等等。为了理解这样的差异，我们还可以用儿童和成人的差异作比较。看起来，在大多数情况下，儿童给定系统的改变比成人更容易，心里系统的弹性或固化似乎是整体人格的基本特征。再次，与不同系统对应的内容是不同的。这第三点差异似乎主要由个人的过往经验所决定。比如，古希腊4岁儿童的心理系统和今天纽约4岁儿童的心理系统是大不相同的。

我们的实验研究显示，最常见的低能儿童的特点是，其心理系统相对固化，不太有弹性。这一理论的基础是基于对低能儿童的实验研究，我们研究其满足、意志、记忆、注意和智能。[1] 容我不在此赘述我们的全部例证，上述例证足以显示，从对这类心理素材的研究中，我们已能理解低能

---

[1] 欲求了解这里勾勒的人格理论更详细的描绘及其实验证据，参见本书第七章。

儿童替代行为的种种吊诡的事实。从心理动力论来看,可以这样来界定低能儿童:他们个性结构的分化程度较小,颇像年龄更小的幼儿;但他们的心理系统却不像幼儿那样富有弹性,而是更加固化。心理系统较少分化的现象常用来解释低能儿童所谓的幼稚病(infantilism),但有一点很清楚:低能儿童和幼儿是不一样的。

如果我们接受低能儿童心理系统更固化的理论,我们首先就必须要解释只中断初始行为却不提供第二个任务的实验结果:低能儿童100%地恢复了被打断的任务。继续进行打断的任务显示出了不正常的高频率,其原因是,被堵塞的张力系统维持不变,得不到充分释放的机会。这一实验结果与日常观察的结果一致:低能儿童非常倔强,一旦决定达到一个目标,这个意向就难以改变。低能儿童广为人知的倔脾气是其心理系统固化的结果。

然而,如果在进行第一个任务之后,低能儿童被带进了一个全新的情境,我们就看不到100%恢复第一个任务的行为。相反,低能儿童恢复第一个任务的行为远不如正常儿童。在我们的实验中,我们发现了一个相当极端的结果:低能儿童重拾第一种任务的频率只有20%。

这里的无恢复结果再一次说明,其原因是心理系统的固化。新心理情境非常僵化,不容易变化,难以产生和旧心理情境的联系。这类低能儿童的典型特征是一心不能二用:要么完全处在这一种情境中,要么完全处在那一种情境中。心理系统固化理论使我们能解释,为什么在有些情况下恢复旧情境的程度高得不正常,在另一些情况下又低得不正常。与此相似,我们还能用它解释上文提及的悖论。

替代行为是否具有替代价值? 这个问题在心理动力系统方面可以这样来表述:一个系统对应初始任务,另一个系统对应第二个任务。如果第二个任务即第二种活动的完成具有对第一个系统的替代价值,那么,这两种系统就必须密切相关,第二个系统的调动就必然调动第一个系统;换言之,两个系统必须是一个动态的整体。正常儿童的心理系统有足够的流动性,两个系统的相似性足以使两者产生特殊的关联。如果受试者接到的第二个任务和第一个任务类似,第一个心理系统就会发生变化,使新的心理系统成为旧心理系统的一部分。这两个系统似乎并没有完全汇聚成一个无分化的整体系统,但我们的确看到一个单一的系统,两部分之间有一个动态的墙壁。如果一部分调动起来,由于内在边界的力度,这个系统就被调动起来了。

低能儿童接到第二个任务时,由于他心理系统的固化,第一个系统保持不变,为了执行第二个任务,另一个独立的系统随即确立。于是,第二个系统的调动并不能启动第一个系统,换言之,第二个任务不具有替代价值。

如果这一理论是正确的,那么,如果我们能找到一条路径在初始系统里开发出第二个任务,该理论就能确定低能儿童心理的替代性满意机制。实际上,自发地从初始活动过渡到一个替代活动时,替代性满意机制就会常常出现;在戈茨沙特的实验里,在我们描绘的例证中,就可以看到这样的机制。低能儿童只有一个系统,因此,第二个任务的替代价值必须特别大。由于他们的众多心理系统固化,所以在这些情境中,那个总系统并没有分化为略有不同的两部分,唯有正常儿童的心理系统才分化为两部分。因此,替代行为产生的结果不一样:它更加彻底地调动低能儿童的整个系统,正常儿童整个系统被调动的程度就不那么彻底了。于是,正常儿童的替代行为很容易启动,但其替代价值并不完美。低能儿童身上出现两种现象:两个系统完全分离,使第二个活动没有替代价值;即使两个任务有一点点联系,他的替代性满意度也是很高的。这种全有或全无的现象对低能儿童至关重要,不仅表现在替代活动中,而且表现在其他领域(比如在智能行为中)。

除了两种活动的联系程度以及第二个任务的难度外,替代行为的现实、非现实程度对于替代价值也至关重要。替代常常不是以现实行为的形式出现的,而是以空中楼阁或白日梦的形式出现的。在许多替代活动中,说话或姿态取代了现实的举动。这种替代活动有替代价值吗?对梦境理论和精神病替代行为的理论而言,这个问题同样重要。通过说话和思维的实验而不是通过现实行为的实验来研究替代行为的效应,很不容易。马勒(Mahler)做了以下类型的实验:受试者做手工时被打断,他不得不想如何继续完成这件手工作品；在受试者不能到达目标时，实验者要他讲一个他能达标的故事。这样的场域很复杂，我只能探讨一小部分。马勒发现，总体上，替代行为越现实，替代价值就越大。至于行为的现实程度如何，那不由替代行为单独决定，决定其现实程度的是替代行为与初始行为的关系。他发现，我们必须区别活动的内在目标和外在目标；替代行为越接近初始行为的内在目标，第二个任务的现实程度就越高，其替代价值就越大。面对智力问题的任务时，一般来说，受试者在思考中寻求解决办法以释放张力，仅仅这样做是不够的；更重要的是，他要表现出实际的解决办法。这就显示，对事件的现实程度或非现实程度而言，社会因素至关重要。除非受试者能告诉实验者替代任务的解决办法，否则，初始心理系统就不能得到足够的释放。因为只有在社会认可的情况下，现实程度才是充分的。

非现实替代行为与某些游戏问题关系密切。根据皮亚杰的理论，儿童的世界概念有神秘性。对儿童而言，幻想与现实、谎言与真实的界线并不分明。我们必须问，就心理需求而言，非现实的事件是否真能使儿童感到满意。斯里奥伯格就此进行了相当全面的实验，他发现，不能泛泛地说，非现实的东西能替代现实的东西。你给儿童一颗糖果替代品而不是真的糖果，给他一把纸做的剪刀而不是真的剪刀，他是否会感到满意呢？那取决于情境的特殊性。考夫卡(Koffka)说，我们必须区分游戏情境和严肃情境。游戏情境不是很固化，你可以说它很"松散"。一些替代行为只能在游戏情境里发生；在游戏情境里，目标的固化程度不如在严肃情境里的固化程度。在严肃情境里，儿童拒绝游戏那样的替代行为。有趣的是，反过来也是同样的道理。游戏情境里的儿童常常不接受替代游戏行为的活动。实验证明，替代活动的可能性取决于总体情境的松散性，这个道理同样适用于成年人。

替代价值的一个重要因素是那一刻需求的强度。斯里奥伯格的实验显示，如果用真实的剪刀的时间够长，儿童就容易接受橡皮泥剪刀。一般地说，需求越强烈，替代活动的替代价值就越大。

表 6-1 替代行为实验结果一览表

（数字为初始活动无恢复百分比）

	初始任务	无替代活动的实验	有替代活动的实验	
			第二任务 容易	第二任务 困难
1	马赛克	10	0	58
	橡皮泥（狗）	20	15（蛇）	70（球）
2	马赛克		初始任务和第二任务 分隔	连接
			15	57
3	7~8岁低能儿	18	68	
	8岁低能儿	0	5	
4	不同的任务	80	（新情境）	（第二个任务几乎与第一个任务相同）
	纸上画画	40	14	
	做纸盒	25	初始任务目标达到	初始任务目标未达到
		25	77	25
		25	讲故事	
			100	19
5	画画		边想边讲	只想不讲
		17	14	0

另一方面，需求的强度增加，接受替代行为的倾向无疑就会增加。这一规律清楚地表现在登博的实验里。他的研究发现，强烈的情绪紧张导致无意义的行为，比如扔圆环去套衣帽钩。他证明，这种自发情境总是冲突情境的结果，他用动力论来解释，替代目标如何获得正诱发力。我们知道，如果一个人有一个目标，该目标就有心理场的功能，就会从某些物件诱发出一个诱发力。比如，如果有个人想把一件物品包裹起来，突然，纸张和绳子就具有正诱发力了。苛勒论述了工具使用情境中的定向状态。登博的研究显示，诱发场产生诱发力，诱发力是达到目标的手段；而且，如

果张力足够强大,与初始目标有关系的其他目标就会应运而生。

我们在本章开篇时看到,就心理系统而言,替代活动和工具的使用之间存在着令人吃惊的关系。现在,我们还看到,从心理环境来看,工具的使用和替代活动的关系密切,因为两者都是从同一个诱发场里诱发出来的。最后,关于自发性替代行为,我们可以把我们考察的主要结论表述如下:替代行为越不符合新的目标,越不与初始的内在目标在同一种路径内,其替代价值就越大。

第七章 低能的动力学理论

近几十年来,教育学取得了长足进步,德克罗利①富有洞见的著作非常重要,这些成果对正常儿童的行为研究产生了决定性的影响。精神病理学对心理学尤其心理学理论的重要性日渐增加。然而,了解心理病理本身特别困难。下文的讨论将尝试提出低能动力论的一些基本原理。我们清醒地意识到,我们提出的仅仅是一个理论框架。这一局限实乃必然,因为我们考察的仅仅是许多低能类型的一种。从动力论的观点看,低能类型有许多种类,该理论依托的仅仅是对某一程度低能的实验研究。然而,在当前个性类型的实验研究中,可能仅局限于研究某一类型低能的不同行为表现,研究这些行为彼此关系的动力学理论,似乎是最重要的。在此基础上,我们将判定哪些概念适用于研究个性差异的一般问题,这样的研究路子似乎比覆盖各种类型的分类研究效果更好。当然毫无疑问,低能的动力学理论必须同时研究一般个性理论的基本问题。

低能并非只是"孤悬的智能疾病",它涉及整体的个性,这是一个常识

---

① 德克罗利(O. Decroly,1871—1932),比利时教育家、心理学家、医生,新教育代表人物。主要著作有《论个性心理学与实验心理学》和《新教学法》——译者注。

问题。① 然而,我们止步于这个一般的洞见,没有再向前迈进一步。最为重要的是,我们极少对总体的个性作出正面的描绘。

我认为,对低能者智能真正富有洞见的实验研究尚未完成。用检测方法判定某些领域的研究固然重要,然而它却不能说明低能者的底层心理过程。至于低能者的底层心理和正常人有何差异,这样的检测也难以给人启示。与其他心理学门类一样,只有超乎测试"成绩"的概念而窥见心理过程的本质,我们才能洞悉低能者的心理过程。此外,有的时候,低能者在某些方面(比如社会行为)的测试成绩还胜过正常人。

如果我们试图超越测试成绩的概念,来探究心理过程的性质,我们就不得不考虑低能者的智力活动和正常人的区别。

第一节 低能儿童的顿悟

对低能者智力的探究遭遇了未曾预料到的重重困难。

过去 20 年间的研究至少确定了智能活动基本性质的轮廓,尤其确定了创造性思维的轮廓。从动力学来看,顿悟涉及场域的重组②,在许多方面和所谓模糊形貌的转换关系密切。感知和思维两个领域内部的总体关系发生了变化,起初看似孤立的部分成为统一整体的构造成分。独立的部分或者不再独立,或者与其他整体的依附部分结成新的整体。简言之,在场域整体组建的过程中,场域的结构发生了变化,而且通常是发生突然的变化。在这一变化的因果关系中,定向的力量发挥了重要的作用。

从这种智力活动理论出发,若有人问低能儿童思维的特殊性究竟在哪里,他就必须首先确定,低能者的顿悟似乎始终具有正常人本性的一切基本属性。毫无疑问,低能者能看见整体,而且他们看见的整体同样明显。③ 不能说低能者不能够从事智能活动,也不能说其心理活动不那么深刻,而且,思维活动中典型的"啊哈"式顿悟无疑也发生在低能者身上。实

---

① 实际上,比奈(智力测验大师——译者注)对低能者性格的研究非常感兴趣。
② See KÖHLER, *Intelligenzprufungen an Menschenajten* (*The Mentality of Apes*), and *Das Wesen der Intelligenz*, *Kind und Umwelt*, Berlin, 1930.
③ 稍后我们将看到,他们悟到的整体性甚至更为明显。

际上,他们似乎常常有这种更强烈的体悟,似乎比正常儿童更喜欢这样的感觉。低能儿童能领会俏皮话,而且比正常儿童更喜欢俏皮话。与正常儿童和类人猿一样,低能儿童的顿悟涉及场域里所有关系的转化。

由此看来,从动力论来看,低能者和正常人的区别是外在的区别。一般地说,智力活动典型的场域结构的变化在两者身上发生的原因有所不同,其心理场域结构的变化并不是由相同的事件引发的。低能儿童的变化是其他事件引发的,这些事件是所谓更容易的任务,或更原始形态的任务。有人指出,低能儿童和正常儿童唯一质的区别似乎是,低能儿童的思维更具象、更感性。[1]

第二节 实验问题的设计

在过去的三年里,我们深入研究了低能的特征,不是靠直接研究智能的方法,而是靠研究意志和需求的领域。在许多方面,这些领域与个性深层特征的关系更密切,而不是与精神活动特征的关系更密切。即使低能是总体个性特征的表现,这样的研究似乎也不可能使我们最终洞察低能儿童智力困难的原因。

很难从智力测试的结果去推导智力动力差异的问题。主要的困难是,通过智力测试去判定个体差异要借助一些活动,而我们对这些活动的心理性质和一般规律了解得并不充分。[2] 因此,我们谨慎选用实验方法,其底层的心理过程及其规律始终是我们最熟悉的。与此相似,我们首先研究低能程度比较轻而不是比较重的个案。显然,这有悖于一般的原理:研究应尽可能从差异入手。指引我们目前研究路径的是出于以下考虑:如果研究低能儿童的方法和研究正常儿童的方法相同,结果很可能是,研究者为两种儿童提供的心理情境就会截然不同,以至于造成完全不同的动力论关系。很可能会出现这样的局面,在一个儿童的心理情境中会发

---

[1] Cf. W. ELIASBERG, Die Veranschaulichung in der Hilfsschule, *Zeitscchr. f. exper. Pad.* t 1926, 27, pp. 134—145.

[2] Cf. LEWIN, *Die Entwicklung der experimeniellen Willenspsychologic und die Psychotherapie*, Hirzel, Leipzig, 1929, p. 28.

生相当大的冲突,而在另一个儿童的心理情境中不会有任何冲突。只有在真正可比的心理情境中,你所比较的行为差异才不至于仅仅是外表的差异,你才可以考虑,在同一类型活动中表现出来的差异才是受试者动力论差异的结果。

我们的受试者来自柏林低能儿童的学校,年龄在6至12岁之间,大多数的智商属于"摩仑"(moron)级,少数属于"痴愚"(imbecile)级。① 对不同年龄的正常儿童所做的对照实验由相同的主持人主持。

实验关注的要点是:(1)满足的心理过程,(2)未满足需求的表现(被中断行为的恢复),(3)替代行为即补偿行为的替代价值。实验的挑选自然受某些工作假设的指引,我们首先简略介绍针对满足的实验结果。

第三节　低能儿童和正常儿童的心理满足

主持人要求儿童不停地画月亮(图7-1)。主持人的指令是,"月亮是圆的,有两只眼睛,一个鼻子,一个嘴巴。"主持人在一张纸上画了一个月亮。儿童要不停地画月亮,直到他受够了。他可以在任何时候停下不画。但像卡斯腾(Karsten)的实验一样,② 这场实验本身就含有继续画下去的压力。(当然,主持人给不同儿童的压力要尽可能相同。)根据卡斯腾

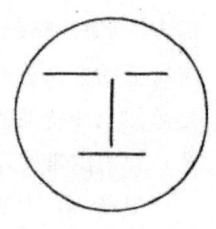

图 7-1

和弗伦德(Freund)③实验所揭示的心理满足的一般规律,由于不断地重复,任务起初的正诱发力或中性诱发力最终变为负诱发力。在这些实验中,满足点达到以后,中断的行为一般不会立即发生,一般会再继续进行一会儿,直到那一活动获得了一定的负诱发力。停下来以后,实验人问儿童,你是否想继续画,画他自己想画的东西(自由画)。如果他愿意,实验

---

① "摩仑"(moron,智商51~70),"痴愚"(imbicile,智商26~50),两者科学而严谨的译文难觅,暂且以此区别两类低能儿童——译者注。
② See A. KARSTEN, Psychische Sättigung, *Psychol. Foscch.*, 1928, 10, 142 ff.
③ See A. FREUND, Die psychische Sättigung im Menstruum und Intermenstruum, *ibid.*, 1930, 13, 198 ff.

人就给他纸和笔,他想画多久就画多久。

我们习惯性地认为,低能儿童有重复动作的显著倾向,同时其持续性很小。因为我们知道,满足和需求的动因关系密切,所以判定低能儿童满足的变动过程就相当重要。画月亮的任务对 9～10 岁和 10～11 岁的低能儿童并不是特别困难,而 8～9 岁低能儿童画月亮的数量肯定少于正常儿童。

实验结果见表 7-1。在满足实验里,与 8～9 岁正常儿童对照组相比,低能儿童画画的总时长(画月亮+自由画的时间)比正常儿童略短一些(41 分钟比 58 分钟),但正常组和低能组个人的时长有相当大的重叠。9～10 岁低能儿童画画的时长(59 分钟)和 8～9 岁正常儿童画画的时长相同,但比 9～10 岁正常儿童时长的平均值(75 分钟)短得多。10～11 岁低能儿童时长的平均值(77 分钟)和 9～10 岁和 10～11 岁两组正常儿童的平均值(79 分钟)几乎相等。

表 7-1　正常儿童(N)和低能儿童(R)心理满足对照表

年龄		满足的时间(秒)			满点 (分钟)	每分钟 画月面数	每 100 分钟次数	
		画月亮数	自由画数	总数			停顿次数	其他活动次数
8～9 岁	R	33	8	41	27	4	30	20
8～9 岁	N	55	3	58	35	8	8	8
9～10 岁	R	56	3	59	30	7	30	17
9～10 岁	N	55	20	75	27	7	15	3
10～11 岁	R	75	2	77	40	7	23	21
10～11 岁	N	45	33	79	35	8	8	8

考虑到低能儿童坚持力和注意力差的特点,这一结果令人吃惊:至少在 9～11 岁这个年龄段里,正常儿童和低能儿童心理满足的情况几乎没有差别。即使在感到满足的时间差异比较大的情况下,两个对照组平均时间的一致性也令人吃惊。三组低能儿童感到满足的时间点分别是 27 分钟、30 分钟和 40 分钟;三组正常儿童感到满足的时间点分别是 35 分钟、27 分钟和 35 分钟。

可见,在这种活动中,正常儿童和低能儿童在总体上感到满足所需的时间并没有本质的区别。① 然而,满足的进程却表现出一些典型的差异。首先给人印象的是,10~11岁低能儿童几乎把全部时间(75分钟)都花在画月亮上,这一活动感到满足的时间点达到以后,他们不愿意继续自由画画,几乎没有例外。② 相反,正常儿童画月亮感到满足的时间点很快就到来(45分钟),但他们都愿意继续自由画画。由此可见,在这个年龄段里,低能儿童在同一种活动里的坚持性超过正常儿童;然而一旦满足以后,他们就不再愿意和这个领域的任何活动维持任何关系了。③ 不过,低能儿童在琐细的技术问题上更频繁地表现出微小的变化(如改变画作的位置和顺序)。

除了变异的倾向外,感到满足的另一个典型表现是次生行为,所谓次生行为主要是指,在活动不中断情况下发生的行为。在次生行为发生的频率上,正常儿童和低能儿童之间似乎没有很大的差异。然而,三个年龄段的低能儿童停顿休息和插入其他行为的频率要高得多,他们肯定会在主要活动中插入大段的其他行为。三个年龄段低能儿童每100分钟停顿休息的次数分别是30、30和23;三个年龄段正常儿童相应的休息次数分别是8、15和7。插入行为的数值,三个年龄段的低能儿童分别是20、17和21,三个年龄段的正常儿童分别是8、3和8。

我们发现,满足实验第一个综合结果是,在8~9岁这个年龄段,正常儿童和低能儿童在总体复合行为(月亮画+自由画)达到满意的速度上没有重大差异。然而,在满意的进程上,两个对照组表现出了典型的差异:继续画的意愿和满足的到来发生冲突,使低能儿童停顿休息和插入其他

---

① 8~9岁低能儿童会比较快地得到满足,原因可能是,任务对于他们的难度超过了正常儿童。他们画月亮的平均数是每分钟4幅,正常儿童作画的平均数则是每分钟8幅。卡斯腾的研究发现,在其他条件相同的情况下,比较专注于核心任务时,达到感到满足的时间就快,在我们这个实验里,比较困难的任务就应该这样看。
② 低能儿童不愿意继续自由画画,可能是受害怕失败的影响吧。
③ 外表上,8~9岁年龄段的儿童表现刚相反:低能儿童转入自由画画变异性的时间早于正常儿童,6岁年龄段的儿童也是这样的。但我倾向于相信,如果考虑动力因素,正常儿童和低能儿童的表现并没有真实的矛盾。

行为的次数增多。换言之,低能儿童要么执行手头的任务;要么完全中断任务,或停顿,或转向另一种活动。正常儿童感到满意的进程的连续性要高得多。他们应对冲突时表现得更灵活,表现出更退让的方式。他们会迅速寻找到一个办法,借助于次生活动或其他手段,安然度过冲突,不会在表面上放弃继续完成任务的意向。相反,低能儿童的行为在表面上要突兀得多,更加表现出"非此即彼"的倾向。

正常儿童的行为更灵活,原因可能是,他们更愿意看到满足实验主持人要求的可能性,这使他们能规避实际的任务。这样的洞见的确有重要的作用,但用纯智力差异进行解释则是错误的。两个对照组儿童行为的灵活性随机直接展开,没有经过特别刻意的考虑。

我不得不相信,有一个更加重要的低能者属性在这里起作用。换言之,心理基质里的功能固化是低能儿童智力产生困难的真正原因。在探讨这一理论之前,我们先简略介绍一下中断行为恢复的实验和替代行为的实验。

第四节 被中断行为的恢复,替代行为的价值

如果你用任何借口打断正在执行任务的受试者,让他做完第二件事情,最后留一点时间(比如一分钟)给他自己用,通常他自然而然要回头去做第一件事情。我们从奥甫桑吉纳的实验结果[①]中获悉,在有些情况下,在执行某些任务时,恢复完成初始行为的现象很常见;即使受试者知道,恢复这一初始行为并不符合实验主持人的意愿。

柯普克用8~9岁的低能儿童[②]和同龄的正常儿童做实验(表7-2)。正常儿童中断行为的恢复率是79%,这个结果和奥甫桑吉纳的实验结果比较吻合;在同样条件下,低能儿童中断行为的恢复率是100%。第一项任务完成以后,31个参与实验的低能儿童在30秒内恢复中断的行为,无

---

① See OVSIANKINA, Wiederaufnahme unterbrochener Handlungen, *Psychol. Forcch.*, 1928, II, 302 ft.

② 这些低能儿童被纳入"摩仑"(moron,智商51~70)级,其中6人偏近"痴愚"(imbicile,智商26~50)级。

一例外。由此可见,在低能儿童身上,和被中断行为对应的心理张力系统以恢复第一个任务的方式顽强地表现出来,其规律性令人吃惊。稍后,我们将探讨其个中原因。

以里斯纳[①]和马勒[②]的研究为基础,柯普克用类似的手法研究替代价值。

里斯纳布置的第二个任务在内容和心理基质的类型上都类似于第一个任务。结果表明,第二种活动(我们称之为替代行为)对主要活动的替代价值随第二种行为的性质、难度和表现方式而变化。替代功能越大,完成主要行为的需求就越得到释放,与之对应的心理张力系统得到的释放就越彻底。

因此,替代行为——而不是全然不同的行为被插入时,根据受试者恢复主要活动频次减少的次数,你就可以测定替代行为的替代价值。

表 7-2 正常儿童(N)和低能儿童(R)替代活动的替代价值

年龄段		n	恢复频次百分比		n	恢复频次百分比	
			无替代行为	有替代行为		同等替代	隐蔽的诱发力
7~8岁	N	34(Ⅰ)	79	33			16(Ⅶ)
8~9岁	R	31(Ⅰ)	100	94	15(Ⅲ)	100	
7~8岁	N	15(Ⅱ)	80	33			
8~9岁	R	31(Ⅱ)	100	90	13(Ⅳ)	93	0
7~8岁	R				6(Ⅴ)	86	
8~9岁	R				8(Ⅵ)	80	
11~12岁	R	16(LⅨ)	80	20			

n=受试者人数;( )=所用程序

[①] K. LISSNER, Die Entspannung von Bedürfuissen durch Ersatzhand lungen, *Psychol. Forsch.*, 1933, 18, pp. 218—250.

[②] W. MAHLER, "Ersatzhandlungen verschiedener Realtatsgrades," *Psychol. Forsch.*, 1933, 18, pp. 27—89.

通过对 8～9 岁低能儿童和 7～8 岁正常儿童的比较得出如下结果。在设定的实验条件下,①正常儿童的替代行为具有很高的替代价值,所以其初始行为的恢复从无替代行为时的 79％ 直降到 33％；与之相比,低能儿童初始行为的恢复只从 100％ 降到 94％。② 由此可见,对低能儿童而言,替代活动的替代价值几乎就是零。在以后的实验中,柯普克逐渐增加主要活动和替代活动的相似性,直到两者极端相似：主要活动的指令是"画动物",替代活动的指令是"在另一张纸上画同样的动物"；主要活动的指令是"用石头修桥",替代活动的指令是"用石头修一座相同的桥"。虽然两种活动极端相似,但替代价值却很低(初始行为的恢复率在 86％ 和 100％ 之间)。但在这些情况下,初始行为的恢复并不是那么快,中断 3～4 分钟以后才开始恢复。

这些实验结果与日常的观察相吻合,一旦低能儿想定一个目标,他就表现出特别僵硬的固化特征。他们常常坚持做一件事情,限定一种方式,明确限定在"此刻",这一点给人留下极其深刻的印象。与之同龄或稍小的正常儿童很容易偏离既定行为,但想要让低能儿童偏离原有的选择是极其困难的。由此可见,低能儿童的意志比正常儿童似乎更坚强、更固化。

低能儿童意志特别固化的特征不仅表现在面对短期目标上,而且表现在生活习惯中。低能儿童的刻板和固执常给人留下很深的印象,远远超过正常儿童表现出来的固执。他们的鞋子要以固定的样子摆在床前,不能变；衣服上的纽扣必须按既定的顺序钉上；他们极端怀疑新的食物,即使肚子饿了,晚餐时也不吃通常在午餐时才吃的食物。

这些经验与低能儿童替代活动的实验结果相吻合,与此相对,另有一些情况似乎恰恰相反。小把戏和小游戏对低能儿童似乎比对正常儿童更加有效,原因可能是,低能儿童的智力稍差。但低能儿童更容易在任务尚

---

① 任务的难度尽可能适应儿童的能力。比如：用橡皮泥做动物,用纸做汽车,用棍子和圆环做汽车。

② 换句话说,31 个低能儿童中,只有 2 人没有恢复初始任务,49 个正常儿童中,却有 33 个人恢复初始任务。

未完成时就感到满足。① 实际上,有时一个纯粹的姿态就足以使他们感到满足。如果他不能把球扔得很远,他可能会满足于举起手臂做一个用力扔的动作。再举一例,许多低能儿童阳刚的姿势与真实动作的功能高度吻合。② 拉扎尔把这些儿童称为"手势儿童"。③ 戈茨沙特④的实验研究说明,若初始任务太困难,低能儿童很容易满足于在一个较低的层次上完成比较简单的任务。

实验结果和日常生活观察都证明了一个看似矛盾的现象,这种现象给人留下了深刻的印象。一方面,低能儿童表现出固化的倾向,特别固执,就功能意义而言,这使替代行为难以发生;另一方面,他们又表现出明显的替代行为倾向,很容易满足于替代行为。这一看似矛盾的现象既表现在低能儿童身上,也表现在正常儿童身上。而且,这两种极端的现象体现在同一个儿童身上。

下文介绍的理论试图深入探究其基本的动力因素,指明了破解这一矛盾现象的办法,还能破解低能儿童身上其他典型的悖论。

第五节 个性动力差异的一般理论

如前所示,低能问题是一个个体差异问题。如果从动力论来看这些个体差异,以下几个思考题就会冒出来。作为一个动力系统,个人或多或少是一个统一体,或多或少是自足(封闭)的系统。⑤ 差异可能源自三个方面:(1)总体系统的结构,(2)系统的心理基质和状态,(3)系统的意义内容。兹分述如次。

---

① Cf. L. M. TERMAN, *The Mealurement of InLelligenee*, Houghton Mifflin, Boston, 1916, p. 203.
② Cf. G. WEISS, Kindertypen in aufgabefreien und aufgabegebundenen Situationen, *Zeitschr. f. Kinder for sh.*, 1930, 36, pp. 343ff.
③ "手势儿童"绝非总是低能儿童。
④ GOTTSCHALDT, *Ber. d. C. Kong. f. Heilpdd.*, Munchcn, 1931, pp. 130—143.
⑤ See LEWIN, Zwei Grundtypen von Lebensprozessen, *Zeitschr. f. Psychol*, 1929, 113, 220 ff.

一、个性结构差异

(一)个性分化差异

儿童和成人最根本的动力差异之一是其心理场域和系统的分化程度不同。事实上,在成人身上,各种生活场域(专业、家庭、友情等)和需求层次的分化十分广泛,而一岁婴儿却难以表现出广泛的需求。成人通常很容易区分边缘和中心,幼儿表现出的分层需求少得多。可见在这个方面,幼儿是一个整体系统,动力上表现出更强的格式塔完形。个性分化的功能差异可用以下拓扑图来表现,图 7-2a 是儿童个性拓扑图,图 7-2b 是成人个性拓扑图。

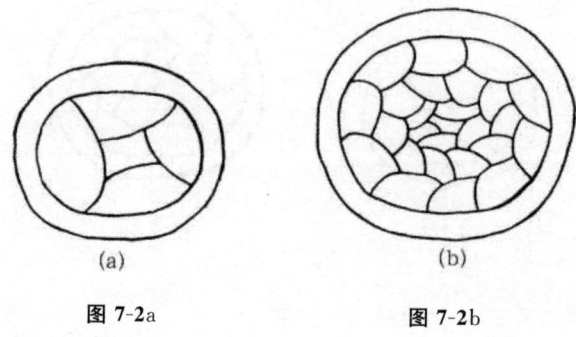

图 7-2a   图 7-2b

(二)个性结构类型

除了分化程度差异之外,在分化类型上当然也存在着重大的个体差异。比如,个人的整体结构可能会和谐或不和谐。个人子系统之间的动力关系绝不是同等密切的。相对封闭的子系统划界的方式存在着巨大的个体差异:哪些部分比较发达?哪些部分不那么发达?子系统间划界的程度是否相对统一?个性组成部分是否相互隔离?个性分割的现象是个性结构类型非常典型的一例。

二、心理基质和心理系统状态的差异

(一)心理基质差异

结构多样性(个性分化差异和个性结构类型)并没有穷尽个性的差

异。因此,在结构同等的情况下,结构变化的难易度可能会大不相同。此外,变化既可能是突兀的,也可能是渐进的。在这一点上,我们可以论述心理动力的柔性、弹性、刚性、脆性或流动性。

总体上应该说,婴儿不仅心理分化较少,而且更容易退让。① 同龄儿童的心理基质似乎有很大的差异。心理基质的特性构成个人深层差异的特性,在遗传上起着重大作用。

心理系统结构容易变化的程度有差异,如果用子系统边界的粗细程度来表现这样的差异,儿童和成人的差异总体上就如图 7-3a 和图 7-3b 所示。

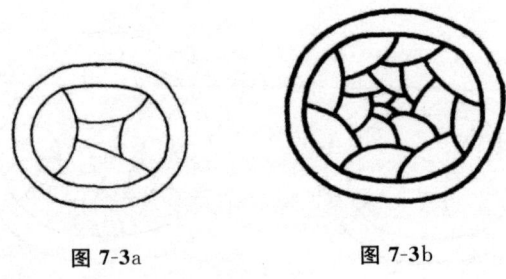

图 7-3a   图 7-3b

(二)心理系统的张力状态

除了心理系统的心理基质差异之外,心理系统的状态尤其是张力状态也必须予以考虑。比如,在满足需求时,张力状态的发生既可能快,也可能慢。也可能,除了暂时状态的多样性以外,个人各子系统的张力之间通常还存在着持久的差异。(广义的心理基质特征包括这段文字和以上三段文字中介绍的特征。)

个人不同心理系统里心理基质的特征绝不是完全整齐划一的。非现

---

① 有些事实——幼儿确立某些习惯的固化特征,似乎有悖于这个年龄段更有弹性的假设。然而从一般生物学观点看,我宁可坚持幼儿心理心理基质更容易流动的假设;我相信,我能用其他方式解释这种互相对立的事实。

实层面的系统具有更大的流动性。① 同一个人身上新旧场域之间可能存在重大的差异。因此,我们说一个人身上的心理基质常量的差异时,有必要就其身上同质的部分进行比较。

三、心理系统意义里内容的差异

即使两个人的心理结构和心理基质特征完全相同,与两人心理系统对应的内容也有可能不同,而且可能构成决定性的心理差异。即使两个人的心理结构和心理基质特征大致相同,如一个俄罗斯大草原上的四岁小儿和一个洛杉矶唐人街上的四岁中国小儿也表现出重大的个体差异,因为他们的目标和理想不同,他们生活场域的意义也不一样。内容的多样性对历史影响的依存度大于心理基质特征和心理结构对历史影响的依存度。

第六节 低能的动力论

一、理论思考

总体上介绍过不同个体的动力论差异后,我们回过头来讲低能(即相当常见的低能类型)的性质问题。我们将从诸多方面考虑这个问题。

二、分化程度

一般地说,在类似条件下成长的8岁低能儿童的心理分化赶不上同龄的正常儿童。低能儿童不仅心智水平较低,而且情感更原始,更幼稚。至于结构蓝图,除了其他差异外,低能儿童的结构分化程度比较低。在这个方面,8岁的低能儿童类似年龄比他小的正常儿童(图7-4)。

通常被称为幼稚症的复杂现象可能主要归因于这种低度分化。幼稚症思维更大的具象性也可能与这种思维的原始性有关系,其意义是动力分化的缺乏。

三、心理基质特征

低能儿童的分化程度对应年龄比他小的正常儿童,但他并不完全类

---

① Cf. J. F. BROWN, Die dynamischen Eigenschaften der Realitats-und Irrealitatschichten, *Psychol. Forsch.*, 1933, 18, pp. 1—26.

似比他小的正常儿童。我们认为,同等分化程度的低能儿童和正常儿童最主要的动力差异是,低能儿童的心理系统比较僵硬,动态重组的能力比较低(图 7-4①)。

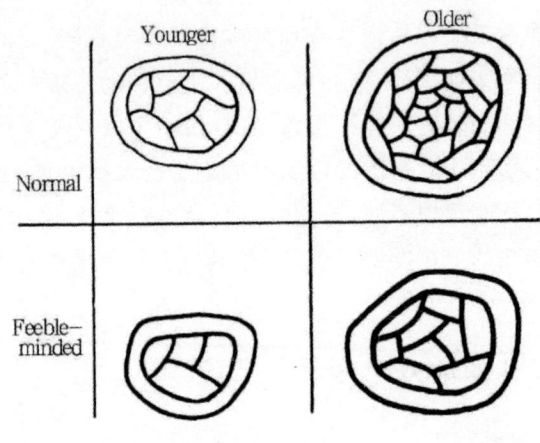

图 7-4

说明:纵坐标上下两个词分别为正常儿童的和低能儿童的,横坐标左右两个词分别为年龄较小儿童的和年龄较大儿童的。

四、应用轮廓

总体上,低能儿童被认为心理系统比较僵硬,流动性较低,这一情况已经被大量的观察所证实。

五、意志目标的固守与固执

如前所示,低能儿童的僵硬和固守②令人印象深刻,他们往往坚守固化的目标和习惯。在一定程度上,低能儿童的僵硬是孤立无助的表现。他总是遭遇不测,他总是比正常儿童更多地发现,他不能信赖他生活其中的世界。察看新情境、看透新情境对他而言比正常儿童要困难得多。像

---

① 和图 3 一样,图 4 里边界线的粗细表示系统内结构变化的难易程度。
② 所谓固守(pedantry)意思是坚守严格的规律性、形成僵硬习惯的倾向,在不必要的程度上和不恰当的情况下仍然坚守的倾向。

处在无助情境里的正常儿童一样,他尝试用熟悉的办法摆脱困境,坚守他相信的手段。在这个程度上,固守也可能是他较低智力的次生效应,是他不善于把握世界的结果。

然而,这一段解释显然是不充分的。低能儿童既不感到孤立无助、也不感到走投无路时,我们也能看到他们顽强固守的倾向。更准确地说,这里似乎有一个很深层的原生的僵化性,这种僵化性特征不仅表现在陈旧的习惯里,而且也表现在新的意志目标里。这种对初始选择目标的固守必然导致柯普克实验里那种恢复被中断目标的行为。

六、替代价值的悖论

我们假设,低能儿童心理系统的重组相对困难。这便使我们能够解释替代行为实验里矛盾的结果。

如果替代活动有替代价值,那就必须满足动力论的假设。如果探究这样的动力论假设,我们就必须确定与此相关的内在心理系统。我们将未完成的初始任务标记为 A,将替代任务标记为 B。替代行为的完成(即 B 的释放)和初始任务的满足(从动力论上来说就是初始任务 A 的释放)必须具备一个条件:A 和 B 的关系非常紧密,B 的释放立即导致 A 的释放。换句话说,A 和 B 必须是一个动力整体里相互依存的部分(图 7-5),而不是两个相互排斥的孤立系统(图 7-6)。在图 7-5 所示的结构里,从动态关系看,A 和 B 的边界相对模糊,它们是一个整体系统的组成部分。只有在这样的情况下,替代行为才具有替代价值。①

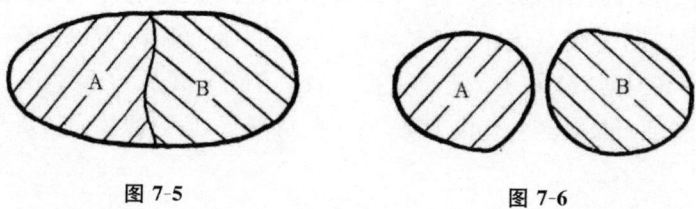

图 7-5　　　　　　　　图 7-6

---

① 在其他条件相同的情况下,由 B 的释放而导致 A 的释放更加完全,第二个行为的替代价值就更高。倘若 A 和 B 所处的整体系统之外还有一个包围它的更强大的共同的外围墙壁,那么,A 和 B 之间的张力就不太依靠相邻的系统。

实际上，里斯纳发现，替代价值的实现很大程度上取决于从第一种活动到第二种活动过渡的类型。如果实验者引进的第二种活动被说成是全新的活动，实际上却是从第一种活动演绎而来的，那么，在其他条件相同的情况下，其替代价值就小得多。蔡加尼克[①]和比伦鲍姆[②]的研究显示，心理系统的相互关系对其张力的释放（直接的释放或借助其他系统的释放）极其重要。他们还验证了足以显示整体心理系统关系的实验手段。

在柯普克研究替代行为的实验情境中，两个任务的相似性就足以显示两个心理系统的关系。儿童接受的替代任务和初始任务有足够的关系时，新生的系统似乎不像是与第一个系统完全分离的，反倒像是从第一个系统生发出来的，至少它和第一个系统关系密切。偶尔，两个系统的密切关系只能在实验中发生。[③] 通常，类似图7-5的总体结构在实验中生成。

两个心理系统容易被重组是另一个必要条件，借此，两个任务的相似性构成总体结构生成的基础，也成为替代价值存在的基础。如果转化的潜能小，前述情况下整体的形成就会困难重重，与第二个任务对应的系统B更可能以独立系统（如图7-6）的面目出现。如果系统B不以独立系统的面目出现，它就会与系统A结成一个动态统一体，但其间的困难会更大。这里的替代价值小，实际上柯普克发现，这就是低能儿童的情况。

与此同时，我们对低能儿童心理基质的基本预设是，其流动性很小。基于此，我们就可以预料，在某些情况下，低能儿童的替代价值比正常儿童大，而不是小。比如，倘若实验者使低能儿童的第二个任务与第一个任务形成动态的联系，那么，由于系统转化相对困难，系统的整合程度就很高，由此而产生的替代价值就特别高。为求得这个结果，可以从第一个任务中演绎出第二个任务。上文业已提及一个看似矛盾的事实：有些情况下，低能儿童极难产生替代满足；另一些情况下，他们的替代满足却很容

---

① See B. ZKIGARNIK, Uber das Behalten von erledigten und unerledigten Handlungen, *Psychol. Forsch.*, 1927, 9, pp. 1—85.

② See G. BIRENBAUM, Das Vergessen einer Vornahme (isolierte seelische Systeme und dynamischc Gesamtbereiche), *Psychol. Forsch.*, 1930, 13, pp. 218—284.

③ See BIRENBAUM, *op. cit.*

易发生。戈茨沙特的例证显示,在第一个任务太困难时,低能儿童自动转向比较容易的任务。不能搭建一个高塔时,他满足于搭建一个矮塔。大量迹象表明,第二个任务产生于第一个任务时,两个任务从动力论的角度来看是没有分隔的。然而,如果两个张力系统没有分隔,那它就应该只有一个张力系统。如此,第二个任务的替代价值对低能儿童就很高,实际上比对正常儿童的替代价值高。这是戈茨沙特实验推导出来的结论,我们的基本设想也支持这一结论。我们还必须详细思考这个结论,因为对智力问题而言,这一结论至关重要。

七、系统的心理基质特征和整体的形成

如果正常儿童身上发生自发性替代行为,比如顺从性替代行为,①那么,新目标通常并不完全等同于旧目标。此时,旧目标并没有完全转化为新目标,而是维持了一定的独立性,比如,它仍然是一个"理想的目标"。这种情况下的正常儿童常常形成一个类似于图7-5的结构:一个相对单一的总体系统随之产生,其中含有两个可分辨、弱分隔的子系统;两个子系统之间有一堵功能上虚弱的墙壁。因此,一个子系统张力的释放必将引起另一个子系统张力的释放,虽然其释放并不完全(张力释放中并未发生深层的转化)。②

倘若两个子系统的心理基质特征特别僵化,一个总体系统分化为两个弱势分隔子系统的情况就不那么容易发生。如果两股力量足够大,就会形成两个分化的系统A和B(图7-6);相反,A和B就不分离而结为一体(图7-7)。在这样的情况下,特别大的替代价值(从外部看如此)随之发生,因为从动力论的角度来看,有一个全然无分化的系统,一个强势的格式塔。因为每一次张力的释放都直接涵盖整个系统。

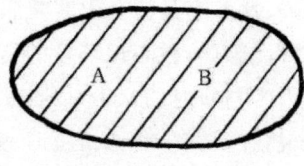

图7-7

从系统动力僵化及其对无分化总体系统形成的影响来看,替代价值

---

① See DEMBO,*op. cit.*
② Cf. Hoppe,Erfolg und Misserfolg,*Psychol. Forsch.*,1930,14,pp.1—62.

的悖论可以被视为必然的结果。因此,低能儿童在多种领域里非此即彼的行为就应该被视为必然的结果。这一非此即彼的特征依托的是这样一个事实:我们看见,由于其心理基质特征,低能儿童身上强势的动力论格式塔结构超过正常儿童。换言之,我们看见的是更加单一的、无分化的系统;然而,它们一旦分离开来,就形成完全分隔的系统。

低能儿童的总体系统中缺乏弱势的格式塔结构。在这些总体系统中,两个或两个以上的子系统虽然或多或少地分离,但它们合成了动力上连接的统一体。

我认为,低能儿童的基本特征之一是,在包罗一切的总体系统里,在绝对分隔和绝对连接的两种状态之间,缺乏连续不断的分级的过渡状态。这就清楚地说明,为什么在许多领域,我们发现了低能儿童行为里看似极端明显的矛盾现象。

八、心理基质特征和心理环境

在考察心理动力的心理基质特征对经验和行为的影响时,我们必须记住,这些特征不仅是内在心理系统的特征,而且,因为心理环境受心理的影响[①]它们同样是心理环境及其变化的特征。在很大程度上,环境里事物和时间的诱发力与感知场域的意义和结构特征都受到心理因素的影响,这并不是完全由客观刺激因素决定的,客观刺激因素也不是单一的因素。因此,在心理环境的结构和变化里,我们不仅感觉到了需求和兴趣的内容与暂时的状态,而且感觉到了心理系统的僵化和不变。然而,一般来说,在研究事物或情境时,我们指向的是其诱发力固化的程度,而不是张力系统的变化或被释放的心理系统的变化。

从心理环境的概念出发,低能儿童的行为表现为非此即彼的特征和心理基质,这是心理基质普遍固化的效应。如上所述,低能儿童全部恢复被打断的任务,无一例外。从刚才提及的立场出发,我们应该说一说未完成任务诱发力的强大的固化性。然而,只有在低能儿童不离开任务的心

---

① 个人的心理动力世界应该包含他的内在心理系统和运动系统,而且要包含其心理环境,这一原理被反复强调,但尚未被充分利用。

理环境时,上述实验条件下的诱发力才有效。在给定条件下,①如果让儿童在另一个层面上执行第二个任务(已打断第一个任务),这就几乎足以将第一个任务的恢复率降到零。在这一点上,正常儿童的行为与低能儿童截然不同。这样的情境可以表述为:低能儿童要么处在此情境,要么处在彼情境,其非此即彼的程度高于正常儿童。分隔的情境在很大程度上是对立而封闭的总体系统,低能儿童的行为顺应这种封闭情境的场力。

从意志心理学来看,转化的困难意味着听凭暂时情境的摆布,下文即将考察这一困难效应对智力的影响。一方面,这一影响可能因外部情况的不同而产生不同的外部效应。比如,它可能表现为当事人的无可奈何,找不到解决办法。(偷窃或性的频繁诱惑可能和这种情境密切相关。)在其他情况下,情境里很小的变异性和较强的分隔性产生比较有力的坚持性、比较投入的目标追求,以及特别高度的专注。另一方面,即使因为外部的影响引起情境发生了微小变化,那也是很大的干扰。因为对受影响的人而言,变化了的情境必然以更大的强度倾向于完全封闭的系统,完全取代了第一种情境里的事实。换句话说,对正常儿童而言,两个或两个以上同时存在的分层情境要困难得多。实际上,低能儿童对干扰是极其敏感的。

我们在满足实验里业已提到,这种非此即彼的特征在低能儿童身上会产生更加频繁的行为停顿。因此,它们完全停止活动的情况比正常儿童频繁得多。

前已述及,低能儿童特别倔强和顽固。在他们坚决的态度里起重要作用的是刚才提到的事实:相对隔绝的系统难以形成,联系不太强、相对分隔的情境却随之产生。这些事实和低能儿童遭遇的困难密切相关,他们被迫停留在冲突情境里了。

决策之前典型的冲突情境是一种悬而未决的状态:这种情境与各种可能选择对应的情境充分呈现出来,同时却必须充分地分离开来。由于上述原因,悬而未决的事情对低能儿童特别困难;也许,他那种顽固劲和

---

① 在其他情况下,低能儿童也可能恢复并不在场的任务。

单一、封闭情境的倾向有一定的关系。

在维持分层情境中,低能儿童遭遇了同样的困难,这使他们难以掩饰而做假。这样的困难表现方式多种多样,以游戏而论,低能儿童的行为看似直来直去,但这一特征并不寻常。

无助和恐惧可能会妨碍低能儿童逃离冲突情境,相比而言,正常的、比较容易变通的儿童容易找到逃离冲突情境的办法。如果一切刚好相反,低能儿童被迫困在悬而未决的冲突之中,他就会极其痛苦。强烈的情绪反应随即发生,或强烈的压抑倾向随即出现。[1]

九、智力缺陷

通过以上探讨,我们学到了一种恰当理解低能儿童的路径,那就是理解低能儿童的智力机制。

上已提及,顿悟涉及场域里整体关系的变化:两件起初独立的事情成为一个整体里相互依存的部分;起初单一的整体分为相互依存的部分;最常见的情况是场域的重组,不同整体里的组成部分结构同时松弛,互相组合而成新的整体。有利于整体之间关系重组的因素可能是场域里的客观变化,比如苛勒实验里香蕉和棍子空间距离的缩短。但这样的重组尤其取决于场域里总体的动态心理特征,或个人的动态心理特征。[2] 这就意味着,心理系统不充分的流动性必然妨碍智力行为的产生,换言之,这妨碍场域里结构性整体的转化。

考虑智力行为及其困难涉及相当复杂的重组时,我们迄今探讨的心理基质特征对智力活动也是极其重要的。

---

[1] 登博(Dembo)的实验结果显示,愤怒在总体上和包围场域的一个障碍所造成的情境有关,它使人无路可逃。这使我们看到愤怒和无助的关系,这对我们理解低能具有特别重要的意义。

[2] 张力特别大时难以顿悟。与此相关的最重要因素是,如果主导总体系统的力量大到足以维持平衡态,促成整体间关系变化的力量就难以产生影响。稍后,我们将介绍促成同一方向变化的另一种情况。

卢普提及低能儿童画画时遭遇困难的典型例子。① 我觉得,这些例子对我们在这里的研究特别重要。如果向低能儿童展示标有巢房1、2、3的蜂巢示意图(图7-8),让他接着画巢房4、5、6、7……他会觉得非常困难,我们可以证明,这些困难不是手工操作的困难。我们经常看到,他画的巢房结构很松散、分离(图

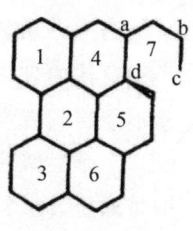

图 7-8

7-9a②)。如果我们探究巢房松散和分离的结构,即所谓格式塔的瓦解,我们会看到以下的现象:他可能会画到巢房7,画出a、b和c三段线。那么,线段d的处境呢?他画巢房7时,该巢房显然必须有一根左下方的分界线,但这条线又是巢房5的分界线。如此,线段d同时是两个整体的依存部分,而且它在两个整体里的性质是全然不同的。再者,在这种构建活动中,儿童实际作画时必然觉得,这段线是一个相对独立的整体。由此可见,我们清楚看到,线段d基本上是三个整体:(1)一根独立的线段,(2)巢房5一个独立的部分,(3)巢房7一个独立的部分。这个情况和上文描绘的替代活动里的冲突情境密切相关。只有充分区分和清楚理解线段d在两个整体里不同的性质,这幅画才能成功。倘若儿童作画时受巢房5和7的影响,倘若线段d被固化为巢房5的构造成分,同时又成为巢房7的边界线,他就会因受到束缚去画一条新的界线,让它成为巢房7左下方的边界线。

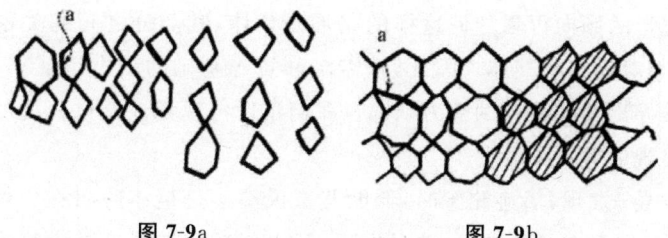

图 7-9a　　　　　图 7-9b

---

① See H. RUPP, tlber Optische Analyse, *Psychol Forsch*., 1923, 4, pp. 262—300.
② 图 7-9a 和图 7-9b 均取自卢普。图 7-9b 是实验结束后有主持人制作的,图 7-8 插入图 7-9a 的目的是要凸显受试儿童绘画的结构。

图 7-9a 和图 7-9b 说明:图 7-9a 和图 7-9b 清楚地显示了既定模式里小型整体的分离状态。两幅图里的线段是两倍粗线条,这是因为低能儿童不能将其视为两个整体同时共用的一部分。

一个类似的情况是,把一个正方形划分为小正方形时,低能儿童不是用贯通正方形的纵横直线来划分,而是在其中画小的正方形,如图 7-10 所示。在临摹比奈智力测验里的菱形时,这种方法和其他两个因素一道发挥作用,低能儿童把菱形当作圆形复制,在圆形上画上一些棱角(图 7-11)。

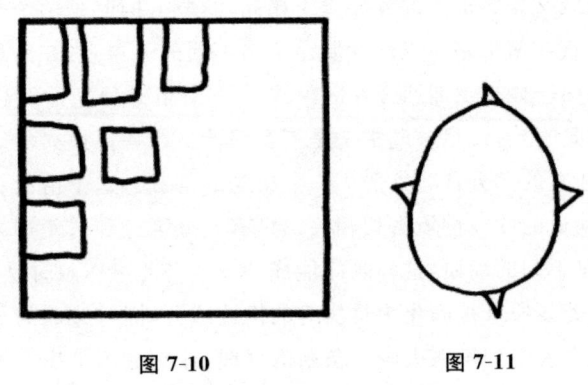

图 7-10　　　　　图 7-11

由此可见,低能儿童执行智力任务有困难,相比而言,他偏爱强势格式塔完形的倾向很强烈。这样的完形是整体,其部分之间的关系非常紧密,是相对隔绝的整体。因此,从需求和意志基础的动力特征来看,我们可以推导出低能儿童的智力缺陷。我们稍后再说个性分化程度与强势格式塔出现的关系。

罗夏[①]发现,墨迹测验时,低能儿童说墨迹是整体的回答少得多。贝克[②]证实罗夏实验的结果,并且发现,智力年龄和墨迹是否为整体的回答

---

① See H. ROHRSCHACH, *Psychodiagnodik*, Bern, 1921.
② See S J. BECK, The Rohrschach Test as Applied to a Feeble-minded Group, *Arch. Psychol*, No. 136, 1932.

之间关系不大,但关系的确是存在的,换句话说,低能儿童把不清楚的场域说成是整体。

低能儿童从部分出发而不是从整体出发,有人根据这个倾向反驳我们的主张,我们认为,强势格式塔对低能儿童的意义特别重要。我在这里简单说一说这个问题。

首先必须明确,"X感知整体的倾向胜过Y"这种泛化的判断形式是毫无意义的,即使是倾向于感知马赛克点的人也能感知到整体。我们只能说,在给定刺激因素的作用下感知到什么样的整体,这样的区分才有意义。比如,在罗夏测验中,回答说墨迹是整体图形时,正常儿童知道绝不是指纸张和墨迹组合的整体,而是指墨迹的整体,并且只能是指墨迹的整体。正常儿童的回答不能被视为是整体构造成分的回答。

这里姑且不断言,偏重整体的描绘是何原因:是教育类型抑或是其他因素造成的。可以说,对低能儿童而言,充分看透范围拓宽后的情境比较困难,甚至正常儿童也难以看透拓宽后的情境。事实上,这是完成智力任务时最常见的困难之一,在这里,延伸基本上要被当作结构的特征来感知。如果断言幼儿或低能儿童见树不见林,那会使人误入歧途。毋庸置疑,幼儿、原始人和动物很大程度上能体会到情境的总体特征。更准确地说,幼儿体会到的客观时空的延伸是一个连续的情境,或者是情境中一个相对封闭的整体,他们感知的整体并不对应成人感知到的全局,和成人感知到的特殊整体也不对应。和成人相比,幼儿偶尔会觉得这个全局的客观延伸性比较大,但在多数情况下,他们觉得这样的延伸性比较小。儿童察看扩展情境的困难较大,首先是因为成人最大限度地把整体看成是分层的结构。换言之,成人觉得,分层复杂、清楚分化的整体可以成为下一级的整体。但绝不意味着,幼儿只见树不见林,相反,强势格式塔在他的感知中起着主宰的作用。毋庸置疑,在这个方面,低能儿童的感知更接近比他们小的儿童。

十、具象特征

低能儿童心理系统的流动性比较小,他们形成和改变格式塔完形的困难比较大。因此,我们能理解,在场域重组时,低能儿童比正常儿童需要的条件多一些,他们需要那种"啊哈"原来如此式的顿悟。另一个问题是,我们是否可以用这样的思路来理解他们思维方式的特征:具象性和原始性。

也许,思维的原始性可以说是具有强势格式塔完形的倾向。由此可以推导,一般的格式塔特征在低能儿童的思维里起到相对重要的作用。然而,我们不宜将这一特征直接归于心理系统的固化,更准确的说法也许是较低的个性分化,已如前述。实际上,具象性和原始性倾向似乎是幼稚型或未分化个性的普遍特征。由此可见,这也许是幼儿与低能儿童共同的结构特征所产生的结果。

也许,我们不得不确认,具象性倾向并不仅仅是幼儿思维的原始性。这是因为在低能儿童身上,抽象思维非常困难,而同龄的正常儿童并不表现出这一特殊的具象性。我们的基础研究显示,有一条路子能帮助我们推导出低能儿童抽象思维的困难。

上文业已提及,低能儿童思维和行为的具象性主要表明,每个物件和事件的意义很大程度上都源于当前的情境,意义是情境不可分割的一部分。因此,一般所谓的抽象,即根据事物关系而进行的群组的构建就更加困难了。除了强调事物依存于实际情境外,具象性理论含有另一层意思,某些群组的构建受到特别的影响。这些群组的类型和现实层面没有直接的关系,而是和更加富于幻想的、观念的、非现实的层面有关系。这种状况和低能儿童心理结构的特点可能有直接的关系。

和正常儿童的总体行为相比,甚至和某些类型的精神病儿童相比,我们这里所研究的低能儿童给人的印象是想象力相对缺乏。这并不是说,低能儿童没有思想。他对具体的事实记得又好又准,这一点并不罕见。但他在思维和游戏中映现出来的是想象力的缺乏,他不具备玩想象力丰富的游戏应具有的典型的丰富性和流动性。

罗夏智力测验说明了低能儿童想象力的缺乏,贝克借用罗夏的墨迹测试得到了同样的结果。受试的儿童很少把墨迹描绘为流动的图形,贝克由此断言,"这一发现显示,低能儿童很少有创造性的想象力。"正如罗夏本人所言,究竟什么心理过程在此起作用,这个问题还不清楚。

我们认为,富于幻想的行为特征的动力论基础在于行为与心理环境和个性层面的关系,我们把这些层面称为非现实层面。现实程度的差异决定了心理生活空间的维度以及个性的维度。比如非现实贴近梦境、游戏和理想目标。我觉得,非现实层面发展的程度,它们在个性整体结构里的地位,以及现实层面和非现实层面关系的类型对个性的总体特征关系重大,尤其对个人的想象力和创造力特别重要。

我们从布朗的研究中获悉,非现实层面的动力特征特别富有流动性。如果说心理系统流动性比较小是低能儿童的特征,在正常儿童中流动性特别高的那些心理层面是低能儿童受损的心理层面,就可以理解了。由此,非现实层面相对缺乏的后果必然是,总体行为里的想象力降低,思维的具象性增强。

是否应该说低能儿童的心理发展滞后,其非现实层面的流动性相对而言比较低,抑或应该说低能儿童个性中非现实层面有功能错位? 只有准确地研究低能儿童非现实层面发展的具体情况,才能得出正确的答案。正常儿童不同层面的形成一开始就有现实层面分化的结果,在分化的过程中,现实层面和非现实层面实际上是不能分离的。对低能儿童发展过程的相应研究应能提供重要的信息,据此,我们就能理解个性不同部分发展的一般问题,这将为我们提供一种重要的实用工具,我们能够借此诊断低能和发育迟缓的区别。

这个方法引导我们了解低能儿童的发展,这是从我们的基本设想中得出的结论。

十一、幼稚症

低能儿童的显著特点之一是和同龄的正常儿童相比,低能儿童的精神发育滞后,这就是所谓的幼稚症。低能儿童的迟钝不仅发生在智力领域,[1]但智力迟钝是其核心,正常儿童和低能儿童的智力差异大致可以说

---

[1] 瓦林报告(Wallin, *Clinical and Abnormal Psychology*, Houghton Mifflin, Boston, 1927),低能儿童第一颗牙齿长得晚,囟门的闭合也比较晚;摩根报告(Morgan, Physiological Maturity of Feeble-minded Girls, *Tr. School Bull*, 1926, 27, 23, 231 ff.),低能女童的月经初潮也来得晚。

成是心理年龄的级差。毋庸置疑,低能儿童的行为在许多方面像年龄较小的儿童,不仅表现在智力上,而且反映在心理广度、知识储备和注意力上,①也反映在情绪的稳定度上。

研究幼稚症时,我们必须记住,智力迟钝不是低能儿童的特有现象,它还常常发生在敏感型和冲动型的精神病人身上。

从动力学来看,尤其与智力迟钝相关的是个性整体系统的分化程度小。既可能是各部分分化程度都小,也可能是在某些重要领域的分化较小。因此我们断言,低能最基本的现象之一是整个人或重要领域的分化程度都小于正常人。

在研究整体系统分化的动力因素过程中,我们得出了以下结论。分化无疑是环境条件的一个应变量,也是个人特征的应变量。至于是否可以说分化速度的快慢带有遗传倾向,这个问题当前还不能回答。然而,心理基质特征与系统的分化速度有关系,这个问题倒是值得考虑。

A 和 B 两个系统在分化程度和结构类型上可能相当,但在心理基质的特征上可能相异。而且,在这两种情况下,影响分化的力量可能强度相同,指向类似。(就我们眼下的目的而论,这些力量系统是内部力量抑或是外部环境的力量,这个问题无关紧要。)在此情况下,我们可以肯定地说,变化方面的高度功能性僵化必然会妨碍整体系统的分化。如果低能儿童的心理基质特征特别稳固,直接推导的结论就是,在其他条件相同的情况下,他的发展必然会慢一些。

心理系统的分化速度源于心理基质特征,这一事实与低能儿童和正常儿童发展(用智力年龄计算)的差异吻合,两者的差异并不会因年龄的增长而维持不变,而是总体上有所增加。实际上,智力年龄差异的增加非常明显,低能儿童的智商维持不变,或有所降低。这种可能性也是有的:低能儿童心理系统的分化速度之所以比较慢,不仅取决于其心理基质特征,而且是因为,影响其分化的力量也相对较弱。②

---

① 实际上,比奈试图确定智力差异和注意力的直接关系。
② 不同个体的心理基质特征大致相符,唯有影响分化的力量是有所不同的,这是可以理解的。在这种情况下,幼稚症也会发生。

然而却不能因此断言,总体上,系统分化越容易,系统的流动性就越大。我们关心的问题是持久的分化,或相对稳定的分化。如果总体系统流动性很大,短暂分化的发生就相对容易,很小的力量也会导致结构的变化,结果,总体个性分化的永久性结构就不会产生。① 这样的动力关系似乎是某些典型的精神病幼稚症的特征。②

因此,从教育学来看,相比精神病儿童,轻度低能的儿童常常感到有收获,容易感到满意,这就可以理解了。低能儿童在心理分化上的进步可能相当慢,而且常常有倒退的情况,但总的分化建构似乎维持了比较高的稳定性。

由此可见,对总体心理系统的持久分化而言,有利的条件不是心理基质固化程度的最大值,也不是其最小值,而是其最佳值。这个最佳值随着促进分化力量的大小而有所变化。

在此必须强调指出,系统固定性太大和流动性太大都会导致低能型的行为。这样的动力论描述是否适用于所谓兴奋型的低能儿童,这个问题值得商榷。

十二、分化的程度,易感性,智力流动性

刚才介绍的心理基质特征与发展速度的关系似乎有力地说明了我们的基本主题。另外,从动力论角度来看,有几种与分化程度相关的事实难以看清,我们不想忽略这几个难点。

(一)几个理论难点

上文业已提及,正常幼儿应被视为柔性、流动、分化程度相对较小的系统。然而毫无疑问,在许多方面,幼儿似乎更固化、固执,甚至比稍大的儿童难以受到影响,当然会比成人难以接受影响。低能儿童和幼儿都硬要坐在"自己的"椅子上吃饭,其固执态度明显。如果一岁婴儿因为没有

---

① 如果流动性完全,永久性结构意义上的分化是不可能的(生物体身上绝不可能看到完全稳定的平衡态)。有机体的完全流动性不会被承认,完全僵化性也不会被承认。

② Cf. LEWIN, Filmaufnahmen über Trieb- und Affektausserungen psychopathischer Kinder.

坐在"自己的"椅子上吃饭而不高兴,一般地说,让他吃东西比让稍大的孩子吃东西更困难。因此,即使你希望坚守儿童流动性较大的论点(这个论点本身很可能是成立的①),在稳定的心理基质特征难以设想的情况下,低能儿童与固化和僵化密切相关的行为也可能发生。

你不妨考虑重构理论,将分化缺乏的现象置于核心,而不是将心理基质特征置于核心;你不妨尝试放弃心理基质特征有差异的设想。至于流动性小应该被赋予首要意义还是次要意义,这个问题不会使我们为难,因为动力论研究的总是系统特征的整体性,所以流动性小之类的问题不再被视为重要问题。然而,除了特别的困难外,局限于分化程度的理论不能被视为论述充足的理论。根据这一概念,低能儿童可以被视为与发展较慢的儿童完全类似的儿童。另外,应该承认,幼稚症即分化程度较低的一些类型不应该被称为低能。

另一个困难与分化程度有关。当面对需要理解不同的任务时,儿童有时会产生困难,比如绘画时记不住成行的数字,完成类似的任务也会遭遇困难,②这种困难不仅见于低能儿童,而且也见于年龄较小的幼儿。于是,你可以推理说,儿童心理的相对流动性应该有助于感知场域分化的形成。

我们的实验发现,我们对心理系统之间动力关系的洞察,尚不足以对这里的问题作出完整的回答。然而近年来,学界对个体差异在各个领域、各种关系中的表现作了详尽的描绘,分化程度的差异、子系统交流程度的差异、子系统变化性的差异的研究都硕果累累。有鉴于此,我想就如何解决其中的理论难点再补充一些意见。

首先,应该强调指出,低能儿童的分化程度比较低,这是基于我们的基本论点自然而然得出的结论。因此,低能儿童表现出年龄较小的正常儿童的某些特征,这些特征是因为分化缺乏而产生的。

---

① 试比较弹性概念,如 C. BUHLER, *Kindheit und Jugend*.
② Cf. H. ROHRSCHACH, *op. cit.*; S. J. BECK, *op. cit.*; W. PETERS, Die Entwick-lung der Wahrnehmungsleistungen beim Kinde, *Zeitschr. f. Psychol.*, 1927, 103, pp. 129 – 184.

其次,一般的观察似乎证明,低能儿童固化特征的程度超过了年龄较小的正常儿童偶尔表现出来的固化特征的程度。

但最重要的是,我们必须探究正常儿童固化特征所具有的真正的动力论意义。

(二)正常儿童的固化

幼儿的行为可能固化,他可能希望老是坐在同一张椅子上吃饭。但无论这固化行为有何含义,它都不是整个童年期的特征,比如其不是一岁以下婴儿的特征。婴儿对某些异常的情境尚不敏感,比如,你怀抱婴儿走动,不会有什么困难,携带三四岁的幼儿走动却不那么容易。三四岁的幼儿已经生活在要求和禁令的世界里,非常明确的必要性附加在某些事物和某些行为上。儿童特别强调并坚守这一意义,也许,这和他们在坚实的现实层面上建立最初的安全岛有关系吧。但成人并非总能清楚地看见这个关系,而且,这个关系常常带有魔幻的特征。

很可能,低能儿童的固化特征具有类似的基础。不过,当某种联系不具有合理的透明性时,低能儿童就比较快地倾向于魔幻的特征并充满了恐惧。在其他心理条件相同的情况下,若要回答心理基质特征的问题,那就要进行固化特征程度的比较研究。

(三)易感性

在其他情况下,年龄越小,儿童越不易受到影响,年龄与易感性的关系似乎颇为不同。如果饥饿的婴幼儿不吃有营养的东西,原因是他不喜欢那种食物的味道,唯一的可能就是爸妈常常用蛮力强迫他吃。6个月的婴幼儿不喜欢稀粥的味道时,他会扭头、撅嘴,最后会把粥吐出来。

面对婴幼儿,成人心理干预的办法乏善可陈。成人可以试图转移其注意力,以改善其情绪,可以拿走吸引他注意力的物件,借以激发他相反的行为。适用于年龄较大的儿童的鼓励和劝说在婴幼儿身上不起作用。

婴幼儿心理系统存在比较大的动力固化吗?我认为,这样的解释似乎是不正确的。这里的情境总体上应该这样来描绘:儿童有明显的愿意与不愿意的倾向,也就是说,主导的场力在起作用,成人在试图改变儿童。在这样的情况下,改变婴幼儿比较容易,改变年龄较大的儿童比较难。如果要理解在这里起作用的基本动力因素,那就必须强调指出,只有在特定情况下,年龄较大的儿童才比婴幼儿难以改变。转移婴幼儿注意力的办法在年龄较大的儿童身上不起作用。因此,我们必须说,在有些情况下,婴幼儿比年龄较大的儿童难以改变,在另一些情况下,婴幼儿又相对容易改变。

这一吊诡的情境似乎与婴幼儿缺乏分化的情况有关系。相比年龄较大的儿童和成人而言,婴幼儿是一个更富于动态的整体。其整体系统的组成部分仍然紧密相连,他们做一切事情都全身心调动,且调动的程度特别高。同时,婴幼儿的整体性意味着,他内在心理系统和外在身体系统的联系都特别紧密,所以个性和心理环境的动态边界就相对薄弱。这意味着,婴幼儿的需求直接改变其心理环境,而心理环境的变化又直接而有力地影响着他的身心状况。

人与环境的整体性以及人与环境之间的壁障不太坚固,这就产生了双重的后果,并且使儿童容易受到影响。如果你用这样或那样的手段改变婴幼儿的心理环境,他就被暴露在业已改变的环境中,而他的防卫机制却寥寥无几。另外,婴幼儿环境的图像直接和他的暂时状况吻合,在这样的情况下,使他变化却更加困难。① 比如,婴幼儿愤怒时,整个世界都充斥着愤怒。如果你不能用一个强有力的事情来改变总体情景的性质,他的愤怒情绪就会维持下去,难以改变。

在这里,系统的整体性还会导致非此即彼的效应,和上文所述系统固化产生的结果类似。如此,在某一方面,心理基质特征更大的固化性和系统的整体性之间就存在功能上的对应性。心理基质特征的固化性和心理分化程度的轻微性都有利于强式格式塔完形的兴起,这就导致了非此即彼的效应。

低能儿童将心理基质的相对固化性和总体个性特别低的分化程度集

---

① 此外,在易感性(susceptibility)问题上,社会场特别的组织形式自然也是特别重要的。

于一身,①(如上所见,这样的低分化程度本身也可以被视为心理发展固化的结果。)这种二合一的特征必然以非此即彼的方式起作用。实际上,在低能儿童身上,我们可以看到一个突出的特征,即刚才所述的易感性那种吊诡的现象:在某些情况下,他很容易受到影响;在另一些情况下,他又很难受到影响。在比奈对低能儿童的分类中,这种情况可能在起作用,他把低能儿童分为反叛型和温顺型。

(四)个性的分化与领悟力的流动

在某些方面,理解年龄较大的儿童的行为比较容易。这可能和另一个因素有关:他们的感知世界和经验世界的分化程度比较大。在客观条件相同的情况下,经验环境分化的程度似乎与个性分化的程度有很紧密的关系。这一关系在儿童早期感知世界的发展中显而易见,在稍后的感知成就的发展中也很明显。在一个彻底的现实领域构造中,一般来说,个体在该领域的分化特征也随之发展,因此至少在某种程度上,进行更明确分化的可能性是存在的。②

较大的分化即较丰富的内在层次资源,只要其他的力量不起反作用,由此产生的结果必然是更丰富多样的构想和观察世界的方式。这种情况的结果是,在现有的领悟方式中,另一个人会发现,他试图在比较多的领域里去作一些变革。即使没有他人的影响,场力不足以强加一种特定观念的情况下,分化程度比较高的人也会发现,他从观念上去领悟一个情境时会有更多的可能性。如果总体情境不令人满意(比如目标遭遇障碍的迂回实验),在其他条件同等的情况下,高分化儿童的观念改变、场域的重组就会比较快地发生。发生场域重组是最好的规避困难的方法,抑或是

---

① 系统相对稳定未必就意味着系统之间没有交流。虽然重新组合和交流的程度并不是互相独立的,但两者却必须区别开来。
② 这个关系的原因并不那么简单。如果一头扎进这个问题,那会离题太远。无论如何,(根据个性与心理环境动力分化缺乏的事实),一个分化程度比较高的人的世界图像的分化程度必定是比较高的,这个事实有意义重大。如此,个人的感知在结构完全的整体中就获得了一定的地位。此外,我倾向于相信,在感知图像最大限度的结构细部和个人感知分化的程度之间,存在着一定的关系,这个关系具有决定性的意义。

创造性的洞见,那就要看有关领域分化的类型和程度,也取决于其他的个性特征。无论如何,一定程度的个性分化会促成场域的重构,这是思想洞见的必要条件。从总体上说,个性分化会产生更多、更丰富多样的行为方式。

由此可见,在某些条件下和一定程度上,面对一种情境或一件任务时,整体系统较高的分化程度和个性较大的流动性之间有一种功能上的对应关系。换言之,具体结构特征和具体基质特征之间有一种对应关系。

从以下诸方面考虑,也可以得出同样的结论。假设 A 和 B 代表基质特征类似、交流程度同等(中等)的两个系统;又假设两个系统都分别含有子系统 a 和 b,而 a 和 b 又尽可能相同;再假设 A 的分化不如 B。在这些情况下,由于 B 比 A 的子系统多,由于总系统内在的变化,子系统 a 变化的可能性就比子系统 b 多一些。

通过内在力量而实现的重组发生在观念的随意变化中。因此,对分化程度高的人而言,需要集中注意力的任务(至少在某种程度上[①])就比较容易完成;在这样的任务里,场域结构的改变或维持是通过调动内在资源实现的。如果总系统不仅含有更多的子系统,而且有质的分化(儿童发展的实际情况就是这样的),那么,无需多少证明就可以确定,影响子系统的可能性就大大提高了。特别重要的是,现实层面和非现实层面的发展,心理基质特征层面的发展,都促成了更丰富的动态可能性。

低能儿童智力低下,注意力差,之所以如此,很可能是因为,他们的总系统分化程度小,分化程度小又是较小的次生流动性产生的结果。实际上,在这里,较小的次生流动性可能更为重要,系统基质固化的直接影响反而会小一些。

较高的内部分化和外部流动性有一定的对应关系。如果这一概念正确,那么,在某些情况下,甚至在低能儿童身上,实际行为更大的流动性会随着年龄的增长而表现出来。即使实际的基质特征不变,即使随着年龄增长而发生的变化指向更大程度的固化,然而,足够快的个性分化应该使

[①] 子系统自发变化的危险似乎构成一种对立的因素。

行为的丰富多样性增加。我倾向于认为,低能程度发展比较慢的趋势始终在证明我们这个结论。无论如何,从这个观点看这一问题,低能儿童的智力发展始终在进步就完全可以理解了。

心理基质较大的固化程度和总系统较大的完整性之间有着功能上的对应关系,表现在(1)强式的、分化相对低的格式塔完形(系统),(2)行为的次生流动性。功能上的对应关系是正常儿童智力发展随年龄而增长的主要原因之一。① 智力逐渐增长,心理系统的流动性虽不必增加,却有一个逐渐固化的过程。此外,功能上的对应关系还可以解释,为什么(由于总系统轻微的分化)低能儿童较大的基质刚性和年龄较小的儿童在智力上的易感性很相似,还可能解释两者之间在许多方面的相似性。

基于以上诸多思考,低能动力论主要特征的轮廓就勾勒出来了。毋庸赘言,大量细致的问题还需要讨论。换言之,如果我们尝试在总体上从动力论的角度来研究人的各种差异,我们就必须提出大量的问题;只有靠实验和对不同个体类型的比较,我们才能回答这些问题。然而,理论在走向成熟之前,即使想通过实验回答问题也是不太可能的。

十三、老年性痴呆

有时,不同类型的精神病症和脑损伤效应伴有固化的行为,这使人想起低能儿童的行为。无疑,行为固化的原因五花八门,我们暂时不考虑精神病症和脑损伤效应。如上所见,个性分化的程度是一个因素,一些子系统的封闭也可能是另一个因素。而且,登博对愤怒的研究显示,在某些情况下,紧张增加的结果可能是更大程度的暂时统一性和整体行为的原始性,也可能是某种固化和弱智,还会造成相当重度的低能。至于这是否真是基质特征(系统的流动性)的变化,是要必须提及的问题。

毋庸置疑,心理系统的流动性和个人总体的生物学机制有着极为密切的关系。这里,我们不想斩钉截铁地假设,心理系统的流动性和任何具体的生化、激素或生长过程有关。不过,我们将简略地思考一下个人身

---

① 可以列举的其他重要因素还有:增大了的知识储备和能力,尤其是世界图像的进一步分化。

体上发生的一种普遍的生物学变化,它和我们的基本论断相吻合。这种变化名为老年性痴呆。

一般地说,正常儿童强大的基质弹性至少会让位于更大的牢固性。随着年龄的增长,这个发展过程最终会导致明显的固化、流动性的缺乏和弹性的流失,这个趋势无须广征博引就可以证明。上文业已指出,系统基质特征正在进行的固化过程与个人日益增加的分化过程有所交叉。至于智力成就,两者的组合过程最明显的初始效应是,经验场里的构建机制增强了,与分化相关的智力流动性加大了。然而,如果随年龄而增加的固化过程比分化过程的速度快,智力流动性就会降低;如果心理基质稳定性很高,固化就会导致低能。如果分化不随年龄而加大,结构就会匮乏,子系统就会流失。在这个方面,固化的结果就特别明显。

另外,个体之间存在着巨大的差异,持久的分化在速度、广度和年龄极限上都有差异,心理基质固化的速度和广度也有差异。在具体的个案中,我们必须研究不同的心理子系统在个人行为中是如何运行的。

大体上,如果心理基质的固化随年龄而增加,如果这里考量的低能类型有相对固化的特征,那么顺理成章的结果是,如上所述,不仅分化过程必然比较慢,而且分化过程必然较早结束。这个结论与许多研究者的观察非常吻合。"低能儿童的智力发展不仅比正常人慢,而且发展停止得比较早,衰退开始得比较早。"[1]

由此可见,我们在这里阐述的理论得出了一个令人吃惊的统一的观点,这个观点不仅涵盖了个体差异——包括低能儿童、正常儿童的差异,在一定程度上也包括精神病人的差异,而且,这个观点还涵盖了个体在年龄增长过程中出现的差异。另外,这一理论还容许我们推导出一种个性类型与另一种个性类型在不同年龄段的基本相似性,使我们能用统一的方式去领会各种领域里许许多多不同的行为;用不同的方式分别考察时,这些行为是五花八门的,而且似乎常常是矛盾的。

---

[1] See R. PINTNER, Feeblemindedness, in CARL MURCHISON, *Handbook of Child Psychology*, 1st ed., 1931, Chap. XIX, p.611. 他旁征博引,支持这一结论。他参照的研究者动用了大量的受试者,有些实验多达几百人。

最后,有一点我不想忽略的是,我们在这里提出的理论试图在方法论上规避以下困难:无论类别划分得多么详尽,都会遇到困难;因为这些困难,分类的结果在某些方面实在是不令人满意的。各种各样的困难似乎绝不局限于心理学,一切学科里都会遇到各种困难。唯有在描绘人的个体差异时,你才能超越分类法去采用建构法,我们所做的正是这样的尝试。这里提出的建构主义理论不是为了确定三五种纯粹的类型及其过渡形态,而是从基本动力论的概念出发,从一开始就容纳了一个原则,以便建构和推导出无穷无尽的个体差异。

十四、小结

本章开篇讲述了正常儿童和低能儿童心理满足的实验研究,接着讲述了被中断行为的恢复以及替代情境的替代价值,提出了一类低能现象的动力论。

低能儿童的行为是从心理系统的心理基质的动力特征衍生出来的,心理系统隐含着个性的结构特征,个性心理分化的程度和速度各有不同,结构各有特色。我们讨论了个性特征在智力、注意力、意志等领域的影响。最后,我们介绍了个性特征与正常儿童心理结构的关系,及其与老人的关系。

第八章 实验研究概述

本概述旨在让读者对我们的实验研究作一个简要的扫描。首先意在标定方向,为有意进一步仔细研究的人提供方便。因此,我们用系统的观点进行描绘,但我们以简要的历史概述开篇,这也许会有可取之处。

第一节 历史概述

我的文章《行为和情绪心理研究》(Investigations in the Psychology of Action and Emotion)报告了意志测量和基本联想律的实验,我最初的目的是超越阿赫的意志测量,使之更精确。我们发现,除其他不足外,基本联想律的基本动力概念有一些错误,其表现是将耦合或其他约束力当作能量或张力的储藏所。我发现,实验过程中发生的这些现象绝不像人们惯常设想的那样简单,相反,它是非常复杂的,不稳定的。显然,我们必须寻找意志心理学中比较简单而稳定的现象,到一般认为特别复杂的事实里去寻找这样的现象。

接着登场的是感知心理学的一系列调查,我的研究即为其中之一。[1]我尝试从感知系统各层次的力量里去推衍深层感知。我还研究了空间位置的逆转,[2]这个问题不仅与感知场结构的关系极为密切,而且与意志问题也密切相关。

我有幸在柏林师从马克斯·韦特海默[3],与沃尔夫冈·苛勒[4]共事十余年,我对这两位杰出学者的感激之情不言自明。格式塔理论的基本思想是我们在意志、情感和个性领域里一切研究的基础。我们那几篇文章里之所以没有明确讨论格式塔理论,常常是因为它是我们实验研究不言自明的基础。

历史地看,率先系统地研究个性结构、动力论以及心理环境的是蔡加尼克[5],后人在这方面的一切研究都以此为基础。她筚路蓝缕,在事实和假设的丛莽中拓荒,她如指南针般实用的概念迄今尚未完全被他人超越。在判断具体个案时,她异常清晰的概念和敏锐出色的心理配合一致,这使她的尝试成为可能。

稍后诸家的实验均重视登博将愤怒作为动力论问题的研究。[6] 蔡加尼克展开自我批评式的研究,并四面出击,借以证明:即使复杂的、表面上似乎不能用严格的动力论来分析的问题也可以用实验来展示;成功和失败、愿望水平、替代或补偿、现实和非现实、冲突、社会关系、个性结构的变化等复杂问题也是可以用建构主义来展示的。她的研究给人留下了深刻

---

[1] See K. LEWIN and K. SAKUMA, Die Sehrichtung monokularer und binokularer Objekte bei Bewegung, und das Zustandekommen des Tiefenellektes, *Psychol. Forsch.*, 1925, 6, pp. 298—357.

[2] See K. LEWIN, Ueber die Umkehrung der Raumiage auf dem Kopf stehender Worte und Figuren in der Wahrnehmung, *Psychol Forsch.*, 1923, 4, pp. 210—261.

[3] 马克斯·韦特海默(Max Wertheimer, 1880—1943),德国心理学家、格式塔心理学之父——译者注。

[4] 沃尔夫冈·苛勒(Wolfgang Kohler, 1887—1967),德国心理学家、格式塔心理学的主要创始人之一——译者注。

[5] 布鲁玛·蔡加尼克(Buma Zeiganik, 1901—1988),俄国心理学家,师从卢因——译者注。

[6] Der Arger ais dynamisches Probiem, *Psychol. Forch.*, 1931, 15, 1144.

的印象,并且证明了,在心理过程的动力论里,环境与个性问题密不可分。在她的研究中,拓扑学概念的实用性和多产性首次得到证明。自然,读者会怀念蔡加尼克等人研究里的量化评估,因为那是以后的研究者不可或缺的研究要素。不过,根据我的经验,只要进行足够的量化分析再加一点坚持,我们总是可以对一个场域作彻底的量化研究。对登博研究的问题进行详细的量化分析就在我们身边展开:霍普、法扬斯和罗森菲尔德研究成败和愿望水平,柯普克、里斯纳和马勒研究替代行为,布朗、马勒和斯里奥伯格研究现实和非现实,维赫研究社会场。我相信,社会场的研究对广阔的社会心理学具有十分重大的意义。

第二节 系统扫描

粗略地说,我们可以区分心理学里两个不同意义的"为什么"。

1. 为什么在给定的暂时情境里,即在某一环境(E)、某一状态里的某人(P)会有这样的行为(B)? 如此,我们就可以用下列公式来表示这个问题,将个人的行为表现为总体情况里的函数:$B=f(PE)$。

2. 更偏重历史的问题是,为什么此时此刻的此情此景有这样的结构,为什么此时此刻的此人处在这样的状态或情境里?

更重要的是更加清楚地把这两个为什么分离开来,比如在联想心理学和弗洛伊德理论中就有必要区分这两个问题。我们实验的重心放在第一个为什么上。诚然,在实验研究的实践中,这两个问题常常紧紧纠缠在一起。所以,若要创造足够明白的情境,那就需要给实验情境构建某种历史结构。

根据我们一般的概念设想和方法论假设,我们所有的研究几乎都既涉及个体差异,又关心一般规律性问题。一般来说,我们的重心放在一般规律性问题上。

至于内容,没有任何行为仅仅被归之于人或心理环境,也不会反被归之于这两种因素或多或少的结合。更准确地说,每一种行为都被视为某人在某一心理情境里暂时的结构。可见,几乎所有的研究都关注这两个为什么的问题。如此,以下的分类只显示这两个问题表述的重心。

第三节　心理系统的一般规律

一、张力系统(需求,目的)

奥甫桑吉纳的文章《被中断活动的恢复》[1]证明,目的或意向的效果是形成一种准需求,从动力论来看,准需求就是一种张力系统。张力系统趋向于张力的释放,进行达到目的的活动。奥甫桑吉纳的实验手法基本上是这样的:一种活动被打断,稍许间隔,主持人为受试者提供相对自由的情境。结果是被中断活动的频繁恢复(见表 8-1)。

表 8-1　被中断活动的恢复研究

中断时长（分钟）	CI(仿佛偶然的情境)					DI(主持人提问打断活动的情境)					
	R_1	TR	R	R?	NR	恢复的百分比	R_i	TR	R	R?	NR	恢复的百分比 cent	恢复+倾向恢复的百分比
0~2	3		18			100	3		15			100	100
2~4			14			100			19		1	95	95
4~8			8			100		1	17		5	74	78
8~20			3			100		1	13		4	74	78
20~40			1						5	1		92	92
超过 40									2	1		83	83
不确定									1		5		
总计	3		44			100	3		71	2	15	79	82

说明:在左半部题名 CI 的实验里,中断仿佛是偶然发生的;右半部题名 DI 的实验里,主持人提出问题,受试者的第一个任务被打断。表左侧第一列是活动中断的时长(以分钟计)。

在 CI 之下的几列显示受试者被打断时的不同反应,根据时长分类。RI 表示不中断,TR 表示倾向于中断,R 表示恢复活动,R? 表示存疑的恢复,NR 表示无法恢复,最后一列是恢复活动的百分比。存疑恢复活动 R? 的百分比是折半计算的。

---

[1] See The Resumption of Interrupted Activities, *Psychol. Forsch.*, 1928, 11, pp. 302-379.

经实验研究,影响活动频繁恢复的因素有:(1)活动的类型;(2)活动被中断时所处的阶段;(3)中断延续的时长;(4)中断行为的性质;(5)中断结束时未完成的任务是否存在;(6)受试者的态度。

追求目标的张力系统得到释放时,恢复活动(即重复)未必发生。这说明,恢复活动对准需求的性质至关重要;又说明,替代性满足能产生同样的效果,而且一般地说,另一个人未完成活动的出现不会产生继续完成的倾向。

在《论已完成活动与未完成活动的维持》一文里,[1]蔡加尼克主攻的问题与奥甫桑吉纳的问题相同,但分析手法不一样。如果从动力论来看,目的或意向与张力系统相对应,系统的张力状态就将在意料之中,这不仅表现在维持活动的倾向上,而且表现在更好地维持活动上。她发现,未完成活动的记忆要好得多(表 8-2)。她证明,更好记忆的原因不是打断受试者的震撼效应,而是受试者被要求回忆时心理系统的状态。她调查的影响因子有:(1)任务的结构;(2)对任务的兴趣;(3)对实验者的主观态度;(4)受试者的年龄段:儿童、少年或成人。

她证明,张力系统可能被人体足够强大的张力变异破坏,这样的变异可能是自然的情感变异,也可能是人为的情感变异,见表 8-3;她还证明,在疲劳状态下(由心理系统发生的流动性引起),比较稳定的系统不会出现。她主攻的问题是非张力系统的形式的强固程度。(这个问题是 Kaulina 一篇未刊稿主攻的课题,也是 Schwarz 研究的重要组成部分。)她的研究显示,更全面的系统的整体结构至关重要;只有在单一心理系统充分分离的情况下,已完成的活动才比未完成的活动记得更加牢靠。

比伦鲍姆的文章《论意向的遗忘》[2]显示,与主要任务(或核心需求)对应的意向或目的几乎不会被忘记。至于重要性稍差些的目的——比如在纸条上写名字(或日期)并将其作为主要任务,忘记的比例会比较大。忘记(未执行)主要取决于一个条件:与目的对应的心理系统是否嵌入了主

---

[1] See On the Retention of Completed and Uncompleted Activities, *Psychol Forsch.*, 1927, 9, pp. 1—85.

[2] See On the Forgetting of an Intention, *Psychol Forsch.*, 1930, 13, pp. 218—284.

要任务或目标。如果这个心理系统嵌入了任务或目标,它又是如何嵌入的?

表 8-2 未完成活动的记忆(RU)与已完成活动(RC)的记忆的比率(RU/RC)

比率排序	受试者姓名	活动				小组平均值			
		ΣR	RU	RC	$\dfrac{RU}{RC}$	ΣR	RU	RC	$\dfrac{RU}{RC}$
1	Wd.	7	6	1	6				
2	Be.	9	7	2	35				
3	St.	13	10	3	33				
	Jf.	8	6	2	30	9.1	7	21	35
5	M.	8	6	2	30				
	Eu.	12	9	3	30				
7	Pl.	7	8	2	25				
10	Paj.	9	6	3	20				
	Gin.	9	6	3	20				
	Hf.	6	4	2	20				
	Pt	15	10	5	20				
	Ml.	12	8	4	20	108	7	38	19
14	Dm	11	7	4	175				
	V.	11	7	4	175				
16	Git.	11	7	4	175				
	Dm. E.	13	8	5	16				
	Kur.	15	9	6	15				
	Jn.	10	6	4	15				
19	Rm.	15	9	6	15				
	Gld.	10	6	4	15				
	Jic.	10	6		15				
	Ml. E.	12	7		14	133	78	55	1.4

续表

比率排序	受试者姓名	活动				小组平均值			
		ΣR	RU	RC	$\dfrac{RU}{RC}$	ΣR	RU	RC	$\dfrac{RU}{RC}$
23	Kur.	19	11	8	14				
	Hn.	12	7	5	14				
25.5	Glk.	16	9	7	13				
	Jnk.	14	8	6	13				
28	Gl.	12	6	6	10	113	57	57	1.0
	Wlt.	12	6	6	10				
	Schn.	10	5	5	10				
	Sim.	11	5	6	0.8				
	St	11	5	6	0.8				
30.5	Fr. Fr.	9	4	5	0.	90	40	50	0.8
32	Sim. H.	7	3	4	0.75				
算术平均值		11.1	6.8	4.25	19				

符号说明:ΣR=能记忆的活动数;RU=能记忆的未完成活动数;RC=能记忆的已完成活动数;RU/RC=未完成活动的记忆与已完成活动的记忆的比率。

表 8-3 兴奋的受试者未完成活动的记忆与已完成活动的记忆的比率(RU/RC)

受试者	未完成活动的记忆(RU)	已完成活动的记忆(RC)	两种记忆的平均值(RU/RC)
I	3	4	0.75
I	4	5	0.8
2	6	7	0.9
4	7	9	0.8
5	4	4	1.0
6	2	4	0.5
平均值	4.3	5.5	0.78

表 8-4 意向实现研究

	任务	E	SE	F	实现意向的百分比
重要任务前	1. 重要任务 A	36		1	97
	2. 重要任务 B	37			100
	3. 重要任务 C	36		1	97
	4. 重要任务 D	36		1	97
	5. 重要任务 E	36		1	97
	平均值:任务 1～5	36.2	0	0.8	97.6
重要任务	6. { I. 喜欢的诗歌或 / II. 画五边形或 / III. 写评论 }	10	11	16	27
	7. II 或 III 或 I	13	8	16	35
	8. II 或 III 或 I	16	4	17	43
重要任务后	9. 猜姓名	16	5	16	43
	10. 构词	16	6	15	43
	11. 勾勒图形	8	5	24	22
	12. 拼合图案	7	5	25	19
	平均值:任务 7～12	12.7	5.5	18.8	34.2

说明:E=实现意向的受试者人数;SE=稍后实现意向的受试者人数;F=忘记意向的受试者人数。

新兴的系统是动态上相对独立的整体,抑或是一个更全面的区域系统里的依附成分?比伦鲍姆研究了这两种可能性的诸多因素。在很大程度上,整体系统的特殊结构以及整体性的完整程度(即强弱意义上的动力论格式塔完形),可以凭借事件的时间结构和内容的内在关系(图 8-4)用实验来判定。在某些情况下,整体系统的结构可能在事件发生以后改变。研究进一步发现,单个系统的张力以及整体系统的结构(以及由此而频发的遗忘率)取决于个人总体的紧张状态和情感状态。

表 8-4 a 替代活动的难度(用工作时间计量)及其与初始任务的相似性

任务	初始任务	益智游戏 替代活动				猜谜 替代活动				翻译 替代活动			
		相似的		不同的		初始任务	相似的		不同的		初始任务	相似的		不同的	
		容易	困难	容易	困难		容易	困难	容易	困难		容易	困难	容易	困难
任务数	44	13	11	9	11	43	13	11	9	10	39	11	10	9	9
平均工作时间(秒)	194	70	<687	32	<323	340	211	<744	223	<690	399	312	<603	236	<559
	76.7	37.4	370.4	22.8	101.2	119.2	73.2	289.5	145.8	222.3	124.9	84.8	187.5	55.6	181.2
替代价值 RWS/RS^4		1.8 < 2.2		1.3 < 1.5			1.4 < 3		0.9 < 1.3			2.3 < 2.8		1.2 < 1.4	

表 8-4 a 说明:
1. 取自 Lissner, op. cit., Table 6. p. 237。
2. 我们用执行任务所需的时间来计量难度。虽然初始任务未完成就被打断了，但计量它们的难度也可以用时间来表示。猜谜是在10秒钟内被打断的，翻译是在文本的某一点上被打断的，即使益智游戏也有足够的相似性，如果挑选相当准确的停顿点，也可能使其停顿。
3. 无疑，活动难易的平均值既是绝对的，也是相对的。平均值差异相当大，原因是个体差异无限大。评价指标不损害替代活动做起来比初始活动要快，64例比59例者替代活动被描绘为容易或困难。如果活动难易值与同一人的初始活动和替代活动，那就要注意：容易的替代活动比初始活动要快一点，62例比59例需要更多的时间。
4. 本表替代价值特别清楚且无一例外地显示:(1)困难的替代活动的替代价值大于容易的替代价值;(2)同等难度的相似的替代价值大于不相似的替代价值;(3)容易而相似的活动的替代价值大于困难且无有替代活动(RS)时中断活动恢复的频率和有替代活动(RWS)时中断活动恢复的频率之比;无替代活动(RS)时中断活动恢复的频率。
替代价值是两种活动恢复频率之比；无替代活动(RS)时中断活动恢复的频率。

二、替代

本节的研究重点是替代活动或补偿性活动或使心理系统得到释放的问题。

里斯纳,在《替代活动对心理需求的释放》[1]中研究了替代活动对初始活动具有替代价值的条件(表 8-4a)。替代活动插入之后,如果被打断的活动没有得到恢复,替代活动就成了它的价值的标准。她发现,困难活动的替代价值比容易活动的替代价值高出许多。初始活动与替代任务的相似度增加,替代价值随之增加。其间涉及的心理系统的联系程度起到了关键的作用,围绕这个问题,柯普克对低能儿童和正常儿童做了比较研究。

表 8-5 低能儿童和正常儿童替代活动的比较

	未完成的任务			用替代活动完成的任务			未完成的任务			用替代活动完成的任务		
个案数	24	24	18	24	24	23	12	12	11	12	12	12
	TSR	SR	RI	TSR	SR	RI	TSR	SR	RI	TSR	SR	RI
百分比	19	33	28	17	4	15	58	8	9	25	6	24
∑R 百分比	65			29			67			42		
RAN/RAS	2.2						1.6					

表 8-5 说明:SR=自发性恢复;TSR=自发性恢复倾向;RI=接收补充指令后的恢复;∑R= SR+TSR+RI;RAN=未完成行为的恢复;RAS=替代行为完成后的恢复;n=个案数。

补充性指令(当实验快结束时,主持人发出指令,可以同等选择已完成任务和未完成任务)如次:"完成以下任务之一。"回应这个中性问题时,选择未完成任务的倾向是张力持久的又一个证明。

TSR,∑R 和 RI 栏里的数字显示不同类型恢复活动的个案数,无论

---

[1] See Discharge of Needs by Substitute Activities,*Psychol Forsch*.,1933,18,pp.27—89.

受试者表现出一种或多种倾向。在ΣR栏里,虽然每个受试者可能不止用一种方式恢复任务,但只有其中之一纳入了本表的计算,因此就可能出现这样的情况:SR(自发性恢复的次数)少于 SR+TSR+RI 的总数。

马勒在《不同现实层面的替代活动》(*Substitute Activities of Different Degrees of Reality*)中使用的实验手法与里斯纳类似,研究的是成人和儿童不同现实层面(思维、言语、行为)替代活动的替代价值(表 8-5)。总体上,现实程度比较高的替代活动的替代价值比较高。然而,至关重要的是替代行为与初始任务内在目标的关系。只有替代活动足以达到受试者内心目标时,替代的满足才会发生(表 8-6)。马勒研究解题任务和完成任务的差异,显示创造社会认可事实的重要意义:现实程度与替代活动的替代价值有关。

表 8-6　替代活动与替代价值

	未完成的任务			用替代活动完成的任务(达到行为目标)			未完成的任务			用替代活动完成的任务(达到行为目标)		
个案数	24	24	19	24	24	24	12	12	10	12	12	12
	TSR	SR	RI	TSR	SR	RI	TSR	SR	RI	TSR	SR	RI
百分比	27	25	24	4	0	10	42	25	15	50	8	33
ΣR 百分比	60			13			75			75		
RAN/RAS	4.6						1					

三、成功与失败:愿望层次

与心理系统的结构和现实程度差异相关的研究有以下一些实验。

霍普,《成功与失败》。[①] 这个问题具有重大的实用意义,但我们迄今对成败经验及其运行规律不甚了了。霍普证明,这类经验的发生不是活动结果的简单功能,而是取决于诸多因素,主要取决于结果与愿望(现实和理想的目标)水平的关系,取决于活动结果的归属,它应当归属于自我

---

① See Success and Failure, *Psychol Forsch.*, 1930, 14, pp.1−62.

的表现。他证明,这些经验仅限于比较狭窄的、有一定困难的场域,其基本决定因素是个人能力的局限。在非常困难和非常容易的任务中,成败经验是不会产生的(图 8-1)。

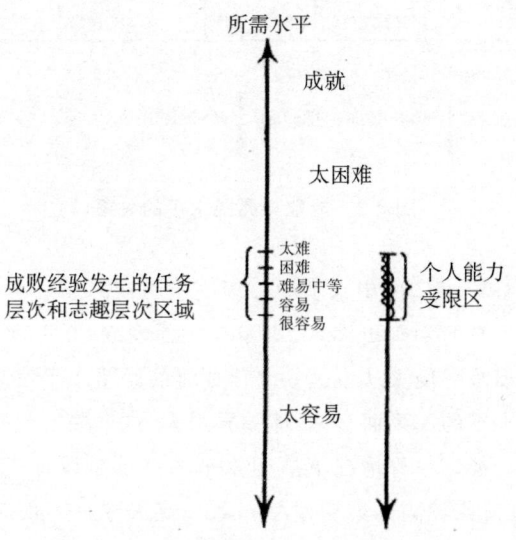

图 8-1　成败与愿望层次的关系(1)

有的时候,我们有可能确定受试者对愿望水平的不同态度,并就不同人的态度进行比较。如此,我们可以研究成败取代愿望水平("现实目标",图 8-2)的影响,以及对理想目标现实程度的影响。对愿望水平的替代、替代目标的形成,以及成功或失败以后自发中断的倾向,都取决于特定的冲突情景。实验结果表明,愿望水平和社会个体的自觉意识有密切关系。研究还发现,个体之间深层次的差异是非常明显的。

弗兰克著有《一任务完成水平对另一任务愿望水平的影响》[1]、《愿望

---

[1] See The Effect of the Level of Performance in One Task on the Level of Aspiration in Another, *Jour. Exper. Psychol*, *in press*.

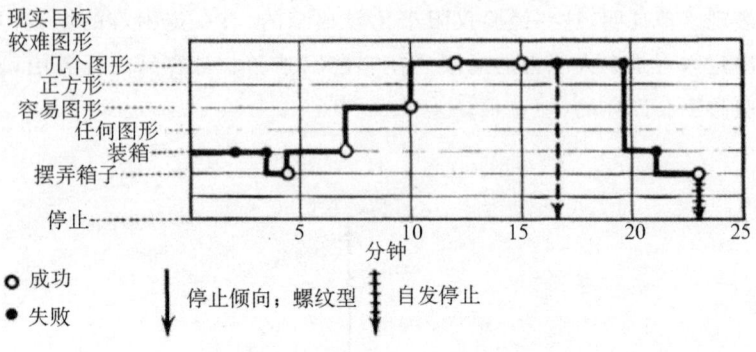

图 8-2 成败与愿望水平的关系(2)

水平的个体差异》①、《愿望水平的心理决定因素》②等。与霍普相比,弗兰克研究愿望水平的手段更客观、更量化。他发现,在一些情况下,在一件任务里的表现水平使人从事另一个任务时的愿望水平发生变化。就愿望水平和表现水平的关系而言,个体差异很大,这个关系似乎表征着可靠而普遍的个性特征。一种情况下愿望水平的高低是以下三种倾向的结果:(1)尽可能维持比较高的愿望水平;(2)规避失败;(3)使愿望水平与合乎实际的未来表现尽可能相吻合。

朱克纳特在《表现与愿望水平》③中研究一个领域的成败对另一个领域里愿望水平替代的影响,她采用大大改进后的手法去判断达到愿望水平的情况。参与实验的学生数以百计,结果显示,一个领域的成功对替代另一个领域的愿望水平产生重要影响,使之上扬或下行。不过,其先决条件是,两个领域必须有明确的动力关系,而且第二个领域里的愿望水平并不是固化不变的。

---

① See Individual Differences of Certain Aspects of the Level of Aspiration, *Amer. J. Psychol*, 1935, 47, pp. 119—129.

② See Some Psychologcal Determinants of the Level of Aspiration, *Amer. J. Psychol*. 1935, 47, No. 2.

③ See Performance and Level of Aspiration, *Psychol Forsch.*, *in press*.

法扬斯在《婴幼儿的成功、坚持与活动》①中研究 1～4 岁幼儿和 6～12 个月婴儿的成败,发现了相当大程度的替代水平;典型的情况是,相当消极的儿童可能会因成功的驱动而走向相当积极的行为,相当积极的儿童可能会因失败的影响而退守为相当消极的行为。她探讨成败与尴尬和退场的关系。看起来,对儿童来说,替代目标的达到、安慰或鼓励在很大程度上相当于真正的成功(图 8-3)。量化研究的结果说明,达到目标在心理上对婴儿(图 8-4)的意义有别于对幼儿的意义。罗森菲尔德的研究证实了法扬斯的结论并使之更加清楚。

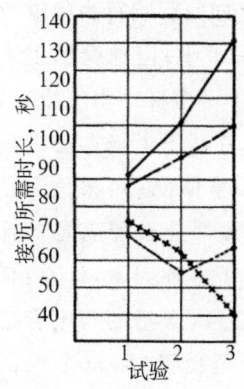

说明:成功、鼓励、替代和失败对时长的影响比较。具有正诱发力的物件悬挂在儿童的眼前,可望而不可即;用跑表计量他努力拿到物件所花的时间,此为"时长",用坐标表示。

实线(—)表示伴随鼓励的成功;从第 1 到第 3 场实验,时长增加了 48%。

虚线(...)表示成功,时长增加了 25%。

十字形虚线(+++)表示替代活动的成功,时长减少了 6%。

图 8-3

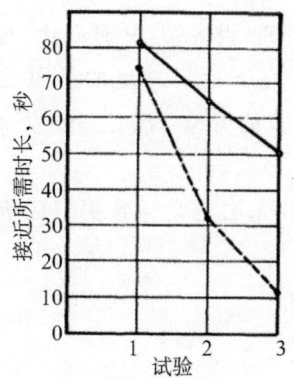

说明:说明:成功(—)和失败(...)对儿童的影响
图 8-4

---

① See Success, Persistence and Activity in the Infant and the Small Child, *Psychol Forsch.*, 1933,17,pp. 268-305.

罗森菲尔德《成败经验的个体发生》[1]一文显示了,儿童达标的经验与成败的经验有何不同,这些经验又如何与不同的发展层次相关联。成败经验发展的一个重要因素是日益分化的目标结构的发展。

四、心理满足

上述问题论及张力系统的动态,与此有别的一个问题是新张力系统自发生成的条件,以及新目标如何与较早的一个目标联系。对替代愿望水平的研究有利于这个问题的解决。这个领域一个独特的问题是心理满足问题。

卡斯腾《心理满足》[2]一文研究的是,行为的重复如何影响行为的继续这一倾向,其实验手法大致是:受试者必须反复做一件事;但他受够了不想继续时有停止的自由,实验所使用的活动尽可能丰富多样。由于重复,原先行为的正诱发力变成了负诱发力。最后,受试者试图退场。心理满足的进程用一些典型性标准予以确认,计有:变化、整体(感知和行为整体)的消解、漫不经心、遗忘。研究显示,虽然疲劳常常是心理满足的征兆,但心理满足有别于疲劳。心理满足的快慢取决于多种因素,计有:任务的结构、当事人的紧张状态、任务的边缘性或核心性(合意的与不合意的任务使人比较快地感到心理满足,中性的任务则稍慢)以及个人的性格。

卡斯腾对相邻领域的共同满足做了量化研究(表 8-7),又对变化、对总场域的心理满足进行了研究(表 8-8)。研究了达到满足的条件之一——"真重复"的发生。他还探讨了在多次重复的情况下满足不能发生的条件。

此外,他的研究结果证明了这样一个命题:未必总是导致更好的表现,更好的表现是联想律期待的结果。

---

[1] See The Ontogeny of Experiences of Success and Failure, *Psychol Forsch.*, in preparation.

[2] See Psychical Satiation, *Psychol Forsch.*, 1928, 10, pp. 142—254.

表 8-7　共同满足,第一天受试组 α

受试者	部分区域总数	部分区域总数之三分之一	部分区域总数之前三分之一			部分区域总数之中三分之一			部分区域总数之后三分之一		
			总时耗		笔画组数	总时耗		笔画组数	总时耗		笔画组数
			分	秒		分	秒		分	秒	
Tr.	3	1	38	15	569	18		476	8	15	70
Ha.	4	1.3	13	30	314	7	45	199	6	45	31
So.	7	2.3	25	30	645	14	30	532	7		174
J.	21	7	10	10	357	6	45	188	3	35	56
Fa.	28	9	5	20	130	4		40	4		78
平均数			18	30	403	10	12	287	5	55	82

表 8-7 说明:受试者按一定节奏(3.5)画笔画,直到即使遇到实验人的压力时也不想再继续画下去。于是,实验人叫他用另一节奏(4.4)画笔画,直到他自发停笔。如此,实验人换另一节奏叫他画,直到他自发停笔。如此等等,直到受试者不为所动,什么样的节奏也不能使他再继续画下去。每一个节奏被视为一个部分区域。如表所示,受试者 Tr. 只需要完成 3 个部分区域就可以达到整个区域的满足。相反,受试者 Fa. 却需要 28 个部分区域才可以达到整个区域的满足。3 个"三分之一"是部分区域总数的均等划分。"笔画数"表示笔画组数量。

表 8-8 显示,满足单个区域所必需的活动量增加时,整体区域满足所必需的部分区域的数量随之减少。

朗格在《幼儿园儿童的行为统一体与游戏》[①]一文中考察了一家蒙台梭利幼儿园,研究不同年龄儿童从事各种游戏的时长,并对决定游戏类型及其停止的各种因素进行研究。

---

① See Action Unities in the Occupations of the Kindergarten,*Psychol Forsch*.,in preparation.

表 8-8　受试组,第一天(1)

(1)排序	受试者	明显得到满足的部分区域	部分区域满足时间的均值
1	Tr.	3	21 分 30 秒
2	Ha.	4	7 分
3	So.	7	7 分
4	J.	21	0 分 58 秒
5	Fa.	28	0 分 29 秒

表 8-8　受试组,第一天(2)

(2)排序	受试者	明显得到满足的部分区域	部分区域满足时间的均值
1	Tr.	3	372
2	Ha.	4	136
3	So.	7	193
4	J.	21	29
5	Fa.	28	9

第四节　环境问题[①]

心理环境(E)属性依托的因素之一是人(P)的状态,可用公式 $E = f(P, X, Y\ldots)$ 来表述。诱发力尤其与张力系统的状态紧密相关。

一、一般拓扑结构与动力论

决定心理环境结构的特别重要的因素有:(1)拓扑关系(不同区域的连接方式,动力边界的存在等);(2)力量场(场内各点力量的指向和力度)。

法扬斯《距离对婴幼儿诱发力强度的意义》[②]研究的问题是:诱发力

[①] 关于环境力量更为透彻的叙述,请参见本书第三章。
[②] See The Significance of Distance for the Strength of a Valence in Infants and Young Children, *Psychol Forsch*., 1933, 17, pp. 215－367.

与儿童的空间距离加大时,与诱发力对应的力量强度是否会减弱。参与实验的婴儿和学龄前儿童从不同的距离尝试得到一个目标物。她就受试儿童抵达目标的各种路径所需的时长进行比较,考察了包括积极和消极、直接和间接路径之间的关系(图 8-5)。

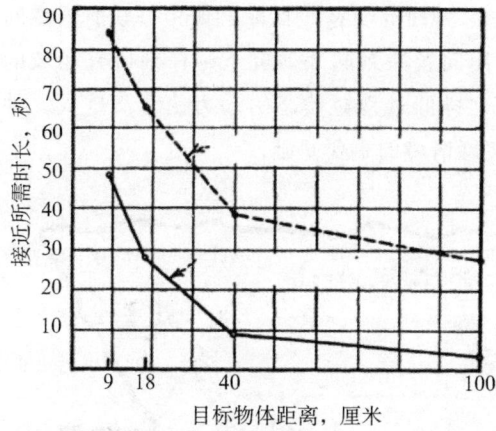

说明:说明:一个有正诱发力的物件悬挂在婴儿面前,与其眼睛平行,婴儿坐在桌前,物件在他伸手可达的地方。"积极路径"和"消极路径"的时长(目测),用跑表进行计量,图中的坐标线是测量的结果。
虚线(...)表示一切路径;实线(_)表示积极路径。

图 8-5　距离对诱发力的影响

她发现,婴儿在实验过程中,随着距离的增加,场力的强度显著减少;相反,学龄前儿童在实验过程中,在主持人研究的距离内,却不见场力的强度减少。两者的差异部分取决于不同年龄儿童生活空间大小的差异,更大程度上是因为社会空间对于较大儿童具有更大的意义。接着,她研究了"物件"场到社会场的变化、害羞时新环境的结构、冲突情境对表情的影响等问题。她在方法论上的重要发展是提出一些特殊的标准,借此,障碍物强固差异引起的驱力差异就可以区分了。她显示,这些约束性力量是驱力强度的函数。

登博在《作为动力问题的愤怒》[①]中分析目标不能达到时,情境拓扑结构的变化(人与目标之间动力障碍的形成,外围障碍的形成),展示目标达到时拓扑结构对行为模式的影响。

我们用心理生活空间的维度来表现不同的现实程度(图 8-6),不同现

---

① See Anger as a Dynamic Problem, *Psychol Forsch*., 1933, 15, pp. 1—114.

实程度的决定性意义就显而易见了。除了拓扑结构、场力,她还研究了场力的分布及其变化。她图示了冲突情境里的场力结构,显示了冲突情境对现实层次行为(波动,各种各样的退场)的影响,以及进入非现实层次的倾向(奇异的解决办法)。登博用诱发场(inducing fields)的概念来表征社会权力关系,借用这些场域的性质来推导主持人与受试者较量的发生与形式(图 8-7)。借用同一概念,她研究与替代目标出现相关联的困难问题,把替代目标问题与工具使用问题联系起来研究。她仔细研究场域的去结构化过程和同质化过程,这样的过程对愤怒的动力论意义重大。她的实验研究成果成为我分析奖惩情境的重要基础。

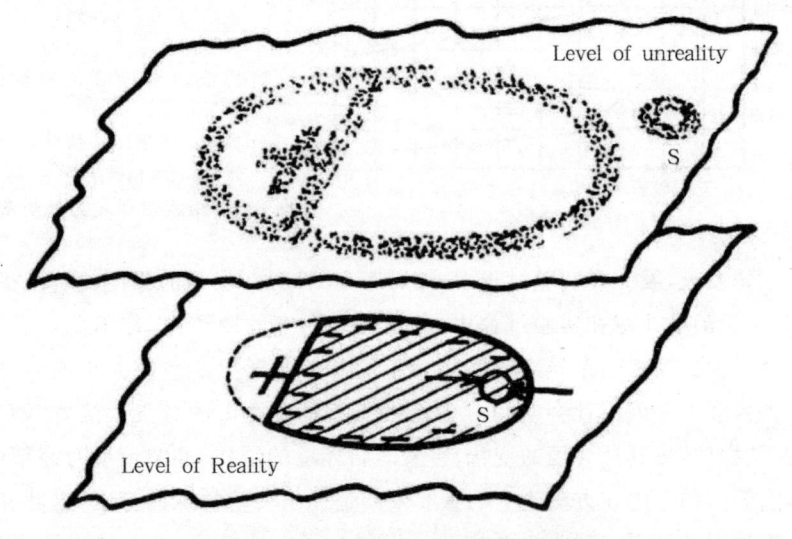

图 8-6　心理生活空间的现实程度

说明:S=受试者;level of reality=现实层次

二、现实与非现实

布朗在《论现实和非现实层次的动力论特征》[①]中用实验来检测这样

---

① See On the Dynamic Properties of the Levels of Reality and Unreality, *Psychol Forsch.*, 1933, 18, pp. 1—26.

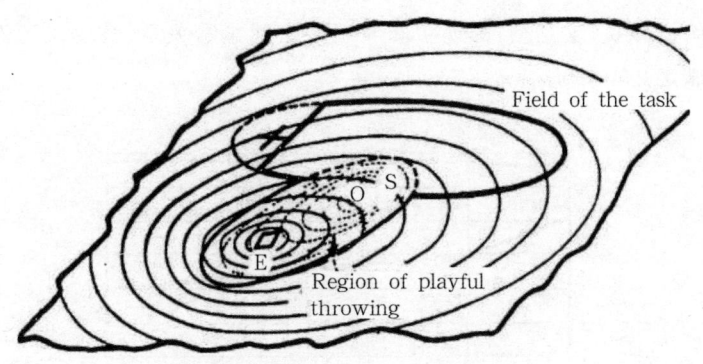

图 8-7　主持人与受试者较量的诱发场

说明：外围障碍不仅包含任务场，而且包含与实验人作对的场域。（实验的任务是扔圆环套瓶子。实验人故意刺激受试者，她干扰的动作有抓住儿童扔出的圆环、挪动瓶子等。受试者立即将其视为游戏，便有了与实验人斗争的基础，而单纯的受试者没有这样的斗争基础。）在这个意义上，与实验人斗争的场域对应"任务场域的特殊区域"。如果受试者在任务场域的斗争中继续占上风，该场域里的矢量和障碍就不复存在，因为它们依靠的是实验人的场力。

一个设想：低现实层次比高现实层次具有更大的流动性。他研究不同层次的张力系统释放的速度，借用蔡加尼克的手法，尤其注意比较对应严肃任务和非严肃任务的系统的释放有何差异。他发现，严肃任务系统张力的持久性大得多（图 8-8），因而与流动性较差的媒介对应。专项的实验显示，执行任务过程中的注意力与强度并不决定这一结果。

在里斯纳和马勒的实验研究里，现实层次和非现实层次的差异也在起作用。

斯里奥伯格在《论游戏的动力学》[①]中研究替代问题，尤其儿童游戏里的替代活动问题。

他发现，物件或行为的替代价值有赖于若干因素，但决定性因素是：儿童所处的是游戏情境还是严肃情境。他探讨了这样一个问题：决定儿

---

① See On the Dynamics of Play, *Psychol Forsch.*, 1934, 19, pp. 122—181.

童魔幻世界观(皮亚杰)的现实和非现实之间紧密关系,是否决定着他的需求满足。

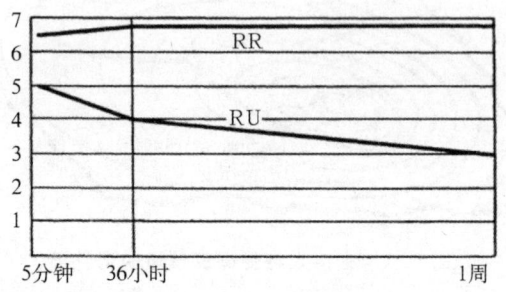

图 8-8　替代活动在现实层次和非现实层次的记忆比较

说明:PR＝能记住的现实任务;UR＝能记住的非现实任务

三、社会场

维赫在《儿童在陌生场域里的行为》①中研究一个特殊社会场对儿童行为的意义。儿童有时独自进入一个陌生人所在的房间;有时被母亲带进一个陌生人所在的房间;有时,陌生人来到他家。维赫将这一陌生场域的强度分为 6 级。除了儿童的个性特征和陌生人的个性特征之外,这个场域的强度是陌生人的空间距离、其逗留的时长及其言行举止的函数。场域强度的级别和儿童行为的样式的相关系数是可以确定的。研究结果显示出令人吃惊的显著的量化规律(表 8-9)。儿童若呆立不动,那就表示他受到最强大的压力;他可能哭叫,试图逃跑,尽可能跑到妈妈身边或者他觉得舒服的地方,那就对应着比较小的压力(图 8-9)。儿童的其他行为也以很强的规律性表现出来:在陌生人的高压下,儿童表现拘谨;在弱小压力下,他表现得太兴奋或太强势。只有进一步减轻压力,他才产生自然而不拘束的行为。

---

① See The Behavior of the Child in Strange Fields, *Wiehe* in preparation.

表 8-9 儿童在陌生人面前的行为

行为		社会场强度的级别					
		5 N=21	4 N=38	3 N=59	2 N=52	1 N=51	0 N=22
1. 倾听	unh h	100% 0	100% 0	100% 0	100% 0	100% 0	100% 0
2. 注视	a	40	10	0	0	0	0
	o sh	30	10	0	0	0	0
	une	30	0	0	0	0	0
	unc	0	20	10	0	0	0
	oem	0	60	30	10	0	0
	d	0	0	30	40	40	0
	unh	0	0	30	50	60	100
3. 背向	a	60	30	0	0	0	0
	v w	30	30	0	0	0	0
	une	10	20	0	0	0	0
	w	0	20	30	0	0	0
	he	0	0	40	20	0	0
	o st	0	0	30	30	0	0
	oem	0	0	0	60	40	0
	unh	0	0	0	40	60	100
4. 微笑	a	100	60	30	0	0	0
	o sh	0	20	0	0	0	0
	unc	0	20	50	0	0	0
	c	0	0	20	40	0	0
	oem	0	0	0	40	40	0
	s un	0	0	0	20	60	100

行为		社会场强度的级别					
		5 N=21	4 N=38	3 N=59	2 N=52	1 N=51	0 N=22
5. 说话	a	100	80	50	20	0	0
	o sh	0	20	20	0	0	0
	we	0	0	20	30	0	0
	I	0	0	10	0	0	0
	d	0	0	0	0	20	0
	oem	0	0	0	30	50	0
	s un	0	0	0	20	30	80
6. 招呼	a	100	90	50	20	0	0
	unc	0	10	20	20	0	0
	i	0	0	30	0	0	0
	d	0	0	0	30	20	0
	oem	0	0	0	30	40	100
	s un	0	0	0	0	40	0
7. 表达愿望	a	100	90	50	20	0	0
	v we	0	10	10	0	0	0
	unc	0	0	20	30	0	0
	i	0	0	20	20	10	0
	c	0	0	0	40	60	100
	oem	0	0	0	0	30	0
8. 给东西或扔东西	a	100	100	0	30	50	80
	o sh	0	0	60	40	0	0
	unc	0	0	30	0	0	0
	i	0	0	10	0	0	0
	oem	0	0	0	30	30	0
	s un	0	0	0	0	10	20

行为		社会场强度的级别					
		5 N=21	4 N=38	3 N=59	2 N=52	1 N=51	0 N=22
9. 身体接触	a	100	100	50	30	10	0
	o sh	0	0	30	20	10	0
	unc	0	0	0	0	0	0
	he	0	0	10	30	10	0
	i	0	0	10	10	0	0
	sub	0	0	0	10	10	0
	oem	0	0	0	0	30	0
	s un	0	0	0	0	30	100
10. 待在附近	a	100	100	60	40	20	0
	o sh	0	0	30	20	0	0
	unc	0	0	10	20	10	0
	up	0	0	0	20	10	0
	oem	0	0	0	0	30	0
	s un	0	0	0	0	30	100
11. 提问	a	100	100	80	50	0	30
	i	0	0	20	20	20	0
	unc	0	0	0	30	20	0
	s un	0	0	0	0	60	70
12. 展示能力	a	100	100	80	0	20	50
	unc	0	0	10	10	0	0
	sub	0	0	10	0	0	0
	oem	0	0	0	70	50	0
	s un	0	0	0	20	30	50

行为		社会场强度的级别					
		5 N=21	4 N=38	3 N=59	2 N=52	1 N=51	0 N=22
13. 炫耀	a	100	100	60	0	30	40
	une	0	0	20	0	0	0
	unc	0	0	20	10	0	0
	oem	0	0	0	70	40	0
	s un	0	0	0	20	30	60
14. 提要求	a	100	100	60	40	0	0
	o sh	0	0	20	0	0	0
	v we	0	0	20	30	0	0
	wo	0	0	0	30	0	0
	c	0	0	0	0	0	0
	aff	0	0	0	0	10	20
	oem	0	0	0	0	30	0
	we	0	0	0	0	40	50
	s un	0	0	0	0	20	30
15. 情感性回应	a	70	100	60	30	0	20
	v we	0	0	20	0	0	0
	o sh	0	0	10	20	10	0
	we	0	0	10	50	60	0
	oem	0	0	0	0	30	80
	s un	30	0	0	0	0	0

代码说明:a=缺席;aff=情感联系;c=自信;d=拉开距离;he=犹豫;i=间接;oem=过分强势;o sh=情感反应或要求过度;o st=开始;P=个性的;sub=替代活动;s un=无拘束;unc=无把握;une=不过分;up=无个性;v we=很微弱;we=微弱;wo=强势要求

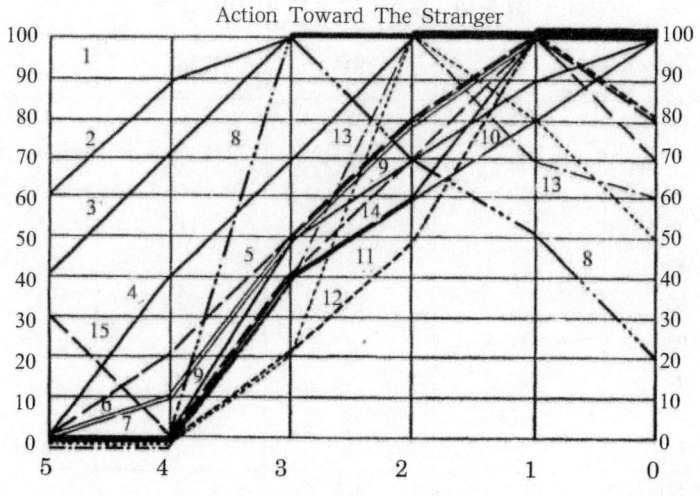

图 8-9　面对陌生人的行为

说明:社会场的力度

横坐标表示不同社会场力度下不同行为发生的百分比。

纵坐标罗列了 15 种不同的行为,分别是:1. 倾听;2. 注视;3. 背向;4. 微笑;5. 说话;6. 招呼;7. 表达愿望;8. 给东西或扔东西;9. 身体接触;10. 待在附近;11. 提问;12. 展示能力;13. 炫耀;14. 提要求;15. 情感性回应。

第五节　整体人的结构与状况

几乎上述一切研究都对整体人的状态和结构作出了贡献。蔡加尼克显示了单纯张力状态对疲劳状态的依存关系(表 8-10),还显示了整体人的情感状态。比伦鲍姆显示了疲劳状态和整体人情感状态对张力状态的依存关系(表 8-11)。卡斯腾研究了整体人的分层,如此,比较核心和比较边缘的内在心理分层对满足过程的意义。霍普、法扬斯和朱克纳特研究了成败经验与整体人状态和性格的关系。

表 8-10 疲劳受试者的 RU/RC 比率

受试者名	R	RU	RC	$\dfrac{RU}{RC}$
A	11	6	5	1.2(5)①
H	9	(4/9)	(5/11)	0.98(1)
S	9	4	5	0.8
F	9	4	5	0.8
K	7	3	4	0.75
Lk	7	3	4	0.75(1.75)
Ph	11	4	7	0.57
E	12	4	8	0.5(1.66)
E	6	2	4	0.5
Fr	6	2	4	0.5(1.5)
平均值	8.7	3.6	5	0.74

说明:R=记忆总数;RU=能记忆的未完成活动数;RC=能记忆的已完成活动数

表 8-11 受试者对张力状态的依存关系

活动	受试者(单纯—兴奋):基本实验				同一组 7 人,在指令下测速度			
	E	SE	F	E%	E	SE	F	E%
1. 匹配……	4	1	2	57	7			100
2. 画五边形	3	2	2	43	6		1	86
3. 描写城市……	5	2		71	7			100
4. 猜名字	3	1	3	43	7			100
5. 造词	2	2		29	7			100
6. 诗歌……	3	3	1	43	6	1		86
7. 写提纲……		1	6	0	4		3	57
8. 辨认首字母书写的学者	5	1	1	71	7			100
9. 写专题文章……	4	1	2	57	6		1	86
平均值……	3.2	1.5	2.2	46	6.3	0.1	0.6	90.5

说明:E=已完成意向;SE=稍后完成的意向;F=被遗忘的意向

---

① 括号里的数字表示同一组受试者 6 个月后再次实验的结果。

一、个性结构的实验简化:回归

登博对愤怒的研究广泛而深入,涉及整体人及其结构变化的问题。比如,愤怒可能以与实际情况极其不同的截然相反的方式表现出来。她的研究涵盖若干领域:各种纯情绪表现、情绪行为、情绪强度标准和情绪爆发的动力学。内在心理系统和外界环境分层边界的功能性牢固度具有决定性意义。浅表情绪比深层情绪更容易产生情绪的表达,登博解释了这一吊诡的现象(图 8-10 和图 8-11)。

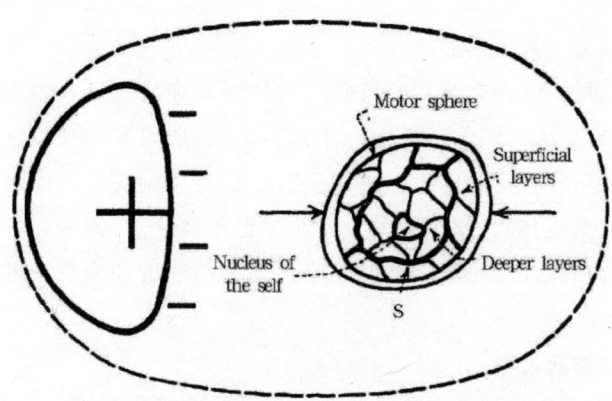

图 8-10　浅表情绪下的心理环境和个性的结构

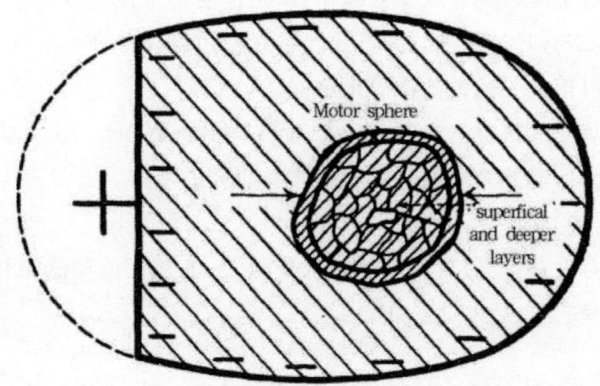

图 8-11　深层情绪下的心理环境和个性的结构

她密切关注情绪紧张加剧时个性结构的细腻变化,仔细研究内在心理系统和外界环境的边界移位问题,特别注意运动中枢的变化。研究结果是人的去分化,即走向更原始性的变化,也就是走向一个动态结构分化较少的统一体;我认为,这具有特别重大的意义。与这个去分化过程携手并进的是环境结构的简单化,这对情绪爆发具有决定性意义。于是,情感上去分化后的成人的世界景观和未分化的儿童的世界景观的共同特征,就这样产生了。登博介绍了儿童的同质性,探讨了整体人的情绪和疲劳方面的差异。

二、经期与月经间期

弗洛伊德在《经期与月经间期的满足》[1]中研究经期与月经间期对做事满足速度产生的影响。由于个体差异很大,所以参与他经期与月经间期的研究是相同的一批人。结果发现,受试者感到满足的速度有非常显著的差异(图 8-12)。这个倾向上的差异更值得注意,因为同一批受试者面对同样而有限的任务时,她们在感到满足的速度和表现上并没有规律性的差异。

三、精神病儿童

一些并非很系统的实验以精神病儿童为研究对象,研究显示,一些类型的儿童比同龄的正常儿童更迅速地感到满足。

我们的实验研究方式饶有趣味;满足速度的个体差异、同一人在不同条件下(经期与月经间期)的行为差异,以及边缘任务和中心任务的差异,最后都可以用统一的方式推导出来。

普遍规律的研究产生动力论概念(结构性、流动性、紧张状态等),这些概念成为低能儿童和精神病儿童实验研究的基础。

四、低能儿童

柯普克发现,在替代活动的替代价值上,正常儿童和低能儿童表现出重大的差异。

---

[1] See On Satiation in and Between Menstrual Periods, *Psychol Forsch.*, 1930, 13, pp. 198-217.

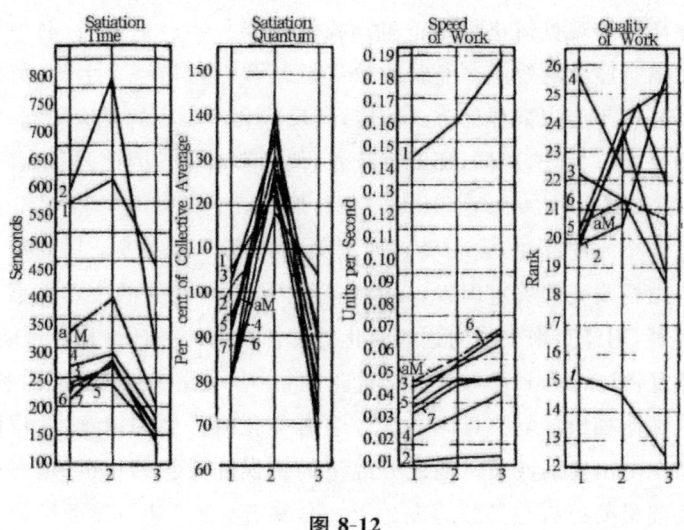

图 8-12

说明:实线(—)表示 7 种不同任务的价值;虚线(…)表示所有任务价值的平均值。

埃尔福特、萨托普和沃尔曼研究正常儿童和低能儿童的满足速度。以此为基础,我们可以准确判定一类低能儿童的动力学特征(见本书第七章)。如上所述,几乎在我们所有的研究里,你都可以发现个体差异的特殊决定因素。

五、执行任务的模式、环境的感知结构和认知结构

本书最后应该提及三个研究项目,它们不太符合本书附录"概述"的分类。它们研究的核心问题是围绕内在心理系统和外部心理环境之间的那个层次,该层次的性质决定研究的问题,你可以把运动任务和感知过程归之于这个层次。这些问题和通常所谓的学习经验密切相关,所以在介绍这三种研究项目之前,有必要先说一说我们对"经验"问题的总体立场。

我研究基本联想律的结果[1]有时遭人误解,他们说我认为"经验"不重要。我论述满足、成败效应、再学习时重犯错误等问题的文章说明,这样

---

[1] See LEWIN, Das Problem der Willensmessung und das Grundgesetz der Assoziation. *Psychol. Forsch.*, 1922, 1, pp. 191–302; 1922, 2, pp. 65–140.

的批评离我的观点何止相差千里。我的研究只不过是证明,联想的概念不足以描写经验的效应。经验的效应总是含有这样一个事实:情境再现时,个人(P)不会以同样的方式回应,其反应和上一次的反应不同;如果他两次的反应行为(B)相同,那就意味着,他没有改变。因此,根据普遍规律 $P=f(BE)$,如果 $B1=B2$,而且 $E1=E2$,那么,P1 就应该等于 P2。经验的效应总是个人的改变,或环境心理意义的改变。经验理论只能涉及个人和环境结构改变的决定因素,以及主导环境力量改变的决定因素。我倾向于怀疑,用经验来表述的这些变化的总体场的统一理论是否可能成立。

施瓦茨(Schwarz)《再学习时重犯的错误》一文[①]在新发现的基础上,施瓦茨试图描绘反复执行同一任务略有变化时产生的困难,并试图判定这些情况下出错的性质。他区分混淆的错误和重犯的错误,他将执行任务所需能量的源头与任务的表达形式分离开来,尤其与任务所依托的限制性力量分离开来。他发现,两种错误从动力论来看其性质是截然不同的。两者的发生都处在这样的情境:在学习过程中,特定形式的系统业已确立,且已相当固化。他详细论述了行为统一体及其不同形式,行为统一体的生成和变化;另外,他还讨论了执行任务的诱发力的意义。

福勒(Forer)在《德克罗利的阅读学习方法研究》[②]中针对5~6岁儿童学习字母、语词和句子的记忆保持进行了研究,她研究三种记忆:(1)记忆的书写形式;(2)其意义;(3)其形式与意义的协调。总体上,她的研究显示,一组异质的形式和意义比同质的形式和意义更容易学会。句子和语词的形式大致学得同样好,字母形式的记忆保持得略好一些。然而,语词和句子的意义比字母的意义记得好;此外,指涉事物的语词比指涉活动或属性的语词记得更牢。书写形式与所指物体在空间并置时,儿童保持记忆的优势胜过成人。我觉得,这一差异和五六岁儿童的梦幻世界图像有关系,因为在这个年龄段,书写形式所指的是物体而不是概念。

---

① See On Relapses in Relearning, *Psychol. Forsch.*, 1923, 2, pp. 86—158, and 1933, 18, pp. 143—190.
② See Investigation of the Decroly Method of Learning Reading, *Zeitschr. für Kinderforsch.*, 1933, 42, pp. 11—44.

福格特(Voigt)在《距离定向的精确度》①中,研究感知场内执行任务的定向。受试者用电光笔射击各种靶子,不瞄准,但射击的距离有变化。他发现,在一定的距离内,射击角度的准确性随着射击距离的增加而增加(图 8-13)。射击成绩的精确度取决于感知场的结构和调动的运动器官(右手射、左手射或双手射)。他的研究展示了运动场的意义,所谓的运动场就是包含人和靶子的统一体。他还研究了射击活动的学习问题。

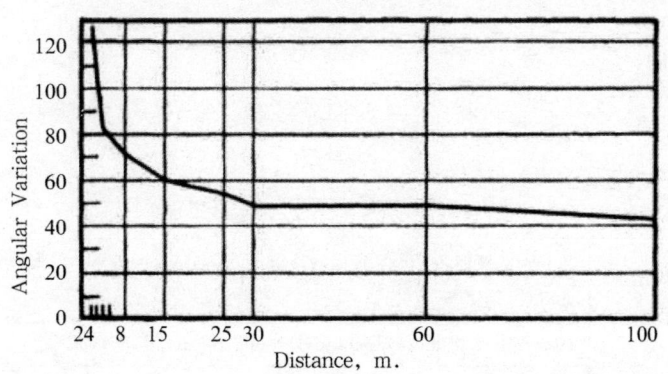

图 8-13

说明:纵坐标为射击角度的变化,横坐标为射击距离(单位:米)的变化。

① See Precision of Direction at a Distance, *Psychol*, *Forsch*. ,1932,16,pp. 70—113.

附录：心理学家实验研究问题一览表

（左列问题用传统的关键词来表示）

（实验研究最详实的主持人用斜体字排印）

行为,活动	Schwarz(整体), Voigt(定向), Zeigarnik and Ovsiankina(类型). 动态关系 见需求、情绪等
愤怒	Zeigarnik, Karsten, Ovsiankina, Hoppe, Fajans, II, *Dembo*.
注意	Karsten, Dembo, Fajans, I and II, Schwarz, Wiehe.
态度	Zeigarnik, Ovsiankina, Karsten, Schwarz, Freund. Brown
性格	Ovsiankina, Hoppe, Dembo, Fajans, I and II, Wiehe.
补偿	见"替代"
冲突	Ovsiankina, Zeigarnik, Karsten, Biren-baum, Hoppe, *Dembo*, Jucknat, Fajans, *I and II*, Rosenfeld, Schwarz, *Wiehe*.
深度	Lewin and Sakuma, Voigt.
发展	见"儿童心理学问题"
害羞	Fajans, II, Karsten, Jucknat.
情绪	Zeigarnik, Karsten, Ovsiankina, Biren-baum, Hoppe, Fajans, II, Dembo, Freund, Wiehe.
经验	见"学习"、"满足"、"成功"
失败	见成功
幻想	Zeigarnik, Dembo.

疲劳	Dembo, Brown, Hoppe, Mahler.
力量	见环境结构、冲突
格式塔	See Whole, unity
体姿,手势	Fajans, II, Hoppe, Dembo. 亦见"非现实"
目标	Hoppe, Dembo, Jucknat (ideal and real goal, level of aspiration), Mahler (inner and outer goal of action), Karsten
习惯	Lewin (measurement of the will), Schwarz, Karsten, Freund, Jucknat, Hoppe
幻觉	Dembo
理想	Hoppe, Jucknat, Dembo. 亦见"非现实"
工具	Dembo(替代), Voigt(定向), Hoppe(效应归属)
个体差异	Köpke(低能), Zeigarnik, Ovsiankina, Karsten, Fajans, II, Freund
意向	Voigt(定向的意义). 亦见"目的"、"需求"
重犯错误	见习惯
学习、再学习、遗忘	Schwarz, Voigt, Forer, Karsten
记忆	Lewin (measurement of the will), *Zeigarnik*, Schwarz, Birenbaum, Jucknat, *Brown*, *Forer*
需求	Zeigarnik, Ovsiankina, Birenbaum, Hoppe, Karsten, Mahler, Rosenfeld, Jucknat, Lissner, Freund, Lewin(意志测量)
感知	见"深度"
坚持	Karsten, Hoppe, Freund, Birenbaum
整体人的结构	Dembo, Köpke, Karsten(分层)
个人	Freund, Hoppe, 亦见"个体差异"、"儿童心理学问题"
游戏	Dembo, Schlossberg 亦见"非现实"
儿童心理问题	Zeigarnik, Ovsiankina, Fajans, I and II, Mahler, Wiehe, *Rosenfeld*, Jucknat, *Forer*
目的	Zeigarnik, Ovsiankina, *Birenbaum*, Brown, Hoppe
阅读	Forer
现实	见"非现实"

烦躁不安	见"情绪"、"冲突"、"满足"
餍足	*Karsten*,Freund
满足	见"需求"
自我意识	Hoppe,Fajans,II,Jucknat
自我控制	见"冲突"、"情绪"、"成功"
技能	Voigt,Schwarz
社会关系	*Dembo*,Wiehe,Hoppe,Jucknat,Fajans,*I and II*
环境结构	Voigt(与定向相关),Forer,Dembo(世界观),Zeigarnik,Ovsiankina,Fajans,I(环境力量),Zeigarnik,Hoppe,Fajans,II(拓扑结构). 亦见"冲突"、"社会关系"
抗争	*Dembo*,Wiehe,Karsten
替代	Hoppe,Dembo,Mahler,Jucknat,Fajans,II
成功	Dembo,*Hoppe*,Fajans,I and II,Jucknat
迷信	Dembo
非现实	*Brown*,*Dembo*,Fajans,II,Mahler,Hoppe,Forer,Schlossberg
诱发力	Ovsiankina,*Karsten*,Dembo,*Fajans*,I(与距离),亦见"冲突"、"需求"
整体,统一体	Voigt(视觉整体与表现),Forer(语词与意义的区分),Birenbaum,Zeigarnik(整体,张力系统的统一性),Dembo(整体人的结构),亦见"成功"、"替代"
意志	见"目的"、"需求"、"冲突"
世界观	Forer,Dembo,Hoppe,亦见"非现实"

人名索引

A

Ach, N., 纳齐斯·阿赫

Adams, D. K., 亚当斯

Adler, A., 阿尔弗雷德·阿德勒

Alverdes, F., 阿尔维德斯

Aristotle, 亚里士多德

B

Bacon, F., 培根

Bartelt, 巴特尔特

Ballmer, 巴尔默

Beck, S. J., 贝克

Binet, A., 比奈

Birenbaum, G., 比伦鲍姆

Blanchard, M. B., 布兰卡

Bogen H, 博根

Brown, J. F., 布朗

Bruno, G., 布鲁诺

Buhler, C., 布勒

Burks, K., 伯克斯

Burks, B. S., 伯克斯

Busemann, A., 布斯曼

C

Cassirer, E., 卡西尔

Coghill, G. E., 柯格希尔

Conrad, H. S., 康拉德

Crozier, W. J., 克罗齐尔

D

Decroly, O. J., O. J. 德克罗利

Dembo, T., 登博

Dexcler, 德克斯勒

Dohme, A., 多姆

Drosches, 多罗希

E

Eliasberg, W., 埃利亚斯伯格

Erfurth, 埃尔福特

F

Fajans, S., 法扬斯

Faraday, M., 法拉第

Forer, S., 福勒

Frank, J., 弗兰克

Frankel, F., 弗兰克尔

Freeman, F N., 弗里曼

Freud, S., 弗洛伊德

Freund, A., 弗伦德

G

Galileo, I, 伽利略

Gesell, A., 格塞尔

Goethe, J. W., 歌德

Gottschaldt, K, 戈茨沙特

Green, G. H., 格林

Grisch, 格里希

H

Hauck, E., 霍克

Hegel, G. W. F., 黑格尔

Hermann－Cziner, A., 赫尔曼－齐纳尔

Hetzer H., 赫泽

Homburger, A., 洪博格

Hoppe F., 霍普

Huang, I., 黄

J

Jaensch E. R., 让舍

James, W., 詹姆斯

Jennings, H. S., 詹宁斯

Joel, E., 约耳

Jones, H. E., 琼斯

Jucknat, 朱克纳特

K

Karsten, A., 卡斯腾

Katz, D., D. 卡茨

Katz, R., R. 卡茨

Kaulina, 考利纳

Kepler J 开普勒

Koffka, K., 考夫卡

Kohler, W., 苛勒

Köpke 柯普克
Kramer 克莱默
Kügelgen, W. von, 屈戈尔根
L
Lange, 朗格
Lau, E. G., 劳
Lazar, 拉扎尔
Lévy-Bruhl, L., 列维－布鲁尔
Lewin, K., 勒温
Lipmann, O., 李普曼
Lissner, K., 里斯纳
Loeb, J., 洛布
M
Mach, E., 马克
Mahler, V., 马勒
McDougall, W., 麦道孤
Montessori, M., 蒙台梭利
Morgan, 摩根
Miller, G. E., 米勒
Murchison, Cari, 莫奇森
O
Ovsiankina, M., 奥甫桑吉纳
P
Peters, W., 彼得斯
Piaget, J., 皮亚杰
Pintner, R., 平特纳
Poincaré, H., 彭加莱
Poppelreuter, W., 波普尔路特
Q

Rohrschach, H., 罗夏
Rosenfeid, M., 罗森菲尔德
Rubin, E., 鲁宾
Rupp, H., 卢普

S

Saathop, 萨托普
Sakuma, K., 佐久问
Schurz, K., 舒尔茨
Schwarz, G., 施瓦茨
Selz, O., 塞尔兹
Simon, T., 西蒙
Sliosberg, S., 斯里奥伯格
Sommer, R., 索默
Stern, C., 斯特恩
Stern, W., 斯特恩

T

Taine, H., 泰纳
Terman, L. M., 特曼
Thorndike, E. L., 桑代克
Tolman, E. C., 托尔曼
Tolstoy, L. N., 托尔斯泰

U

Ucko, 乌柯
von Uexkull, 冯·于克斯屈尔

V

Voigt, G., 福格特

W

Wallin, J. E. W., 瓦林
Watson, J. B., 华生

Weiss, G., 怀斯
Wertheimer, M., 韦特默
Wiehe, F., 维赫
Winkler, 温苛勒
Wohrmann, 沃尔曼
Wolf, K., 沃尔夫
Wundt, W., 冯特

Z

Zappert, J., 扎珀特
Zeiganik, B., 蔡加尼克

主题索引

A

Achievement, inadequacy of concepts of, 成就,概念之不足
Action wholes, development of in child, 儿童行为整体的发展
Adult, authority of, 成人的权威
 struggle against, 对成人权威的抗拒
 example of, 成人权威示例
 flattery and deceit as forms of, 作为成人权威的恭维和欺骗
 relation to adult's field of power, 成人权威与成人权力场域的关系
Affectivity, 情感性,易感性
Age of defiance, 对抗成人的年龄段
 dynamic explanation of, 对抗年龄的动力论诠释
Aha-experience in feeble-minded, 低能人"啊哈"原来如此的顿悟经验
"Almost" situation, "几乎"情境
Ambiguous figures, 模棱两可的数字
Anger, 愤怒,生气
 relation of substitute activity to, 愤怒与替代活动的关系

Anthropomorphism, 拟人式
"Arrangement," as evasion of barter, 作为规避交易的"安排"
Artistic expression, 艺术表达
Aspiration, level of, 愿望水平
as affected by performance in another task, 受另一件任务影响的愿望水平
relation to substitute activity, 愿望水平与替代活动的关系
to success and failure, 愿望水平与成败的关系
satisfaction of feeble-minded with lower level of, 低能儿童满足于较低的愿望水平
Association, 联想
law of, 联想律
not a cause of psychical events, 联想不是心理事件的原因
relation to will, 联想与意志的关系
theory, 联想理论
Average, contrast with the concrete situation, 平均的情况,与具体情况的反差

B

Barrier, acquisition of negative valence by, 负诱发力获得的障碍
in interest situation, 兴趣情景里的障碍
properties of, firmness, 障碍的牢固性
reality of, 障碍的现实
in punishment situation, 惩罚情景里的障碍
punishment situations lacking in, 缺乏障碍的惩罚情景
representation of, 障碍的表征
task, as, 作为任务的障碍
types of, physical-corporeal, 心理—身体的障碍类型
sense of honor, 荣誉感障碍
sociological, 社会学意义上的障碍

Behavior, as function of environment and person, 行为是环境和个性的函数

Boundaries, firmness of, 边界,边界的牢固

functional weakness of, in young child, 幼儿边界机能的虚弱

C

Classification, 分类

abstract, 抽象分类

contrast with constructive method, 分类与建构主义方法的对比

dichotomous, 二元分类

functional, 功能分类

Command, 指令 (see Punishment; Reward)

Compensation, 补偿 (see Substitution)

Comprehension, relation to differentiation of the person, 领悟,领悟力与个性分化的关系

Concepts, 概念

Aristotelian, 亚里士多德概念

classificatory, 分类概念

conditional-genetic, 条件-遗传的概念

constructive, 建构性概念

dynamic, 动力论概念

of energy, 能量概念

Galilean, 伽利略概念

Concepts-genotypic, 概念-遗传型的

Historic-geographic, 历史地理的概念-遗传型的

phenotypic, 表现的概念-遗传型的

in transition, 过渡中的概念-遗传型的

evaluative, 评价性的概念-遗传型的

Conflict, definition of, 冲突,冲突的定义

types of, 冲突定义类型

Constraint, 约束,限制
in punishment situation, 惩罚情景中的约束
Convergence, theory of, 融合论
Coupling, 耦合(see Association)
Creativeness, relation to level of unreality, 创造性,与非现实层次的关系

D

Daydreams, 白日梦
example of, 白日梦示例
Deception, 欺骗
difficulty of in feeble-minded, 低能儿童欺骗的困难
Defiance, 对抗
age of, dynamic explanation, 对抗年龄,对抗年龄的动力论解释
Despair, 绝望
Determination, intrinsic, 内在的决定
by whole situation, 总体情况的决定
Detour, 迂回
relation to field forces, 迂回与场力的关系
Devaluation, of adult's ideology, 成人意识形态的贬值
Development, of the person, 个性的发展
Differentiation of psychical systems, relation of rate to material property of mobility, 心理系统的分化,心理系统分化速度与流动性心理基质的关系
Direction, 方向
Discipline, 纪律
Distance, psychological, dependence of valence on, 心理距离,心理距离取决于诱发力
functional determination of, 心理距离的函数判定
Division of personality, 个性的分割
Domination, of child by adult, 成人对儿童的支配

Dreams, 梦
Drives, 驱力
(See also Tension system)
E
Ego, stabilization of, 自我,自我的稳定
Eidetic images, 清晰的形象
Embarrassment, 尴尬,害羞
relation to failure, 尴尬与失败的关系
Emotional outburst, 情绪爆发
Encouragement, 鼓励
Encysting, 自闭
Energy, 能量
relation to force, 能量与力量的关系
sources of, 能源
Enuresis, 尿床
Environment, psychological, relation, 心理环境关系
to individual and law, 心理环境与个体和法律的关系
statistical investigation of, 心理环境的统计数字研究
structure of, 心理环境的结构
dependence on momentary state of person, 心理环境对个人状态的依附
(See also Field.)
Equilibrium, tendency toward, 平衡倾向
Exactness, 精确
Experimental investigations, survey of, 实验研究概述
Experimental techniques, 实验技法 (see Interrupted activity, resumption of)
F
Failure, 失败
conditions determining, 失败的决定条件

effect of consolation, 失败的安慰效应
on duration of action, 失败对行为时长的影响
relation to difficulty of task, 失败与任务难度的关系（See aso Success）
Fantasy, 幻想
Fatigue,effect on tension in system, 疲劳,疲劳对心理系统张力的影响
Feebleminded,concreteness in, 低能,低能的具体表现
differentiation and mobility of comprehension, 低能儿童领悟力的分化与流动性
dynamic theory of,structure of, 低能结构的动力论
comparison with normal,representation of, 低能与正常表征的比较
degree of differentiation, 低能的分化度
material properties, 低能的心理基质属性
experimental methods,selection of, 低能儿童选择的实验方法
experimental results,satiation, 低能儿童满足的实验结果
Feeble-minded,experimental results, 低能儿童的实验结果
satiation,course of, 低能儿童满足进程
"either-or" behavior, 低能儿童"非此即彼"的行为
secondary actions, 低能儿童实验里的次生行为
technique, 低能儿童实验里的技法
total vs. part satiation, 低能实验结果里的总体满足对部分满足
resumption of interrupted action,substitute value, 低能实验里中断行为的恢复,其替代价值
technique, 低能实验的技法
variation in similarity of substitute actions, 低能实验里替代行为相似性里的变异性
formulation of experimental problem, 低能实验问题的表述
infantilism, 低能实验的幼稚型
relation of rate of differentiation to material properties, 低能儿童心理

  基质属性与分化速度的关系

intelligence defects, 低能儿童的智力缺陷（see Intelligent activity）

lack of graded transitions of dynamic connections in, 低能儿童动态关系分级过渡的缺乏

material properties and psychical environment, 低能儿童的心理基质和心理环境

material properties of systems and formation of wholes, 心理系统的心理基质属性和整体的形成

pedantry and fixation of goals, 低能儿童目标的固守与僵化

relation to development of strong Gestalts, 低能与强势格式塔发展的关系

to lack of differentiation, 低能儿童与分化缺失的关系

to level of unreality and lack of imagination, 低能与非现实层次和想象力缺失的关系

to smaller degree of differentiation, 低能与低度分化的关系

to undeveloped level of unreality, 低能与非现实低度发展的关系

senile dementia, earlier cessation of differentiation in feebleminded, 老年性痴呆，低能儿童分化的早期中止

substitute value, paradoxes of, 替代价值的悖论

dependence of, on dynamic connections of task, 低能儿童对任务动力关系的依附

susceptibility to influence, 低能儿童的易感性

dependence on field conditions, 低能儿童对场域条件的依靠

test approach, its inadequacy, 低能测试法的不足

theory of in application, 低能实验的应用理论

whole personality involved, 低能实验涉及的整体个性

Field, psychological, difference from objective situation, 心理场，与客观情景的区别

Field, functional determination of, direction in, 场域，其函数判定，其

    方向
problems of, 场域问题
reorganization(transformation) of, in feebleminded, 低能儿童的场域
    重组(转化)
in intellectual tasks, 智能任务里的场域
insight as, 作为洞见的场域
on plane of unreality, 非现实层面的场域
in prohibition situation, 禁令情景中的场域
relation to differentiation of the person, 场域与个性分化的关系
role of directed forces in, 场域里定向力的作用
topological representation of, 场域的拓扑学表达
Field of force, 力量场
convergent field, 会聚场
definition of, 力量场的定义
illustration of, 力量场的示例
influence on development, 力量场对儿童心理发展的影响
social, 社会力量场
Flattery, 恭维
Forces, 力,力量
constraining, 力的控制
dependence on valences, 力量对诱发力的依靠
driving, 驱力
environmental(field), 环境(场)力
definition of, 力量的界定
fundamental properties of, 力量的基本属性
direction, 力的方向
strength of, 力度
relation to energy, 力量与能量的关系
to needs, 力与需求的关系

Freedom of movement, dependence on sphere of power, 行动自由,对权力场的依靠
restriction of, 行动自由受限制
in prohibition, 行动自由被禁止
relation to constraint, 行动自由与约束的关系

G

Genotype, 遗传类型
Gestalt, 格式塔
contrast with summative conglomerate, 格式塔与累积组合体的对比
strong, 强势格式塔
relation of, to degree of differentiation of person, 格式塔与个性分化程度的关系
theory, 格式塔理论
Gesture, 手势,体姿
in feebleminded, 低能者的体姿
"gesture children," "手势儿童"
"Global" method of reading and writing, "整体"读写教学法
Goal, distinction between inner and outer, between "real" and "ideal," 目标,内外目标之别,"现实"目标与"理想"目标之别
in relation to substitute activity, 目标与替代活动的关系
striving toward, 奔向目标
(See also Valence)
Going-out-of-the-field, 退场
in anger, 愤怒时退场
encysting as, 作为退场的自闭
prevention of, by barrier, 用障碍预防退场
in punishment situation, 惩罚情境里的退场
relation to failure, 退场与失败的关系
suicide as, 作为退场的自杀

types of, 退场的类型

H
Habit, 习惯
Heredity and environment, 遗传与环境
Homogenization, 均质化

I
Ideology, 意识形态
relation to level of unreality, 意识形态与非现实的关系
transformation of, 意识形态的转化
Imagination, 幻想,想象力
lack of in feeble-minded, 低能者想象力的缺乏
relation to level of unreality, 想象力与非现实层次的关系
Imbedding, 嵌入
transformation of interest by, 嵌入引起的兴趣转变
Impudence, 放肆,粗鲁
Independence, 自主性,独立性
of decision, 决策的自主
Individual differences, relation of, to dynamic theory of the person, 个体差异,与个性动力论的关系
to general law, 个体差异与一般规律的关系
Inducing fields, 诱发场
Induction, 诱导
of child's goals by adult, 成人对儿童目标的诱导
of valence, 诱发力的诱导
Infantilism, 幼稚症,幼稚病
of psychopathic types, 精神病型的幼稚
Inferiority, feeling of, 自卑感
Ink-blot figures, 墨迹测验
Insight, definition of, 顿悟,其定义

difference in, between feebleminded and normal, 低能儿童与正常儿童顿悟的差异
nature of, as reorganization, 顿悟作为重组的性质
Intellectual tasks, solution of, 智力任务的解决
Intelligence quotient, dynamic theory of constancy of, 智商,智商恒定的动力论
Intelligence testing, imitations of, 智力测验,其模拟
Intelligence activity, defects of, in feeble-minded, 低能儿童智力活动的缺陷
similarity of, in normal and feebleminded, 正常儿童和低能儿童智力活动的相似性
theory of, 智力活动理论
Intention, forgetting of, 意向,其遗忘
Interest, genuine transformation of, 兴趣,兴趣的真实改变
interest situation, 兴趣情景
natural vs. artificial, 自然兴趣对人为兴趣
Interrupted activities, resumption of, 被中断活动的恢复

L

Law, concept of, 规律,其概念
general validity of, 规律的普遍有效性
relation to individual differences, 规律的普遍有效性与个体差异的关系
to individual and environment, 规律的普遍有效性与个人和环境的关系
Lawfulness, 规律性,合乎规律性
criteria of, 合乎规律的标准
exceptions, 合乎规律的例外
frequency, 频率,频发性
of individual event, 个人事件的合乎规律性
statistical character of, 合规律性的统计学特征
Level of aspiration, 愿望水平 (see Aspiration)

Life-space, 生活空间

dependence upon temporal displacement of goals, 生活空间取决于目标的暂时替代

structure of, in levels of varying reality, 生活空间在各种现实层次上的结构

Life-time, extension of, in child, 儿童生活时间的延展

Locomotion, psychological, 心理移动

M

Magical features of child's word, 儿童语词的魔幻特征

Means, 手段

Memory, 记忆(see Retention)

Milieu, 环境

Mobility of psychical systems, 心理系统的流动性

Montesson system, 蒙台梭利教育学体系

Moral disgrace, 道德耻辱

Morality, 道德

Motor actions, 运动行为

N

Need, 需求

environmental structure and, 环境结构与需求

(See also Tension system)

Negativism, 违拗, 抗拒

O

Obedience, 服从

Obstinacy, in feeble-minded, 低能儿童的顽固性

P

Pedantry, 固守

definition of, 固守定义

in feeble-minded, 低能儿童的固守

in normal child,　　正常儿童的固守
Perception,　　感知
　　role in guidance of action,　　感知指引行为的作用
Persistence,in feeble-minded and normal,　　低能儿童和正常儿童感知持久性
and rigidity of will in feeble-minded,　　低能儿童的感知持久和意志固化
Person,conditions determining tension in,　　个人,决定个人紧张状态的条件
dependence upon historical factors,　　个人对历史因素的依靠
development of structure of,　　个性结构的发展
differences,in content of meaning of the systems,　　心理系统意义内容里的个体差异
in structure,　　个性结构
Person,dynamic theory of,　　个性,个性动力论
material differences(ease of change of structure),　　个性的心理基质差异(结构改变容易)
representation of,　　个性的表征
relation to problem of individual differences,　　个性与个体差异的关系
simplification of structure of,　　个性结构的简化
states of tension,　　个体的紧张状态
conditions determining tensions in,　　决定紧张状态的条件
difference of,in different regions of,　　不同区域的个性差异
stratification of,　　个性的分层
structure of,in child,　　儿童的个性结构
Play,　　游戏
distinction between play and serious situations,　　游戏与严肃情景的区别
dynamics of,　　游戏动力论
relation to substitution,　　游戏与替代的关系
Power,sphere of,of child,interference in by prohibition,　　儿童的权力

  场,禁令对儿童权力场的干扰

control of child by adults, in situations without barriers,　成人在无障碍情境中对儿童的控制

Pressure,　压力

resulting in bodily rigidity,　身体僵硬产生的压力

social,　社会压力

Process differential,　过程的微分

Prohibition,　禁令（see Punishment; Reward）

Property, development of concept of,　财产概念的发展

Psychical material,　心理基质(see Person, dynamic theory of)

Psychical systems,　心理系统

interconnections of,　心理系统的相互关系

rate of differentiation of,　心理系统分化的速度

relation of motorium to,　运动系统与心理系统的关系

segregation of,　心理系统的隔离

Psychological environment,　心理环境(see Field)

Psychological law,　心理规律,心理定律

relation to individual differences,　心理规律与个体差异的关系

Psychological present,　心理在场

danger of too narrow a,　心理在场狭隘的危险

extension of,　心理在场的延伸

Psychological situation, constancy of,　心理情景的恒常性

a necessity for comparative experimentation,　心理情景对比较实验的必要性

relation of behavior to,　心理情景与行为的关系

Psychological situation, representation of,　心理情景的表征

total, concrete importance of,　心理情景总体表征的重要性

Psychopathic child,　精神病儿童

comparison with normal and feebleminded children,　精神病儿童与正

常儿童和低能儿童的比较

sensitivity to environment,　　精神病儿童对环境的敏感
Punishment, psychological situation in, characteristics of, constraint,
　　惩罚,心理情景里的惩罚,典型的惩罚,约束情境里的惩罚
command with threat of,　　带威胁指令的惩罚
comparison with transformation of interest,　　惩罚与兴趣转变之比较
degree of reality of,　　惩罚的真实度
function of certainty of anticipation,　　预期必受惩罚的功能
of intellectual maturity,　　心智成熟的惩罚
transformation of,　　惩罚的转变
devaluation of,　　惩罚的贬值
kinds of behavior in, acceptance of punishment,　　惩罚行为的类别,接受
　　惩罚
action against barrier,　　抗拒障碍
encysting,　　自闭
escape tendencies,　　逃避惩罚的倾向
execution of command,　　执行指令
flight into unreality(emotional outburst),　　遁入非现实(情感爆发)
struggle with adult,　　对成人的抗争
nature and disposition of valences,　　诱发力的性质和倾向
prohibition with threat of,　　用惩罚性威胁的禁令
topological representation,　　惩罚的拓扑表征
state of tension,　　惩罚的张力状态（See also Reward）
types of conflict situation in,　　惩罚里的冲突情境类别
Purpose intention,　　目的意向
(See also Tension system)

R

Rationalization,　　合理化
Reading, Decroly method of learning,　　阅读,德克罗利阅读法

Reality, basis of, resistance of objective barriers, 现实,现实的基础,客观障碍对现实的抗拒
will of other persons, 他人意志的现实
degrees of in anger, 愤怒程度的现实
Reality, dependence of, upon situation freedom, 现实,对现实的依靠,对情景自由的依靠
dynamic properties of level of, 现实层次的动力属性
education for, 为现实的教育
(See also Unreality)
Regression, 回归
Reorganization, 重组
Representation, topological, 拓扑表征
Responsibility, relation to freedom, 责任,与自由的关系
Restless behavior, 焦燥不安行为
dependence of form of, on topology of situation, 焦燥行为对情景拓扑结构的依靠
Retention, of competed and uncompleted activities, 记忆保持,已完成活动和未完成活动的记忆保持
Reward, psychological situation in, 奖赏里的心理情景 (see Punishment)
combination of punishment with, and similarity of situation with that of punishment, 奖惩结合,奖赏情景与惩罚情景的相似性
command with prospect of, 带有奖赏希望的指令
comparison with punishment situation, 奖赏与惩罚情景的比较
with transformation of interest, 带有兴趣转变的奖赏
disposition of valences, 诱发力的倾向
prohibition with prospect of, 有奖赏希望的禁令
types of behavior in, 奖赏行为类型

S

Satiation, 餍足,满足
consatiation, 共同满意
in menstruum and intermenstruum, 月经期和月经间期的餍足
in normal and feeble-minded, 正常儿童和低能儿童的餍足(See also Feebleminded, satiation in)
School, atmosphere, 学校的氛围
marks, 学校的标记
Self, 自我
boundaries of, 自我的边界
Self-consciousness, 自我意识
relation to level of aspiration, 自我意识与愿望水平的关系
Self-control, 自我控制
Senile dementia, 老年性痴呆
Situation, total concrete, 总体的具体情景
Social fields(see Fields, social), 社会场
Social pressure, 社会压力
Social standing, 社会地位
Sphere of power(see Field of power), 权力场
State of tension, 张力状态,紧张状态
definition of, 其定义
factor in a dynamic theory of the person, 作为个性动力论因素的张力状态
in punishment situation, 惩罚情景里的张力状态
relation to forgetting of an intention, 张力状态与意向遗忘的关系
Statistics, 统计学
limitations of, 统计学的局限
Steering process, 定向过程
Stereotypy, in feebleminded, 低能儿童的定型

Stimulus, as source of energy, 作为能量源的刺激
Strangeness, in social field, 社会场里的陌生情境
Structure, environmental, 环境结构
mental, 心理结构
Struggle, 抗争（see Audit）
Sublimation, 升华
Substitute activity, value, attainment of inner goal, 替代活动，其价值、内在目标的实现
conditions of, 替代活动的条件
degree of reality of substitute activity, 替代活动的真实度
difference between normal and retarded children, 正常儿童与迟钝儿童替代活动的差异
difficulty of substitute task, 替代任务的难度
dynamic connection of substitute and original task, 替代任务和原有任务的动态关系
intensity of need, 需求的强度
level of aspiration, 愿望水平
in feeble-minded children, 低能儿童的替代活动
relation of content and material of substitute task to original, 替代任务的内容和心理基质与原有任务的关系
similarity of substitute task, 替代任务的相似性
Substitution, dynamic theory of, 替代的动力论
experiments on, 替代的动力论实验
explanation of paradoxes of, in feeble-minded, 低能儿童吊诡行为之解释
relation to discharge of tension, 替代活动与紧张情绪释放的关系
to play, 替代活动与游戏的关系
to tools, 替代活动与工具的关系
Substitution, summary of experimental results, 替代，实验结果小结
Success, relation to persistence of activity in infant, 成功，成功与婴儿

活动坚持的关系

difference from achievement in children, 儿童成功与成就的差异(See also Failure)

Suicide, 自杀

Survey of experiments, 实验概述

T

Teology, natural, 自然目的论

Tension, state of, 张力状态(see State of tension; Tension system)

Tension system, conditions determining nature of discharge, 张力系统,决定紧张情绪释放的条件

discharge of, 紧张情绪的释放(Sec also Person)

Terminology, 术语

Tools, 工具

relation to substitute activity, 工具与替代活动的关系

Topology, 拓扑学

Transformation of interest, 兴趣的转变

differences from reward situation, 兴趣转变与奖赏情景的差异

by imbedding, 靠嵌入实现的兴趣转变

of psychical systems, 心理系统的兴趣转变

of values, 价值的兴趣转变

(See also Field)

U

Unity of the mind, 心理的统一性

Unreality, level(plane) of, 非现实层次

action of gesture, 体态动作的非现实层次

characterized by fluidity of medium, 以媒介流动为特征的非现实层次

development of separation from reality in the child, 儿童区分非现实和现实能力的发展

as dimension of psychical field, 作为心理场一维的非现实

example of, 非现实示例
of future events, 未来事件的非现实性
stratification of, 非现实的分层(See also Reality)

V

Vagabonding, 流浪
Valence, 诱发力(卢因语)
definition of, 诱发力的定义
dependence on distance, 诱发力对距离的依靠
on need, 对需求的依靠
examples of, 诱发力示例
induction of, 诱发力的感应
magnitude as function of distance, 诱发力作为距离函数的量级
Valence, shifts in, 诱发力的变化
transformation of, by imbedding, 靠嵌入完成的诱发力转变
Vector, definition of, 矢量，矢量定义

W

Wholeness, degree of, 整体程度
Will, measurement of, 意志的测量
rigidity of in feeble-minded, 低能儿童的固化特征
Withdrawal, 退缩(see Going-out-of-the-field)

A Dynamic Theory of Personality

Preface

The present book is a collection of originally independent articles which were written at different times and for quite different occasions. Hence, the reader will find some of the fundamental ideas recurring throughout the book. The selection has been made in order to give a picture of the fields thus far studied, the psychology of the person and of the environment, and at the same time to indicate their connections with the various applied fields, especially child psychology, pedagogy, psychopathology, characterology, and social psychology.

Only a few years ago one could observe, at least among German psychologists, a quite pessimistic mood. After the initial successes of experimental psychology in its early stages, it seemed to become clearer and clearer that it would remain impossible for experimental method to press on beyond the psychology of perception and memory to such vital problems as those with which psychoanalysis was concerned. Weighty "philosophical" and "methodological" considerations seemed to make such an undertaking a priori impossible. The first positive experiments in this direction seemed only to confirm the belief that the experimental psychology of (will, emotion, and character was condemned to rest content with surface facts and to leave all deeper problems to schools and speculation, incapable of experimental test.

Working in this field I felt that I had begun a task methodologically and technically sound and necessary, the broader elaboration of which could not be expected for decades. Nevertheless it soon became clear that though these problems are difficult, they are by no means impossible to solve. One had only to clear out a number of hoary philosophical prejudices and to set his scientific goal high enough to arrive at explanation and prediction. Today it can no longer be doubted that the questions set, for example, by psychoanalysis are readily accessible to experimental clarification if only appropriate methods and concepts are employed. Indeed, it seems some what easier to advance to dynamic laws in the field of needs and emotions than in the psychology of perception. My visit to American universities during the last year has shown me that, in spite of all the differences of historical background, the belief in these possibilities is giving rise to many experiments. The relations to psychopathology and to comparative psychology give promise of becoming especially fruitful. Naturally I know how near the beginning we stand. But the development seems to be proceeding much more rapidly than I had hoped. The reason for this is, above all, the historical position of psychology, which is ripe for a "Galileian" mode of thought.

I have been asked whether I approve of the name "topological psychology" for this type of research. I have no objection to it so long as the following points are emphasized. I am convinced that psychology is today in a position to grow beyond the "schools" in the old sense of the word. To contribute to this growth is a major goal of our work which uses, so far as possible, the language of mathematics. For this language is less equivocal than any other and at the same time "objective" and "unspeculative," since it expresses only the structural order of things and events. However, I do not limit myself to concepts of topology. Furthermore, the use of mathematical language is only an expression of a more general "constructive" method whose chief characteristic is its greater ability to bridge the gap between theory and particular fact. Nevertheless, topology remains the basic mathematical discipline for the presentation of dynamics in the whole field of psychology, and I am more and more convinced that it will become, beyond this, a solid framework for a dynamic sociology.

Doctors D. K. Adams and Karl Zener have undertaken the great labor of translating the articles into English. Only those who know the difficulties of this sort of translation in scientifically new fields will appreciate the extent to which I am indebted to them.

ITHACA, NEW YORK,   KURT LEWIN.
March, 1935

Translators' Preface

Several of the terms used in this translation may be better understood if the German terms which they are designed to translate are indicated. The adjectives *psychisch and seelisch* have both been translated "psychic"or"psychical"because it seems to us that events, processes, and structures that are properly called psychical do not become *psychological* until they have been operated upon in some way by the science of psychology or by psychologists. An ambiguity is thus avoided which could give rise to unnecessary misunderstandings and which, in the case of physics, has done so. Thus the expression "the physical world" is ambiguous because it may mean "the material world of experience" or "the world of physics," two radically different things.

The word *Seele* has been translated, with much misgiving, by "mind. " We had thought to translate it by "soul," in the belief that the time was ripe for a reintroduction of the latter word into the technical English terminology of psychology. It seemed impossible that there should be any confusion of the psychological "soul," deduced as it is from concrete behavior, with the "soul" of theology, the properties of which cannot be derived from or tested by concrete behavior. But a sampling of opinion among American psychologists was against the use of this more accurate translation. It is consequently necessary to point out that "mind" as here used ("the totality of psychical systems") is not to be taken in any narrowly intellectualistic sense but rather in a meaning approximating that of McDougall. In his later papers Lewin uses the term *psychologische Person* (translated by "psychological person") in what seems to be essentially the same sense as *Seele* in the earlier articles.

Other translations which might require comment are explained either in the text itself or in notes.

Acknowledgment is due Professor Murchison, Director, and the Clark University Press for permission to reprint Chapters I and III, which originally appeared in the *Journal of General Psychology*, Volume 5, pages 141-177, and in Murchison's *Handbook of Child Psychology*, respectively.

The monograph *Die psychologische Situation bei Lohn und Strafe* (Chapter IV of this book) was first published by Hirzel of Leipzig in 1931. The "Theorie des Schwachsinns"(Chapter VII of this book) was published in *Hommage au Dr. Decroly* by Les Usines reunies Scheerders van Kerchove a St. -Nicholas- W. ,Belgium in 1933. "Erziehung zur Realitat" (Chapter V of this book) was published in *Die Neue Erziehung* in 1931. We have to thank the publishing house of Julius Springer, Berlin, for permission to translate the portion of *Vorsalz, Wille und Bedurfnis* which appears in Chapter II and for the use of most of the figures in Chapter VIII. The latter have been redrawn after certain of those in the long series of articles edited by Professor Lewin in the *Psycholo-*

gische Forschung. We also wish to thank Mr. Charles E. Stuart for generous assistance in preparing the drawings.

                                                              D. K. ADAMS.

                                                               K. E. ZENER.

DURHAM, NORTH CAROLINA,
March, 1935.

Chapter I
The Conflict Between Aristotelian and Galileian Modes of Thought In Contemporary Psychology[1]

In the discussion of several urgent problems of current experimental and theoretical psychology I propose to review the development of the concepts of physics, and particularly the transition from the Aristotelian to the Galileian mode of thought. My purpose is not historical; rather do I believe that certain questions, of considerable importance in the reconstruction of concepts in present-day psychology, may be clarified and more precisely stated through such a comparison, which provides a view beyond the difficulties of the day.

I do not intend to infer by deduction from the history of physics what psychology ought to do. I am not of the opinion that there is only one empirical science, namely, physics; and the ques-

---

[1] *Jour. Gen. Psyrhol*, 1931, 5, 141-177, edited by Carl Murchison.

tion whether psychology, as a part of biology, is reducible to physics or is an independent science may here be left open.

Since we are starting from the point of view of the researcher, we shall, in our contrast of Aristotelian and Galileian concept formation, be less concerned with personal nuances of theory in Galileo and Aristotle than with certain ponderable differences in the modes of thought that determined the actual research of the medieval Aristotelians and of the post-Galileian physicists. Whether some particular investigator had previously shown the later sort of thinking in respect to some special point or whether some very modern speculations of the relativity theory should accord in some way with Aristotle's is irrelevant in the present connection.

In order to provide a special setting for the theoretical treatment of the dynamic problems, I shall consider first the general characteristics of Aristotelian and Galileian physics and of modern psychology.

General Character of The Two Modes of Thought

In Physics

If one asks what the most characteristic difference between "modern" post-Galileian and Aristotelian physics is, one receives, as a rule, the following reply, which has had an important influence upon the scientific ideals of the psychologist: the concepts of Aristotelian physics were anthropomorphic and inexact. Modern physics, on the contrary, is quantitatively exact, and pure mathematical, functional relations now occupy the place of former anthropomorphic explanations. These have given to physics that abstract appearance in which modern physicists are accustomed to take special pride.

This view of the development of physics is, to be sure, pertinent. But if one fixes one's attention less upon the style of the concepts employed and more upon their actual functions as instruments for understanding the world, these differences appear to be of a secondary nature, consequences of a deeplying difference in the conception of the relation between the world and the task of research.

Aristotelian Concepts

Their Valuative Character. As in all sciences, the detachment of physics from the universal matrix of philosophy and practice was only gradually achieved. Aristotelian physics is full of concepts which today are considered not only as specifically biological, but preeminently as valuative concepts. It abounds in specifically normative concepts taken from ethics, which occupy a place between valuative and nonvaluative concepts: the highest forms of motions are circular and rectilinear, and they occur only in heavenly movements, those of the stars; the earthly sublunar world is endowed with motion of inferior types. There are similar valuative differences between causes: on one side there are the good or, so to speak, authorized forces of a body which come from its tendency toward perfection ($\tau\epsilon\lambda$os), and on the other side the disturbances due to chance and to the opposing forces ($\beta\iota\alpha$) of other bodies.

This kind of classification in terms of values plays an extraordinarily important part in medieval physics. It classes together many things with very slight or unimportant relation and separates things that objectively are closely and importantly related.

It seems obvious to me that this extremely "anthropomorphic" mode of thought plays a large role in psychology, even to the present day. Like the distinction between earthly and heavenly, the no less valuative distinction between "normal" and "pathological" has for a long time sharply differentiated two fields of psychological fact and thus separated the phenomena which are fundamentally most nearly related.

No less important is the fact that value concepts completely dominate the conceptual setting of the special problems, or have done so until very recently. Thus, not till lately has psychology begun to investigate the structural (Gestalt) relations concerned in perception, thus replacing the concept of optical illusion, a concept which, derived not from psychological but from epistemological categories, unwarrantedly lumps together all these "illusions" and sets them apart from the other phenomena of psychological optics. Psychology speaks of the "errors" of children, of "practice," of "forgetting," thus classifying whole groups of processes according to the value of their products, instead of according to the nature of the psychological processes involved. Psychology is, to be sure, beyond classifying events *only* on the basis of value when it speaks of disturbances, of inferiority and superiority in development, or of the quality of performance on a test. On all sides there are tendencies to attack actual psychological processes. But there can hardly be any doubt that we stand now only at the beginning of this stage, that the same transitional concepts that we have seen in the Aristotelian physics to lie between the valuative and the nonvaluative are characteristic of such antitheses as intelligence and feeble-mindedness or drive and will. The detachment of the conceptual structure of psychology from the utilitarian concepts of pedagogy, medicine, and ethics is only partly achieved.

It is quite possible, indeed I hold it to be probable, that the utility or performance concepts, such as a "true" cognition versus an "error," may later acquire a legitimate sense. If that is the case, however, an "illusion" will have to be characterized not epistemologically but biologically.

Abstract Classification. When the Galileian and post-Galileian physics disposed of the distinction between heavenly and earthly and thereby extended the field of natural law enormously, it was not due solely to the exclusion of value concepts, but also to a changed interpretation of classification. For Aristotelian physics the membership of an object in a given class was of critical importance, because for Aristotle the class defined the essence or essential nature of the object and thus determined its behavior in both positive and negative respects.

This classification often took the form of paired opposites, such as cold and warm, dry and moist, and compared with present-day classification had a rigid, absolute character. In modern quantitative physics dichotomous classifications have been entirely replaced by continuous gradations. Substantial concepts have been replaced by functional concepts. [1]

Here also it is not difficult to point out the analogous stage of development in contemporary psychology. The separation of intelligence, memory, and impulse bears throughout the characteristic stamp of Aristotelian classification; and in some fields, for example, in the analysis of feelings (pleasantness and unpleasantness), or of temperaments, [2] or of drives, [3] such dichotomous classifica-

---

[1] E. CASSIRER, *Substanzbegriff und Funktionsbegriff, Untersuchungen über die Grundfragen der Erkenntniskritik*, B. Cassirer, Berlin, 1910.

[2] R. SOMMER, Uber Personlichkeitstypen, *Ber. Kong. f. exper. Psychol*, 1925.

[3] LEWIN, *Die Entwicklung der experimentellen Willenspsychologie und die Psychotherapie*, S. Hirzel, Leipzig, 1929

tions as Aristotle's are even today of great significance. Only gradually do these classifications lose their importance and yield to a conception which seeks to derive the same laws for all these fields, and to classify the whole field on the basis of other, essentially functional, differences.

The Concept of Law. Aristotle's classes are abstractly defined as the sum total of those characteristics which a group of objects have in common. This circumstance is not merely a characteristic of Aristotle's logic, but largely determines his conception of *lawfulness and chance*, which seems to me so important to the problems of contemporary psychology as to require closer examination.

For Aristotle those things are lawful, conceptually intelligible, which occur *without exception*. Also, and this he emphasizes particularly, those are lawful which occur *frequently*. Excluded from the class of the conceptually intelligible as mere chance are those things which occur only *once*, individual events as such. Actually since the behavior of a thing is determined by its essential nature, and this essential nature is exactly the abstractly defined class (*i. e.*, the sum total of the common characteristics of a whole group of objects), it follows that each event, as a particular event, is chance, undetermined. For in these Aristotelian classes individual differences disappear.

The real source of this conception may lie in the fact that for Aristotelian physics not all physical processes possess the lawful character ascribed to them by post-Galileian physics. To the young science of physics the universe it investigated appeared to contain as much that was chaotic as that was lawful. The lawfulness, the intelligibility of physical processes was still narrowly limited. It was really present only in certain processes, for example, the courses of the stars, but by no means in all the transitory events of the earth. Just as for other young sciences, it was still a question for physics, whether physical processes were subject to law and if so how far. And this circumstance exercised its full effect on the formation of physical concepts, even though in philosophical principle the idea of general lawfulness already existed. In post-Galileian physics, with the elimination of the distinction between lawful and chance events, the necessity also disappeared of proving that the process under consideration was lawful. For Aristotelian physics, on the contrary, it was necessary to have criteria to decide whether or not a given event was of the lawful variety. Indeed the regularity with which similar events occurred in nature was used essentially as such a criterion. Only such events, as the celestial, which the couire of history proves to be regular, or at least frequent, are subject to law; and only in so far as they are frequent, and hence more than individual events, are they conceptually intelligible. In other words, the ambition of science to understand the complex, chaotic, and unintelligible world, its faith in the ultimate decipherability of this world, were limited to such events as were certified by repetition in the course of history to possess a certain persistence and stability.

In this connection it must not be forgotten that Aristotle's emphasis on frequency (as a further basis for lawfulness, besides absolute regularity) represents, relative to his predecessors, a tendency toward the extension and concrete application of the principle of lawfulness. The " empiricist," Aristotle, insists that not only the regular but the frequent is lawful. Of course, this only makes clearer his antithesis of individuality and law, for the individual event as such still lies outside the pale of the lawful and hence, in a certain sense, outside the task of science. Lawfulness remains limited to cases in which events recur and classes (in Aristotle's abstract sense) reveal the essential nature of the events.

This attitude toward the problem of lawfulness in nature, which dominated medieval physics and from which even the opponents of Aristotelian physics, such as Bruno and Bacon, escaped only gradually, had important consequences in several respects.

As will be clear from the preceding text, this concept of lawfulness had throughout a quasi-statistical character. Lawfulness was considered as equivalent to the highest degree of generality, as that which occurs very often in the same way, as the extreme case of regularity, and hence as the perfect antithesis of the infrequent or of the particular event. The statistical determination of the concept of lawfulness is still clearly marked in Bacon, as when he tries to decide through his *tabula praesentia* whether a given association of properties is real (essential) or fortuitous. Thus he ascertains, for example, the numerical frequency of the cases in which the properties warm and dry are associated in everyday life. Less mathematically exact, indeed, but no less clear is this statistical way of thinking in the whole body of Aristotelian physics.

At the same time—and this is one of the most important consequences of the Aristotelian conception—regularity or particularity was understood entirely in *historical* terms.

The complete freedom from exceptions, the "always" which is found also in the later conceptions of physical lawfulness, still has here its original connections with the frequency with which similar cases have occurred in the actual, historical course of events in the everyday world. A crude example will make this clearer: light objects, under the conditions of everyday life, relatively frequently go up; heavy objects usually go down. The flame of the fire, at any rate under the conditions known to Aristotle, almost always goes upward. It is these frequency rules, within the limits of the climate, mode of life, etc. , familiar to Aristotle, that determine the nature and tendency to be ascribed to each class of objects and lead in the present instance to the conclusion that flames and light bodies have a tendency upward.

Aristotelian concept formation has yet another immediate relation to the geographically-historically given, in which it resembles, as do the valuative concepts mentioned above, the thinking of primitive man and of children.

When primitive man uses different words for "walking," depending upon its direction, north or south, or upon the sex of the walker, or upon whether the latter is going into or out of a house, ① he is employing a reference to the historical situation that is quite similar to the putatively absolute descriptions (upward or downward) of Aristotle, the real significance of which is a sort of geographic characterization, a place definition relative to the earth's surface. ②

The original connection of the concepts with the "actuality," in the special sense of the given historic-geographic circum-

---

① L. LÉVY-BRUHL, *La Mentalité primitive*, Alcan, Paris, 1922, (5th ed. , 1927).

② In the following pages we shall frequently have to use the term "historic-geographic. " This is not in common usage, but it seems to me inaccurate to contrast historic and systematic questions. The real opposition is between "type" (of object, process, situation) and "occurrence. " And for concepts that deal with occurrence, the reference to absolute geographic space-coordinates is just as characteristic as that to absolute time-coordinates by means of dates.

At the same time, the concept of the geographic should be understood in such a general sense as to refer to juxtaposition, correlative to historical succession, and as to be applicable to psychical events.

stances, is perhaps the most important feature of Aristotelian physics. It is from this almost more even than from its teleology that his physics gets its general anthropomorphic character. Even in the minute particulars of theorizing and in the actual conduct of research it is always evident not only that physical and normative concepts are still undifferentiated, but that the formulation of problems and the concepts that we would today distinguish, on the one hand, as historic[①] and, on the other, as nonhistoric or systematic are inextricably interwoven. (Incidentally, an analogous confusion exists in the early stages of other sciences, for example in economics.)

From these conceptions also the attitude of Aristotelian physics toward lawfulness takes a new direction. So long as lawfulness remained limited to such processes as occurred repeatedly in the same way, it is evident not only that the young physics still lacked the courage to extend the principle to all physical phenomena, but also that the concept of lawfulness still had a fundamentally historic, a temporally particular significance. Stress was laid not upon the general validity which modern physics understands by lawfulness, but upon the events in the historically given world which displayed the required stability. The highest degree of lawfulness, beyond mere frequency, was characterized by the idea of always, eternal ($αει$ as against $επι\ το\ πολυ$). That is, the stretch of historic time for which constancy was assumed was extended to eternity. General validity of law was not yet clearly distinguished from e-

---

① There is no term at present in general use to designate nonhistoric problem formulations. I here employ the term "systematic," meaning thereby, not "ordered," but collectively nonhistoric problems and laws such as those which form the bulk of present-day physics (see p. 12).

ternity of process. Only permanence, or at least frequent repetition, was proof of more than momentary validity. Even here in the idea of eternity, which seems to transcend the historical, the connection with immediate historic actuality is still obvious, and this close connection was characteristic of the "empiricist" Aristotle's method and concepts.

Not only in physics but in other sciences—for example, in economics and biology—it can be clearly seen how in certain early stages the tendency to empiricism, to the collection and ordering of facts, carries with it a tendency to historical concept formation, to excessive valuation of the historical.

Galileian Physics

From the point of view of this sort of empiricism the concept formation of Galileian and post-Galileian physics must seem curious and even paradoxical.

As remarked above, the use of mathematical tools and the tendency to exactness, important as they are, cannot be considered the real substance of the difference between Aristotelian and Galileian physics. It is indeed quite possible to recast in mathematical form the essential content of, for example, the dynamic ideas of Aristotelian physics (see page 16). It is conceivable that the development of physics could have taken the form of a mathematical rendition of Aristotelian concepts such as is actually taking place in psychology today. In reality, however, there were only traces of such a tendency, such as Bacon's quasi-statistical methods, mentioned above. The main development took another direction and proved to be a change of content rather than a mere change of form.

The same considerations apply to the exactness of the new physics. It must not be forgotten that in Galileo's time there were no clocks of the sort we have today, that these first became possible through the knowledge of dynamics founded upon Galileo's work. ①Even the methods of measurement used by Faraday in the early investigations of electricity show how little exactness, in the current sense of precision to such and such a decimal place, had to do with these critical stages in the development of physics.

The real sources of the tendency to quantification lie somewhat deeper, namely in a new conception by the physicist of the nature of the physical world, in an extension of the demands of physics upon itself in the task of understanding the world, and in an increased faith in the possibility of their fulfillment. These are radical and far-reaching changes in the fundamental ideas of physics, and the tendency to quantification is simply one of their expressions.

Homogenization. The outlook of a Bruno, a Kepler, or a Galileo is determined by the idea of a comprehensive, allembracing unity of the physical world. The same law governs the courses of the stars, the falling of stones, and the flight of birds. This homogenization of the physical world with respect to the validity of law deprives the division of physical objects into rigid abstractly defined classes of the critical significance it had for Aristotelian physics, in which membership in a certain conceptual class was considered to determine the physical nature of an object.

Closely related to this is the loss in importance of logical dichotomies and conceptual antitheses. Their places are taken by more and more fluid transitions, by gradations which deprive the dichotomies of their antithetical character and represent in logical form a transition stage between the class concept and the series

---

① E. MACH, *Die Mechanik in ihrer Entwicklung*, Leipzig, 1921.

concept. ①

Genetic Concepts. This dissolution of the sharp antitheses of rigid classes was greatly accelerated by the coeval transition to an essentially functional way of thinking, to the use of conditional-genetic concepts. For Aristotle the immediate perceptible appearance, that which present-day biology terms the *phenotype*, was hardly distinguished from the properties that determine the object's dynamic relations. The fact, for example, that light objects relatively frequently go upward sufficed for him to ascribe to them an upward tendency. With the differentiation of phenotype from *genotype* or, more generally, of descriptive from conditional-genetic ② concepts and the shifting of emphasis to the latter, many old class distinctions lost their significance. The orbits of the planets, the free falling of a stone, the movement of a body on an inclined plane, the oscillation of a pendulum, which if classified according to their phenotypes would fall into quite different, indeed into antithetical classes, prove to be simply various expressions of the same law.

Concreteness. The increased emphasis upon the quantitative which seems to lend to modern physics a formal and abstract character is not derived from any tendency to logical formality. Rather, the tendency to a full description of the concrete actuality, even that of the particular case, was influential, a circumstance which should be especially emphasized in connection with present-day psychology. The particular object in all departments of science not only is determined in kind and thereby qualitatively, but it posses-

---

① E. CASSIRER, *op. cit.*
② LEWIN, *Gesetz und Experiment in der Psychologie*, Weltkreis verlag, Berlin Schlachtensee, 1927.

ses each of its properties in a special intensity or to a definite degree. So long as one regards as important and conceptually intelligible only such properties of an object as are common to a whole group of objects, the individual differences of degree remain without scientific relevance, for in the abstractly defined classes these differences more or less disappear. With the mounting aspirations of research toward an understanding of actual events and particular cases, the task of describing the differences of degree that characterized individual cases had necessarily to increase in importance and finally required actual quantitative determination.

It was the increased desire, and also the increased ability, to comprehend concrete particular cases, and to comprehend them fully, which, together with the idea of the homogeneity of the physical world and that of the continuity of the properties of its objects, constituted the main impulse to the increasing quantification of physics.

Paradoxes of the New Empiricism. This tendency toward the closest possible contact with actuality, which today is usually regarded as characteristic and ascribed to an antispeculative tendency, led to a mode of concept formation diametrically opposed to that of Aristotle, and, surprisingly enough, involved also the direct antithesis of his "empiricism."

The Aristotelian concepts show, as we have seen above, an immediate reference to the historically given reality and to the actual course of events. This immediate reference to the historically given is lacking in modern physics. The fact, so decisively important for Aristotelian concepts, that a certain process occurred only once or was very frequently or invariably repeated in the course of history, is practically irrelevant to the most essential questions of modern physics. ①This circumstance is considered fortuitous or merely historical.

The law of falling bodies, for example, does not assert that bodies very frequently fall downward. It does not assert that the event to which the formula $s=1/2gt^2$ applies, the "free and unimpeded fall" of a body, occurs regularly or even frequently in the actual history of the world. Whether the event described by the law occurs rarely or often has nothing to do with the law. Indeed, in a certain sense, the law refers only to cases that are never realized, or only approximately realized, in the actual course of events. Only in experiment, that is, under artificially constructed conditions, do cases occur which approximate the event with which the law is concerned. The propositions of modern physics, which are often considered to be antispeculative and empirical, unquestionably have in comparison with Aristotelian empiricism a much less empirical, a much more constructive character than the Aristotelian concepts based immediately upon historical actuality.

In Psychology

Here we are confronted by questions which, as problems of actual research and of theory, have strongly influenced the development of psychology and which constitute the most fundamental grounds of its present crisis.

The concepts of psychology, at least in certain decisive respects, are thoroughly Aristotelian in their actual content, even though in many respects their form of presentation has been somewhat civilized, so to speak. The present struggles and theoretical difficulties of psychology resemble in many ways, even in

---

① So far as it is not immediately concerned with an actual "History of the Heavens and the Earth" or a geography.

their particulars, the difficulties which culminated in the conquest over Aristotelian ways of thinking in physics.

Aristotelian Concepts

Fortuitousness of the Individual Case. The concept formation of psychology is dominated, just as was that of Aristotelian physics, by the question of regularity in the sense of frequency. This is obvious in its immediate attitude toward particular phenomena as well as in its attitude toward lawfulness. If, for example, one show a film of a concrete incident in the behavior of a certain child, the first question of the psychologist usually is: "Do all children do that, or is it at least common ?" And if one must answer this question in the negative the behavior involved loses for that psychologist all or almost all claim to scientific interest. To pay attention to such an "exceptional case" seems to him a scientifically unimportant bit of folly.

The real attitude of the investigator toward particular events and the problem of individuality is perhaps more clearly expressed in this actual behavior than in many theories. The individual event seems to him fortuitous, unimportant, scientifically indifferent. It may, however, be some extraordinary event, some tremendous experience, something that has critically determined the destiny of the person involved, or the appearance of an historically significant personality. In such a case it is customary to emphasize the "mystical" character of all individuality and originality, comprehensible only to "intuition," or at least not to science.

Both of these attitudes toward the particular event lead to the same conclusion: that that which does not occur repeatedly lies outside the realm of the comprehensible.

Lawfulness as Frequency. The esteem in which frequency is held in present-day psychology is due to the fact that it is still considered a question whether, and if so how far, the psychical world is lawful, just as in Aristotelian physics this esteem was due to a similar uncertainty about lawfulness in the physical world. It is not necessary here to describe at length the vicissitudes of the thesis of the lawfulness of the psychic in philosophical discussion. It is sufficient to recall that even at present there are many tendencies to limit the operation of law to certain "lower" spheres of psychical events. For us it is more important to note that the field which is considered lawful, not in principle, but in the actual research of psychology—even of experimental psychology—has only been extended very gradually. If psychology has only very gradually and hesitantly pushed beyond the bounds of sensory psychology into the fields of will and affect, it is certainly due not only to technical difficulties, but mainly to the fact that in this field actual repetition, a recurrence of the same event, is not to be expected. And this repetition remains, as it did for Aristotle, to a large extent the basis for the assumption of the lawfulness or intelligibility of an event.

As a matter of fact, any psychology that does not recognize lawfulness as inherent in the nature of the psychical, and hence in all psychical processes, even those occurring only once, must have criteria to decide, like Aristotelian physics, whether or not it has in any given case to deal with lawful phenomena. And, again, just as in Aristotelian physics, frequency of recurrence is taken as such a criterion. It is evidence of the depth and momentum of this connection (between repetition and lawfulness) that it is even used to define experiment, a scientific instrument which, if it is not directly opposed to the concepts of Aristotelian physics, has at least become significant only in relatively modern times. ①Even for Wundt repetition inhered in the concept of experiment. Only in recent years has psychology begun to give up this requirement, which withholds a large field of the psychical from experimental investigation.

But even more important perhaps than the restriction of experimental investigation is the fact that this extravagant valuation of repetition (i. e. , considering frequency as the criterion and expression of lawfulness) dominates the formation of the concepts of psychology, particularly in its younger branches.

Just as occurs in Aristotelian physics, contemporary child psychology regards as characteristic of a given age, and the psychology of emotion as characteristic of a given expression, that which a group of individual cases have in common. This abstract Aristotelian conception of the class determines the kind and dominates the procedure of classification.

Class and Essence. Present-day child psychology and affect psychology also exemplify clearly the Aristotelian habit of considering the abstractly defined classes as the essential nature of the particular object and hence as an explanation of its behavior. Whatever is common to children of a given age is set up as the fundamental character of that age. The fact that three-year-old children are quite often negative is considered evidence that negativism is inherent in the nature of three-year-olds, and the concept of a negativistic age or stage is then regarded as an explanation (though perhaps not a complete one) for the appearance of negativism in a given particular case!

Quite analogously, the concept of drives—for example, the

---

① The Greeks, of course, *knew* of experiment.

hunger drive or the maternal instinct—is nothing more than the abstract selection of the features common to a group of acts that are of relatively frequent occurrence. This abstraction is set up as the essential reality of the behavior and is then in turn used to explain the frequent occurrence of the instinctive behavior, for example, of the care of infant progeny. Most of the explanations of expression, of character, and of temperament are in a similar state. Here, as in a great many other fundamental concepts, such as that of ability, talent, and similar concepts employed by the intelligence testers, present-day psychology is really reduced to explanation in terms of Aristotelian essences, a sort of explanation which has long been attacked as faculty psychology and as circular explanation, but for which no other way of thinking has been substituted.

Statistics. The classif ficatory character of its concepts and the emphasis on frequency are indicated methodologically by the commanding significance of statistics in contemporary psychology. The statistical procedure, at least in its commonest application in psychology, is the most striking expression of this Aristotelian mode of thinking. In order to exhibit the common features of a given group of facts, the average is calculated. This average acquires a representative value, and is used to characterize (as mental age) the properties of"the"two-year-old child. Outwardly, there is a difference between contemporary psychology, which works so much with numbers and curves, and the Aristotelian physics. But this difference, characteristically enough, is much more a difference in the technique of execution than in the actual content of the concepts involved. Essentially, the statistical way of thinking, which is a necessary consequence of Aristotelian concepts, is also evident in Aristotelian physics, as we have already seen. The difference is that, owing to the extraordinary development of mathematics and of general scientific method, the statistical procedure of psychology is clearer and more articulate.

All the efforts of psychology in recent years toward exactness and precision have been in the direction of refinement and extension of its statistical methods. These efforts are quite justified in so far as they indicate a determination to achieve an adequate comprehension of the full reality of mental life. But they are really founded, at least in part, on the ambition to demonstrate the scientific status of psychology by using as much mathematics as possible and by pushing all calculations to the last possible decimal place.

This formal extension of the method has not changed the underlying concepts in the slightest: they are still thoroughly Aristotelian. Indeed, the mathematical formulation of the method only consolidates and extends the domination of the underlying concepts. It unquestionably makes it more difficult to see the real character of the concepts and hence to supplant them with others; and this is a difficulty with which Galileian physics did not have to contend, inasmuch as the Aristotelian mode of thought was not then so intrenched and obscured in mathematics (see page 9).

Limits of Knowledge. Exceptions. Lawfulness is believed to be related to regularity and considered the antithesis of the individual case. (In terms of the current formula, lawfulness is conceived as a correlation approaching $r = \pm 1$.) So far as the psychologist agrees at all to the validity of psychological propositions, he regards them as only regularly valid, and his acceptance of them takes such a form that one remains aware of a certain distinction between mere regularity and full lawfulness; and he ascribes to biological and, above all, to psychological propositions (in contrast to physical) only regularity. Or else lawfulness is believed to be only the extreme case of regularity, [1] in which case all differences (between lawfulness and regularity) disappear in principle while the necessity of determining the degree of regularity still remains.

The fact that lawfulness and individuality are considered antitheses has two sorts of effect on actual research. It signifies in the first place a limitation of research. It makes it appear hopeless to try to understand the real, unique, course of an emotion or the actual structure of a particular individual's personality. It thus reduces one to a treatment of these problems in terms of mere averages, as exemplified by tests and questionnaires. Anyone to whom these methods appear inadequate usually encounters a weary skepticism or else a maudlin appreciation of individuality and the doctrine that this field, from which the recurrence of similar cases in sufficient numbers is excluded, is inaccessible to scientific comprehension and requires instead sympathetic intuition. In both cases the field is withdrawn from experimental investigation, for qualitative properties are considered as the direct opposite of lawfulness. The manner in which this view is continually and repeatedly advanced in the discussion of experimental psychology resembles, e-

---

[1] As is well known, the concept of possible exceptions and the merely statistical validity of laws has very recently been revived in physical discussion. Even if this view should finally be adopted, it would not in any way mean a return to Aristotelian concepts. It suffices here to point out that, even in that event, it would not involve setting apart within the physical world a class of events on the basis of its degree of lawfulness, but the whole physical universe would be subject only to a statistical lawfulness. On the relation of this statistical view to the problem of precision of measurement, see Lewin, *Gesetz und Experiment in der Psychologie* Weltkreisverlag, Berlin, 1927

ven to its particulars, the arguments against which Galileian physics had to struggle. How, it was urged at that time, can one try to embrace in a single law of motion such qualitatively different phenomena as the movements of the stars, the flying of leaves in the wind, the flight of birds, and the rolling of a stone downhill. But the opposition of law and individual corresponded so well with the Aristotelian conception and with the primitive mode of thinking which constituted the philosophy of everyday life that it appears often enough in the writings of the physicists themselves, not, however, in their physics but in their philosophy. ①

The conviction that it is impossible wholly to comprehend the individual case as such implies, in addition to this limitation, a certain laxity of research: it is satisfied with setting forth mere regularities. The demands of psychology upon the stringency of its propositions go no farther than to require a validity "in general," or "on the average," or "as a rule." The "complexity" and "transitory nature" of life processes make it unreasonable, it is said, to require complete, exceptionless, validity. According to the old saw that "the exception proves the rule," *psychology does not regard exceptions as counterarguments so long as their frequency is not too great.*

The attitude of psychology toward the concept of lawfulness also shows clearly and strikingly the Aristotelian character of its mode of thought. It is founded on a very meager confidence in the lawfulness of psychological events and has for the investigator the added charm of not requiring too high a standard of validity in his

---

① To avoid misunderstanding, the following should be emphasized: when we criticize the opposition of individual and law, as is customary in psychology, it does not mean that we are unaware of the complex problems of the concept of individuality.

propositions or in his proofs of them.

Historic-geographic Concepts. For the view of the nature of lawfulness and for the emphasis upon repetition which we have seen to be characteristic of Aristotelian physics, in addition to the motives which we have just mentioned, the immediate reference to the concerned actuality in the historic-geographic sense was fundamental. Likewise, and this is evidence of the intimacy in which these modes of thought are related, presentday psychology is largely dominated by the same immediate reference to the historic-geographic datum. The historical bent of psychological concepts is again not always immediately obvious as such, but is bound up with nonhistoric, systematic concepts and undifferentiated from them. This quasi-historical set forms, in my opinion, the central point for the understanding and criticism of this mode of concept formation.

Although we have criticized the statistical mode of thought, the particular formulas used are not ultimately important to the questions under discussion. It is not the fact that an arithmetic mean is taken, that one adds and divides, that is the object of the present critique. These operations will certainly continue to be used extensively in the future of psychology. The critical point is not that statistical methods are applied, but how they are applied and, especially, what cases are combined into groups.

In contemporary psychology the reference to the historic-geographic datum and the dependence of the conclusions upon frequency of actual occurrence are striking. Indeed, so far as immediate reference to the historic datum is concerned, the way in which the nature of the one-, two-, or three-year-old child is arrived at through the calculation of statistical averages corresponds exactly to Bacon's collection of the given cases of dryness in his *tabulae praesentiae*. To be sure, there is a certain very crude concession made in such averages to the requirements of nonhistoric concepts: patently pathological cases, and sometimes even cases in which an unusual environment is concerned, are usually excluded. Apart from this consideration, the exclusion of the most extreme abnormalities, the determination of the cases to be placed in a statistical group is essentially on historic-geographic grounds. For a group defined in historic-geographic terms, perhaps the one-year-old children of Vienna or New York in the year 1928, averages are calculated which are doubtless of the greatest significance to the historian or to the practical school man, but which do not lose their dependence upon the accidents of the historic-geographic given even though one go on to an average of the children of Germany, of Europe, or of the whole world, or of a decade instead of a year. *Such an extension of the geographic and historic basis does not do away with the specific dependence of this concept upon the frequency with which the individual cases occur within historically-geographically defined fields.*

Mention should have been made earlier of that refinement of statistics which is founded upon a restriction of the historic-geographic basis, such as a consideration of the one-year-old children of a proletarian quarter of Berlin in the first years after the War. Such groupings usually are based on the qualitative individuality of the concrete cases as well as upon historic-geographic definitions. But even such limitations really contradict the spirit of statistics founded on frequency. Even they signify methodologically a certain shift to the concrete particulars. Incidentally, one must not forget that even in the extreme case of such refinement, perhaps in the statistical investigation of the only child, the actual definition is in terms of historic-geographic or at best of sociological categories; that is, according to criteria which combine into a single group cases that psychologically are very different or even antithetical. Such statistical investigations are consequently unable as a rule to give an explanation of the dynamics of the processes involved.

The immediate reference to the historically given actuality which is characteristic of Aristotelian concept formation is evident also in the discussion of experiment and nearness to life conditions. Certainly one may justly criticize the simple reaction experiments, the beginnings of the experimental psychology of the will, or the experiments of reflexology on the ground of their wide divergence from the conditions of life. But this divergence is based in large part upon the tendency to investigate such processes as do not present the individual peculiarities of the particular case but which, as "simple elements" (perhaps the simplest movements), are common to all behavior, or which occur, so to speak, in everything. In contrast to the foregoing, approximation to life conditions is often demanded of, for example, the psychology of will. By this is usually meant that it should investigate those cases, impossible to produce experimentally, in which the most important decisions of life are made. And here also we are confronted by an orientation toward the historically significant. It is a requirement which, if transferred to physics, would mean that it would be incorrect to study hydrodynamics in the laboratory; one must rather investigate the largest rivers in the world. Two points then stand out: in the field of theory and law, the high valuation of the historically important and disdain of the ordinary; in the field of experiment, the choice of processes which occur frequently (or are common to many events). Both are indicative in like measure of that Aristotelian mixing of historical and systematic questions which carries with it for the systematic the connection with the abstract classes and the neglect of the full reality of the concrete case.

Galileian Concept Formation.

Opposed to Aristotelian concept formation, which I have sought briefly to characterize, there is now evident in psychology a development which appears occasionally in radical or apparently radical tendencies, more usually in little half steps, sometimes falling into error (especially when it tries most exactly to follow the example of physics), but which on the whole seems clearly and irresistibly to be pushing on to modifications that may ultimately mean nothing less than a transition from Aristotelian to Galileian concept formation.

No Value Concepts. No Dichotomies. Unification of Fields.

The most important general circumstances which paved the way for Galileian concepts in physics are clearly and distinctly to be seen in present-day psychology.

The conquest over *valuative*, anthropomorphic classifications of phenomena on bases other than the nature of the mental process itself (see page 3) is not by any means complete, but in many fields, especially in sensory psychology, at least the chief difficulties are past.

As in physics, the grouping of events and objects into paired opposites and similar logical dichotomies is being replaced by groupings with the aid of serial concepts which permit of continuous variation, partly owing simply to wider experience and the recognition that transition stages are always present.

This has gone furthest in sensory psychology, especially in psychological optics and acoustics, and lately also in the domain of smell. But the tendency toward this change is also evident in other fields, for example, in that of feeling.

Freud's doctrine especially—and this is one of its greatest services—has contributed largely to the abolition of the boundary between the normal and the pathological, the ordinary and the unusual, and hereby furthered the *homogenization* (see page 10) of all the fields of psychology. This process is certainly still far from complete, but it is entirely comparable to that introduced in modern physics by which heavenly and earthly processes were united.

Also in child and animal psychology the necessity is gradually disappearing of choosing between two alternatives—regarding the child as a little adult and the animal as an undeveloped inferior human, or trying to establish an unbridgeable gap between the child and adult, animal and man. This homogenization is becoming continually clearer in all fields, and it is not a purely philosophical insistence upon some sort of abstract fundamental unity but influences concrete research in which differences are fully preserved.

Unconditional General Validity of Psychological Laws. The clearest and most important expression of increasing homogeneity, besides the transition from class to serial concepts, is the fact that the validity of particular psychological laws is no longer limited to particular fields, as it was once limited to the normal human adult on the ground that anything might be expected of psychopathies or of geniuses, or that in such cases the same laws do not hold. It is coming to be realized that every psychological law must hold without exception.

In actual content, this transition to the concept of strict exceptionless lawfulness signifies at once the same final and all-embracing homogenization and harmonization of the whole field that gave to Galileian physics its intoxicating feeling of infinite breadth, because it does not, like the abstract class concepts, level out the rich variety of the world and because a single law embraces the whole field.

Tendencies toward a homogeneity based upon the exceptionless validity of its laws have become evident in psychology only very recently, but they open up an extraordinarily wide perspective. ①

The investigation of the laws of structure—particularly the experimental investigation of wholes—has shown that the same laws hold not only within different fields of psychological optics but also in audition and in sensory psychology in general. This in itself constitutes a large step in the progress toward homogeneity.

Further, the laws of optical figures and of intellectual insight have turned out to be closely related. Important and similar laws have been discovered in the experimental investigation of behavioral wholes, of will processes, and of psychological needs. In the fields of memory and expression, psychological development appears to be analogous. In short, the thesis of the general validity of

---

① The association psychology contains an attempt at this sort of homogeneity, and it has really been of essential service in this direction. Similarly, in our time reflexology and behaviorism have contributed to the homogenization of man and animal and of bodily and mental. But the Aristotelian view of lawfulness as regularity (without which it would have been impossible to support the law of association) brought this attempt to nothing. Consequently, the experimental association psychology, in its attempt at the end of the nineteenth century to derive the whole mental life from a single law, displayed the circular and at the same time abstract character that is typical of the speculative early stages of a science, and of Aristotelian class concepts.

Indeed, it seems almost as if, because of the great importance of frequency and repetition for Aristotelian methodological concepts, the law of association was designed to make use of these as the actual content of psychological principles, inasmuch as frequent repetition is regarded as the most important cause of mental phenomena.

psychological laws has very recently become so much more concrete, particular laws have shown such capacity for fruitful application to fields that at first were qualitatively completely separated, that the thesis of the homogeneity of psychic life in respect to its laws gains tremendously in vigor and is destroying the boundaries of the old separated fields. ①

Mounting Ambitions. Methodologically also the thesis of the exceptionless validity of psychological laws has a far-reaching significance. It leads to an extraordinary increase in the demands made upon proof. It is no longer possible to take exceptions lightly. They do not in any way "prove the rule," but on the contrary are completely valid disproofs, even though they are rare, indeed, so long as one single exception is demonstrable. The thesis of general validity permits of no exceptions in the entire realm of the psychic, whether of child or adult, whether in normal or pathological psychology.

On the other hand, the thesis of exceptionless validity in psychological laws makes available to investigation, especially to experiment, such processes as do not frequently recur in the same form, as, for example, certain affective processes.

From the Average to the Pure Case. A clear appreciation of

---

① For this section compare especially M. Wertheimer, Untersuchungen zur Lehre von der Gestalt, II, *Psychol. Forsch.*, 1923, 4, 301-350, W. Köhler, *Gestalt Psychology*, Liveright, New York, 1929. K. Koffka, *The Growth of the Mind : An Introduction to Child Psychology* (trans. by R. M. Ogden), Harcourt, Brace, New York; Kegan Paul, London, 1924, (2d ed. , 1928), and Lewin, *Vorsatz Wille und Bedurfnis , mit Vorbemerkungen uber die psychischen Krafle und Energien und die Struktur der Seele*, Springer, Berlin, 1926. A review of the special researches is found in W. Kohler, Gestaltprobleme und Anfänge einer Gestalttheorie, *Jahresber. d. ges. Physiol.*, 1924.

this circumstance is still by no means habitual in psychology. Indeed, from the earlier, Aristotelian point of view the new procedure may even seem to conceal the fundamental contradiction we have mentioned above. One declares that one wants to comprehend the full concrete reality in a higher degree than is possible with Aristotelian concepts and yet considers this reality in its actual historical course and its given geographical setting as really accidental. The general validity, for example, of the law of movement on an inclined plane is not established by taking the average of as many cases as possible of real stones actually rolling down hills, and then considering this average as the most probable case. ① It is based rather upon the frictionless rolling of an ideal sphere down an absolutely straight and hard plane, that is, upon a process that even the laboratory can only approximate and which is most improbable in daily life. One declares that one is striving for general validity and concreteness, yet uses a method which, from the point of view of the preceding epoch, disregards the historically given facts and depends entirely upon individual accidents, indeed upon the most pronounced exceptions.

How physics arrives at this procedure, which strikes the Aristotelian views of contemporary psychology as doubly paradoxical, begins to become intelligible when one envisages the necessary methodological consequences of the change in the ideas of the extent of lawfulness. When lawfulness is no longer limited to cases which occur regularly or frequently but is characteristic of every

---

① In psychology it is asserted, often with special emphasis, that one obtains, perhaps from the construction of baby tests, a representation of the "general human," because those processes are selected which occur most frequently in the child's daily life. Then one may expect with sufficient probability that the child will spontaneously display similar behavior in the test.

physical event, the necessity disappears of demonstrating the lawfulness of an event by some special criterion, such as its frequency of occurrence. Even a particular case is then assumed, without more ado, to be lawful. Historical rarity is no disproof, historical regularity no proof of lawfulness. For the concept of lawfulness has been quite detached from that of regularity; the concept of the complete absence of exceptions to laws is strictly separated from that of historical constancy (the "forever" of Aristotle). ①

Further, the content of a law cannot then be determined by the calculation of averages of historically given cases. For Aristotle the nature of a thing was expressed by the characteristics common to the historically given cases. Galileian concepts, on the contrary, which regard historical frequency as accident, must also consider it a matter of chance which properties one arrives at by taking averages of historical cases. If the concrete event is to be comprehended and the thesis of lawfulness without exception is to be not merely a philosophical maxim but determinative of the mode of actual research, there must be another possibility of penetrating the nature of an event, some other way than that of ignoring all individual peculiarities of concrete cases. The solution of this

---

① The contrast between Aristotelian and Galileian views of lawfulness and the difference in their methods may be briefly tabulated as follows:

	For Aristotle	For Galileo
1. The regular is	lawful	lawful
The frequent is	lawful	lawful
The individual case is	chance	lawful
2. Criteria of lawfulness are	regularity frequency	not required
3. That which is common to the historically occurring cases is	an expression of the nature of the thing	an accident, only historically conditioned

problem may only be obtained by the elucidation of the paradoxical procedures of Galileian method through a consideration of the problems of dynamics.

Dynamics

Changes in the Fundamental Dynamic Concepts of Physics

The dynamic problems of physics were really foreign to the Aristotelian mode of thought. The fact that dynamic problems had throughout such great significance for Galileian physics permits us to regard dynamics as a characteristic consequence of the Galileian mode of thought. [1] As always, it involved not merely a superficial shift of interest, but a change in the content of the theories. Even Aristotle emphasized "becoming," as compared with his predecessors. It is perhaps more correct to say that in the Aristotelian concepts statics and dynamics are not yet differentiated. This is due especially to certain fundamental assumptions.

Teleology and Physical Vectors.

A leading characteristic of Aristotelian dynamics is the fact that it explained events by means of concepts which we today perceive to be specifically biological or psychological: *every object tends, so far as not prevented by other objects, toward perfection*, toward the realization of its own nature. This nature is for Aristotle, as we have already seen, that which is common to the class of the object. So it comes about that the class for him is at the same time the concept and the goal ($\tau \epsilon \lambda$os) of an object.

This teleological theory of physical events does not show only that biology and physics are not yet separated. It indicates also

---

[1] E. MACH, *The Science of Mechanics* (Eng. trans., 2d ed., rev.), Chicago, 1902.

that the dynamics of Aristotelian physics resembles in essential points the animistic and artificial mode of thought of primitive man, which views all movement as life and makes artificial manufacture the prototype of existence. For, in the case of manufactured things, the maker's idea of the object is, in one sense, both the cause and the goal of the event.

Further, for Aristotelian concepts the *cause* of a physical event was very closely related to psychological "drives": the object strives toward a certain goal; so far as movement is concerned, it tends toward the place appropriate to its nature. Thus heavy objects strive downward, the heavier the more strongly, while light objects strive upward.

It is customary to dismiss these Aristotelian physical concepts by calling them anthropomorphic. But perhaps it would be better, when we consider that the same fundamental dynamic ideas are today completely dominant in psychology and biology, to examine the actual content of the Aristotelian theses as far as possible independently of the style of their presentation.

It is customary to say that teleology assumes a direction of events toward a goal, which causal explanation does not recognize, and to see in this the most essential difference between teleological and causal explanation. But this sort of view is inadequate, for the causal explanation of modern physics uses directed quantities, mathematically described vectors. Physical force, which is defined as "the cause of a physical change," is considered a directed, vectorial factor. In the employment of vectorial factors as the foundation of dynamics there is thus no difference between the modern and the Aristotelian view.

The real difference lies rather in the fact that *the kind and direction of the physical vectors in Aristotelian dynamics are completely determined in advance by the nature of the object concerned*. In modern physics, on the contrary, *the existence of a physical vector always depends upon the mutual relations of several physical facts*, especially upon the relation of the object to its environment. ①

Significance of the Whole Situation in Aristotelian and Galileian Dynamics.

For Aristotelian concepts, the environment plays a part only in so far as it may give rise to "disturbances" forced modifications of the processes which follow from the nature of the object concerned. The vectors which determine an object's movements are completely determined by the object. That is, they do not depend upon the relation of the object to the environment, and they belong to that object once for all, irrespective of its surroundings at any given time. The tendency of light bodies to go up resided in the bodies themselves; the downward tendency of heavy objects was seated in those objects. In modern physics, on the contrary, not only is the upward tendency of a lighter body derived from the relation of this body to its environment, but the weight itself of the body depends upon such a relation.

This decisive revolution comes to clear expression in Galileo's classic investigations of the law of falling bodies. The mere fact that he did not investigate the heavy body itself, but the process of "free falling or movement on an inclined plane," signifies a transition to concepts which can be defined only by reference to a certain sort of situation (namely, the presence of a plane with a certain inclination or of an unimpeded vertical extent of space

---

① Naturally this applies also to internal causes, which involve the mutual relation of the parts of a physical system.

through which to fall). The idea of investigating free falling, which is too rapid for satisfactory observation, by resorting to the slower movement upon an inclined plane presupposes that the dynamics of the event is no longer related to the isolated object as such, but is seen to be dependent upon the whole situation in which the event occurs.

Galileo's procedure, in fact, includes a penetrating investigation of precisely the situation factors. The slope of the inclined plane, that is, the proportion of height to length, is defined. The list of situations involved (free falling, movement on an inclined plane, and horizontal movement) is exhausted and, through the varying of the inclination, classified. The dependence of the essential features of the event (for example, its velocity) upon the essential properties of the situation (the slope of the plane) becomes the conceptual and methodological center of importance.

This view of dynamics does not mean that the nature of the object becomes insignificant. The properties and structure of the object involved remain important also for the Galileian theory of dynamics. But the situation assumes as much importance as the object. *Only by the concrete whole which comprises the object and the situation are the vectors which determine the dynamics of the event defined.*

In carrying out this view, Galileian physics tried to characterize the individuality of the total situation concerned as concretely and accurately as possible. This is an exact reversal of Aristotelian principles. The dependence of an event upon the situation in which it occurs means for the Aristotelian mode of thought, which wants to ascertain the general by seeking out the like features of many cases, nothing more than a disturbing force. The changing situations appear as something fortuitous that disturbs and obscures the essential nature. It was therefore valid and customary to exclude the influence of the situation as far as possible, to abstract from the situation, in order to understand the essential nature of the object and the direction of its goal.

Getting Rid of the Historical Bent.

The actual investigation of this sort of vectors obviously presupposes that the processes involved occur with a certain regularity or frequency (see page 6). For otherwise an exclusion of the differences of the situation would leave no similarities. If one starts from the fundamental concepts of Aristotelian dynamics, the investigation of the dynamics of a process must be more difficult—one might think here of emotion in psychology—the more it depends upon the nature of the situation concerned. The single event becomes thereby unlawful in principle because there is no way of investigating its dynamics.

The Galileian method of determining the dynamics of a process is directly opposed to this procedure. Since the dynamics of the process depends not only upon the object but also, primarily, upon the situation, it would be nonsensical to try to obtain general laws of processes by excluding the influence of the situations as far as possible. It becomes silly to bring in as many different situations as possible and regard only those factors as generally valid that are observed under all circumstances, in any and every situation. It must, on the contrary, become important to comprehend the whole situation involved, with all its characteristics, as precisely as possible.

The step from particular case to law, from "this" event to "such" an event, no longer requires the confirmation by historical regularity that is characteristic of the Aristotelian mode of thought. This step to the general is automatically and immediately given by the principle of the exceptionless lawfulness of physical events. ① What is now important to the investigation of dynamics is not to abstract from the situation, but to hunt out those situations in which the determinative factors of the total dynamic structure are most clearly, distinctly, and purely to be discerned. *Instead of a reference to the abstract average of as many historically given cases as possible, there is a reference to the full concreteness of the particular situations.*

We cannot here examine in great detail why not all situations are equally useful for the investigation of dynamics, why certain situations possess a methodological advantage, and why as far as possible these are experimentally set up. Only one circumstance, which seems to me very seldom to be correctly viewed and which has given rise to misunderstandings that have had serious consequences for psychology, requires elucidation

We have seen above how Galileian concepts separated the previously undifferentiated questions of the historical course of events on one side and of the laws of events on the other. They renounced in systematic problems the immediate reference to the historic-geographic datum. That the procedure instituted does not, as might at first appear, contradict the empirical tendency toward the comprehension of the full reality may already be clear from our last consideration: the Aristotelian immediate relation to the historically regular and its average really means giving up the attempt to understand the particular, always situation-conditioned event. When this immediate relation is completely abandoned, when the place of historic-geographic constancy is taken by the

---

① It is impossible here to go more fully into the problem of induction. (Cf. Lewin, Gesetz und Experiment in der Psychologie.)

position of the particular in the whole situation, and when (as in experimental method) it is just the same whether the situation is frequent and permanent or rare and transitory, only then does it become possible to undertake the task of understanding the real, always ultimately unique, event.

The Meaning of the Process Differential.

Methodologically there may seem to result here another theoretical difficulty which can perhaps be better elucidated by a simple example than by general discussion. In order that the essentials may be more easily seen, I choose an example not from familiar physics but from problematical psychology. If one attempt to trace the behavior of a child to psychical field forces, among other things—the justification for this thesis is not here under discussion—the following objection might easily be raised. A child stands before two attractive objects (say a toy T and a piece of chocolate C), which are in different places (see Fig. 1). According to this hypothesis, then, there exist field forces in these directions (a and b). The proportional strength of the forces is indifferent, and it does not matter whether the physical law of the parallelogram of forces is applicable to psychical field forces or not. So far, then, as a resultant of these two forces is formed, it must take a direction (r) which leads neither to T nor to C. The child would then, so one might easily conclude according to this theory, reach neither T nor C. [1]

---

[1] I am neglecting here the possibility that one of the field forces entirely disappears.

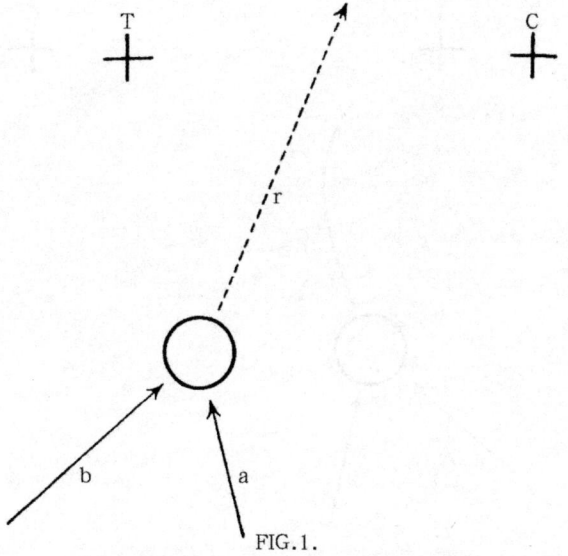

FIG. 1.

In reality such a conclusion would be too hasty, for even if the vector should have the direction *r* at the moment of starting, that does not mean that the actual process permanently retains this direction. Instead, *the whole situation changes with the process*, thus changing also, in both strength and direction, the vectors that at each moment determine the dynamics. Even if one assumes the parallelogram of forces and in addition a constant internal situation in the child, the actual process, because of this changing in the situation, will always finally bring the child to one or the other of the attractive objects (Fig. 2). [1]

---

[1] Even if the distances of the attractive objects and the strength of their attractions were equal, the resulting conflict situation would lead to the same result, owing to the lability of the equilibrium.

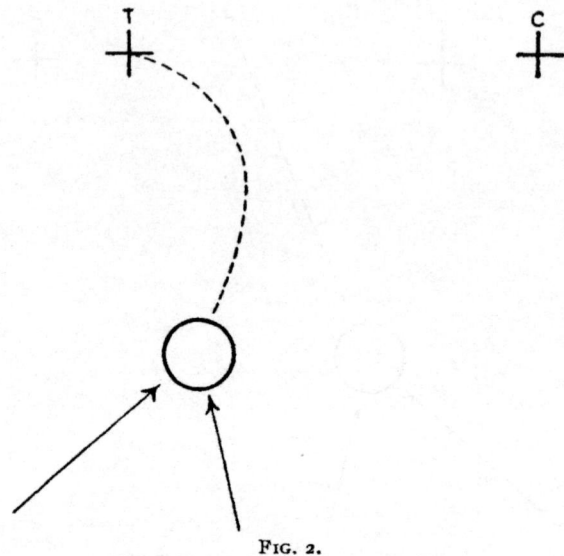

FIG. 2.

What I would like to exhibit by this example is this: if one tries to deduce the dynamics of a process, particularly the vectors which direct it, from the actual event, one is compelled to resort to process differentials. In our example, one can regard only the process of the first moment, not the whole course, as the immediate expression of the vector present in the beginning of the situation.

The well-known fact that all, or at least most, physical laws are differential laws[①] does not seem to me, as is often supposed, to prove that physics endeavors to analyze everything into the smallest "elements" and to consider these elements in the most perfect possible isolation. It proceeds rather from the circumstance that physics since Galileo no longer regards the historic course of a process as the immediate expression of the vectors determinative

---

① H. POINCARE, *La Science et l'hypothèse*, Paris, 1916.

of its dynamics. For Aristotle, the fact that the movement showed a certain total course was proof of the existence of a tendency to that course, for example, toward a perfect circular movement. Galileian concepts, on the contrary, even in the course of a particular process, separate the quasi-historical from the factors determining the dynamics. They refer to the whole situation in its full concrete individuality, to the state of the situation at every moment of time.

Further, for Galileian concepts, the forces, the physical vectors which control the situation, are proved by the resulting process. However, it is valid to exclude the quasi-historical in order to get the pure process, and therefore necessary to comprehend the type of process by recourse to the process differential, because only in the latter, and hence unmixed, is it expressed. This recourse to the process differential thus arises not, as is usually supposed, from a tendency to reduce all events to their "ultimate elements," but as a not immediately obvious complementary expression of the tendency to derive the dynamics from the relation of the concrete particular to the concrete whole situation and to ascertain as purely and as unmixed with historic factors as possible the type of event with which this total situation is dynamically related.

Experimentally also it is important to construct such situations as will actually yield this pure event, or at least permit of its conceptual reconstruction.

Methodological.

It remains to examine more closely the logical and methodological consequences of this mode of thought. Since law and individual are no longer antitheses, nothing prevents relying for proof upon historically unusual, rare, and transitory events, such as most physical experiments are. It becomes clear why it is very illuminating, for systematic concepts, to produce such cases, even if not exactly for the sake of their rarity itself.

The tendency to comprehend the actual situation as fully and concretely as possible, even in its individual peculiarities, makes the most precise possible qualitative and quantitative determination necessary and profitable. But it must not be forgotten that only this task, and not numerical precision for its own sake, gives any point or meaning to exactness.

Some of the most essential services to knowledge of the quantitative, and in general of the mathematical, mode of representation are (1) the possibility of using continuous transitions instead of dichotomies in characterization, thereby greatly refining description, and (2) the fact that with such functional concepts it is possible to go from the particular to the general without losing the particular in the general and thereby making impossible the return from the general to the particular.

Finally, reference should be made to the method of approximation in the description of objects and situations, in which the continuous, functional mode of thought is manifest.

Fundamental Dynamic Concepts in Psychology

The dynamic concepts of psychology today are still thoroughly Aristotelian, [①] and indeed the same internal relations and motives seem to me here displayed, even to the details.

Aristotelian Ideas: Independence of the Situation; Instinct.

In content, which is easiest to exhibit and indeed hardly

---

① The same holds, incidentally, for biology, which I cannot here especially examine, although I regard psychology in general as a field of biology.

requires exposition, psychological dynamics agrees most completely with Aristotelian concepts: it is teleology in the Aristotelian sense. The traditional mistake of regarding causal explanation as an explanation without the use of directed forces has notably retarded the progress of dynamics, since psychological dynamics, like physical, cannot be understood without the use of vector concepts. It is not the fact that directed quantities are employed in psychological dynamics that gives it its Aristotelian character, but the fact that the process is ascribed to vectors connected with the object of investigation, for example, with the particular person, and *relatively independent of the situation*.

The concept of instinct in its classical form is perhaps the most striking example of this. The instincts are the sum of those vectors conditioned by predispositions which it is thought must be ascribed to an individual. The instincts are determined essentially by finding out what actions occur most frequently or regularly in the *actual life* of the individual or of a group of like individuals. That which is *common* to these frequent acts (*e. g.*, food getting, fighting, mutual aid) is regarded as the *essence* or essential nature of the processes. Again, completely in the Aristotelian sense, these abstract class concepts are set up as at once the goal and the cause of the process. And indeed the instincts obtained in this way, as averages of historical actuality, are regarded as the more fundamental the more abstract the class concept is and the more various the cases of which the average is taken. It is thought that in this way, and only in this way, those "accidents" inherent in the particular case and in the concrete situation can be overcome. For the aim that still completely dominates the procedure of psychology in large fields is founded upon its effort to free itself of the connection to specific situations.

Intrinsic Difficulties and Unlawfulness.

The whole difference between the Aristotelian and Galileian modes of thought becomes clear as soon as one sees what consequences, for a strict Galileian view of the concept of law, follow from this close and fixed connection of the instinct to the individual "in itself." In that case the instinct (*e. g.*, the maternal) must operate continually without interruption; just as the explanation of negativism by the "nature" of the three-year-old child entails for Galileian concepts the consequence that all three-year-old children must be negative the whole day long, twenty-four hours out of the twenty-four.

The general Aristotelian set of psychology is able to dodge these consequences. It is satisfied, even for proof of the existence of the vectors which should explain the behavior, to depend upon the concept of regularity. In this way it avoids the necessity of supposing the vector to be existent in every situation. On the basis of the strict concept of law it is possible to disprove the hypothesis, for example, of the existence of a certain instinct by demonstrating its nonexistence in given concrete cases. Aristotelian concepts do not have to fear such disproofs, inasmuch as they can answer all references to concrete particular cases by falling back on mere statistical validity.

Of course these concepts are thereby also unable to explain the occurrence of a particular case, and by this is meant not the behavior of an abstractly defined "average child," but, for example, the behavior of a certain child at a certain moment.

The Aristotelian bent of psychological dynamics thus not only implies a limitation of explanation to such cases as occur frequently enough to provide a basis for abstracting from the situation, but leaves literally any possibility open in any particular case, even of frequent events.

Attempts at Self-correction: the Average Situation.

The intrinsic difficulties for dynamics which the Aristotelian mode of thought brings with it, namely, the danger of destroying the explanatory value of the theory by the exclusion of the situation, are constantly to be observed in contemporary psychology and lead to the most singular hybrid methods and to attempts to include the concept of the situation somehow. This becomes especially clear in the attempts at quantitative determination. When, for example, the question is raised and an attempt made to decide experimentally how the strengths of various drives in rats (perhaps hunger, thirst, sex, and mother love) compare with each other, such a question (which corresponds to asking in physics which is stronger, gravitation or electromotive force) has meaning only if these vectors are ascribed entirely to the rat and regarded as practically independent of the concrete whole situation, independent of the condition of the rat and its environment at the moment. Such a fixed connection is, of course, ultimately untenable, and one is compelled at least in part to abandon this way of thinking. Thus the first step in this direction consists in taking account of the *momentary condition of the drive* with regard to its state of satiation: the various possible degrees of strength of the several drives are ascertained, and their maximal strengths are compared.

It is true, of course, that the Aristotelian attitude is really only slightly ameliorated thereby. The curve expresses the statistical average of a large number of cases, which is not binding for an individual case; and, above all, this mode of thought applies the vector independently of the structure of the situation.

To be sure, it is not denied that the situation essentially determines the instinctive behavior in the actual particular case, but in these problems, as in the question of the child's spontaneous behavior in the baby tests, it is evident that no more is demanded of a law than a behavioral average. The law thus applies to an average situation. It is forgotten that there just is no such thing as an "average situation" any more than an average child.

Practically, if not in principle, the reference to the concept of an "optimal" situation goes somewhat further. But even here the concrete structure of the situation remains indeterminate: only a maximum of results in a certain direction is required.

In none of these concepts however are the two fundamental faults of the Aristotelian mode of thought eliminated: the vectors determining the dynamics of the process are still attributed to the isolated object, independently of the concrete whole situation; and only very slight demands are made upon the validity of psychological principles and the comprehension of the concrete actuality of the individual single process.

This holds true even for the concepts immediately concerned with the significance of the situation. As mentioned before, the question at the center of the discussion of the situation is, quite in the Aristotelian sense, how far the situation can hinder (or facilitate). The situation is even considered as a constant object and the question is discussed: which is more important, heredity or environment? Thus again, on the basis of a concept of situation gotten by abstraction, a dynamic problem is treated in a form which has none but a statistical historical meaning. The heredity or environment discussion also shows, even in its particulars, how completely these concepts separate object and situation and derive the dynamics from the isolated object itself.

The role of the situation in all these concepts may perhaps be best exhibited by reference to certain changes in painting. In medieval painting at first there was, in general, no environment, but only an empty (often a golden) background. Even when gradually an environment did appear it usually consisted in nothing more than presenting, beside the one person, other persons and objects. Thus the picture was at best an assembling of separate persons in which each had really a separate existence.

Only later did the space itself exist in the painting; it became a whole situation. At the same time this situation as a whole became dominant, and each separate part, so far indeed as separate parts still remain, is what it is (e. g. , in such an extreme as Rembrandt) only in and through the whole situation.

Beginnings of a Galileian Mode of Thought.

Opposed to these Aristotelian fundamental ideas of dynamics there are now signs in psychology of the beginnings of a Galileian mode of thought. In this respect the concepts of sensory psychology are farthest advanced.

At first, even in sensory psychology, explanations referred to isolated single perceptions, even to single isolated elements of these perceptions. The developments of recent years have brought about, at first slowly but then more radically, a revolution in the fundamental dynamic ideas by showing that the dynamics of the processes are to be deduced, not from the single elements of the perception, but from its whole structure. For it is impossible by a consideration of the elements to define what is meant by figure in the broader sense of the word. Rather, the whole dynamics of sensory psychological processes depends upon the ground1 and beyond it upon the structure of the whole surrounding field. The dynamics of perception is not to be understood by the abstract Aristotelian method of excluding all fortuitous situations, but this principle is penetrating today all the fields of sensory psychology—only by *the establishment of a form of definite structure in a definite sort of environment*. ①

Recently the same fundamental ideas of dynamics have been extended beyond the special field of perception and applied in the fields of higher mental processes, in the psychology of instinct, will, emotion, and expression, and in genetic psychology. The sterility, for example, of the always circular discussion of heredity or environment and the impossibility of carrying through the division, based upon this discussion, of the characteristics of the individual begin to show that there is something radically wrong with their fundamental assumptions. A mode of thought is becoming evident, even though only gradually, which, corresponding somewhat to the biological concept of phenotype and genotype, tries to determine the predisposition, not by excluding so far as possible the influence of the environment, but by accepting in the concept of disposition its necessary reference to a group of concretely defined situations.

Thus in the psychological fields most fundamental to the whole behavior of living things the transition seems inevitable to a Galileian view of dynamics, which derives all its vectors not from single isolated objects, but from the mutual relations of the factors in the concrete whole situation, that is, essentially, from the momentary condition of the individual and the structure of the psychological situation. *The dynamics of the processes is always to be derived from the relation of the concrete individual to the concrete situation*, and, so far as internal forces are concerned, from the mutual relations of the various functional systems that make up the individual.

---

① E. RUBIN,*Visuelwahrgenommene Figuren*,Gyldenalske,Copenhagen,1921.

The carrying out of this principle requires, to be sure, the completion of a task that at present is only begun: namely, the providing of a workable representation of a concrete psychological situation according to its individual characteristics and its associated functional properties, and of the concrete structure of the psychological person and its internal dynamic facts. Perhaps the circumstance that a technique for such a concrete representation, not simply of the physical but of the psychological situation, cannot be accomplished without the help of topology, the youngest branch of mathematics, has contributed to keeping psychological dynamics, in the most important fields of psychology, in the Aristotelian mode of thought. But more important than these technical questions may be the general substantial and philosophical presuppositions: too meager scientific courage in the question of the lawfulness of the psychical, too slight demands upon the validity of psychological laws, and the tendency, which goes hand in hand with this leaning toward mere regularity, to specifically historic-geographic concepts.

The accidents of historical processes are not overcome by excluding the changing situations from systematic consideration, but only by taking the fullest account of the individual nature of the concrete case. *It depends upon keeping in mind that general validity of the law and concreteness of the individual case are not antitheses, and that reference to the totality of the concrete whole situation must take the place of reference to the largest possible historical collection of frequent repetitions.* This means methodologically that the importance of a case, and its validity as proof, cannot be evaluated by the frequency of its occurrence. Finally, it means for psychology, as it did for physics, a transition from an abstract classificatory procedure to an essentially concrete constructive method.

That psychology at present is not far from the time when the dominance of Aristotelian concepts will be replaced by that of the Galileian mode of thought seems to me indicated also by a more external question of psychological investigation.

It is one of the characteristic signs of the speculative early stage of all sciences that schools, representative of different systems, oppose each other in a way and to an extent that is unknown, for example, in contemporary physics. When a difference of hypotheses occurs in contemporary physics there still remains a common basis that is foreign to the schools of the speculative stage. This is only an external sign of the fact that the concepts of that field have introduced a method that permits step-by-step approximation to understanding. Thereby results a continuous progress of the science which is constantly more narrowly limiting the consequences for the whole structure of differences between various physical theories.

There seems to me much to indicate that even the development of the schools in contemporary psychology is bringing about a transition to a similar sort of constant development, not only in sensory psychology but throughout the entire field.

Chapter II
On The Structure of The Mind[1]

On the Causes of Psychical Events

The relations to which theory has heretofore looked in experimental psychology, when seeking the causes of a psychical event, belong almost exclusively to one quite specific type of relation. This is a real connection which one may designate as *adhesion* of any sort of object or collection of objects or processes. The fact that certain single objects are connected with each other, or that a whole event sticks together in the sense of adhesion, is given as the cause of a psychical event.

The most pronounced case of such a type of connection is presented by the association between two psychical objects in the sense of the old association theory. The objects a and b have en-

---

[1] An excerpt from *Vorsalz, Wille und Bedürfnis, mit Vorbemerkungen uber die psychischen Krafte und Energien und die Struktur der Seele*, pp. 21-39. For use of the word "mind" see translators' note.

tered into an association by reason of earlier contiguity. And this association phenomenon is claimed to be the cause of the fact that on the occurrence of experience a, experience b results.

But even when experience is not regarded as the cause of the association and forces are assumed which do not obey the laws of association, such as the determining tendency [1] or any sort of natural coherence, [2] the following fundamental type is still retained: *the stimulus possesses an adhesion with certain reactions*. And this adhesion is regarded as the cause of the course of the event.

In psychology these couplings were conceived for the most part as mechanically rigid connections in the sense of an association of individual stimulations with established reactions. In opposition to this, the idea is beginning to gain ground that usually we have to do not with rigid connections of distinct pieces or elements but with temporally extended wholes (of the type, for example, of a melody), the moments or phases of which can be explained only by the whole. Recently a deplorable misconception of the fundamental ideas of Gestalt theories has sometimes occurred. This misconception may be stated as follows: The cause of the process b is not to be seen in its rigid coupling with the preceding independent event a. Rather, if a forms a dependent moment of a more comprehensive whole, it carries that whole with it. Thus, indeed, no chain-like coupling of member to member, but the connections of the parts in the whole, is regarded as the "cause" of the

---

[1] N. ACH, *Über den Willensakt und das Temperament*, Quelle u. Meyer, Leipzig, 1910.

[2] G. E. MÜLLER, *Komplextheorie und Gestalttheorie*, Vanderhoeck u. Ruprecht, Göttingen, 1923.

event.①

The experimental investigation of habits (association) has shown that the couplings created by habit are never, as such, the motor of a psychical event.② Such a conception is also erroneous when the essential fact of the process of habit formation and of practice is taken to be, not the formation of piecemeal associations, but the re-formation and new formation of definite action unities. Rather, certain psychical energies, that is, tense psychical systems which derive, as a rule, from the pressure of will or of a need, are always the necessary condition of the occurrence—in whatever way—of the psychical event. It hardly requires special mention that this does not mean that on the one side there are psychical Gestalten, and on the other psychical energies without any definite psychical locus.

Sometimes the habit, for example in "compulsive habits," may with the waxing of the needs breed new psychical energies. Sometimes it may bring about access to energies which have not theretofore been available to the act involved; when in drug addicts, for example, originally single and occasional pleasurable experiences are "absorbed into the vital needs"③ and ever broader and deeper strata of the person are drawn into this addiction.

---

① Thus, there is still no reference to any such thing as the tensions in a dynamic whole.

② LEWIN, *Zeitschr. f. Psychol.* , 1917, 77, 212-247; Psychol. Forsch , 1922, 1, 191-302; 1922, 2, 65-140. SIGMAR, Ü)ber die Hemmung bei der Realisation eines Willensaktes, *Arch f. d. ges. Psychol.* , 1925, 52, 92.

③ E. JOËL and F. FRÄNKEL, Zur Pathologie der Gewöhnung, II in *Theraple der Gegenwart* , 1926, 67, 60. Further *Der Kokainismus* , Springer, Berlin, 1924. Cf also W. MCDOUGALL, *Social Psychology* , Methuen, London, 1908.

In the case, however, of a mere "habit of execution"①(that is, the fusion, formation, or re-formation of certain actions) it is in principle impossible to regard them as the cause (in any full sense) of the psychical events. ②

These propositions, first valid for habit and association, can be generalized to every kind of coupling. For *connections are never causes of events*, wherever and in whatever form they may occur. Rather, in order that the bound or coupled complex move, in other

---

① LEWIN, *loci. cit.*
② That one must assume further factors besides associations as the causes of psychical events has long been said. Among experimental investigations which have advanced in this direction, should be mentioned, above all, those of Ach (*op. cit*) and Poppelreuter (Über die Ordnung des Vorstellungslaufes, *Arch. f. d. ges Psychol.* 1913, 3, 371). Selz (*Die Geielze des geordneten Denkvelaufs*, Spemann, Stuttgart, 1913, and *Zur Psychologie des produktiven Denkens und des Irrtums*, Cohen, Bonn, 1922) exhibited the significance of nonassociative forces, the determining tendencies, chiefly in the field of particular intellectual processes. He also remarked that "even in investigations of memory the existing determinations can by no means always be neglected" (*op. , cit. , pp.* 283-290). To be sure, as late as 1920 the same author in a polemic against attacks from the side of association psychology (Komplextheorie und Gestalttheoric, *Zeitschr. f. Psychol*, 1920, 83, 215), expressly remarks, for example, that the actualization of complexes of knowledge "can also occur without a determination directed upon them," which together with a number of other statements seems to me unequivocally to mean that association as one possible cause of psychological events cannot be denied. Since Selz recently (Zur Psychologie der Gegenwart, *Zeitschr. f. Psychol.* , 99, 166 ff.) refers to the above and similar sentences in raising questions of priority I should like merely to remark without going into these questions that I should be very glad if I might interpret these references to mean that Selz, in any event at present, regards the fundamental thesis of my work as experimentally proven; namely, that not only must other causes of psychical events be recognized besides association but that association presents in principle no motor for psychical events.

words that a process occur (and this holds also for purely machine systems), energy capable of doing work must be set free. *One must therefore inquire of every psychical event whence the causal energies come.*

To say that couplings are not to be regarded as sources of energy is by no means to say that there are no couplings, or that their presence or absence is unimportant. They are, indeed, not sources of energy for events, but the form of the event depends in large degree upon them. Thus, for example, the re-formation of certain common action unities plays a very important role. (To be sure, if we are to advance to laws, the practice must be given up of subsuming every case in which an earlier occurrence can be established under the concept of "experience." Instead of this senseless conglomerate, a number of phenomena will have to be distinguished which obey laws of very different nature: the enriching or changing of the fund of knowledge; the learning and practicing of tasks of different kinds; and, of essentially different nature, the process which one may characterize as fixation of impulses or needs.)

When the concept of energy is used here and when later those of force, of tension, of systems, and others are employed, the question may be left quite open as to whether or not one should ultimately go back to physical forces and energies. In any event, these concepts are, in my opinion, general logical fundamental concepts of all dynamics (even though their treatment in logic is usually very much neglected). They are in no way a special possession of physics but are seen, for example, in economics (although up to the present less precisely developed), without requiring the assumption that therefore one must derive economics in some way from physics.

Quite independently, then, of the question of the ultimate derivability of psychology from physics, the treatment of causal dynamic problems compels psychology to employ the fundamental concepts of dynamics, not, as frequently in the past, promiscuously, but in the development of a differentiated concept-formation in dynamic fields. Physical analogies may often be drawn without damage to clarification. On the other hand, it is always necessary carefully to avoid certain very easy errors, for example, in the adequate comprehension of the psychical field forces; and it must always be kept in mind that we have to do with forces in a *psychical* field and not in the physical environment.

On the question of the psychical sources of energy, the following should be noted briefly.

The stimulus itself may perhaps be considered in many perceptual processes as being at the same time and to a certain degree the source of energy for the process in the sensory sector (e. g. , in the field of vision). In actual behavior and emotions, however, as when one undertakes a journey upon the receipt of a telegram or becomes furious at a question, the physical intensity of the stimulus obviously plays no essential role. Hence it has been customary to speak of a "release, " of a process which has been represented by the analogy of the explosion of a keg of powder by the discharging spark.

This conclusion will nevertheless have to be fundamentally changed in two directions.

1. Since the conception of the perceptual world as a sum of sensory elements must be given up, perception presenting us rather with actual things and events, which have definite meaning, the stimulus to perception (*e. g.* , the disfigured countenance of a

wounded soldier) must be assessed not according to its physical intensity but according to its psychological reality. This sort of perceptual experience may carry with it immediately certain purposes or create certain needs which were not before present. To discuss whether and if so to what extent such perceptual experiences are themselves to be regarded as sources of energy is probably not very fruitful in the present state of research. In any event, there may occur reorganizations [*Umschichtungen*, literally "restratifications"] through which available [*arbeitsfähige*] energy becomes free; in other words tense psychical systems may arise which were not present before, at least in this form. Nevertheless, there is much evidence that the essential amount of energy of a psychical process does not flow out of the momentary perceptions themselves.

2. This is, to be sure, not equivalent to saying that we have here to do with a "release" in the sense of the function of the spark in the cartridge or the driving rod in the steam engine.

a. When, for example, a child wants to get to a certain object, perhaps a piece of chocolate, the direction of the process will change if a sharp edge or a cross dog threatens the path or if some other barrier is present. In the simplest case the child will make a detour and then strive toward the object in a new direction. In brief, the totality of the forces present in the psychical field, including the attractive object, will control the direction of the process, according, indeed, to laws which may be established in detail. Thus far then we have to do only with the well-known and fundamental fact that *forces control the course of a process*.

It holds no less for psychology than for physics that no unequivocal (definite) relation obtains between the magnitude of the forces and the amount of energy of the process. On the contrary, relatively slight forces may, when the whole field is appropriately formed, control relatively large amounts of energy. Conversely, large forces and tensions may go hand in hand with slight energies. Thus a relatively slight change in the kind or direction of these forces may direct a process permanently into other paths. (This plays a very large part in, for example, the technique of social dominance.)

In every process *the forces in the inner and outer environment are changed by the process itself*. This change of the forces controlling the processes may, however, be of very different degree in different processes, so that in many processes this change is not essential to the course of the process itself, while in others the course of the process itself is fundamentally influenced thereby.

The latter case, with which psychology frequently has to deal, is a process of the following type. Every movement starting upon the perception of certain objects changes at the same time the position, relative to the individual, of the field forces controlling the behavior. It can thus prescribe new directions for the process, for example, the child is driven out of his original direction by obstacles. Thus there occurs a *steering* of the process by the perceptual field. [1]

A continuous control of the process by the forces of the outer psychological environment occurs when the activities are not (or are in only slight degree) autochthonous, or when the forces inherent in the course of the process as such are small relative to the

---

[1] W. KÖHLER, Gestaltprobleme und Anfänge einer Gestalttheorie, *Jahresbericht d. ges. Physiol.*, 1922-1924, 537 ff. Compare also as a concrete example from tes oculomotor system: K. Lewin and K. Sakuma, Die Sehrichtung monokularer und binokularer Objekte bei Bewegung und das Zustandekommen des Tiefeneffektes, *Psychol. Forsch.*, 1925, 6, 339.

field forces. For example, a child is faced by a disagreeable situation in which he is threatened from different sides. If, instead of thrusting through with a single impulse and without succeeding on the other hand in inwardly insulating himself against his impressions, he moves slowly through this field of positive and negative valences, ① then the steering of the process by the field forces comes to full expression even in every little phase of the movement.

As a rule, however, the action process is not to be regarded as such a continuous flow. Rather, it proceeds typically in successive action steps which themselves form largely autochthonous wholes: for example, the running toward the chocolate as far as the first obstacle, the pause for reflection, the angry reaching with the arm, another pause, a detour around the barrier. In such an action process with a marked whole character (when, that is, the forces which inhere in it as an autochthonous process are large as against the forces of the field) no continuous control of each individual phase of the autochthonous action unity by the forces of the field occurs. But the steering by the field forces still holds in the large, especially for the succession of the action wholes, a circumstance of fundamental significance in, for example, the theory of detour behavior.

Whether the control of the process by the field of force occurs in this latter manner or in the sense of a continuous steering depends, on the one hand, upon the integral firmness and the forces of the action process itself and, on the other hand, upon the strength of the forces in the field. Hence, changes in either of these circumstances lead to essential changes in the course of the

---

① For the meaning of this term, see p. 77 (with note).

process. At all events, the steering processes are of fundamental significance for the whole field of impulsive and controlled behavior.

(The concept of steering is, to be sure, used in a still narrower sense: for cases in which a relatively independent steering process changes the forces of the field continuously in such a way that a second simultaneously occurring process is thereby steered in its course. A physical example of this is the amplifying tube.)

b. Objects which, like the chocolate in the above example, form the goal of the process are also to be regarded primarily as objects from which a force, steering the process, goes out in the same way as from a sharp edge, from a breakable object, or from the symmetrical or asymmetrical disposition of objects on both sides of the path taken by the child. [1]But they may in addition have been the occasion for the evocation of those needs out of which, as a reservoir of energy, the process in this case ultimately flows (which does not need to hold in the case of, for example, the sharp edge). If the child had been supersatiated with sweets, the whole process would not have occurred. To this extent, then, the chocolate has here also a second function.

The presence or absence of this sort of reservoir of energy, that is, of certain needs or need-like tensions, makes itself noticeable again and again in various forms in the whole field of the psychology of will and impulse. It plays a part when the interest in or effort toward a goal ceases with *satiation* of the psychical need in-

---

[1] Cf. A. HERMANN-CZINER, Zur Entwicklungspsychologie des Umgehens mit Gegenständen, *Zeitschr. f. angew. Psychol.*, 1923 22, 337, BARTELT andLAU, Beobachtungen an Ziegen, *Psychol. Forsch.*, 1924, 5, 340. DEXLER, Das Gestaltprinzip und die moderne Tierpsychologie, *Lotos*, 1921, 69, 143.

volved; when an intended act, after its completion (or the completion of a substitute act), is not repeated upon the occurrence of a second similar occasion; when a well-established act fails to occur even upon the occurrence of the habitual stimulus, if certain energies do not impel the individual to the act. Finally, this fact has basic significance for the problems of the *affective* process. The close connection described above (Sec. *a*) between the perceptual field and the course of the process must not let us forget that *the forces which control the course of the process remain without effect or simply do not arise when no psychical energies are present, when there exists no connection with tense psychical systems which keep the process in motion.*

The occasions which set need energies free may, as in the above examples, be decisive forces for the special course of the process. Precisely this double function is frequently realized in psychology. It is closely related to a group of especially marked reformations of the field by the process of the activity itself.

c. The attainment and eating of the chocolate are especially significant for the change of the field forces because the coming into possession of the chocolate and the beginning of the satiation process imply not only a change in the position of the field forces but at the same time a profound change of the psychical tensions which produce the behavior.

The perception of an object or event can thus:

1. Cause the formation of a definite tense psychical system which did not previously exist, at least in that form. Such an experience immediately produces an intention, or awakens a desire, which was not previously present.

2. An already existing state of tension, which may go back to a purpose, a need, or a half-finished activity, is interested in

[*spricht an*] a certain object or event, which is experienced as an attraction (or repulsion), in such a way that this particular tense system now obtains control of the motorium. We shall say of such objects that they possess a "*valence.*"

3. Valences of this sort operate at the same time (as do certain other experiences) as field forces in the sense that they steer the psychical processes, above all the motorium.

4. Certain activities, caused in part by valences, lead to satiation processes or to the carrying out of intentions and hence to the reduction of the tensions in the basic system involved to an equilibrium at a lower level of tension.

The particular processes by which the sight of the chocolate (*Sec. a*) causes the behavior cannot here be discussed in detail. It might be that the available energy already present in a psychical system momentarily in a state of tension is simply helped to break through to the motorium. Or it might be that, upon the presence of the valence, a system which until then has not been capable of work undergoes a radical transposition [*Umlagerung*] of such kind that now energy becomes free. One might even think at times of resonance phenomena and so on. It is nevertheless improbable that discharges in the special sense of the pure machine-like discharge play a considerable role. The fact that impulses show, as a rule, an inner, real [*sachliche*] relation to the special psychical energy sources on which they draw speaks against this assumption.

There are, naturally, all transitional degrees between valences which set free available energy and the field forces which control the remainder of the process. This does not affect the necessity of inquiring always as to the energy sources of the process involved.

This holds also for cases of steering in the narrower sense of the word. Here also one may not neglect the fact that the slight forces and energies necessary for steering are not identical with the energies of the steered system and that the effect fails to occur if the flow of energy to the primary process fails. (Analogy: failure of the plate circuit in an amplifying tube)

We cannot here discuss the possible sources of psychical energy as to content. At all events, the needs and the central goals of the will are important in this connection. Nevertheless some general questions, which are appropriate here, as to the structure of psychical energetic systems must be considered.

Psychical Energies and the Structure of the Mind

It is customary, at present, again to emphasize somewhat more strongly the unity of the mind. This occurs doubtless as a protest against the atomistic dissection of the mind into piecemeal discrete sensations, feelings, and other experiences. The question of unity of the mind is, however, still very ambiguous, and in order to avoid misunderstandings we shall later (see page 61) have to mention a number of questions which might be raised in this connection. Suffice it here to note that we propose to discuss not the whole problem complex indicated by the ambiguous term "unity of the mind," but rather a definite problem concerning the psychical energies.

First, the following general considerations should be noted: Exactly when problems of wholeness are central, one must beware of the tendency to make the wholes outwardly as extensive as possible. Above all, it must be clear that concrete research must always go beyond vague generalities to inquire about the structure [*Strukturicrtheit*] of the wholes concerned into subwholes, and about the special boundaries of the superordinate systems determining the particular case.

There is an inclination, probably correct, to regard the unity of the whole region of the psychical which makes up an individual as relatively greater than the unity of physical nature. But the proposition "Everything is related to everything else," which by no means adequately portrays the conditions in physical nature, ① is also not wholly valid for the unity of the mind, although in both cases it contains an element of truth.

Twenty-five years ago I awoke, happy that I did not have to go to school that day, I flew a kite, came home late to lunch, ate a great deal of dessert, and played in the garden; these and all the other experiences that filled the following days and weeks may be reproduced under certain circumstances (perhaps in hypnosis) and are hence in that sense not dead. Doubtless, indeed, the whole of childhood experience may have a decisive significance for all development and consequently also for present behavior; moreover, certain special experiences may still have a very acute significance for present psychical processes. Thus each single everyday experience of the past may somehow influence the present psychic life. But this influence is in most cases to be evaluated in just the same way as the influence of some specific changes in a fixed star upon the physical processes in my study: *it is not that an influence exists but that the influence is extremely small, approximately zero.*

This lack of influence is by no means peculiar to experiences widely separated in time. I look out the window and notice the movements of a column of smoke from a chimney. To be sure, such an experience may in a special case profoundly influence the

---

① W. KOHLER, *Die physischen Gestalten*, Weltkreisverlag, Erlangen, 1920.

rest of the psychic life; but in general every psychical event is by no means related to each of the thousands of other daily little experiences. Behavior would not be changed or would be changed imperceptibly if a great many of our experiences did not occur or occurred in other ways.

The proposition "In the psychical, everything is related to everything else" is inadequate, however, for other reasons than that it is necessary to separate the significant from the insignificant. It does not suffice to say instead: "To be sure, not every experience, but certainly every profound or significant one, is related to all other psychical events." Even such a quantitatively improved proposition, so to speak, remains inadequate.

The relations of psychical events to each other and the breadth of influence of each single experience upon the other psychical processes depend not simply upon their strength, indeed not even upon their real importance. The individual psychical experiences, the actions and emotions, purposes, wishes and hopes, are rather *imbedded in quite definite psychical structures, spheres of the personality, and whole processes*. One may, for example, be interrupted in the midst of a conversation by a telephone call about some relatively indifferent matter which is settled in a few words. In this case the total situation may lead to a more rapid completion of the telephone conversation. But the individual experiences, wishes, and purposes which dominated the preceding conversation and which dominate it again upon its resumption are as a rule practically insignificant for the telephone conversation, unless unusually strong tensions are involved.

Whether, and if so how, two psychological events influence each other depends to a large extent upon whether they are imbedded in the same or in different total processes or upon the *re-*

lation which these different psychical complexes have to each other. Thus an experience, weak in itself, may be of essential significance to a perhaps temporally relatively distant psychical event, while much stronger experiences which belong to another system may be practically without effect even upon temporally nearer processes.

The context which is built up in memory is also not dependent upon relations of intensity and time but is dominated by its actual belongingness to the same total process. ①

This belonging to quite definite psychical systems is also in high degree characteristic of the dynamically basic psychical tensions and energies.

The individual psychical needs or the tensions which result from certain processes and experiences often have, of course, a certain connection with each other. Thus it may happen, for example, that affective energies out of one system may go over into another (perhaps those resulting from events in vocational life into processes in family life) and come to expression in the latter. Thus it may happen, also, that the satiation of a need produces consatiation of functionally adjacent needs. The intimacy of this communication varies greatly, however, among different tense psychical systems. The general tendency to communication seems also to vary in strength in certain psychical conditions and in different individuals. Nevertheless it must not be forgotten that each dynamic psychical system does not have clear communication with every other, but that the communication in many cases is extremely weak, indeed practically nonexistent.

---

① W. POPPELREUTER, Über die Ordnung des Vorstellungslaufes, Arch. f. d ges. Psycho. ,1912,25,208-349.

If there were not this sometimes astoundingly complete segregation of different psychical systems from each other, if there were instead a permanently real unity of the mind of such kind that all the psychical tensions present at a given time had to be regarded as tensions in a uniform, unitary, closed system, no ordered action would be possible. Only the really extreme exclusion of the majority of all the simultaneously present psychical tensions, some of which are frequently much stronger, and the practically exclusive connection of the motor sphere with one special region of inner tensions make an ordered action possible. This exclusion for the purpose of a definite action does not always occur by means of temporary elimination of all the other tensions present in the mind; the psychical tensions arise of themselves in definite psychical structures or regions which have already been formed, or are then formed, by means of certain dynamic processes which we shall not here discuss.

Let us summarize the considerations of this section: The mind is often considered to be the very prototype of unity. The unity of consciousness, the unity of the person, are often used as the basis and self-evident presupposition of far-reaching speculations; and the integration of the individual, especially in its psychical aspects, seems closely connected with the special nature, the absolute uniqueness, which it is customary to ascribe to an individual.

Upon closer examination, however, we find here a whole range of problems of unity. The question of the unity of consciousness is not identical with the question of the unity of the whole region of psychical forms and processes, of tense and not-tense psychical systems, the totality of which may be designated as the mind. Further, it is at least questionable whether that which may be called the ego or self, ① the unity of which is important for many problems, is not merely one system or complex of systems, a functional part region within this psychical totality (see page 61).

We are speaking here not of this problem of the unity of the self but only of the problem of the dynamic homogeneity of the mind.

Further, the psychical totality which is Mr. X is at least different from that of Mr. R. and from that of the child Q. This difference, which constitutes the individuality (*Eigenart*) of the person involved, his individuality in the sense of that which sets his nature apart from the individuality of other individuals, is probably evident in some way as always the same special, characteristic individuality, in each of its processes, parts, and expressions. Questions of individuality in this sense, that is, such questions as whether such identical characteristics of all the processes in the given mind are demonstrable and in what they consist (a basic question for individual psychology), are also here excluded. Such individuality or uniqueness of all that belongs to the same psychical totality (mind) might also be present even if the latter presented no firm unity, for example, if each of these totalities were comparable to a whole physical world and did not possess the unity of a physical organism or even of a single homogeneous closed system. We are not here discussing the question of the identical characteristics of processes which belong to the same psychical totality but solely the question of the causal-dynamic homogeneity of the mind, the question of the presence of relatively segregated energetic systems.

---

① Cf. W. JAMES, *Principles of Psychology*, Holt, New York, 1890.

Finally, it should be noted that the existence of relatively segregated psychical energetic systems has nothing to do with the distinction of various psychical abilities such as memory, will, or understanding. On the contrary, the repudiation of sharp boundaries between these fields of inquiry is actually a presupposition of the present line of thought.

The next result of these considerations is as follows. Doubtless there exists in certain spheres, for example, within the motorium, a relatively high degree of unity. But however high one may estimate the degree of unity in a psychical totality, the recognition that within the mind there are regions of extremely various degrees of coherence remains an exceedingly important condition of more penetrating psychological research. We have to do not with a single unitary system but with a great number of such strong configurations (*starken Gestaltern*), some of which stand in communication with others and thus form component parts of a more inclusive weak configuration [*schwache Gestalt*]. Other psychical structures, again, may show no real connection worth mentioning. The difference between the conception of the mind as a single whole, uniform in all its parts, and the conception of the mind as a sum of experiences is only formal and not in any way relevant to research. It is necessary, however, to recognize the natural structure of the mind, its psychical systems, strata, and spheres. It is necessary always to determine where we have to deal with wholes and where not.

The formation of definite psychical systems is related in part to the ontogenctic development of the mind. It therefore also shows, as does that development, a specifically historical component.

The Tendency to Equilibrium: The Dynamic Firmness of Boundaries and Relative Segregation of Psychical Systems

The following considerations lead to similar conclusions as to the structure of the psychical in dynamic respects.

The psychical processes may often, by the use of certain points of view, be deduced from the tendency to equilibrium (as may biological processes in general, as well as physical, economic, or other processes). The transition from a state of rest to a process, as well as change in a stationary process, may be derived from the fact that the equilibrium at certain points has been disturbed and that then a process in the direction of a new state of equilibrium sets in.

In carrying through this line of thought, however, one must pay special attention to certain points.

1. The process moves in the direction of a state of equilibrium only for the *system as a whole*. Part processes may at the same time go on in opposed directions,① a circumstance which is of the greatest significance for, for example, the theory of detour behavior. It is hence important to take the system whole which is dominant at the moment as basis. Indeed, the concrete task of research will often consist precisely in the search for this determinative system, its boundaries and its internal structure. From these the particular events may then be directly deduced by means of the above-mentioned general proposition.

2. A state of equilibrium in a system does not mean, further, that the system is without tension. Systems can, on the contrary, also come to equilibrium in a state of tension (e. g., a spring under tension or a container with gas under pressure). The occurrence

---

① KOHLER, *Die physischen Gestalten.*

of this sort of system, however, presupposes a certain firmness of boundaries and actual segregation of the system from its environment (both of these in a functional, not a spatial, sense). If the different parts of the system are insufficiently cohesive to withstand the forces working toward displacement (*i. e.*, if the system shows insufficient internal firmness, if it is fluid), or if the system is not segregated from its environment by sufficiently firm walls but is open to its neigh-boring systems, stationary tensions cannot occur. Instead, there occurs a process in the direction of the forces, which encroaches upon the neighboring regions with diffusion of energy and which goes in the direction of an equilibrium at a lower level of tension in the total region. The presupposition for the existence of a stationary state of tension is thus a certain firmness of the system in question, whether this be its own inner firmness or the firmness of its walls.

We are here using the concept of the firmness of a system solely in a functional-dynamic sense without thereby making any special assertions about the material of the system concerned. Naturally, the firm walls of a system may be composed of a surrounding system in a state of tension. In this case the above-described presuppositions hold again for both systems as a whole.

The occurrence of such tense systems is very characteristic of psychical processes, at least after infancy. A tendency may readily be observed toward immediate discharge of tension (to a state of equilibrium at the lowest possible state of tension). Such an equilibrium, perhaps through the fulfillment of a wish, is, however, often not immediately possible because of the character of the total situation. It may be that the equilibration can only gradually be established, for example, by means of long-continued effort, or it may be that it is for the time wholly unattainable. Then there arises, at first, a stationary tense system which may, when a very profound disturbance of equilibrium is involved, embrace broad psychical strata. The child to whom an important wish is denied may throw itself upon the ground and remain there in a state of tension, rigid as if transfixed by despair. As a rule, however (or after some time), there results a special tense system. The unfulfilled wish, for example, or the half-finished activity does not cripple the whole motorium or charge the entire mind with tension, but there remains a special tense system which may not appear in experience for a long time and which may influence the course of the other psychical processes only slightly. On appropriate occasion, however, it may assert itself most strongly (e. g. , by the resumption of the half-finished activity).

In many such tense systems, even when a direct equilibration of tension (e. g. , by fulfillment of the wish or completion of the activity at a later time) does not occur, a discharge may yet eventually result. It may be that the equilibration of tension results from a substitute completion (compensation) ; or it may be that the segregation of the system is not so complete as to exclude equilibration with the adjacent systems (somewhat in the nature of diffusion). Very frequently, however, the tensions of such special systems persist over long periods or may be, at most, only reduced. Hence *there arc systems of very considerable functional firmness and isolation in the psychical.*

In the adult, at least, there exists as a rule a great number of relatively separate tense systems which are influenced, to be sure, by a general discharge of the whole person but which can only rarely be actually discharged thereby, and then usually incompletely. They form reservoirs of energy for action, and without their very considerable independence ordered action would be impossible.

The experimental investigations of half-finished activities [1] also show impressively that the mind is dynamically by no means a perfectly closed unity. If, for example, in a series of experimental tasks several are interrupted by the experimenter before completion, there only seldom results a general state of tension which increases with each new unfinished task, and in these few cases only a slight general tension occurs. Instead of a single total state of tension, which pushes toward discharge in any random way (e. g., by further work on already finished tasks), there results a number of relatively independent tense systems which demonstrate their separateness in various directions. Only in the case of very strong tensions does the state of tension usually extend itself far over the neighboring regions.

The problem of whether the psychical is a single homogeneous system in which practically everything is related to everything else or whether relatively separate dynamic systems are present, is, incidentally, not identical with the problem of the unity of the self, which becomes acute in the phenomenon of split personality, although the two problems have certain relations to each other.

The question thereby raised is extremely difficult and far reaching. Its concrete discussion necessarily presupposes a much more advanced state of the experimental investigation of psychical structure. The following remarks, which are to be regarded merely as a groping beginning, grow out of the effort to avoid certain easy misinterpretations and at the same time to indicate some theoretical possibilities to the discussion of which we are repeatedly brought by the concrete experimental work on our problems.

---

[1] Cf. OVSIANKINA and ZEIGARNIK, below, Chap. VIII, p. 242

It would be natural from Gestalt theoretical considerations to understand the self in terms of the psychical totality perhaps as its structural individuality. As a matter of fact, some such notion is basic to the concept of character, for the adequate conception of which one must start, not from the presence of certain isolated properties (traits), but from the whole of the person. If from this beginning one comes to the problem of the psychical dynamic systems, the attempt will in all probability be made to identify the self with the whole of the psychical totality.

A number of facts, however, drive one in the opposite directioji to the view that a special region, within the psychical totality, must be defined as the self in the narrower sense. Not every psychically existent system would belong to this central self. Not every one to whom I say "*Du*," not all the things, men, and environmental regions which I know and which may perhaps be very important to me, belong to my self. This selfsystem would also have in functional respects—this is most important—a certain unique position. Not every tense psychical system would stand in communication with this self. Tensions which have to do with the self would also have functionally a special significance in the total psychical organism (see the next section), and it is possible that within this region differently directed tensions would tend to equilibrium considerably more strongly and that relatively isolated dynamic systems within it could much less readily occur.

One would have recourse to such a hypothesis or to similar ones only when weighty facts of dynamics, for example, in the field of emotion, drive him to it. It is necessary here only to note that the distinction of relatively separate psychical systems leaves open various possibilities for the question of the unity and homogeneity of the self.

In summary, the following should at all events be remarked. We have seen above that it is necessary for the investigation of causal relations and dynamic relations to pay especial attention to the psychical tensions and sources of energy. *These psychical tensions and energies belong to systems which are in themselves dynamic unities and which show a greater or less degree of abscission.* The structure of the dynamic system involved and the presence (in greater or less degree) or the absence of communication with various other psychical systems, as well as every change in boundary conditions, are hence of the greatest significance for the psychical process, for the equilibration of psychical tensions, and for the flow of psychical energy.

In the treatment of problems of the psychical energies and tensions one must therefore never forget that they have a position in definite psychical systems and hence must be treated from those points of view (Gestalt theoretical) which are valid for such systems.

Psychical Processes as Life Processes

In the treatment of the psychical sources of energy as dynamic systems which are in variously close communication with each other, one must not forget that in dealing with psychical processes one is dealing with life processes. This circumstance had naturally to be left in the background of the preceding discussion since in the present status of the problem of the psychical forces and energies we must at first be concerned with settling some general primitive questions. Hence in order to avoid misunderstandings it should be emphasized at least briefly.

The mere distinction of different degrees of communication between the dynamic systems will probably not suffice for the adequate description of the psychical structure. One will probably have to distinguish also layers or strata [*Schichten*] of different functional significance.

For example, the special significance which the motor process possesses for the equilibration of psychical tensions, the way in which the motorium may come into communication with certain psychical systems, and the circumstances under which this communication changes give to the motor sphere a relatively unique functional position. Similarly one may inquire as to the functional significance of conscious thought or of clear imagery. (Even within the perceptual process one will probably have to go beyond the inadequate distinction between central and peripheral processes to the distinction of special functional strata.)

Further, changes clearly of the types of development, of maturation, of growth, and of regulation play a great role.

This holds hardly less of the psychical energy sources also, for example, of the psychical needs. The needs show a marked ontogenesis. This is true not only specifically, of such needs as the sexual, but also generally. The typical small child enjoys throwing things down; later he pushes the things under the carpet; as a somewhat older child, he likes to hide and to play "hide and seek"; even certain lies of children are often largely "hiding." Or the young child likes at first to open and shut a certain little box; later still, sitting on the arm of his mother, he prefers to open and shut a door; still later, when he can walk, this door game is frequently extended indefinitely and he likes in addition to open and close all drawers. In these cases and in similar ones it is necessary always to follow not only the development of ability in certain performances but also the development of the inclinations, the needs, the interests. ① In following the concrete need and the individual child it is important to note the development in the content of the need, where an increase occurs and where a decrease, where an originally broad need is narrowed down to a certain small sphere of valences, and where, on the other hand, a quite special inclination extends to neighboring regions. In this connection one cannot depend upon the identity of the performance as the sole criterion of belonging to the same need. Outwardly quite different acts may belong close together in respect to their sources of energy, while outwardly quite similar acts, perhaps playing with dolls (or with building blocks, etc), may be differently based in the two-year-old child and the four-year- old child.

Such developments frequently show a rhythm like, for example, the biological development of the egg: they occur in steps which are within themselves largely autonomous. The concepts of maturation and of crisis become essential.

Superimposed upon the ontogenetic development is the quicker rhythm of the waxing and waning of the inclinations and needs (psychical satiation and return to an unsatiated condition).

Physiology, among the fundamental problems of which the energetic economy of the organism belongs, has been treated up to the very recent past as a "physics of life." Energy exchange has been studied most exactly, but it was forgotten that these processes are here imbedded in the organism, and so the really biological problems of energy processes were neglected. With the peculiar position which energy exchange, as a moment of the life process, acquires in biology, certain specific problems are presented; the

---

① K. G. LAU, *Beiträge zur Psychologie der Jugend in der Pubertatszeit*, 2d ed. , Beltz Langensalza, 1924.

attempt has been made to designate these by the term *"Mittel organischen Geschehen"*

An analogous danger and an analogous difficulty, which become clear in carrying through the problems on concrete material, exist for the psychological problems of energy as well. For example, it is shown that certain systems with certain tensions and velocities of equilibration may be deduced from the degree of communication with adjacent regions of the system concerned and from the relation of their tensions; and in the treatment of these one can in principle succeed with the abovementioned or related basic concepts of energy processes. But there also occur, occasionally, rather abrupt regulation phenomena (*e. g.*, the sort of thing usually spoken of as the intervention of self-control or a willing), which cannot be deduced from the principles originally taken as basis, principles which have proved adequate up to this point. In such cases the transition to more comprehensive regions (which, when treated as total systems, may clear up what was at first puzzling) is sometimes useful. It cannot here be discussed whether the explanation may always be attained in this way, by recourse to wholes of varying extent and varying strength, or whether the processes of psychical growth and maturation require the use of essentially other conceptual structures than those above described. For here we are faced with questions which embrace the whole field of life. [1] In any case the same concept of the dynamic whole in the pregnant sense of the dynamic Gestalt will play a decisive role, and a broad field is indicated to psychological experimental research which promises to yield important clarification toward the solution of the general problems of life.

---

[1] Cf. K. LEWIN, *Der Begriff der Genese*, Springer, Berlin, 1922.

Chapter Ⅲ
Environmental Forces In Child Behavior And Development[1]

We have here to deal only with the psychological influence of the environment. This does not mean that the somatic effects of environment, for example, of nutrition or climate, do not have great psychological significance. On the contrary, the somatic as well as the psychological influence of the environment is constantly operating on the entire child.

Introduction

It has long been recognized that the psychological influence of environment on the behavior and development of the child is ex-

---

[1] Reprinted from CARL MURCHISON, *Handbook of Child Psychology*, Clark Univ. Press, Worcester, Mass., 2d ed. rev., Chap. 14, 1933, by permission.

tremely important. ① Actually, all aspects of the child's behavior, hence instinctive and voluntary behavior, play, emotion, speech, expression, are codetermined by the existing environment. Some recent theories, notably those of Watson and Adler, assign to environment so predominant an influence upon development that hereditary factors are usually neglected. ② Stern's theory of convergence emphasizes, on the contrary, that a predisposition and an environmental influence must operate in the same direction in order to effect a particular mode of behavior. ③

Average and Individual Milieu.

The fact of environmental influence has been thoroughly established in various ways in recent years by the psychological study of various environments. For example, the intelligence of country children has been compared with that of city children, ④

---

① H. TAINK, Dc l'Intelltgcncc (2 vols) Paris, 1870 (3d ed., 1878) On Intelligence (trans, by T. D. Haye and rev. with additions by the author, 2 vols.), Holt &- Williams, New York, 1889.

② J. B. WATSON, *Behaviorism*, People's Instit. Publ. Co., New York, 1924-1925 (rev. ed., Norton, New York, 1930); A ADLI-R, *Über den nervosen Charakter. Grundznge cincr vergleichenden Individualpsychologie und Psychotherapie*, Bergmann, Munich and Wiesbaden, 1912 (4th ed., 1928). *The Neurotic Constitution: Outlines of a Comparative Individualistic Psychology and Psychotherapy* (trans by B. Glueck and J. E. Lind), Moffat, Yard, New York, 1917.

③ W. STERN, *Psychologie der frnhen Kindheit, bis zum sechslen Li'bcnijahre*, Quelle &- Meyer, Lcipzig, 1914 (6th ed., rev., 1930). *Psychology of Early Childhood, up to the Sixth Year of Age* (trans, from the 3d German ed. by A Harwell), Holt, New York, Allen, London, 1924 (2d ed., rev., 1930).

④ E HAUCK, Zur difTerenticllen Psychologie des Industrie- und Landkindes, *Jenacr Beitr. z. Jugend- und Erzichnngspychol*. Beltz, Langensals, 1929, H E JONES, H S CONRAD, and M. B. BLANCHARD, Environmental Handicap in Mental Test Performance, *Univ. Calif, Psutbl. Pychol*, 1932, 5, 63-99.

and the significance of size of family and position among siblings has been investigated. ① Research upon foster children ② and twins③ has also played an important part. In the case of identical twins one can be sure of equivalent hereditary capacities and dispositions. Similarities in conduct in the face of differences in environment may thus yield important information as to the kind and strength of the effects of environment, on the one hand, or of heredity, on the other.

Present-day investigation of the environment uses primarily statistical methods. The average of as many school records as were obtainable for only children is compared, for example, with that of eldest, middle, and youngest children in families of three. Particular environmental factors may be excluded to a certain degree, for example, in the investigation of the effect of size of family or of position in the series of siblings, by including only children of approximately the same economic status. These investigations have brought to light a wealth of interesting facts; for example, that in certain social levels in Germany the number of children optimal for school achievement is three or four, but that in proletarian families, on the contrary, only children display, on the average, the

---

① A. BUSFMANN, Die Familie als Erlebnismilieu des Kindes, Zsch. f. Kinderforsch, 1929, 36, 17-32.

② B. S. BURKS, The Relative Influence of Nature and Nurture upon Menial Development; A comparative study of foster parent—foster child resemblance, 27th Yearbook, N. S. S. E, 1928, Pt. i, 219-316; F. N. FREEMAN, et al., The Influence on the Intelligence, School Achievement and Conduct of Foster Children, 27th Yearbook, N. S. S. E., 1928, Pt. 1, pp. 103-218.

③ A. GESELL, The Developmental Psychology of Twins, in A Handbook of Child Psychology, ed. by C. Murchison, Worcester, 1st ed., 1931.

best records. ①

Valuable and indispensable as these facts are, they can rarely offer more than hints toward the problem of the forces of the environment. For, in the investigation of the fundamental dynamic relations between the individual and the environment, it is essential to keep constantly in mind the actual total situation in its concrete individuality. The statistical method is usually compelled to define its groups on the basis not of purely psychological characteristics but of more or less extrinsic ones (such as the number of siblings), so that particular cases having quite different or even opposed psychological structure may be included in the same group. Especially to be emphasized, however, is the following consideration: the calculation of an average (e. g. , of "the one-year-old child") is designed to eliminate the "accidents" of the environment; the determination of the "average situation" (e. g. , of the average effect of the situation of being an only child) is to exclude individual variations. But the very relation that is decisive for the investigation of dynamics—namely, that of the position of the actual individual child in the actual, concrete, total situation—is thereby abstracted. ② An inference from the average to the concrete particular case is hence impossible. The concepts of the average child and of the average situation are abstractions that have no utility whatever for the investigation of dynamics. ③ The use of the average and the curve of distribution is unexceptionable

---

① A. BUSEMANN, *op. cit.*
② LEWIN, Conflict between Aristotelian and Galileian Modes of Thought in Psychology, *Jour. Gen. Psychol.* , 1931, 5, 141-177 (Chap I of this volume).
③ Thus the environment researches become, in general, the more fruitful the more attention is paid to a comprehension of the concrete total situation instead of to the number of cases.

where the object is to obtain a numerical value to characterize the position of a given individual in a group. For the discovery of dynamic laws, however, it does not suffice to segregate a single property or a phenotypically defined event, without regard to the structure of the total situation, and then to treat statistically as many as possible of the situations that display this characteristic.

The laws of falling bodies in physics cannot be discovered by taking the average of actual falling movements, say of leaves, stones, and other objects, but only by proceeding from so-called pure cases. Likewise in psychology the forces of the environment and the laws of their operation on child behavior can be discovered only by proceeding from certain total situations that are simple but well defined in their concrete individuality. Only in this way, which usually implies experiment and systematic variation of conditions, can general propositions be made which will hold good even for the actual individual child and the concrete particular case.

It may, of course, be questioned whether it is possible to speak scientifically (*i. e.*, with conceptual rigor) of dynamic properties, especially of forces of the psychological environment. ① Saying, for example, that bad treatment oppresses the child, or that praise exalts it, may obviously have a merely figurative significance.

In biology the tropism theory of Loeb attempted to establish in a scientifically precise way dynamic relations between environmental stimulation and the behavior of certain animals. It has, however, been shown that the circumstance of the animals' learn-

---

① The speculative philosophical grounds which might be urged against such an attempt are not considered here. In America they are usually of a physical nature, in Germany partly physical and partly *geisteswissenschaftlich*.

ing implies essential modification, [1] and, moreover, that their behavior depends pnon their momentary "mood."[2]

The biologists at present have in part gone back to an indeterministic or at least a nondynamic point of view according to which it is impossible to talk of a strictly lawful operation of environmental forces upon the individual. The influence of the environment is reduced essentially to the principle of trial and error. That is, the occurrence of the elementary actions is, so far as their relations to the environment are concerned, essentially accidental. The theory thus displays marked Darwinistic traits: it excludes the problem of a direct dynamic relation between environment and individual and limits the effect of the environment to the evocation of agreeable or disagreeable experiences. This theory may be regarded as an attempt to avoid the uncomfortable concept of environmental forces in a psychological sense and to derive an explanation of all behavior so far as this may be possible from the organism itself.

In child psychology also the principle of trial and error is regarded as fundamental for the development of child behavior. [3] On the other hand, it has recently been emphasized, first, that besides "experience" intrinsic maturation has fundamental significance for

---

[1] H. S. JENNINGS, *Behavior of the Lower Organisms*, Columbia Univ. Press, New York, 1906.

[2] F Au ERDES, *Neue Bahnen in der Lehre vom Verhalten der niederen Tiere*, Springer, Berlin, 1922.

[3] K. BtUiLKR, *Die geistige Entitleklung des Kindes*, Fischer, Jena, 1918 (new ed., 1929).

The Mental Development of the Child, Harcourt, Brace, New York, Kegan Paul, London, 1930.

child development [1] and, secondly, that besides blind trial and error there is insightful behavior. [2] In the case of insightful behavior the conduct of the individual is again brought into immediate relation to the special structure of the situation.

Individual, Environment, and Law.

Before we consider in detail the question of the psychological forces of the environment, we must discuss briefly the relation of the concepts environment, individual, and law. Environment is understood psychologically sometimes to mean the *momentary situation* of the child, at other times to mean the milieu, in the sense of the chief characteristics of the permanent situation. The following considerations apply to both concepts.

The actual behavior of the child depends in every case both upon his individual characteristics and upon the momentary structure of the existing situation. It is not possible, however, as is increasingly obvious, simply to single out one part to be attributed to the environment and another to be ascribed to the individual. But even when the primitive question, "Which is (in this case) more important, heredity or environment?" is given up, and the thesis is advanced that heredity and environment must work in the same direction in order to effect a certain mode of behavior, it is still assumed that hereditary dispositions may be defined as tendencies toward certain real modes of behavior without reference to a particular environment. Actually, reference to a specific environment, indeed, to an aggregate of specific environments, is indispensable to the concept of predisposition: a predisposition or indi-

---

[1] W. STERN, *Psydiologie der fruhcn Kindheit, bis zitm sechsten Lebensjahre*; K. KOFFKA, *The Growth of the Mind*; K. BUHLER, *op. cit.*

[2] K. KOFFKA, *op. cit.*

vidual characteristic of the person (P_a) (see page 72) cannot be defined by one specific mode of behavior, but only by an aggregate of modes of behavior of such kind that different environmental situations (E_1, E_2,...) are correlated with the modes of behavior (B_α, B_β,...) they elicit. The individual characteristics of a person as regards both predisposition and momentary state are thus to be defined not phenotypically but genotypically in dealing with dynamic problems.

The variations in behavior (B_α, B_β,...) with the same individual characteristics may be extremely large. A child that is negative in one situation may be shy in another and at ease in a third. Thus Kramer found in 100 per cent of his cases that bestial children lost their bestial behavior so completely wrhen brought into an appropriate environment that they might better be characterized as dainty.

Sensitivity to environment varies considerably in different individuals. In general it is greater in psychopathic than in normal children. [1]

In order for one individual characteristic[2](P_a) to be differentiated from another (P_b) it must be associated with different modes of behavior (B) in the same situations (E_1, E_2, E_n).

---

[1] A. HoMHURG. ER, *Vorlesungen ubcr Psychopathologie des Kindesalters*, Springer, Berlin, 1926.

[2] These considerations apply equally to a single characteristic or personality trait and to the whole personality.

$$P_a \begin{cases} E_1 \rightarrow B_\alpha \\ E_2 \rightarrow B_\beta \\ E_3 \rightarrow B_\gamma \\ \cdot \quad \cdot \\ \cdot \quad \cdot \\ \cdot \quad \cdot \\ E_n \rightarrow B_v \end{cases} \qquad P_b \begin{cases} E_1 \rightarrow B_\varepsilon \\ E_2 \rightarrow B_o \\ E_3 \rightarrow B_\alpha \\ \cdot \quad \cdot \\ \cdot \quad \cdot \\ \cdot \quad \cdot \\ E_n \rightarrow B_\mu \end{cases}$$

Thus, on the whole, different individuals may often display the same (or very similar) modes of behavior (B). Watson and Adler emphasize this similarity, and probably the ultimately possible modes of behavior of very many people might indeed show a considerable, if not a complete, measure of agreement. But this similarity of possible behavior does not imply similarity of the individuals, because it requires different situations to bring out (approximately) similar behavior. ① Neither similarity nor difference in behavior (B) permits of direct unequivocal inference of similarity or difference of individual characteristics or of situation factors. Inference of an individual characteristic (P) is possible only when the environmental situations (E) agree, inference of the situation only when the individuals agree. ②

In such cases, to be sure, the inference is unequivocal. Indeed, psychological laws really say the same thing in another way: from a certain total constellation—comprising a situation and an

---

① These situations must, in general, be the more different the more different he individuals.

② Even if the Watson-Adler thesis that the overwhelming majority of mankind is capable of most tasks were right, it would imply neither similarity of endowment nor the decisive importance of environmental factors.

individual—there results a certain behavior, $i.\ e.$, $(E_1, P_a) \rightarrow B_a$, or in general: $B = f(PE)$.

In reality, *the dynamics of environmental influences* can be investigated *only simultaneously with the determination of individual differences* and with *general psychological laws*. The discovery of psychological laws, on the other hand, yields important insights into the significance of environmental factors and individual characteristics. It will be plain from these considerations what vital importance the systematic especially the experimental—investigation of environmental changes with the same individual ① has for the study of the environmental forces.

Environmental Structure and Needs.

An analysis of environmental factors must start from a consideration of the total situation. Such an analysis hence presupposes an adequate comprehension and presentation in dynamic terms of the total psychological situation as its most important task.

Loeb's theory, by and large, identifies the biological environment with the physical environment: the dynamic factors of the environment consist of light of specific wave length and intensity, gravity, and others of similar nature. ② Others, notably von üexkiill, have shown, on the contrary, that the biological environment is to be characterized quite differently, namely, as a complex of foods, enemies, means of protection, etc. The same physical situation must thus be described for different species of animals as a

---

① Only in the same individual or in identical twins can one be sure of dealing with the same individual characteristics.

② W. J CROZIER, The Study of Living Organisms, Chap. II, *The Foundations of Experimental Psychology* (ed. by C. Murchison), Clark Univ. Press, Worcester, Mass., 1929, pp. 45-127.

specifically different phenomenal and functional world ["*Merk- und Wirkwelt*"].

In child psychology, also, the same physical environment must be quite differently characterized according to the age, the individual character, and the momentary condition of the child. The life-space of the infant is extremely small and undifferentiated. This is just as true of its perceptual as of its effective space. ① With the gradual extension and differentiation of the child's life-space, a larger environment and essentially different facts acquire psychological existence, and this is true also with respect to dynamic factors. The child learns in increasing degree to control the environment. At the same time and no less importantit becomes psychologically dependent upon a growing circle of environmental events.

When, for example, one breaks a doll a few feet away from a baby, the latter is unaffected, while the same procedure with a three-year-old usually calls forth energetic intervention.

The later extension of the child's space-time beyond the room and the family circle also means not only an intellectual survey of wider relations but, above all, an extension of the environmental objects and events upon which the child is psychologically immediately dependent.

The mere *knowledge* of something (*e. g.* ,of the geography of a foreign country, of the economic and political situation, or even of immediate family affairs) does not necessarily change the

---

① E. LAU, Beiträge zur Psychologic der frühen Kindheit II. *Zeittschr. Kinderforieh.* , 1931, 31, 481-501; C. BÜHLER, Kindheit und Jugend: Genese des Bewusstseins, *Psychol. Monographien*, 3, Hirzel, Leipzig, 1928. *From Birth to Maturity*. (In preparation.) S. FAJANS, Die Bedeutung der Entfernung fur die Stärke eines Aufforderungscharakters beim Säugling und Kleinkind, *Psychol. Forsch.* , 1933, 17, 213-267.

child's life-space more than superficially. On the other hand, psychologically critical facts of the environment, such as the friendliness or unfriendliness of a certain adult, may have fundamental significance for the child's life-space without the child's having a clear intellectual appreciation of the fact.

For the investigation of dynamic problems we are forced to start from the psychologically real environment of the child.

In the "objective" sense, the existence of a social bond is a necessary condition of the viability of an infant not yet able itself to satisfy its biologically important needs. This is usually a social bond with the mother in which, functionally, the needs of the baby have primacy.

But social facts, as essential constituents of the *psychobiological* environment, very early acquire dominant significance. This does not mean, of course, that when the child of three months reacts specifically to the human voice and to a friendly smile [1] the relation to certain individuals has already become a stable constituent of the child's psychological environment. The age at which this will occur depends essentially upon the individual endowment and the experiences of the child.

The fact that certain activities (*e. g.*, playing with certain toys) are allowed and others forbidden [2] (*e. g.*, throwing things or touching certain objects belonging to grown-ups) begins very early certainly before the age of two to play an important dynamic part in the structure of the child's environment. With the growth

---

[1] C. BÜLER and II. HKTZKR, Das erste Verständnis von Ausdruck im ersten Lebensjahr, *Zeitschr. f. PsychoL*, 1928, 107, 50-61; H. HETZER and K. WOLF, Babytests, *Zeilschr. f. Psychol*, 1928, 107, 62-104.

[2] G. WEISS, Aufgabegebundenes und aufgabefreies Verhalten von Fürsorgezöglingen, *Zeitschr f Kinderjorsch*, 1930, 36, 195ff.

of the child social facts usually acquire more and more significance for the structure of the psychological environment.

Social facts such as friendship with another child, dependence upon an adult, etc. , must also be regarded, from the dynamic point of view, as no less real than physical facts. Of course, in the description of the child's psychological environment one may not take as a basis the immediately objective social forces and relations as the sociologist or jurist, for example, would list them. One must, rather, describe the social facts as they affect the particular individual concerned. ① For the objective social factors have no more an unambiguous relation to the psychological individual than objective physical factors have. Exactly the same physical object may have quite different sorts of psychological existence for different children and for the same child in different situations. A wooden cube may be one time a missile, again a building block, and a third time a locomotive. What a thing is at any time depends upon the total situation and the momentary condition of the child involved. Similar considerations hold also for the social factors.

In this dependence there becomes clear a matter of fundamental psychological importance, namely, *the direct relationship between the momentary state of the individual and the structure of his psychological environment*. ② That the psychological environment, even when objectively the same, depends not only upon the individual character and developmental stage of the child concerned but also upon its momentary condition becomes clear when

---

① LEWIN, Vectors, Cognitive Processes and Mr. Tolman's Criticism, *Jour. Gen Psychol.* ,1933,8,318-345.

② Ibid. ; LEWIN, *Vorsatz, Wille und Bedurfnis mil Vorbemcrkungen ubcr die psychischen Kraftc und Encrgicn und die Struktur der Seele.*

we consider the relation between environment and needs.

Beside the quasi-physical and quasi-social environment, a mental task or a phantasy must sometimes be characterized from the dynamic point of view as environment. Activities (e. g., a game) may have the character of a region into or out of which the child may go. In the same sense a mathematical problem may have this character. The description of the child's environment would be incomplete without including the whole world of phantasy which is so important for the child's behavior and so closely connected with its ideals and with its ideal goals.

In the environment there are, as we have seen, many objects and events of quasi-physical and quasi-social nature, such as rooms, halls, tables, chairs, a bed, a cap, knife and fork, things that fall down, turn over, can start and go of themselves; there are dogs, friends, grown-ups, neighbors, someone who rarely gets cross, and someone who is always strict and disagreeable. There are places where one is safe from rain, others where one is safe from adults, and still others where one may not go under any circumstances. All these things and events are defined for the child partly by their appearance but above all by their *functional possibilities* (the *Wirkwelt* in von Uexküll's sense). The stairs are something that one can (or cannot yet) go up and down, or something that one climbed yesterday for the first time. Thus history, as the child has experienced it, is also a psychologically essential constituent of the things of the environment.

With all these, however, there remain certain critical properties of the psychobiological environment still undescribed Objects are not neutral to the child, but have an immediate psychological effect on its behavior. Many things attract the child to eating, others to climbing, to grasping, to manipulation, to sucking, to raging at them, etc. These imperative environmental facts we shall call them valences ① [*AuffordcruHgscharaktcrc*] determine the direction of the behavior. Particularly from the standpoint of dynamics, the valences, their kind (sign), strength, and distribution, must be regarded as among the most important properties of the environment.

The valence of an object usually derives from the fact that the object is a means to the satisfaction of a need, or has indirectly something to do with the satisfaction of a need. The kind (sign) and strength of the valence of an object or event thus depends directly upon the momentary condition of the needs of the individual

---

① These valences arc not to be confused with what is generally understood by "stimulus," as the term is used in speaking of a stimulus-reaction process. The effect of the valence corresponds dynamically much more nearly to a command, a summons, or a request.

A fairly precise translation of *Auffordernngwharakter* is the term "demand value," which Tolman [K. C. TOLMAN, *Purposive Behavior*, Applcton-Century, New York, 1932] uses for the same concept. In order to avoid unnecessary misunderstandings, Professor Tolman and Lewin have agreed to use the same term and at Tolman's suggestion have chosen "valence"

[There is no good English equivalent for *Aufforderungscharakter* as the author uses it. "Positive *A uffordcrungscharaktere*" and "negative *Aufforderungscharakters*" might be accurately rendered by "attractive characters" and "repulsive characters," were it not desirable, for various reasons, to have a neutral term. Perhaps the most nearly accurate translation for the expression would be "compulsive-character," but that is cumbrous and a shade too strong. In consultation with the author it has been decided to do a very little violence to an old use of the word "valence" (see the New English Dictionary). It should be noted that, in contrast to chemical valence, which is only positive, psychological valence or a psychological valence may be either positive (attracting) or negative (repelling), and that an object or activity loses or acquires valence (of either kind) in accordance with the needs of the organism. —Translators' note.]

concerned; the valence of environmental objects and the needs of the individual are correlative. ①(Concerning induced valence, see page 97.) Even with objective identity of environment, the strength and the appearance of the valences are quite other for a hungry child than for a satisfied one, for a healthy child than for a sickly one.

The correlation between valence and environment leads to a fundamental change in the latter with the changing needs of increasing age. The objects bearing valences are different for the baby, the toddler, the kindergartener, and the pubescent. ②

The valences change also with the *momentary state of* the needs. When the need for nourishment, for playing with a doll, or for reading history is in a hungry or unsatisfied condition, a bit of food, a doll, or the history book attracts the child, that is, has a positive valence; whereas, when this need is in a stage or state of satisfaction, the object is indifferent to the child; and, in the stage of oversatiatkm of the need, it becomes disagreeable to the child, that is, it acquires a negative valence. ③

Since the psychological environment, especially for the child, is not identical with the physical or social environment, one cannot, in investigating environmental forces, proceed from the physi-

---

① LEWIN,*Vorsatz*,*Wille und Bedurfnis mit Vorbemerkungen uber die psychischen Krafte und Energien und die Struktur der Seele*.
② LEWIN, Vectors,Cognitive Processes and Mr. Tolman's Criticism,*Jour. Gen. Psychol.* ,1933,8,318-345.
③ A. KARSTEN, Psychische Sattigung, *Psychol. Forsch.* , 1928, 10, 142-254; D KATZ, Psychologische Probleme des Hungers und Appetits, insbesondere beim Kinde,*Zeitschr f. Kinderforsch.* , 1928, 34, 158-197; LEWIN, Die Bedeutung der "psychischen Sättigung" für einige Probleme der Psychotechnik, *Psychotechn. Zeitschr.* ,1928,3,182.

cal forces as Loeb, for example, does in biology. If we start primarily from the psychobiological environment and pay due attention to its dependence upon the actual momentary condition of the individual involved, it is quite possible to discover universally valid principles of the dynamic effects of the environment. To be sure, it will always be necessary to keep in mind the total structure of the existing situation. ①

Psychological environmental forces [Umweltkräfte] may be defined empirically and functionally, excluding all metaphysical problems, by their effect upon the behavior of the child. ②They are equally applicable to the momentary situation and to the permanent environment of the child.

In summary: to understand or predict the psychological behavior (B) one has to determine for every kind of psychological event (actions, emotions, expressions, etc.) the momentary whole situation, that is, the momentary structure and the state of the person (P) and of the psychological environment (E). $B = f(PE)$. Every fact that exists psychobiologically must have a position in this field and only facts that have such position have dynamic effects (are causes of events). The environment is for all of its properties (directions, distances, etc.) to be defined not physically but *psychobiologically*, that is, according to its quasi-physical, quasi-social, and quasi-mental structure.

It is possible to represent the dynamic structure of the person

---

① By situation is meant the psychological situation, with particular reference to its dynamic properties.

② The fundamental concepts of psychological dynamics are thus for the present to be defined purely from the point of view of psychology and biology. Whether they agree in their formal logical structure with the fundamental dynamic concepts of physics need not here be discussed.

and of the environment by means of mathematical concepts. The coordination between the mathematical representation and its psychodynamic meaning has to be strict and without exception.

We shall first describe the psychological field forces and their mode of operation, without consideration of the question whether the object in any particular case has acquired its valence through some previous experience or in some other way.

The Region of Freedom Of Movement. Forces And Fields of Force

The first presupposition for the understanding of the child is the determination of the psychological place at which the child concerned is and of his region of freedom of movement, that is, of the regions that are accessible to him and of those regions that psychologically exist for the child but are inaccessible to him by reason of the social situation (prohibition by the adult, limitation by other children, etc.) or because of the limitations of his own social, physical, and intellectual abilities. Whether his region of freedom of movement is large or small is of decisive significance for the whole behavior of the child. ①

One can characterize these possible and not possible psychodynamic locomotions (quasi-bodily, quasi-social, and quasimental locomotions) at every point of the environment with the help of the concept of topology, which is a nonquantitative discipline about the possible kinds of connections between "spaces" and their parts.

The basis for the coordination between mathematical and psychodynamic concepts so far as environmental questions are

---

① F WIKHE, *Die Grenzen des Ichs*. (In preparation.) LEWIN, *Die psychologische Situation bci Lohn und Strafe*, Hirzcl, Leipzig, 1931(Chap. IV of this volume).

concerned is the coordination of topological path and psychodynamic locomotion. The topological description determines which points the different paths lead to and which regions these paths cross. The region which a child cannot reach one can characterize by means of barriers between these regions and their neighboring regions. The barrier corresponds as a dynamic concept to the mathematical concept of boundary. One must distinguish between different strengths of barriers.

Fundamental Properties of Field Forces.

To determine not only which locomotions (paths) are possible but which of the possible locomotions will occur at a given moment one has to use the concept of *force*.

A force is defined through three properties: (1) direction, (2) strength, and (3) point of application. The first and second properties are to be represented through the mathematical concept *vector*. The point of application is indicated in the figures (as is the custom in physics) by the point of the arrow.

Dynamically the force is correlated with psychobiological locomotions in a one-to-one correspondence. "The real locomotion must occur in every case according to the direction and the strength of the resultant of the momentary forces" and " In any case of locomotion there exists a resultant of forces in its direction."

The direction which the valence imparts to the child's behavior varies extremely, according to the content of the wants and needs. Nevertheless, one may distinguish two large groups of valences according to the sort of initial behavior they elicit: the positive valences ($+$), those effecting approach; and the negative ($-$), or those producing withdrawal or retreat.

The *actions* in the direction of the valence may have the form of uncontrolled impulsive behavior or of directed voluntary activity; they may be "appropriate" or "inappropriate."

Those processes which make an especially goal-striving impression are usually characterized dynamically by a reference to a positive valence. ①

One has to distinguish between driving forces, which correspond to positive or negative valences, and *restraining* forces, which correspond to barriers.

Direction of the Field Force. That the valence is not associated merely with a subjective experience of direction, but that a directed force, determinative of the behavior, must be ascribed to it, may be seen in the fact that a change in the position of the attractive object brings about (other things being equal) a change in the direction of the child's movements.

An especially simple example of an action in the direction of a positive valence is illustrated in Figs. 1 and 2. A sixmonths-old infant stretches arms, legs, and head toward a rattle or a spoonful of porridge in accordance with the direction of the vector (V).

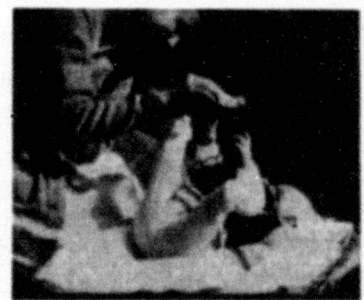

FIG.1.

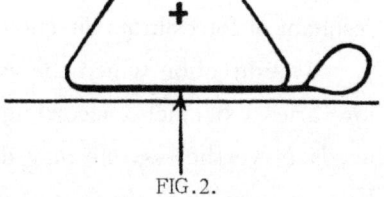

FIG.2.

---

① See below, p. 120.

The direction of the field forces plays an important part in such intelligent behavior as has to do with detour [*Umweg*] problems. The child perhaps wants to get a piece of chocolate on the other side of a bench (see Fig. 3). The difficulty of such a problem consists primarily not in the length of the detour (*D*) but in the fact that the initial direction of the appropriate route does not agree with that of the vector from the valence. The detour is the more difficult, other things being equal, the more the barrier makes it necessary for the child in making the detour to start off in a direction opposed to the direction of the valence (Fig. 4).

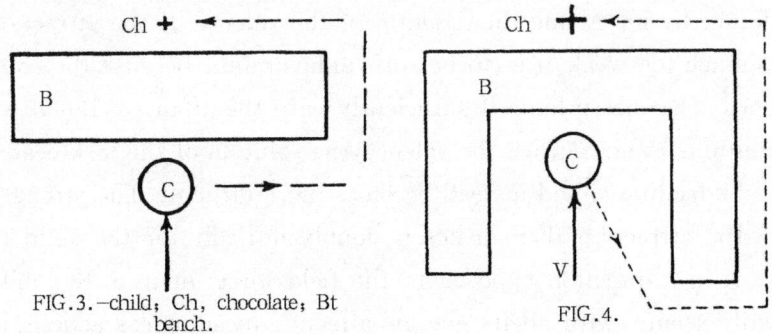

FIG.3.—child; Ch, chocolate; Bt bench.

FIG.4.

The situation is similar when the child wants to take a ring off a stick, while the stick stands so that the ring cannot be pulled directly toward the child, but must first be moved upward or away from himself. Similar factors are operative when a child at a certain age may have difficulties in sitting down on a chair or a stone. The child approaches with his face toward the stone (*s*). In order to sit down he must turn around, that is, execute a movement opposed to the direction of the

FIG.5.

field force (Fig. 5). ①

When the child finds the solution of such a detour problem, it happens by reason of a restructuring of the field. ② There occurs a perception of the total situation of such a kind that the path to the goal becomes a unitary whole. The initial part of the route, which objectively is still a moment away from the goal (see Fig. 4), thereby loses psychologically that character and becomes the first phase of a general movement toward the goal. ③

How critically important the question of *direction* is in this case is indicated by the fact that one cannot force a solution of the detour by increasing the *strength* of the valence. If the attraction is much too weak, it is, to be sure, unfavorable, because the child does not concern himself sufficiently with the affair. ④ But if we continue to strengthen the valence, the solution of the task ceases to be facilitated and instead becomes more difficult. The strength of the attraction then makes it doubly difficult for the child to start in a direction opposed to the field force. Instead, the child will execute, with all its energy, affective meaningless actions in

---

① LEWIN, Die Auswirkung von Umweltkräften, *Proc. 9th Int. Cong. Psychol.*, 1929, 286-288.

② W. KÖHLER, *The Mentality of Apes* (trans. by E. Winter), Harcourt, Brace, New York, 1925.

③ Frequently this transformation is not immediately complete, and the first part of the route retains a sort of double character.

④ Bogen found, even among school children who were working on such tasks voluntarily, that solutions were found more frequently if the valence of the goal was strengthened by the addition of a piece of chocolate (see H. BOGEN and O. LIPMANN, *Naive Physik*. Arbeiten aus dem Institut für angewandte Psychologie in Berlin. Theoretische und experimentelle Untersuchungen über die Fähigkeit zu intelligentem Handeln, Barth, Leipzig, 1923).

the direction of the valence (see page 96). ① Above all, that relative detachment and inward retirement from the valence which are so favorable to perception of the whole situation and hence to the transformation [*Umstrukturierung*] of the total field, which occurs in the act of insight, are made much more difficult (see page 152). For the same reason, the prospect of an especially intense reward or punishment may impede the solution of intellectual tasks.

To older children of normal intelligence the preceding examples of detour problems ofter no difficulty, because they already have a sufficient survey of such situations or corresponding experiences. For them, it no longer requires a special act of intelligence in order that, instead of the spatial directions, the *functional* directions become decisive for the movement.

We may at this point remark a circumstance of general importance: direction in the psychobiological field is not necessarily to be identified with physical direction, but must be defined primarily in psychological terms. The difference between psychological and physical direction appears more prominently in older children. When the child fetches a tool or applies to the experimenter for help, the action does not mean, even when it involves a physical movement in a direction opposite to the goal, a turning away from the goal but an approach to it. Such indirect approaches are more rare among babies. This is due to the slighter functional differentiation of their environment and to the fact that *social* structure has not yet the overwhelming significance for them that it has for ol-

---

① The impulsive struggles of Thorndike's cats may have been due in part to such a situation (see E. L. THORNDIKE, *Animal Intelligence*, Macmillan, Nenr York, 1911).

der children.

Fajans[1] found, for example, that in a certain situation in which three-and-four-year-old children usually applied to the experimenter for help (indirect approach), the corresponding turning of the baby to its mother was more a withdrawal from failure than a seeking for help.

In the cases mentioned, the direction of the field forces is determined by objects which, by reason of visual or auditory distance perceptions, have a definite place in the environment. In the case of newborn children, it is possible to speak of such precisely directed field forces only in so far as the psychological environment has sufficient structure and solidity.

Directed action in response to certain forms of tactile stimulation may be observed very early. Touching the child's cheek with the nipple may elicit a turning of the head in the corresponding direction.

Also among older children the (psychological) *separation of the self from the valence* remains in many respects a necessary condition for the directedness of the action upon the valence. Fairly often the action does not proceed immediately to the use of the object, but the field force disappears (or is at least very much weakened) as soon as the object comes into the "possession" of the individual involved. An example from our films: a nine-month-old child before which two rattles are laid does not begin to play after getting one of them, but is interested only in the rattle that he does not have. The close relation between directed field forces and the separation of the self from the goal object can also be demon-

---

[1] S FAJANS, Erfolg, Ausdauer und Aktivität beim Säugling und Kleinkind, *Psychol. Forsch*, 1933, 17, 268-305.

strated in various ways with older children.

Strength of the Field Forces. For the strength of the valences, internal factors, especially the actual momentary state of the child's needs, are of crucial significance. [①] In addition, the strength of the field force going out from a valence depends also upon the position of the valence relative to the individual and upon the presence or absence of other valences.

Fajans[②] has shown that, other things being equal, the strength of a valence increases with its apparent proximity, at least in certain cases. This is expressed by both the duration and the intensity of the efforts toward the goal. (In these experiments actual attainment of the goal was impossible.)

In a group of babies approximately ten months old, for example, the average total duration of approaches in the first three minutes at distances of 9, 40, and 100 cm. was respectively 75, 39, and 27 sec. In a group of three-year-olds the average total duration of approaches in the "near" experiment was 58 sec., in the "far" experiment 28 sec.

The activity, as well as the duration of approaches, increases with the degree of proximity of the valence. The reason for this is different for younger and for older children.

Again one may not, to be sure, simply assume that psychological distance corresponds to physical distance. In the first place, a difference in apparent distance is significant only within a rather narrowly limited range, in accordance with the smallness of the child's life-space; and this range, as the work of Fajans shows, is

---

① A. KARSTEN, *op. cit.*
② S. FAJANS, Die Bedeutung der Entfernung für die Stärke eines Aufforderungscharakters beim Säugling und Kleinkind, *Psychol. Forsch.*, 1933, 17, 213-267.

considerably smaller for the one-year-old than for the three-year-old child. Just as visual extent in perceptual space (e. g. , with reference to the law of apparent size) increases with age, ① so the life-space of the child increases and differentiates in dynamic respects. Difference in distance cannot be purely physically defined also because the range in which the child almost gets the desired object has qualitatively a special character. This "almost"situation has an especially marked significance, for example, with reference to experiences of success and failure, and cannot be reckoned simply as a smaller distance (see page 88).

An obvious discrepancy between spatial and psychological distance was observed in a group of four-year-old children who experienced the situation less as an objective task than as a social relationship with the experimenter. They were simply faced by an adult who would not give them a doll. For these children the kind and duration of approach remained independent of the distance of the valence. Indeed, for the social route to the valence (by way of the experimenter), the psychological distance is the same in any case.

With older children the intellectual appreciation of the functional and particularly the sociological relations (perhaps of their dependence upon the might of other children and of adults) is so far developed that physical distance usually plays a much smaller part in such situations. ②

Weiss found in her Fraenkel experiments (see page 75) with rather uninhibited five-year-old children that the distance of the

---

① E. LAU, *op. cit.*
② Of course, where very strong valences are concerned or very fundamental needs, primitive physical distance usually plays a considerable role, even with adults.

toys on the table was no longer important to the choice made; the child fetches what he wants. To be sure, when inhibitions are present, the distance again plays a considerable role, even with older children.

With increasing age temporally distant events also acquire increasing significance. To the psychological situation belong not only those facts that are actually perceptible and objectively present, but also a range of past and future events. A censure or a commendation may long remain a present psychological fact for the child, and an expected event may have psychological reality in advance of its occurrence.

As an example of the increase in the strength of the valence with temporal proximity, it may be pointed out that, among the inmates of homes for delinquent children, reform schools, and similar institutions, it is not infrequently observed that they become especially difficult just before their discharge. We noted this paradoxical behavior, so sharply opposed to their own interests, ① especially in previously well-behaved individuals. The essential reason was found to be the following: Even for the youth who is at first well behaved in the home (H) the wish for freedom (F) is an important motive of his behavior. At first this freedom is a distant half-imaginary goal, and, most important, good conduct in the home is the way that shall ultimately lead him there. Now that his discharge is approaching, the longed-for, but until now uncertain, world of freedom is just ahead (Fig. 6). The boundary of the home thereby acquires in much greater degree the character of a marked barrier (B) which separates the youth from his almost attained goal. Hence the home acquires a pronounced negative valence. E-

---

① It not infrequently happens that the prospective discharge is thereupon revoked.

motional and rebellious actions are further facilitated by the very high state of tension (see page 95) and by the fact that the youth already feels half free. ① In a topologically similar experimental situation with infants an increase of affectivity occurred in 85 per cent of the cases when the Held forces in the direction of the goal behind the barrier were strengthened and the general state of tension thereby raised. ② In many cases the impatience of children can be explained by a similar structure of the environment.

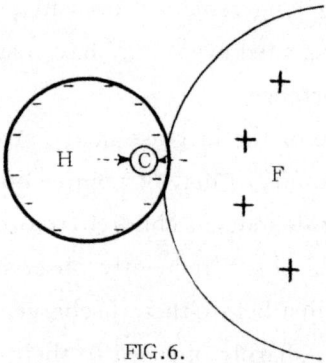

FIG.6.

The experiments of Fajans show that the restraining forces corresponding to the barrier increase when the strength of the valence behind the barrier is increased (see page 90).

Constellations of Forces. Conflict.

The ways in which different valences may interact in a situation are naturally very numerous. I select for discussion the case of conflict because of its special significance.

Conflict is defined psychologically as the opposition of ap-

---

① It has happened that a prisoner sentenced to three years tried to escape within a week of his discharge

② S. FAJANS, Erfolg, Ausdauer und Aktivitat, beim Säugling und Kleinkind.

proximately equally strong field forces. There are three basic cases of conflict, so far as driving forces are concerned.

1. The child stands between two positive valences (Fig. 7). He has to choose perhaps between going on a picnic (P) and playing (Pl) with his comrades. In this type of conflict situation decision is usually relatively easy. As a result of the fact that after the choice is made the goal chosen often seems inferior (for reasons to be described later), oscillation does sometimes occur.

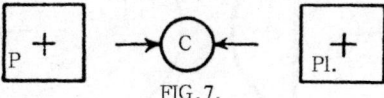

FIG. 7.

2. The child faces something that has simultaneously both a positive and a negative valence (Fig. 8). He wants, for example, to climb a tree (Tr), but is afraid. This constellation of forces plays an important part in cases in which a reward is offered for an activity (e. g. , a school task) which the child does not want to execute. ①

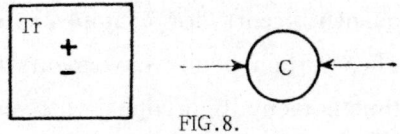

FIG. 8.

Conflict situations of this type usually develop rather quickly also in the detour experiments mentioned above, in the experiments of Fajans, or in other situations in which the attainment of the goal is impeded by some barrier. At first the child sees a difficult barrier (B) between himself and his goal (G). which hinders the completion of actions in the direction of the field forces (Fig. 9). But after the child has run against the barrier several times

---

① For these and the following remarks, see Chap IV, below.

and perhaps hurt himself, or had the wounding experience of failure, the barrier itself acquires a negative valence (Fig. 10). Beside the positive, there comes into existence a negative vector, and we have the Type 2 conflict situation. The negative vector usually increases gradually in strength and finally becomes stronger than the positive. Accordingly, the child goes out of the field.

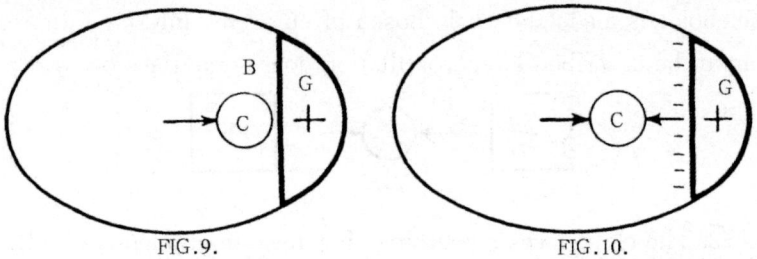

FIG.9.   FIG.10.

This withdrawal [*Aus-dem-Felde-Gehen*] either may be physical, as when the child retreats, turns away, or possibly leaves the room or place, or may be an inward going out of the field, as when the child begins to play or to occupy himself with something else.

It not infrequently occurs, for example in embarrassment, that the child makes certain bodily movements toward the goal but at the same time is mentally occupied with something else. In such cases the bodily act has the character of a more or less set gesture. ①

In such situations the withdrawal is at first almost always merely temporary. The child turns away, only to return after a while for another try at the barrier. ② A final and permanent withdrawal usually occurs only after several temporary withdrawals, the duration

---

① LFWIN, Kindlicher Ausdruck, *Zeitschr. f. pad. Ptychol*, 1927, 28, 510-526; S FAIANS, Erfolg, Ausdauer und Aktivitat bcim Saugling und Kleinkind.
② SFAJAN'S, *ibid*.

of which increases until finally the child does not return.

Unusual persistence in such a situation is not necessarily an indication of activity. On the contrary, active children usually go out of the field earlier than passive children. It is not the duration but the kind of approach that is significant for activity. ①

Related to this is the fact that under certain circumstances the single actions in such a conflict situation are longer with the infant than with the young child, ② although in general the duration of action unities increases with the age of the child. ③

3. The third type of conflict situation occurs when the child stands between two negative valences, for example, when it is sought by threat of punishment (P) to move a child to do a task (T) he does not want to do (Fig. 11).

There is an essential difference between this and the conflict situation described under 1. This becomes clear when one proceeds to represent the total distribution of forces in the field of force.

Field of Force. The field of force indicates which force would exist at each point in the field if the individual involved were at that point. To a positive valence there corresponds a convergent field (Fig. 12).

As a simple example of the structure of the field of force in a conflict situation of Type 2, a case from one of my films may be adduced: a three-year-old boy wants to fetch a rubber swan out of the water to the beach, but is afraid of the water. To the swan (S) as positive valence there corresponds a convergent field (Fig. 13). This field is overlaid by a second field which corresponds to

---

① *Ibid.*
② A HOMBURGER, *op. cit.*
③ C BÜHLER, op. cit.

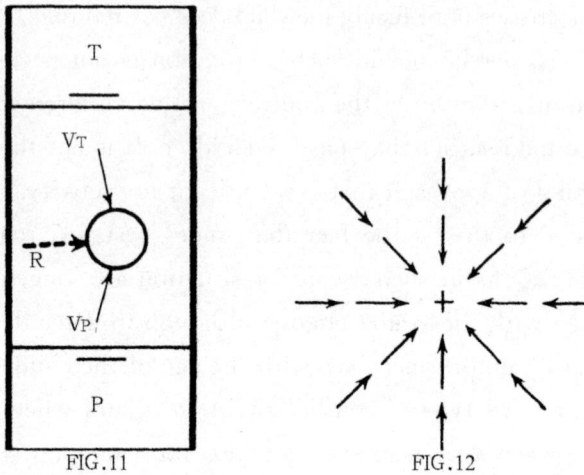

FIG.11   FIG.12

the negative valence of the waves. It is important that here, as frequently in such cases, the strength of the field forces which correspond to the negative valence diminishes much more rapidly with increasing spatial distance than do the field forces corresponding to the positive valence. From the direction and strength of the field forces at the various points of the field it can be deduced that the child must move to the point P where equilibrium occurs. (At all other points there exists a resultant which finally leads to P.) Corresponding to the momentary oscillations of the situation, above all to the more or less threatening aspect of the waves, this point of equilibrium approaches and retreats from the water. Indeed, this oscillation is reflected in the child's approaches to and retreats from the water.

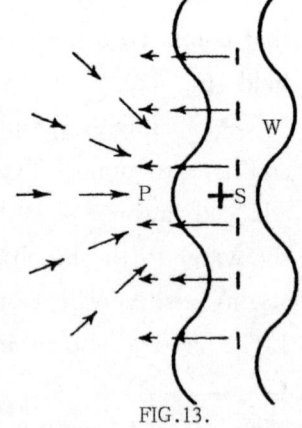

FIG.13.

If we return now to Type 3 of the conflict situation and compare it with Type 1, the chief difference is shown in Figs. 14 and 15: in both cases two central fields overlap. But while in Type 1 a stable equilibrium exists at the point P (Fig. 14) so far as sidewise movements (on line S) are concerned, in Type 3 this equilibrium is labile (Fig. 15). That is, there exists in the case of threat of punishment (Fig. 11) a situation which evokes a tendency to break out toward the side, in accordance with the strong sidewise resultant (R) of the two vectors (V_p and V_t). Consequently the child always goes out of the field unless other circumstances prevent it. Hence, if the threat of punishment is to be effective, the child must be so inclosed by a barrier (B) that escape is possible only by way of the punishment or by way of doing the disagreeable task. ① That is, in addition to requiring the execution of the task, it is necessary to limit the child's freedom of movement, thus creating (by physical or social means) a more or less constrained situation.

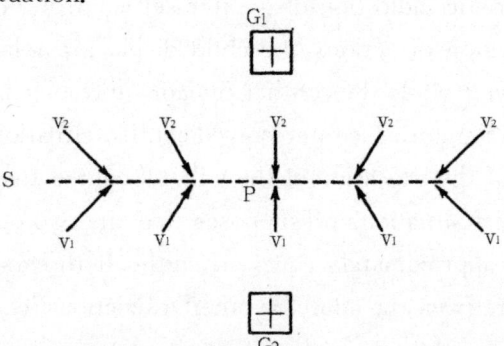

FIG 14. (From K. Lewin, Vectors, Cognitive Processes, and Mr. Taiwan's Criticism, Jour. General PsychoL, 1933, 8, 323.)
'Driving force corresponding to goal (G).
....line of equilibrium.

---

① The barrier may derive its firmness psychologically from the power of the adult, from the child's sense of honor, or from some other such factor (see Chap. IV, below).

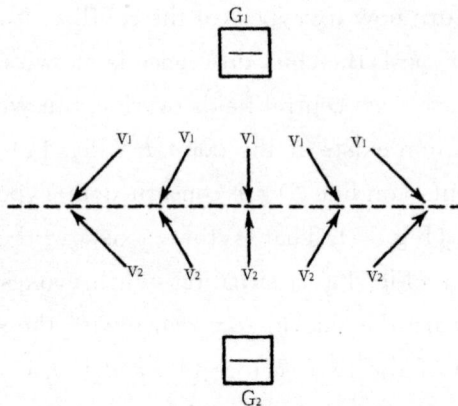

FIG. 15. (From K. Lewin, Vectors, Cognitive Processes, and Mr. Tolman's Criticism, Jour. Genetal PsychoL, IQ33, 8, 323.)
>Driving force corresponding to goal (G).
....line of equilibrium.

With the young child, the opposition of two approximately equal field forces in the conflict situation leads typically (so far as it is not an unstable equilibrium) to a relatively rapid alternation of actions in the direction of each of the two field forces in turn. It is a characteristic indication of greater self-control when, instead of this oscillation of action, the child displays a relatively calm type of behavior while the conflict remains unresolved. [1]

Ability to endure such unresolved conflict situations is an important aim of the education of the will. Of course, the occurrence of such conflict situations presupposes that the two opposed field forces are of approximately equal strength. If threats of punishment, pressure from the adult, or other restrictions leave the child little enough freedom, no real conflict situation can develop.

---

[1] The principle that self-control is not a consequence but a condition of obedience finds a theoretical justification in these considerations; see M. MONTESSORI, *Selbsttätige Erziehung im fruhen Kindesalter* (trans. by O. Knapp), Hoffman, Stuttgart, 1913.

If a situation becomes hopeless, that is, if it becomes as a whole inescapably disagreeable, the child, despairing, *contracts*, physically and psychically, under the vectors coming from all sides and usually attempts to build a wall between himself and the situation. This is expressed both in the typical bodily gestures of despair (crumpling up, covering the eyes with the arms, ① etc. ; see Fig. 16) and by a sort of encysting (Fig. 17) of the self: the child becomes obdurate.

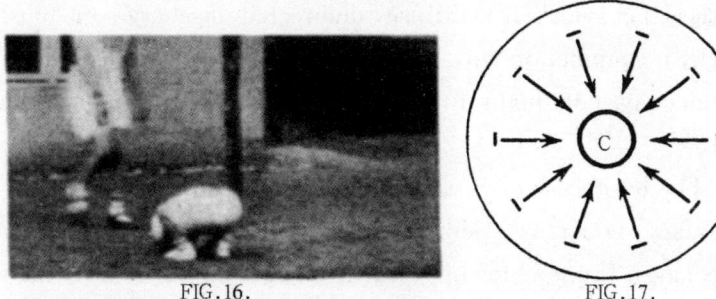

FIG.16. FIG.17.

State of Tension.

The opposition of the two field forces in a conflict situation leads indirectly, as may be deduced in detail, to an increase in the total state of tension② of the child, especially when there is an outer barrier. (See the constrained situation with threat of punishment in Fig. 11)

Especially with children, in whom the psychological delimitation between self and environment is still slight (see page 106),

---

① See Lewin; appendix to W. STERN, *op. cit.* The experiments of Fajans also show how in cases of great embarrassment the field forces drive the child, on the one hand, to turn away, to forget, to go (bodily or psychically) out of the field, or, on the other hand, to increased passivity.

② Tension is defined as the opposition of field forces in every direction.

any increase in environmental tension is usually immediately reflected. This sensitivity may be seen in the fact that a tearful or a cheerful mood in the environment, travel preparations, the mother's bad humor, or any other excitement usually transfers to the child even when every effort is made to conceal the circumstances from him.

In the simplest case, an increase in the general state of tension is expressed by restless behavior [*Unruhehandlungen*]. Restless behavior is a diffuse, undirected discharge of tension which, in conjunction with the directed forces of the particular situation, may culminate in affective outbursts, such as fits of rage. ①

The basic case of restless behavior is unambiguously clear in the infant and has very similar forms in pleasant and in unpleasant expectancy. If one holds out a rattle or nursing bottle near the baby (the psychological situation corresponds to that shown in Fig. 2), he stretches with arms, legs, and mouth in the direction of the valence. He does not remain calmly in this position, however, but begins to wave his arms and legs about.

With somewhat older children the least intense form of restless behavior, corresponding to an increase in the general state of tension, is a rapid change of occupation. An example: a three-year-old child in a Montessori kindergarten was very fond of drawing, but one day the director was unable to supply the requisite paper. Thereupon there occurred a number of varieties of *substitute behavior*; the child caressed the pencils, watched the drawing of older children, etc. Finally the child took up other occupations, but the average time he stayed with them was only 3.5 min. as against

---

① T. DEMBO, Der Ärger als dynamisches Problem, *Psychol. Forsch.*, 1931, 15, 1-144.

14. 6 min. on the preceding and 12. 3 min. on the following day. The increased tension resulting from the impassable barrier between the child and his goal had thus produced a fourfold increase in the frequency of his changes of occupation.

Ucko has demonstrated an analogous increase in frequency of change with older children in an experimental investigation of similar situations. ① In addition, the increase in tension made the occupation more superficial.

Although marked restless behavior is essentially a diffuse discharge, its *form* depends upon the topology of the particular situation. For example, if the restless behavior is produced by the fact that there is a barrier between the child and the positive valence, the restless movements occur so that so far as possible there is no increase in the child's distance from the positive valence. In other words, the restless movements occur in the line of equilibrium; that is, when approach is prevented by a barrier, they take a direction perpendicular to that of the field vector.

In the case of the child who has difficulty in sitting down on a stone (Fig. 5) this may lead to circling the stone. If a sufficiently strong positive valence is enclosed by a circular fence (F, Fig. 18), the restless behavior (R) (apart from actions in the direction of the valence) may take the form of circling the barrier. ② If, on the other hand, the child is inside and the valence outside the circular barrier, the typical behavior is a very slight oscillation along the side toward the valence (Fig. 19).

---

① In these experiments the tension was produced by interrupting the child in his favorite occupation.

② K. LEWIN, Die Auswirkung von Umweltkräften, *Proc. 9th Int. Cong. Psychol*, 1929, 286-288.

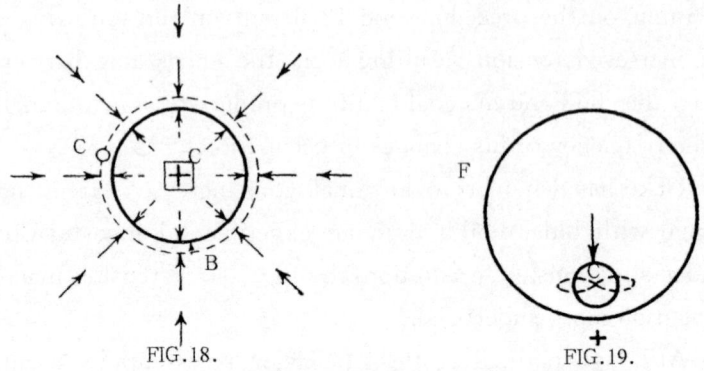

FIG. 18.   FIG. 19.

FIG. 18. (From K. Lewin, Vectors, Cognitive Processes, and Mr. Tolman's Criticism, Jour. General Psychol., 1933, 8, 323.)
Dnving foice corresponding to goal (G).
——'Restraining force corresponding to barrier (/*).
....line ot equilibrium.

Induced Valences

As already mentioned, the valences correspond in part directly to the momentary needs of the child. A positive or negative valence may, however, be induced in an object or event by other environmental factors. This fact is of special importance in children.

Social Fields.

It is a fundamental fact of childhood that the child's environment is not subject to his own control. The child faces a host of demands and difficulties. Difficulties arise from physical facts of the environment and the limitations of the child's own abilities: an object that he wants to lift proves to be too heavy, a staircase down which he wants to crawl too steep, or the pencil does not go over the paper as it should. Still more important are social factors, especially the authority or power of adults and of other children.

In the life of the neonate these social powers are first effective as sheer physical mastery (the child is bathed, dried, made to drink, etc.). But very soon their influence upon the child's psychological environment acquires increasing significance. The adult forbids or permits the handling of certain objects, characterizes behavior as good or bad, praises and blames.

For the infant of a few weeks or months the valences depend essentially upon his own needs and their momentary condition. If he does not want a food he cannot be moved by psychological means to eat it. ① He simply spits it out. With the older child the possibility of influencing him by psychological means is disproportionately greater. The disagreeable act may be imbedded in a game or in another action unity, and its meaning (and hence its valence) thereby radically changed.

The possibility of direct influence is correlated with the increasing psychological reality for the child of social facts, especially of the powers of others. ② Many objects in the environment, many modes of conduct, and many goals acquire a positive or a negative valence or the properties of a barrier, not directly from the needs of the child himself, but through another person. This induction may be brought about by an expressed prohibition or command. More important, however, is the effect of example, that is, of that which the child sees characterized by the behavior of adults as positive or negative for them. Even the very young child usually has a very fine sensitivity to social evaluations and forces.

The negative valence of a forbidden object (O, Fig. 20) which in itself attracts the child thus usually derives from an inducing field of force of an adult (A). If this field of force loses its psycho-

---

① Apart from simple distraction.
② Dynamically considered, these spheres of influence constitute fields of force for the child.

logical existence for the child (*e. g.*, if the adult goes away or loses his authority) the negative valence also disappears.

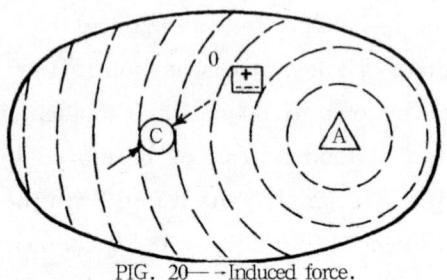

PIG. 20——Induced force.

In addition to the sphere of power of the adult, the behavior and spheres of power of other children or of a group of children are of critical importance for the kind and strength of induced valences.

The strength and extent of the fields of force of other people in the child's environment vary greatly, depending especially upon the economic situation, the character of the parents, the number, sex, and kind of children in the family and among friends.

As a rule, the domain in which the child's environment is "free" (*i. e.*, essentially, dependent only on his *own* sphere of power) is relatively small. Too strong or too extensive alien spheres of power may lead to a real oppression of the child or to a particularly violent revolt. This is equally true in cases of too great strictness and of too great fondness. In either case the child has not enough life-space in which the valences and other dynamic properties of his psychological environment may be determined by his own needs. Wiehe,[1] in an experimental investigation of the effect of a strange room or a strange person, distinguishes various

---

[1] F. WIEHE, *op. cit.*

degrees of strength of such a field, which degrees can be correlated quantitatively with distinct kinds of behavior, among others with the different kinds and degrees of approaches to and withdrawals from a strange person. The degree of strength of such a social field of force is, excluding the individuality of the child and of the stranger, a function of the spatial distance of the strange person, the duration of his presence, and his behavior. The strongest degree of pressure is expressed by the child's becoming motionless; a somewhat weaker, in his crying and showing a tendency to run away, where possible, to the neighborhood of the mother or to another field in which he feels at home. In the other actions of the child also a very strong pressure of strangeness [*Fremdheitsdruck*] evokes inhibited, a somewhat weaker pressure overexcited or overemphasized, behavior. Only a further reduction of the pressure leads to a natural free behavior (see Chap. VIII, Fig. 9, page 261).

As an example of the effect of alien fields of force upon the child, let us consider the significance of the level of the external demands made upon him. Experiences of success and failure have, as Adler correctly emphasizes, an extremely marked effect upon the child's encouragement and discouragement, and hence upon his later performance. In experiments on success and failure with three- to four-year-old children Fajans found the following: if one distinguishes four grades of activity (from very active to very passive), the child's activity on the same act may be reduced three grades by failure.[①] On the other hand, the activity of passive children could be increased by about the same amount. The effect upon the general selfconsciousness is also considerable.

Hoppe[②] has shown that the occurrence of success and failure experiences depends upon the momentary "level of aspiration" [*Anspruchsniveau*], and that this level of aspiration is in turn related to the ability of the individual: with "quite too hard" and "quite too easy" tasks no experience of success or failure occurs. The child, for example, has no essential experience of failure when it cannot do something that only adults or much older children can do. Nevertheless, the level of aspiration is by no means determined *solely* by the ability of the individual. On the contrary, a level of aspiration decidedly above (or below) the child's real ability may be produced by the demands of adults or by the performances of comrades. For this reason there may develop a feeling of inferiority (or of superiority) which may be severely prejudicial to the child's general conduct and actual achievements.

Fajans found that the effects of failure could be materially reduced by a verbal consolation of the child (Fig. 21). Here again the significance of the social field for the consciousness of self is evident. The offer of a substitute satisfaction [*Ersatzbefriedigung*] is even more effective than such consolation.

Even for children of from six to nine months, success or failure changes the degree of activity and the duration of action toward the goal. But at this age the repetition itself, after a success,

---

① This holds chiefly for repetition of the same act within a certain interval of time. Adams (D. K. ADAMS, Experimental Studies of Adaptive Behavior in Cats, *Comp. Psychol Monog.*, 1929, 6, No. 26, pp. 41, 47, 92, etc.) has reported marked reduction in the duration of activity with failure of cats in puzzle boxes.

② F. HOPPE, Erfolg und Misserfolg, *Psychol. Forsch.*, 1930, 14, 1-62.

leads to a diminution in the duration of actions toward the goal (Fig. 22).

Jucknat, [1] in an experimental investigation of some hundreds of school children, found that success and failure in one region may, under certain circumstances, change the level of aspiration in other regions: namely, when the two regions have sufficient dynamic connection and when the child's goal level in the region concerned is not too firmly fixed.

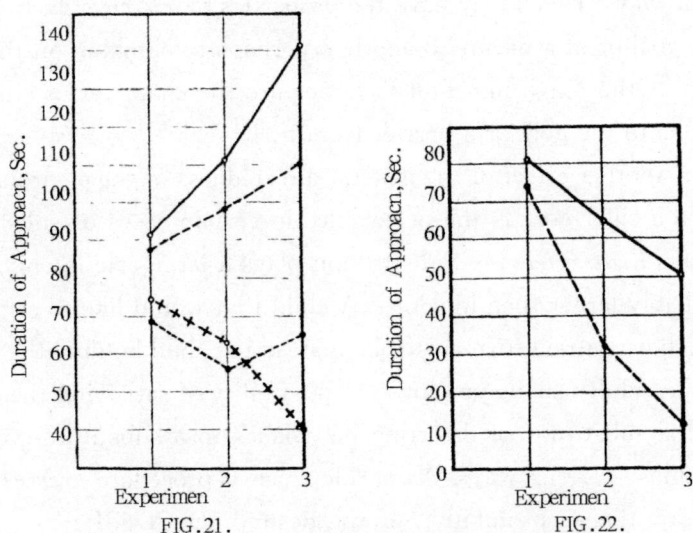

FIG. 21.—Comparison of the effects of success,4(encouragement, substitution, and failure upon the duration of approach [Zuwendungsdauer].
——Success with concomitant encouragement. Increase in duration of approach from first to third experiment [Vt−rtnch] 48 per cent
... Success. Increase in duration of approach == 2S per cent
. . Substitute success. Diminution in duration of approach = 6 per cent
Failure. Diminution in duration of approach = 48 per cent
FIG. 22.—Effect of success (——) and failure (......) upon the infant.

---

[1] JUCKNAT, Leistung und Anspruchsniveau. (In preparation.)

Means and Substitutes.

An object or event possessing special emphasis may also, like a social field, induce an effect upon the environment.

A strongly accented goal so transforms the situation that practically all objects acquire a reference to this goal. ① A building block that has just been a locomotive for the child becomes a hammer when he desires to drive a stick into a hole. An object that becomes a *tool* may thus possess a derived valence. In the same way a bench may have the properties of *a barrier* in front of one goal or of a means to another, perhaps to climbing on the table. ② Other environmental facts acquire the character of either a means to the goal or a barrier from it.

Another effect of the general directedness of the environment upon a chief goal is the occurrence in certain cases of substitute goals [*Erastzziele*]. ③ Substitution plays a large role in children, probably larger than in adults. A child that would like to stroke a dog, but is afraid to, may stroke instead the child holding the dog. ④ The adult usually employs the possibility of satisfying the child with a substitute, of diverting his wishes to a substitute goal, in the most various ways. As a rule, such a procedure creates less friction than a prohibition of the desired act. A different conse-

---

① This is not merely an extension of an agreeable character to a larger field. On the contrary, quite different, both positive and negative valences and other kinds of shifts may be induced in surrounding objects by a positive valence.

② T. DEMBO, *op. cit*; W. KOHLER, *The Mentality of Apes*.

③ We are not here concerned with the theory of substitution which plays an especially important part in Freudian theory, except as it touches the question of *environmental forces*. See T. Dembo, *op. cit*.

④ LEWIN, K. , *Die Entwicklung der experimentcllen Willenpsychologic und die Psychotherapie*, Hirzel, Leipzig, 1929.

quence of a prohibition (by reason of certain total structures which cannot here be discussed) is an implicit or overt counterreaction, the so-called negative behavior of the child, which is the more fundamental in that the whole psychological emphasis of the desired act is considerably enhanced by the adult's prohibition. ①

Such processes are very often significant in pretending or play-acting behavior. A child would like to strike another child but contents himself with a threat; he would like to throw a ball very high and makes an exaggerated gesture.

With certain children, those Lazar has called "gesture children," the tendency to substitute a mere gesture for a real performance or a serious action is so strong as to constitute an essential character trait.

For children in general, the serious and the playful, reality and make-believe are much more fluid, less sharply distinct than for adults. This fact is related to a property of the psychological environment which we must discuss briefly.

Strata of Reality In The Environment

The psychological environment of the adult shows a rather marked differentiation into strata of various degrees of reality. The plane of reality may be characterized briefly as the plane of "facts" to which an *existence independent of the individual's own wishes* is ascribed. It is the realm of realistic behavior, of insuperable difficulties, etc.

The more unreal planes are those of hopes and dreams, often of ideology. A stratum of greater unreality is dynamically charac-

---

① It is possible that the proposition that "action and reaction are equal" holds also for psychological dynamics.

terized as a more fluid medium. ① Limits and barriers in such a stratum are less firm. The boundary between the self and the environment is also more fluid. In a plane of unreality "one can do what he pleases." ②

A complete description of the psychological environment must always set forth the structure not only of the level of reality but also of the levels of unreality. If conditions on the plane of reality become too disagreeable for any reason, for example, as a result of too high tension, there arises a strong tendency to go out of the level of reality into one of unreality (flight into dream, into phantasy, ③ or even into illness).

These facts hold in principle equally for the adult and for the child. Nevertheless, it is characteristic of the child's psychological environment (a) that the differentiation of various degrees of reality is much less marked and (b) that transitions between the levels of reality and unreality occur much more easily than in adults.

The psychological environment of the small child can be characterized neither as a real nor as an unreal world, but the two strata are still relatively undifferentiated. Jaensch ④ and his students have shown for sensory psychology that the eidetic images [*Amchauungsbilder*] of children have the properties still undifferenti-

---

① J. F. BROWN, Über die dynamischen Eigenschaften der Realitats- und Irreal; tätsschichten, *Psychol. Forsck.*, 1933, 18, 1-26.
② T. DEMBO, *op. cit.*
③ See below, pp. 145ff.
④ E. JAENSCH, *Übcr den Aufbau der Wahrnehmungswelt und die Grundlagen der menschlichen Erkenntnis*, Barth, Leipzig, 1927.

ated of both the perceptions and the imaginings of adults. Piaget [1] has shown that the child's conception of the world, especially his ideas of causation, is still essentially "magical" and "animistic," that name and thing, act and magic word, are not yet clearly separated. [2]

These properties of the child's perceptions and intellectual view of the world are only an expression of the general fact that in the child's psychological environment the differentiation between the levels of reality and unreality is still slight. This fact is further displayed in the peculiar seriousness of the child's play. From it derives the relative lack of distinction between wish and reality that is expressed, for example, in the very tenuous distinction between "falsehood" and "truth."[3] The great "suggestibility" of children is related to the same fact. For not only are the child's psychical processes closely dependent upon his present physical condition (e. g., illness), but, which is more often overlooked, the reverse also holds. Bodily condition may be very greatly influenced—especially in children—by the psychological. Thus it is that a small child's pain ceases when one blows on the spot and that the horse may be "gone" when someone "throws him out the window."

The relatively slight differentiation between strata of reality and of unreality may still be noted in puberty: sometimes beside

---

[1] J. PIAGET, La causalité physique chez l'enfant, Paris, Alcan, 1927. The Child's Conception of Physical Causality (trans. by M. Gabain), Harcourt, Brace, New York, Kegan Paul, London, 1930.

[2] See also D. KATZ and R. KATZ. Gcsprache mit Kindern. Untersuchungen znr Sozialpsychologie und Padagogik, Springer, Berlin, 1928.

[3] C. STERN and W. STERN, Errinnerung, Aussage und Lüge in der ersten Kindheit. (Monog, u. d. seel Entwick. d. Kindes, Vol. 2), Barth, Leipzig, 1910.

the real life a second life of phantasy is led for years, the events of which have the greatest significance for the child. Even for adolescents ideologies still in general possess much more real forces than for adults.

It would, of course, be false to believe that a differentiation between real and unreal strata is completely lacking in the child. ① This is primarily true in the field of his real needs, both somatic and psychological. Even though the child may, under certain circumstances, be satisfied with an imaginary sweet instead of a real one or treat a piece of wood better than a real doll, there are still very early indications of differentiation, at least in many respects, between reality and unreality.

Sliosberg ② found that such an unreal object is accepted as a substitute only when the child is in a play situation.

Play.

The following circumstances constitute in my opinion the foundation for a dynamic theory of play: whether a given behavior (e. g. , game X in the sand box) is to be characterized as playful or nonplayful cannot be determined from the standpoint of the adult but solely in terms of the child's own lifespace. The fundamental dynamic property of play is that it has to do with events which belong in one respect to the level of reality, namely, in so far as they are activities visible also to other persons (e. g. , as against daydreams). But at the same time play behavior is much less

---

① Piaget's thesis may have to be limited even for the child's intellectual concept-world (see I. HUANG, Children's Explanations of Strange Phenomena. *Psychol. Forsch.* , 1930, 14, 63-182; K. BÜHLER, *op. cit*)

② S. SLIOSBERG, Zur Dynamik des Ersatzes in Spiel- und Ernstsituationen. *Psychol. Forsch.* , 1934, 19, 122-181.

bound by the laws of reality than is nonplay behavior; both the goal setting and the execution are in much greater degree subject to the pleasure of the person. This dynamic fluidity, in respect of which the play field approximates the dynamics of unreality, is evident, among other ways, in the changeableness of the meaning of things and of the child's own person (playing roles), which goes far beyond what is possible in the level of reality. The play field is hence a region more or less limited as regards reality which shows even in its content a most immediate relation to the unreality of air castles and wish ideals. ①

The various games may be differentiated according to their dynamic fluidity. They vary rather considerably in the degree of their dynamic fluidity, and the "rules of the game" may be so strict that the game may, dynamically, approach the rigidity of reality.

A strong tendency to go out of reality into unreality occurs, especially when an overstrong pressure dominates the former.

The course of differentiation depends not only upon the individual characteristics of the child, but also in essential ways upon the situation and lot of the particular child. Among proletarian children this stratification usually develops earlier. ② An early and sharp separation of reality and unreality seems to be unfavorable to the child's development. Important as a sufficiently clear separation of these planes is, the kind of relation obtaining between them remains decisive of, among other things, all creative behavior and determines whether the ideal goals, which belong dynamically to the level of unreality, more or less directly condition behavior in the plane of reality.

---

① See below, Chap. IV.
② H. HETZER, Kindheit und Armut, *Psychol. d. Fursorge*, 1, Hirzel, Leipzig, 1929.

Boundaries of the Self

Closely related to the slighter differentiation of the child's psychological environment into real and less real or unreal planes is a second factor: for the child, the boundary between the self and the environment is less defined than for the adult. This circumstance is of critical significance to the operation of the environment upon the child.

The individual is dynamically a relatively closed system. How strongly the environment operates upon the individual will therefore be determined (apart from the structure and forces of the situation) by the functional *firmness of the boundaries* between individual and environment. The internal structure of the *child* individual is characterized dynamically by a relatively slight differentiation among the psychological regions [*Bereiche*] and by slight functional firmness in the boundaries of the various psychological systems. ①

In other words, the child, to a greater extent than the adult, is a dynamic unity. ② The infant, for example, acts first with its whole body and only gradually acquires the ability to execute part actions. ③ The child learns only gradually to separate voluntarily certain parts of its environment, to concentrate.

---

① This is not the place for a more comprehensive discussion of the internal structure of the personality.
② A "strong Gestalt" in Köhler's sense (see W. KÖHLER, Gestalt Psychology.)
③ Coghill's (*Anatomy and the Problem of Behavior*, Macmillan, New York, Cambridge Univ. Press, Cambridge, 1929; Individuation versus Integration in the Development of Behavior. *Jour. Gen. Psychol.*, 1930, 3, 431-435) important researches have shown that in embryological development even the reflexes are formed by a gradual differentiation of reactions which originally involved the whole organism. See also Lewin, Kindlicher Ausdruck.

Analogously to this relatively slight delimitation among the various inner psychological systems, the functional firmness of the boundary between his own person and the psychological environment is also in general less with the child than with the adult. This is expressed, for example, by the fact that the "I" or self is only gradually formed, perhaps in the second or third year. Not until then does the concept of property appear, of the belonging of a thing to his own person. ① The same relative indistinctness of the limits of the self is apparent in the fact that external impressions touch the central nucleus of the child's personality decidedly more readily than is the case with adults. Conversely, needs or other tensions of the inner psychological systems burst through very easily in the form of impulsive behavior and uncontrolled affective demonstrations (see the examples on pages 94 and 95).

The slighter firmness of the boundary between self and environment has a direct bearing upon the slighter separation of real from unreal strata (see page 103). For it (the former) implies that the psychological environment of the child is more intimately connected with and responsive to his momentary needs and wishes.

The functional firmness of the limiting layer between the child and the environment varies greatly, even in the same child, in different situations and toward different persons. This is equally true of the child's receptivity or inaccessibility toward external impressions, and of the ease with which internal states, especially tensions, come to expression.

It has been found in the course of psychopathological investigations that in certain circumstances children are more readily in-

---

① W. STERN, *op. cit.*

duced to talk openly of personal matters when they are naked. ①
Children also are usually inclined to talk more freely about experiences otherwise kept back when they are going to bed in the evening. ②

The functional firmness of the wall between the self and the environment depends not only upon the age but also upon the individual characteristics of the person. It is especially slight among certain psychopathic children. ③ The cause of this may be a greater fluidity and at the same time a slight (relative to chronological age) degree of differentiation of the person. This fluidity is also apparent in the dynamics of the environment, so far as the latter is psychologically determined. Feeble-minded children are also characterized by a relatively slight degree of differentiation of the person (see Chap. VII, page 194).

As distinguished from the above described psychopathic children, certain types at least of the feeble-minded are characterized by a slight fluidity of the psychical systems. Thiinflexibility leads to an "either-or" behavior that is evident in a sphere of the psychology of the will in an especially strong fixation of certain va-

---

① James has emphasized the close relation between clothing and the psychological person as a social being. It is hence (and on other grounds) understandable that under certain circumstances nakedness diminishes the firmness of the psychological wall between child and environment.

② Cf. D. KATZ and R. KATZ, *op. cit.* The greater frankness of children shortly before going to sleep may be related to a beginning of the partial dissolution of the boundary between reality and unreality that is characteristic of sleep and dreaming. (See also G. H. GREEN, *The Daydream. A study of development*, Univ. London Press, London, 1923.)

③ LEWIN, Filmaufnahmen über Trieb- und Affektausserungen psychopathischer Kinder (verglichen mit Normalen und Schwachsinnigen), *Zeitschr. f. Kinderforsch.*, 1926, 32, 414-447.

lences and modes of behavior (stubborness, pedantry). The immobility of the psychological systems and of the psychological structure of the environment is at the same time a decisive dynamic cause for the difficulties of these children in intellectual fields.

Even when a marked separation of the self from the environment has already occurred there may exist a particular dynamic union between the self and other persons, for example, the mother of some friend. This union may be expressed in various ways, among others by the child's behaving worse with the mother than with other people, by outspoken protest against even a temporary absence of the mother, by turning to the mother—"hiding behind her skirts"—in any disagreeable situation. In such cases the presence or absence of the mother changes the total structure of the psychological environment essentially, especially the child's feeling of security or insecurity. As a consequence of the close psychological relationship between the mother and the child's own person, the real abilities of the mother, her effectiveness as against the things and persons of the environment, have for the child the functional significance of an extension of his own security and power against the environment. A departure of the mother thus means to the child a weakening of his strength against the environment. ①

The animistic character of the child's view of the world may also be related to the fact that his psychological environment generally has *personal* fields of force as prominent dynamic features of its structure.

Not only other persons but other objects may have a close

---

① The tendency of children to take a doll or some favorite toy along to bed is another expression of the close union of these objects with the self.

psychological relation with the self of the child. To the "I" in this sense there belong not only the child's own body but certain toys, a particular chair, etc. Such objects are dynamically somewhat like his own body in that they represent points of special sensitivity to invasions by environmental forces. Whether an object belongs to the self or to the outside world depends, according to Wiehe,① among other things upon the present needs and internal tension systems of the child and changes with them. It happens, for example, that the destruction of an incomplete production of the child, in consequence of its belonging to the self, is felt by him as a violent invasion ; while destruction some time after completion of the task leaves him quite unaffected. An internal discharge of tension is usually accompanied by a loosening of the appurtenances of the self, and this is especially marked in children.

The Influence of Environmental Forces on Development

The same factors that are critical for the momentary situation are also characteristic cf the *total milieu* of the child over longer periods of his life. Their effects upon the development of the child's personality and his whole behavior are similar to the effects of the forces described in the momentary situation upon his momentary behavior. Particular features of the environment are usually less important than its total character in determining its effect upon development and, more particularly, upon the rate and mode of differentiation of the child's personality. Overly harsh or severe surroundings may lead to the child's encapsulating or insulating himself from the environment. The child becomes stubborn and negativistic (see pages 94 and 95). Optimal environmental

---

① F. WIEHE, *op. cit.*

conditions, for example, optimal tension level, vary considerably with different individuals. It is a well-known fact that infants and young children who grow up in an institution generally show a slower development in many respects than children who grow up in a family.

It is already clear from the circumstances just discussed what great significance a change of environment may have for the child's development. The so-called difficulties of training are not infrequently related to the particular requirements of the parents, to their characters, and to the way they get along together. These difficulties disappear as soon as the child has been for some time in a suitable environment. To be sure, the difficulties usually begin all over again after a return to the old environment.

Enuresis is not infrequently treated successfully by changing environment. [1] Of course, the improvement is often only temporary. Grisch describes the disappearance of a voluntary dumbness with change of environment.

Up to now we have been describing the effects of the present situation upon development. These effects cease with a change in the situation. Nevertheless, the operation of the environment always produces, as a consequence, a more or less marked change in the individual himself, and thus changes his basis of reaction to all later situations. This influence of the present situation upon future possibilities of conduct, which is particularly significant to development as a process considerably extended in time, is due not only to the child's acquisition of certain intellectual experiences but, above all, to the fact that his whole person is changed in certain specific ways.

---

[1] J. ZAPPERT, Kritisches über Enuresis nocturnis, *Arch. f. Kinderhk.*, 1926, 79, 44- 69.

This indirect operation of present upon future situations may be expressed in favorable as well as in unfavorable ways. Its importance is especially great in view of a condition which might be termed the *circular causal relation* [*zirkuläre Rückkoppelung*] *between self and environment*. A feeble-minded child, for example, is at a disadvantage among his comrades in two ways. In the first place, he cannot do a task (*e. g.*, corking a bottle, writing with a pencil) even when the conditions are so arranged as to be actually the same for the feeble-minded child and his normal playmate (*e. g.*, when both are gotten to grasp the pencil or cork and bottle in the same way). In practically all cases in practical life, however, there is a second difficulty: when the more intelligent child is given a task, he knows that he must look for the mode of manipulation that involves the least difficulties under the conditions given. The less intelligent child has a narrower field and sees less into the internal relations of the environment. He does not find out, perhaps, that it is most convenient to hold the bottle as near the mouth as possible. More generally, he is less likely to discover the easiest way of solving the problem.

The less intelligent child is thus not only less able, but the actual demands made upon him by apparently the same problem are usually really greater than those made upon the intelligent child. The poorer solution of the weaker child thus usually has the double character of an *inferior performance of a more difficult task*.

If, now, the less gifted child experiences a failure, he will, as we have seen, attack subsequent problems less intensely. The increased fear of failure creates, wholly apart from the child's inferior ability, a situation psychologically still more unfavorable. In the new situation the already weaker child will thus fail or give up all the more readily. He stands usually before a (psychologically considered) harder task, and his total situation is, owing to his earlier experiences, more unfavorable.

Quite analogous cumulative series due to this vicious circle may be seen in psychopathic children or in other children that have difficulties in social groups. The overexcitable or socially disagreeable child is not only less competent in his social situation, and thus makes his task harder, but also the other children reject him, drive him to a defensive attitude, etc. The child soon gets himself into a social situation, originating perhaps in some quite trivial conflicts, that would tax the capacities of a child of high social endowment. Similar developments of a circular causal relationship between capacity and environment are basic, for example, to stammering. [1] Conversely, not the least advantage of the gifted child consists in the especially favorable environmental conditions that he usually creates for the future.

I consider it one of the fundamental tasks of pedagogy so to constitute the situation of children in difficulties that the severe injuries usually occasioned by the circular causal relation may be avoided or undone. For here at least lie genuine pedagogical possibilities which do not require changing the child's "abilities."

---

[1] A. HOMBURGER, *op. cit.*

Chapter IV
The Psychological Situations of Reward and Punishment

In the following presentation, the problem of reward and punishment will not be discussed in its entire scope. To raise the pedagogical question of the possibility of entirely avoiding reward and punishment is to pass over into the fundamental dialectical problem of authority in education. Consequently, a positive or negative attitude toward a system of pedagogy based on reward and punishment as essential educational principles is less a problem of psychology than of *Weltanschauung*.

In this discussion I intend to limit myself chiefly to a psychological problem, or, from the pedagogical point of view, a technical one: namely, that of *utilizing the prospect of reward or punishment as a means* of bringing about or suppressing certain definite behavior in the child.

Reward and punishment are not to be regarded here as sociological or juridical but as psychological categories. Hence an identical action may be in one case a punishment, in another a reward, according to the total situation in which the child is placed.

The prospect of reward or punishment only arises when the

child is required to perform an action, to behave in a certain way, other than that which at the moment he prefers. The child must solve a problem, do a piece of work, or otherwise engage in some activity toward which he is antagonistic, indifferent, or too slightly interested to make the necessary sacrifices. He must solve a problem in arithmetic but does not like to calculate. He is to eat a certain food distasteful to him.

If the activity desired by the educator possesses in itself a sufficient attraction for the child reward and punishment are unnecessary. The child will be prompted by his own needs to move in the desired direction.

Reward or punishment must, therefore, lead the child either to carry out a given command or to respect a given prohibition ; to refrain, that is, from carrying out some natural or desired activity.

The situation involving either reward or punishment is then to be contrasted with that in which the behavior of the child is dominated by an original or derived interest in the thing itself. ①

From a purely psychological point of view the question may

---

① I restrict myself in discussing the general situation of reward and punishment to those cases in which the child actually experiences the reward as reward, the punishment as punishment. I thus refrain from considering here those cases in which punishment is for any reason desired by the child, as, for instance, where it relieves an unendurable situation, or offers the child the possibility of associating with a particular person, or the like. Again, under reward, I do not consider cases where a child, to his surprise, is rewarded for something that he actually wanted very much to do. The discussion is based, in part, upon our experimental investigations. Cf. F. Hoppe, Erfolg und Misserfolg, *Psychol. Forsch.* , 1930, 14, 1- 62; S. Fajans, Die Wirkung von Erfolg und Misserfolg auf Ausdauer und Aktivität beim Säugling und Kleinkind, *Psychol. Forsch.* , 1933, 17, 213-267; T. Dembo, Der Arger als dynamisches Problem, *Psychol. Forsch.* , 1931, 15, 1-144; and an investigation by Ucko upon the effect of prohibition (in preparation) .

be raised as to which is more favorable for the performance of a definite task: interest in the thing itself, or the prospect of reward or punishment. At first sight natural interest might be judged the more favorable on the ground that the need of the child directly provides sufficient psychical energy, which might be lacking in the other situation. It would, however, be hasty to maintain the thesis that greater psychical energy is available in the case of natural interest. Sufficiently strong punishment or a longed-for reward may under certain circumstances bring into play much greater and more persistent forces than would interest in the thing itself.

The attempt to prove the psychological superiority of the "naturalness" of interest in the one situation as against its "artificiality" in the other involves the use of concepts which, to say the least, need much more precise formulation if they are to be psychologically unambiguous. Even in those cases in which the child is interested in the thing itself, the interest is probably derived: a natural interest of the child in figures or letters may, for instance, derive in a particular case from an interest in various street-car lines, in house numbers, or in store signs.

And, even though the child is of himself interested in numbers or letters, this interest may be designated as "natural" only with reservations. It has developed from living in a definite metropolitan milieu and is in any case somehow mediate and derived from more original needs. This holds for most instances even though the interest involved is quite lively.

From the above point of view reward and punishment might appear solely an attempt of the pedagogue to bring about intentionally an indirect accentuation of interest when it had not occurred in the child's past. Actually, one frequently finds the opinion held in child and developmental psychology (and not only in reflexology) that with small children the important function of reward and punishment is to bring about associatively the desired emphasis. Such a view would obscure the deep psychological difference between an interest pedagogy and one based on the application of reward and punishment. This confusion, though quite convenient for many educators, would be considered psychologically fatal by others.

To understand the nature and scope of the processes in question, it is necessary to achieve a penetrating insight into the *structure of the concrete psychological situation*. The behavior of a child in response to reward and punishment can be as little derived from isolated stimuli or separate psychological processes as can any other type of behavior— as little, for that matter, as the psychological meaning of any environmental influence. The child's behavior is not sufficiently characterized by being ascribed to a "natural" or derived need. Rather, an understanding of the effect of an environmental interference or of an actual act is possible only when the process concerned is considered in its relation to the whole present concrete situation. Indeed, conceptual derivation of the actual occurrence is possible only through consideration of the relations existing between a specific individual and the particular structure of the present situation. [1]

In work and play, in expression, action, emotion—everywhere the actual occurrence is conditioned by the present structure of the environment. By environment is here meant not only the momentary situation in the narrower sense of the word but also the inclu-

---

[1] LEWIN, The Conflict between Aristotelian and Galileian Modes of Thought in Contemporary Psychology, Chap. I above; Zwei Grundtypen von Lebensprozessen, *Zeitschr. f. Psychol.*, 1929, 113, 209 ff.

sive psychological life-space ordinarily referred to as milieu. The task of scientifically representing the psychological environment is thus of fundamental significance. It is especially so for the most important problem of psychology, namely, the explanation of psychological dynamics. Nevertheless, there has existed up to the present a great lack of proper tools for the purpose. This discussion, aside from its special theme, may be taken as an elementary example of the application of a method which I regard as an essential step in the fulfillment of this task.

In the following analysis of the situation I shall attempt to develop a precise topological *representation* of its total structure and of those factors most generally important for dynamics. The results will be presented directly, and, trusting in the immediate intelligibility of the terms, I shall not attempt here to justify the designation of certain psychological characteristics of the situation as "barriers," others as "vectors"(forces), or others as "areas."

Herein exists the proper task of research, and here lie great difficulties of representation, however simply they may appear in result. In such topological representation one need not consider separate particulars of the *situation* in relative isolation, as one is too tempted to do in purely verbal description. Rather the procedure used forces one to start out primarily from the present total situation as a unity. For this reason, and on account of the conceptual precision of such a means of representation, one must always, in using it, consider a whole range of implicit codetermined consequences.

On the other hand, and for the same reasons, such a representation permits one in a peculiarly high degree to unify a mass of apparently unrelated or contradictory details and to clarify their mutual relationships. I shall limit myself in the following to a discussion of the main features of the momentary total situation. These provide also the basis for an understanding of the differentiated stratification of many particular cases.

I shall first briefly discuss a few properties of the situation determined by interest in the thing itself, and then consider the psychological situation in reward and punishment. There, situations involving a command will be considered first.

This is not the place to consider whether psychology is justified in using the concepts of mathematical topology, a nonmetrical qualitative science of relationships of a very general nature. I should like to emphasize, however, that the problem is not that of representing the physical-geographical, nor yet the objective sociological situation, but rather the structure of the psychological situation, that is, the situation as it exists for the child. I scarcely need to remark that the vectors used in the following representations do not stand for physical forces.

The Interest Situation

Dynamically considered, the structure of the situation in which a child turns toward an occupation (e. g., playing with a doll) because of interest in the occupation or task itself is relatively simple. The situation is dominated by an attraction, or in our terms, by a positive valence (Fig. 1). ① The child (C) sees a doll. Playing with

FIG.1.

---

① We shall indicate a positive valence by +, a negative by —. It is important to note that valence may be possessed by any psychological object—a concrete physical object, a social ideal, an activity, a way of acting, a state (sleeping), or any kind of goal.

the doll (D) momentarily possesses for the child positive valence. There exists a psychical field force, a vector, proceeding from the child in the direction of the activity of playing with the doll. If this attraction is strong enough relative to the other psychical forces existing in the situation, an action of the child in this direction will occur.

How does the child behave when such action in the direction of the attraction encounters difficulties? How does he act, for instance, when a bench blocks his progress toward the doll, or when an adult's prohibition or the sphere of power of another child hinders his attainment of this goal? Psychologically such a difficulty, be it physical or social, constitutes a barrier (B, Fig. 2) between the child and the doll. Such a barrier will hinder the activity of the child in the direction of the goal ; usually it does not completely stop the child, but acts in such a way as to force him out of the original direction. [1] The child will, perhaps, try to go around the bench, to "get around" the adult, or to borrow the doll from his playmates "at least for a while."

To summarize, occurrences conditioned by interest in the goal itself exhibit the following characteristic dynamic properties. If the child is forced out of its original direction by difficulties (Fig. 3) , the direction of the field force also changes in accordance with the changed local relations between individual and goal. Further, the change of direction is of such a character that *a vector in the direction of the goal* constantly arises and initiates the corresponding be-

---

[1] What occurs in a concrete instance depends upon the firmness and form of the barrier, and upon its direction relative to the direction of the field vectors. Above all, it depends upon whether the barrier completely encloses the goal, or leaves open possible avenues of approach.

havior. The behavior thus makes a pronounced goal-seeking impression. A natural teleology reigns.

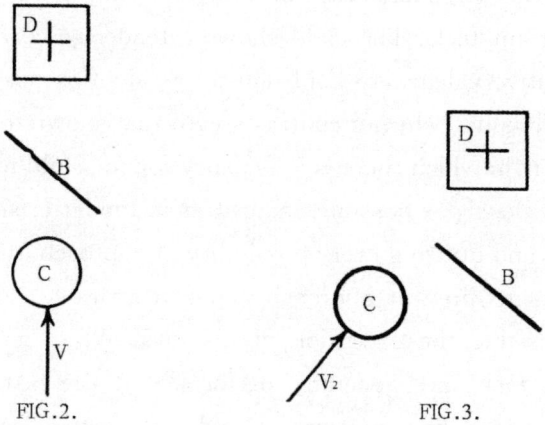

FIG.2.   FIG.3.

What is ordinarily designated as teleology and taken as the criterion of the behavior of living beings is in large part nothing other than an expression of the following fact: a positive valence controls the situation in such a way that with changes in the position of the person the direction of the field forces changes in the manner just described.

Command With Threat of Punishment

Nature and Disposition of Valences.

In the reward or punishment situation the occupation, or more generally, the behavior required of the child possesses, as mentioned above, not a positive but a negative valence. The child, for example, has no desire to fill a page with the letter "i," or he does not wish to calcu-

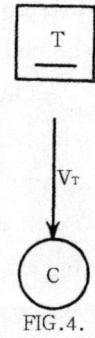

FIG.4.

late. Thus a vector (V_T) in the sense of a thrust away from the task operates upon the child (Fig. 4).

From this circumstance follow several simple but pedagogically important facts. The child shows a tendency, corresponding to the negative valence, to hold himself as aloof as possible from the task. Thus his behavior contrasts with that shown in the interest situation, in which there is a tendency for the child to approach the task as closely as possible. Instead, as in the latter situation, of welcoming and utilizing every possibility of approach, the child actively seeks to prevent approach and endeavors to postpone as long as possible the execution of his task. When no escape is open, such tasks are generally performed at the last moment. There exists also the tendency to abandon the task as soon as possible.

If despite his disinclination we wish to get the child to calculate, it is necessary to turn him from his present occupation, perhaps some kind of play, toward the arithmetic task. Dynamically this means that by some method a field force must be produced, oppositely directed to the previous force (V_T), and strong enough to overcome it.

One such method is threat of punishment. It is essentially indifferent whether the character of the punishment is apparent to the child as such or is concealed.

One may say: If you don't do your arithmetic you will be whipped; you will not be allowed to go on the picnic; you will get a bad mark; you must stay after school. In these cases one makes use of a second negative valence, a further unpleasantness. Further, in order to procure a field force opposed in direction to the vector proceeding from the first negative valence, the second negative valence must be placed behind the child.

The fundamental situation in threat of punishment is represented topologically in Fig. 5. The child finds himself between two negative valences, the arithmetic task (T) and the punishment (P). If the threat of punishment is to be effective, the vector (V_p) proceeding from it must not only be strong enough to overcome vector V_T even when the child comes into immediate contact with the unpleasant task, but also continue to hold the child within the field of this task. [1]

The following abstract consideration will help to clarify the difference between the foregoing and the interest situation. If in the latter the child is obstructed by a difficulty, the direction of the vector immediately changes, as we saw, in such a way that the child continues to act in the direction of the original goal. If in the punishment situation the child is similarly forced away by a difficulty, he will immediately tend to take a direction opposite to that of the task to be completed.

If one is to bring about a renewed movement in the direction of the undesired task, the second negative valence, the punishment, must acquire such a position that it is again opposed to the present direction of the vector (V_T, Fig. 6). In this situation there is thus lacking the pedagogically important property of the interest situation, according to which the child when thrust away by difficulties resumes of himself the direction of the task (see Fig. 3), providing the difficulties are not too unpleasant.

Even, however, without special difficulties in the performance of the task, in the threat-of-punishment situation there exists from the beginning and as a constant condition a dynamic configuration

---

[1] Once the child is in the field of the task, other factors also come into play (see pp. 136 f.).

in which the child is forced away from the task. The negative valence of the task itself works dynamically like a difficulty barrier. In many respects it hinders approach with even greater strength. The situation is further complicated by the presence of a second negative valence, creating a conflict situation for the child.

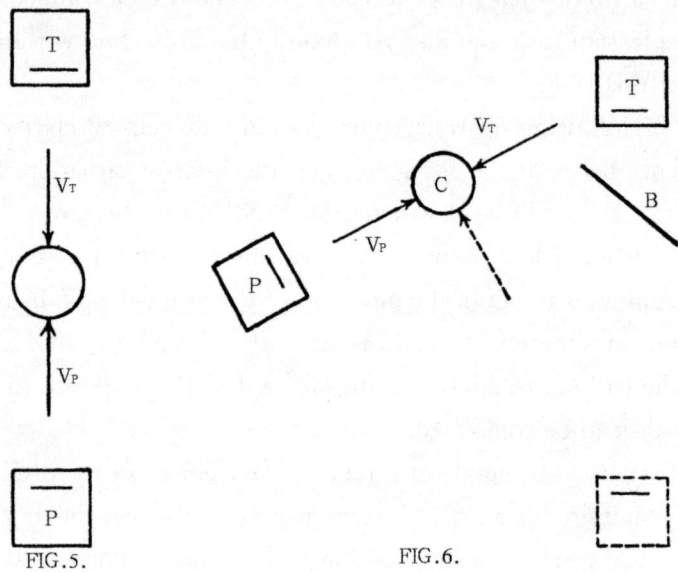

FIG.5.　　　　　　　FIG.6.

Types of Conflict.

A conflict is to be characterized psychologically as a situation in which oppositely directed, simultaneously acting forces of approximately equal strength work upon the individual. Accordingly, three fundamental types of the conflict situation are possible.

1. The individual stands between two positive valences of approximately equal strength (Fig. 7). An instance of this sort is that of Buridan's ass starving between two stacks of hay.

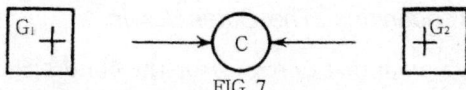
FIG.7.

In general this type of conflict situation is solved with relative ease. It is usually a condition of labile equilibrium. Approach to one attraction is in itself often sufficient to give it predominance. The choice between two pleasant things is generally easier than that between two unpleasant unless questions are involved which cut deeply into the life of the individual.

Such a conflict situation can upon occasion also lead to an oscillation between two attractions. It is of considerable importance that in these cases a decision for one goal alters its valence in such a way as to make it weaker than that of the renounced goal.

2. The second fundamental type of conflict situation occurs when the individual finds himself between two approximately equal negative valences. The punishment situation just discussed (Fig. 5) is a characteristic example which we shall examine more fully in a moment.

3. There exists finally the possibility that one of the two oppositely directed field vectors derives from a positive, the other from a negative valence. In this case conflict arises only when both positive and negative valences are in the same place. A child may wish, for instance, to stroke a dog which it fears, or to eat a forbidden cake. In these cases there exists the conflict situation represented in Fig. 8. We shall have occasion later to go into such a situation in more detail.

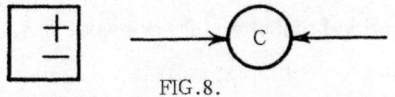
FIG.8.

Escape Tendencies. The Outer Barrier.

Threat of punishment creates for the child a conflict situation of the type represented in Fig. 5. The child stands between two negative valences and the corresponding field forces. In response to such a pressure on both sides the child necessarily reacts with the tendency to avoid both unpleasant things. Thus there exists an unstable equilibrium. The situation is such that the slightest sidewrse displacement of C must produce a very strong resultant (VR) perpendicular to the direction punishment-task (Fig. 9). Thus the child in avoiding both the task and the punishment will try to get out of the field (in the direction of the dotted arrow in Fig. 9).

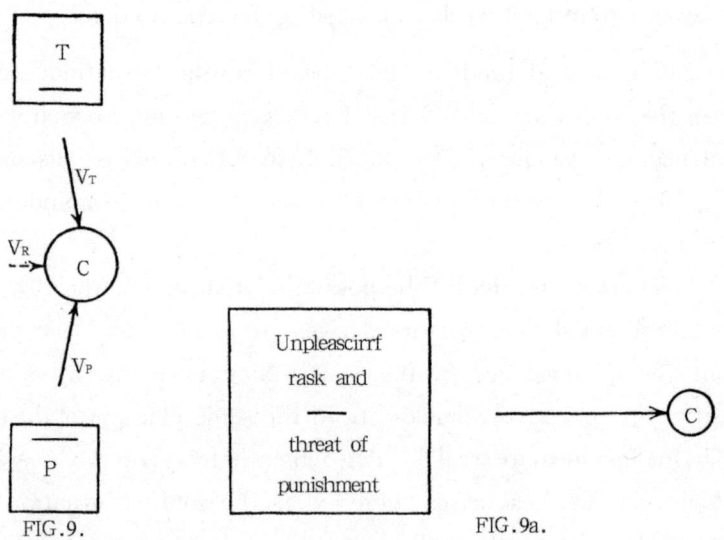

FIG.9.   FIG.9a.

It may be added that the child does not always come into the threatened-punishment situation in such a way that it stands immediately between punishment and unpleasant task. Often the child may find himself at first entirely outside the whole affair. For instance, he may be required on pain of punishment to finish an unpleasant school task within a fortnight. In this case punishment and task constitute a relatively unitary, undifferentiated whole which is doubly unpleasant to the child (see page 169). The child will have nothing to do with the disagreeable affair. In this situation (Fig. 9a) there exists a strong tendency to flight, often resulting more from the threat of punishment than from the unpleasantness of the task itself. More precisely, it may result from an increased unpleasantness of the total complex due to the threat of punishment.

The most primitive attempt to avoid simultaneously task and punishment is a bodily going-out-of-the-field, running away, hiding. Frequently going-out-of-the-field takes the form of postponing for several minutes or hours the performance of the task. In cases of repeated, severe punishment a new threat may result in an actual attempt by the child to run away from home. Fear of punishment frequently plays a role in the early stages of childish vagabonding. [1]

Another form of going-out-of-the-field consists in engaging in some other task. Often the child seeks to *conceal* his going-out- of-the-field by choosing an occupation against which as such the adult can find no objection. Thus the child may take up another school task more pleasing to him, execute some previously given commission, or the like.

Finally, the child occasionally escapes both punishment and unpleasant task by *deceiving* the adult more or less crassly. In ca-

---

[1] G. HOMBURGER, *Psychopathologie des Kindesalters*, Berlin, 1926, p. 508.

ses where the adult has difficulty in checking up, the child may claim to have carried out the task even when he has not, or he may say (a somewhat more refined form of deceit) that a third person relieved him of the unpleasant task or that for some other reason its execution became unnecessary.

The conflict situation resulting from threat of punishment thus creates a very strong tendency to go out of the field (see Figs. 5 and 9). With the child, such a *going-out-of-the-field*, varying according to the topology and field forces of the situation, *necessarily occurs unless especial measures are taken to prevent it*. If the adult wishes the child to undertake the task despite its negative valence, mere threat of punishment is not sufficient. The adult must see to it that the child cannot leave the field. The adult, that is, must erect some sort of *barrier* which will effectively prevent such escape. He must so erect the barrier (B) that the child can gain freedom only by carrying out the task or by incurring the punishment (Fig. 10[①]).

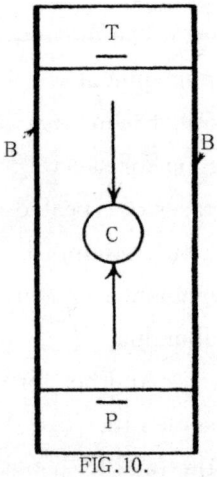

FIG. 10.

Actually, threats of punishment intended to get the child to carry out some definite task are always so framed that they, together with the field of the task and that of the pun-

---

① In this and later diagrams barriers will be represented by thick lines. Thin lines will be used to bound qualitatively definite areas, for example, the area of the task where the boundaries do not possess psychologically very great dynamic firmness. It is both possible and necessary to distinguish different degrees of firmness of boundary (cf. G. Bircnbaum, Das Vergessen einer Vornahme, *Psychol. Forsch.*, 1930, 13, 218-284). We may, however, limit ourselves here to a schematic differentiation of two degrees.

ishment, completely enclose the child. The adult is forced so to construct the barriers that no "hole" remains through which the child may slip out. Should the adult be too unskilled, or should his power in this respect be insufficient, the child will slip through if aware of the slightest hole in the barrier.

The most primitive type of such barriers is the physicalcorporeal: the child may be shut up in a room until he has finished the task. ①

In general, however, the barriers are *sociological*. ② The barriers surrounding the child are the instruments of power possessed by the adult in virtue of his social position and the inner relationship existing between him and the child. Such a social barrier is no less real than a physical one.

Barriers resulting from social factors may restrict the child's freedom of movement to a narrow spatial area. The child, for instance, is not locked in but is forbidden to leave the room before

---

① It should also be mentioned that with' a child definite, narrow limits must be set for the completion of the task (see p. 128). In diagramming the situation one is limited to the psychological present (for reasons that cannot here be discussed in detail, cf. Chap. II). The sequence of occurrences must thus be represented diagrammatically as a succession of situations. Time restrictions are therefore to be shown in the single representation only in so far as they are sensed by the child in the present situation as limitations of its freedom of movement.

② For the most part the concepts and occurrences that constitute the psychological field are determined by social rather than by physical facts.

completing the task [1] In other cases the external freedom of movement is practically unrestricted but the adult keeps the child under constant surveillance. He is not allowed out of sight. Since, ordinarily, the child cannot be followed about constantly, the adult often makes use of the child's world of magic. The capacity for constant control of the child is assigned to the policeman or to the bogey man. A God that knows everything the child does, from whom no escape is possible, is not infrequently used to the same effect. Secret eating of sweets may, for instance, be controlled in this way.

Often the barners are directly constituted by life in a given social milieu, by the customs of the family in which one lives, or by the organization of the school.

For effectiveness it is essential that the social barrier possess a sufficiently real firmness. If at a particular point it is not resistant enough the child will break through. For instance, if the child knows that a threatened punishment is only verbal or if he can rely with some certainty upon the probability of being able to wheedle the adult out of executing the punishment, he will instead of completing the task trust to the possibility of breaking through the barrier. A similar weakness of barrier exists when a mother delegates the responsibility of watching over the child's completion of a task to a nurse, teacher, or elder child, who, unlike herself, does not possess sufficient resistance to prevent the child from going out of the field.

---

[1] Restriction of one's freedom of movement is itself frequently used as a punishment. Even then the confinement is often effected by nonphysical, social, or quasi-magical means. The child, for instance, may be placed in a corner, or bound to the leg of a chair by a thread of twine. (Cf. W. von Kügelgen, *Jugenderinnerungen cines alten Mannes*, Stuttgart o. J.)

Along with physical and social barriers there exists a third type, closely dependent upon social facts but differing in important respects from the last-mentioned examples. One may appeal, for instance, to the child's pride ("Remember you are not a street urchin!""You're not a bad boy!") ; or to the social standards of a group ("Remember you are a girl!""... a boy!") . One turns in such cases to a definite system of ideology, to goals and values recognized by the child himself. Such an appeal to the ideology contains a threat : danger of exclusion from the group. At the same time, and most importantly, this ideology constitutes an outer barrier. It defines for the individual the boundaries of freedom of action recognized by the ideology. Many threats of punishment are effective only so long as the individual feels bound to these limits. If he no longer recognizes the ideology, that is, the moral limitations of the group, threats of punishment frequently become ineffective. The individual refuses to allow his freedom of action to be confined within these limits.

The strength of barrier necessary in a specific case depends upon the nature of the child and upon the strength of the negative valences of task and punishment. The *more intense the negative valence, the firmer must be the barrier*. For the stronger the barrier, the stronger is the sidewise directed resultant force. Thus the greater the pressure the adult must exert upon the child to bring about the desired behavior, the firmer, the less penetrable must be the barrier erected.

The Constrained Character of the Situation.

The barrier surrounding the punishment situation constitutes not only an enclosure against the surrounding environment, but also a more or less decided restriction of free movement on the part of the child. This restriction not only means that the child must carry out the specified task but constitutes at the same time a *general* limitation of freedom of movement.

This fact is perhaps most clear in those instances in which the child is locked in his room. Even, however, in cases where apparently only the performance of a definite action is required and the child is given freedom in its other movements, the actual barrier effects a general restriction of freedom of movement. If this were not so, but the play area—topologically the space enclosed by the barrier (Fig. 11)—were allowed to become as large as desired, the child would have the opportunity of engaging for as long as he cared in as many occupations as he wished before accomplishing the task. In reality the child would of course take advantage of this possibility. Thus while remaining within the field he would be able, as regards reward and punishment, to go out of the field. Expressed in other terms, the barrier would recede psychologically to a great distance, becoming thereby unreal.

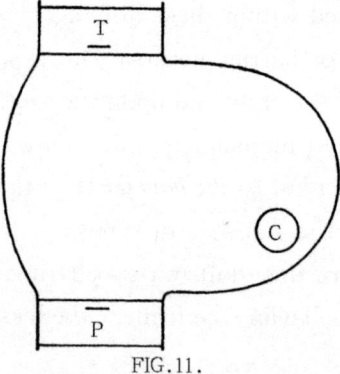

FIG.11.

The extent of freedom of movement left the child by physical or social barriers is certainly of importance psychologically and pedagogically; but it must be strongly emphasized that *threat of punishment always and necessarily gives rise to the structure of a constrained situation.* The constrained aspect of the situation is prominent in proportion to the sharpness of pressure the adult must exert in order to get the child to carry out the task. Constraint depends not only, on the fact that in these cases the barrier must be particularly firm and lacking in holes, but also on the tendency of the adult to restrict the barrier in order to avoid weak places and to reduce to a minimum the play space left the child. The sharper the threatened punishment the greater, ordinarily, is the general restriction on the life of the child and the stronger is the tendency of the adult to revert to primitive physical barriers. The more the child's milieu is founded on threats of punishment and the severer these punishments are the more the milieu as a whole assumes the constrained character of a prison or reformatory marked by bars, locked rooms, and constant surveillance.

The barrier surrounding the punishment situation need not always be erected for the special instance. The area within which the child can move, his sphere of freedom, is itself limited corresponding to his restricted sphere of power. The sphere of power of the single adult and above all of the organization of adults who control the communal life is all powerful and ordinarily completely surrounds the sphere of freedom of the child. Only definite areas exist in the child's life within which it can find respite from the threat of immediate adult interference. The life of the child in a secret gang, friendship and conversation with other children, or certain play zones may constitute such areas. But even these afford the child freedom and inaccessibility for only a definite time. Indeed, the fact that the child's physiological conditions of life, its nourishment and shelter, are controlled by the adult causes the sphere of movement of the child to lie as a rule in the sphere of power of the adult.

Whether a threat of punishment necessitates in addit'on *special barriers is a question of the particular instance.* Very often a slight threatened punishment makes such an increased limitation necessary. Frequently the adult's mode of living or the conditions and habits required by living in a house, which previously had not been sensed as restrictions, acquire for the child as a result of threatened punishment the meaning of a barrier limiting his freedom of movement.

Punishment Situations without Barriers.

In certain cases despite a threat of punishment special barriers are not demonstrable. The child, though standing before an unpleasant task, even one of decidedly negative valence, may yet complete it without any apparent barrier to prevent his going-out-of-the-field. There may even appear to be no threat of punishment. The admonition of the adult to perform the task seems sufficient to cause the child obediently to complete it.

We are not considering here cases in which the child performs the task out of love of the adult. These would fall under the problem of reward. Rather, we are concerned with situations in which behind the admonition there stands an unexpressed threat of punishment. Precisely in a milieu in which the child's attitude toward the adult is foreign and hostile he may behave as though undertaking the unpleasant task of his own free will. The erection of particularly narrow barriers may thus be unnecessary. Indeed in just such milieux it is not infrequently pointed out with pride that the child is left much freedom, that it is not narrowly restricted.

A representation of this type of situation by the topology shown in Fig. 10 would not be exactly correct. The enclosure of the field through a barrier expresses topologically the fact that the psychical field is completely surrounded. But in addition it indicates that a special region, the barrier, acts as a *bounding zone* of an inner sphere, the area which it encloses. This inner sphere within which the child is free to move may as we mentioned before be large or small. The freedom within this area is certainly not to be considered as equal to the freedom in a sphere without an outer barrier. Rather, because of the barrier the character of the entire field and its dynamic peculiarities are changed qualitatively in important respects. In a moment we shall consider these in more detail. In the punishment situations mentioned above, however, there exists a relatively free sphere of activity, an inner sphere, which is to be distinguished from the barrier felt as such. Even when the child is confined within a room he can, if recalcitrant and innerly unbroken, do essentially what he pleases.

In the situation just sketched, however, such a particular barrier and inner sphere are actually lacking. The power of the adult and his threats of punishment have so penetrated the whole life-sphere of the child that areas in which he can move freely and independently are as good as nonexistent. It is unnecessary to hinder the child's going-out-of-the-field by the erection of an outer barrier because the function of this barrier has spread out over the whole field. The child finds himself in a field completely controlled at every point by the power of the adult (Fig. 12①).

---

① The psychological field corresponding dynamically to the sphere of power of the adult (A) will be schematically represented in this and later figures by concentric circles. Actually, of course, the field of force of the adult will not pervade the sphere of action of the child in such a homogeneous fashion but will be of different density in different places. For our present purposes, however, we need not consider this inequality.

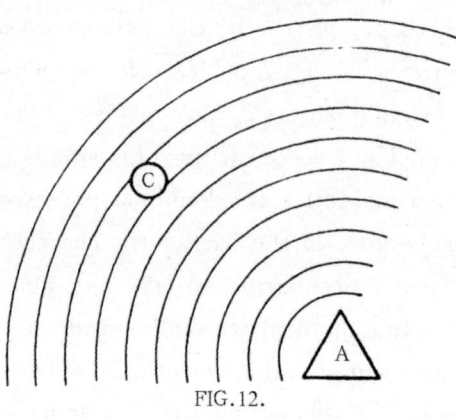

FIG. 12.

Naturally such a condition is never completely attained. If the child is to live at all he must retain the possibility of a minimal independence of movement. The condition which we have in mind does not correspond simply to the situation in which the free sphere of action within the outer barrier is made as small as possible. Nor can it be created simply by such a restriction of the sphere of action. It is more apt to occur when the adult either by particularly severe punishments or through a definite ideology so dominates the child that he dare not resist. The child may thus carry out unpleasant tasks unhesitatingly because *at every point within his sphere of action Ic is internally controlled* by the wishes of the adult. This dependence may go so far that special threats of punishment are unnecessary. In extreme cases it is scarcely necessary for the adult even to mention his wishes.

How far such penetration of the entire field by a regime of punishment is possible depends, of course, not only upon the milieu but also upon the nature of the individual child. But even in cases where there is no extreme restriction of the child's freedom of movement it is important to keep in mind whether the structure of the total situation corresponds to the topology represented by

Fig. 9 or to that shown in Fig. 12. ①The latter case must be especially emphasized since it is in precisely the most severely constrained situations that this characteristic is particularly noticeable. Since in these instances inner domination of the child plays a decisive role the actual force exercised by the adult is difficult to recognize. Yet the less apparent its action from without in, the stronger it is. In many cases which are to be regarded throughout as forced actions there may in a superficial and even in a rather exacting examination appear to be exhibited exactly those characters so typical of the dynamically opposite situation. I refer to the apparent free will characteristic of the child when it acts from interest in the task itself, freely following its needs in a situation actually without barriers.

Consideration of the situation outlined above is complicated by the fact that instances occur in which such a complete penetration of the child's life-sphere and its transformation into a constraint-situation is caused by the adult's overweening love and constant protection. In this way as well the child may be placed in an overpowering field of force.

Leaving the above case in which erection of a special outer barrier is unnecessary, we shall return to a discussion of the typical punishment situation. Even this is to be characterized as a constrained situation, especially when, as previously mentioned, the inner sphere is very small. That such an outer barrier produces the

---

① Naturally there exist transitional and mixed cases. One may think of Fig. 12 as showing an extension of the barrier throughout the entire field. This is a possible notion since the barrier is conceived throughout as functionally denfined.

characteristics of constraint becomes clearer when a situation of this kind is compared with one in which not threat of punishment but interest in the task itself is the dominant factor. In such cases (see Figs, 1 to 3) it is unnecessary to erect an outer barrier since the positive valence itself continually leads the child back to the task. Neither is it necessary to limit in any respect the freedom of movement of the child. In contrast to that of punishment, the total situation can remain free and unconstrained.

State of Tension.

The situation involving threat of punishment was in its general topology characterized by the opposition of two negative valences (the task on one hand, the punishment on the other) and by the outer barrier hindering sidewise escape. For a general characterization of the situation it is necessary in addition to determine the state of tension in the field.

We have seen above that a conflict is thus produced; in consequence of two negative, oppositely placed valences, two opposed vectors (V_T and V_P.) work upon the child (Fig. 10). These vectors are not two isolated forces in an otherwise uninfluenced field, but lead to an increase in the state of tension within the total situation.

This means that the vectors operating on the child are not limited to those from task and punishment. Instead there exist opposed field forces of approximately equal strength affecting movements in every other direction. At *all positions* in the field the child is subject to an increased *general pressure*.

That this increased total tension in the field is a necessary consequence of the two negative valences in the punishment situation is readily deduced from our general principles. [1]We have already discussed the production by vectors V_T and V_P of a strong resultant (V_R) directed sidewise in the direction of the outer barrier (Fig. 9). Otherwise expressed, the conflict situation results in a tendency to go out of the field. If, however, the child attempts to move in the direction of this resultant he strikes the outer barrier. He may break through. If he does so the topology of the total situation is changed and the punishment becomes ineffective. This case will be discussed later. On the other hand the barrier may hold fast. The barrier itself then acquires a negative valence. This may result from a variety of causes: the child has hurt himself, perhaps bodily by running against the barrier; he has experienced his own impotence; or the like. Nonphysical barriers, furthermore, consist largely of prohibitions and act directly as barriers in virtue of their negative valence.

Thus in so far as the punishment situation is maintained there proceeds from the barrier a vector $(V_B$, Fig. 13) opposed in direction to the previous resultant (V_R). Movement in the direction of this resultant leads to conflict; that is, two oppositely directed field forces are acting along the same line.

The same dynamic situation is created when the child seeks to go through the barrier at any point. Opposed field forces exist for the child at every point in the field acting in every direction (Fig. 14[2]); a state of tension exists in the field. [3]

---

[1] The following discussion of the relation between certain field forces and tension in the total field although based upon the punishment situation has a general psychological significance for a whole group of similar situations.

[2] The crosshatching represents the condition of tension.

[3] As a dynamic concept, tension is defined as oppositely directed vectors.

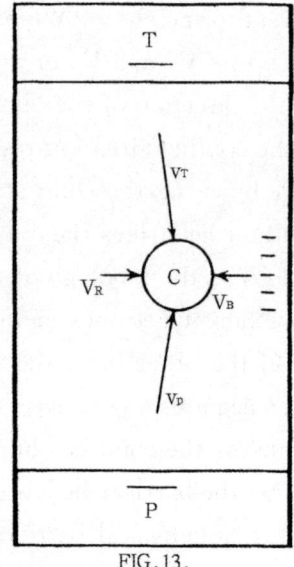
FIG. 13.

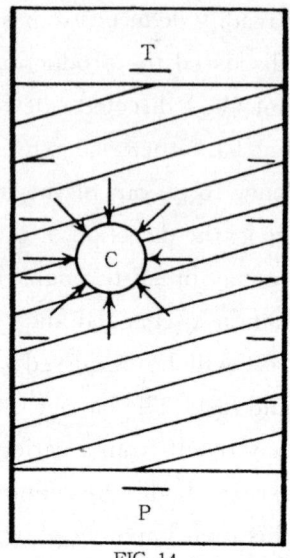
FIG. 14.

The degree of tension in the field depends obviously upon the strength of the negative valences of punishment, task, and barrier. An important influence in determining the strength of the negative valence of the punishment is the child's previous experience in the present or earlier instances of collision with the barrier. For example, the negative valence of the punishment is very strong when the child has previously been severely punished for attempting to go out of the field. The negative valence of the barrier in its acute effect upon the individual case is, however, largely dependent on the strengths of the negative valences of task and punishment. In the last analysis the minimum firmness of barrier and minimal threat of punishment necessary for making such a threat effective depend upon the strength of the negative valence of the task.

Modes of Behavior in the Punishment Situation.

In the previous section we have discussed the general characteristics of the topology and field forces existent when an attempt is made, by threatened punishment, to force the child to act in a certain way. We shall now briefly consider the possibilities of actual behavior that exist for the child in such a situation.

Execution of the Command. Through threat of punishment the child is induced to perform the task, that is, to show the desired behavior. The vector (VP) proceeding from the punishment shows itself stronger than the opposed vector (VT, Fig. 15). The outer barrier remains sufficiently firm. Thus the child enters the field of the task. Completion of the task signifies for the child the way to freedom, escape from the punishment.

Once the child has entered the field of the task the situation may be fundamentally altered. The circumstance that the task no longer stands over against the child but is rather a field in which he finds himself may suffice to bring about this transformation. Sometimes the affair is not so bad as it had appeared in advance. A small child, for instance, may not want to eat a new food but notices at the first bite that it does not taste so bad as expected.

The fact that the child because of threatened punishment enters a field so unpleasant in appearance is in itself, however, not favorable to such a transformation toward pleasantness. On the contrary it may often result in the task's remaining unpleasant. Frequently, moreover, the child is already familiar with the actual unpleasantness of the task.

Standing-within-the-task is in any case psychologically quite a different situation from that of threat of punishment.[1]

Acceptance of the Punishment. The situation in which the vector proceeding from the task is stronger than the negative valence of the punishment (Fig. 16) is in a sense the opposite of the preceding. If in this case the outer barrier is sufficiently strong the child will take the punishment. He goes into the field of punishment because punishment constitutes a way to freedom, similar to that offered by the task in the previous case.

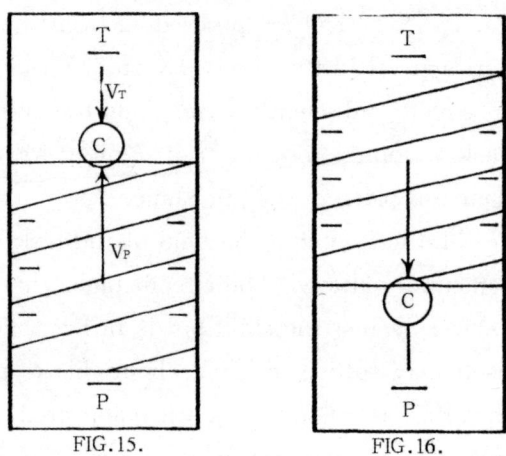

FIG. 15.   FIG. 16.

The following is an example of this type of behavior.

A father says to his three-year-old son, "If you do not gather up your things you will be whipped." The child goes to his father, turns his back to receive the blow and says, "All right!" It is clear that the child had construed his father's remark to mean that he was presented with two possibilities of action.

---

[1] In the World War it could be clearly observed that returning to the front constituted a much more unpleasant situation than being at the front.

It is to be noted that the youngster had never received a whipping. Some time before a switch had been procured and had been used as a threat. The pedagogical atmosphere in the home was, however, characteristically free and lively and the acquisition of the switch rather an isolated event.

It is possible, moveover, that curiosity may have played a role in the decision of the child since during the Christmas holidays a short time before there had been a good deal of reference to the switch, as well as to Santa Claus.

Again the situation underwent transformation for the child as he took the punishment. He noticed that the actual experience of the punishment was in reality not so bad as the ideology of the adult had made it appear in advance.

As punishment for too uproarious conduct, a girl of ten years was confined in a small dark room by her teacher, with whom she generally stood well. The child sat on a vacuum cleaner, pounded lustily with her feet, and sang. To the teacher's astonishment the girl, upon being released, was pleased and answered back jokingly without noticeable embarrassment.

The child had actually succeeded in transforming the punishment into a playful occasion. The real unpleasantness was not very great once she had decided not to take the punishment in a moral sense (see page 138).

The child in experiencing various punishments builds up a certain knowledge of the actual degree of unpleasantness of different punishments. He views a threatened punishment no longer from without but from within, weighing the unpleasantness of the task against that of the punishment. He becomes callous to the punishment and thus less sensitive to threats. An important step in this direction occurs when the child attempts at least retrospectively to minimize the degree of reality of the punishment and the moral degradation which accompanies it.

An intelligent, lively girl of six years who had been going to school for three months tilted back on her chair. As a punishment the teacher made her kneel. When the child returned home she did not appear in the least sad and said to her mother, "I like to kneel."

This particular event stood in a larger context for both teacher and child. The teacher thought it advisable to proceed against the child with stricter disciplinary measures. The child, although at first very much delighted with school, began to withdraw into herself, and her attitude toward the punishment was at the same time an expression of an incipient struggle against the teacher's sphere of power That this transformation in the school atmosphere really bore heavily upon the child and that her indifference toward it was quite superficial manifested itself clearly in her total behavior. She became afraid of the dark, had nightmares, and cried at night in her sleep, "Don't always look at me so, teacher!"

More important than experiencing the degree of unpleasantness of the task is the circumstance that in such cases the execution of the punishment is apt to lead to a revolution in the ideology of the child. His system of values may become transformed. The adult always represents the punishment as something bad, morally degrading. This moral disgrace is ordinarily a major source of the negative valence of the task.

Related to the above is the fact that public punishments are particularly shunned. That social standing is thus injured by punishment is not only of importance to adults but is one of the main grounds for children's fear of punishment.

A certain five-year-old boy was ill. Whenever he was naughty the little negro puppet which hung over his bed was turned with its face to the wall. Thus the fact of his naughtiness was apparent to everyone who came into the room. This exposure acted as a decided sharpening of the already painful circumstance that the beloved negro puppet must hang with its face to the wall. Incidentally, the youngster himself never attempted to turn back the puppet although it hung just above his bed.

Once a transformation of values occurs, however, once punishment loses for the child its aspect of disgrace the strength of its negative valence decreases considerably. There then stands behind the threat only the specific unpleasantness of the present punishment. Timidity before the entire sphere of punishment no longer exists. No longer does the child think anything of being punished. Eventually he may reach the point of view that failure to perform the task is more worthy of pride than is its completion.

The following circumstance is dynamically important in the origin of such a transformation. If the negative valence of the task is so strong that the child prefers punishment, the latter as the lesser evil becomes relatively positive. This shift of relative position is made more difficult by the fact that something belonging to a morally inferior sphere must now appear as being in some way superior to the morally unobjectionable action desired by the adult. When this occurs the unique moral position of the punishment sphere is at one point and thus, in principle, broken down.

The child who attempts to gain freedom by going topologically through the punishment generally finds himself, however, *disillusioned*. Ordinarily the adult is not content merely to inflict the punishment but demands anew the completion of the hated task. At the same time he often threatens a more severe punishment (P_2).

Thus acceptance of the punishment docs *not* actually mean for the child a way to freedom. He finds himself afterwards (Fig. 17) still in the same constrained situation facing the prospect of increasing punishments, which in general finally make him docile. This is probably significant in explanation of the fact that punishment is relatively seldom chosen by the child.

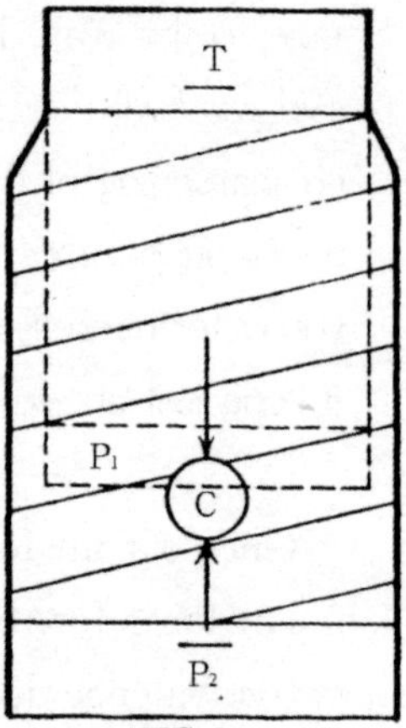

At times, however, punishment actually constitutes a way to freedom. It may be that the adult cannot bring himself to resort to more extreme measures, or perhaps the task in question cannot be executed later on.

FIG.17.

The following is an instance in which acceptance of the punishment really constituted an escape from the constrained situation. W. von Kügelgen at the age of five years was sent to a girls' school. The femininity of the girls was so repulsive to him that on the second day he told his mother that he would not return to school. "Finally, amazed at such staunch resistance she played her trump card and asked me which I would choose, a 'crop of whippings,' as she expressed it, or returning to school. And with that she lost the battle One thought of the faces of the girls and their gentle ways stopped any hesitation. I chose the 'crop.' The punishment was appropriately severe, yes, as I remember it, beyond expectation. Yet it was not to be compared with the detestable dungeon of girls. I was now free. And my mother never presented to me again a similar alternative."①

Action against the Barrier. The third behavioral possibility in the punishment situation, along with performance of task and acceptance of punishment, is action in the direction of the barrier.

In this case the vectors proceeding from task and punishment are too great and the child moves in the direction of the resultant (V_R). There may, then, ensue either a blind, uncontrolled charge against the barrier (the child locked in a room may knock his head and legs against the walls), or a considered attempt to break through. The exact procedure employed by the child in specific cases depends naturally upon the nature of the existing barrier. He may attempt to gain freedom through flattery, defiance, or deceit.

If the barrier is very firm, there is no way out for the child. Under these conditions and with sufficiently strong tension in the total field, there may develop tendencies toward suicide. Suicide then appears as the last remaining possibility of going-out-of-the-field.

As a result of her parents' strictness, Martha, ten years of age, lived in constant terror of poor grades at school.②"The fear of poor marks was especially evident shortly before Easter when the

---

① W. VON KÜGELGEN, *op. cit.*
② A. DOHME, Beitrag zur Psychologie und Psychopathologie typischer Schulkonflikte auf den verschiedenen Altersstufen, *Zeitschr. f. Kinderforsch.*, 1930, 36, 458.

question of promotion was to be decided It was so strong that the child often cried out in her sleep, ran to her mother's bed, and wanted to stay with her because she was afraid. Her parents treated Martha very sternly. Once the mother threatened, 'If you are not promoted you need not come back home! "After this utterance the child entertained thoughts of suicide." The tendency to better her position with her parents by particular neatness was also observable. She "helped about the house more than was required of her, in order to make her mother happy."

Most of these attempts to break through evince not only the escape tendency but also more or less open strife with the adult.

These aspects are related to a condition which we shall proceed to discuss more in detail.

Struggle with the Adult. We have already mentioned that as a rule the outer barrier is essentially social in nature and rests upon the actual power of the adult over the life-sphere of the child. When, then, the child turns against the outer barrier he directs himself in the last analysis against the will and power of the adult to whom the erection of the barrier is due.

In addition, the threatened punishment and finally the task itself is set by the adult. All the vectors and barriers controlling the situation may in the end be traced to the adult who is responsible for maintaining them. Were only the power of the adult to collapse, the whole situation would fall to pieces; task, punishment, and barrier would cease to exist. All valences determining the situation thus derive dynamically from the circumstance that the field is controlled by the adult (Fig. 18). The field of force corresponding to the sphere of power of the child is not strong enough to maintain itself against the sphere of power of the adult. The struggle of the child is an attempt to make a stand against this superior force.

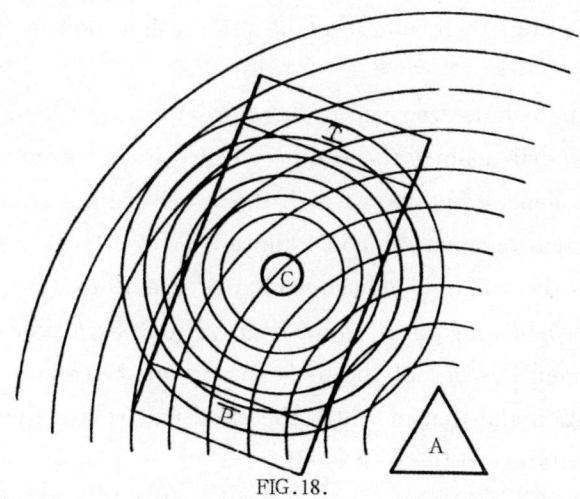

FIG.18.

We have previously spoken (see page 131, Fig. 12) of the domination of the total field by the adult. We were concerned there with peculiarly crass types of constrained situation, in which threat of punishment was effective seemingly without especial barriers. We now see that quite generally the punishment situation is related to the situation there discussed.

Nevertheless, there exists a considerable difference between the former situation and the one here considered. It is possible that, although the outer surrounding barrier is extraordinarily firm due to the actual power of the adult, the child may yet possess within the enclosed area distinct freedom of movement. Threat of punishment, here, is directed specifically toward one task. Not every point in the total situation assumes the character of constraint, as in the examples sketched above.

The actual connection of the adult with task, punishment,

and barrier may not be intellectually quite clear to the child, but owing to the very fine sensitivity of even small children to social relations within their sphere of life, this connection is clearly enough felt.

The punishment situation, therefore, tends to produce an action of combat against the center whence issue dynamically the negative valences and upon which the whole painful situation depends, namely, against the adult himself.

Thus the *threat of punishment creates necessarily a situation in which child and adult stand over against each other as enemies*. Herein lies one of the most important differences between this situation and that in which the child undertakes the task because of interest in the task itself.

The nature of the struggle, as well as the direction in which it takes place, may vary extraordinarily and depends upon the character of the child, of the adult, and upon the peculiarities of the momentary situation. In essence the strife of the child may be directed against the task, against the punishment, or against the barrier thwarting the attempt to go out of the field.

In a direct struggle against the task, the child, as previously mentioned, may advance difficulties which the adult must recognize. The notebook has disappeared, the pen is broken, other pressing assignments must be prepared, and so on. Not infrequently the struggle is carried on by means which Adler[1] would designate as "arrangements." That is to say, the difficulty which the adult must recognize consists in the fact that the child has developed a headache, a phenomenon that is frequently to be ob-

---

[1] Cf. ALFRED ADLER, *Über den nervosen Charakter*, Bergmann, Wiesbaden, 1912. (English trans, *The Neurotic Constitution*, Moffat, Yard, New York, 1917.)

served before school examinations.

The struggle may be directed more specifically against the punishment. Among children a favorite method of anticipating blows at school is to put on particularly thick clothes. A helpful illness is a good defense against punishment. Even flattery, standing in well with the adult, may have the character of such a struggle. The exercise of every form of cheating and deceit occurs more readily in proportion as the situation acquires for the child the character of strife. In such a strife the child may use without hesitation methods which it would probably not employ in any but a hostile atmosphere.

A simple example of an attempt to evade punishment by *deeption* after the deed is described by Schurz. [1] Schurz received a poor mark on his report card. "Whether it was due to shame over my failure or to fear of my father's severity, the fact was that on Saturday when I came home I tried to make my father think that the chaplain had forgotten to write on my card, or something of the sort. My uncertain behavior convinced my father at once that something was wrong. A few questions brought me to confess the true state of affairs The following conversation then occurred: ' You have neglected your duty and have tried to hide the truth from me. Don't you think you deserve to be whipped?'

"'Yes. But please let us go into the cow-shed where no one can see or hear us.' The request was granted. I underwent my chastisement in the seclusion of the cow-shed. It was not severe, and no one knew anything of it. My father forgave me and treated

---

[1] KARL SCHURZ, *Lebenserinnerungen*, cited by BAÜMER and DROESCHES, *Vonder Kinderseele*, Leipzig, 1908, p. 236.

me as before. But the bitter consciousness of having been humiliated deservedly remained with me some time as a heavy burden. For a long while I avoided the cow-shed, the scene of my shame, whenever possible."

The tendency discussed above to attempt to prevent one's punishment from becoming public is clearly shown in this illustration.

Finally, the struggle may center specifically against the outer barrier, which hinders going-out-of-the-field.

Whether they are directed especially against the task, the punishment, or the barrier, all of these fighting activities characteristically show a *double aspect*, conditioned by both the structure of the situation and the dynamic source of the field forces. They are at the same time a flight from and a struggle against the adult. Actually the child can go out of the field only by going through the barrier, task, or punishment, and in the last analysis all these are only different embodiments of the adult himself.

If the total milieu is such that the child must frequently count upon threatened punishments, he may carry on the strife against the adult beyond the specific punishment situation, attempting in this way to shake or undermine his power. Here belong the struggle between teacher and pupils, the so-called problem of discipline, and the endless variety of active and passive obstruction which children are accustomed to raise against those parents and teachers who lay especial emphasis on authority.

Encysting. Defiance. Going-out-of-the-field need not result in breaking through the boundaries of the punishment situation. It may also be achieved by a sort of *encysting* of the child within the field. Without actually leaving the field the child attempts to make himself unassailable, at least for a time; to erect a wall between both task and punishment, and himself. Functionally and in meaning, such an encysting is in many respects equivalent to going-out-of-the-field.

The encysting is usually the more marked the higher the tension and the less the prospect of escape. The child mentioned above (page 140) who entertained thoughts of suicide from fear of not being promoted showed this encysting. "Martha had no chum. Aside from playing with her girl classmates on the way home from school she remained alone Neither did she have any friends among the children of the neighborhood. She played only occasionally with them, preferring to associate with smaller children"[1]

Closely related to encysting, indeed a special form of it, is the *defiance* reaction.

The child withdraws into himself. He does not, however, attempt to avoid the strong pressure of the environment, to evade every unpleasant contact. Rather, encysting here consists in taking up a defiant, fighting attitude toward the environment. [2] As it is displayed for instance in the case of a new punishment threatened immediately after previous punishment (see example on page 140), the defiance reaction is both a convulsive summing up of one's forces and self-assertion in a tense hostile situation. It signifies an insensitivity toward the threat and at the same time a struggle against the field of power of the adult. The insensitivity results chiefly from the fact that the values and demands set up by

---

[1] A. DOHME, *loc. cit.*
[2] Cf. FAJANS, *loc. cit.*, and WINKLER, *Der Trotz*, Munich, 1929.

the foreign field of force are no longer recognized as binding for the individual concerned. Along with encysting and strife, defiance involves also a certain revolution in the child's ideology.

In children defiance frequently occurs as a first sign of independence, of breaking through the social field that until then has been overpowering. With suppressed, passive children the first welcome sign of activity often consists in being impudent.

Flight into Unreality. Emotional Outburst. Among the various types of actual behavior which may occur in the punishment situation, there remain to be discussed certain processes which have a direct relation to the state of tension in the situation, namely, flight into unreality and emotional outburst.

In the psychological life-sphere in addition to the plane of reality there usually exist various *levels of unreality*. Unreality (the plane of dreams, of so-called imagination, of gesture) is roughly characterized by the fact that in it one can do as he pleases. Dynamically there is a lack of firm barriers and a large degree of mobility. ① And the boundaries between the ego and the environment are also fluid.

The degree of reality of psychological processes and inventions is such a fundamental category that it is to be used as a special third dimension for all more exact representations of the psychical environment (see Fig. 18). A consideration of this dimension in a more detailed presentation of the problems of reward and punishment

---

① J. F. BROWN, Über die dynamischen Eigenschaften der Realitats—und Irrealitatsschichten, *Psychol. Forsch.*, 1933, 18, 1-26.

would undoubtedly be very important. It is closely related to questions of morality and to the general ideology of the child.

If the condition of tension in the situation of threatened punishment becomes too unpleasant without prospect of a way out, there arises a strong tendency to go out of the field by fleeing from the plane of reality into that of unreality. One succeeds, of course, in going out of the unpleasant field not bodily, but only psychologically.

The differentiation of the psychical environment into levels of reality and unreality is at first not clear in the child. This condition expresses itself in the magical structure of his conception of the world,①in play, and in the lack of a firm boundary between truth and falsehood, dream and reality, gesture and action. Furthermore, transition from reality to unreality occurs readily.

Fear of punishment may not only dominate dreams, but may lead eventually to enuresis and similar phenomena. ②It may also result in intensive daydreams.

Within the level of unreality those things upon which the unpleasantness of the plane of reality rests are removed. The child is no longer in a constrained situation in the power of the adult, but is free. The unpleasant task is finished or put aside. The child himself is dominant, not the adult. When definite needs and wishes are sharply blocked on the plane of reality, a sort of substitute satisfaction③of just these needs may occur in the level of unreality of

---

① J. PIAGET, *La représentation du monde chez l'enfant*, Alcan, Paris, 1926. (English trans. , *The Child's Conception of the World*, Harcourt, Brace, New York, 1929.)
② Cf. HOMBURGER, *op. cit.* , and DOHME, *loc. cit.*
③ In psychoanalytic theory substitution, as is well known, plays a great role. Concerning the dynamics and types of substitution processes, see Dembo, *op. cit.*

play or daydream.

The following literary example, to be presented rather fully, illustrates not the conflict situation between unpleasant task and punishment but rather the fluctuating situation after the misdemeanoi, the fear of coming punishment. The topology of the situation in the second part of the story corresponds closely to that of the punishment situation. The child, locked in his bedroom, faces the threatened punishment in a situation of decided constraint.

Nikolaj [1] received a failing mark in his history lesson under Teacher Lebedew, because he had learned nothing. He feared censure and punishment from his tutor, St. Jerome, whom his brother had at first deceived about the mark. Furthermore, he had run out of the room for a while during the hour. This was discovered by Mimi, his sister's governess, who would tell his grandmother about it. Thirdly, Nikolaj had secretly opened a brief case containing letters of his father and in doing it had broken the small key. He therefore anticipated a punishment from his loved father.

"'Mimi's complaint! The bad mark! And the key! Nothing worse could have happened. Grandmama—for Mimi's tale, St. Jerome—for the zero, Papa— for the key. ... And all this will come down on my head not later than tonight !' 'What will happen to me?'

'A-ah! What have I gotten into?' I said to myself walking up and down on the white rug of the work room. 'Eh,' I said to myself, taking the candy and cigars, 'what must come, must come!' And so I ran back into the house.

This fatalistic sentiment which I learned in my childhood from

---

[1] L. N TOLSTOY, *Lebensstufen*, Diederichs, Leipzig, 1903, pp. 255 ff.

Nikolaj has exercised a soothing, momentarily quieting effect upon me in all the heavy hours of my life. As I entered the room I was in a somewhat excited and unnatural but completely gay frame of mind.

After dinner the games began and I participated in them in the liveliest manner. We were playing 'cat and the mouse.' Tn my awkwardness I bumped the governess of the Family Kornakow who was playing with us, stepped acci dentally upon her dress and tore it. I saw that all of the girls, especially Sonit schka, were prepared to enjoy with the greatest pleasure the way in which the governess with angry expression hurried into the girls' room to sew her dress, and I made up my mind to repeat for them the pleasurable incident.

As a result of this amiable intention, I commenced as soon as the governess came back to our room to prance around her. Persisting in this game long enough I snatched a favorable moment to again entangle myself in her clothes and tear them. Sonitschka and the children of the countess could scarcely keep from laughing. My own pride was flattered to the last degree. But st. Jerome, who must have seen through my game, came up, wrinkled his forehead (which I could barely stand) and said that my playfulness did not become me, and if I did not behave better it would end badly in spite of the celebrations of the day.

"I found myself, however, in the excited condition of one who has already lost more in play than he has in his pocket, who fears to settle his accounts, and who in his despair keeps playing new cards without hope of regaining them in order to prevent himself from coming to consciousness. I laughed up at him impudently and left him standing"

Dynamically the situation described is to be characterized somewhat as follows (Fig. 18a). The *fields of force* dominating the life-space of the child (C) are, above all, those of the father (F), of the grandmother (G), and of the tutor, St Jerome (J). The child experiences the field of power of St. Jerome as hostile Now, however, because of his own guilt the fields of his father and grandmother possess vectors directed against him. These latter are the persons to whom the child feels most closely bound, who have control of the house, and from whom in the last analysis the sphere of power of the tutor, St. Jerome, derives. At present all these fields have acquired a threatening significance for the child.

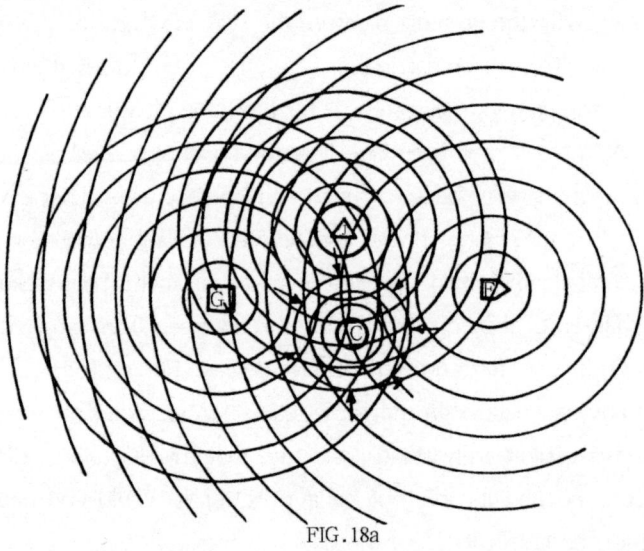

FIG. 18a

As a result of these threats from all sides the inner tension of the child is extraordinarily great. His first reaction consists in going-out-of-the-field in the direction of unreality. The child comforts himself in attempting a fatalistic weakening of reality ("What is to come, will come!"). Naturally this is not sufficient to relieve the tension, which is intensified by the gaiety of the celebration occurring on the plane of reality. Pronounced restless activity and emotional outbreaks ensue.

This affectivity soon leads to a new severe clash with the tutor St. Jerome, who meantime has discovered the bad mark and has exposed the boy in public. The child hits the tutor and is thereupon locked in the attic.

In despair and full of fear of the coming punishment the boy sits in the room. The level of reality (LR) in his situation is to be represented approximately as follows (Fig. 18b).

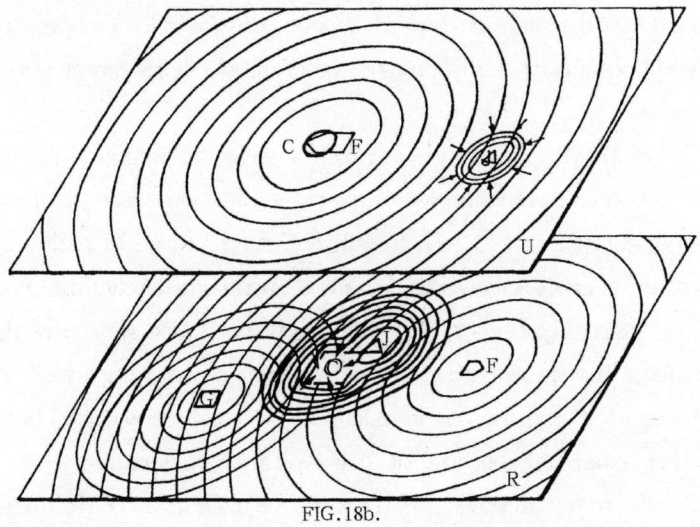

FIG. 18b.

Out of the whirl of the preceding scenes he is brought into an externally quiet environment. It is, however, at the same time a situation of pronounced bodily constraint, a physical prison. This prison is an expression of the hostility of St. Jerome and simultaneously an expression of the strength of this inimical sphere of power. In the social level of reality the child's own field of force is wholly inferior to this hostile power. St Jerome himself had locked the child in the bedroom. The heaviness of the situation is the more oppressive since acutely hostile actions of the highest authorities, the father and grandmother, are to be anticipated in the near future.

In spite of the extraordinary state of tension there occur no true emotional outbreaks, as had happened shortly before. Outwardly the child appears rather quiet. This behavior may in part result from the fact that the child, now alone and left to himself, possesses whithin the prison a definite even though narrowly limited freedom. The following considerations are probably more important. If pressure from the environment becomes so great and so all sided that the situation appears without possibility of escape (such conditions are typical of despair) a certain bodily rigidity frequently results. [1]

In this prison situation in which a bodily going-out-of-the-field is impossible the tension within the plane of reality leads to an inner gomg-out-of-the-field, to a transition from the plane of reality into that of unreality. Lively imagining and daydreams occur. The affective tension expresses itself within the plane of unreality by restless thinking The special structure of the level of unreality which thus shows itself, and the events occurring in it, are reproduced below rather extensively because of their typical characteristics.

"I did not weep but it was as though a stone lay on my breast. Thoughts and ideas flew with accelerated speed back and forth in my confused imagination. But the memory of my misfortune constantly interrupted their strange chain, and I fell back again in an endless labyrinth of uncertainty over my fate.

"It soon came to me that there must surely be some unknown cause of the universal lack of love, yes, even hate, shown me (I

---

[1] LEWIN, Kindliche Ausdrucksbewegungen, in W. STERN, *Psychologic der fruhen Kindheit*, 6th ed., Quelle u. Meyer, Leipzig, 1930, p. 502 (English trans., *Psychology of Early Cht'dhood*, Holt, New York, 1930).

was at that moment firmly convinced that everyone from grandmother to the coachman Philip hated me and rejoiced in my present sorrow) Perhaps, I said to myself, I am not, after all, the son of my Father and Mother, Volodja's brother, but an unfortunate waif, a foundling kept from pity And indeed this foolish thought not only provided me a certain doleful comfort but seemed fully probable It was an ecstasy to think that the cause of my unhappiness was not my guilt but my fate from birth, a destiny resembling that of the unfortunate Karl Iwanowitsch.

"And talking on to myself, I asked why this secret remain concealed now that I had seen through it Tomorrow morning, I thought, I will go to papa and say, 'Papa, in vain you hide from me the secret of my birth I know it ' He will reply, 'What is to be done, my dear child? Sooner or later you would surely have discovered it—You are not my son—I have, however, taken you as a son and if you prove yourself worthy of my love, I shall never desert you. ' And shall answer, 'Tapa, although I have no right to give you this name, still I will use it this one time more. I have always loved you and will love you. I shall never forget that you have been my benefactor. Yet I can remain no longer in this house. Here no one loves me, and St. Jerome has sworn to destroy me. Either he or I must leave your house. I cannot answer for myself. I so hate this man that I am capable of anything. I shall kill him. Yes, I swear it Papa, I will kill him. ' Papa reasons with me but I put out my hand and say to him, 'No, my friend, my benefactor, we cannot live under one roof. Let me go, I embrace him and say, I know not why in French, ' *Oh, man père, oh mon bien faiteur, donne-moi pour la dernière fois la bénédiction el que la wlonté de Dieu sot faite*!' And I sat on the chest in the dark room and wept, sobbing loudly at this thought. Suddenly I thought again of the shameful punishment awaiting me. Reality came back to me in its true light and the pictures of my imaginatiorn faded instantly."

The subjective oppression of the situation is not least dependent upon the fact that it is traceable to the child's own guilt. The first flight into unreality consists in a separation of these guilty occurrences from his own ego. As frequently occurs after failure [1] one's own responsibility for the unpleasant state of affairs is shifted by rationalization. Fate, for whom no one can answer, is to blame The inner alienation of the grandmother and above all of the father, so feared bythe child, is explained by the fact that he is not a real son of his father, but a foundling. The child (suddenly breaking into French) refuses pathetically al consolation and draws the tragic (and thus not guilty) consequence: he leaves the house, he thinks, "I shall soon die." The flight from the prison is com-pletcd, even though on the plane of unreality.

Gradually there occurs a general *trutural reorganization of the plane of unreality*. This continues until the child possesses in this plane what he lacks in reality, especially until his social position is radically changed and indeed com pletcly reversed.

"Soon I saw myself free, far from our house. I was a hussar entering battle. From all sides the enemy pressed down upon me. I drew my sabre, killing the first assailant with one stroke. Another stroke sufficed for the second, and another for the third. Finally exhausted from wounds and fatigue I sank to earth crying, 'Victory!' The general rode by, and asked, 'Where is—he oui deliverer?' All pointed to me. He fell on my neck, crying through tears ol joy, 'Victory!' Later, convalescing, I was walking along the Twer-Boulevard. I was a general! The Czar met me and asked, Who is this

---

[1] HOPPE, *op. cit.*

wounded youngster? The famous hero, Nikolaj,' he was told. The Czar approached me,'I thank you. Ask of me what you will. I will grant you anything. Bowing respectfully and leaning on my sabre, I replied, I am fortunate, mighty Czar, to havte been able to spill my blood for my country. I would gladly have offered my life, Since, however, you are so gracious as to grant me a request, permit me to destroy my enemy, the foreigner, St. Jerome. I approached St. Jerome threateningly, 'You are to blame for my unhappiness. Kneel!' Suddenly, however, the thought came to me that the real St. Jerome might enter with a rod at any minute. Again I saw myself not as a general saving his country, but as a most deplorable, pitiable creature.

"Soon the thought of God came to me and I asked why he should be punishing me. I had not neglected to pray, morning and evening. Why then should I suffer? I can definitely say that the first step toward the religious doubts of my boyhood days occurred at this instant. It was not because unhappiness drove me to grumbling and disbelief but because the thought of the injustice of Providence came to me. And in that twenty-four hours of solitude and complete mental confusion the thought was like an evil seed that, falling after a rain in loose earth, quickly sprouted and took root. Soon I imagined that I should surely die, and pictured vividly St. Jerome's astonishment when he would find my lifeless body in the attic. I remembered the tale of Natalja Sawischa, that the soul of the expired lingers about the house for forty days. In thought I wandered after death unseen through the rooms of my grandmother's house, hearing Ljubotschka's whining, the complaints of grandmother, and Papa speaking with August Antonowitsch. 'He was a good boy,' Papa would say with tears in his eyes. 'Yes,' St Jerome would counter, 'but a great rogue. ' 'You should have respect for the dead' Papa censured. You were the cause of his death. You intimidated him. He could not stand the humiliation you caused. ... Out of my house, miserable one!

"St Jerome sank to his knees, begging forgiveness. Then the forty days were over and my soul flew to heaven. I saw there something wonderfully beautiful, white, transparent, and felt that it was my Mother."

The situation in unreality is a complete reversal of that in reality. The child's own field of force that had just shown itself quite weak on the plane of reality (LR, Fig 18b) becomes, on the plane of unreality, thanks to his heroic behavior, the socially dominant field. At the same time the particularly painful separation from his beloved father is overcome. Whereas in reality the socially most powerful field of force (that of the father, F) is turned against the child, in unreality because of this reunion it stands at his disposal; the father fulfills the punishment of St Jerome.

The previous daydream had also created on the plane of unreality a very similar situation. There it was the Czar, the most powerful person in the world, whose field of force was placed at the disposition of the boy. Both imaginal situations led to the destruction of St. Jerome, whose power in reality was keeping the boy prisoner in the attic. On the plane of unreality the child is not weak and imprisoned, but powerful and free. The most powerful victorious enemy of the actual moment, on the contrary, is impotent and defeated.

The imaginal picture stretching into unearthly power and freedom climaxes in the reunion with the dead mother.

We shall not examine later occurrences on the plane of reality. The child refuses to make apology to the teacher. A final attempt at actual flight from the house is frustrated by the father.

If the opposed vectors controlling the conflict situation are very strong, the tension may result in diffuse discharge, that is, in an *emotional outburst*. This is illustrated in the above example. The child raves, cries out, weeps. When this happens in the punishment situation, it generally occurs when a momentary attempt at flight is frustrated.

Even if no marked emotional expression occurs, as in the story above, the increased state of tension may decidedly influence the quality of work. We shall consider a case of especial pedagogical interest, the solution of intellectual tasks. Intellectual tasks undoubtedly require for their solution a certain tension, a vector in the direction of completion of the task. It is unnecessary to discuss again (see pages 120 f.) the fact that positive valence of the task itself provides a more favorable condition for the solution of intellectual tasks than aversion to the task. In the former case despite the occurrence of difficulties, that is, barriers, in the course of its solution a child continues to work in the direction of the task.

It is to be noted further that a conflict situation, especially when it leads to a strong total tension, is peculiarly unfavorable to the solution of intellectual tasks. In its general psychological structure the solution of an intellectual problem consists essentially in a transformation of the Gestalt relations within the sphere of the problem, in a mental "clicking," so to speak. ① A necessary condition for the occurrence of such "clicking" is that the individual achieve a view of the field as a whole. The decisive transformation of the structure of the field also requires that the person be able to stand above the situation. He must have the possibility of

---

① W. KÖHLER, *Intelligenzprüfungen an Menschenaffen*, Springer, Berlin, 1924. (English trans., *The Mentality of Apes*, Harcourt, Brace, New York, 1925.)

gaining some distance from the task. Only thus is it possible to see the total system of relations instead of simply several isolated facts in the field.

If the child is in a conflict situation with a strong state of tension he feels himself to be standing under the situation, that is, without a view from above. This obviously constitutes an unfavorable condition for calm intellectual solution of the problem.

We have completed our discussion of the topology of the situation involving threat of punishment in the case of a command. We shall not proceed immediately to threat of punishment in the case of a prohibition but shall first consider the situation arising when there is a prospect of reward.

Command With Prospect of Reward

Pedagogically, reward appears as the opposite of punishment.

Nevertheless, the general situations in which reward and punishment occur are in certain respects similar. As in the case of punishment, the prospect of reward is only offered when the child is to be led to a type of behavior which the natural field forces of the moment will not produce. The child is to do something which he does not wish to do or to refrain from doing something he desires to do. We shall first consider the situation in which the child is to be gotten by reward to carry out an undesired task.

Nature and Disposition of Valences and Barriers.

The child (C) is again placed opposite a task (T) of negative valence. Whereas in threatened punishment the attempt is made to overcome the vector proceeding from the task by means of a second negative valence, in the present situation a positive valence is utilized. This may be a good mark, a toy, a piece of candy, a promotion, being praised as a good child, or the like. Since the attraction proceeding from the positive valence must overcome the repulsion of the task, the reward (R) must be in the same direction as the task (T). It must also be placed behind the task (Fig. 19).

Thus we are again confronted with a conflict situation. As we have seen, this means that two approximately equal oppositely directed field forces are working on the child. In this case the conflict situation is of the third type discussed above (page 123).

The vector (V_R) proceeding from the reward must again be stronger than that proceeding from the task (V_T), and its strength must vary with the unpleasantness of the task.

Such a situation would, however, by no means suffice to get the child to complete the task. To the child, attracted by the reward, the unpleasant task constitutes a barrier, lying between him and the goal (G). In this respect the topology corresponds to that of the situation in which a difficulty prevents the child from attaining his goal (Fig. 2). As a rule R in such a situation, where the goal is blocked, the child attempts to get around the barrier. It is the situation in which the *Umweg* (detour) typically occurs. Or the child may attempt to find a weak spot in the barrier. Thus, as in the case of punishment, the child may attempt, when the prospect of a reward is offered, to reach the attractive goal (*e. g.*, candy) without fulfilling the task (Fig. 20). Unless measures are taken to insure that such an evasion of the task is not possible, he will, for example, attempt to obtain the reward from the adult by flattery or by an effort to conceal his failure to finish the task.

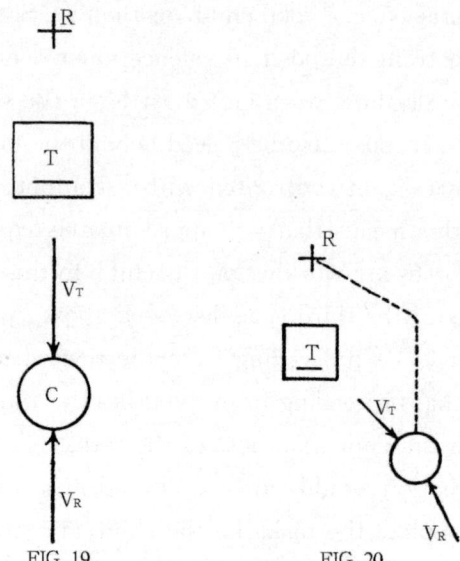

FIG. 19.   FIG. 20.

Thus it is also necessary in the reward situation so to erect barriers that access to the reward is possible only through carrying out the task (Fig. 21).

One may represent this situation without using particular barriers. The fact that the reward may be reached only through the task is also represented if the task is pictured as a zone surrounding the reward (Fig. 22). Topologically the two representations are in many respects equivalent. In both, the zone of the reward (R) is entirely enclosed. The representations differ in that in Fig. 22 the enclosing zone is relatively homogeneous, consisting only of the task, whereas in Fig. 21 it consists partly of the task, partly of the special barrier (B). In most cases Fig. 21 probably represents the situation more accurately. There are usually special barriers, firm conduct of the adult, for example. Generally a series of other precautions, physical and social, are also necessary to insure that the child will attain the reward only through completing the task.

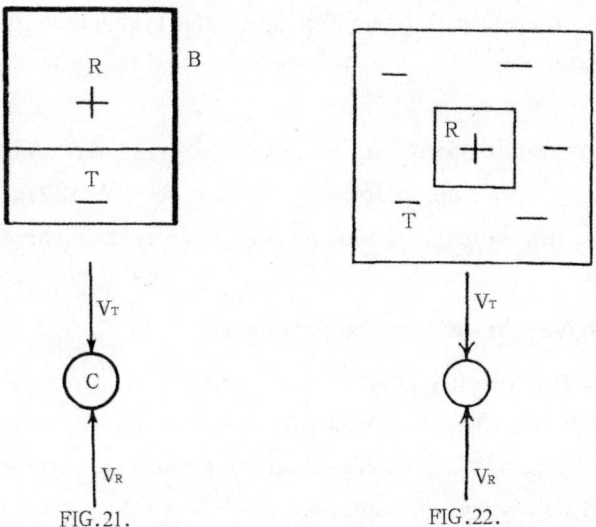

FIG.21.   FIG.22.

Comparison of the Total Situations Underlying Reward and Punishment.

Important parallels appear in the comparison of the total situations of expected reward and expected punishment. Both are conflict situations, and there occur in both general consequences of conflict: increase in tension and tendency to deviate from the direction of the task. In both cases there is lacking the natural teleology characteristic of the interest situation (see page 120).

Certain differences, however, exist. In considering them, we shall not be primarily concerned with the moral aspects of reward or punishment, nor with their effect upon self-consciousness, nor the encouragement or discouragement incidental to their occurrence. One major difference lies in the fact that with threat of punishment the child is surrounded by a barrier, whereas in the reward situation he stands outside the ring constituted by both barrier and task. Thus a prospect of reward does not restrict the child's freedom of movement as a whole. Rather, within the life-sphere of the child only one specific object, the reward, is made unattainable (until, of course, it is reached through completion of the task).

Further, when prospect of reward is presented merely in order to bring about completion of a task (see page 130), the situation lacks the constraint characteristic of the punishment situation.

Behavior in the Reward Situation.

1. If the reward possesses an attraction strong enough to counterbalance the unpleasantness and duration of the task and if the remaining barriers surrounding the reward are strong enough, the child will carry out the task.

Nevertheless, as with punishment, there is lacking here also, the natural teleology characteristic of the interest situation (where the child constantly orients himself toward the actual goal of the task). Frequently upon approach or actual entrance into the field of the task, the child's movement quickly reveals a discrepancy between the direction of the task's goal and of the reward (Fig. 23). The child veers in the direction of the reward during the completion of his task. He will break off the task as soon as possible, perhaps before completion, if only the reward can be attained.

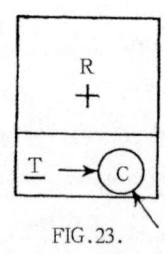

FIG.23.

2. If the unpleasantness of the task is stronger than the reward, the child will abandon the reward, analogously to taking the punishment.

Frequently there occurs a relative shift and reevaluation of worths (see page 138). Often the reward is given a moral tone.

And not infrequently this moral tone signifies a social elevation of the good child above his comrades. Renunciation of the reward usually means that the child at least in the given instance stands outside the ideology in which the reward (a good mark, for example) is considered morally desirable.

There exist, however, important differences between the situation just sketched and that of punishment. In consequence of the lessened condition of constraint in the reward situation the processes are on the whole of an easier character. Further, the moral revaluations that occur when the child accepts punishment as the lesser evil are in part of different type from those that occur when the child abandons a reward or gives up an ambition to achieve a good mark.

Only rarely does reward follow a definite action of the child as a factually necessary consequence, independent of the adult's will. [1] Such situations are psychologically related in important respects to those in which behavior is determined by interest in the thing itself.

3. With strong unpleasantness of task and strong attraction of reward the child may attempt to break through the barrier, to participate, for instance, in an excursion promised as reward even though his task be unfinished.

This situation resembles in certain respects that of punishment. To be sure, a break through the barrier leads in this case to reward rather than to freedom. But a parallel exists in that the

---

[1] Punishment may also, under certain circumstances, possess the character of a natural sanction against transgression of a command or prohibition.

barrier here also rests essentially upon the power of the adult. Breaking through has thus the character of a struggle with the adult. Corresponding to the lack of a pronounced condition of constraint, the strife is generally less bitter. In addition there exists a stronger tendency to conduct the struggle by flattery or some other accepted method, since the child is striving to induce the adult to allow it some pleasure.

Combination of Reward and Punishment.

The reward situation just sketched seldom occurs in this pure form. Usually the adult relies upon a pedagogy neither of reward alone nor of simple punishment, but rather upon a combination of the two, "sugar and the switch."Generally with presentation of a reward there is at the same time a more or less hidden threat of punishment should the reward prove ineffective.

The school system of grading is perhaps the simplest and most characteristic example of this case. A good grade has the character of a reward, a bad one that of punishment, and the total situation is such that one or the other necessarily occurs. when the child is faced with an unpleasant school task which will be graded, the tendency to solve the problem as well as possible derives both from the negative valence of a bad mark and from the positive valence of a good one (Fig. 24).

This simultaneous fear of punishment and hope of reward is characteris-

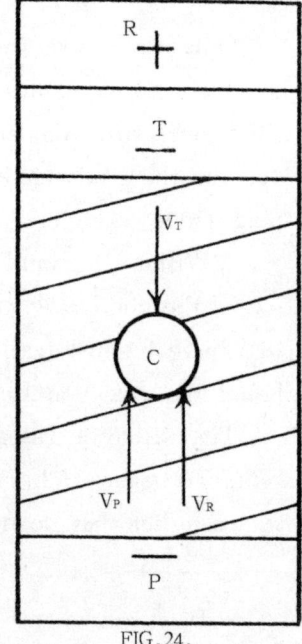

FIG.24.

tic of many situations of the type in question.

Prohibition With Threat of Punishment

So far we have discussed cases in which threat of punishment or prospect of reward has served the purpose of getting the child to perform a definite action, that, for instance, of completing a definite task. Let us now briefly consider the topology of those cases in which prohibition rather than commanded performance of a desired action is to be insured. We shall discuss first prohibition with threat of punishment.

There occur cases of threatened punishment in which one might as well speak of command as of prohibition. If a teacher threatens a child with punishment should he fail to behave, the child is faced in the first place with a prohibition of certain unmannerly actions (laughing, acting "fresh," and so on). In addition, he is expected to display a group of well-intentioned positive types of action, a minimum of which may not be evaded in fulfilling the prohibition. Thus a command also exists. Although the following cases may not always lend themselves to unequivocal classification in one or another definite group, it is preferable to proceed from such definite fundamental cases for the elucidation of psychological dynamics.

The child is faced by a desired goal, a positive valence. For a negative valence to be effective as an opposing force it must lie in the same direction as this goal. Thus arises a conflict situation of the third type (see page 123), similar to that existing when a command is presented with prospect of reward.

The most obvious representation of the situation, therefore, would be analogous to Fig. 21 or to Fig. 22 : threat of punishment stands as an opposing force before the desired goal (DG, Fig. 25). ①

The behavior of the child testifies that to a certain extent this representation actually fits the situation. A two-year-old child has been forbidden to pick flowers in the garden. Consider his behavior as he hesitates before a flower, saying threateningly to himself, "No, no." Such conduct gives the impression that the threat of punishment really stands as a barrier in front of the desired goal.

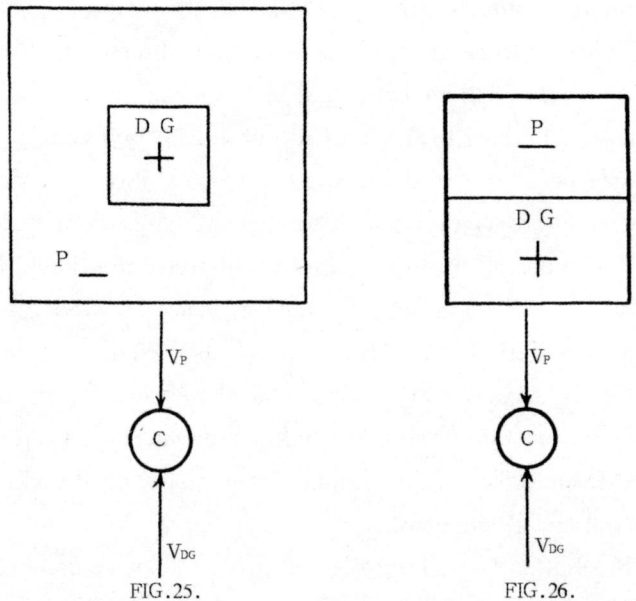

FIG.25. FIG.26.

Nevertheless punishment does not stand before the wanted goal in the same way as the unpleasant task before the reward. Punishment is not something that temporally precedes the attain-

---

① In Fig 25 the representation of the topology is analogous to that of Fig. 22. A representation analogous to Fig 21 would in this case be less adequate.

ment of the goal. It is not a possible way to the goal, but stands rather temporally behind it.

In attempting to represent this temporal relation it is, nevertheless, not possible to place the punishment forthwith behind the desired goal, as in Fig. 26. For this would represent the goal as immediately attainable by the child, who would then be free to move away from the punishment. Actually should the child carry out the desired activity he would thereby incur the punishment. Once he enters the field of the desired goal he finds himself surrounded by the punishment. The situation after entrance into the desired activity (the second phase) may be represented topologically as in Fig. 27. The child, as it were, stands in a cage from which he strives to escape by all available methods.

The further fact that the child cannot escape punishment by lingering in the field of the goal is not represented, although such attempts are sometimes observed. The punishment is here not a barrier preventing transition of the child to another activity. Generally nothing stands in the way of such a shift. Rather, punishment comes to the child without the necessity of his moving in a definite direction.

A certain transformation of its topology is thus characteristic of the prohibition situation. Before acting (first phase Fig. 28) the child sees the threat of punishment (TP) as an obstacle between him and the desired goal. This obstacle, however, is essentially different from the barriers we have previously discussed. It can be passed without any present difficulty or unpleasantness. It does not thus represent the actual, real punishment but only reflects the barrier that acquires full reality after entrance into the desired activity. Thus in the first phase the barrier has more or less the unreality of all future events, of everything whose advent is not yet certain.①

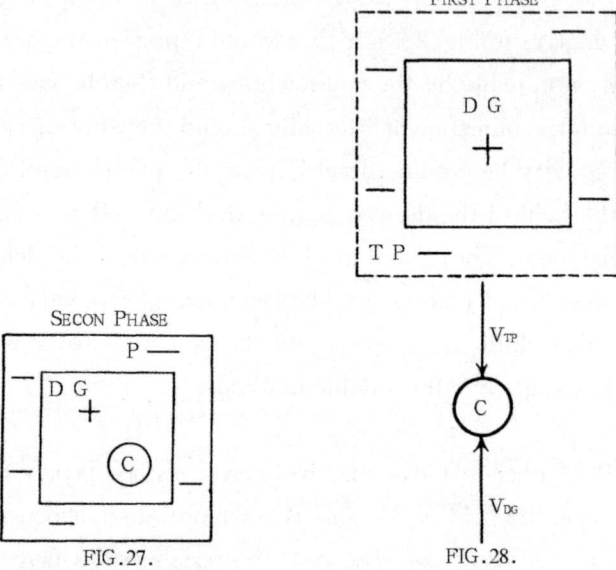

FIG. 27.   FIG. 28.

In the case of command with threat of punishment a definite time is set within which the command must be executed.② This furnishes as we have seen an element of constraint; the child is surrounded by a barrier (Fig. 10). In the case of prohibition with threat of punishment such a temporal limitation need not exist. The constrained character is in general less pronounced. The child

---

① For the significance of degrees of reality in dynamics, see Hoppe, op. cit., and Dembo, *op. cit*. The fact that the unreality of future events is not quite the same as that of thought is left unconsidered here.

② Or the command may be conditional. A definite action, for instance, is to be carried out upon occurrence of certain conditions. Thus, "If someone comes you are to say, 'Good day,' nicely."

remains free to move except in the definitely bounded area of the forbidden action. The constrained character of the situation, however, increases if the forbidden area is very large or if it touches a central life-sphere (as when association with a loved friend or indulgence in a favorite occupation is forbidden).

Digression on the Degree of Reality of Punishment.

The degree of reality of reward or punishment plays a large role in determining the actual behavior of the child. This degree of reality depends upon a whole group of factors. Above all it is a function of the certainty with which the child anticipates punishment or reward (thus indirectly of the actual power of the adult, his sympathy, and so on). It depends equally upon the character and upon the momentary condition of the child (e. g. , immersion in his own dreams and the degree of reality of his conception of the world). I remember quite exactly my childish attitude toward whips. Since I never experienced whippings at home the cane-handled switch at school always had for me something of the incomprehensible and unreal, although it was not infrequently used. This unreality was so strong that once when I was forced to face it the situation filled me with amazement. The teacher was astonished, as I observed with surprise and without crying the lively pain of the separate blows.

The importance of the degree of reality of punishment is shown above all in the fact that children who once have experienced a punishment are wont to behave quite differently in the face of a threatened repetition from whose who have never experienced it. The reason that the burned child shuns the fire, that one who has been severely punished generally shows less resistance in the face of a new threat of punishment, is not to be sought merely in an associative coupling with pain. More essential is an increase in the degree of reality of the punishment, the transformation of the punishment from an imagined, possible occurrence in a level of unreality into part of the plane of reality. We have already mentioned that such transformation of the degree of reality does not always result in increased fear of punishment but may lead to devaluation of the punishment and eventually to release from the previous ideology. Descent from levels of unreality to the plane of reality makes things not only harder, but also more naked, simple, and more easily surveyed in their whole extent.

A certain *transformation* in time of the *degree of reality* is to be observed in all the reward and punishment situations we have discussed. With increasing nearness punishment and unpleasantness of task both become more real. Occurrences within this interval may lead to sudden shifts in the degree of reality of either. Punishment of another child by the adult, even mention of some other punishment anything making the adult seem particularly dangerous or harmless are examples of such occurrences. Such shifts often play an essential role in determining the time and nature of the child's decision. Should the degree of reality of punishment and task differ too greatly a pronounced conflict situation does not generally arise. [1]

In the event of incompletion of the task in the situation of command with threat of punishment, the punishment continues to gain in reality as it approaches. In the last discussed instance of prohibition with threat of punishment, the punishment is typically an *ex post facto* affair, especially when the forbidden goal of de-

---

[1] We may recall that one of the necessary conditions for the origin of a true conflict situation is the approximate equality of opposed vectors.

sire (perhaps some attractive sweets) is present and therefore possesses a very much higher degree of reality. "Opportunity makes the thief." It is also naturally characteristic of these situations that there exists a relatively great difference between the degrees of reality of the positive and negative valences. Herein often lies the child's chief difficulty in making a stand against the attraction.

Related to the fact that punishment is psychologically farther oil than satisfaction of the desire is the circumstance that a certain intellectual maturity is a necessary condition of the effectiveness of such threatened punishments. The world of a little child is of small extent temporally as well as spacially. Events which can be surveyed in direction of past or future and which as part of the momentary situation determine the behavior of the child develop in the first year of the child's life from initially very small temporal extents. Not until a sufficiently large temporal span becomes a psychologically real present for the child can a threat of punishment be effective by reason of such a topology. ①

A general property of threat of punishment frequently becomes noticeable in the last-mentioned situation and is to be related to natural differences in the degrees of reality of punishment and desired goal. It is precisely because of threat of punishment that an originally neutral event first acquires *positive* attraction. ② Corresponding opposed shifts in valences may also be observed in

---

① We shall discuss later (p. 169) still another possible effect of punishment.
② I do not here refer to cases in which the punishment as such possesses positive valence.

commands. These processes are closely related to phenomena of defiance. Here lies a realm of fundamental psychological significance. I shall go into it only in so far as it bears upon the topology of the situation in general.

Prohibition isolates a definite area from the life-sphere of the child in that it surrounds this area with a barrier. It delimits the zone of free movement of the child. Thus there occurs an interference in the sphere of power of the child. This naturally releases an opposed action, in which the child seeks to assert himself against the sphere of power of the adult. The perverting effect of a command and above all of a prohibition upon the valence of an object is from this point of view to be understood as a struggle for freedom of movement in the life-space of the child. Here lies also the explanation of why, at just the age of two to three years, these reactions of defiance are particularly frequent. [1]An especially pronounced stabilization of the ego of the child takes place at this time, showing itself, for example, in the development of the concept of property.

With respect to degree of constraint the prohibition situation with threat of punishment is related to the command situation with prospect of reward. On the whole the child retains freedom of movement. Only one definite area, that of the desired goal, is enclosed. Nevertheless when the occurrence is viewed not by itself but as included in the total surrounding situation, the condition of

---

[1] Charlotte Bühler speaks of "an age of defiance." The fundamental processes underlying the defiance reaction may well be of a general nature They are not, of course, to be explained merely in terms of the age level itself. Our observations and experimental investigations of infants appear to indicate that the defiance reaction represents an expression in the social sphere of a very general psychological law, equivalent to the proposition "action equals reaction".

constraint in the former case is somewhat more pronounced. The adult's domination of the field appears more clearly in the foreground.

Prohibition With Prospect of Reward

The situation involving prospect of reward for refraining from some action is rather special in nature. The reward promised is always contingent upon continued avoidance of the action *within definite time limits*. Either this action may attract directly (e. g. , the eating of sweets) or for some more * indirect reason it may be difficult to avoid. Thus rewards are often resorted to in an attempt to combat enuresis; they may be promised to a pair of siblings for cessation from their frequent teasing.

The situation is thus characterized by a positive valence or an equivalent pressure toward a definite action. The reward, a second valence introduced by the adult, is supposed to prevent the child from acting in the direction of the first valence. Thus there exists a conflict situation of the first type (Fig. 7).

The relations are rarely so simple. Generally there is the prospect not only of reward for abstinence, but of punishment for indulgence. Furthermore, as a rule the first valence increases in strength with the passage of time. It is often easy to resist for a brief period but difficult to hold out over a longer one. The following special example, although simple, represents the topology of a whole group of similar situations. A child learning to swim attempts the full length of the pool; his goal is to swim one hundred p meters. This goal attracts him exceedingly. At certain distances along the edge of the pool there are ropes to which he may hold. The child has rested on them in earlier attempts. He now faces the problem of swimming past all these attractive resting places to the end of the pool.

In this case the topology of the psychological situation corresponds quite well to that of the physical-geographical. The child is attracted by the resting place immediately in front of him (R_1, Fig. 29), and at the same time by the desired but distant goal (to swim one hundred meters). As the task grows increasingly difficult and the fatigue of the child increases, the danger that he will yield to the attraction of the nearest resting place becomes ever greater (Fig. 30).

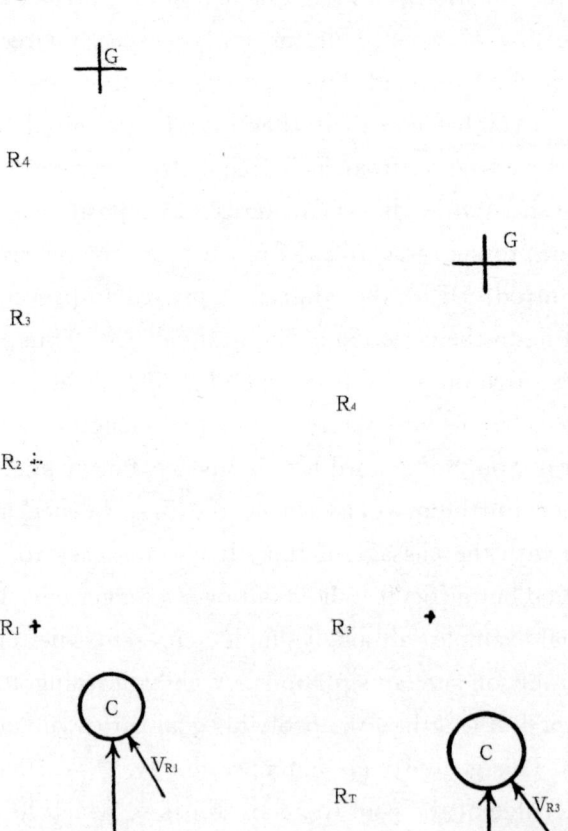

FIG. 29.　　　　　　　　　FIG. 30.

From a certain distance the attraction of the final goal itself generally increases in strength as it is approached. The ultimate behavior will differ according to the relative strengths of the vectors and the condition of the child.

In promising a reward for abstinence from an activity during a definite period, one has also generally to reckon with the existence of a series of attractions tempting toward a transgression of the prohibition. The child receives the reward only when it has successfully steered past all these attractions.

Reward, Punishment, And Genuine Transformation of Interest

Having completed our general discussion of the structure of the situation underlying reward and punishment, we may now turn to a problem closely related both psychologically and pedagogically. We have previously indicated that utilization of reward and punishment becomes an acute problem only when one desires a form of behavior not prompted by natural inclination. In such cases there exists together with these two possibilities of bringing about the desired behavior a third, namely awakening an interest, producing an inclination. This possibility is one particularly stressed by modern pedagogy. The problem arises as to how the situation involved is to be characterized psychologically. A penetrating discussion of this important and theoretically very interesting problem would require much space. Here I must perforce restrict myself to a few remarks.

Interest in an object or activity not previously interesting may be awakened in many ways: by example, by imbedding the task in another context (for instance, carrying out arithmetic problems by playing salesman), and by a variety of other methods. Not infrequently interest in an object depends upon the personality of a definite teacher.

The question naturally arises as to whether these situations are essentially different from those involving prospect of reward or punishment.

At first sight, and indeed from a psychological point of view, it might appear that the situation in which, for instance, the child calculates only because he likes to play at selling is similar to that of reward. The activity of calculating possesses a negative valence, but playing at selling, the goal behind it, leads the child to calculate. The situation would thus correspond to that of Fig. 21.

Such cases doubtless exist. In them, however, the psychological essential of the third mentioned possibility, transformation in valence of the *thing itself*, is not attained. The characteristic topology of the reward situation remains unaltered: the negative valence of calculating persists unchanged, and there merely arises next to it a second positive valence. Thus fundamentally there has occurred no true transformation in the valence of calculating.

From the psychological point of view, however, one can scarcely begin to speak of an interest pedagogy unless the valence of the activity in question is successfully and truly changed.

The objection is easily raised that in practice such a shift in valence of the thing itself is rarely attained, that in any case one must always add something to the situation in order to bring about the transformation of interest. Without ignoring the great practical difficulties involved, and without intending to imply that such a transformation of valence may always be achieved, I should still like to emphasize that the "addition" of new moments may have effects other than those just indicated.

If an activity, undesired in itself, is related to something else that the child likes (*e. g.*, a primer is decorated with pretty pictures), the pleasant and the unpleasant, though standing next to each other, may remain unconnected. There exist, however, imbeddings of a task or activity of such a sort that the meaning, and together with it the valence, of the task completely changes. A child that does not like a certain food eats it without ado if the goblin on the end of the spoon is to be buried, or if the spoon, as train, is to enter the station of the mouth. In such cases the original action, eating, becomes a dependent part of a more inclusive activity whole and eventually merely a superficial layer of the other activity. It is a fact fundamental to the psychology of action and need as well as to that of sensation that the psychological reality, and the effect of such dependent parts, is primarily determined through the *whole* in which they are imbedded. ①

It is because of this condition that imbedding a separate task in another mental sphere (*e. g.*, taking an activity from the sphere of school tasks into the sphere of action for a practical purpose) may radically change the valence of the activity.

Whether or not establishment of another connection actually leads to a transformation of valence thus depends essentially upon whether there has thereby been created a true whole, a dynamic Gestalt, or merely a summative conglomerate. ② Between summa-

---

① For references, see K. KOFFKA, Psychologie der optischen Wahrnehmung, Handuch der normalen uid pathologischen Physiologic, 1931, 12, 2 Hefte, 1215-1271; and KoHLER, *Gestalt Psychology*, Liveright, New York, 1920. For an especial experimental investigation of wholes in behavior and in systems of needs, see BIRKNBAUM, Das Vcrgessen ciner Vornahme, *Psydiol. Forsch.*, 1930, 13, 218 ff.

② Cf. the concept of *Und-Summe* in M. WFRTHE. IMKR, *Psychol Forsch.*, 1921, 1, p. 47; 1923, 4, P. 301.

tive togetherness and the completely unified whole of a strong Gestalt, in which parts completely lose their independence, there exists a continuous transition (dynamically weak Gestalten). Indeed this is of essential significance for our problem of the transformation of interest. One would expect that for a child taking no joy in learning to write the alphabet, a change of valence would occur more quickly when he is allowed as soon as possible to write meaningful communications in sentence form than when he is provided with a primer with decorative drawings bordering its pages. [1] For in the first case the letters lose their psychological separateness more readily.

If, however, separate letters constitute too great a difficulty for the child, the writing of each letter will become an independent task and the structural transformation of the meaning of the total activity will be hindered

Change in valence of a task or of an activity thus becomes possible when one imbeds the "same accomplishment" (externally regarded) in another behavior whole or in another mental sphere. (It is thus important, *e. g.*, that a given piece of work be part of the preparation for a birthday celebration, that some other work be for this or that teacher, and so on.) Pedagogically applied this means that for the small child the *total atmosphere* of the school is not only important but possesses almost a constitutive significance for the dynamics of the separate activities.

We have contrasted transformation of interest in the thing it-

---

[1] Here lies one of the chief advantages of the "global" method of reading and writing developed by Decroly.

self with situations involving reward and punishment. To neglect the existence of transition cases would, however, be both false and too schematic. Both threat of punishment and the prospect of reward may in definite instances and to a certain degree lead to a transformation in valence of the thing itself. Threat of punishment may make less valued the forbidden object. Reward may lead the child to regard the thing not at first wanted as something to be valued for its own sake.

This spread of valence from reward and punishment to the thing itself plays a role particularly in the young child, corresponding with the general weakness of functional boundaries between his mental systems. [1] Reward and punishment, when they are externally tacked on, may thus act as a simple strengthening of command or prohibition even though they possess for the child no understandable justification. With older children, however, transformation in valence of the thing itself occurs only when the command or prohibition is recognized as actually justified; when, that is, the behavior is brought into relationship with some whole which attracts or repels the child as something valuable or worthless. Resort to threat of punishment or promise of reward to support a command or prohibition is expressive of the fact that the command or prohibition is not factually justified or not sufficiently so. Thus in fact the threat of punishment acts antagonistically to transformation in valence of the thing itself. This opposed effect is clearest when the arbitrariness, lack of factual justification of the reward or punishment, is combined with an unjust accusation of a particular child.

---

[1] See Chap. III.

Chapter V
Education For Reality[①]

On the subject Education for the Present I do not wish to discuss the certainly very interesting questions of the position of the aims and methods of Montessori education in the social, economic, and political total situation of the present, nor what education has to perform in this respect. I wish, rather, to inquire into education for present-day life essentially in a *psychological* sense.

I remember a conversation with a Montessori teacher. She told of a student who, in her sixth semester, did not yet know what she ought to study, and added: "In a child that had gone through the Montessori system that would be impossible."

Those who know the Montessori system will understand what was meant by that. The teacher was, she thought, speaking

---

① From *Die Neue Erziehung*, 1931, No. 2, pp. 99-103. An address given in February 1931 at a convention on problems of the Montessori method. This does not imply that the author would defend the orthodox Montessori method.

of a person who oscillated between various possibilities and desires and was unable at the right moment to carry out the right act. She fails in the face of the present because she is unable to choose among the things the world offers and to reach a clearheaded decision. The child in the Montessori school learns precisely and primarily this: to decide himself, and to choose freely between possibilities which are given him. This is doubtless one of the most positive aspects of Montessori education.

The American student usually has, as a result of the total environment in which he has grown up, the ability to decide, to stand with both feet on the ground of reality, in higher degree than the German student; the present-day German student in greater degree than the student before the War. Desirable as this attitude is, it has, nevertheless, a danger to which attention may again be drawn today: the present in which one lives very easily becomes all too narrow, the mode of life [*Praxis*] all too superficial, the level of aspiration all too low, the facts all too naked.

Those familiar with the discussions of the Montessori problems will see at once a relation to the question of the atrophy of imagination through suppression of play. I do not wish to discuss the demand to nurture the imagination of the child because imagination in itself is something beautiful. Even a quite realistic consideration of the requirements for life in the present must recognize an intrinsic problem in this demand.

Extension of Psychological Life-Space and -Time

This becomes still clearer when the question of education for the present is subject to discussion.

If one starts out from the psychology of the small child, one has at first to regard this task as downright paradoxical. It is, indeed, a chief characteristic of the young child, say of the six-months- old infant, to be essentially the present and nothing but the present. With a variation of Hegel's dictum one might say, "The child is essentially present."[*Das Kleinkind ist wesentlich itzt.*] The world of the child is not only spatially small (the cradle, the events of the nursery), but also temporally only slightly extended. His units of action are small in scope and of brief duration. Past and future play little part, and that only for short periods, in his psychological environment. *The demand for a life in the present is hence realized to extreme degree in the young child.*

The related demand for *independent decision* in the present is, in a certain sense, also realized to extreme degree in the infant. The infant acts in accordance with his momentary needs: what does not taste good to him he does not eat; if one attempts to compel him he spits out the porridge.

An education for the present seems here to be in no sense necessary. The pedagogical task seems, rather, to be precisely the opposite, extension of the narrow horizon of the present in spatial (including social) and temporal directions. For today Goethe's saying is still valid—"Who cannot give an account of three thousand years remains in the darkness of inexperience, can live only from one day to another."①

This development in spatial-temporal extension rests, so it might seem, essentially upon the fact that the child, through experience, learns to survey ever larger relations. The adult would then have the task of furthering and accelerating this natural process. It

---

① Wer nicht von drei Tausend Jahren sich weiss Rechenschaft zu geben Bleib im Dunkel unerfahren, mag von Tag' zu Tage leben.

is today common property of pedagogical theories (although this demand is represented in variously radical degree and the practical tasks are still extremely great) that such a leading out from the narrowness of the child world is not possible by the simple procedure of acquiring and retaining knowledge but presupposes the autonomous activity and productivity of the child as a natural basis.

But a pedagogy that sees in the extension of the psychologically present life-space of the child only an *intellectual* problem overlooks a quite decisive consideration.

The extension of the child world beyond the momentary present into the future consists partly, to be sure, in the fact that the perceptual wholes in which the world is presented are gradually extended, that the intellectual survey becomes more embracing: the child experiences, for example, that some time after the lightning, the thunder comes; that he is scolded when he upsets a cup. In many respects more fundamental, however, is the development of *action wholes*; the child no longer strives solely for present things, not only has wishes that must be realized at once, but his purposes grasp toward a tomorrow. When he is somewhat older, not only events several months past but also events several months in the future play a considerable role in present behavior. The *goals* which determine the child's behavior *are thrown continually further into the future*. A decisive extension of the psychologically present life-space of the child is based upon this temporal displacement of goals.

This presents, however, a pedagogically important problem. When the perceptual space of a child is extended from his crib to the room and the street, from hours to days and months, it is still, chiefly, a spatial (social) or temporal extension within the same level of reality. But the action goal that reaches out into the future is at the same time somewhat more *unreal*. It is something that comes out of the realm of wishes and dreams, as a rule an ideal goal, that does not yet possess so full a reality as a present event. A far-ranging wish goal brings, at the same time, an extension of the life-space in another dimension; it signifies a reference to another, an unreal level of the psychological environment, and this reference is usually, indeed, more pronounced the more distant the goal. Even in adults the bold, far-seeing plan stands close to Utopia and fantasy, and there is danger of diversion into unreality.

Levels of Reality and Unreality.

A word on the difference between levels of reality and unreality. ①Considered from the point of view of psychological dynamics, unreality, the land of dreams and air castles, presents a soft and easily movable medium. It is characterized by the fact that in it one can do whatever he wishes. Unreality is not limited to things of thought; ② an action may also be unreal. The child in the kindergarten who has been forbidden for some reason to draw, watches the other children draw or strokes the crayons. The mere *gesture*, the phrase, and in a certain sense even the substitute (compensatory) act belong no less to the level of unreality than do dreams.

The stratification into levels of greater and less degrees of reality is a general property of the psychological environment of the person. The adult flees into unreality when the level of reality becomes too tense and disagreeable. Of the greatest significance for

---

① Cf. DEMBO, Der Arger als dynamisches Problem, *Psychol. Forsch.*, 1931, 15, 1-144; HOPPE, Erfolg und Misserfolg, *Psychol. Forsch.*, 1930, 14, 1-62; LEWIN, above, pp. 145-153.

② There is also a realistic thinking.

his whole behavior, and a basic fact for pedagogy, is the degree of reality of the stratum in which the center of gravity of the life of a particular individual lies.

In the child the strata of reality and unreality are still only slightly separated. His thinking, for example, shows traces of magic. To what extent and in what way the separation of reality from unreality is brought about is a crucial question for the life of the child. That this separation occur in a clear and clean-cut way is one of the most essential pedagogical postulates. This is not merely an overcoming of the child's magic-animistic view of the world and certainly not an essentially intellectual process. The separation derives chiefly, rather, from the sphere of action and rests upon the experiences of the child concerning anything that does not go as he wants it to.

There are essentially two general conditions upon a basis of which reality as a psychological fact for the child is formed : (1) the will of *another person*; and (2) the resistance of *things* against his own will.

Social Fields of Force

In the infant the forces of the psychological environment are determined essentially by *his own needs*. By a process of development (which I cannot here discuss more fully) in the course of the first year of life a psychological environment is formed, the attractions and fears, the possibilities and difficulties of which are determined for the most part, not by the child's own needs, but by the fact that the child lives in the *social field of force* of other persons. The will of the parents and comrades induces for the child certain goals, valuations, friendships, and enmities. It is, above all, through these spheres of power of other people that reality and unreality are separated for the child.

Almost always the will of an adult is the strongest and hardest reality in the child's life. Indeed, there exists in the adult, thanks to the actual superiority of his sphere of power, the natural inclination to make his wishes the decisive principle of reality for the child. Pedagogically expressed, the child has to obey. The more a pedagogy is based on obedience the more this outside will becomes the supporting scaffold of the child's reality. Even in such cases reality and unreality are separated for the child, indeed the separation is then usually fairly simple. Self-control in the face of reality is also learned by the child in this way; but this discipline rests upon the fact that the adult leads the child. A constraint situation is established, the most striking expression of which is the harness or halter for kindergarten children that one still sees occasionally on the street. If, in such a situation, the sphere of power of the adult, his position of authority, should for any reason collapse, the structure of the level of reality on which the life of the child rests psychologically must also collapse. This occurs when the child becomes independent, usually at the latest, with puberty. Such a collapse is usually bad for the child especially because the constraint situation in which he has lived is not only an inimical pressure but at the same time the crutch of his existence.

The child lived in a present which, thanks to the immediate relation of his goals and values to those of the adult, reached formally, to be sure, far beyond the narrow situation of the moment, and in which he arrived at a separation of reality from unreality. But the level of reality collapses because it lacks a fundamental relation to his owrn needs. What that means becomes clear when one considers the other conditions upon which reality and unreality may be psychologically separated, namely, the resistance of things to the execution of one's own will.

Objective Barriers

The second way to the separation of reality and unreality, the child's experience of objective difficulties in attaining the goal chosen by himself, is in many respects pedagogically opposed to the first; that is, an intensive experience of a reality independent of his own wish occurs only when the wish for the goal is strong. The formation of a recognized stratum of objective realities and necessities, which is certainly pedagogically desirable, presupposes the existence of a total situation in which the child has the possibility to set himself goals and to act freely according to his own needs and his own judgment. *Objectivity cannot arise in a constraint situation; it arises only in a situation of freedom.* Intensive needs of the child's own and freedom to set goals are pedagogically not an inhibition but a necessary condition to a happy separation of reality and unreality.

To be sure, it is necessary that the child who has chosen his own goal be not spared the difficulties of attaining it, neither the difficulties conditioned by social life nor those of physical materials. On the other hand, these difficulties should not be so overwhelming that the child gives up entirely setting goals of his own or flees out of the all too disagreeable reality into unreality.

We know how precisely this consideration, free choice of occupation on the one side, self-control on the basis of the special structure of the materials of the occupation on the other side, belongs to the fundamental principles of Montessori education. That the particular difficulties due to the nature of the material used frequently become visibly clear may permit the child to experience the objectivity of the difficulties in an especially fortunate way. Thus one may hope that the barriers to the attainment of a goal, which are usually not understood by the child and hence easily slip into the realm of the indeterminate, the fearful and uncanny, the unreal, may be used in a construction of a clear level of objective reality. For the child in the kindergarten to follow even for some hours his own individual rhythm I believe to be entirely appropriate for most children; since the rhythm of psychological needs in respect of satiation and satisfaction varies so unpredictably from child to child, from day to day, only if the child can actually follow his own needs can we expect that strong tension toward the goal, which constitutes a favorable condition for the development of a marked level of reality.

Even later it remains important that certain intervals of occupation according to one's own choice and own rhythm be provided. Although, to be sure, the incorporation in the social group becomes in many respects more dominant and the question of the formation of an objective level of reality within the personal relation acquires an increased importance, the conditions become much more complicated by reason of multiple imbedding. Thus one of the pedagogically most difficult problems is to give a functionally proper place in the psychological life-space of the child to that middle level between psychological reality and unreality which is commonly called fantasy and which is related in the most intimate way to, for example, the gesture and artistic expression of all sorts. For the requirement of a clear and clean-cut separation of reality from unreality and of a life in the level of reality cannot mean that the level of unreality is to be banished entirely from the psychological life-space of the child or that any functional connection between the planes of psychological reality and unreality is to be destroyed. For the breadth of the present life-space and the adequacy of realistic behavior depend in a far from unimportant degree upon the kind and depth of the relations between these levels.

Freedom and Responsibility

Education for the present cannot mean an education for living in a momentary situation. The problem of the extension of the psychological life-space of the child, which reaches beyond intellectual and didactic problems, is related most intimately to the psychological separation of the levels of reality and unreality. The development of a level of reality which shall provide a sound basis clear through to adulthood requires that the free life-space of the child be not too small. The separation of reality and unreality seems usually to occur earlier in proletarian children; but we know that this is not always an advantage, that an all too hard environment leads to stunting. Analogously, an early separation of reality and unreality is produced by the construction of an authoritative, obediencedemanding, constraint situation; but the arbitrary and overdone separation of these levels carries with it the danger of concealed substitute satisfactions and a later collapse of the whole level of reality. Only in a sufficiently free life-space in which the child has the possibility of choosing his goals according to his own needs and in which, at the same time, he fully experiences the objectively conditioned difficulties in the attainment of the goal, can a clear level of reality be formed, only thus can the ability for resnonsible decision develop.

Chapter VI
Substitute Activity and Substitute Value

Experimental studies of the dynamic laws of the behavior and structure of personality have forced us to consider more and more complicated problems. Instead of investigating the single psychological systems which correspond to simple needs and desires, we have to deal with the interrelationships of these systems, with their differentiation and transformations, and with the different kinds of larger wholes built up from them. These interrelationships and larger wholes are very labile and delicate. Yet one must try to get hold of them experimentally because they are most important for understanding the underlying reality of behavior and personality differences. In doing this we often find facts which Freud first brought to our attention, thereby rendering a great service even though he has not given a clear dynamic theory in regard to them. One such fact is that of substitution.

Freud uses the concept of substitution extensively to explain both normal and abnormal behavior. Moreover, sublimation, which is closely related to substitution, is according to him an important foundation of our whole cultural life. We find substitution in very different forms. There is, for instance, the man who dreams of a palace and brings a few pieces of marble into his kitchen. There is the man who cannot buy a piano, but who collects piano catalogs. Again we find the delinquent boy who knows that he will not be allowed to leave his reform school but who asks for a traveling bag as a birthday present. And the little boy who threatens and scolds the larger boy whom he cannot beat on the playground. These and a hundred other examples make us realize how important and far reaching the problem of substitution is in regard to psychological needs as well as with reference to bodily needs such as hunger and sex. The greater the need, the stronger seems to be the tendency to substitution. Even the great field of children's play has a peculiar relationship to substitution, either of objects or of activity.

Everyone recognizes, I believe, that at present we have no theory which really explains the dynamics of substitution. Freud avoids giving a definition of substitution and, according to the opinion of prominent psychoanalysts, he develops no real theory for it.

If one asks about the necessary and adequate conditions for the appearance of substitute action and about its effects, one meets a paradoxical fact. Substitute actions arise often in situations in which one cannot reach a certain goal, situations in which a psychobiological tension exists. Let us take an example from the work of Dembo on anger. The subject who takes part in the experiment has been trying for a long time to throw rings over a bottle, but without success. At last in tears she goes to the door and slings the rings over some coat hooks. Another example is that of the subject who cannot reach the flower which is her goal. She suddenly grabs another ilower which stands in a vase nearby.

These events, which at first appear quite understandable, seem less simple when considered from the standpoint of the dynamics of the situation. Obviously the substitute action springs from the tension system which corresponds to the original action. One would expect, therefore, that the tension system of the original action would be discharged through the substitute action, either completely or in part. Yet in many cases the person only becomes more dissatisfied and more emotional as is clearly evident in the experiments we have made. But if the main system is not discharged through the substitute action it is not easy to understand, from the standpoint of dynamics, why the substitute action should arise at all.

For the investigation of this and other dynamic questions we have carried on a series of experiments with adults, feebleminded children, and psychopathic children. I shall give a few of the results of these experiments.

If one tries to define the range over which substitution may occur, one meets with great difficulty. If, for example, in experiments on the effect of a prohibition, one takes a doll away from a child and the child begins to make doll clothes, one would call this a substitute activity. But if the child begins to play with a train, one is not sure. One person would say that it is a substitute activity and another that it is not, that the child would have played with the train even if the doll had not been taken away. How similar must the original and the subsequent action be in order that one may say surely that the latter is a substitute action? Another example: If the subject throw the rings, not over the bottle, but over a block which is nearby, it is probable that this is a substitute act. But if he playfully puts the rings first over one arm and then over the other, or if he spins the rings on the floor, are these substitute actions or simple restless actions?

It is impossible to escape this difficulty by limiting the concept of substitution to acts which are very similar in content to the original action; for, without doubt, there are substitute actions which are very dissimilar in form to the original act. We know, for example, from the work of Fajans, that a doll may be a real substitute for a child who has been unable to reach a piece of candy. Or the child may accept his mother's sympathy as an equally genuine substitution. On the other hand, we shall see that two actions can be very similar, without one serving as a substitute for the other. In regard to examples from psychoanalysis it is important that the similarity of two facts is not sufficient evidence for the statement that one is a substitute for the other. Whether a substitute is present or not cannot be decided from the *external* appearance of the events. It is necessary in each individual case to see whether the two facts have a certain *dynamic* connection.

From the dynamic point of view one can speak of substitution only in cases in which the substitution is connected with the tension system corresponding to the original goal, that is, only if the substitute action springs from this original system. According to this dynamic point of view, one finds an unexpected relation between substitution and the use of *tools* or other means of reaching a goal. If one wishes to give information to someone and the telephone is out of order, one sends a telegram; if the child cannot take a direct path to his objective, he tries to reach it by a roundabout route. In all such cases, in which the carrying out of an intention is changed according to environment, a new action springs from the psychological system which corresponds to the original goal.

Experiments have shown that indeed we find a fluid transition between the use of new tools or new ways and the special substitute action. If, for example, the subject uses a stick to place the rings over the bottle, this use of tools changes the meaning of the task so that we have a new task. If we use the concept of substitution in a broad sense, we can speak of the use of tools from the psychological point of view as a substitute goal or substitute action. We shall return to the question of similarity later. At first we shall speak of substitution only when the new action arises from the original tension system and when, at the same time, the new goal is sufficiently different from the original goal. It is necessary to distinguish between different kinds of substitution. But here we shall limit ourselves to the question of whether, and if so under what conditions, a substitute action brings substitute satisfaction.

We have tried experimentally to determine whether a tension system can be discharged through a substitute action. We know from the work of Ovsiankina that if an activity which has been begun is interrupted there is a strong tendency to resume it as a result of the tension system which corresponds to the quasi-need of completing the task. In our experiments on substitution the subject, after the interruption of the first activity, receives a second task which seems to serve as a substitute for the first activity. If, for example, the original task is to make a dog out of plasticine, the second task might be to make another animal or a ball out of plasticine. If one interrupts the telling of a story, the subject might be asked to draw a picture for the conclusion; or if the subject is interrupted in the drawing of some picture, he may he asked to complete the picture by telling a story.

We have investigated cases in which the relationship between the original and substitute activities lies in the action on material of the same kind and cases in which the *content* of the activity is similar but the *material* is different. If the second activity actually has value as a substitute, the tension system of the original interrupted activity must be discharged wholly or in part. Therefore, the subject will resume the original task less often if the second task has substitute value and can bring about a substitute satisfaction. And, on the other hand, the subject will resume the original task more often if the second task has no substitute value. In some cases the experimenter does not give the second task directly, but creates a situation which offers the possibility of spontaneous substitution.

Lissner[1] found, in fact, that there are cases in which the second activity has substitute value and the resumption of the original activity occurs less often. It was soon clear that not only was the similarity of the two tasks important for the substitute value, but also the *degree of difficulty* of the substitute action. For example: if after the interruption of the task of putting mosaic blocks together the second task of making a mosaic pattern was easy, the resumption was 100 per cent, that is, the substitute value was zero; but if the second task of mosaic pattern was difficult, the resumptions dropped to 42. [2] In order that a greater degree of substitution may correspond numerically to a higher percentage, we shall give the results in terms of nonresumption. According to this rotation, the above case of easy substitute action has a nonre-

---

[1] K. LISSNER, Die Entspannung von Bedürfnissen durch Ersatzhandlungen, *Psychol. Forsth.*, 1933, 18, 218-250.

[2] *Ibid.*, p. 231, Table 4.

sumption value of 0 per cent; and the difficult substitute action has a value of 58 per cent. Another example: the original task which the subject has to do is to make a little dog out of plasticine. The second task is to make another animal. If the second animal is something easy to make, like a snake, the substitute value is smaller (15 per cent) than if it is difficult (70 per cent). We can say, therefore, that the substitute value of the second task is the stronger the more difficult the task. The difficulty of the task is very important for substitute value because it is related to the standard which the person sets for himself. The substitute value is, therefore, related to what we have called the level of aspiration.

Whether or not the substitute action in a particular case is in direct dynamic *contact* with the original task is very important for the substitute value. We find very little substitute value if the two activities are psychologically *separated* through special circumstances of the situation. Such isolation can sometimes be realized by having the experimenter say at the time of interruption: "Now we shall do an entirely new task." With the same task, the substitute value can be strong if one develops the substitute out of the original task. In a particular case the percentage of nonresumption in a situation of isolation was 15; whereas in a situation of contact between the two tasks, the percentage was 57. ①

The great significance of the kind of connection between the two systems corresponding to the original and substitute tasks shows up, above all, in experiments with feeble-minded children. KÖpke and Zeigarnik find with so-called *Hilfschuler* (retarded children of moron level) seven to eight years old the following

---

① *Ibid.*, p. 240, Table 8a.

facts; if one gave no substitute action, the feeble-minded in all cases resumed the interrupted activity; that is, the nonresumption was 0 per cent. With normal children a year younger nonresumption was 18 per cent. If one gave a substitute task the nonresumption in the case of feeble-minded was 5 per cent; whereas in the case of normals it was about 70 per cent. This means that the substitute value of an action which was very strong for the normals was negligible for the feeble-minded. KÖpke increased the similarity between the original and the second activity to identity. For example, if the original task was to draw an animal on red paper, the second task was to draw the same animal on green paper. Or, if the original task was to build a bridge, the second task was to build another bridge like the first. In this case, the nonresumption by feeble-minded children was never more than 20 per cent. This very significant numerical result appears to conflict with other experiences. One often sees that the feeble-minded child, if he cannot reach a goal, is easily satisfied with an achievement short of his aim. Gottschaldt has observed the same thing in special experiments. If a feebleminded child wants to build a high tower of blocks and finds difficulties, he is comparatively easily satisfied with a substitute action, such as building a small tower or some other simple structure. That the feeble-minded child is easily satisfied with substitute actions can be further seen in cases like the following. A young feeble-minded child wishes to throw a ball very far. He docs not succeed, but he is happy because he made such a vigorous movement. The feeble-minded child has a tendency to be satisfied with a gesture if the real action is impossible. Lazar has a special term for such children; he calls them "gesture children."Thus, there are doubtless many cases in which the feeble-minded child is much more easily satisfied with a substitution than a normal child. On the other hand, our experiments show that in some cases the substitute value is much less with feeble-minded children than with normal children. In order to clear up the contradiction between these two kinds of cases, we must study the nature of the psychological systems in feeble-minded children. Certainly, all cases of feeble-mindedness have not the same psychological nature. I shall speak only of the most common type.

At present, the general assumption is that feeble-mindedness not only is a defect of intelligence, but also indicates a difference in the make-up of the personality. On the whole, however, one cannot yet define this type of personality. We have worked on this question in recent years in different ways, and I shall try to give a short description of the theory that has resulted.

From the dynamic point of view, the difference between persons is based on three points. The person, dynamically, is a totality of systems. First, one can distinguish the structure of the totality, that is, the *degree* of differentiation of the systems and the *kind* of differentiation of systems in this totality. The one-year-old child, for example, is dynamically not so differentiated into separate systems as a thirty-year-old man. In the child we do not have so many systems. The connection between different things is closer, and we do not have such markedly differentiated strata between the periphery and the center. Second, with the same structure the dynamic *material* of the systems may be different. The systems can be more or less rigid, more or less fluid, and so forth. For this kind of difference also we can use the example of the child and the adult. It seems that the possibility of changing a given system is easier in the child—in most cases—than in the adult. The elasticity or the rigidity of the systems seems to be a very basic and important characteristic of the whole person. The third point is the differences of *content* which correspond to the different systems. With the same structure and same material, the content may be different. This third point seems determined chiefly by the history of the person. For example, the content of the systems of a four-year-old boy among the ancient Greeks was quite different from that of a four-yearold in New York City today.

For the most common kind of moron, according to our experiments, it seems to be typical that the psychological systems are comparatively *rigid*, not easily flexible. I shall not enumerate all our evidence for this theory, which is based upon experiments on satiation, will, memory, attention, and intelligence in the feeble-minded. [1]It may be sufficient to show that from this kind of psychological material, we can understand even the paradoxical facts of substitution in morons. From the dynamic point of view, this kind of child is defined as a person who has a less differentiated structure, like that of a younger child. But the systems are not so flexible as in the young normal child; they are more fixed. The smaller degree of differentiation is the explanation of what we generally call the *infantilism* of these morons. But it is clear that these feeble-minded are not the same as the younger normal children.

If we accept the theory that the systems are more rigid, then, in the first place, we can explain the results of the simple interruption experiments in which no substitute task was given; the fact, namely, that the feeble-minded resume the interrupted task in 100 per cent of the cases. This abnormal frequency of resumption is a consequence of the fact that a tension system, once it is built up,

---

[1] For a more complete statement of the theory of the person here sketched, and of the experimental evidence upon which it is based, see below, Chap. VII.

stays unchanged without being diffusely discharged. This experimental result agrees with the observations of daily life that feebleminded children are often extremely stubborn and that it is relatively difficult for such a child to change his goal after he has set himself toward it. This well-known stubbornness is a result of the rigidity of his psychological systems.

We do not, however, find 100 per cent resumption if the child is brought after the first task to a totally different situation. On the contrary, the resumption then occurs much less often than with a normal child. In such cases in our experiments, we find again a rather extreme result, namely, 20 per cent resumption.

The reason for the nonresumption in this case is again the rigidity of the psychological systems. The new psychological situation is so rigid that it cannot be changed readily enough for a connection with the old situation to be brought about. It is typical of this kind of feeble-minded that they cannot do two things at the same time. They are either totally in one situation or totally in another. The theory of rigidity of the systems enables us, therefore, to explain why there is in some cases an abnormally high degree of resumption, in other cases an abnormally low degree of resumption. In a similar way, we can use this theory to explain the paradox which we have mentioned before.

The question whether the substitute action has substitute value presents itself in respect to the psychological, dynamic systems as follows: One system corresponds to the original task; and one corresponds to the second task. If the completing of the second task, that is, of the substitute activity, is to have substitute value for the first system, then the two systems must be so connected that the discharge of the second system at the same time discharges the first system; that is, the two systems must be one dynamic whole. In normal children, the systems are fluid enough so that the similarity of the two tasks suffices to effect a special kind of connection between the two systems. When the subject receives a second similar task, the first system changes so that the new system will be a dynamical part of the old. These two systems appear to be not entirely dissolved into one, undifferentiated whole; but we have one unitary system with a dynamic wall between the two parts. If one part is discharged, then, according to the strength of the inner boundary, the whole system may be discharged.

When the feeble-minded child receives the second task, the first system remains, as a result of its rigidity, unchanged; and for the second task a separate system is established. So it happens that the discharging of the second system does not discharge the first; that is, the second task has no substitute value.

If this theory is right, it must be possible to set up, in feeble-minded children, a substitute satisfaction if we find a way to develop the second task out of the original system. In fact, this often happens when the child spontaneously proceeds from the original activity to a substitute, as in the experiments of Gottschaldt and in the cases about which we have spoken before. We have only one system. Therefore, the substitute value must be particularly great. As a result of the rigidity of the systems we do not have in these cases the differentiation of the whole system into two parts, slightly separated from each other, as are those of normal children. Therefore, the substitute action will discharge the whole system in the feebleminded child more completely than in the normal child. So it happens that with normal children we can bring about rather easily a substitute action, but the substitute value is not perfect. With feeble-minded children either we have a complete separation of the two systems so that a second activity has no substitute value, or, if the two tasks are connected at all, the substitute satisfaction is perfect. Such all-or-none functioning in feeble-minded persons is important not only in substitution but in other fields (*e. g.*, in intelligent acts).

Besides the degree of connection and the previously mentioned degree of difficulty of the second task, the degree of reality and unreality of the substitute action is important for the substitute value. The substitute often does not occur in the form of a real action, but in the form of an air castle or a *daydream*. In many cases of substitution, speaking or *gesture* takes the place of a *real* act. Has this kind of substitute real substitute value? This question is also important for the theory of dreams and for substitution in psychopathic cases. It is not easy to make experimental investigations upon the effect of this unreal substitution through speaking and thinking, in place of real action. Mahler has made experiments of this type : a piece of handwork was interrupted and the subject had to think how he would complete the work; or if a person could not reach a goal he was asked to tell a fairy story in which he attained his goal. This field is very complicated and I can discuss only a part of it. Mahler found that, in general, the substitute value is stronger the more real the substitute action is. But what degree of reality an action has cannot be determined by the kind of substitute action alone, but always by observation of the relationship between the substitute action and the original action in a particular case. Mahler found that one must distinguish between the *inner goal* and the *outer goal* of an activity and that the degree of reality of the second task, and with it the substitute value, is the greater the more nearly the substitute action approaches the inner goal of the original action. In tasks which have the character of an intellectual problem it is generally not enough for the discharge of the tension that the subject find the solution in thinking; it is important that he express the solution in reality. In this way it is shown that social factors are very important in determining the real or unreal character of an event. Only when it is possible for the subject to inform the experimenter of the solution of the substitute task is an adequate discharge of the original system possible. For only in case of social recognition is the degree of reality sufficient.

The question of unreal substitution has a close relationship to certain problems of play. According to the theory of Piaget, the child's conception of the world has a mystical character. For the child, name and thing, fantasies and reality, lies and truth are not clearly separated. One must ask whether for psychological needs also an unreal event can give real satisfaction to the child. Sliosberg, who has carried out comprehensive experiments on this question, found that it is impossible to make the general statement that the unreal can be substituted for the real. Whether a child is satisfied or not when one gives him make-believe candy for real candy, paper scissors for real scissors, depends in each case on the special character of the situation. We must, as Koffka has said, distinguish between the play situation and the serious situation. The play situation is not so rigid; one may call it "loose. "Certain kinds of substitution are possible only in a play situation, in which objects have not so fixed a character as in a serious situation. In the serious situation the child usually refuses the play substitute. It is interesting that the opposite is also true. The child in the play situation will often refuse a real action as a substitute for the play action. Experiments show that for adults also the possibility of a substitute depends upon the looseness of the whole situation.

An important factor for the substitute value is the momentary intensity of the need. The experiments of Sliosberg show that the child more easily accepts the plasticine scissors, for example, after he has played long enough with the real ones. Generally, the stronger the need the less the substitute value of a substitute action.

On the other hand, the tendency for substitute action, without doubt, will increase as the tension of the need increases. This was particularly clear in the experiments of Dembo, in which the strong affective tension leads to such nonsense action as throwing rings over the coat hooks. Dembo has shown that such spontaneous substitution is always a result of a conflict situation and has given a dynamic theory of how the substitute goal receives its positive valence. We know that if a certain goal exists for a person, this goal works as a psychological field which induces a derived valence in certain other objects. For example, if one wishes to wrap up something, then, suddenly, paper and string assume a positive valence. KÖhler has spoken of the directed state of the situation in the use of tools. Dembo has shown that an inducing field exists, which gives valences as means for reaching the goal; moreover, if the tension is strong enough, other goals are induced which have a certain relation to the original goal.

In the beginning we saw that, as far as psychological systems are concerned, a surprising relation exists between substitution and the use of tools. Now we see also that from the point of view of the psychological environment the use of tools and substitution are closely related because both are induced by the same inducing field. Finally, we can formulate our main results in regard to non-spontaneous substitution: the substitute value is the greater the more the substitute action corresponds, not to a new goal, but to another way of reaching the original inner goal.

SUMMARY OF EXPERIMENTS ON SUBSTITUTION
Figures indicate percentages of nonresumption

	Original Task	Experiments without Substitution	Experiments with Substitution	
I.			Second task is.	
			Easy	*Difficult*
	Mosaic	10	0	58
	Plasticine (dog)	20	15 (snake)	70 (ball)
II.			Original and second task are.	
			Isolated	*Connected*
	Mosaic		15	57
III.				
	Normal children 7 to 8 years	18	68	
	Feeble-minded 8 years	0	5	
			(New situation)	(Second task nearly identical with first)
		80	14	
IV.			Goal of the original task is	
			Reached	*Not reached*
	Different tasks	40	77	
		25		25
			Telling	
	Figuring on paper	25	100	
	Paper box	25		19
V.			Thinking	
			With telling	*Without telling*
	Figuring	17	14	0

Chapter VII
A Dynamic Theory of The Feeble−Minded

During the last few decades, advances in pedagogy, of which Decroly's penetrating work constitutes not the least, have been decidedly influenced by study of the behavior of abnormal children. Psychopathology has continually gained in significance for psychology, particularly for psychological theory. Yet a true understanding of the psychopathological processes themselves is often peculiarly difficult. The following discussion attempts to develop the fundamentals of a dynamic theory of feeble-mindedness. We are aware that we are presenting only the outlines of a theory. This is so of necessity since we shall consider exclusively one relatively frequent type among the many, dynamically perhaps quite varied, kinds of feeble-mindedness. And the experiments upon which the theory is based have been carried out on only one particular degree of feeble-mindedness. Yet at present in a psychological investigation of the varied types of personality, it seems to me most important to attempt as strict as possible a theory of the dynamic relation between the different behavioral manifestations of one type, and then to determine which of the dynamic concepts thus evolved are applicable to the general problem of personality differences. Such a course seems more fruitful than to continue suggesting new classificatory divisions for the entire range of types. Without doubt, however, a dynamic theory of feeble-mindedness must at the same time deal with the basic problems of a general *dynamic theory of the person*.

It is common knowledge that feeble-mindedness is not merely an "isolated disease of the intellect" but involves the total personality. [1]We have, however, progressed little beyond this first general insight. In particular we lack a positive characterization of this peculiarity of the total personality.

As I see it, a truly penetrating experimental investigation of the intellectual processes of the feeble-minded remains to be achieved. Determination by test procedures of deficient accomplishment in certain fields, important as this is in itself, has thrown little light upon the nature of the underlying processes. Nor has it illuminated the differences between them and the intellectual processes of the normal individual. As in other branches of psychology here also insight into the nature of the processes involved can only be won by pushing beyond mere concepts of achievement. Moreover, certain performances, social behavior for instance, may upon occasion be better achieved by the feeble-minded than by a person of normal intelligence.

If one attempts to transcend the concepts of achievement and

---

[1] Indeed Binet was keenly interested in the problem of the character of the feeble-minded; cf. A. Binet et T. Simon, L'Intelligence des imbeciles, *L'Annie psychologique*, 1909, 15, i ff.

to inquire into the nature of the psychological processes themselves, he is of course first forced to consider what distinguishes the intellectual activity of the feeble-minded from that of the normal person.

The Act of Insight in The Feeble-Minded

In an attempt of this sort one is confronted by unexpectedly great difficulties.

Investigations of the last twenty years have established at least the outlines of the fundamental nature of intellectual activity, especially of creative thinking. Dynamically the act of insight consists in a *reorganization of the field* (Köhler [1]), closely related in many respects to the transformation of so-called ambiguous figures. In the fields both of perception and of thought there is a shift in the totality of internal relations. Forms that appear at first as isolated totalities become part of a unified whole. Dependent parts become independent or unite with originally dependent parts of other wholes to form new wholes. Briefly, the structure of the field as regards its grouping into wholes undergoes a transformation, usually an abrupt one. In the causation of this transformation definite directed forces play an essential role.

If, proceeding from this theory of intelligent activity, one asks wherein the peculiarity of feeble-minded thinking lies, he must first establish that acts of insight in the feeble-minded appear throughout to have in all fundamental properties the *same nature* as in the normal individual. It is certain that the feeble-minded see

---

[1] KöHLER, *Intelligenzprufungen an Menschenajfen (The Mentality of Apes)*, and Das Wesen der Intelligenz, *Kind und Umwelt*, Berlin, 1930.

wholes and that these wholes are not less pronounced. ①It cannot be maintained that the feeble-minded do not engage in intelligent activity or that the process as such is less intensive. Moreover the "Aha-experience" typical of the act of thinking undoubtedly occurs in the feeble-minded. Indeed, they appear often to experience it more intensively and to rejoice in it more than do normal children. Morons and imbecile children may experience jokes and enjoy them keenly. Equally with the normal child and the anthropoid, the act of insight in the feeble-minded consists in a transformation of the whole relations in the field.

There remains then this difference, quite an external one from the dynamic point of view: the transformation of field structure typical of the experience of wit or of intelligent activity in general is not occasioned in the feeble-minded by the same events which produce it in normal children of the same age. It is caused by other events, the so-called easier tasks, or more primitive jokes. The only qualitative distinction that seems to have been pointed out between the process of the two groups is that the feeble-minded think more concretely and perceptually. ②

Formulation of The Experimental Problem

During the last three years we have attempted to gain insight into the peculiarities of the feeble-minded, not by the direct route of investigating intelligence, but by experimental investigations in the spheres of will and needs. In many ways these spheres are

---

① We shall see later that it may plausibly be maintained that they are even more pronounced.

② Cf. W. ELIASBERG, Die Veranschaulichung in der Hilfsschule, *Zeitschr. f. exper. Päd.* t 1926, 27, 134-145.

more directly related to the deeper peculiarities of personality than are intellectual processes. If then feeblemindedness be an expression of a peculiarity of the total personality it seems not unlikely that through such investigations insight may finally be obtained into the causes of the intellectual difficulties themselves.

One major difficulty in reasoning from the results of intelligence testing to the problem of dynamic differences is the fact that in testing procedures individual differences are determined by means of activities the psychological nature and general laws of which are not sufficiently known.① We have, therefore, utilized throughout those experimental procedures in which the underlying processes and their laws are best known to us. For similar reasons we have first investigated relatively light rather than pronounced degrees of feeble-mincledness. This is apparently contrary to the general principle that investigation should begin with differences as crass as possible. Our present approach has been guided by the following consideration. If one uses the same procedure with idiots as with normal children it is very probable that the difference in psychological situations created for normal and for idiot children will be so great that completely different dynamic relations will exist. It may well happen, for instance, that for the one a difficult conflict may arise, whereas for the other none may ensue. Only when truly *psychologically* comparable situations exist may one compare differences in behavior in more than an external way or consider such differences in the same type of activity as the effects of dynamic differences of the person.

The experimental subjects consisted of pupils from different

---

① Cf. LEWIN, *Die Entwicklung der experimentellen Willenspsychologic und die Psychotherapie*, Hirzel, Leipzig, 1929, pp. 28.

schools for the defective in Berlin, ranging in age from six to twelve years. The majority were classed as moron, a few as imbecile. Control experiments were carried out by the same experimenters on normal children of various ages.

The experiments chiefly concern: (1) the process of satiation, (2) the expression of an unsatisfied need (resumption of an interrupted action), and (3) the substitute value of a substitute (compensatory) action. The selection of experiments was naturally guided by certain working hypotheses. We shall first present briefly the results of the experiments on satiation.

Psychical Satiation In Feeble-Minded and Normal Children

The children were asked to draw moon faces continuously (Fig. I; "The moon, the moon, the moon is round; it has two eyes, a nose, and mouth"). A moon face was copied for the child on a sheet of notebook paper. The child then had to draw moon faces "until he had enough of it." He was free to stop at any time. But the situation in itself contained, as in the experiments of Karsten,[1] a weak pressure toward continuing to draw. (The experimenter must of course endeavor to maintain this pressure as equal as possible with different children.) According to the general laws of psychical satiation, of which the fundamentals are known from the experiments of Karsten and Freund,[2] the initially positive or neutral valence of the task gradually changes with repetition into indifference and finally into a negative valence. In these

---

[1] A. KARSTEN, Psychische Sattigung, *Psychol. Forsch.*, 1928, 10, 142 ff.
[2] A. FREUND, Die psychische Sättigung im Menstruum und Intermenstruum, *ibid.*, 1930, 13, 198 ff

experiments breaking off generally did not occur immediately upon reaching the satiation point. The child usually worked for a while after the satiation point had been reached until the activity acquired a certain degree of negative valence. After stopping, he was asked by the experimenter if he would not like to continue, drawing anything he chose (free drawing). If so, paper and pencil remained at his disposal for as long as he wished to go on.

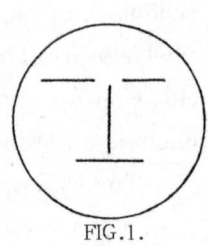

FIG.1.

One is accustomed to attribute to the feeble-minded a pronounced inclination toward repetition and at the same time small persistence in working. Since satiation, as we know, is closely connected with the dynamics of needs, it appeared important to determine its course with the feeble-minded. The task presented no special difficulties to the nine- to tenand to the ten- to eleven-year-old feeble-minded. Only the eight- to nine-year-olds drew decidedly fewer moons than the normals of equal age.

The result in the main is as follows (Table I): the total duration of the satiation experiment (moon faces plus free drawing) is on the average shorter with the eight- to nine-yearold morons than with normal children of equal age (41 as against 58 min.). Times for individual children of the normal and feeble-minded groups, however, overlap considerably. The average time (59 min.) of the nine- to ten-year-old morons is the same as that of the eight- to nine-year-old normals, and shorter, but not decidedly so, than the average of the nine- to ten-year-old normals (75 min.). The average of the ten- to eleven-year-old feeble-minded (77 min.) is almost identical with that (79 min.) of the normal nine- to ten- and ten- to eleven-year-olds.

Table I—Psychical Satiation In Normal (N) And Rktardi. D (R) Children

Age, years		Satiation time, minutes			Satiation point, minutes	Moons per minute	Number per too minutes of	
		Moons	Free drawing	Total			Pauses	Other activities
8 to 9	R	33	8	41	27	4	30	20
	N	55	3	58	35	8	8	8
9 to 10	R	56	3	59	30	7	30	17
	N	55	20	75	27	7	15	3
10 to 11	R	75	2	77	40	7	23	21
	N	45	33	79	35	8	7	8

Considering the notion of little persistence and capacity for concentration on the part of the feeble-minded, it is surprising that at least in the case of the nine- to eleven-year-olds no essential difference in total time exists. Even when the comparison is made between times at which satiation first clearly appears, the averages show surprisingly good agreement. In the three age groups of the feeble-minded this satiation point occurs on the average at 27, 30, and 40 min. respectively; in the groups of normal children at 35, 27, and 35 min.

The times required for total satiation in such activities by normal and subnormal children thus appear on the whole not to differ essentially. ① The *course of satiation*, however, shows certain typical differences. One is first struck by the fact that with

---

① One may refer the quicker satiation of the eight- to nine-year-old feebleminded to the fact that the task was more difficult for them than for the normal children. The feeble-minded drew on the average only four moons a minute as against eight for normals of the same age. According to Karsten, other things being equal, satiation is more rapid with more accentuated central tasks and the more difficult tasks here must be so regarded.

the ten- to eleven-year-old morons nearly the entire time (75 min.) is taken up with the drawing of moon faces, and that after satiation of this activity they refuse almost without exception to continue with free drawing. ① Normal children, on the other hand, are satiated with drawing moon faces much sooner (after 45 min.). Yet all of these children were ready to continue with free drawing. Thus on the average the feebleminded of this age displayed more persistence in one and the same activity than did the normal children. Once satiated, however, they would have nothing more to do with any part of the sphere. ② They showed much more frequently, however, small technical variations (in respect, for instance, to position or serial order of drawings).

Together with the tendency toward variation, a typical manifestation of satiation is the appearance of secondary actions, that is, actions which are carried out on the side without interruption of the major activity. In frequency of secondary actions there appears to be no important difference between the normal and the feeble-minded. With the feeble-minded, however, and in all three age groups, there occur much more often *pauses for rest and interposed actions*, which definitely interrupt the main activity. The number of pauses for rest per 100 min. in the feeble-minded, grouped by age, is 30, 30, and 23; in the normal, 8, 15, and 7. The corresponding values for interposed actions are 20, 17, 21 for the feeble-minded; 8, 3, 8 for the normal children.

---

① This refusal may also have been influenced, on the part of the feeble-minded, by a fear of failing in free drawing.

② The eight- to nine-year-olds show externally the opposite : the feeble-minded go over earlier than do the normal into the decided variations of free drawing. The same holds with the six-year-olds. I incline to believe, however, that no actual contradiction exists when dynamic questions are considered (see below)

As a general result of the satiation experiments we find that in ages eight to eleven there exist between normal and moron no significant differences in rate of satiation of the total complex (drawing moon faces plus free drawing). Typical differences do occur, however, in the course of satiation: conflict between the wish to continue drawing and the beginning of satiation leads in the feeble-minded to many more pauses for rest and interposed actions. That is, the moron child is either definitely engaged in the task in hand or he interrupts this activity *completely* by a pause or a shift to another occupation. The course of satiation in the normal child is far more continuous. He responds to the conflict in more elastic, yielding fashion. He more readily finds a way, with the aid of secondary activities or by other means, to steer through the conflict without externally giving up continuation of the task. The behavior of the feeble-minded is much more abrupt, more "either-or."

The cause of the more elastic behavior of the normal child may be sought in his readier survey of the possibilities of satisfying the demands of the experimenter, thus enabling him really to evade the actual task. Although in point of fact this greater insight plays a role, a purely intellectualistic interpretation would be false. The elastic and inelastic behavior of the two groups proceeds quite directly and without particular deliberation. ①

I am constrained to believe that a much more fundamental property of the feeble-minded is here operative; namely, a functional rigidity, an immobility of the psychic material, which itself constitutes the true cause of the intellectual difficulties. Before go-

---

① Of greater importance, rather, is the fact that the feeble-minded much more readily feels himself inadequate to the social situation, that he fails to stand aoove it.

ing into this theory the experiments on resumption of interrupted actions and on substitution will be briefly presented.

Resumption of Interrupted Actions. Substitute Value of Substitute Actions

If on any pretext one interrupts the execution of a task in which a subject has become inwardly engaged, occupies him in another way, and then after completion of this second task finally leaves him to himself for a short time (say half a minute), the subject ordinarily returns spontaneously to the first task within this period. We know from the work of Ovsiankina ① that this resumption is very frequent in certain situations and with certain tasks even when the subject knows that a resumption is not in line with the wishes of the experimenter.

Köpke has carried out similar experiments with eight- to nine-year-old feeble-minded②and with seven- to eight-year-old normal children (Table II). The frequency of resumption with normal children was 79 per cent (in good agreement with the figures of Ovsiankina); with the feeble-minded under the same conditions 100 per cent. After finishing the second task, the 31 feeble-minded children investigated returned without exception to the interrupted one, and within 30 sec. Thus in the feeble-minded the tension system corresponding to the interrupted action worked itself out with an astonishing regularity in a resumption of the task. We shall discuss the reasons for this later.

---

① OVSIANKINA, Wiederaufnahme unterbrochener Handlungen, *Psychol. Forsch.*, 1928, II, 302 ft.

② Twenty-five of these children were classed as morons, six as slightly imbecile

Proceeding from the work of Lissner[1] and Mahler, [2] Köpke used a similar technique in the investigation of substitute value.

Table Ⅱ—Substitute Value of Substitute Activities In Normal (N) And Retarded (R) Children

Age, years		n	Frequency of resumption in per cent		n	Frequency of resumption in per cent	
			Without substitute	With substitute		Identical substitute	Concealed valence
7to8	N	34(I)	79	33			
8to9	R	31(I)	100	94	15(Ⅲ)	100	16(Ⅶ)
7to8	N	15(Ⅱ)	80	33			
8to9	R	31(Ⅱ)	100	90	13(Ⅳ)	93	o
8to9	R				6(V)	86	
	R				8(Ⅵ)	80	
12t13	R	16(LX)	80	20			

n = number of subjects
( ) = procedure used

Lissner gave her subject as second activity a task similar to the interrupted one in content or in type of material. It became clear that the substitute value of the second activity (which we shall name the substitute action) for the main activity varied according to the nature, difficulty, and mode of presentation of the second action. The greater its functional substitute value the greater is the relief of the need for completion of the main action and the more complete is the discharge of the tension system correspond-

---

[1] K. LISSNER, Die Entspannung von Bedürfuissen durch Ersatzhand lungen, *Psychol. Forsch.*, 1933, 18, 218-250.

[2] W. MAHLER, "Ersatzhandlungen verschiedener Realitatsgrades," *Psychol. Forsch.*, 1933, 18, 27-89.

ing to it. One can therefore test the substitute value by determining how much less often the subject returns to the main activity when a substitute rather than a completely heterogeneous action is interposed.

Comparison of eight- to nine-year-old feeble-minded with seven- to eight-year-old normal children gave the following result. Under conditions①in which the substitute action had such a high substitute value with the normal children that the percentage of resumption sank from 79 (in experiments without a substitute action) to 33, the resumption with the feebleminded sank only from 100 to 94. ②With the feeble-minded the substitute value was thus almost zero. Köpke then gradually increased the similarity of the main and substitute activities until they were practically identical: for the task"paint an animal" was substituted the task "paint the same animal again on another sheet of paper"; for "build a bridge out of stones" was substituted "build the same bridge out of stones." In spite of this extremely high similarity the substitute value remained low (resumption remained at 86 to 100 per cent). In these cases, however, resumption was not so prompt, taking place only after 3 to 4 min.

These experimental results accord with certain observations of daily life. Once a feeble-minded child has in mind a definite goal he often shows a peculiarly rigid fixation on it. It is extremely striking with what rigidity these children often insist on carrying out a definite action in precisely one way and exactly "now," and

---

① Tasks were used which as far as possible were adapted in degree of difficulty to the capacities of the children. Examples: to model an animal out of plasticine, to assemble an automobile out of paper strips, to build an automobile out of rods and rings.

② In other words: whereas only 2 out of 31 feeble-minded children did not return to the original task, 33 of the 49 normal children did not resume it.

how difficult it is to sway them from their preference even with conditions under which a normal child of the same or somewhat younger age would be relatively easily moved. Thus the *will* of the feeble-minded often appears stronger, certainly more *rigid* than that of the normal child.

This peculiar rigidity of the will expresses itself not only in facing momentary goals but also in so-called habits. Feebleminded children frequently impress one with their pronounced stereotypy [1] and pedantry, far exceeding the commonly observed pedantry of normal children. Thus their shoes must stand before the bed in exactly one way; the buttons on a piece of clothing must be fastened in one definite order; the child is extremely suspicious of new foods, and even when hungry he may refuse at supper time a food generally eaten at lunch.

In contrast to these experiences, which agree with the experimental results on substitution in the feeble-minded, are others which seemingly imply the opposite. The circumstance that tricks and diversions for instance are likely to be more effective with the feeble-minded than with the normal child is due, perhaps, to his lesser intellectual capacities. But the feebleminded child is much more readily satisfied with an incomplete solution of a task, indeed often a pure gesture appears to suffice. If he finds it difficult to throw a ball far, he may be quite satisfied in raising his arm as though to throw in a forceful manner. To illustrate further, the masculine gestures of many of these children have in high degree

---

[1] *Cf.* L. M. TERMAN, *The Measurement of Intelligence*, Houghton Mifflin, Boston, 1916, p203.

the function of real acts. ①Lazar characterizes such children as *Gestenkinder.* ② Also the experimental findings of Gottschaldt③show that the feebleminded are relatively easily satisfied with completing a simpler task at a lower level of aspiration when the original task is too difficult.

Experimental results and observations of daily life thus testify with equal impressiveness to an apparent contradiction: on the one hand the feeble-minded show an especial rigidity and tendency toward fixation which makes the occurrence of substitute actions, in the functional sense, very difficult; on the other, there is revealed a pronounced tendency toward substitute actions and a tendency to be readily satisfied with them. Not only is this true of two different groups of children. Both extremes are characteristic of one and the same child.

The theory to be discussed below attempts to penetrate to the essential dynamic factors involved and seems to point to a way of solution of this and a series of other paradoxes typical of the feeble-minded.

General Theory of The Dynamic Differences Among Persons

As previously mentioned, the problem of feeble-mindedness is one of individual differences. If these individual differences are regarded from a dynamic point of view the following general considerations arise. As a dynamic system the individual is more or less

---

① Cf. G. WEISS, Kindertypen in aufgabefreien und aufgabegebundenen Situationen, *Zeitschr. f. Kinderforsch.* ,1930,36,pp. 343 ff.

② These are by no means always feeble-minded children.

③ GOTTSCHALDT,*Ber. d. V. Kong. f. Heilpdd.* ,Munchen,1931,130-143.

unitary and more or less self-contained (closed). ① Differences may derive from a diversity of (1) structure of the total system, (2) *material* and state of the system, or (3) its meaningful *content*.

Differences in Structure of the Person.

Degree of Differentiation. One of the most fundamental dynamic differences between small child and adult is the degree of differentiation in their various psychical regions and systems. The fact that various life-spheres (profession, family, friendships with definite persons, and so on) as well as different needs are much more differentiated in the adult than in the one-yearold child scarcely demands extensive demonstration. In the adult it is generally not difficult to distinguish more peripherally and more centrally located regions. The young child shows far less pronounced *stratijication*. Thus in this respect he is a much more unitary system, dynamically a stronger Gestalt. A topological representation of the functional differences of the total personality in respect to degree of differentiation corresponds to the differences between Fig. 2 *a* (child) and Fig. 2 *b* (adult).

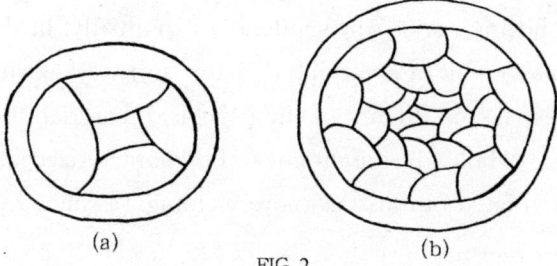

(a)　　　　　　　　　(b)
FIG.2.

---

① LEWIN, Zwei Grundtypen von Lebensprozessen, *Zeitschr. f. Psychol*, 1929, 113, 220 ff.

Types of Structure. Together with differences in degree of differentiation, there certainly exist between different individuals important differences in the type of differentiation. The total structure may for instance be relatively harmonious or inharmonious. The dynamic connections between various part systems of the person are by no means equally close. Great individual differences exist with reference to *the way* this delimitation of relatively closed subordinate wholes occurs: which parts are more strongly and which parts more weakly developed, whether the degree of demarcation among the subordinate wholes is relatively uniform or whether separate parts of the personality are particularly isolated. The phenomenon of division of personality is an example of a very special type of structure.

Differences in Psychical Material and in State of the Systems.

Differences in Material. Diversities in structure (in degree of differentiation and in type of structure) do not exhaust the possible differences within the personality. Thus with identical structures, the *ease* with which they *change* may differ decidedly. Further, the shifting may occur suddenly or gradually. In this connection one may speak of a varying dynamic softness, elasticity, hardness, brittleness, or fluidity of the psychical material.

On the whole the infant must be characterized as not only less differentiated but also as more yielding. ①Among children of

---

① Certain facts, such as the strong fixation of the small child on certain habits, appear to speak against the hypothesis of a generally greater plasticity at this age. I prefer, however, from general biological points of view, to maintain the hypothesis of easier mobility of the psychical material and believe that I can otherwise explain the opposed facts (see pp. 228ff).

the same age there appear to exist great differences in material. The special properties of one's psychical material must constitute a very deep individual peculiarity of the person and play a decided role in heredity.

If differences in ease of structural change within the system are indicated by variation in thickness of the boundaries separating its various parts, the differences between small child and adult correspond in general to those between a and b, Fig. 3.

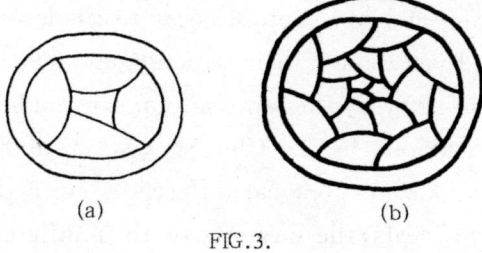

(a)　　　　　　　(b)

FIG. 3.

States of Tension in the Systems. Along with the material properties must also be considered properties of the state of the systems, especially their state of tension. In the satisfaction of a need, for instance, this state of tension may change slowly or rapidly. It is also quite probable that together with the diversity of momentary states there exist also enduring differences in the average tension in the systems of the total person. (By material properties in the broad sense we mean to include the properties discussed in the present as well as in the previous three paragraphs.)

The material properties of the different systems within the same individual are by no means completely uniform. The systems of the plane of unreality possess a greater degree of fluidity, [1] and

---

[1] *Cf.* J. F. BROWN, Die dynamischen Eigenschaften der Realitats-und Irrealitatschichten, *Psythol. Forsch.*, 1933, 18, 1-26.

important differences may exist between young and old part regions of the person. In so far, therefore, as we speak of individual differences in the material constants of the person as a whole, it is necessary to compare *homogeneous* parts within the total person.

Differences in Content of Meaning of the Systems.

Even though the structure and the material properties of two individuals are the same, the content corresponding to the systems may be different and constitute decisive psychological differences of the person. Even though their structure and material properties should be approximately the same, a fouryear- old boy in the Russian steppes and one in the Chinese quarter of San Francisco would show important personal differences since the content of their goals and ideals, the meaning of their different spheres of life, are different. In higher degree than material properties and structural plan, these diversities of content depend upon historical influences.

A Dynamic Theory of The Feeble-Minded

Theoretical Considerations

In returning from general discussion of the possible dynamic differences among persons to the problem of the nature of the feeble-minded (to, *i. e.*, a relatively frequent type of the feebleminded) the following is to be considered.

Degree of Differentiation.

The feeble-minded child of, say, eight years is in general less differentiated than the eight-year-old normal child brought up under otherwise similar conditions. Not only is his level of intelligence lower but on the whole it is to be designated as more primitive, more infantile. In respect to structural plan, aside from other differences of structure, the feeble-minded is to be designated as less differentiated. In this respect he resembles a younger normal child (Fig. 4).

The complex of phenomena ordinarily designated as infantilism may be due chiefly to this small degree of differentiation. The greater concreteness of thinking may also be related to this primitiveness in the sense of lack of dynamic differentiation. ①

Material Properties.

Even though a feeble-minded child corresponds in degree of differentiation to a younger normal child he is not to be regarded as entirely similar. We conceive the major dynamic difference between a feeble-minded and a normal child of the same degree of differentiation to consist in a greater stiffness, a smaller capacity for dynamic rearrangement, in the psychical systems of the former (Fig. 4②).

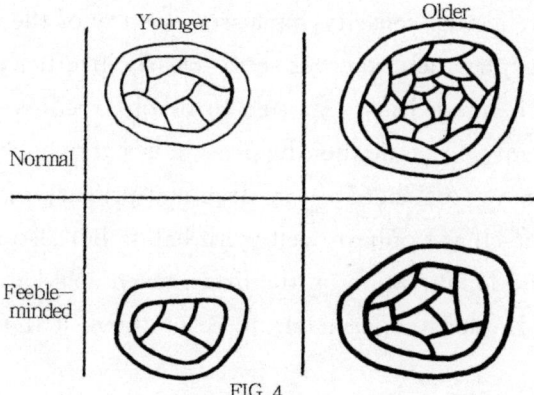

FIG. 4.

---

① See below, pp. 222ff.
② As in Fig. 3 increase in thickness of the boundary lines represents decrease in ease of structural change within the system.

A pplication in Outline

That on the whole the feeble-minded is to be characterized as dynamically more rigid, less mobile, is attested by a large number of observations.

Pedantry and Fixation of Volitional Goals.

As previously mentioned, it is striking with what inflexibility and pedantry [①] the feeble-minded is accustomed to cling to a fixed goal or habit.

In part this inflexibility of the feeble-minded is an expression of his helplessness. Mishaps occur to him oftener. He finds more frequently than the normal child that he cannot trust the world in which he lives. It is far more difficult for him to survey a new situation and to see through it adequately. Therefore he inclines, as does the normal child in situations of helplessness, to try ways which are well known to him, to cling to means which he trusts. To this extent pedantry also may be a secondary effect of his smaller intellectual capacity, his lesser mastery of the world.

This explanation however seems clearly insufficient. Pedantry in the feeble-minded is very often to be observed even when the child certainly feels neither helpless nor overwhelmed. Rather there seems to exist here a very deep and primary rigidity, which manifests itself not only in well-worn habits but also in new volitional goals. This fixation on the first chosen goal led without exception in Kopke's experiments to resumption of the interrupted goal.

---

① By pedantry is meant the tendency to insist upon strict regularities and to develop inflexible habits to an unnecessary degree and under inappropriate circumstances.

Paradoxes of Substitute Value.

The assumption of a relatively difficult rearrangement of psychical systems in the feeble-minded permits us to account for the paradoxical results of the substitution experiments.

If one inquires into the dynamic assumptions that must be fulfilled in order for a substitute activity to have substitute value, the following is to be established with reference to the inner psychical systems. Let the uncompleted primary task be designated A, the substitute task, B. Satisfaction of the primary task (dynamically, discharge of A) by the completion of the substitute action (*i.e.*, by discharge of B) occurs when, and only when, the two systems A and B are so related that the discharge of B brings with it an immediate discharge of A. That is to say, A and B must be relatively dependent parts of one dynamic whole (Fig. 5) and cannot therefore be mutually isolated systems (Fig. 6). Only when the structure is as represented in Fig. 5, where A and B are, dynamically, relatively weakly bounded parts of one total system, can the substitute action have substitute value. [1]

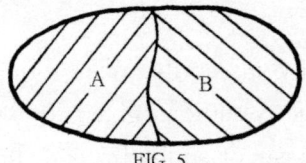
FIG.5.
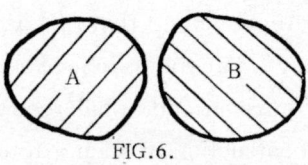
FIG.6.

Actually Lissner[2] found that the substitute value depends

---

[1] The discharge of A by B may be, other things being equal, more complete and thus the substitute value ot the second action higher, if the total system A and B is bounded from other systems by a strong common outer wall. In this case the state of tension of A-B is less dependent upon that of the neighboring systems.

[2] K. LISSNER, *ibid*. p. 240. Table 8.

significantly upon the type of transition from the first to the second activity. If the second activity is introduced by the experimenter as, so to speak, an entirely new experiment the substitute value is, other things being equal, much less than when the second activity is developed out of the first. The investigations of Zeigarnik ① and Birenbaum②have already shown the fundamental importance of the interconnections of psychical systems for their tension and discharge (directly or by the discharge of other systems). They have also indicated the means by which one may experimentally produce definite relations between whole psychical systems.

In the situations utilized in the substitution experiments of Köpke, a certain degree of similarity between the two tasks was adequate to bring about a sufficient connection between the two systems. When these children were presented with a substitute task sufficiently related to the initial one, the system which arose did not seem to be completely separated but appeared rather to grow out of the first or at least to develop in close connection with it. Occasionally such a close connection between the two systems first arose only during the course of the work. ③As a rule a structure similar to that of Fig. 5 results.

That the psychical systems be easily susceptible of re-formation is an additional requisite under the conditions given for the construction of such a totality on the basis of similarity and thus also for the existence of substitute value. If the capacity for trans-

---

① B. ZKIGARNIK, Uber das Behalten von erledigten und unerledigten Handlungen, *Psychol. Forsch.* ,1927,9,1- 85.

② G. BIRENBAUM, Das Vergessen einer Vornahme (isolierte seelische Systeme und dynamischc Gesamtbereiche), *Psychol. Forsch.* ,1930,13,218-284.

③ See BIRENBAUM, *op. cit.* , concerning the course and conditions underlying the formation of such totalities.

formation be small, the building of such totalities under the previous conditions will occur with difficulty, if at all. System B, corresponding to the second task, will then be more likely to appear as an independent system (corresponding to Fig. 6). If not it will unite with A to form a dynamic unity only with greater difficulty. The substitute value will be small. Actually Köpke found this to be the case with feeble-minded.

At the same time it may be predicted from our basic assumption concerning the slight mobility of the psychical material of the feeble-minded that with them, under certain circumstances, the substitute value must be greater than with the normal, rather than less. For instance, if with the feeble-minded one should succeed in bringing the second task into dynamic connection with the first, the relative difficulty of transformation of the system must give it a particularly high degree of unity, thus resulting in a high substitute value. This might be attained by developing the second task out of the first. We have already referred to the seemingly paradoxical fact that along with instances of extreme difficulty of substitute satisfaction there occur in the feeble-minded others in which substitute satisfaction appears readily. In the cases mentioned by Gottschaldt, when the first task was too difficult for the child he *spontaneously* turned to easier tasks. On failing in the construction of a high tower he contented himself with a lower one. There is much indicating that in such spontaneous growth of the second task out of the first the two activities dynamically are unseparated. If, however, the tension systems are not divided, there exists actually only one tension system. Thus the substitute value will be high; higher, indeed than with the normal. This inference is supported by a consequence adduced from our fundamental assumption, a consequence which we must consider somewhat in detail, since it is of essential significance for the specifically intellectual problem.

Material Properties of Systems and the Formation of Wholes.

In normal individuals if there occurs spontaneous substitution, for instance of the type of substitution of resignation, ① the new goal in general is dynamically not completely identical with the old. The original goal is not wholly transformed into the new one, but often maintains a certain independence, for example an "ideal goal." In such cases there frequently develops in normal children a dynamic structure similar to that of Fig. 5: one relatively unitary total system arises in which are distinguishable two, although weakly divided, part systems. That is, a wall exists between the two part systems even though it is a weak one functionally. Discharge of the one system will therefore cause a substantial though not a complete discharge of the other (in so far as a deeper transformation does not occur during discharge). ②

If the systems are particularly rigid in respect to their material properties, such a differentiation of one total system into two weakly divided parts would less easily occur. If the forces in question are strong enough two separate systems, A and B (Fig. 6), are more likely to result, or A and B will remain completely undivided (Fig. 7). In these cases a very high substitute value (externally viewed) must ensue because there exists a dynamical-

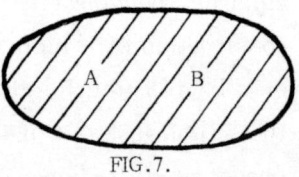

FIG.7.

---

① See DEMBO, *op. cit.*

② It frequently does. Cf. Hoppe, Erfolg und Misserfolg, *Psychol. Forsch.*, 1930, 14, 1-62.

ly undifferentiated system, a strong Gestalt, and because therefore each discharge of tension must directly embrace the whole system.

From this dynamic rigidity of systems and its effect on the formation of differentiated total systems the paradoxes of substitute value may be derived as necessary consequences. Thus, in general, is to be understood the either-or behavior so characteristic of the feeble-minded in a variety of fields. This either-or characteristic rests upon the fact that in the feebleminded, because of their psychical material properties, we encounter, in higher degree than with the normal, strong dynamic Gestalten. That is, we encounter in higher degree unitary, internally undifferentiated systems which, in so far as they are separated, are separated completely.

There is a relative lack of weak Gestalten, those organizations in which two or more part systems constitute a dynamically connected unity although at the same time remaining separated to a greater or less degree.

One of the fundamental properties of the feeble-minded is, in my opinion, the paucity of continuously graded transitions between absolute separation and absolute connection in more inclusive dynamic wholes. This state of affairs makes clear why in so many fields one finds in the behavior of the feebleminded extreme apparent contradictions.

Material Properties and the Psychical Environment.

In surveying the consequences of a person's dynamic material properties for experience and behavior, one must remember that these properties are characteristic not only of the internal psychical systems but equally of the psychical environment and of its changes, in so far as the latter are psychologically conditioned. ① Not only such facts as valences of environmental objects and events but also the meaning and structural peculiarities of the perceptual field depend significantly upon psychobiological factors of the individual concerned and are not completely or univocally determined by the objective stimulus factors. Thus not only the content and momentary state of needs and interests, but all dynamic properties of the person, the rigidity and unchangeability of his systems, make themselves felt in the structure and changes of the psychical environment. Ordinarily, however, in treating particular objects or situations, one refers to the degree of fixation of their valence rather than to the transformation of tense or discharged psychical systems.

Regarded from this conception of the psychical environment, the behavior of the feeble-minded reveals the same either-or structure, as effect of the general rigidity of the psychical material. We mentioned above that the retarded pupils returned, without exception, to the interrupted task. From the standpoint just developed we should speak of a strong fixation of valence on the uncompleted work. This valence, however, will only remain effective under the conditions of the previous experiment as long as the feeble-minded does not leave the immediate psychological environment of the task. Under the given conditions, ② allowing the child to carry out the second task (interrupting task) on another table suf-

---

① The principle that within the dynamic world of a definite individual is to be included not only his inner psychical systems and motorium but equally his psychical environment is one that has been repeatedly emphasized but so far insufficiently needed. *Cf.* W. Köhler, *Gestalt Psychology*, and LEWIN, *Vorsatz, Wille und Bedurfnis*.

② Under other conditions the feeble-minded also may very well return to tasks which are not present.

fices to reduce almost to zero the frequency of returns to the first task. The behavior of normal children contrasts decidedly with this. The situation may be formulated thus: in higher degree than the normal the feeble-minded is *either in the one or in the other situation*. Separate situations are in much higher degree opposed closed wholes, and the feeble-minded acts according to the field forces of these closed situations.

From the point of view of a psychology of the will, difficulty of transformation [*Umstrukturierung*], the effect of which upon the intellectual processes we are to consider immediately, signifies a *deliverance* of the person to the mercies of the momentary situation. According to the circumstances, this may have externally different effects. It may, for instance, appear as helplessness, as incapacity to find a way out. (The frequency of seductions to stealing, or within the sexual sphere, may well be closely related to this situation.) Under other circumstances the small changeability and relatively strong segre - gation of the situation result in great persistence and energy in the pursuit of a definite goal, to a particularly high concentration. On the other hand, if even a small change in the situation is occasioned by an external influence, it will constitute a much more profound interference. For in these persons the changed situation must, in much higher degree, tend to appear completely closed, supplanting entirely the facts of the first situation. That is to say, the formation of two or more simultaneously existent stratified situations will be much more difficult than in the normal individual. As a matter of fact the feebleminded are thus generally extremely sensitive to distractions.

As previously mentioned in connection with the satiation experiments, this either-or characteristic results much more frequently in the introduction of pauses by the feeble-minded. Thus they completely interrupt their work more often than do normal children.

The peculiar resoluteness and *obstinacy* of the feeble-minded have already been referred to. An essential role in their determination is played by the facts just discussed, namely, the more difficult formation of relatively separated systems and the occurrence of less weakly connected but relatively separated situations. These are very intimately related with the great difficulty encountered by the feeble-minded when he is forced to *remain in a conflict situation*.

The characteristic conflict situation before decision[1] is a state of suspension in which the situations corresponding to various possible decisions are sufficiently present but must at the same time be kept sufficiently apart. On account of the reasons mentioned, the maintenance of this state of suspension is peculiarly difficult for the feeble-minded, and his obstinacy may be associated with this tendency toward univocal, dynamically closed situations.

The same difficulty in maintaining stratified situations makes it hard for the feeble-minded to dissimulate. This is expressed in most varied ways. In play for instance it often gives the total behavior of the feeble-minded an uncommonly appealing appearance of moral rectilinearity.

Helplessness and fear may prevent the feeble-minded from escaping a conflict out of which a normal, more mobile child would find a way with relative ease. If, despite all tendencies to the contrary, the child is forced by superior circumstances to remain in an unresolved conflict he generally suffers very acutely. Strong emo-

---

[1] See Chaps. III and IV.

tional reactions or suppressions result. ①

Intelligence Defects.

In these considerations we have achieved an approach to the understanding of fecble-mincledness in its proper sense, that is, the intellectual processes of the feeble-minded.

As we have previously mentioned, the act of insight consists essentially in a change in the whole-relations in the field. Two initially quite independent facts become dependent parts of an interconnected whole; an originally unitary whole splits into relatively independent parts; or, by far most frequently, a re-formation of the field occurs such that parts of different wholes simultaneously become loosened and combine with other parts to form new wholes. Such re-formation of the whole-relations may be favored by objective shifts in the field (for instance, decreasing the spatial distance between banana and stick in Kohler's experiments). It is most particularly dependent, however, upon the general dynamic psychological properties of the given field, or of the particular person. ② *This means then that an insufficient general mobility of the psychical systems must hinder the occurrence of intellectual acts*, that is, the occurrence of certain transformations of the structural unities in the field.

---

① Dembo has shown that generally anger is connected with the presence of an outer barrier creating a situation without escape for the person concerned. This enables us to see the relation of anger and helplessness, which may be of particular significance in the understanding of the feeble-minded.

② This state of affairs, illustrated by the difficulty of achieving insight with too great a stage of tension, is related, among other things, to the fact that forces working toward shifting of whole-relations can effect little if the total system is dominated by strong forces maintaining a condition of equilibrium. We will refer later to another circumstance working in the same direction.

That the same material properties of the person hitherto discussed are of extreme significance for ease of intellectual activity will become even clearer upon consideration of certain rather complicated re-formations typical of intellectual acts and their difficulties.

Rupp[①] mentions several examples of typical difficulties in drawing by the feeble-minded, which seem to me to be particularly significant in the present connection. If a feeble-minded child is presented with a honeycomb pattern (Fig. 8) of which the cells 1,2, and 3 are given, and asked to continue in the sequence 4, 5, 6, 7... , he encounters great difficulties which, can be shown not to be manual. Frequently there occurs a loosening up and isolation of the individual cells (Fig. 9a[②]). If we inquire into the cause of this isolation of the cells, or as we may say, the Gestalt disintegration (see above), we find the following. The child may have proceeded as far as cell 7, and have drawn lines a, b, and c. What now is the situation with regard to line d? For the child at work on cell 7 it is obvious that the cell must possess a boundary line below to the left. This line is however also the upper right boundary of cell 5. The line d is thus simultaneously a dependent part of two different wholes and indeed has a quite different character in the two. Further, in such constructive activity it is necessary at the moment of actual drawing to perceive the separate line as a relatively independent whole.

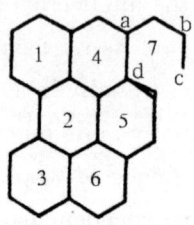

FIG.8.

---

① H. RUPP, tlber Optische Analyse, *Psychol. Forsch.*, 1923, 4, 262-300.
② Figures 9a and 9b are from Rupp, *op. cit.*, p. 267, Figs. 4f and 4, respectively. The cross-hatching in Fig. 9b was intentionally inserted afterward by the experimenter in order to bring out the structure of the drawing.

Thus, fundamentally, one must see with sufficient clearness three wholes: d as, (1) an independent line (to be drawn, for instance, in a definite direction from a definite point), (2) a dependent part of cell 5, and (3) a dependent part of cell 7. The situation is closely related to that of conflict with substitution previously described. The drawing can succeed only when the different characters of d in the two wholes are sufficiently differentiated and clearly appreciated. If, at the time, the child is dominated only by whole 5 or 7 and if d is sufficiently fixated as belonging to the already completed whole 5, as constituting its upper right boundary, then in bounding cell 7 he will be constrained to draw a new line, its lower left boundary.

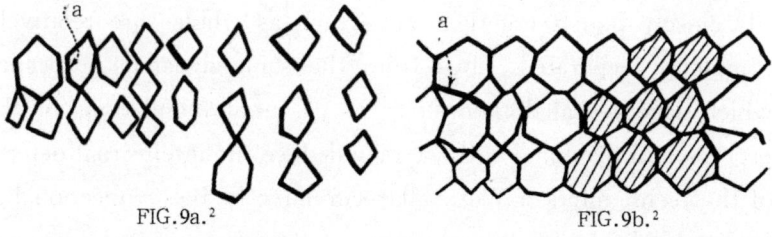

FIG. 9a.[2]   FIG. 9b.[2]

Figures 9a and 9b show clearly this isolation of the smaller wholes of the given pattern The line a in both figures is an example of doubling a line, a condition which results from the inability to see the line simultaneously as part of the two different wholes.

A similar situation occurs when, instead of solving the task of dividing a square into smaller ones by drawing parallel lines through the entire figure, the feeble-minded solves it by making a row of smaller squares as in Fig. 10. It plays a role, together with two other factors, when in the copying of the Binet rhombus the figure is reproduced as a circle with added corners (Fig. 11)

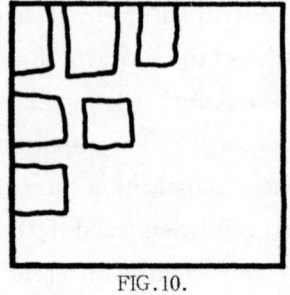
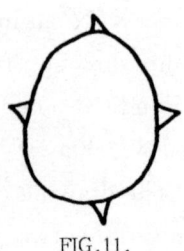

FIG.10.   FIG.11.

The cause of difficulties of the feeble-minded in such intellectual tasks thus rests upon the fact that in the feeble-minded there is a much greater tendency toward the formation of strong Gestalten, that is, of unities whose subordinate parts are extraordinarily closely bound together and which as wholes are relatively completely separated. Thus from the same dynamic properties which have revealed themselves as essential foundations of the processes of need and will, we may deduce the intellectual defects of the feeble-minded. We shall recur later to the connection between the degree of differentiation of the person and the appearance of strong Gestalten.

Rohrschach[1] found that on presentation of ink -blot figures the feeble-minded gave decidedly fewer whole answers. Beck[2] confirmed this finding and discovered a small yet decided correlation between mental age and the tendency to give whole answers, that is, to describe the unclear field as a whole.

From this tendency to proceed from parts rather than from

---

[1] H. ROHRSCHACH, *Psychodiagnostik*, Bern, 1921
[2] S J. BECK, The Rohrschach Test as Applied to a Feeble-minded Group, *Arch. Psychol*, No 136, 1932.

wholes an objection might be developed against our thesis of the special importance of the strong Gestalt in the feeble-minded I shall therefore deal briefly with this question

It must first be made clear that the thesis, "X tends to pen eive wholes in greater degree than Y," is in this generalized form absolutely meaningless Even though there existed persons who perceived only a "mosaic of points," they would be perceiving wholes. One can only meaningfully distinguish what particular wholes will be perceived with given constellations of stimuli For example, the whole answers of normal children with Rohrschach by no means referred to the piece of paper with the ink blot but only to the ink blot. Yet they are not considered as part answers.

Here we may leave it open whether type of instruction or any other factor is responsible for the preference of these wholes in description. Certainly one may say that it is frequently harder for the feeble-minded, even as for the younger normal child, to sufficiently see through extended situations. This is indeed one of the most frequent difficulties in the solution of intellectual tasks. *Extension* is here essentially to be conceived in the sense of a property of structure; it would be completely misleading to assert that the small child or the feeble-minded see only parts and no wholes. It can no longer be doubted that small children, primitive people, and animals depend to a particularly high degree upon the total character of situations. Rather the objective temporal and spatial extension of that which will be experienced by a young child as one connected situation, or as one relatively closed whole within a situation, often fails to correspond with that which would appear to the adult as the total situation or a special whole within it. This objective extension of the total situation is occasionally greater with the small child, very frequently however less than with the adult. The child's greater difficulty of surveying extended situations derives above all from the fact that with the adult the maximal degree of differentiation of wholes appears to be higher. That is to say, with the adult more complexly stratified yet clearly differentiated wholes may develop as subordinate wholes. This means, however, that the small child by no means sees only parts, but that with him, on the contrary, strong Gestalten play a much more dominating role. It may scarcely be doubted that in this respect the feeble-minded stands closer to the younger child.

Concreteness.

Because of the slighter mobility of his psychical systems and his greater difficulty in developing and changing Gestalten, one is enabled to understand why the feeble-minded requires other conditions than the normal individual in order to achieve a reorganization of the field, an intellectual Aha-experience. There remains the further question as to whether the specific concreteness and primitiveness of their way of thinking is to be understood in terms of these same considerations.

Primitiveness of thinking may perhaps be referred to the tendency toward development of strong Gestalten. From this one might infer that the general Gestalt characteristics play a relatively greater role with the feeble-minded. Yet rather than tracing this peculiarity of the feeble-minded directly to the rigidity of his systems it is probably more correct to refer it to his smaller degree of differentiation as a person, to which we have already referred. Indeed the tendency to concreteness and primitiveness appears to be a general feature of the childlike or otherwise undifferentiated person. It may thus be the effect of that structural property which the feeble-minded has in common with the young child (see page

209).

One will probably have to recognize in the tendency toward concreteness more than merely the primitiveness of the younger child. For this difficulty concerning abstract thinking still appears pronounced in the feeble-minded at an age at which the normal child of equivalent mental age no longer shows this peculiar concreteness. Our general groundwork indicates a way in which this peculiarity of the feeble-minded may be derived.

Concreteness of thinking and action in the feeble-minded signifies chiefly, as previously mentioned, that every object and event derives its meaning in peculiarly high degree from the present situation, that it is not a separable part of the situation. Thus abstraction, by which one generally means construction of groups according to certain factual relations of the individual objects, is rendered more difficult. Tn addition to emphasizing in general the dependence of the particular object on the actual situation, the thesis of concreteness implies that certain types of group construction are especially hindered. These are the types of grouping which are not directly in the level of reality, but more imaginal, conceptual, unreal. This condition may be related to very specific properties in the structure of the feeble-minded.

Compared with the total behavior of normal or even of certain psychopathic types of children, that of the particular kind of feeble-minded which we are considering strikes one by its relative lack of imaginativeness. This does not mean that the feeble-minded child has no ideas. Not infrequently he possesses a good and accurate memory for concrete facts. But his thinking and play as well reflect a poor imagination. He lacks a certain richness and a particular kind of mobility characteristic of imaginative play.

This lack of imagination on the part of the feeble-minded is revealed in the above mentioned investigations of Rohrschach[1] and Beck,[2] utilizing the Rohrschach ink-blot figures. From the fact that the figures relatively seldom were described as in motion, Beck concludes," This finding indicates that the feebleminded have very little capacity for creative fantasy." Just what psychological processes play a role here is, as Rohrschach himself emphasizes, rather unclear.

We regard the dynamic basis of the peculiarity of imaginative behavior as consisting in the relation of these occurrences to levels in the psychological environment and in the person, levels we have designated by the term unreality. Differences in degree of reality determine a dimension in the psychological life-space [3] and in the person. The levels of unreality stand, for example, in close relation to dreams, play, and ideal goals. *The degree of their development, their position in the whole structure of the person, and the type of connection between these levels of reality and unreality appear to me to be of fundamental significance for the total character of a person, in particular for his imagination and creativeness.*

We know from the investigation of Brown[4] that the dynamic properties of the levels of unreality are characterized by especial fluidity. If now relatively small mobility of psychical systems is characteristic of feeble-mindedness it is understandable that those

---

① H. ROHRSCHACH, *op. cit.* , pp. 94 ff.
② S. J. BECK, *op. cit.* , p. 72.
③ See Chap. IV, p. 145.
④ J. F. BROWN, *op. cit.*

psychical levels which in the normal individual are characterized by a particularly high fluidity will suffer particularly in the feeble-minded. Thus the consequence of a relative lack of development of the levels of unreality must be a lowered imaginativeness in total behavior, an increased concreteness of thinking.

Whether one must speak only of a lack of development and relative nonfluidity of the levels of unreality or whether the function of these levels within the total person is displaced can be determined only from a precise investigation of the particularities of development of levels of unreality in the feebleminded. In the normal child formation of levels of different degrees of reality is the effect of a differentiation from beginnings in which the planes of reality and unreality cannot actually be separated. An investigation of the corresponding development in the feeble-minded should yield important information concerning the general problem of the development of different parts of the total person and perhaps furnish also an important practical instrument for the differential diagnosis between feeble-mindedness and late development.

This suggestion leads us to the consequences for the development of the feeble-minded which result from our basic assumption.

Infantilism.

One of the most tangible peculiarities of the feeble-minded is his retardation in comparison with normal children of like age, that is, his infantilism. The slow development of the feeble-minded child occurs by no means only in the intellectual sphere. ① The fact of retardation is so central that, for instance, the difference in intelligence between normal and feebleminded can roughly be characterized by its degree, that is, by mental age. It is scarcely to be doubted that the feebleminded behaves in many respects like a younger child, not only with regard to intelligence but also with reference to the breadth of his mental horizon, his store of knowledge, his attention,' ② his emotional instability.

In a theory of infantilism one must keep in mind that retardation is not a specific peculiarity of the feeble-minded but also occurs frequently, for instance, in psychopathic types, especially the sensitive and impulsive.

Dynamically retardation may be related especially to a *smaller degree of differentiation* of the total systems of the psychical person, be it in all parts or in certain important spheres. We have, accordingly, to state as one of the most essential facts concerning the feeble-minded that the rate of differentiation of the total person, or of important spheres, is smaller than with the normal individual.

Inquiry concerning the dynamic conditions upon which the rate of differentiation of such a total system depends leads us to the following considerations. Differentiation is certainly a function of the conditions of the environment as well as of the individual peculiarities of the person. At present we cannot answer the ques-

---

① Wallin(*Clinical and Abnormal Psychology*, Houghton Mifflin, Boston, 1927) reports the later appearance of the first tooth and the later closing of the fontanelle; Morgan (Physiological Maturity of Feeble-minded Girls, *Tr. School Bull*., 1926, 27, 23, 231 ff.), that menstruation occurs later with feeble-minded.

② Binet, indeed, attempted to bring differences of intelligence in direct relation to processes of attention.

tion whether one may properly speak of an inherited predisposition for a faster or slower rate of differentiation. The question, however, as to the relation existing between material properties and rate of differentiation of a system may well be raised.

Two systems, A and B, may be equal in respect to their degree of differentiation and their type of structure, yet differ with regard to their material properties. Further, in both cases the forces effecting differentiation may be equally strong and similarly directed. (For our present purpose it does not matter whether these are inner forces of the system or forces of the environment.) In such a case one may say unequivocally that a high functional *rigidity* with respect to changes must *hinder differentiation* of the total system. If, then, the material properties of the feeble-minded are to be characterized as particularly immobile, the direct deduction may be made that his development must, other things being equal, be slower. ①

This derivation of the rate of differentiation from material properties agrees very well with the fact that the difference in development (measured in years of mental age) between a feeble-minded and normal child does not remain constant with change in age but in general increases. Indeed, this increase is so decided that the intelligence quotient remains constant or actually decreases. Naturally it is very possible not only that the slower rate of differentiation rests upon peculiarities of material properties but that

---

① A more precise dynamic derivation would have to proceed from the relation between the strength of the forces pressing toward re-formation and of those necessary for the reorganization of a definite material.

the forces effecting differentiation are also relatively weak. ①

One may not, however, assert that in general differentiation of a system occurs the more readily the more fluid the system. We are concerned with the problem of an enduring, or in any case a relatively stable differentiation. If the total system is very fluid momentary differentiation may occur relatively easily, but the slightest force will again alter the structure so that development of a differentiated permanent structure of the total person does not result. ②Such dynamic relations seem to us to be characteristic of the infantilism of certain *psychopathic* types. ③

It is thus understandable why from the pedagogical point of view work with the milder grades of feeble-minded is often more fruitful and satisfying than work with psychopathic children Single advances in differentiation may occur much more slowly with the feeble-minded and of course there are with them also frequent relapses, but the construction in general seems to possess a higher degree of stability.

Thus the favorable condition for enduring differentiation of the total psychical systems of a person is neither a maximal nor

---

① It is quite conceivable that there are instances in which the material properties of different persons correspond in the rough and only the forces effecting differentiation differ. In such cases also infantilism must result.

② With a completely fluid system, differentiation in the sense of an enduring structure would be impossible (we never encounter the state of completely stable equilibrium in a living being). Such a complete fluidity in an organism could be as little admitted as complete rigidity.

③ *Cf*. LEWIN, Filmaufnahmen liber Trieb- und Affektausserungen psychopathischer Kinder.

minimal but rather an optimal degree of material rigidity, varying according to the strength of forces working toward differentiation.

It must be emphasized at this point that not only too great inflexibility but also too great fluidity of the system must lead to feeble-minded types of behavior. It might be worthwhile to test the applicability of such a dynamic characterization to the so-called erethetic feeble-mindedness.

Degree of Differentiation, Susceptibility to Influence [Beinflussbarkeit], Intellectual Mobility.

The connection just discussed between material properties and rate of development seems to me to speak quite forcibly for the correctness of our fundamental thesis. On the other hand, there are several kinds of facts related to degree of differentiation which are difficult to see through, dynamically. We do not wish to neglect pointing out these difficulties.

Several Theoretical Difficulties. As mentioned, the young normal child is to be considered as a relatively slightly differentiated as well as a relatively soft, mobile system. Yet there can be no doubt that in many respects the small child appears to be more fixated, pedantic, yes, even more difficult to influence than an older child or indeed the adult. Not only the feebleminded but also the small child demands with striking rigidity to sit on "his" chair while eating. If for some reason or other it does not please a one-year-old child to eat, it is generally much harder to move him to do so than it is an older child. Thus even though one wishes to continue holding to the thesis of greater mobility of the child (in it-

self quite probable ①) it becomes apparent that behavior quite closely related to the fixation and rigidity of the feeble-minded may occur under circumstances in which an immobile material is not to be thought of.

One might consider reconstructing the theory so as to place at the center lack of differentiation rather than material properties, or one might attempt to dispense altogether with the assumption of a difference in material. The question of whether slight mobility is to be given a primary or secondary significance would not disturb us greatly, since in a dynamic theory dealing always with the totality of the properties of a system such questions are no longer seen as of much importance. Aside from special difficulties, however, a theory that would restrict itself to differences in degree of differentiation cannot be regarded as sufficient fundamentally. According to such a conception the feeble-minded would be conceived of as entirely similar to a person with slower development. Such a view is, however, undoubtedly false. Furthermore infantilism, that is, a smaller degree of differentiation, admittedly occurs with types which are not to be designated as feeble-minded.

Another difficulty is connected with the problem of differentiation. Failure in the face of differentiated tasks involving comprehension, as for instance in drawing, in retention of rows of numerals, and similar tasks, ② is found not only with feebleminded but also with small children. Yet one might reason that their relative mobility should rather facilitate the formation of differentia-

---

① Compare the concept of plasticity, for instance, with C. BUHLER, *Kindheit und Jugend*.

② *Cf.* H. ROHRSCHACH, *op. cit.*; S. J. BECK, *op. cit.*; W. PETERS, Die Entwicklung der Wahrnehmungsleistungen beim Kinde, *Zeitschr. f. Psychol.*, 1927, 103, 129-184.

ted perceptual fields.

Our present experimental findings and insight into the general dynamics of the connection between psychical systems are not sufficient to yield a complete answer to the problems here in question. But the distinctions between degree of differentiation, degree of communication among part systems, [1] and the degree of their changeability have shown themselves so fruitful to us in recent years in the characterization of individual differences in such diverse spheres and in such varied connections that I should like to add a few considerations with reference to the solution of the difficulties involved.

In beginning, it should be emphasized that the relatively small differentiation of the feeble-minded follows from our fundamental thesis. Therefore the feeble-minded must show certain characteristics of the normal younger child, namely those which are specific effects of lack of differentiation.

Further, general observation seems to me to speak for the view that the degree of rigidity with the feeble-minded goes significantly beyond the occasional fixation observable in younger children.

Above all, however, one must inquire into the real dynamic meaning of fixation in the normal child.

Pedantry in the Normal Child. Whatever pedantry in the small child, for example, his wish always to sit on the same chair at table, may signify, it is by no means characteristic of the entire young child of, say, less than one year. At this age the child is still

---

[1] Through these concepts, particularly that of the degree of communication, the complex of facts referred to by E. R. Jaensch in the distinction between integrated and disintegrated types can probably be comprehended in sharper dynamic concepts.

quite insensitive to unusual situations of certain kinds. One can, for instance, take him on trips with fewer difficulties than a child of three or four. The child of three or four years already lives in a world of commands and prohibitions. A very definite must is often attached to certain things and types of behavior. This meaning is particularly stressed and held to by the child, probably in connection with the development of initial islands in a firm level of reality. This connection is, however, not always easily transparent to the adult, and often it is infected with magical features.

It is very possible that the pedantry of the feeble-minded is similarly based. Yet when some connection is not rationally transparent to him the feeble-minded must incline the sooner to magic ideas and fears. The question of material peculiarities here can only be answered by means of a comparative investigation of the degree of fixation under otherwise equal psychological conditions.

Susceptibility to Influence. In other cases in which the child appears to be influenced with greater difficulty the younger he is, the relations seem to be essentially different. If the hungry infant refuses his nourishment because he does not like its taste, there often remains only the possibility of brute force. The six-months-old child who does not savor his porridge turns his head away, purses his lips together, and eventually spews it out.

With the very small child the adult has fundamentally only a few methods of psychological interference. He can attempt to divert the child, to better his emotional state, or try to provoke a contrary action on the part of the child by apparent withdrawal of the object in question. The varied possibilities of encouragement and persuasion applicable to an older child are lacking.

Does there exist actually a greater dynamic rigidity of the psychical systems of the small child? To me such an interpretation appears false. The situation in question is as a whole to be characterized as one in which there exist for the child pronounced inclinations or disinclinations, that is, definite dominating field forces, together with an attempt by the adult to change the child. Under certain conditions this change is more difficult to effect in the small than in the older child. If one is to understand the basic dynamic factors operative it must be emphasized that it is only under very definite conditions that the smaller child is harder to change. The primitive method of diversion becomes generally ineffective with somewhat older children. One must then state that *under certain conditions the small child is harder, under other conditions easier to change than the older child*.

This paradoxical situation seems to be directly related to the lack of differentiation of the small child. In a higher degree than older children or adults the small child is a dynamic whole. The different parts of the total system are still so closely connected that in a peculiarly high degree the small child engages with his entire person in everything that he does. At the same time this unity means that the inner psychical and the bodily systems of the total person are particularly closely connected and that the dynamic boundary between person and psychological environment is relatively weak. [1] This means, for instance, that in the small child the needs of his person alter directly the character of his psychological environment and also that a change in the psychological environment affects more directly and strongly the total state of the person.

This wholeness and the slight firmness of the wall between person and environment have a double consequence for the ease

---

[1] See Chap. III.

with which the child may be influenced. If, by one means or another, one succeeds in altering the psychological environment of the child, then the small child is exposed with fewer defences to the changed environment. On the other hand, the total picture of the environment of the small child conforms much more directly to his own momentary state and under certain conditions it will be more difficult to bring about such an alteration. ① For instance, if the small child is angry, the whole world is momentarily flooded with anger. If one is not successful in evoking an occurrence strong enough to change the character of the whole situation, the child will remain relatively unchangeable.

The greater wholeness of the total system leads here also to an either-or effect, similar to that which we have discussed as resulting from the rigidity of systems. Thus *in a certain respect there exists a functional equivalent between greater material rigidity and greater wholeness of the total system*. Both material rigidity and slight differentiation must favor the origin of stronger Gestalten, thus leading to an either-or effect.

The feeble-minded combine both a relatively high material rigidity and a specially small degree of differentiation of the total person ② (which, as we have seen, may itself be conceived as an effect of rigidity on development), which must work in the same way with regard to the either-or effect. Actually in the feeble-minded one may observe in a striking manner the above discussed paradox of susceptibility to influence: under certain circumstances

---

① Further, the special organization of the social field is naturally of particular significance for susceptibility to influence.

② Relative immobility of systems does not necessarily mean that these systems are not in communication with each other. Reformability and degree of communication are to be distinguished even though not independent of each other.

he is influenced with ease, under others with particular difficulty. This circumstance may have played a role in Binet's classification of the feeble-minded into rebellious and tractable types.

Differentiation of the Person and Mobility of Comprehension.

The fact that in certain respects it is easier to gain access to an older child is related further to the greater differentiation of the older child's worlds of perception and experience. Under objectively equal conditions, the degree of differentiation of the experienced environment appears to stand in closest connection with the degree of differentiation of the person concerned. This connection is apparent in the early development of the perceptual world[1] and also in the later development of perceptual achievements. [2] Together with the thorough structuring of a factual sphere, there grow generally the differential characteristics of the features of individual facts in the sphere and thus, at least to a certain extent, the possibility of more differentiated distinction. [3]

From the greater differentiation, the greater wealth of inner levels, there must thus result for the given person a greater richness of ways of conceiving and observing, in so far as other forces

---

[1] Cf. K. KOFFKA, *The Growth of the Mind*.

[2] Cf. W. PETERS, *op. cit.*

[3] It would lead too far afield to enter here into the problem, not wholly a simple one, of the cause of this relation. In any case an important role is played by the fact that the world picture of a more differentiated person is itself more differentiated (according to the lack of dynamic separation between the psychical person and the psychical environment). The individual perceptual fact thus acquires a position in a completely structured whole. I incline to believe that in addition a general relation between the maximal degree of structural detail in a perceptual picture and the degree of differentiation of the receptor is of decided significance.

do not work antagonistically. The result of this situation is that a second person finds comparatively more spheres from which he may attempt to evoke a change in the existing way of comprehension. Even without the influence of someone else, the more differentiated person will have more possibilities of differently conceiving a given situation if the strength of the field forces do not impose a definite conception. If, for any reason, the total situation is unsatisfactory (if, for instance, access to a goal is barred, as in the detour experiments), a change in conception, a re-formation of the field, will occur, other things being equal, earlier in the more differentiated child. Whether this re-formation of the field occurs as the most painless evasion of the difficulty or as creative insight may depend upon the kind and degree of differentiation with respect to the factual sphere concerned and upon other personal peculiarities. In any case a certain degree of differentiation of the person will facilitate the restructuring of the field necessary for intellectual insights. In general it will make possible a greater richness of differing modes of behavior.

Thus under certain conditions and to a certain extent there exists a functional equivalence between a higher degree of differentiation of the total system and a greater mobility of the person in the face of a given situation or task. There exists, that is, an equivalence between a specific characteristic of structure and a definite material property.

The same conclusion is reached as the result of the following considerations. Let A and B represent total systems of similar material properties and with equal (medium) degrees of communication. Further, both systems contain part systems a and b respectively, which in themselves are as similar as possible. A is on the whole, however, less differentiated than B. Under these circumstances, because of the greater diversity of part systems in B, there will exist many more possibilities of a change of b than of a through inner shifts in the total system.

Such re-formation through inner forces occurs in voluntary changes of conception [Auffassung]. The tasks of voluntary concentration and attention, tasks, that is, in which a change or maintenance of field structure is to be brought about by inner means, are therefore (at least within certain limits[1]) easier for a person of higher degree of differentiation. It requires little demonstration to establish that possibilities of influencing the separate part systems are significantly raised if the difference in differentiation of the total system consists not only in the number of part systems but (as actually occurs in the development of the child) also in qualitative differentiation within the total system. In particular, the development of levels of reality and unreality, of levels, that is, differing in material properties, contributes richer possibilities dynamically.

It is quite possible that a determining role in the intellectual weakness of the feeble-minded and in their poor capacity for voluntary concentration, is played by precisely this smaller differentiation of the total system in consequence of the associated *slighter secondary mobility*. Indeed it may here be more important than the direct effect of the material rigidity of the system.

If our conception of a certain equivalence between higher degree of differentiation and external mobility be correct, then under certain conditions, even with the feeble-minded, a greater mobility of actual behavior should make itself noticeable with an increase in

---

[1] The danger of spontaneous changes in the part systems seems to constitute an antagonistic factor.

age. Even though the actual material properties do not change, or, indeed, though the change with age is in the direction of greater rigidity, yet a sufficiently faster advance of differentiation should increase the wealth of possible varieties of behavior. I incline to believe that the development of the slighter degrees of feeble-mindedness confirms this conclusion throughout. In any case the absolute advance of intellectual achievements on the part of the feeble-minded becomes fully understandable from this point of view.

The functional equivalence between greater material rigidity of the systems and a greater wholeness of the total system in respect to (1) the formation of strong, relatively undifferentiated Gestalten (systems), and (2) the secondary mobility of behavior is one of the major causes of the normal child's increase in intellectual achievement with age. ① This occurs without increase in fluidity of the psychical systems, but rather despite a more probable gradual stiffening. This equivalence explains, further, why (because of a slighter differentiation of the total system) the feeble-minded, in spite of his greater material rigidity, is so similar to the younger child in susceptibility to influence, in intelligence, and in many other respects.

With these considerations the sketch of a dynamic theory of the feeble-minded is outlined in its main features. It scarcely need be emphasized that an abundance of detailed questions remains to be discussed or that a theory which attempts to proceed from the totality of dynamically possible differences of the person as a whole must raise a host of problems to be answered only by ex-

---

① As additional important factors the increased store of knowledge and abilities and, above all, the greater differentiation of the world picture are to be mentioned.

periment and by comparison of very different individual types. But before theoretical penetration has achieved a certain degree of maturity it is often impossible even to formulate the questions which should be answered by experiment.

Senile Dementia.

We refrain from consideration of the different kinds of mental disease or the effects of brain injuries which sometimes are accompanied by a kind of rigidity reminiscent of the behavior of the feeble-minded. Certainly the cause of behavioral rigidity may vary. Not only, as we have seen, is the degree of differentiation of the total person of influence, but the encapsulation of certain part systems remains a possible causal factor. The work of Dembo[1] on anger has shown, furthermore, that increase in state of tension may, under certain conditions, lead to greater momentary unity and primitiveness of the total behavior and may result in a certain fixation and weakness of intelligence which appears rather feeble-minded. The question as to whether a change is actually one of *material* property (the systems' mobility) must therefore be raised each time.

It cannot be questioned that dynamic mobility of the psychical systems is related in the closest fashion to the total biological constitution of the person concerned. We do not wish here to make definite assumptions concerning its relation to any specific biochemical, endocrine, or growth processes. We shall, however, briefly consider a general biological change in the total person which agrees peculiarly well with our fundamental thesis. This is the change designated as *senile dementia*.

The great material plasticity of the normal small child gives

---

[1] T. DEMBO, *op. cit.*

way, generally at least, to greater firmness. That with increasing age this development may lead finally to decided rigidity, lack of mobility, and inelasticity scarcely demands extensive demonstration. It has previously been pointed out that this progressive stiffening of the system's material properties is cut across by an increasing differentiation of the total person. In respect to intellectual achievements by far the most apparent initial effects of the combined processes are the increased structuration of the field of experience and the greater intellectual mobility associated with differentiation. Should stiffening, however, proceed faster than differentiation with increasing age intellectual mobility of behavior must decrease and in cases of high degree of material immobility lead to appearances of feeble-mindedness. In this respect the effect must be particularly striking if, with age, instead of increase in differentiation there occurs an impoverishment of structure, a loss of part systems.

There exist, moreover, great individual differences in the tempo, extent, and age limits of enduring differentiation as well as in the tempo and extent of stiffening of the psychical material. In concrete instances one must lay most weight upon how the different part systems of the person individually behave.

In general if a stiffening of psychical material occurs with age and if the type of feeble-mindedness here considered is characterized by relative rigidity, then it follows not only that the process of differentiation must proceed more slowly, as discussed above, but also that it must *cease earlier*. This conclusion agrees very well with observation. "The mental development of the feeble-minded is not only slower than that of the normal individual, it also ceases earlier and begins to decline earlier. "[1]

The theory here propounded thus permits a surprisingly unified view not only of those individual differences which are related to differences of the person in the feeble-minded, in the normal, and to a certain extent in the psychopathic, but also of those resting upon *development in age*. Further, it permits us to deduce the fundamental similarity of one type with other age levels of a different type and to comprehend in a unitary fashion a great multiplicity of kinds of behavior in very different fields, which, taken separately, are very diverse, often apparently contradictory.

Finally, I do not wish to neglect pointing out that the theory here presented attempts to avoid *methodologically* those difficulties which all classificatory divisions, however different in detail, must contend with and because of which these divisions are in certain respects so unsatisfactory. These difficulties of all classifications appear by no means only in psychology but in every science. They seem to be superable only when in the characterization of individual differences of the total person one passes beyond classificatory to constructive methods. We have made such an attempt. The constructive theory here presented does not lead to a distinction of three, four, or five pure types and their transitions, but, proceeding from certain basic dynamic concepts, contains from the beginning a principle for the construction and deduction of an endless variety of personal differences.

---

[1] R. PINTNER, Feeblemindedness, in CARL MURCHISON, *Handbook of Child Psychology*, ist ed. , 1931, Chap. XIX, p. 611. Pintner supports this assertion by reference to a number of investigations by various authors who used large numbers of subjects, in some cases over periods of ten years.

Summary

Proceeding from comparative experimental investigations on normal and feeble-minded children of psychical satiation, resumption of interrupted actions, and substitute value of substitute actions, a dynamic theory of a definite type of feeblemindedness has been developed.

The behavior of the feeble-minded is deduced from certain dynamic material properties of the psychical systems, which themselves imply specific structural peculiarities of the total person with respect to its degree and rate of differentiation and special kind of structure. The effects of these peculiarities of the person in the fields of intelligence, attention, will, and so on, have been discussed, and finally their relations to the structure of the person of the normal small child and of the senescent.

Chapter VIII
Survey of The Experimental Investigations

The following synopsis is designed to give the reader a very brief survey of our experimental investigations. It is planned, above all, to orient those who wish to go on to a closer acquaintance with these investigations. The description is therefore essentially from the systematic point of view. It may be desirable, however, to introduce it with a few historical remarks.

Historical Remarks

The point of departure for *Untersuchungen zur Handlungs- sund Affektpsychologie* [Investigations in the Psychology of Action and Emotion] was the investigation of the measurement of the will and the fundamental law of association, [1] the original aim

---

[1] K. LEWIN, Das Problem der Willensmessung und das Grundgesetz der Assoziation. *Psychol. Forsch.*, 1922, 1, 191-302; 2, 65-140.

of which was to make more precise Ach's attempts to measure the will. This investigation showed that the fundamental law of association (apart from other defects) errs in its basic dynamic concepts in so far as it treats couplings or other constraining forces as constituting also reservoirs of energy or tensions. Also it became clear to me that the phenomena occurring in these experiments were by no means so simple as was customarily assumed, but quite complicated and unstable. It was evident that one had to look for the simpler and essentially stabler phenomena of will psychology in facts which were generally considered especially complicated.

There followed a series of investigations in the field of the psychology of perception. In one of these [1] I attempted to derive the perception of depth from certain constellations of forces in different layers of the perceptual system. The investigation of the reversal of spatial position [2] treats a problem which stands in the closest relation not only to the structure of the perceptual field but also to the problems of the will.

Fortunately I experienced Max Wertheimer's teaching in Berlin and collaborated for over a decade with Wolfgang Kohler. I need not emphasize my debts to these outstanding personalities. The fundamental ideas of Gestalt theory are the foundation of all our investigations in the field of the will, of affection, and of the personality. In the few articles in which the problems of general Gestalt theory are not explicitly discussed, this is solely because they have become the selfevident foundation of experimental

---

[1] K. LEWIN and K. SAKUMA, Die Sehrichtung monokularer und binokularer Objekte bei Bewegung, und das Zustandekommen des Tiefeneffektes, *Psychol. Forsch.*, 1925, 6, 298-357.

[2] K. LEWIN, Ueber die Umkehrung der Raumlage auf dem Kopf stehender Worte und Figuren in der Wahrnehmung, *Piychol. Forsch.*, 1923, 4, 210-261.

practice.

Historically the first experimental investigation of the series on the structure and dynamics of the personality and of the psychological environment is that of Zcigarnik. ① All later experimental investigations are built upon this. It was an attempt to break a first path through a primeval forest of facts and assumptions, using as compass concepts the practical utility of which was still wholly untried. The coincidence on the part of B. Zeigarnik of unusual conceptual clearness with great psychological acuity in the judgment of particular cases made this attempt possible.

Among the later experimental investigations a similar fundamental significance attaches to Dembo's investigation ② of anger as a dynamic problem. She shows, by means of a self-critical investigation versatile in attack, that even rather complicated problems (success and failure, level of aspiration, substitution or compensation, reality and unreality, conflict, social relations, changes in the structure of the person), problems which at first seem to lie beyond any possibility of a dynamically strict and yet experimentally demonstrable presentation, are capable of such a presentation with the aid of a constructive psychology. Her investigation is an impressive illustration of the fact that in a dynamic theory of psychological processes the problems of the environment and of the person are inseparably bound up together. It turned out that the investigation of this emotion extended itself necessarily to an investigation of certain environmental structures. In this research the utility and fertility of topological concepts for the presentation of

---

① Über das Behalten erledigter und unerledigter Handlungen, *Psychol. Forsch.* , 1927, 9, 1-85.
② Der Ärger als dynamisches Problem, *Psychol. Forsch.* , 1931, 15, 1-144.

complicated environmental structures was demonstrated for the first time. The reader will naturally miss the quantitative evaluation which is an essential component of Zeigarnik's and of all the other researches of the series. But according to my experience the thorough quantitative investigation of a field can always be obtained with some persistence if only the qualitative analysis is sufficiently advanced. A quantitative elaboration of some of the questions attacked by Dembo is already at hand, namely: the problem of success and failure and level of aspiration by Hoppe, Fajans, Rosenfeld; the problem of substitution (compensation) by Köpke, Lissner, Mahler; the problem of reality and unreality by Brown, Mahler, Sliosberg; certain social fields by Wiehe. I hope that the last-named investigation may have a fundamental significance for a broad field of social psychology.

Systematic Survey

One may distinguish roughly two meanings of the question "Why" in psychology:

1. Why, in a given momentary situation, that is, with a given person (P) in a certain state and in a certain environment (E), does precisely this behavior (B) result? The problem is thus to represent the behavior (event) as a function of the momentary total situation ($B = f(PE)$).

2. The more historical question: Why, at this moment, does the situation have precisely this structure and the person precisely this condition or state?

It is important to separate these two questions more clearly than is done, for example, in association psychology and in Freud's theory. The center of gravity of our experimental work lies, as a rule, in the first kind of why. In experimental practice, to be sure, these two kinds of problems are often so closely related that the creation of a sufficiently unequivocal situation requires a certain historical structure of the experimental situation.

In accordance with our general conceptual and methodological assumptions nearly all of our investigations treat not only questions of *individual differences* but problems of general *lawfulness*. The center of gravity lies, as a rule, in the problem of the general laws.

As regards content, no action is referred either to the person on the one side or to the psychological environment on the other; or yet to a more-or-less combination of both factors. Rather, each action is referred to the momentarily obtaining structure of such a person in such a psychological situation. Nearly all the investigations are therefore occupied with both problems. The following classification thus indicates merely the center of gravity of the problem formulations.

General Laws of the Psychological Systems

Tension Systems (Need, Purpose).

Ovsiankina, The Resumption of Interrupted Activities. [1] This article contains proof that the effect of a purpose or intention is the formation of a quasi-need, that is, dynamically, of a tension system. This tension system drives toward discharge and causes activities which serve the execution of the purpose. The technique of the experiments was essentially as follows: an activity was interrupted, and after a certain interval a situation of relative freedom for the subject was created. There resulted a frequent re-

---

[1] *Psychol. Forsch.*, 1928, 11, 302-379.

sumption of the interrupted activity (Table I).

The influence of the following factors, among others, upon the frequency of resumption were investigated: (1) the kind of activity; (2) the phase in which the activity was interrupted; (3) the duration of the interruption; (4) the nature of the act of interruption; (5) the presence or absence of the uncompleted task at the end of the interruption; (6) the attitude and character of the person.

TABLE I[1]

Duration of interruption, minutes	CI						DI						
	R_1	TR	R	R?	NR	R in per cent	R_1	TR	R	R?	NR	R in per cent	R+TR in per cent
0to2	3	.	18	..	.	100	3	.	15	..	.	100	100
2to4	.	..	14	..	.	100	.	.	19	..	1	95	95
4to8	..	.	8	..	.	100	.	1	17	..	5	74	78
8to20	.	.	3	..	.	100	.	1	13	..	4	74	78
20to40	.	.	1	..	.	100	.	.	5	1	..	92	92
Over 40	..	..	.	..	.	..	.	.	2	1	.	83	83
Indeterminate	.	..	.	.	...		.	1	..	..	5	..	..
Total	3	.	44	.	.	100	3	3	71	2	15	79	82

The left half of the table under the heading Cl includes the experiments with interruptions occurring as though by chance. The right half with the heading DI lists the experiments in which the first task was interrupted by asking the subject to do another (disturbing) task. In the first column the duration of the interruption is given in minutes. The six following columns show the number of cases of RI (refusal to be interrupted), TR (tendency to resume), R (resumption), $R?$ (questionable resumption), NR (nonresuption), and R in percentage (total percentage of resumptions), according to the duration of interruption. In calculating the percentage of R, the instances of $R?$ are counted as one half.

---

[1] Ovsiankina, *op. cit.*, Table I, p. 326.

The proof that the resumption (or as the case may be, a repetition of the activity) fails to occur as soon as the tension system is discharged by the attainment of the goal is important for the character of the quasi-needs as tension systems. It is shown that a substitute satisfaction can have the same effect and, further, that the presentation of the half-finished work of another person does not, as a rule, cause a tendency to completion.

Zeigarnik, On the Retention of Completed and Uncompleted Activities. [1] Zeigarnik attacks the same problem as Ovsiankina but with another technique. If a purpose or intention corresponds dynamically to a tense system, it is to be expected that the state of tension of the system should be evident not only in the tendency to completion of the activity but also, for example, in its better retention. Zeigarnik finds, indeed, that *memory* for uncompleted activities is much better (Table II). She proves that it is not the shock effect of the interruption that is the cause of this better retention but rather the state of the psychical systems involved at the time when the subject is asked to recall. The influence of the following things, among others, was investigated in detail: (1) the structure of the task (an activity with a definite end as against a continuous activity); (2) interest in the task; (3) the attitude of the subject toward the experimenter; (4) the differences among children, adolescents, and adults.

Zeigarnik shows that the tension systems may be destroyed by sufficiently strong variations of tension in the whole person (affective variations produced naturally, Table III, and artificially) ; and that in a fatigued state (owing to the then occurring fluidity of the systems) no sufficiently stable systems arise. Zeigarnik at-

---

[1] *Psychol. Forsch.* , 1927, 9, 1- 85.

tacks the important question of the firmness of form of nontense systems. (This question is directly investigated in an unpublished work of Kaulina and plays an essential part in that of Schwarz.) The structure of the more comprehensive system totalities is shown to be essential; only when the single psychological systems are sufficiently separated are completed activities better remembered than uncompleted.

Birenbaum, On the Forgetting of an Intention. [1] It is shown that intentions or purposes which correspond to a main task (or to a central need) are almost never forgotten. With the less important purposes such, for example, as writing the name (or the date) on the sheet of paper used for the main task, the forgetting (nonexecution) depends essentially upon whether and if so how the system corresponding to the purpose is imbedded in that of the main task or main goal.

TABLE II. —[2] The Ratio of The Retained Uncompleted To The Retained Completed Activities $\frac{RU}{RC}$

Rank Order of Subjects

Rank $\frac{RU}{RC}$	Subjoet	Activities				Arithmetic mean by groups			
		ΣR	RU	RC	$\frac{RU}{RC}$	ΣR	RU	RC	$\frac{RU}{RC}$
1	Wd.	7	6	1	6				
2	Be.	9	7	2	35				
3	St.	13	10	3	33				
5	Jf.	8	6	2	30	9.1	7	21	35
	M.	8	6	2	30				
	Eu.	12	9	3	30				
7	Pl.	7	8	2	25				

---

[1] *PsychoL Forsch.* ,1930,13,218-284.

[2] Zeigarnik,*op. cit.* ,Table I,p. 9.

Rank $\frac{RU}{RC}$	Subject	Activities				Arithmetic mean by groups			
		ΣR	RU	RC	$\frac{RU}{RC}$	ΣR	RU	RC	$\frac{RU}{RC}$
10	Paj.	9	6	3	20	108	7	38	19
	Gin.	9	6	3	20				
	Hf.	6	4	2	20				
	Pt.	15	10	5	20				
	Ml.	12	8	4	20				
14	Dm.	11	7	4	175				
	V.	11	7	4	175				
16	Git	11	7	4	175				
	Dm. E.	13	8	5	16				
19	Ml. R	15	9	6	15	133	78	55	1.4
	Jn.	10	6	4	15				
	Rm.	15	9	6	15				
	Gld.	10	6	4	15				
	Jic.	10	6	4	15				
23	Ml. E.	12	7	5	14				
	Kur.	19	11	8	14				
	Hn.	12	7	5	14				
25.5	Glk.	16	9	7	13				
	Jnk.	14	8	6	13				
28	Gl.	12	6	6	10	113	57	57	1.0
	Wlt.	12	6	6	10				
	Schn.	10	5	5	10				
30.5	Sim.	11	5	6	0.8	90	40	50	0.8
	Fr.	9	4	5	0.8				
32	Sim. H.	7	3	4	0.75				
Arithmetic mean		11.1	6.8	4.25	19				

ΣR = number of retained activities.

RU = number of retained uncompleted activities.

RC = number of retained completed activities.

RU/RC = ratio of retained uncompleted to retained completed activities.

TABLE III. ① $\frac{RU}{RC}$ For Excited Subjects

Subject	RU	RC	$\frac{RU}{RC}$
I	3	4	0.75
II	4	5	0.8
III	6	7	0.9
IV	7	9	0.8
V	4	4	1.0
VI	2	4	0.5
Mean	4.3	5.5	0.78

Table IV ②

	Task	E	SE	F	Per cent E
Before Critical Task	1. Match task A	36		1	97
	2. Match task B	37			100
	3. Match task C	36		1	97
	4. Match task D	36		1	97
	5. Match task E	36		1	97
	Mean: Tasks 1 to 5	36.2	0	0.8	97.6
Critical Task	6. { I. Favorite poem or II. Draw a pentagon or III. Write cities	10	11	16	27
	7. II ro III or I	13	8	16	35
	8. III ro I or II	16	4	17	43
After Critical Task	9. Guessing a name	16	5	16	43
	10. Word building	16	6	15	43
	11. Outlining a figure	8	5	24	22
	12. Monogram	7	5	25	19
	Mean: Tasks 7 to 12	12.7	5.5	18.8	34.2

E = number of subjects who executed intention.
SE = number of subjects who subsequently executed intention.
F = number of subjects who forgot intention.

① Zeigarnik, *op. cit.* Table 28, p. 70.

② Birenbaum, *op. cit.*, Table 2, p. 238. A series of five match tasks (different, but of the same general character) is followed by one radically different in content (the critical task, No. 6 above), which is then followed by a heterogeneous series.

Table IVa[1] — The Dependence of The Substitute Value Upon The Decree of Difficulty (Measure in Working Time[2]) of The Substitute Activity and Upon Its Similarity to The Original Activity[3]

Task	Puzzle					Riddle					Translation				
	Original activity	Substitute activity				Original activity	Substitute activity				Original activity	Substitute activity			
		Similar		Different			Similar		Different			Similar		Different	
		easy	hard	easy	hard		easy	hard	easy	hard		easy	hard	easy	hard
n······	44	13	11	9	11	43	13	11	9	10		11	10	9	9
Working time mean.inseconds.	194	70	<687	32	<323	340	211	<744	223	<690	39	312	<603	236	<559
Mean variation	76.7	37.4	370.4	22.8	101.2	119.2	73.2	289.5	145.8	222.3	124.9	84.8	187.5	55.6	181.2
Substitute value: $\frac{RWS}{RS^4}$		18 < 22		13 < 1.5			1.4 < 3		0.9 < 13			23 < 28		12 < 1.4	

1. Lissner.op.cit.,Table 6,p.237.
2. As a measure of the difficulty of the activity we use the time required for its execution. In the case of the original activity also time may be used as a measure of difficulty. even though these activities are interrupted before completion. The interruption occurred at almost exactly the same pont in the execution with the different subjects.The riddle task was regularly interrupted after ten words, the translation task at a certam point in the teix.Even in the case of the puzzle the mode of work was sufficiently similar to permit the selection of a rather precisely defined point for interruption.
3. The difference between the arıthmetic means for *easy* and *hard substitute* activzties is. Without exception. great both absolutely and in comparison to the orıgınal activity.The fact that the mean variation is considerable is due to the inagnitude of the mdividual differences and does no timpair the c,haracterization of the substitute activity as easy or difficult.If one compares original activity and substitute activity for the same subject, the following is to be noted. The easy substitute activities are executed more quickly than the substitute activity in 59 out of 64 cases (even though the original activity is not completed). The difficult substitute activities. on the other hand, require a longer time than the original activity in 59 out of 62 cases.
4. The summary of the substitute values in this table shows particularly clearly and without exception that (r) the substitute value of the more difficult substitute actıvty is greater than that of the easier; (2) the substitute value of simlar substitute activities of the same degree of difficulty is greater than that of dissimilar substitute activities; (3)the substitute value of easy similar activities is greater than that of difficult dissimilar activi ties; (4)the difference between the substitute values is greatest between difficult similar and easy dissimilar substitute activities.

The substitute value is expressed as the ratio of the frequency of resumption of the interrupted activity when no substztute is given (RWS) to the frequency of resumption of the interrupted activity when a substitute is presented (RS).

Birenbaum treats of the factors which determine whether a newly arising system is dynamically a relatively independent whole or a dependent part of a more comprehensive regional system. The special structure of the total system and the degree of its wholeness [*Ganzheitlichkeit*] (in the sense of a stronger or weaker dynamic Gestalt) may be to a large extent experimentally determined by means of the temporal structure of the event and the internal relations of its content (Table IV). Under certain circumstances the structure of the total system may be changed after the event. The tension of the single systems, as well as the structure of the total system (and hence the frequency of forgetting) is found to depend, further, upon the general state of tension and the affective state of the whole person.

Substitution.

The question of the discharge of the psychical systems through substitute or compensatory activities forms the chief problem in the investigation of the following.

Lissner, The Discharge of Needs by Substitute Activities. [1] Lissner investigated the conditions under which a substitute activity has dynamic substitute value for the original activity (Table IV*a*). The nonresumption of interrupted activities after the insertion of a substitute activity was used as a criterion of substitute value (see Chap. VI, page 180). The substitute value of a difficult performance was found to be considerably higher than the substitute value of an easier performance (see page 248). The substitute value increases with the similarity between the original and the substitute task. The degree of connection between the systems in-

---

[1] *Psychol. Forsih.*, 1933, 18, 218-250.

volved plays a decisive role.[1] Köpke investigates this question comparatively on feeble-minded and normal children.

TABLE V[2]

	Tasks not completed			Tasks completed by substitution (subst.=acting)			Tasks not completed			Tasks completed by substitution (subst.=taking)		
n	24	24	18	24	24	23	12	12	11	12	12	12
	TSR	SR	RI	TSR	SR	RI	TSR	SR	RI	TSR	SR	RI
Per cent	19	33	28	17	4	15	58	8	9	25	0	24
ΣR in per cent	65			29			67			42		
$\dfrac{RAN}{RAS}$	2.2						1.6					

SR = spontaneous resumption.
TSR = tendency to spontaneous resumption.
RI = resumed after supplementary instruction.
$\Sigma R = SR + TSR + RI$.
RAN = resumption of acts not completed.
RAS = resumption after completion of substitute act.
n = number of cases.

The supplementary instruction (used with subjects that did not spontaneously resume, at the very end of the experiment, when numbers of both completed and uncompleted tasks were equally accessible) was as follows: "Now do any one of these tasks." The preference for uncompleted tasks in response to this neutral instruction provided in these cases a further criterion for the persistence of the tension.

In the columns $TSR, \Sigma R$, and RI, the figures indicate the total number of cases of resumption of the different kinds, irrespective of whether the same subject showed more than one kind. In ΣR, however, only one resumption of each resumed task is counted for each resuming subject, even though he may have resumed in more than one way. Consequently it may happen that SR is less than $TSR + SR + RI$.

---

[1] LISSNER, *op. cit.*, Table 8, p. 240.
[2] Mahler, Table 4, p. 44.

Mahler, Substitute Activities of Different Degrees of Reality. [1] Mahler, with a similar experimental technique, studied the question of dynamic substitute value especially for substitute activities of varying degrees of reality (thinking; talking; actual doing) in adults and children (Table V). On the whole, substitute activities of higher degrees of reality have greater substitute value. The relation of the substitute act to the inner goal of the original activity nevertheless remains of decisive importance. Substitute satisfaction occurs only when this inner goal is in sufficient degree attained by the substitute activity (Table VI). Mahler investigates the difference between problem tasks and realization tasks and shows the significance of the creation of a socially acknowledged fact for the degree of reality and the substitute value of the substitute activity.

TABLE VI [2]

	Tasks not completed			tasks completed by substitution Gout of act attained			Tasks not completed			tasks completed by substitution Gout of act attained		
n	24	24	19	24	24	24	12	12	10	12	12	12
	TSR	SR	RI	TSR	SR	RI	TSR	SR	RI	TSR	SR	RI
Per cent	27	25	24	4	0	10	42	25	15	50	8	33
ΣR in per cent	60			13			75			75		
$\dfrac{RAN}{RAS}$	4.6						1					

Success and Failure; *Level of Aspiration*.

Related to the structure of the psychological systems and the differences in degree of reality is the experimental work of the following.

---

① Psychol. Forsch. ,1933,18,27- 89.
② Mahler, Table 6, p. 50.

Hoppe, Success and Failure. [1] In spite of the great practical significance of this problem we have hitherto known very little about the occurrence of experiences of success and failure and the laws of their operation. Hoppe shows that the occurrence of these experiences is not a simple function of the result of the activity but depends, among other things, upon the relation of this result to the momentary level of aspiration (real and ideal goal) of the person and upon the ascription of the result of the activity to the self as its own performance. He shows that these experiences are limited to a rather narrow zone of difficulty, which is determined essentially by the limits of the ability of the person. In quite too hard and quite too easy tasks experiences of success or failure do not occur (Fig. 1).

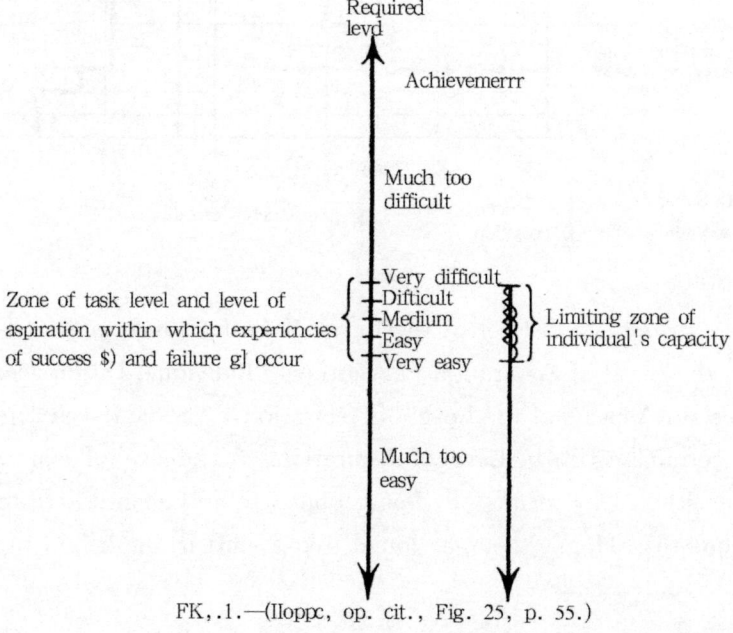

FK,.1.—(Hoppe, op. cit., Fig. 25, p. 55.)

---

[1] *PsychoJ. Forsch.*, 1930, 14, 1-62.

It is sometimes possible to fix upon different altitudes of the level of aspiration and to compare them for different persons. Thus one can investigate the effect of success and failure on the displacement of the level of aspiration ("real goal," Fig. 2) and the degree of reality of the ideal goal. These displacements of the level of aspiration, the formation of substitute goals, as well as the tendency to spontaneous interruption after certain successes and failures, rest upon a definite conflict situation. Close relations were found to obtain between the level of aspiration and the *self-consciousness* of the individual as a social person. Pronounced and apparently very deep-lying individual differences were found.

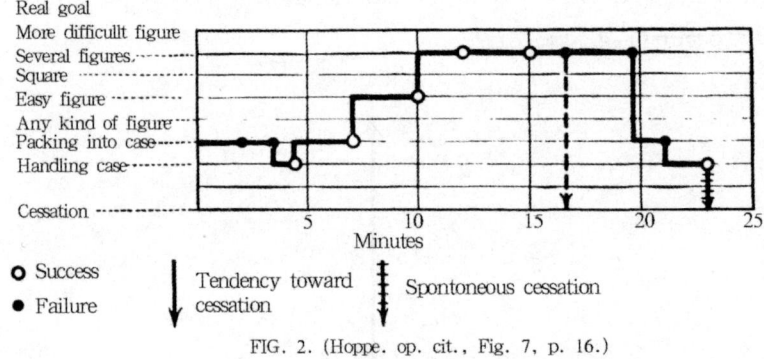

FIG. 2. (Hoppe. op. cit., Fig. 7, p. 16.)

Frank, The Effect of the Level of Performance in One Task on the Level of Aspiration in Another, [1] Individual Differences in Certain Aspects of the Level of Aspiration, [2] Some Psychological Determinants of the Level of Aspiration. [3] The level of aspiration was studied by means of a more objective and quantitative technique than Hoppe's. It was found that a shift in the height of the

---

① *Jour. Exper. Psychol*, in press.
② *Amer. J. Psychol*, 1935, 47, 119-129.
③ *Amer. J. Psychol*. 1935, 47, No. 2.

level of performance in one task causes a shift in the height of the level of aspiration in another task under certain specified conditions. The relation between the level of aspiration and the level of performance differs widely among individuals and seems to represent a reliable and general personality trait. The height of the level of aspiration in a given case is a resultant of the tendencies (1) to keep the level of aspiration as high as possible, (2) to avoid failure, and (3) to hold the level of aspiration in close agreement with a realistic estimate of future performance.

Jucknat, Performance and Level of Aspiration. [1] Jucknat investigated the effect of success and failure in one field upon the displacement of the level of aspiration in another field. She uses an essentially improved technique for the diagnosis of the obtaining level of aspiration. The experiments were carried out with some hundreds of school children and showed that success and failure in one field may importantly displace the level of aspiration in another field, upward or downward. This presupposes, however, definite dynamic relations between the two fields and a not too fixed level of aspiration in the second field.

Fajans, II, Success, Persistence and Activity in the Infant and the Small Child. [2] Fajans investigated success and failure in children of from one to four years and in infants of six months to one year. She found a very considerable displacement of the level of activity of behavior: characterologically rather passive children can be moved by success to a rather active kind of behavior and characterologically rather active children can be reduced by failure to a rather passive kind of conduct. Fajans discusses the relation

---

[1] *Psychol. Forsch.*, in press.
[2] *Psychol. Forsch.*, 1933, 17, 268-305.

of success and failure to embarrassment and to going-out-of-the-field. It appears that the attainment of a substitute goal, a consolation, or an encouragement is, for the child, to a rather considerable degree the equivalent of a genuine success (Fig. 3). The quantitative results suggest that the attainment of a goal means psychologically something essentially other in the infant (Fig. 4) than in the young child. This circumstance is confirmed and more explicitly investigated by the following.

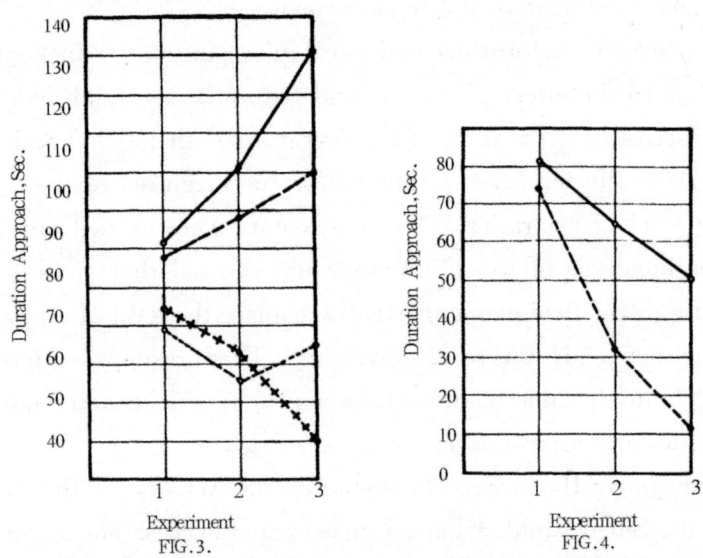

Experiment
FIG. 3.

Experiment
FIG. 4.

FIG. 3.—Comparison of the effects of success, encouragement, substitution and failure upon the duration of approach [Zuwendungfdauer]. A positively valent object was hung out of reach of the child; his cfTorts toward it were timed with a stop watch and are indicated as "duration of approach" upon the ordinates. (Fajans, II, Fig. 7, p. 290.)

—————— Success with concomitant encouragement. Increase in duration of approach from first to third experiment = 48 per cent.
.... Success. Increase in duration of approach = 25 per cent.
.... Substitute success. Diminution in duration of approach = 6 per cent.
+ −f −f + −f Failure. Diminution in duration of approach = 48 per cent.

FIG. 4.—Effect of success (——————) and failure (.........) upon the infant. (Fajans, II, Fig. 2, p. 278.)

Rosenfeld, The Ontogeny of Experiences of Success and Failure. [1]It is shown in what way the experiences of achieving and of non-achieving differ from the experiences of success and failure in children, and how these experiences are related to different developmental levels. An important factor in the development of success and failure experiences is the development of increasingly differentiated goal structures.

Psychical Satiation.

To be distinguished from the above-described questions on the dynamics of the tension system is the question of the conditions under which a new tension system spontaneously arises and how the new goal is related to the earlier goal. This problem has been attacked in the investigations of the displacement of the level of aspiration. A special problem in this field is that of psychical satiation.

Karsten, Psychical Satiation. [2]Karsten investigates the question of how the repeated execution of an act influences the inclination to execute the act yet again. The technique is essentially as follows: the subject must do a certain task repeatedly; he is, however, free to stop as soon as he has enough of it. Karsten used a group of activities as varied as possible. By reason of the repetition, an originally positive valence of the act changes to a negative. Finally the subject tries to go out of the field. The progressive process of satiation is evidenced by such typical criteria as variation, dissolution of the whole (of both perceptual and action unities), inattention, forgetting. Psychological satiation is shown to be different from fatigue although fatigue is frequently a symp-

---

[1] *Psychol. Forsch.*, in preparation.
[2] *Psychol. Forsch.*, 1928, 10, 142-254.

Table VII—Consatiation. First Day, Subject Group α

Subject	Sum of the part regions	Number of part regions per third	First third of the part regions			Second third of the part regions			Third third of the part regions		
			Total time		Amount	Total time		Amount	Total time		Amount
			Minutes	Seconds		Minutes	Seconds		Minutes	Seconds	
Tr.	3	1	38	15	569	18	..	476	8	15	70
Ha.	4	1.3	13	30	314	7	45	199	6	45	31
So.	7	2.3	25	30	645	14	30	532	7	..	174
J.	21	7	10	10	357	6	45	188	3	35	56
Fa.	28	9	5	20	130	4	.	40	4	..	78
Mean			18	30	403	10	12	287	5	55	82

The procedure used in this experiment was to have the subject make strokes in a certain rhythm (3,5) until he would no longer continue even upon slight pressure from the experimenter. He was then asked to make strokes in another rhythm (4, 4), again until spontaneous cessation. He was then asked to make strokes in still another rhythm, again until spontaneous cessation. and thus process was continued until the subject could no longer be moved to make strokes in any new rhythm whatsoever. Each rhythm is regarded as a part region. As may be seen from the table, subject Tr. required the satiation of only three part regions before the whole region was satiated (*i.e.*, making strokes any way at all) was satiated; whereas subject Fa. required the satiation of 28 part regions before the whole region was satiated. The "thirds" referred to in the table are the results simply of the division of the total number of part regions required for the subject into three equal parts. "Amount" means number of stroke groups executed.

[1] Karsten, Table 5, p. 222.

tom of psychical satiation. The speed of satiation depends, among other things, upon the structure of the task, upon the state of tension of the whole person, upon whether the task involved is of a more peripheral or more central character (both agreeable and disagreeable tasks are comparatively more rapidly satiated than neutral ones), upon the character of the person.

The problem of the consatiation [*Mitsättigung*] of neighboring regions is quantitatively investigated (Table VII) as is also the effect of variation upon the satiation of the total region (Table VIII). A condition of satiation is the occurrence of "genuine repetition." Karsten discusses the conditions under which satiation, in spite of many repetitions, fails to occur.

Karsten's results are, in addition, an impressive demonstration of the thesis that repetition by no means always brings with it an improvement in performance such as would be expected from the law of association.

Table VIII shows that with increase in amount of activity necessary to satiate single part regions, the number of part regions that have to be explicitly satiated in order to satiate the whole region decreases.

Table VIII. [1]—Subject Group on The First Day

(1) Rank order	Subject	Number of explicitly satiated part regions	Average satiation time per part region
1	Tr.	3	21 Min.30 sec.
2	Ha.	4	7 Min.
3	So.	7	7 Min.
4	J.	21	0 Min. 58 sec.
5	Fa.	28	0 Min. 29 sec.

[1] Karsten, Table 3, p. 217.

(2) Rank order	Subject	Number of explicitly satiated part regions	Average satiation quantum per part region
1	Tr.	3	372
2	Ha.	4	136
3	So.	7	193
4	J.	21	29
5	Fa.	28	9

Lange, Action Unities in the Occupations of the Kindergarten. [1] *Lange* investigates the duration of occupations in children of various ages under the conditions of a Montessori kindergarten and the various factors which determine the kind of occupations and cessations of activity.

Problems of the Environment[2]

The properties of the psychobiological environment (E) depend, among other things, upon the state of the person (P) involved [$E = f(P, X, Y...)$]. The valences, especially, are directly related to the state of the tension systems.

General Topology and Dynamics.

Of especial importance for the structure of the psychological environment are (1) the *topological* relations (*i. e.*, the mode of connections of different regions, the presence of dynamic barriers, etc.); (2) the *fields of force* (direction and strength of the forces at the various points of the field).

Fajans, I, The Significance of Distance for the Strength of a

---

[1] *Psychol. Forsch.*, in preparation.
[2] A somewhat more thorough survey of the results up to the present concerning environmental forces is found in Chap. III.

Valence in Infants and Young Children. [1]Fajans investigates the special problem of whether the strength of the force corresponding to a valence diminishes as the spatial distance between the valence and the person increases. She used as subjects infants and preschool children who tried to reach a goal object from various distances. She compared the duration of active and passive, direct and indirect, approaches (Fig. 5).

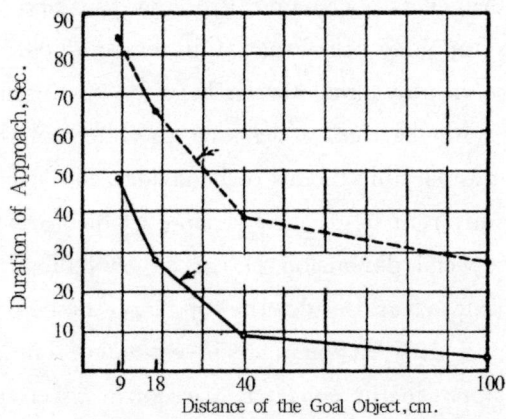

FIG.5.—In these experiments with infants a positively valent object was hung at eye level as the infant sat upon a table at the horizontal distance indicated from his outstretched hand. The total duration of "active approaches" and "passive approaches" (visual regard) was measured with a stop watch and is indicated upon the ordinates. (Fajans, I, Fig. 4,p.239.)
———All approaches (active and passive).
———Active approaches.

She found, in the case of the infants, a clear diminution in the strength of the field forces with increasing distance but no such diminution (within the investigated distances) with the preschool children. This difference rests in part upon the different magnitudes of the life-space at these different ages, in part on the greater significance of social fields for the older children. Fajans follows up the metamorphosis of "thing"[*sachlichen*] fields into so-

---

[1] *Psychol. Forsch.* ,1933,17,215-267.

cial fields, the structure of the new environment in embarrassment, the effect of certain conflict situations on expression, and other questions. Methodologically important is the development of special criteria which permit the discrimination of differences in the strength of driving forces from differences in the firmness of barriers. Fajans shows that the strength of these restraining forces is a function of the strength of the driving forces.

Dembo, Anger as a Dynamic Problem. [1]Dembo analyzes the change in the topology of a situation in which a goal is unattainable (formation of a dynamic barrier between person and goal, formation of an outer barrier) and shows the effect of the obtaining topology on the possible modes of behavior. The decisive significance of the different *degrees of reality*, which are to be represented by a special dimension of the psychobiological life-space (Fig. 6), becomes clear. Besides the topology, the field forces, their distribution and their changes, are investigated. The structure of the fields of force in the *conflict* situation is given, its effect on behavior in the level of reality (oscillation, various kinds of going-out-of-the-field), as well as the tendency to go into the level of unreality (fantastic solutions). Dembo uses the idea of *inducing fields* for the presentation of social power relations and deduces the occurrence and the forms of the struggle between experimenter and subject from the nature of these fields (Fig. 7). She also uses this concept in treating the difficult problems related to the spontaneous occurrence of substitute goals and relates the problem of the substitute goal to that of the use of tools. Dembo follows in detail the process of *destructurization* [*Destrukturierung*] and *homogenization* [*Homogenisierung*] of the field, which is ver-

---

[1] *Psychol. Forsch.*, 1931, 15, 1-144.

y significant for the dynamics of anger. The experimental findings of this investigation form the essential basis for my analysis of the situation of reward and punishment (see Chap. IV, page 114).

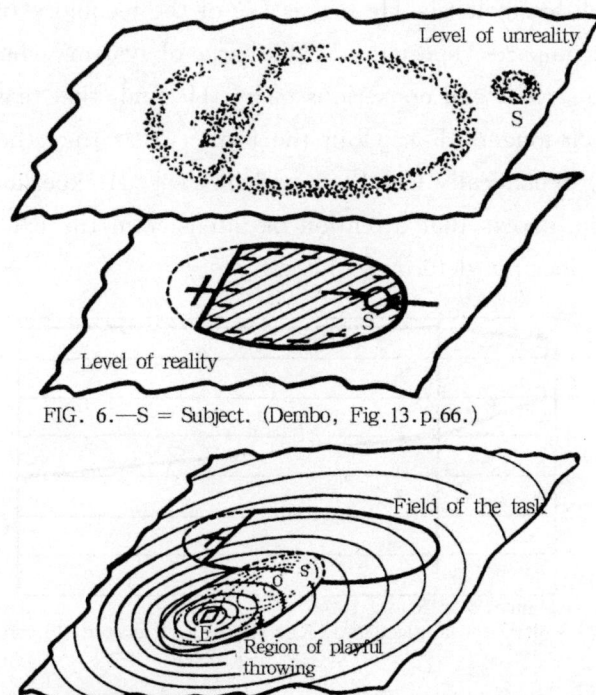

FIG. 6.—S = Subject. (Dembo, Fig.13.p.66.)

FIG. 7. The outer barrier embraces not only the field of the task but also the field ot the struggle with the experimenter. (The task here is to throw rings over a bottle. The experimenter intentionally provokes the subject by catching the thrown rings, moving the bottle, etc. The subject immediately takes this up as a game, which gives him a basis for conducting a struggle with the experimenter, a basis which, as mere subject, he did not have.) To this extent, then, the field of the struggle with the experimenter corresponds to "a special region of the field of the task." If the subject should succeed continually in getting the upper hand in the struggle the field of the task, its vectors and its barriers, would be annulled in so far as these rest upon the field of force of the experimenter. (Dembo, Fig.17.p.82.)
———— Field of force of the experimenter.
　　　　Field of force of the subject.

Reality and Unreality.

Brown, On the Dynamic Properties of the Levels of Reality

and Unreality. [1] Brown tests experimentally the assumption that the less real levels are dynamically more fluid than the more real, by investigating the speed of discharge of tense systems which belong to different levels. He makes use of the technique of Zeigarnik and compares especially the discharge of systems which correspond to serious and nonserious tasks. He finds that tension persists much longer (Fig. 8) in the former, that they thus correspond to dynamically less fluid media. A special experimental arrangement shows that attention or intensity in the execution of the task does not determine this effect.

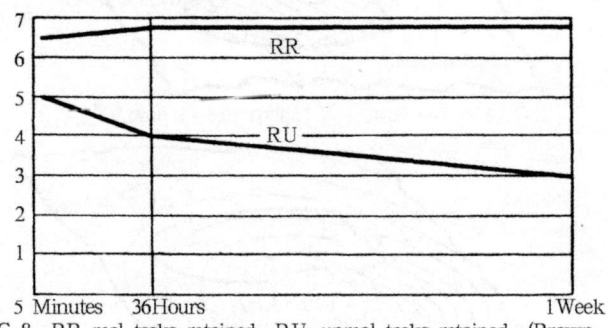

FIG.8—RR real tasks retained. RU=unreal tasks retained. (Brown, Fig.5.P-13.)

The question of the differences between levels of reality and unreality also plays a role in the already mentioned works of Lissner and Mahler.

Sliosberg, On the Dynamics of Play. [2] Sliosberg investigates the problem of substitution especially in the play of the child. It is found, among other things, that the substitute value of an object or an action depends essentially upon whether the child is in a play or in a serious situation. The question is discussed whether the

---

[1] *Psychol. Forsch.*, 1933, 18, 1-26.
[2] *Psychol. Forsch.*, 1934, 19, 122-181.

close connection between reality and unreality which determines the child's magical view of the world (Piaget) is also determinative for the satisfaction of his needs.

Social Fields.

Wiehe, The Behavior of the Child in Strange Fields. [1]Wiehe investigates the significance of a special social field for the behavior of children. The children, sometimes alone, sometimes in the presence of the mother, are brought into a strange room, or a strange person appears in the child's home. Wiehe distinguishes six different degrees of strength of this strange field. The degree of strength is, apart from individual characteristics of the child and of the strange person, a function of the spatial distance of the strange person, of the duration of his presence, and of his conduct. It is possible to correlate the different degrees of the strength of the field with definite modes of behavior of the child. Surprisingly marked quantitative lawful relations resulted (Table IX). The strongest pressure was expressed by the child's becoming motionless; crying and the tendency to run away, where possible to the neighborhood of the mother or into another field where the child feels itself more at home, correspond to a weaker degree of pressure (Fig. 9). The other activities of the child also showed, with great regularity, an inhibited character under high pressure of strangeness and an overexcited or overemphasized character under somewhat weaker pressure. Only a further reduction of pressure led to natural free behavior.

---

[1] In preparation.

Table IX[1]—Action Toward The Stranger

Behavior		Degree of the strengths of the social field					
		5 N = 21	4 N = 38	3 N = 59	2 N = 52	1 N = 51	0 N = 22
1. Listen to	unh	100%	100%	100%	100%	100%	100%
	h	0	0	0	0	0	0
2. Look at	a	40	10	0	0	0	0
	o sh	30	10	0	0	0	0
	une	30	0	0	0	0	0
	unc	0	20	10	0	0	0
	ocm	0	60	30	10	0	0
	d	0	0	30	40	40	0
	unh	0	0	30	50	60	100
3. Turn bodily toward	a	60	30	0	0	0	0
	v w	30	30	0	0	0	0
	une	10	20	0	0	0	0
	w	0	20	30	0	0	0
	hc	0	0	40	20	0	0
	o st	0	0	30	30	0	0
	oem	0	0	0	60	40	0
	unh	0	0	0	40	60	100
4. Smile at	a	100	60	30	0	0	0
	o sh	0	20	0	0	0	0
	unc	0	20	50	0	0	0
	c	0	0	20	40	0	0
	oem	0	0	0	40	40	0
	s un	0	0	0	20	60	100
5. Speak to	a	100	80	50	20	0	0
	o sh	0	20	20	0	0	0
	we	0	0	20	30	0	0
	I	0	0	10	0	0	0
	d	0	0	0	0	20	0
	oem	0	0	0	30	50	0
	s un	0	0	0	20	30	80
6. Address to	a	100	90	50	20	0	0
	unc	0	10	20	20	0	0
	i	0	0	30	0	0	0
	d	0	0	0	30	20	0
	oem	0	0	0	30	40	100
	s un	0	0	0	0	40	0

[1] Wiehe, in preparation.

Behavior		Degree of the strengths of the social field					
		$N=21 \atop 5$	$N=38 \atop 4$	$N=59 \atop 3$	$N=52 \atop 2$	$N=51 \atop 1$	$N=22 \atop 0$
7. Express wishes	a	100	90	50	20	0	0
	v we	0	10	10	0	0	0
	unc	0	0	20	30	0	0
	i	0	0	20	20	10	0
	c	0	0	0	40	60	100
	oem	0	0	0	0	30	0
8. Give or throw something	a	100	100	0	30	50	80
	o sh	0	0	60	40	0	0
	unc	0	0	30	0	0	0
	i	0	0	10	0	0	0
	oem	0	0	0	30	30	0
	s un	0	0	0	0	10	20
9. Make bodily contact	a	100	100	50	30	10	0
	o sh	0	0	30	20	10	0
	unc	0	0	0	0	0	0
	he	0	0	10	30	10	0
	i	0	0	10	10	0	0
	sub	0	0	0	10	10	0
	oem	0	0	0	0	30	0
	s un	0	0	0	0	30	100
10. Stay nearby	a	100	100	60	40	20	0
	o sh	0	0	30	20	0	0
	unc	0	0	10	20	10	0
	up	0	0	0	20	10	0
	oem	0	0	0	0	30	0
	s un	0	0	0	0	30	100
11. Ask personal questions	a	100	100	80	50	0	30
	i	0	0	20	20	20	0
	unc	0	0	0	30	20	0
	s un	0	0	0	0	60	70
12. Demonstrate ability	a	100	100	80	0	20	50
	unc	0	0	10	10	0	0
	sub	0	0	10	0	0	0
	oem	0	0	0	70	50	0
	s un	0	0	0	20	30	50

Behavior		Degree of the strengths of the social field					
		$\frac{5}{N=21}$	$\frac{4}{N=38}$	$\frac{3}{N=59}$	$\frac{2}{N=52}$	$\frac{1}{N=51}$	$\frac{0}{N=22}$
13. Show off	a	100	100	60	0	30	40
	une	0	0	20	0	0	0
	unc	0	0	20	10	0	0
	oem	0	0	0	70	40	0
	s un	0	0	0	20	30	60
14. Make demands	a	100	100	60	40	0	0
	o sh	0	0	20	0	0	0
	v we	0	0	20	30	0	0
	wo	0	0	0	30	0	0
	c	0	0	0	0	0	0
	aff	0	0	0	0	10	20
	oem	0	0	0	0	30	0
	we	0	0	0	0	40	50
	s un	0	0	0	0	20	30
15. Affective reactions	a	70	100	60	30	0	20
	v we	0	0	20	0	0	0
	o sh	0	0	10	20	10	0
	we	0	0	10	50	60	0
	oem	0	0	0	0	30	80
	s un	30	0	0	0	0	0

a＝absent.
aff＝connected with affections.
c＝confident,
d＝discretely,
he＝hesitancy.
i＝indirect,
oem＝overemphasized,
o sh＝overshort.
ost＝only starting.

P＝personal.
s ub＝substitute activity,
s un＝socially unhindered,
unc＝uncertain,
une＝unemphasized.
up＝impersonal.
v we＝very weak,
we＝weak,
wo＝doing with emphasis.

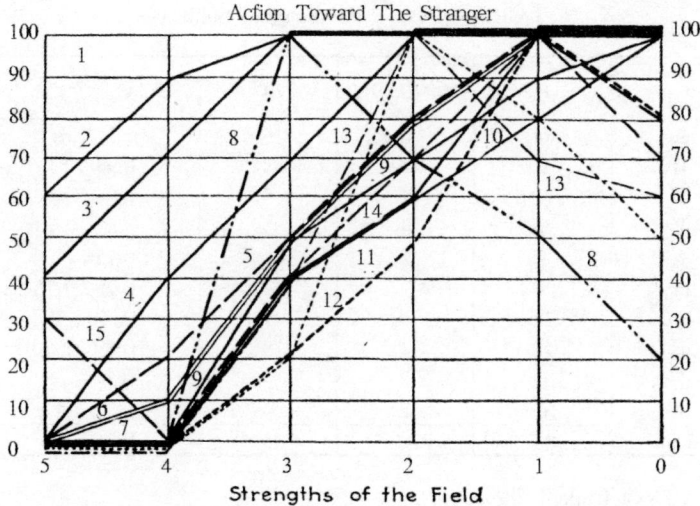

Abscissae represent percent of cases m which fhe different kinds of action occur erf the different strengths of fhe field

1–Listen to 4–Smiling at 7–Express wishes 10–Staying near 13– Show off
2–Look at   5–Speaking to 8–Give or throw 11–Personal questions 14–Make demand
3–Turning   6–Address to 9–Bodily contact 12–Demonstrate ability 15–Affective reaction
FIG. 9.

Structure and State of the Whole Person

Nearly all the investigations described above have also contributed somewhat to the problem of the state and structure of the whole person. Zeigarnik showed the dependence of the single tension upon the fatigue (Table X) and affectivity of the whole person. Birenbaum showed their dependence upon the state of tension (Table XI) of the whole person. In Karsten's investigation the stratification [*Geschichtetheit*] of the whole person and the significance of the more central and more peripheral inner psychological strata for the process of satiation became clear. Hoppe, Fajans, and Jucknat treat of the relation between experiences of success and failure and the state and character of the whole person.

TABLK X[1] $\frac{RU}{RC}$ For Fatigued Subjects

Subject	R	RU	RC	$\frac{RU}{RC}$
A	11	6	5	1.2 (5)[2]
H	9	(4/9)	(5/11)	0.98 (1)
S	9	4	5	0.8
F	9	4	5	0.8
K	7	3	4	0.75
Lk	7	3	4	0.75 (1.75)
Ph	11	4	7	0.57
E	12	4	8	0.5 (1.66)
E	6	2	4	0.5
Fr	6	2	4	0.5 (1.5)
Mean	8.7	3.6	5	0.74

① Zeigarnik, Table 25, p. 66.

② The numbers in parentheses indicate the results of the experiment with the same subjects in the fresh condition six months previously.

Tablk XI[1]

Activity	Subjects (naive-excited): basic experiment				The same seven subjects instructed for speed			
	E	SE	F	E%	E	SE	F	E%
1. Match task···	4	1	2	57	7	···	···	100
2. Draw a pentagon	3	2	2	43	6		1	86
3. Write cities···	5	2		71	7			100
4. Guess a name	3	1	3	43	7	···		100
5. Word building	2	2	3	29	7			100
6. poem···	3	3	1	43	6	1		86
7. Outline······		1	6	0	4		3	57
8. Names of scholars with one intial················	5	1	1	71	7			100
9. Monogram···············	4	1	2	57	6		1	86
Mean················	3.2	1.5	2.2	46	6.3	0.1	0.6	90.5

E = executed intention.

SE = subsequently executed intention.

F = forgotten intention.

① Birenbaum, Table 10, p. 271.

Experimental Simplification of the Structure of the Person: Regression.

The above-mentioned investigation of Dembo on anger goes more extensively into the problems of the whole person and of the change in its structure. Anger, for example, can show itself in extraordinarily different, indeed in opposed, ways. Dembo investigates the different kinds of pure emotional expression and emotional behavior, the criteria of emotional intensity, and the dynamics of emotional outbursts. The functional firmness of the boundaries of the strata between the inner psychical systems and the environment is of decisive significance. The paradoxical circumstance, that superficial emotions lead more readily to emotional expression than the more serious ones, is explained (Figs. 10 and 11).

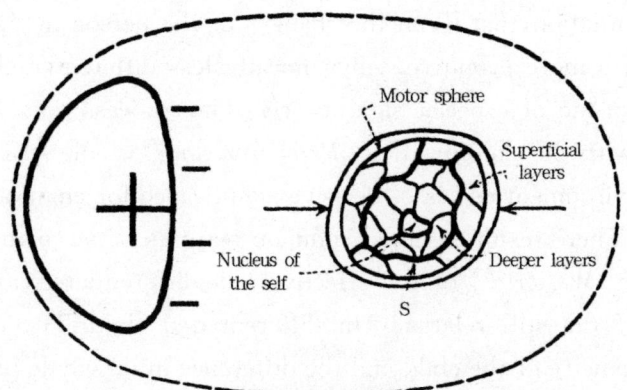

FIG. 10.—Structure of the psychological environment and the person in super-ficialemotion. (Dembo, Fig. 18, p. 109.)

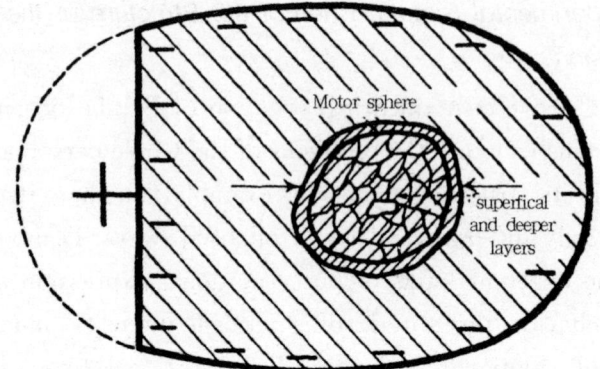

FIG.11.—Structure of the psychological environment and the person in deeper lying emotion. (Dembo, Fig. 19, p.110.)

Dembo follows the change in the finer structure of the person with increasing affective tension, and the displacement of the chief boundary between the inner psychical systems and the environment with special reference to the motorium. The results on de-differentiation, that is, on the changes of the person in the direction of a more primitive, a dynamically less differentiated unity, seem to me of especial significance. This process goes hand in hand with the simplification [*Primitivierung*] of the structure of the environment and is of decisive significance for emotional outburst. There result essential common features between the world picture [*Welibild*] of the affectively de-differentiated adult and that of the still relatively un-differentiated child. The dynamic homogeneity of the child and the difference in its whole person in emotion and in fatigue are discussed.

Menstruum and Intermenstruum.

Freund, On Satiation in and between Menstrual Periods. [1] Freund investigated the influence of the menstrual and intermen-

---

[1] *Psychol. Forsch.* ,1930,13,198-217.

strual periods on the speed of satiation for certain tasks. Because of the great individual differences the same subjects were investigated in both conditions. There resulted a very marked difference in the speed of satiation, which held indeed without exception for every individual (Fig. 12). This difference in inclination is the more noteworthy since there occurred no regular difference in speed or quality of performance when the same subjects were set definitely limited tasks of the same sort.

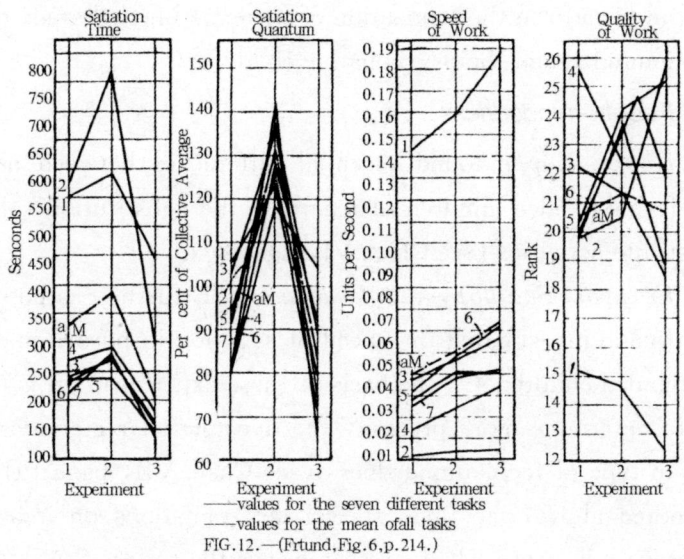

FIG.12.—(Frtund,Fig.6,p.214.)

Psychopathology.

Some not very systematically executed experiments on psychopathic children seem to show that certain types of these children are more rapidly satiated than normal children of the same age. [1]

---

[1] Cf. Lewin, Trieb- und Affektäusserungen psychopathischer Kinder (Motion pictures of psychopathic children compared with normal and feeble-minded children), *Zeitschr. f. Kinderforsch.*, 1926, 32, 414-447.

It may be of interest, as an example of our way of work, that these individual differences in speed of satiation, as well as the difference in the behavior of the same person in different conditions (during and between menstruation) and, finally, the difference between peripheral and central tasks, may be deduced in unitary fashion.

The dynamic concepts (such as degree of structuredness, fluidity, state of tension) which resulted from investigations of the general laws form the foundation of the experimental study of the feeble-minded and the psychopathic child.

Feeble-mindedness.

Köpke. *Köpke* found essential differences between normal and feeble-minded children in regard to the substitution value of substitute activities (see Chap. VI, page 180).

Erfurth, Saathop, and Wöhrmann. Erfurth, Saathop, and Wohrmann investigated the speed of satiation in normal and feeble-minded children. On the basis of these experiments it is possible to determine more precisely the dynamic characteristics of a certain type of feeble-mindedness (see Chap. VII, page 194). As we noted above, one finds special determinations on individual differences in nearly all the researches of the series.

Modes of Execution, Perceptual and Cognitive Structure of the Environment

In conclusion three works should be mentioned which do not fit well into the selected grouping. These investigations center about problems for which the nature of the stratum between the inner psychical systems and the physical environment is chiefly determinative, the stratum to which one may refer the motor tasks [*Ausführungshandlung*] and the processes of perception. Since these questions are closely related to problems of which one usually thinks in speaking of experience in learning, a few words on our general position toward the problem of "*experience*" should precede discussion of these investigations.

The results of the investigation of the fundamental law of association①are sometimes misinterpreted to mean that I hold "experience" to be unimportant. The articles on satiation, on the effect of success and failure, on lapses in relearning, among others, show that such a conception is far removed from my view. It is only that the effect of experience cannot be sufficiently characterized by means of the concept of association. The effect of experience always consists in the fact that a person (P), upon the repetition of a situation, reacts not in the same way but in another way than that in which he reacted the preceding time. If the behavior (B) is really in both cases the same, it means that the person has remained unchanged. (Thus if $B_1=B_2$ and $E_1=E_2$, P_1 must equal P_2 in accordance with the general law: $P=f(BE)$). The effect of experience is always a change of the person or of the psychological meaning of the environment. A theory of experience can consist only in a determination of the various possible changes in the structure of the person, of the environment, and of the forces dominating that environment. I am inclined to doubt that a unitary theory of the whole field of these changes in terms of experience is possible.

Schwarz, On Relapses in Re-learning, I and II. ② Building upon the negative findings of my investigation of association,

---

① LEWIN,"Das Problem der Willensmessung und das Grundgesetz der Assoziation. " *Psychol. Forsch.* ,1922,1,191-302; 1922,2,65-140.

② *Psychol*,*Forsch.* ,1923,2,86-158,and 1933,18,143-190.

Schwarz attempted to formulate, on the newly found basis, the conditions under which a change in a repeatedly executed task presents difficulties and to determine what the nature of the errors occurring under these conditions might be. Schwarz distinguishes between errors of confusion and errors of relapsing. He separates the question of the momentary source of the energy for the execution of the task from the form of its expression and especially from its dependence upon constraining forces. He finds that the two kinds of error are dynamically of essentially different nature. Both occur only when, in the learning process, systems of quite definite form have been built up and have also become sufficiently rigid. He treats in detail the question of action unities, their different forms, their genesis, and their change; he further discusses the significance of the valences for the execution of the task.

Forer, An Investigation of the Decroly Method of Learning Reading. [1] Forer compares the retention of children from five to six years old for single letters, words, and sentences. She investigates their memory for (1) these written forms of different extent; for (2) their significance; and for (3) the coordination of written form and significance. In general, it is shown that a group of relatively heterogeneous written forms and meanings is more easily learned than a homogeneous group. The written form of a sentence and of a word are about equally well, that of a letter a little better, retained. But the meaning of a word and the meaning of a sentence are very much better retained than letters; further, words referring to things are better retained than words referring to activities or to properties. The spatial juxtaposition of the written form and the related object constitutes an essential advantage

---

[1] *Zeitschr. für Kinderforsch.*, 1933, 42, 11-44.

for the retention of children in contrast to that of adults. This difference seems to me to be related to the magical world picture of the child in that, at this age, the written forms designate objects and not concepts.

Voigt, Precision of Direction at a Distance. [1] Voigt treats the problem of the steering of the execution of a task by the perceptual field. His subjects shot with a light-pistol, without taking aim, at targets of various kinds and at varying distances. He found that within certain distances the angular precision of the shooting increased with the distance of the target (Fig. 13). Voigt investigates exhaustively the dependence of these results upon the structure of the perceptual field and upon the motor apparatus used (shooting with the right hand, the left hand, and with both hands). He demonstrates the significance of the motor field [*Handlungsfeld*], which embraces in unitary fashion the person and the goal. Voigt also goes into the question of the learning of that sort of activity.

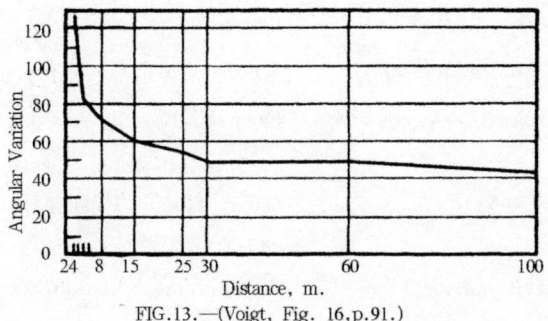

FIG.13.—(Voigt, Fig. 16, p.91.)

---

[1] *Psychol. Forsch.* 1932, 16, 70-113.

Survey of The Experimentally Handled Problems
In Terms of Traditionally Used Key Words

(The names of authors treating a given topic most exhaustively are printed in italics.)

Action, activity(*Handlung*)	Schwarz (wholeness), Voigt (steering), Zeigarnik and Ovsiankina (kinds). On dynamics see Need, Emotion, etc.
Anger(*Arger*)	Zeigarnik, Karsten, Ovsiankina, Hoppe, Fajans, II, *Dembo*.
Attention(*Aufmerksamkeit*)	Karsten, Dembo, Fajans, I and II, Schwarz, Wiehe.
Attitude(*Einstellung*)	Zeigarnik, Ovsiankina, Karsten, Schwarz, Freund. Brown.
Character(*Charakter*)	Ovsiankina, Hoppe, Dembo, Fajans, I and II, Wiehe.
Compensation	See Substitute.
Conflict(*Konflikt*)	Ovsiankina, Zeigarnik, Karsten, Birenbaum, Hoppe, *Dembo*, Jucknat, Fajans, *I and II*, Rosenfeld, Schwarz, *Wiehe*.
Depth(*Tiefe*)	Lewin and Sakuma, Voigt.
Development(*Entwickelung*)	See Problems of child psychology.
Embarrassment(*Verlegenheit*)	Fajans, II, Karsten, Jucknat.
Emotion(*Affekt*)	Zeigarnik, Karsten, Ovsiankina, Birenbaum, Hoppe, Fajans, II, Dembo, Freund, Wiehe.
Experience(*Erjahrung*)	See Learning, Satiation, Success.
Failure(*Misserfolg*)	See Success.
Fantasy(*Phantasie*)	Zeigarnik, Dembo.
Fatigue(*Ermudung*)	Dembo, Brown, Hoppe, Mahler.
Force(*Kraft*)	See Structure of environment, Conflict.

Gestalt(*Gestalt*)   See Whole, unity

Gesture(*Geste*)   Fajans, II, Hoppe, Dembo. See also Unreality.

Goal (*Ziel*)   Hoppe, Dembo, Jucknat (ideal and real goal, level of aspiration), Mahler (inner and outer goal of action), Karsten.

Habit(*Gewohnheit*)   Lewin (measurement of the will), Schwarz, Karsten, Freund, Jucknat, Hoppe.

Hallucination(*Halluzination*)   Dembo.

Ideal(*Ideal*)   Hoppe, Jucknat, Dembo. See also Unreality.

Instrument(*Wcrkzeug*)   Dembo (substitute), Voigt (steering), Hoppe (ascription of the effect).

Individual differences(*Individ ltdIc Untcnthirdc*)   Köpke (feeblemindedness), Zeigarnik, Ovsiankina, Karsten, Fajans, II, Freund.

Intention(*Absicht*)   Voigt (significance for steering). See also Purpose, Need.

Lapse(*Riickfall*)   See Habit.

Learning, relearning, forgetting (*Lcrncn, Umlernen, Verlcrncn*)   Schwarz, Voigt, Forer, Karsten.

Memory(*Gedachtnis*)   Lewin (measurement of the will), Zeigarnik, Schwarz, Birenbaum, Jucknat, Brown, Forer.

Need(*Beditrfnis*)   Zeigarnik, Ovsiankina, Birenbaum, Hoppe, Karsten, Mahler, Rosenfeld, Jucknat, Lissner, Freund, Lewin (measurement of the will).

Perception(*Wahrnehmung*)   See Depth.

Persistence(*A usdauer*)   Karsten, Hoppe, Freund, Birenbaum.

Person, structure of the whole person (*Person, Struktur der Gesamtperson*)	*Dembo*, Köpke, Karsten (stratification) Freund, Hoppe. See also Individual differences, Problems of child psychology.
Play(*Spiel*)	Dembo, Schlossberg. See also Unreality.
Problems of child psychology(*Kinder psychologische Problem*)	Zeigarnik, Ovsiankina, Fajans, I and II, Mahler, Wiehe, *Rosenfeld*, Jucknat, Forer.
Purpose(*Vornahme*)	Zeigarnik, Ovsiankina, *Birenbaum*, Brown, Hoppe.
Reading(*Lesen*)	Forer.
Reality(*Reälitdt*)	See Unreality.
Restlessness(*Unruhe*)	See Emotion, Conflict, Satiation.
Satiation(*Psychische Sättigung*)	*Karsten*, Freund.
Satisfaction (*Befriedigung*)	See Need.
Self-consciousness (*Selbstbewusstsein*)	Hoppe, Fajans, II, Jucknat.
Self-control(*Selbstbeherrschung*)	See Conflict, Emotion, Success.
Skill(*Geschkklichkeit*)	Voigt, Schwarz.
Social relations (*Sociale Beziehungen*)	*Dembo, Wiehe*, Hoppe, Jucknat, Fajans, I and II.
Structure of environment (*Umweltstruklur*)	Voigt (connection with steering), Forer, Dembo (concept of the world), Zeigarnik, Ovsiankina, Fajans, I (environmental forces), Zeigarnik, Hoppe, Fajans, II (topology). See also Conflict, Social relations.
Struggle(*Kampf*)	*Dembo*, Wiehe, Karsten.
Substitute(*Ersatz*)	Zeigarnik, Ovsiankina, Birenbaum, Hoppe, Dembo, Mahler, Jucknat, Fajans, II.
Success(*Erfolg*)	Dembo, *Hoppe*, Fajans, I and II, Jucknat.

Superstition(*Aberglauben*)	Dembo.
Unreality (*Irrealitat*)	*Brown*, *Dembo*, Fajans, II, *Mahler*, Hoppe, Forer, Schlossberg.
Valence(*Aufforderungscharakter*)	Ovsiankina, *Karsten*, Dembo, *Fajans*, I (and distance). See also Conflict, Need
Whole, unity(*Ganzheit*)	Voigt (visual wholeness and performance), Forer (differentiation of word and meaning), Birenbaum, Zeigarnik (wholeness, unity of tension systems), Dembo (structure of the whole person). See also Success, Substitute.
Will(*Wille*)	See Purpose, Need, Conflict.
World, concept of(*Weltbild*)	Forer, Dembo, Hoppe. See also Unreality.

Index of Names

A
Ach, N. , 43, 45, 239
Adams, D. K. , 100
Adler, A. , 66, 72, 100, 142
Alverdes, F. , 69
Aristotle, 1, 2, 5-9, 11, 12, 14, 26, 27, 34

B
Bacon, F. , 6, 7, 9, 20
Bartelt, 50
Baiimer, 143
Beck, S. J. , 221, 223, 224, 229
Binet, A. , 195, 220, 225, 232
Birenbaum, G. , 126, 168, 212, 244, 246, 264, 265, 271-273
Blanchard, M. B. , 67
Bogen, H , 83
Brown, J. F. , 103, 145, 208, 224, 241, 260, 271-273
Bruno, G. , 6, 10
Bühler, C. , 74, 75, 91, 164, 228
Bühler, K. , 70, 105
Burks, B. S. , 67
Busemann, A. , 67, 68

C
Cassirer, E. , 4, 100
Coghill, G. E , 107
Conrad, H. S. , 67
Crozier, W. J. , 73

D

Decroly, O. J. , 168, 194, 270
Dembo, T. , 95, 102, 103, 115, 160,
174, 181, 192, 214, 218, 236, 240,
241, 258-260, 265, 266, 271-273
Dexler, 50
Dohme, A. , 140, 144, 146
Drösches, 143

E
Eliasberg, W. , 196
Erfurth, 268

F
Fajans, S. , 74, 80, 85, 86, 88-90, 94,
100, 101, 115, 144, 182, 241,
252, 253, 257, 258, 265, 271-273
Faraday, M. , 10
Forer, S. , 270, 272, 273
Frank, J , 252, 272, 273
Frankcl, F. , 45
Freeman, F N. , 67
Freud, S , 22, 180, 181, 242
Freund, A. , 198, 267, 268

G
Galileo, 1, 10, 26, 29, 33
Gesell, A. , 67
Goethe, J W , 173
Gottschaldt, K , 186, 189, 205, 213
Green, G. H. , 108
Grisch, 111

H

Hauck, E. , 67
Hegel, G. W. F. , 172
Hermann-Cziner, A. , 50
Hetzer, H. , 75, 106
Homburger, A. , 72, 91, 113, 125, 146
Hoppe, F. , 100, 115, 150, 160, 174,
214, 241, 250-252, 265, 271-273
Huang, I. , 105

J
Jaensch, E. R. , 104, 229
James, W. , 56, 108
Jennings, H. S. , 69
Joël, E. , 45
Jones, H. E. , 67
Jucknat, 101, 252, 265, 272, 273

K
Karsten, A. , 18, 85, 198, 200, 254-
256, 264, 271-273
Katz, D. , 78, 104, 108
Katz, R. , 104, 108
Kaulina, 244
Kepler, J. , 10
Koffka, K. , 24, 70, 1 68, 191, 232, 268
Köhler, W. , 24, 48, 53, 58, 83, 102,
107, 152, 168, 192, 195, 215, 218,
240
Köpke, 185, 202, 204, 211-213, 241,
247, 268, 271-273
Kramer, 71
Kügelgen, W. von, 126, 139, 140

L

Lange, 256

Lau, E. G. , 50, 64, 74, 86

Lazar, 103, 186, 205

Lévy-Bruhl, L. , 8

Lewin, K. , 5, 11, 17, 24, 31, 44, 45, 48, 65, 68, 75-78, 80, 81, 83, 89, 90, 93, 94, 96, 97, 102, 104, 106-108, 117, 148, 197, 206, 215, 227, 239, 240, 267, 269, 272

Lipmann, O. , 83

Lissner, K. , 184, 202, 203, 212, 241, 247, 248, 260, 272, 273

Loeb, J. , 69, 73, 78

M

Mach, E. , 10, 27

Mahler, V. , 190, 202, 241, 247, 249, 250, 260, 271-273

McDougall, W. , 45

Montessori, M. , 94, 96, 171, 172, 177, 256

Morgan, 225

Miiller, G. E. , 43

Murchison, Carl, 66

O

Ovsiankina, M. , 60, 183, 202, 242, 243, 271-273

P

Peters, W. , 229, 233

Piaget, J. , 104, 105, 146, 191, 261

Pintner, R. , 237

Poincaré, H. , 33

Poppelreuter, W. , 45, 55

R

Rohrschach, H. , 221, 223, 224, 229

Rosenfeld, M. , 241, 254, 272, 273

Rubin, E , 40

Rupp, H , 219

S

Saathop, 268

Sakuma, K. , 48, 239, 272, 273

Schurz, K. , 143

Schwarz, G. , 244, 270-273

Selz, O. , 45

Simon, T. , 195

Sliosberg, S, 105, 191, 241, 261, 272, 273

Sommer, R , 5

Stern, C , 104

Stern, W. , 66, 67, 70, 94, 104, 107

T

Taine, H. , 66

Terman, L. M. , 204

Thorndike, E. L. , 84

Tolman, E. C. , 77

Tolstoy, L. N. , 146

U

Ucko, 96, 115, 272, 273

von Uexkull, 73, 77

V

Voigt, G. , 271-273

W

Wallin, J. E. W. , 225
Watson, J. B. , 66, 72
Weiss, G. , 75, 87, 205
Wertheimer, M. , 24, 30, 168
Wiehe, F. , 80, 99, 110, 241, 261-263, 271-273
Winkler, 144
Wöhrmann, 268
Wolf, K. , 75
Wundt, W. , 15

Z

Zappert, J. , 111
Zeigarnik, B. , 60, 185, 212, 240, 241, 243-246, 260, 264, 271-273

Index of Subjects

A

Achievement, inadequacy of concepts of, 195
Action wholes, development of in child, 173
Adult, authority of, 176
 struggle against, 138, 141-144
 example of, 147f.
 flattery and deceit as forms of, 143 relation to adult's field of power, 141f.
Affactivity, 264
Age of defiance, 102f., 110
 dynamic explanation of, 163f.
Aha-experience in feeble-minded, 196, 222
"Almost" situation, 86f.
Ambiguous figures, 195, 221
Anger, 258, 260
 relation of substitute activity to, 260
Anthropomorphism, 2, 28
"Arrangement," as evasion of barrier, 142
Artistic expression, 178
Aspiration, level of, 100, 205, 250-254
 as affected by performance in another task, 252
 relation to substitute activity, 185
 to success and failure, 250
 satisfaction of feeble-minded with lower level of, 205
Association, 43, 269, 270
 law of, 239

not a cause of psychical events, 44f.
relation to will, 239
theory, 43ff.
Average, contrast with the concrete situation, 68

B

Barrier, acquisition of negative valence by, 89f., 134
in interest situation, 119
properties of, firmness, 127
reality of, 128, 160
in punishment situation, 123ff.
punishment situations lacking in, 130-133
representation of, 126
task, as, 122, 154
types of, physical-corporeal, 126
sense of honor, 127
sociological, 126f.
Behavior, as function of environment and person, 71-73, 79
Boundaries, firmness of, 58f.
functional weakness of, in young child, 169

C

Classification, 4, 238
abstract, 4, 15
contrast with constructive method, 238
dichotomous, 4, 10
functional, 5

Command (*see* Punishment; Reward)
Compensation (*see* Substitution)
Comprehension, relation to differentiation of the person, 232-236
Concepts, 8
Aristotelian, 2ff.
classificatory, 4f., 238
conditional-genetic, 11
constructive, 238, 241
dynamic, 27, 35ff., 40, 46ff.
of energy, 46
Galileian, 9ff
Concepts, genotypic, 11
historic-geographic, 8, 9, 19, 30
phenotypic, 11
in transition, 22
valuative, 2, 3
Conflict, definition of, 88
types of, 88-91, 123
Constraint, 161
in punishment situation, 128-133
Convergence, theory of, 66
Coupling (*see* Association)
Creativeness, relation to level of unreality, 224f.

D

Daydreams, 190
example of, 146
Deception, 125, 140, 143
difficulty of, in feeble-minded, 217
Defiance, 144f
age of, dynamic explanation, 163f.

Index of Subjects **595**

Despair, 94
Determination, intrinsic, 28ff. , 38f.
  by whole situation, 36ff. , 49
Detour, 154
  relation to field forces, 82f.
Devaluation, of adult's ideology, 137
Development, of the person, 209-215, 236-238
Differentiation of psychical systems, relation of rate to material property of mobility, 226
Direction, 81-85
Discipline, 144, 176
Distance, psychological, dependence of valence on, 86f. , 257f.
  functional determination of, 86
Division of personality, 207
Domination, of child by adult, 131ff. , 142
Dreams, 103f, 145.
Drives, 15, 38
(See also Tension system)

E

Ego, stabilization of, 164
Eidetic images, 104
Embarrassment, 90, 258
  relation to failure, 253
Emotional outburst, 145-152, 218, 265f.
Encouragement, 253
Encysting, 94, 144f.
Energy, 46, 50f.

relation to force, 48, 239
sources of, 43-65
Enuresis, 111, 146, 164
Environment, psychological, relation to individual and law, 70ff.
  statistical investigation of, 67
  structure of, 73- 80, 269
  dependence on momentary state of person, 76
  (See also Field)
Equilibrium, tendency toward, 58f.
Exactness, 2, 10, 16
Experimental investigations, survey of, 239-273
Experimental techniques (see Interruptured activity, resumption of)

F

Failure, 150, 250-253
  conditions determining, 250ff.
  effect of consolation, 101
  on duration of action, 101
  relation to difficulty of task, 251
  (See also Success)
Fantasy, 74, 76, 104, 178, 259
Fatigue, effect on tension in system, 264
Feeble-minded, concreteness in, 222, 225
  differentiation and mobility of comprehension, 232-236
  dynamic theory of, structure of, 209-238

comparison with normal, representation of, 210
degree of differentiation, 209
material properties, 209f.
experimental methods, selection of, 197f.
experimental results, satiation, 198-202
Feeble-minded, experimental results, satiation, course of, 200
"either-or" behavior, 201, 216
secondary actions, 200f.
technique, 198
total *vs.* part satiation, 199
resumption of interrupted action, substitute value, 202-206
technique, 202
variation in similarity of substitute action, 204
formulation of experimental problem, 196-198
infantilism, 225-227
relation of rate of differentiation to material properties, 226
intelligence defects (*see* Intelligent activity)
lack of graded transitions of dynamic connections in, 215
material properties and psychical environment, 215-218
material properties of systems and formation of wholes, 214f.
pedantry and fixation of goals, 210f.

relation to development of strong Gestalts, 222f.
to lack of differentiation, 223
to level of unreality and lack of imagination, 223
to smaller degree of differentiation, 225
to undeveloped level of unreality, 223
senile dementia, earlier cessation of differentiation in feeble-minded, 237
substitute value, paradoxes of, 211ff.
dependence of, on dynamic connections of task, 215
susceptibility to influence, 227-232
dependence on field conditions, 230ff.
test approach, its inadequacy, 195
theory of, in application, 185-238
whole personality involved, 194f.
Field, psychological, difference from objective situation, 75f.
Field, functional determination of, direction in, 84
problems of, 257-264
reorganization (transformation) of, in feeble-minded, 219-222
in intellectual tasks, 152
insight as, 195f.
on plane of unreality, 150
in prohibition situation, 160
relation to differentiation of the person, 232-236
role of directed forces in, 196

topological representation of, 117f.
Field of force, 80-103, 257ff
convergent field, 91.
definition of, 91 f.
illustration of, 92f.
influence on development, 66-113
social, 97, 102, 175f. , 261-264
Flattery, 140, 143, 154, 157
Forces, 48
constraining, 81, 239, 258
dependence on valences, 88
driving, 81, 239, 258
environmental (field), 77-113
definition of, 79
fundamental properties of, 80- 88
direction, 81- 85
strength of, 85- 88
relation to energy, 48
to needs, 50f.
Freedom of movement, dependence on sphere of power, 99
restriction of, 93, 126, 128f. , 155
in prohibition, 163
relation to constraint, 128ff.

G

Genotype, 11
Gestalt, 240
contrast with summative conglomerate, 168
strong, 206, 215, 247
relation of, to degree of differentiation of person, 221

theory, 240
Gesture, 103, 145, 174, 178, 190
in feeble-minded, 205
"gesture children," 186
"Global" method of reading and writing, 168
Goal, distinction between inner and outer, between "real" and "ideal," 250f.
in relation to substitute activity, 190
striving toward, 81
(*See also* Valence)
Going-out-of-the-field, 190
in anger, 259
encysting as, 144
prevention of, by barrier, 125
in punishment situation, 124f.
relation to failure, 253f
suicide as, 140
types of, 90

H

Habit, 44ff.
Heredity and environment, 71
Homogenization, 10, 22, 24

I

Ideology, 103, 105, 127, 132
relation to level of unreality, 145
transformation of, 137f. , 145, 156, 162
Imagination, 145
lack of, in feeble-minded, 223f

relation to level of unreality, 223f
Imbedding, 54, 178, 244
transformation of interest by, 166-169
Impudence, 145
Independence, 145
of decision, 17f.
Individual differences, relation of, to dynamic theory of the person, 194
to general law, 73, 241
Inducing fields, 192, 259
Induction, 97-100
of child's goals by adult, 175f.
of valence, 192
Infantilism, 188, 225-227
of psychopathic types, 227
Inferiority, feeling of, 100
Ink-blot figures, 221
Insight, definition of, 196
difference in, between feeble-minded and normal, 196, 2i8ff.
nature of, as reorganization, 1951.
Intellectual tasks, solution of, 150
Intelligence quotient, dynamic theory of constancy of, 226f.
Intelligence testing, limitations of, 195, 197
Intelligent activity, defects of, in feeble-minded, 218-222
similarity of, in normal and feeble-minded, 196
theory of, 196
Intention, forgetting of, 244-247
Interest, genuine transformation of, 166-170
interest situation, 118-120
natural *vs.* artificial, 115f.
Interrupted activities, resumption of, 242f.

L

Law, concept of, 5
general validity of, 9, 23, 31
relation to individual differences, 70-73
to individual and environment, 70-73
Lawfulness, 5, 37ff.
criteria of, 6, 7, 14, 15, 26
exceptions, 17, 19, 24
frequency, 7, 14
of individual event, 5, 11-13, 18-35
statistical character of, 7
Level of aspiration (*see* Aspiration)
Life-space, 14
dependence upon temporal displacement of goals, 173
structure of, in levels of varying reality, 178
Life-time, extension of, in child, 172-174
Locomotion, psychological, 61

M

Magical features of child's world, 127, 146, 175, 230, 261, 270
Means, 102

Memory (*see* Retention)
Milieu, 67, 68, 71
Mobility of psychical systems, 218ff.
Montesson system, 171ff. , 177
Moral disgrace, 138
Morality, 145
Motor actions, 269ff

N
Need, 50, 73, 74
environmental structure and, 73-80
(*See also* Tension system)
Negativism, 102f. , 110, 163f.

O
Obedience, 176
Obstinacy, in feeble-minded, 217

P
Pedantry, 109
definition of, 210
in feeble-minded, 204, 210f.
in normal child, 229f.
Perception, 239f, 269
role in guidance of action, 51f.
Persistence, in feeble-minded and normal, 200
and rigidity of will in feeble-minded, 204
Person, conditions determining tension in, 264f.
dependence upon historical factors, 209

development of structure of, 107ff.
209ff. , 236ff.
differences, in content of meaning of the systems, 209
in structure, 206f.
Person, dynamic theory of, 180-187, 206-209
material differences (ease of change of structure), 207
representation of, 208
relation to problem of individual differences, 194, 206
simplification of structure of, 265f
states of tension, 208
conditions determining tensions in, 208
difference of, in different regions of, 208
stratification of, 265f.
structure of, in child, 107ff.
Play, 103, 265f.
distinction between play and serious situations, 191
dynamics of, 261
relation to substitution, 181, 191
Power, sphere of, of child, interference in by prohibition, 163
control of child by adult's, in situations without barriers, 130ff.
Pressure, 133
resulting in bodily rigidity, 148
social, 99f. , 264
Process differential, 32ff.

Prohibition (*see* Punishment; Reward)
Property, development of concept of, 107
Psychical material (see Person, dynamic theory of)
Psychical systems, 55f.
  interconnections of, 57f., 211-215
  rate of differentiation of, 226f.
  relation of motorium to, 63f.
  segregation of, 58f.
Psychological environment (see Field)
Psychological law, 79
  relation to individual differences, 73
Psychological present, 163
  danger of too narrow a, 172
  extension of, 173
Psychological situation, constancy of, a necessity for comparative experimentation, 197
  relation of behavior to, 116f.
Psychological situation, representation of, 117f.
  total, concrete importance of, 69
Psychopathic child, 108
  comparison with normal and feeble-minded children, 257f.
  sensitivity to environment, 72
Punishment, psychological situation in, characteristics of, constraint, 128f.
  command with threat of, 120-153
  comparison with transformation of interest, 166-170
  degree of reality of, 161-164
  function of certainty of anticipation, 161
  of intellectual maturity, 163
  transformation of, 162
  devaluation of, 162
  kinds of behavior in, acceptance of punishment, 126-140
  action against barrier, 140
  encysting, 144
  escape tendencies, 123-128
  execution of command, 135f.
  flight into unreality (emotional outburst), 145-153
  struggle with adult, 141-144
  nature and disposition of valences, 120-122
  prohibition with threat of, 158-164
  topological representation, 159f.
  state of tension, 133f.
  (*See also* Reward)
  types of conflict situation in, 122-123
Purpose, intention, 51
(*See also* Tension system)

R

Rationalization, 150
Reading, Decroly method of learning, 270
Reality, basis of, resistance of objective barriers, 176-178
  will of other persons, 155f.

degrees of, in anger, 258.
Reality, dependence of, upon situation freedom, 177
dynamic properties of level of, 103ff. , 260
education for, 171-179
(See also Unreality)
Regression, 265f.
Reorganization (see Field)
Representation, topological, 41, 117f.
Responsibility, relation to freedom, 178
Restless behavior, 95f.
dependence of form of, on topology of situation, 96
Retention, of completed and uncompleted activities, 243f.
Reward, psychological situation in (see Punishment)
combination of punishment with, and similarity of situation with that of punishment, 153
command with prospect of, 153-158
comparison with punishment situation, 154f.
with transformation of interest, 166-170
disposition of valences, 153
prohibition with prospect of, 164-166
types of behavior in, 156f.

S
Satiation, 254-257, 264f.

consatiation, 55, 256
in menstruum and intermenstruum, 267
in normal and feeble-minded, 268
(See also Feeble-minded, satiation in)
School, atmosphere, 169
marks, 157f.
Self, 61f.
boundaries of, 106-110
Self-consciousness, 101
relation to level of aspiration, 251
Self-control, 94
Senile dementia, 236-238
Situation, total concrete, 243
Social fields (see Fields, social)
Social pressure, 99f. , 264
Social standing, 138
Sphere of power (see Field of power)
State of tension, 88, 94-97
definition of, 134
factor in a dynamic theory of the person, 208
in punishment situation, 133-135
relation to forgetting of an intention, 247
Statistics, 16, 20
limitations of, 68
Steering process, 49f. , 271
Stereotypy, in feeble-minded, 204
Stimulus, as source of energy, 47f.
Strangeness, in social field, 99f. , 26 iff.
Structure, environmental, 93

mental, 52ff.
Struggle (see Adult)
Sublimation, 180
Substitute activity, value, attainment of inner goal, 190, 250
conditions of, 180-193, 247, 250
degree of reality of substitute activity, 249
difference between normal and retarded children, 185ff., 193, 247
difficulty of substitute task, 184
dynamic connection of substitute and original task, 182, 185
intensity of need, 191
level of aspiration, 185
in feeble-minded children, 186
relation of content and material of substitute task to original, 184
similarity of substitute task, 182, 185
Substitution, dynamic theory of, 181, 188ff.
experiments on, 182-193
explanation of paradoxes of, in feeble-minded, 211-213
relation to discharge of tension, 243, 247ff to play, 191
to tools, 183
Substitution, summary of experimental results, 193
Success, relation to persistence of activity in infant, 252f.
difference from achievement in children, 254

(See also Failure)
Suicide, 140
Survey of experiments, 230-273

T

Teleology, natural, 120, 155f.
Tension, state of (see State of tension; Tension system)
Tension system, conditions determining nature of discharge, 242-243
discharge of, 58ff.
(See also Person)
Terminology, 271ff.
Tools, 102, 192
relation to substitute activity, 183
Topology, 117, 241, 257ff.
Transformation, of interest, 166-170
differences from reward situation, 167f.
by imbedding, 166ff.
of psychical systems, 212f.
of values, 138, 156
(See also Field)

U

Unity of the mind, 52ff.
Unreality, level (plane) of, i45ff.
action of gesture, 174
characterized by fluidity of medium, 174
development of separation from reality in the child, 175, 177, 194f.
as dimension of psychical field, 145-

Index of Subjects **603**

174
example of, 146-151
of future events, 160, 174
stratification of, 174
(*See also* Reality)

V

Vagabonding, 125
Valence, 51, 81
definition of, 175
dependence on distance, 86f., 166 on need, 78
examples of, 118
induction of, 175
magnitude as function of distance, 166
Valence, shifts in, 163
transformation of, by imbedding, 167ff.
Vector, definition of, 81

W

Wholeness, degree of, 247
Will, measurement of, 239
rigidity of, in feeble-minded, 204
Withdrawal (*see* Going-out-of-the-field)

中译者后记

《个性动力论》是司马兰和姜颖昳两位女士转战中国传媒大学出版社以后委托我翻译的第五本传播学经典,其余四本是汉英双语版,已于去年推出,它们是:《变化中的时间观念》《传播的偏向》《帝国与传播》和《传播的结构与功能》。

感谢她们对我锲而不舍的支持。

《个性动力论》是选集,英文版编辑工作不尽人意。有鉴于此,为了提高中译本的可读性,我在"编辑"上下了一点功夫,意在为其"增色"。兹将我冒昧的"跨界"编辑工作略呈于此。

(1)英文本目录太简略,只有8章的8个题名。中译者将嵌入正文的三个层次的小节题名在目录中详尽列出,意在厘清作者的思想脉络、各章的篇章结构,借以帮助读者前后对照、跨章节阅读和检索。如今的中译本章节题名逾140个,希望这样的"大动作"能被读者接纳,并被视为译者的"大手笔"。

(2)原书的注释有两类:(A)既提供文献出处,又加上作者的解说和发挥;(B)仅提供文献出处,别无任何信息。经反复琢磨,中译本删去第二类注释,保留第一类注释。

（3）原书第八章的附录"心理学家实验研究问题一览表"有重要的参考价值，中译者将其"升格为"全书的附录，赋予它其余各章所享有的同等地位，以期引起研究者的重视。

（4）库尔特·卢因是心理学家，传播学创始人威尔伯·施拉姆将其奉为传播学四大奠基人之一，并将其《个性动力论》视为传播学奠基作。但《个性动力论》的主题、精要和关怀均为实验心理学和社会心理学，与传播学的读者毕竟有点"隔"，为了不影响中译本读者的阅读速度，我们尽量节制中译者注释，以免扰乱读者的思路。

（5）原书的许多图和表没有"题名"和"说明"，我们予以补充，意在厘清和凸显作者的思想。

（6）可惜，原书"人名索引"只有姓，没有名，为求这一样式的一以贯之，译者只好给所有的人物同等待遇，所以，弗洛伊德、歌德、黑格尔、开普勒、蒙台梭利、皮亚杰、托尔斯泰等大家也只见其姓而不见其名了。

书中近百种图表令我头痛，承蒙深圳大学理科学报郭媛小姐出手"救援"。她耐心仔细、精心制作了大量图表，容我代读者感谢她。

何道宽

于深圳大学文化产业研究院

深圳大学传媒与文化发展研究中心

2014年4月18日

译者简介

何道宽,深圳大学英语及传播学教授、政府津贴专家、资深翻译家,曾任中国跨文化交际研究会副会长、广东省外国语学会副会长,现任中国传播学会副理事长、深圳翻译协会高级顾问,从事英语语言文学、文化学、人类学、传播学研究 30 余年,著作和译作 80 余种,约 2,000 万字(著作 85 万字,论文约 30 万字,译作逾 1,900 万字)。

著作有《凤兴集:闻道·播火·摆渡》《中华文明撷要》(汉英双语版)、《创意导游》(英文版)。电视教学片有《实用英语语音》。

译作约 80 种,要者有:《思维的训练》《文化树》(一、二版)、《理解媒介》(一、二、三版)、《麦克卢汉精粹》《数字麦克卢汉》(一、二版)、《交流的无奈:传播思想史》《麦克卢汉:媒介及信使》(含一二版)、《思想无羁:技术时代的认识论》《传播的偏向》(一、二版)、《帝国与传播》(一、二版)、《游戏的人》(一、二版)、《中世纪的秋天》(一、二版)、《手机》《真实空间》《麦克卢汉书简》《传播与社会影响》《新政治文化》《麦克卢汉如是说》《媒介环境学》(简体字版、繁体字版)、《技术垄断》(简体字版、繁体字版)、《模仿律》《莱文森精粹》《与社会学同游》《伊拉斯谟传》《口语文化与书面文化》《传播学批判研究》《重新思考文化政策》《17世纪的荷兰文明》《裸猿》(一、二版)、《人类动物园》《亲密行为》《作为变革动因的印刷机》《超越文化》(一、二版)、《无声的语言》《传播学概论》(施拉姆)、《新新媒介》(一、二版)、《软利器》《迫害、灭绝与文学》《菊与刀》《理解新媒介:延伸麦克卢汉》《字母表效应》《变化中的时间观念》《文化对话》《媒介、社会与世界》《群众与暴民:从柏拉图到卡内蒂》《互联网的误读》《中国传奇》《初闯中国》《媒介即是按摩》《麦克卢汉的地球村》《驱逐:十九世纪美国排华史》《心理动力论》、《乌合之众》《余音绕梁的麦克卢汉》《指向未来的麦克卢汉》《公共场所的行为:聚会的社会组织》等。

论文50余篇,要者有《介绍一门新兴学科——跨文化的交际》《比较文化之我见》《中国文化深层结构中崇"二"的心理定势》《论美国文化的显著特征》《和而不同息纷争》《多伦多传播学派的双星:伊尼斯与麦克卢汉》《异军突起的第三学派——媒介环境学评论之一》《麦克卢汉:媒介理论的播种者和解放者》《莱文森:数字时代的麦克卢汉,立体型的多面手》等。